The *Rāmāyaṇa* Revisited

The *Rāmāyaṇa* Revisited

EDITED BY MANDAKRANTA BOSE

OXFORD
UNIVERSITY PRESS
2004

OXFORD
UNIVERSITY PRESS

Oxford New York
Auckland Bangkok Buenos Aires Cape Town Chennai
Dar es Salaam Delhi Hong Kong Istanbul Karachi Kolkata
Kuala Lumpur Madrid Melbourne Mexico City Mumbai
Nairobi São Paulo Shanghai Taipei Tokyo Toronto

Published by Oxford University Press, Inc.
198 Madison Avenue, New York, New York 10016

www.oup.com

Library of Congress Cataloging-in-Publication Data
The Rāmāyaṇa revisited / edited by Mandakranta Bose.
p. cm.
Includes bibliographical references and index.
ISBN 0-19-516832-1; 0-19-516833-X (pbk.)
1. Vālmīki *Rāmāyaṇa* I. Bose, Mandakranta, 1938–
BL1139.26.R359 2004
294.5'922046—dc22 2003058112

9 8 7 6 5 4 3 2 1

Printed in the United States of America
on acid-free paper

To my sisters
Mriducchanda and Madhusraba

Preface

Like other pervasive presences one grows up with, until recently the *Rāmāyaṇa* was for me a part of life I took for granted with no expenditure of conscious effort. The passage of years, the repositioning of the *Rāmāyaṇa* in present-day public life, and conversations with friends, colleagues, and students have increasingly drawn me to a more critical engagement with what I see as a foundational text of South and Southeast Asian societies. My studies through the past five years have led me to organize several scholarly gatherings, out of which a modest volume of essays by diverse hands has already appeared in print and the present, fuller collection conceived. In bringing these essays together, my aim was to offer the reader some of the most informed and imaginative work currently under way in major areas of *Rāmāyaṇa* studies, including its design, ideology, and performance. The crop of *Rāmāyaṇa* scholarship in the past two decades has been singularly rich, not only in expanding and developing the fields of research but in questioning received wisdom and discovering fresh instruments of inquiry. In like manner, the present volume attempts to press ahead with revaluations and rediscoveries that, I believe, will animate what I suspect will be a continuing debate on the *Rāmāyaṇa* for a long time to come. The two great epics of India, the *Mahābhārata* and the *Rāmāyaṇa*, have the distinction of never having turned into dead if revered classics, and remain embedded in the living cultures of many Asian peoples, including those in the various Asian diasporas. The essays presented here recognize this contemporaneity of the *Rāmāyaṇa* and engage with it on the many levels of its existence.

Among an editor's many tasks the pleasantest is the acknowledgment of debts, both personal and professional. I have been particularly fortunate in the varied and consistent help I have received from institutions, colleagues, friends, and family, and I take this opportunity to thank them all. I have been fortunate to have received support from many corners, including my colleagues and friends. I would like to acknowledge them all. My first debt of gratitude is to the University of British Columbia for providing research grants that enabled me to make research trips, organize conferences, and publish conference proceedings. My thanks are due in particular to the Peter Wall Institute of Advanced Studies at the University of British Columbia for its generous funding, and to its director, Dr. Ken McCrimmon, who believed in me, helped me finance and organize two international *Rāmāyaṇa* conferences, and gave me invaluable practical advice. Both the past and present directors of the Institute of Asian Research, Dr. Terrence McGee and Dr. Pitman Potter, have helped me beyond the call of mere institutional duty, providing resources for an entire *Rāmāyaṇa* conference and an exhibition, "The *Rāmāyaṇa* in View"; without their support I could not have generated the interest in the *Rāmāyaṇa* at this university that it enjoys today. I must also acknowledge the unfailing support of Dr. Frieda Granot, Dean of Graduate Studies, in all my research ventures. The Museum of Anthropology at the University of British Columbia helped me to organize performances of the *Rāmāyaṇa* on several occasions, and I am grateful to the Museum's director and staff. I would also like to acknowledge with much pleasure a very substantial research grant from the Social Sciences and Humanities Research Council of Canada that has allowed me to enlarge the scope of my work on the *Rāmāyaṇa*.

I record with equal gratitude and much personal warmth the support I have received and continue to enjoy from my students, Tanya Boughtflower, Nandita Jaishankar, Nicki Magnolo, Amandeep Mann, and Daniel Winks. Photographs of temple sculptures were provided by Michael Dowad, for which I am grateful to him. Other photographs that accompany the articles have been mostly provided by the authors, and some are from my personal collection, including reproductions of painted scrolls that I have acquired through the years from village painters of West Bengal. I take this opportunity to thank these often obscure but always vigorous artists.

My husband, Tirthankar Bose, has provided constant help by going through every stage of the book with me meticulously. Without his help this book would not have seen the light. I am grateful to Margaret Case and Rebecca Johns-Danes for their meticulous copyediting. Finally, I would like to thank Cynthia Read and Theodore Calderara of Oxford University Press for taking on the task of steering this book through the complex publication process with patience and understanding.

Note on Transliteration

Non-English words are italicized and marked with diacritics, other than terms that appear in Merriam-Webster's Collegiate Dictionary or have passed into common usage in the critical literature of South and Southeast Asia, such as "guru," "pandit," and "kathakali." Proper names are transliterated according to usage in their language of origin. Exceptions, if any, are stated in notes to individual chapters.

Contents

Contributors, xiii

Introduction, 3

1. Resisting Rāma: Dharmic Debates on Gender and Hierarchy and the Work of the *Vālmīki Rāmāyaṇa*, 19
   Robert P. Goldman

2. Gendered Narratives: Gender, Space, and Narrative Structures in Vālmīki's *Bālakāṇḍa*, 47
   Sally J. Sutherland Goldman

3. *Rāmāyaṇa* Textual Traditions in Eastern India, 87
   William L. Smith

4. Reinventing the *Rāmāyaṇa* in Twentieth-Century Bengali Literature, 107
   Mandakranta Bose

5. Why Can't a Shudra Perform Asceticism? Śambūka in Three Modern South Indian Plays, 125
   Paula Richman

6. Hanumān's Adventures Underground: The Narrative Logic of a *Rāmāyaṇa* "Interpolation," 149
   Philip Lutgendorf

7. "Only You": The Wedding of Rāma and Sītā, Past and Present, 165
Heidi Pauwels

8. When Does Sītā Cease to Be Sītā? Notes toward a Cultural Grammar of Indian Narratives, 219
Velcheru Narayana Rao

9. Representing the *Rāmāyaṇa* on the *Kūṭiyāṭṭam* Stage, 243
Bruce M. Sullivan

10. The "Radio-Active" *Gīta-Rāmāyaṇa*: Home and Abroad, 259
Vidyut Aklujkar

11. Mysticism and Islam in Javanese *Rāmāyaṇa* Tales, 275
Laurie J. Sears

12. Chasing Sītā on a Global/Local Interface: Where Cartographies Collide, Silent Vessels "Tell in Full," 293
Kaja M. McGowan

13. The *Rāmāyaṇa* in the Arts of Thailand and Cambodia, 323
Julie B. Mehta

14. The *Rāmāyaṇa* Theme in the Visual Arts of South and Southeast Asia, 335
Kapila Vatsyayan

Appendix 1 The *Rāmāyaṇa* in Asia, 355

Appendix 2 Variant Names of Main Characters, 359

Index, 361

Contributors

Vidyut Aklujkar has taught Hindi, Indian literature, and Indian mythology at the University of British Columbia, and Sanskrit at Harvard. In addition to several research publications in international journals and anthologies, she has a monograph on the philosophy of language, *The Primacy of Linguistic Units,* Indian Philosophical Quarterly Publication No. 12 from the University of Poona (1987). She has six books to her credit in Marathi, including two edited volumes, one on Konkani idioms and the other, entitled *Videshini,* an anthology of prizewinning short stories written by authors in the Marathi diaspora. For three years she has written a series of articles on language for the Marathi weekly *Saaptaahik Sakaal,* published from Pune, India. She has been an editor and now serves as an editorial counselor on the Marathi quarterly *Ekata,* published from Toronto. She has also served for many years as a final judge on the prestigious literary awards committee for the annual awards given by Maharashtra Foundation in the United States.

Mandakranta Bose is Director of the Centre for India and South Asia Research at the University of British Columbia, where she teaches Eastern religions and women's studies. A fellow of the Royal Asiatic Society of London, she studied at the universities of Calcutta, British Columbia, and Oxford, earning a D.Phil. from the last. Among her recent books are: *Speaking of Dance: The Indian Critique* (Delhi: D. K. Printworld, 2001); *The Dance Vocabulary of Classical India* (Delhi: Indian Books Centre, 1995); *Movement and Mimesis: The Idea of Dance in the Sanskritic Tradition* (Dordrecht: Kluwer Academic Publishers, 1991); a critical edition, *Nartananirṇaya by Puṇḍarika Viṭṭhala* (Calcutta: General Printers, 1991); and two edited volumes, *Faces of the Feminine in Ancient, Medieval and Modern India*

(New York: Oxford University Press, 2000), and *A Varied Optic: Contemporary Studies in the Rāmāyaṇa* (Vancouver: Institute of Asian Research, University of British Columbia, 2000).

Robert P. Goldman is Professor of Sanskrit and India Studies at the University of California at Berkeley. His areas of scholarly interest include Sanskrit literature and literary theory, Indian epic studies, and psychoanalytically oriented cultural studies. He has published widely in these areas, authoring several books and dozens of scholarly articles. He is perhaps best known for his work as the director, general editor, and a principal translator of a massive and fully annotated translation of the critical edition of the *Vālmīki Rāmāyaṇa* (Princeton: Princeton University Press, 1984–). His work has been recognized by several awards and fellowships, including election as a fellow of the American Academy of Arts and Sciences.

Sally J. Sutherland Goldman, Lecturer in Sanskrit, earned her Ph.D. from the University of California at Berkeley in 1979. She teaches Sanskrit at all levels as well as Buddhist Sanskrit, Pali, and Prakrit at the University of California at Berkeley. She is the coauthor of the *Devavāṇīpraveśika: An Introduction to Sanskrit Language*. She is associate editor of the *Vālmīki Rāmāyaṇa* Translation Project, annotator of the first book of the epic, the *Bālakāṇḍa*, and coauthor of the fifth book, the *Sundarakāṇḍa* (Princeton: Princeton University Press, 1992–1996). She is currently working on the sixth and seventh books of the epic. She is the editor of *Bridging Worlds: Studies on Women in South Asia* (New York: Oxford University Press, 1992), a collection of articles on the roles of women in South Asia, and the coeditor of a new volume, *Themes in Indian History: The Sanskrit Epics* (New York: Oxford University Press, forthcoming). Her areas of interest are women's studies, epic and classical Sanskrit literature, *vyākaraṇa* or Sanskrit grammar, and Veda. She has authored a number of articles focusing on these areas.

Philip Lutgendorf earned his Ph.D. at the University of Chicago and is associate professor of Hindi and Modern Indian Studies at the University of Iowa. His research includes north Indian oral performance traditions based on Tulsīdās's *Rāmāyaṇa*, on which he has published a major study, *The Life of a Text: Performing the Rāmcaritmānas of Tulsīdās* (Berkeley and Los Angeles: University of California Press, 1991) and a number of articles. He has coauthored the *Rāmcaritmānas Word Index* (Delhi: Manohar, 1997) with Winand Callewaert. More recently, he has made a special study of the cult of Hanumān, with several articles published and in press, including the forthcoming "Evolving a Monkey: Hanumān, Poster Art and Postcolonial Anxiety" in *Contributions to Indian Sociology*. One of his interests is Indian cinema, on which he runs a Web site: www.uiowa.edu/incinema.

Kaja M. McGowan is Assistant Professor of Art History and Asian Studies at Cornell University in Ithaca, New York. Focusing her research on the reciprocal relationships between neighboring countries in Southeast Asia, she examines the flow of ideas, artistic traditions, and artifacts that link their cultures. She arrived at her current research interests through a study of classical Balinese dance and has come to focus on gender issues as they are revealed in the complex visual symbologies that evolve between the landscape and the human body. Her articles, "Balancing on Bamboo: Women in Balinese Art," in *Asian Art and Culture* (New York: Oxford University Press, 1995), and "Maritime Travelers and Tillers of the Soil: Reading the Landscape(s) of Batur," in *Studies in Southeast Asian Art: Essays in Honor of Stanley J. O'Connor*, edited by Nora A. Taylor (Ithaca: Cornell Southeast Asia Program Publication, Cornell University, 2000), explore these issues.

Julie B. Mehta is the author of *Dance of Life: The Mythology, History and Politics of Cambodian Culture* (Singapore: Graham Brash, 2001) and coauthor, with her husband Harish C. Mehta, of the best-selling biography *Hun Sen, Strongman of Cambodia* (Singapore: Graham Brash, 1999). A gold medalist from Loreto College, Calcutta, she holds degrees in English literature, and specializes in Indian, Thai, and Cambodian culture, art, and religion. Julie Mehta has lived in Southeast Asia for twenty years, has worked as a correspondent in Singapore, Canberra, Phnom Penh, and Bangkok, and has been behind major initiatives to promote cross-cultural understanding in Asia. She now lives in Toronto and is working on two new books on Southeast Asia.

Heidi Pauwels is Associate Professor in the Department of Asian Languages and Literature at the University of Washington in Seattle, where she teaches both modern and old Hindi language and literature, and courses on Hinduism. She studied in Europe (in Belgium with Winand Callewaert and in Germany with Monika Horstmann), India (at the Vrindaban Research Institute), and the United States (in Seattle with Alan Entwistle), and taught at the School of Oriental and African Studies in London (1994–1997). Her publications include two monographs on sixteenth-century bhakti: *Kṛṣṇa's Round Dance Reconsidered: Hariram Vyas's Hindi Ras-Pañcādhyāyi* (London: Curzon Press, 1996), and *In Praise Of Holy Men: Hagiographic Poems by and about Hariram Vyas* (Groningen: Egbert Forsten, 2002), and various articles in scholarly journals and conference proceedings, including comparisons of medieval and contemporary film and television retellings of the stories of Kṛṣṇa and Rāma.

Velcheru Narayana Rao is Krishnadevaraya Professor of Languages and Cultures of Asia at the University of Wisconsin, Madison. Among his many publications are his recent *Hibiscus on the Lake: Twentieth-Century Telugu Poetry from India* (Madison: University of Wisconsin Press, 2003); *Classical Telugu Poetry: An Antholgy*, a volume coauthored with David Shulman (Berkeley and Los Angeles: University of California Press, 2002); *The Sound of the Kiss: Or the Story That Must Never Be Told* (New York: Columbia University Press, 2002); and *A Lover's Guide to Warrangal: The Kridabhiramamu by Vinukonda Vallabharaya* (New Delhi: Permanent Black, 2002). Among his many articles are "A *Rāmāyaṇa* of Their Own: Women's Oral Tradition in Telugu," in *Many Ramayanas* (Berkeley and Los Angeles: University of California Press, 1991) and "The Politics of Telugu Ramayanas, Colonialism, Print Culture, and Literary Movements," in *Questioning Ramayanas* (Berkeley and Los Angeles: University of California Press, 2000), both edited by Paula Richman.

Paula Richman, Irvin E. Houck Professor of South Asian Religions at Oberlin College, specializes in Tamil religious literature. She edited and contributed to *Many Rāmāyaṇas: The Diversity of a Narrative Tradition in South Asia* (Berkeley and Los Angeles: University of California Press, 1991) and *Questioning Rāmāyaṇas: A South Asian Tradition* (Berkeley and Los Angeles: University of California Press, 2001). Her most recent monograph is *Extraordinary Child: Poems from a South Indian Devotional Genre* (Honolulu: University of Hawai'i Press, 1997). She is completing a book on Tamil *Rāmāyaṇas* in the mid-twentieth century, focusing on writers such as E. V. Ramasami, C. Rajagopalachari, Puthumaippittan, Bharati, and Kumudini.

Laurie J. Sears is Professor of History at the University of Washington in Seattle. She is the author of *Shadows of Empire: Colonial Discourse and Javanese Tales* (1996) and the editor of *Fantasizing the Feminine in Indonesia* (1996), both published by Duke University Press, Durham. She teaches Southeast Asian histories and literatures, comparative colonialisms, and postcolonial theories. She is currently finishing two new books: an edited volume entitled *Area, Knowledge, Discipline: Southeast Asian Studies in the Twenty-first Century*, and a monograph entitled *Trauma and Literary Representation in Java.*

William L. Smith teaches in the Department of Indology at the University of Stockholm, Sweden. His chief area of interest is the Eastern Indo-Aryan languages and literatures. His writings include *Rāmāyaṇa Traditions in Eastern India* (Stockholm: Department of Indology, University of Stockholm, 1995); *Bengali Reference Grammar* (Stockholm: Department of Indology, University of Stockholm, 1997); *Patterns in North Indian Hagiography* (Stockholm: Department of Indology, University of Stockholm, 2000); and a work on Śaṅkaradeva (Stockholm: Department of Indology, University of Stockholm, 2001). He has also edited *Maithili Studies: Papers Presented at the Stockholm Conference on Maithili Language and Literature* (Stockholm: Department of Indology, University of Stockholm, 2003). He is currently involved in research on *Mahābhārata* literature in Assamese, Bengali, and Oriya.

Bruce M. Sullivan, Professor of Religious Studies at Northern Arizona University, earned his Ph.D. from the University of Chicago in 1984. His book on the authorship of the *Mahābhārata*, entitled *Kṛṣṇa Dvaipāyana Vyāsa and the Mahābhārata: A New Interpretation* was published from Leiden by E. J. Brill in 1990, with a second edition under the title *Seer of the Fifth Veda* (Delhi: Motilal Banarsidass, 1999). He has coauthored with N. P. Unni two translations and studies of Kerala's Sanskrit drama tradition: *The Wedding of Arjuna and Subhadrā* (Delhi: Nag Publishers, 2001), and *The Sun God's Daughter and King Saṁvarana* (Delhi: Nag Publishers, 1995). He is also the author of the *Historical Dictionary of Hinduism* (1997), the paperback edition of which is *A to Z of Hinduism* (Lanham, Md.: Scarecrow Press, 2001), and articles and chapters on various aspects of Hindu religious traditions.

Kapila Vatsyayan, art historian, literary critic, and institution builder, has made the study of the arts and literatures of India and Southeast Asia her life's work. Her academic life began as a student of English literature in Delhi and Michigan, but broadened into sustained studies in Sanskrit, while her artistic life began with rigorous training in classical Indian dancing. Her 1968 book, *Classical Indian Dance in Literature and the Arts* (New Delhi: Sangeet Natak Akademi, 1968), established her as the foremost authority in the performing arts of India, and was followed by pioneering studies in almost every area of South Asian culture, her contributions to which have been recognized by many honors. Among her many books are *Dance in Indian Painting* (New Delhi: Abhinav, 1982), and The *Square and the Circle in the Arts of India* ([1983], 2nd ed., New Delhi: Abhinav, 1997). President of India International Centre, Delhi, and the first director of the Indira Gandhi National Centre for the Arts in Delhi, Dr. Vatsyayan has held visiting professorships in numerous universities around the world.

The *Rāmāyaṇa* Revisited

Introduction

As an ancient narrative that continues to influence the social, religious, cultural, and political life of modern South and Southeast Asia, the *Rāmāyaṇa* hardly needs to be justified as an object of serious study. But its adaptability to multiple genres, art forms, and social contexts does invite investigation, as does the reliance that countless South and Southeast Asians place on it as a guide to everyday conduct. Not a year passes that at least one of my students of South Asian origin does not tell me how she was exhorted by her mother to try to be like Sītā. Improbable as this reverence seems to me, and hard to reconcile with the dissipation of cultural heritage resulting from distance in space and time, it is a reality of South Asian life. To make such an impression, what forms does the *Rāmāyaṇa* assume as it appears to its countless admirers? In what ways and to what extent do these forms of representation construct the meaning of the epic for its audiences? The diversity of its retellings suggests that the *Rāmāyaṇa* holds different meanings for different audiences. If we are to discover what those varying meanings are and how they arise, then we must take stock not only of the literary text but also of non-literary forms, such as, dance dramas, oral narratives, stage plays, songs, films, and the visual and plastic arts.

The need to widen our investigative approaches is urgent in view of the pace at which recent *Rāmāyaṇa* scholarship is advancing. Even a cursory survey of recent publications shows the degree of sustained attention the *Rāmāyaṇa* is commanding today, from rigorously crafted editorial and translation projects to precisely researched interpretive readings that cover the whole range of public life, from politics to entertainment.[1] Conferences on the *Rāmāyaṇa* are regular events, organized by major academic bodies such as the

Sahitya Akademi of India, and by community organizations such as the International Ramayana Institute of North America. Complementing this scholarly interest, there has been a resurgence of interest in the public domain in the form of stepped-up performances of the traditional Rāmlīlā celebrations of northern India and plays and films derived from the epic.[2] A milestone in the dissemination of the epic in modern times is the television serial *Rāmāyaṇa* produced in 1987 for India's state-run broadcaster, Doordarshan, by Ramanand Sagar. This serial entranced vast audiences and brought public life to a halt during its weekly airing, and it continues to draw loyal viewers on video in India and within the huge Indian diaspora.[3] Sanjay Khan, a major filmmaker, has announced plans for a blockbuster film with the telling title "Maryyada Purushottam" ("The honor of the lord of men") based on the epic. A more somber but equally decisive sign of the grip that the *Rāmāyaṇa* has on the popular mind is its highly effective use as a political reference point in India from the late 1980s.[4] The epic seems well on the way to emerging as an instrument of identity formation, particularly for Hindus within the Indian diaspora, among whom the public chanting of the Tulsīdāsi *Rāmāyaṇa* has spread substantially over the last twenty years.[5] But interest in the Rāma tale is by no means confined to South or Southeast Asian populations and often crops up at unexpected places. For example, the distinctly off-the-track Salt Spring Island, situated off the western shore of Canada, has for many years hosted an annual *Rāmāyaṇa* performance entirely for the delectation of the local community. In the summer of 2002, Vancouver saw a multimedia dance drama on the *Rāmāyaṇa* that became something of a tourist attraction. That the epic has reached the global mass market is attested still better by the production of a technologically brilliant if determinedly Disneyfied cartoon version by a joint Japanese-Indian group, presented at international film festivals in the late 1980s and now making the rounds in a DVD reincarnation.[6]

The recharged social appeal of the *Rāmāyaṇa* has been responsible in large part for the current scholarly focus on its ideological meanings and functions. This interest has led to the recognition, first, that the literary tradition represented by Vālmīki's *Rāmāyaṇa* and its many literary descendants, most notably Tulasīdās's reworking of it in Hindi, Kampaṉ's *Irāmāvatāram* in Tamil, and Kṛttivāsa's *Rāmāyaṇa* in Bengali, has exercised a hegemonic authority in South Asian civil society, generating emulation in narratives and performances. Second, the argument has gained force that this authority is one that is contested by numerous nonhegemonic or counterhegemonic versions.[7] Reading the literary versions as inscriptions of elitist, patriarchal, and generally regressive social and political values, recent scholarship has turned to oral, folk, and regional versions and performance forms as populist, subaltern, or feminist retellings of the epic. Not surprisingly, studies grounded in these perceptions rely upon the methods and theoretical frameworks of postcolonial criticism, subaltern history, and gender studies.[8]

This enlargement of the critical perspective is an increasingly important part of contemporary *Rāmāyaṇa* studies. Within the past three decades, scholarship has made a rapid advance in both volume and depth to engage with retellings of the *Rāmāyaṇa* that have historically arisen out of regional, racial, caste, and gender sensibilities. Much of present-day *Rāmāyaṇa* scholarship aims at uncovering such sensibilities by tracing the resonance between the major versions of the epic and its local retellings, and subjecting them to intense rhetorical, structural, and ideological scrutiny. Studies in the choice of narrative structures and strategies of representation have revealed a dynamic relationship of subscription and resistance to the ethical and political formulas authorized by standard versions. Up to the middle of the twentieth century, *Rāmāyaṇa* scholarship was dominated by textual, philological, and philosophical commentary, and by research on its origins, literary parallels, historicity, and transmission.[9] With that solid platform established, research since the 1970s has been able to turn toward searching assessments of the cultural and political instrumentality of the *Rāmāyaṇa*.

The existence of regional variants of the Rāma tale, including those from beyond the borders of India, is not, of course, a recent discovery, the diversity of Rāma tales having been noted by a number of early scholars.[10] Some of the most enthusiastic and keenly observed reports come from the poet Rabindranath Tagore in the letters he wrote home during his visit to Java in 1927.[11] But from mid-twentieth century onward, research in *Rāmāyaṇa* variants picked up pace, as attested by the proliferation of comparative studies in collections such as *The Rāmāyaṇa Tradition in Asia*, *Rāmāyaṇa in South East Asia*, and *Variation in Rāmāyaṇa in Asia*.[12] By the late twentieth century, it became customary for scholars of South Asian languages and literatures to view the epic not only as a finished literary masterpiece by Vālmīki that had gained a new life at the hands of Tulsīdās, but also as part of the varied folk cultures of India and Southeast Asia. Local versions came increasingly under critical scrutiny and came to be situated in their particular social ethos and cultural idiom. However, until the 1960s the main approaches to the *Rāmāyaṇa* comprised efforts to establish texts, origins, and parallels; to examine philological characteristics, historicity, and moral themes; and occasionally to claim the pervasiveness of Hindu culture. In contrast, the past thirty years or so have seen an accelerating interest in the textual, narrative, and representational diversity of the *Rāmāyaṇa*, which marks it as a hegemonic social text on the one hand and, on the other, as a platform for resistance to that hegemony.

We may note in passing, though, that the notion of the *Rāmāyaṇa* as an oppositional text is not exclusive either to the present time or to folk traditions on the margin. One of the most powerful counter-*Rāmāyaṇas* to date is a self-consciously literate work in the Virgilian epic mode from the mid-ninteenth century in sonorous Bengali blank verse, the *Meghanādavadha kāvya* (1861) by Michael Madhusudan Datta, who mourns Rāvaṇa's defeat and his son Meghanāda's death at the hands of the treacherous "Rāma and his rabble."[13] But the decisive turn of scholarly interest toward counterhegemonic constructions and implications has to be understood as a recent phenomenon. *Rāmāyaṇa* scholarship today is systematically attempting to chart the scale of alternative constructions. In doing so it recognizes that the variety and number of such constructions is so vast as to put into question the authority of centrality traditionally ascribed to such versions as the Vālmīki or Tulsīdāsi *Rāmāyaṇa*, and indeed the validity of electing any version as a master narrative. In regional versions of the *Rāmāyaṇa*, scholars continue to discover how social groups disempowered by caste, race, and gender have capitalized on the narrative lines of the epic to inscribe upon it their own understanding of the world that it celebrates, and sometimes to dispute it.[14] As already noted, of equal social potency and immediate relevance to our own times is the scholarly perception of the political agency of the *Rāmāyaṇa*.

The complexity of the reception, retelling, and transmission of the *Rāmāyaṇa* is compounded by its spread across regions beyond the borders of South Asia over the span of more than a millennium. The peoples of Southeast Asia in particular have developed their own powerful traditions of the Rāma tale in their oral and literary narratives, their art and architecture, their music, dance, and drama.[15] The uses of the *Rāmāyaṇa* have not left social and political practice unaffected, either. The legitimation of Thai monarchies by the dynastic adoption of the name Rāma and by centering dynastic power in a capital named Ayutthya is only one of many indications of the epic's social application. But it is not only by its political uses that the pervasiveness of the *Rāmāyaṇa* in Southeast Asia can be explained. Rather, it is possible that its generic patterns of heroism, justice, and human relations are flexible enough to accommodate and perhaps invite turns in the narrative, choices of episodes, manipulation of character and theme, and modes of representation that are embedded in the particulars of regional histories and thus rendered self-reflexive.

A worthwhile critical task, then, is to comprehend the *Rāmāyaṇa* at once as a foundational text and a cultural phenomenon of protean identities, and to do so across time and space. The present book originated in the conviction that critical approaches to the *Rāmāyaṇa* must look beyond its literary and religious identity to its capacity to serve as the meeting ground of many arts and social practices. Over the past four years, the contributors to this volume have examined this understanding of the epic at a number of scholarly gatherings. Through these exchanges it became apparent that a particularly effective way to capture the complexity of the *Rāmāyaṇa* would be to investigate the construction of meaning and the strategies of such construction across the artistic genres in which it has appeared before audiences in varying contexts. Precisely because contemporary scholarship is concerned with the use of the *Rāmāyaṇa* in molding public life, asserting particular ideological positions, and contesting received wisdom, it must pay particular attention to the forms in which it appears in the public arena. From oral narration to sculpture to film and street theater, the representation of the *Rāmāyaṇa* varies widely and demands careful inquiry.

With this need in view, the essays in this volume engage with and draw upon texts as well as other forms of transmission, such as oral, musical, and dramatic performances; and paintings, scrolls, murals, and sculptures of the *Rāmāyaṇa*. They are dealt with both descriptively and analytically with regard to themes, treatment, techniques, and impact. Both in South Asia and Southeast Asia, the *Rāmāyaṇa* is known to vast audiences as much through the visual and performing arts as through textual and oral forms. It forms the core narrative of classical dance and drama in several Southeast Asian cultural traditions, including those of Indonesia, Thailand, Cambodia, Burma, Malaysia, Laos, and Vietnam, whose ancient, complex, and vibrant performance styles that feature puppetry, masked dances, and dance dramas remain at the center of their cultural life. In many parts of rural India, painted scrolls that depict highlights from the story are presented at village fairs by traveling artists who sing the narrative as they display the painting frame by frame.

The full range of *Rāmāyaṇa* performances is yet to be mapped, but many have been studied in considerable depth.[16] A major temple festival of the Palghat region of Kerala is the *tolapāvakuthu*, a leather-puppet play annually celebrating the life of Rāma over a twenty-one day period.[17] Local performances of this kind are popular with common folk as explications and affirmations of religious messages, on the one hand, and entertainment, on the other. In the more formal tradition of classical theater in India, we find at least one form of *Rāmāyaṇa* performance that is between seven and eight centuries old. This is the *kuṭiyāṭṭam* dance drama of Kerala, with a repertory of three *Rāmāyaṇa* plays. Not all performance styles are as sophisticated as these Keralan exemplars, but stories from the *Rāmāyaṇa* have been told and sung as part of village culture since the fifteenth century in India,[18] while outside India the *Rāmāyaṇa* has been the platform of performance arts of vast complexity and popularity. What are these performance forms? Where and how are they produced? These questions have been addressed in *Rāmāyaṇa* scholarship for a long time, especially in relation to the arts of Southeast Asia. A more recent emphasis is on understanding how the process and the performance of the *Rāmāyaṇa*, their representational modes, and their contents resonate with public life and public concerns, and perhaps shape social and personal values. This critical interest is one that is strongly represented in the present volume.

The geographical areas covered here are South and Southeast Asia, especially India, Indonesia, Thailand, and Cambodia, where the *Rāmāyaṇa* in its various forms has become a part of the cultural idiom, with important implications for social and political life. Southeast Asian subjects of monarchical rule have drawn inspiration from the ancient legend to idealize Rāma as the model ruler, and by extension have reinforced obedience to the monarch, as in Thailand and Cambodia over the past two centuries. More interesting, elsewhere in Southeast Asia religious boundaries have been crossed to draw upon *Rāmāyaṇa* legends for identity formation or moral instruction. In Indonesia the story of Rāma has been fitted into the Islamic tradition, whereas in Thailand and Cambodia the Theravadins have not only identified Rāma and the Buddha as one and the same but have also brought a multitude of Hindu divinities from the *Rāmāyaṇa* into the Theravadin tradition.

Perhaps the surest proof of the "epic" quality of the *Rāmāyaṇa* is its adaptability to many artistic forms and many ethical and political positions, many of them equivocal and some mutually contradictory. Regional cultural imperatives have led to widely differing interpretations of the same episodes and characters, in addition to inventing altogether new ones. The *Rāmāyaṇa* has developed into a text of cultural hegemony, affecting a wide array of modes of expression from academic articles to folk art, sculpture, music, and theater, and adapting in the industrial age to film, comic books, and television across the continents. Its versions across many arts and national domains provide rich material to study cultural transfer, especially where significant departures from the narrative of moral schemes of the central tradition are found, as in retellings of episodes from the epic from women's points of view in recent dance dramas.[19]

Not surprisingly, textual studies in the *Rāmāyaṇa* constitute a substantial scholarly corpus. Comparative studies in the epic's textual history show how significantly, sometimes widely, its contents have varied. But even in this area much work has to be done, particularly with regional *Rāmāyaṇa*s, about many of which information is scarce and critical study uneven. For instance, the Bengali *Rāmāyaṇa* of Kṛttivāsa remains less examined than its phenomenal popularity and longevity among the Bengali-reading public would lead one to expect,[20] and the powerful version by the woman poet Candrāvatī of sixteenth-century Bengal has only recently begun to draw sustained critical attention.[21] This is not to disparage the studies that do exist in these areas, but to acknowledge the urgency of bringing under scholarly scrutiny the seemingly limitless adaptability of the *Rāmāyaṇa* to multiple imaginaries, including those dictated by class, race, gender, and geography. Pursuing this interest in the constant remaking of a cultural icon, the present volume expands its understanding of the "text" to include nonverbal renditions of the epic. Accordingly, one of its aims has been to reach across multiple disciplines to uncover the layering of "texts," showing for instance how the requirements of a performing art such as Indonesian shadow puppetry, or of a plastic art such as sculpture, interact with the narrative materials of the epic.

To take the kathakali dance style as a ready example, we may see how its stylistic conventions dictate the formation of gender identities such that the same emotional state, say grief at separation, appears differently in masculine and feminine personae. How then will the style affect the narration of the reunion of Rāma and Sītā after the fall of Rāvaṇa? How will the audience's understanding of the human drama, its ethical content, be affected by the manner in which the dance presents the episode? Will the style lend itself to Vālmīki's representation of Sītā's vocal outrage at Rāma's coarse rejection of her, or will it alter the episode into a portrayal of a meek Sītā finding solace in compliance, as in Tulsīdās's version? The making of meaning here is clearly problematic because of the moral and political ambiguities inherent in styles of representation and one that will clearly benefit from the availability of both literary and performance analyses. To this purpose it is necessary to correlate the way we understand what we read and the way we understand what we hear or see. That is why we take the position that examining the *Rāmāyaṇa* across a spectrum of art forms affords opportunities for a critical comprehension both deep and wide. This broad view also brings to attention how a literary artifact has evolved as an entire and self-sustaining cultural system. Without claiming to be exhaustive in its disciplinary coverage, this volume has chosen to emphasize approaches that support one another, in the editor's estimate, in uncovering multiple connections between the story, its retellers, and its audiences.

Unquestionably, there are other approaches that may lead to instructive insights in the *Rāmāyaṇa*. An obvious one is the sociological; for instance, the economics of the production of the *Rāmāyaṇa* is organically related to the politics of its dissemination. But not only is a compendium of methodologies impracticable (given the economics of publishing, for one thing!), it is also necessary to concede that the needs of a focused comprehension dictate selectivity. In this editor's judgment, explorations in performance, iconography, narrative design, and gender representation are approaches that dovetail effectively to create such a focus, because each demonstrates the process by which form and substance come together to construct meaning in relation to social, political, and cultural contexts.

Broadly speaking, the contributions to this volume address one or more of three areas of inquiry: the narrative structures of the *Rāmāyaṇa*; the types, techniques, and contents of performances; and the social content—particularly gender implications—of both narrative manipulations and representational forms. Although there are frequent crossovers between these areas, the essays aim at particular emphases. The collection begins with studies that focus on the literary text, first that of Vālmīki and then regional retellings. These are followed by essays that deal with revisions of commonly known narrative elements, whereby particular aesthetic or ethical values have been projected. That similar alterations also appear in performances is demonstrated by studies in dance dramas and musical performances from two regions of India, whereas two essays on the performing arts of Southeast Asia examine the political imperatives that underlie narrative choices and performance techniques. In order to keep in view the vast extent of renderings of the *Rāmāyaṇa*, three broad surveys of the visual and performance arts have been included.

Inevitably, there are overlaps between the studies presented here, because in choosing particular aspects of the *Rāmāyaṇa* the authors are keenly aware of the implications of their findings for other areas. Textual studies, for instance, are also studies in ideas of gender and power, and accounts of performances recognize the importance of narrative traditions. These crossovers are, in my judgment, the best argument for the principle on which this volume has been assembled, that is, the need for correlating separate areas of *Rāmāyaṇa* studies.

The first two articles of the volume are grounded in Vālmīki's *Rāmāyana*, the earliest text of the legend, and examine its relationship with the narrative and ideological tradition it initiated, especially in the context of the implications of its design. In his essay on resistance to the idolization of Rāma, Robert Goldman suggests that the undercutting of the ideological positions within Vālmīki's original narrative that modern studies in the *Rāmāyaṇa* identify as a powerful force in alternative *Rāmāyaṇas* is incipient in the original text itself. Noting the formative influence of the great epics of India on the construction of the South Asian ethos, especially on formulations of gender and power,

Goldman shows how the authority of Vālmīki's text is modulated by its rhetorical strategies. In his study of episodes from Vālmīki's original narrative that are built upon debates, and of the symbiosis of their rhetorical and conceptual texture, Goldman uncovers the narrative process by which ideologies of gender and power are formed. The "forensic encounters" between the major characters of the *Rāmāyaṇa*, Goldman argues, work toward enforcing adherence to the ethical and political ideals that emerge as dominant directives. However, since the narrative falters whenever the opposition embodied in these encounters becomes irreconcilable, Goldman views this as Vālmīki's own problematizing of women's subordination to the patriarchy, and raises the possibility that Vālmīki himself accommodates within his narrative a degree of resistance to hegemony.

The relationship between ideology and narrative design is also examined by Sally J. Sutherland Goldman in her study of the *Sundarakāṇḍa* of Vālmīki's *Rāmāyaṇa*, in which she correlates the representation of gender and space to show how they affect the narrative structure of the epic. Taking as examples Hanumān's heroic leap toward Laṅkā and his encounters with various figures, primarily Surasā and Śikhikā, on the way, Sutherland Goldman finds the episode an intentionally gendered narrative vital to the structural integrity of the *kāṇḍa*. In her view, the physical space in which the various episodes of the epic are set is systematically marked with gender attributes, and this marking is systematic, intentional, and necessary for the internal logic of the narrative.

These articles are followed by three studies, by William Smith, Mandakranta Bose, and Paula Richman, on regional versions of the *Rāmāyaṇa*, beginning with a broad review of eastern versions and continuing with explorations in aspects of particular revisions. William Smith's review of the forms and versions in which the *Rāmāyaṇa* appears in eastern India, specifically in Assam, Bengal, and Orissa since medieval times, shows that although these versions were derived from Vālmīki's Sanskrit poem, they are reflections of local religious and social influences. Tracing both bhakti and and *śākta* sources, such as the *Adhyātma Rāmāyaṇa*, Tulsīdās's devotional *Rāmāyaṇa*, and the *Adbhuta Rāmāyaṇa*, in the eastern *Rāmāyaṇas*, Smith argues that the story of Rāma thereby became the major and most widely accessible repository of religious and social ideas for mass audiences in eastern India.

The eastern tradition is placed within a narrower scope by Mandakranta Bose, who examines the representation of the feminine in Rāma tales in the culture of Bengal. Noting that whole episodes are invented in Kṛttivāsa's fifteenth-century Bengali *Rāmāyaṇa* to ascribe self-defining roles to women, Bose relates these changes to the dominance of the bhakti doctrine sweeping through the region. An even more sustained celebration of the idea of the mystical power of the feminine appears in the *Rāmāyaṇa* of the father-and-son team Jagadram and Ramprasad, in which Sītā is revealed as the embodiment of *devī* and brings about the final conquest of evil by defeating the thousand-headed Rāvaṇa, whom Rāma is unable to subdue. Here, as in Kṛttivāsa, the spiritual stance is that of bhakti, which dominates the Bengali narrative tradition of the Rāmakathā. Yet even within this tradition of devotion, a radically different voice is heard in the retelling of the epic in the eighteenth century by the woman poet Candrāvatī. A deeply religious woman herself, Candrāvatī nonetheless directs her sympathy toward Sītā, going so far as to turn the epic mainly into Sītā's story, but also that of Mandodarī's life and the poet's own as parallel legends of women's suffering. The evident subtext of Candrāvatī's writing is the miserable lot of women in general, which marks a distinctive trend in Bengali *Rāmāyanas*. Bose points out that the questioning of Rāma's actions, of Sītā's treatment in particular, is a common feature of Bengali Rāma tales. Even a retelling as devoted to celebrating Rāma's divinity as the early-nineteenth century bardic version by the renowned rural poet Dasharathi Ray indulges in occasional questioning of Rāma's justice. Later in the nineteenth century, Michael Madhusudan Datta revolutionzed the tradition of retelling the Rāmakathā in his Bengali epic inspired by Homer and Virgil, the *Meghanādavadha Kāvya*, which imported a secularized view into the tradition. His contempt for Rāma remains unmatched, but later Bengali writers have continued to undercut the conventional devotional stance in consistently satirical retellings. Putting to close scrutiny a short story and a farcical play for children, Bose shows how the *Rāmāyana* has been used in Bengal as both an instrument to question received tradition and a storehouse for narrative models.

Regional retellings also form the basis of Paula Richman's essay, in which she examines the interest found across south India in an episode originating in the *Uttarakāṇḍa* attributed to Vālmīki's *Rāmāyaṇa*. Among the actions for which Rāma has been most frequently criticized in south India, she notes, the story of the beheading of Śambūka, a low-caste ascetic, by Rāma stands out for the attention it has drawn. Three twentieth-century plays, one each in Tamil, Telugu, and Kannada, deal with the episode, reflecting in their revaluation of the main characters, their interaction, and the ethical implications of Rāma's action the vigorous debate on caste in south India in the first half of the twentieth century. All three depart from the original story in responding to the killing of Śambūka with horror and clear him from the taint of *adharma*, although in one of them the ending is radically changed from the Vālmīki original, and Śambūka is not killed by Rāma, who is envisioned by the playwright as a wise and compassionate ruler who rises above brahminical prejudice. The other two plays are critical of Rāma, one for his refusal to admit the spiritual equality of men, and the other for what it views as his political use of Śambūka's transgression to shut out low-caste people from institutions of privilege. Different as they are in their stands regarding Rāma, all three plays attempt to explain the complex motivations behind the brahminical prohibition against the practice of asceticism by a low-caste person, and all are ranged against that prohibition. Their treatment of the episode thus implies a critical response to the authority of texts. Describing both the arguments and the stage-history of the plays in detail, Richman develops the idea that the reiteration of the same episode in the plays and their longevity in south India suggests the centrality of caste-bound power relations in the region. With equal force, she points out that these modern dramatizations of the episode reveal the persistence of oppositional strands within the *Rāmāyaṇa* tradition. Here again we may see how the particular historical consciousness of a cultural region may crystallize in response to the *Rāmāyaṇa*, and how in the moral and narrative complexity of the *Rāmāyaṇa*, narrators can find matrices for organizing their own times and worlds, as indeed attested by contemporary authors.

One must, however, tread warily in entwining location and theme, and in identifying types of narrative alterations as distinctive regional characteristics, all the more because regional emphases are often easy to assume. For example, whereas the alternative *Rāmāyaṇas* from eastern India commonly emphasize the plight of women within the power relations authorized by the mainstream Rāma tales, the emphasis in the revisionist versions of south India seem to be on the racial oppression embedded in those relations. Do these regional patterns of emphasis reflect equally distinctive patterns of regional social experience? Are Bengali counternarratives mostly expressions of women's historical disempowerment and resistance, whereas Tamil, Telugu, and Kannada narratives are mostly reflections of the antibrahmanical sentiment of modern south India? Closer scrutiny urges caution, for contrary evidence often springs to mind—for instance, the existence of Telugu women's narrative songs. The fact is that not enough work has yet been done in historicizing regional *Rāmāyaṇa*s to warrant a ready answer, and there are indeed crossovers in patterns of emphasis among regional versions that preclude quick theorizing. In Telugu women's versions, the focus is on Sītā's suffering, not on racial oppression. On the other hand, in the Bengali story that Bose discusses in her essay, the satire targets both male and Aryan self-valorization. Thus, instead of looking for dominant regional characteristics it is perhaps more useful to examine the crossovers of theme and character modeling and the undercurrents that flow across cultural boundaries.

With the next two essays we turn to examples of the correlation between alterations in the narrative and shifts in the interpretation of episodes. These essays, the first by Philip Lutgendorf and the next by Heidi Pauwels, deal with episodes and characters from the *Rāmāyaṇa* in the north Indian tradition, as they appear in textual as well as performance traditions. They also address the gender representation in classical, medieval, and contemporary practices. Philip Lutgendorf focuses on Hanumān and his influence on the devotees of Rāma both in South and Southeast Asia and in the diaspora. Heidi Pauwels discusses in detail the impact of the televised *Rāmāyaṇa* in India and in the diaspora, comparing one of its highlighted episodes with its originals in Vālmīki and Tulasīdās.

The role of the *Rāmāyaṇa* in mirroring and reinforcing dominant ethical ideals is examined by Philip Lutgendorf, who traces the idealization of Hanumān in South and Southeast Asian societies, in textual as well as performance formats such as wrestling. He notes that although Hanumān is idolized as the perfect devotee in view of his celibacy, the misogyny inherent in the ideal of celibacy is recognized in folk retellings. Lutgendorf further shows how this recognition is countered in Southeast Asian folklore by fitting Hanumān into a householder lifestyle in which the human and the simian norms meet, and Hanumān is endowed with a piscine female as wife and a son. In the development of the Hanumān figure, then, we may see a problematic correlation between ascetic, romantic, and misogynist ideals that calls into question assumptions about gender roles and identities.

The relationship between narrative design and gender roles is studied by Heidi Pauwels in her essay, in which she compares three versions of the wedding of Rāma and Sītā as they appear in the Vālmīki *Rāmāyaṇa*, in Tulsīdās's *Rāmcaritmānas*, and the TV version by Ramanand Sagar. She shows how the classical, medieval, and contemporary portrayals differ from each other, and speculates about what meanings the refocusing of the narrative may hold for the cultural authority of contemporary mass media. Pauwels concludes that through the different periods from which she has followed the episode, its focus has shifted from duty to devotion, and from devotion to entertainment, although the message of wifely devotion has, if anything, gained greater currency and has solidified conventional gender paradigms.

The issue of gender paradigms prompts Velcheru Narayana Rao to ask how fixed a fictional character's identity can be when the character is recreated through multiple versions of the narrative. Narayana Rao notes that in comparison to other legendary women of India, such as Draupadī of the *Mahābhārata*, the *gopis* of the *Bhāgavata Purāṇa*, and the women characters of the *Kathā-sarit-sāgara*, Sītā has emerged as the epitome of wifely devotion and self-sacrifice, especially in the twentieth century. Her emergence as a model depends on certain signifiers, a crucial one being her insistence on following Rāma into exile. But can her identity remain inviolate if some of these signifiers are omitted? Just as a change in phonemes in a word changes the word itself, could changes in the array of episodes that feature Sītā change the very idea of Sītā? Drawing upon several retellings of the *Rāmāyṇa* and the more recent tradition of "anti-*Rāmāyaṇa*" texts, Narayana Rao attempts to discover the boundaries that hold together the idea of Sītā even as they permit innovations in representing her.

Innovations in both plot construction and gender representation are examined by Bruce Sullivan with regard to the *kuṭiyāṭṭam* theater of Kerala, in which three classical Sanskrit plays feature prominently. He points out that all of them capitalize on departures from Vālmīki's text and are tailored to the unique features of the *kuṭiyāṭṭam* style of acting, which affect the representation of the story. In this performance idiom, which can be traced back to the tenth century, characters mimic the psychological states and actions of other characters across lines of gender and species (such as Rāvaṇa enacting Sītā's moods, or Hanumān enacting Rāma's), whereby gender identities in particular are loosened from those set by Vālmīki. In his study, Sullivan shows how the *kuṭiyāṭṭam* performance tradition transforms the plot of the epic and challenges the audience to relish complex, multiple-identity characters.

One of the many performance modes in which the *Rāmāyaṇa* has appeared is considered in the next essay by Vidyut Aklujkar, who describes a musical adaptation of the *Rāmāyaṇa* from Maharashtra. Created in the early 1950s for radio audiences, the *Gīta-Rāmāyaṇa* was a series of fifty-six songs in the Marathi language set to music in the classical style. Broadcast every week, the program quickly won large audiences at the time, and more recently it has again become popular at home and abroad. Such was its popularity that the composer began to perform the songs to live audiences and continued to do so through a twenty-five-year stretch. He was followed by other singers elsewhere in India and, more recently, in North America. Attempting to explain the instant success and enduring appeal of the series, Aklujkar balances the creative genius of both the creator and the singer against the intrinsic strengths of the *Rāmāyaṇa*, noting that the musical series has become a defining identifier of the culture that produced it.

With the next two essays we not only move out of Indian forms of the *Rāmāyana* but also move toward understanding its discursive instrumentality in social and political exchange. Whereas Laurie Sears delves into the historical and evolutionary process of the movement of *Rāmāyaṇa* story in Indonesia and its religious and political implications, Kaja McGowan undertakes a topical and contemporary inquiry into the use of the story in East Timor as a framework within which the nation's troubled and erased history is being reconstructed. Sears argues that cross-cultural traffic between Hindu-Javanese social and religious practices, on the one hand, and those of the Muslim immigrants who arrived in the eighteenth century, on the other, have resulted in a synthesis in which Javanese shadow puppeteers not only find audiences for Hindu myths across religious boundaries but also adapt *Mahābhārata* puppets to tell *Rāmāyaṇa* stories. The process, Sears states, subverts the linearity of the *Rāmāyaṇa* but builds a discourse in which the puppets serve as material objects that encode ideas of character, ethics, behavior, and morals.

The use of the *Rāmāyaṇa* as a mediating artifact between politics and semiotics is examined by Kaja McGowan in her essay on the conservation and interpretation of history in East Timor. In its violent history, mapmaking has often turned into a military contest, obliterating the actuality of public experience and history which, McGowan believes, may nonetheless be recovered through silent objects as witnesses. In East Timor, the historical experience of foreign domination and destruction is sought to be recovered, interpreted, and validated within an allegorical framework supplied by the theme of Sītā's abduction by Rāvaṇa, which is conveyed through a unique artistic medium, that of intricately embossed shell casings depicting the *Rāmāyaṇa* episode. McGowan argues that this ekphrastic entry into sites of domination and contest from which conventional language has been erased has been made possible by the availability of the *Rāmāyaṇa* as a narrative model.

The place of the *Rāmāyaṇa* in the performing arts of Southeast Asia is assessed by Julie Mehta in her survey of the performance traditions of Thailand and Cambodia, which traces their roots, their evolution, and their impact on contemporary cultural and social life. While the epic has been the single richest source of inspiration for sculpture, it exists in a more dynamic relationship with the indigenous cultures of Southeast Asia in dance dramas. Mehta observes that though these performance forms are deeply rooted in the original Indian narrative, their plot and characters are altered to fit the specific psyche and artistic traditions of the Thai-Khmer social milieu. This has occasionally resulted in significant deviations from the Indian sources in the construction of plot and character, leading to substantially different ethical points of view.

As a wrap-up to the volume, Kapila Vatsyayan's essay offers a wide-ranging inquiry into the role of the *Rāmāyaṇa* in shaping the arts of South and Southeast Asia since early times, which leads her to a many-layered argument about the nature of the formative role of the *Rāmāyaṇa* in artistic production; of the relationship between the literary, visual, and kinetic arts; of the criteria for the selection of themes and narrative elements in the arts; and of the interdependence of content and medium. Along with an extensive inventory of the visual and plastic arts, especially painting and sculpture, in India, Cambodia, Thailand, Laos, Malayasia, Burma, Java, and Bali, she lists literary versions in different languages and from religious traditions other than the Hindu, such as the Buddhist and the Jain. Noting that across the vast terrain of Asian arts the representation of the *Rāmāyaṇa* has varied widely, and that attitudes to themes and protagonists have changed over time even as the presence of the epic remains unchallenged, Vatsyayan suggests that this process of dynamic cultural negotiation may revolve around an indispensable thematic core to generate countless variants. As a parallel to this process, she posits an interaction between a regionwide model and its local retooling. This view of a dynamic of diversity leads her to ask whether the varied expressions of the epic reveal a specifically Asian aesthetic. As a supplement to her observations, Vatsyayan provides in an appendix an inventory of the visual and plastic arts, especially painting and sculpture, of India, Cambodia, Thailand, Laos, Malayasia, Burma, Java, and Bali, as well as of literary versions in different languages and from different religious traditions, such as Buddhist and Jain, in addition to the Hindu heritage.

As acknowledged at the beginning of this introduction, the essays presented here neither cover the entire field they explore nor offer the last words on their subjects. But as parts of a joint venture, they attempt to demonstrate the critical importance of correlating the varied identities of a work of the epic imagination. In doing so, these studies not only take fresh critical positions but reaffirm the centrality of the *Rāmāyaṇa* to humanist scholarship. Vālmīki's ancient prediction still holds true:

Yāvaccandradivākarau dyuloke pracariṣyataḥ /
Tāvad Rāmāyaṇikathā bhūloke pracariṣyati//

> As long as the sun and the moon reign in the sky, the story of Rāma will continue to reign on earth.

It is hoped that the present volume will help to extend this singular longevity of the *Rāmāyaṇa* by probing the sources of its vigor.

NOTES

1. Leaving aside the wealth of journal articles, the full, book-length works over the past twenty years include: Brockington 1984; Goldman et al. 1984–in progress;

Hart and Heifetz 1988; Lutgendorf 1991; Smith 1988; Thiel-Horstmann 1991; Richman 1991 and 2001; and van der Veer 1988.

2. A full inventory of dramatic and film renditions of Rāma tales is not yet available, but stage and film versions have been made by major figures in the performing arts such as Uday Shankar, Shanti Bardhan, Rukmini Devi Arundale, and Utpal Dutt. Critical work on the Rāmlīlā is more substantial, and the recent literature includes Parkhill 1993; Schechner and Hess 1993; Bonnemaison and Macy 1990; Kapur 1990; Sax 1990; and Hess 1983. Although Sooraj Barjatya's 1995 hit film, *Hum aapke hain kaun?* (Who am I to you?) was not a *Rāmāyaṇa* remake, it closely paralleled an idealized pattern of family relationships and values.

3. V. Dalmia-Luderitz 1991.

4. Davis 1996; Lutgendorf 1995; Pollock 1993; Datta 1993; and Thapar 1989.

5. My emphasis on the public nature of this subscription is deliberate and reflects some doubt as to private engagement with the *Rāmāyaṇa*; almost none of the households canvassed in Vancouver in 2002 reported possession of a copy.

6. *The Legend of Prince Rama: Ramayana.* Produced by Nippon Ramayana Films and directed by Yugo Sako and Vijay Nigam. An international venture, the DVD is marketed by a Malaysian company from Kuala Lumpur and carries the announcement, "Ramayana Goes Where Aladdin Never Dared"!

7. As illustrated, for instance, in Thiel-Horstmann 1991; Singh and Datta 1993; and Richman 2001.

8. See, for instance, Kumar 1995.

9. As an example of such labors we may cite the work of Nilmadhab Sen, who published eighteen articles between 1949 and 1957, sixteen of them on grammar. Camille Bulcke's work on recensions of the Vālmīki *Rāmāyaṇa*, Edward W. Hopkins's on narrative parallels, and M. V. Kibe's on the historicity of Laṅkā, remain models of scholarship.

10. For some early notices, see Sen 1920; Raghuvira and Yamamoto 1938 and Raghavan 1961. Suniti Kumar Chatterji discussed *Rāmāyaṇas* from India, China, Japan, and Southeast Asia extensively in his Bengali writings scattered through numerous periodicals from the late 1920s onward and collected as a posthumous "résumé" in *The Rāmāyaṇa*, 1978. Extensive studies in comparative mythology were done by Sukumar Sen, especially in his Bengali work, *Rāmakathāra Prāk-Itihāsa*, 1977.

11. Rabindranath Tagore 1961.

12. Raghavan 1980; Sahai 1981; and Srinivasa Iyengar 1983.

13. The phrase is Datta's own, from a letter to his friend Rajnarayan Basu, c. 1861. On Datta's oppositional stance, see C. Seeley, "The Raja's New Clothes: Redressing Rāvaṇa in *Meghanādavadha Kāvya*," in Richman 1991. Clifford Hospital discusses a similar elevation of Rāvaṇa to heroic status in C. N. Srikantan Nayar's Malayalam play, *Laṅkālakṣmī nāṭakam*; see C. Hospital, "Rāvaṇa as Tragic Hero: C. N. Srikantan Nayar's *Laṅkālakṣmī*," in Thiel-Horstmann 1991.

14. See, among others, V. Narayana Rao, "A *Rāmāyaṇa* of Their Own: Women's Oral Tradition in Telugu," in Richman 1991. Substantial work on women's *Rāmāyaṇas* was outlined by Nabaneeta Dev Sen in her Radhakrishnan Memorial Lectures at Oxford University in May 1997 (unpublished).

15. Useful surveys are offered in Raghavan 1980; see especially H. B. Sarkar, "The Migration of the *Rāmāyaṇa* Story to Indonesia"; Amin Sweeney, "The Malaysian *Rāmāyaṇa* in Performance"; J. R. Francisco, "The Ramayana in the Philippines"; Chamlong Sarapadnuke, "*Rāmāyaṇa* in Thai Theatre"; Kamala Ratnam, "The Ramayana in Laos"; S. Sahai, "The Khvay Thuaraphi"; U Than Han and U Khin Zaw, "*Rā-*

māyaṇa in Burmese Literature and Arts"; and J. Tilakasiri, "*Rāmāyaṇa* in Sinhala Literature and Its Folk Version."

16. My own survey of the *Rāmāyaṇa* in the performing arts of India is in its initial stage.

17. The festival has been extensively documented and examined by Blackburn 1996.

18. A valuable discussion of the correlation of the dramatic and the visual appears in a study of the *yātrā* performances of (mainly) rural Bengal by Abanindranath Tagore 1969. Rabindranath Tagore's nephew, Abanindranath (d. 1951) was the leading figure of the Bengal School of art.

19. For instance, a dance based on the life of Sītā by Mallika Sarabhai, and *Sītāyaṇa*, a dance drama by the Canadian dancer Menaka Thakkar.

20. A notable exception is a study by Tony K. Stewart and Edward C. Dimock, "Krttibāsa's Apophatic Critique of Rāma's Kingship," in Richman 2001.

21. Dev Sen 2000.

REFERENCES

Blackburn, Stuart H. *Inside the Drama-House.* Berkeley and Los Angeles: University of California Press.

Bonnemaison, S., and C. Macy. 1990. "The Ramlila in Ramnagar." *Design Quarterly* 147.

Brockington, John. 1984. *Righteous Rāma: The Evolution of an Epic.* Delhi: Oxford University Press.

Chatterji, Suniti Kumar. 1978. *The Rāmāyaṇa: Its Character, Genesis, History, Expansion and Exodus.* Calcutta: Prajñā.

Dalmia-Luderitz, V. 1991. "Television and Tradition: Some Observations on the Serialization of the *Rāmāyaṇa.*" In *Rāmāyaṇa and Rāmāyaṇas,* edited by M. Thiel-Horstmann. Wiesbaden: Otto Harrasowitz.

Datta, P. K. 1993. "VHP's Ram: The Hindutva Movement in Ayodhya." In *Hindus and Others,* edited by Gyanendranath Pandey. New Delhi: Viking.

Davis, R. H. 1996. "The Iconography of Rama's Chariot." In *Contesting the Nation: Religion, Community, and the Politics of Democracy in India.* Philadelphia: University of Pennsylvania Press.

Dev Sen, N. 2000. "Candrāratī *Rāmāyaṇa*: Feminizing the Rāma-Tale," in M. Bose, ed., *Faces of the Feminine in Ancient, Medieval, and Modern India* (New York: Oxford University Press, 2000).

Goldman, Robert P., et al., eds. and trans. 1984–in progress. *The Rāmāyaṇa of Vālmīki: An Epic of Ancient India.* Princeton: Princeton University Press.

Hart, George L., and Hank Heifetz, eds. and trans. 1988. *The Forest Book of the Rāmāyaṇa of Kampaṉ.* Berkeley and Los Angeles: University of California Press.

Hertel, B. R., and C. A. Humes, eds. 1993. *Living Banaras.* Albany: State University of New York Press.

Hess, Linda. 1983. "*Ram Lila*: The Audience Experience." In *Bhakti in Current Research, 1979–1982,* edited by M. Thiel-Horstmann, Berlin: Dietrich Reimer.

Kapur, Anuradha. 1990. *Actors, Pilgrims, Kings and Gods: The Ramlila at Ramnagar.* Calcutta: Seagull.

Kumar, Nita. 1995. "Class and Gender Politics in the Ramlila." In *The Gods at Play,* edited by William Sax. New York: Oxford University Press.

Lutgendorf, Philip. 1991. *The Life of a Text: Performing the Rāmcaritmānas of Tulsidas.* Berkeley and Los Angeles: University of California Press.

———. 1995. "Interpreting Ramraj: Reflections on the 'Ramayana,' Bhakti and Hindu Nationalism." In *Bhakti Religion in North India: Community Identity and Political Action,* edited by D. Lorenzen. Albany: State University of New York Press.

Parkhill, Thomas. 1993. "What's Taking Place: Neighbourhood *Rāmlīlās* in Banaras." In B. R. Hertel and C. A. Humes, eds., *Living Banaras.* Albany: State University of New York Press.

Pollock, Sheldon. 1993. "*Rāmāyaṇa* and Political Imagination in India." *Journal of Asian Studies* 52.2 (May).

Raghavan, V. 1961. *Some Old Lost Rāma Plays.* Annamalainagar: Annamalai University.

———, ed. 1980. *The Rāmāyaṇa Tradition in Asia.* New Delhi: Sahitya Akademi.

Raghuvira and Chikiyo Yamamoto. 1938. *Rāmāyaṇa in China.* Nagpur: International Academy of Indian Culture.

Richman, Paula, ed. 1991. *Many Rāmāyaṇas: The Diversity of a Narrative Tradition in South Asia.* Berkeley and Los Angeles: University of California Press.

———. 2001. *Questioning Rāmāyaṇas: A South Asian Tradition.* Berkeley and Los Angeles: University of California Press.

Sahai, S., ed. 1981. *Rāmāyaṇa in South East Asia.* Gaya: Centre for South East Asian Studies.

Sax, William. 1990. "The Ramnagar Ramlila: Text, Performance, Pilgrimage." *History of Religions* 30.2.

Schechner, R., and L. Hess. 1993. "Crossing the Water: Pilgrimage, Movement and Environmental Scenography of the *Ramlila* of Ramnagar." In B. R. Hertel and C. A. Humes, eds., *Living Banaras.* Albany: State University of New York Press.

Sen, Dineshchandra. 1920. *The Bengali Ramayanas.* Calcutta: University of Calcutta.

Sen, Sukumar. 1977. *Rāmakathāra Prāk-Itihāsa* [The prehistory of the Rāma legend]. Calcutta: Jijñāsā.

Singh, K. S., and B. N. Datta, eds. 1993. *Rama-Katha in Tribal and Folk Traditions of India.* Calcutta: Anthropological Survey of India, and Seagull Books.

Smith, W. L. 1988. *Rāmāyaṇa Traditions in Eastern India: Assam, Bengal, Orissa.* Stockholm: Department of Indology, University of Stockholm.

Srinivasa Iyengar, K. R., ed. 1983. *Variation in Rāmāyaṇa in Asia.* New Delhi: Sahitya Akademi.

Tagore, Rabindranath. 1961. *Java Yatrira Patra* [Letters from a traveler in Java]. In *Rabindra Racanāvalī* [Collected works], centenary edition, vol. 10. Calcutta: Government of West Bengal.

Thapar, R. 1989. "The Ramayana Syndrome." *Seminar* 353.

Thiel-Horstmann, M., ed. 1991. *Rāmāyaṇa and Rāmāyaṇas.* Wiesbaden: Otto Harrasowitz.

Van der Veer, Peter. 1988. *Gods on Earth: The Management of Religious Experience and Identity in a North Indian Pilgrimage Centre.* London: Athlone Press.

I

Resisting Rāma: Dharmic Debates on Gender and Hierarchy and the Work of the *Vālmīki Rāmāyaṇa*

Robert P. Goldman

The great epics of India have been a source of almost continual fascination on the part of Indologists since knowledge of the Sanskrit language and its rich literary and religio-philosophical history became widely available to European scholarship at around the turn of the nineteenth century. Even now, at the turn of the twenty-first century, that fascination shows no sign of slackening. On the contrary, Indian epic studies seem to have been undergoing a revival or sorts with the recent appearance of an abundance of new translations, monographs, and collections of scholarly papers concerned with one or both of the poems or with their reworkings, retellings, and transformations into a variety of languages and sociopolitical contexts.[1]

Some of these works, particularly some of the essays collected by Richman and Bose, have come to grips with the important role these texts have had in South Asian constructions and institutions that involve gender, power, hierarchy, and authority. Yet, for all of this profusion of important scholarly production, only a relatively small proportion of this work has attempted to subject the epics to a close and careful rhetorical analysis in an effort to shed light on the ways in which these texts came to have the considerable influence on the formation of social attitudes and structures with and for which they are so often alternately credited and condemned, depending on the political stance of the authors.

A number of recent studies of the *Rāmāyaṇa*, for example, have focused on the important and neglected topic of folk and vernacular versions of the Rāma story in which the hegemonic discourses of patriarchy and social hierarchy that lie close to the heart of Vālmīki's

Rāmāyaṇa are contested or resisted in a variety of subaltern and/or regional retellings. Studies in this arena have recently appeared in a number of collections and monographs such as Paula Richman's *Many Rāmāyaṇas* and her *Questioning Rāmāyaṇas*, Monika Thiel-Horstmann's *Rāmāyaṇa and Rāmāyaṇas*, and William Smith's *Rāmāyaṇa Traditions in Eastern India*.

One assumption underlying many of these studies is that Vālmīki's monumental epic speaks monovalently for the brahmanical elites of ancient and medieval India, making little room available for discourses that run counter to the hegemonic and comprehensive regimes of patriarchal dominance and the *varṇāśramadharma* (the duties of members of each *varṇa* in the four stages of life). In this way, the *ādikāvya* ("first poem," the *Rāmāyaṇa*) is understood to be in significant contrast with the closely intertextual *Mahābhārata*,[2] where culturally normative regimes of power, gender, religion, and social hierarchy are at times powerfully ambiguous and contested. Under no circumstances would it be correct to attempt to underestimate the significance of this contrast. On the other hand, there are a number of what might be called "leakages" from the supposedly hermetic value system of Vālmīki that provide the narrative space within which the epic story with all of its moral and social didacticism can both move forward and engage its audience. This leakage affords, as well, an opportunity for us to read the epic "against the grain," as it were, and to try thereby to recover some of the voices that the dominant discourse pushes to the margins.

The present essay then will examine some episodes in Vālmīki's poem in which characters representing varying degrees of "subalternity" question or contest the dominant ideology of the poet and his central hero. It will argue that a close and careful reading of the debates that are framed within the narrative, as well as some of its silences, will illuminate the ideological underpinnings of this monumental work and its role in the formation of the culture and society of South Asia. In short, I will attempt to take the poem's debates seriously, listening carefully to the substantive points and rhetorical strategies of the poet and his characters while paying close attention to the social realities that underlie them. In this way I will try to unpack the ideologies of gender and power that lend the epic much of its social and historical impact. In so doing, I hope to be able to add to our understanding of what, with a bow to Obeyesekere, I call the "work" of the epic.[3] By this I refer not so much to the kind of symbolic remove through which dreams and cultural productions enable individuals and societies to work through tabooed or repressed psychic formations as to the workmanlike forensic strategies by means of which the epic poet is able to dramatize, work through, and disseminate his representation of some of the most critical concerns of the traditional culture of India's elites.

It must be understood, in undertaking such a reading of the epic, that the effort is necessarily bedeviled, like any subaltern reading of an elite document, by the problems inherent in reading an author against him or herself and seeking to read, in some cases, between the *ślokas*. Moreover, if we have learned anything from the long history of textual exegesis and the much shorter one of modern cultural studies, no text really speaks unambiguously for itself, and all readings of all texts are themselves contingent acts of interpretation. This must be even more the case with a text like the *Vālmīki Rāmāyaṇa*, concerning whose authorship virtually nothing of a genuinely historical nature is known and which is, in any case, a text that cannot be confidently ascribed to a single author or even a single historical period. For the epic has grown with the culture it has served, adding and changing episodes and passages, incorporating and preserving ideologies and, above all, serving as the foundation for a massive cultural edifice of commentary, interpretation, refiguration, and performance that is one of the most characteristic features and indeed one of the wonders of Indian civilization.

If, with regard to social norms, the *Mahābhārata* is an epic of violation, of irreducible conflicts between cultural imperatives and the subversion of them, and a brooding meditation on rupture and decay, the *Rāmāyaṇa* stands in sharp contrast to it as a paean to conformity, obedience, and as a handbook of social integration. This difference is the basis for the differential treatment of the poems in the traditional South Asian and specifically Hindu contexts. Yet it is the *Rāmāyaṇa*'s very quality of social normativity, and its resulting status as the family text par excellence and the ideal medium for the acculturation of children, that makes even its smaller leakages all the more significant and noticeable.

From a structural perspective, the epic poem in its received form seems almost to play with the issues of normativity and transgressivity in its very framing narrative; in the poem's *upodghāta* or narrative preface, we see the two sharply juxtaposed and creatively combined to make the epic poem, in form and substance, possible.

The preface opens with one of the culture's most elaborate and well-known celebrations of the idealized South Asian male. Here Vālmīki, a forest sage, but not yet the "first poet," questions the divine seer Nārada as to the existence in the world of their time of an ideal man in terms of his moral, physical, and intellectual qualities.

> *ko nv asmin sāmpratam loke guṇavān kaś ca vīryavān /*
> *dharmajñaś ca kṛtajñaś ca satyavākyo dṛḍhavrataḥ //*
> *cāritreṇa ca ko yuktaḥ sarvabhūteṣu ko hitaḥ /*
>
> *vidvān kaḥ kaḥ samarthaś ca kaś caikapriyadarśanaḥ //*
> *ātmavān ko jitakrodho matimān ko 'nasūyakaḥ /*
> *kasya bibhyati devāś ca jātaroṣasya saṃyuge //*[4]

> Is there a man in the world today who is truly virtuous? Who is there who is mighty and yet knows both what is right and how to act upon it? Who always speaks the truth and holds firmly to his vows? Who exemplifies proper conduct and is benevolent to all creatures? Who is learned, capable, and a pleasure to behold? Who is

> self-controlled, having subdued his anger? Who is both judicious and free from envy? Who, when his fury is aroused in battle, is feared even by the gods? (*VR* 1.1.2–4)

After a moment's thought, Nārada responds with ten verses in which he identifies the Kosalan king Rāma as such a person, elaborating on Vālmīki's terms in such a way as to leave his audience in no doubt that what is to follow will be nothing less than a kind of ancient Indian *Book of Virtues*.[5]

The seer follows his dense description of Rāma's qualities with a terse account of his tragic career, a brief description of his utopian reign, and an account of the differing benefits that accrue to the members of the four great *varṇas* of Aryan social classes from hearing his story.[6] All of this takes him fewer than sixty verses.

But if the substance of the epic is laid out in this, its opening chapter (*sarga*), saturated with the all-important notion of dharma, its form is to emerge only through a rupture in the fabric of the normative. For immediately after hearing the edifying tale of Rāma and its soothing conclusion, the sage makes his way through the beautiful forest to a pleasant ford (*tīrtha*) on the banks of the nearby Tamasā River for his ritual bath. There he becomes enraptured by the natural beauty of the place until his attention becomes focused on a charming pair of mating cranes. But his delight suddenly turns to horror as a tribal hunter emerges from the woods to shoot and kill the male bird. Witnessing this violent disruption of the quiet sylvan scene and hearing the piteous wailing of the hen-crane, the sage is filled with a mixture of pity and rage. Denouncing this transgression (*adharmo 'yam*) of the norms of civilized conduct, Vālmīki utters his famous curse through which his grief (*śoka*) is transmuted into a new medium of expression, *śloka*, poetry. Through the intercession of Lord Brahmā, this new form, born of a moment of rupture and violation, will serve as the medium for the poetic rendering of Nārada's tale, even as it foreshadows its underlying theme of separation and its central aesthetic-emotive tenor, of pity, *karuṇarasa*.[7]

With this by way of my own *upodghāta*, let me now turn to a discussion of some of the seminal passages in the longer poem in which this dialectic of norm and transgression is articulated in a series of dialogues or debates in which the violation of some central norm of dharmic conduct is posed as a kind of *pūrvapakṣa* (premise) and the norm itself put forward to trump it as it were in the form of a *siddhāntapakṣa* (conclusion). These are not, I should note at the outset, merely dummy debates designed to provide an opportunity for the reiteration of a series of cultural clichés. Rather they offer us a glimpse into some significant social and ethical tensions that the epic was designed, in part, to resolve.

These debates involve a variety of parties who represent different genders and positions within the traditional pattern of hierarchical relationships. In most but not all cases, they are resolved in favor of the figure with higher status, and in most but again not all cases, the position most closely congruent with dharma will prevail. In several cases, however, the questions of status and dharma are sufficiently complex or debatable to make the arguments interesting. In a number of cases, the debates hinge upon and are in a sense fundamentally about hierarchy as the critical element in the formulation of the hegemonic discourses of *varṇāśramadharma* and gender.

Several of these debates do not involve Rāma directly but serve to establish some critical parameters of dharma and social relations before the narrative of the epic proper even begins. An instructive example is the confrontation between Rāma's father, the aged King Daśaratha, and the fearsome king turned brahman seer, the irascible Viśvāmitra, when the latter comes to request the deputation of young Rāma to guard his sacrifice from the depredations of the *rākṣasas*.[8] The episode involves the clash of public duty and personal emotion that so often bedevils the heroes of the Indian epics. Here Daśaratha's overprotective concern for the darling child of his old age leads him to attempt to rebel against two of the most powerful rules of the patriarchal culture of honor that so deeply saturates the epics. These are unquestioning deference and obedience to brahmanical renunciants and unhesitating adherence to one's given word.

The episode begins with the arrival of the irascible sage Viśvāmitra at the Kosalan court. The king is, naturally, delighted at the honor bestowed upon him by the visit of so august a personage, and greets him with an extravagant encomium. He compares the sage's arrival to the falling of rain in a desert and the birth of a son to a childless man. He declares that the sage's visit is proof that he himself has lived a virtuous life and that it represents nothing short of the fruition of his very birth.[9] So effusive, in fact, is the king's welcome that he unthinkingly goes too far, promising to fulfil faithfully any request the sage might make of him without even pausing to ascertain the actual purpose of his visit. He tells Viśvāmitra, "You should not hesitate about what you wish done, Kauśika. I will carry it out fully, for you are as a god to me."[10]

Now apart from the dramatic foreshadowing here of the account of how Daśaratha will get into even more trouble over his predilection for writing this kind of blank check, the episode to this point is merely one more example of the nearly hysterical deference to the holy man that becomes the norm in Sanskrit literature. What follows, however, is a pointed illustration of the kinds of rupture in the standard models that actually drive the epic narratives.

Delighted with this deferential reception, and yet perhaps anticipating Daśaratha's discomfort, the sage praises the king and adjures him to be true to his promise (*satyapratiśravaḥ*). He then reveals that he has come to demand that Rāma accompany him to the wilderness to fight off the dreaded *rākṣasa* minions of the demon king Rāvaṇa.[11] But once the king hears what the sage actually wants, he forgets all about his generous promise. He first begs that Rāma be spared this dangerous duty and finally flatly refuses to hand him over.[12] Viśvāmitra is infuriated by the retraction of his promise and rebukes him sharply, crying, "First you promise something, then you want to take back the promise! This turnabout is unworthy of the House of the Rāghavas. If you think that this is proper, your majesty, then I will go just as I came, and you Kākutstha, may rejoice with your kinsmen as one whose word is false (*mithyāpratijñaḥ*)."[13]

To emphasize that the displeasure of a powerful person like Viśvāmitra is not to be taken lightly, the poet notes in the following verse that "Now when wise Viśvāmitra was seized with fury in this way, the whole earth shook and fear gripped the gods."[14]

The situation has now come to a moment of crisis for which the poet is not yet prepared, and he must therefore act to defuse this potentially explosive conflict. He does so through the introduction of yet another immensely powerful patriarchal figure, Daśaratha's venerable family priest (*purohita*) and Viśvāmitra's ancient archrival, the sage (*ṛṣi*) Vasiṣṭha. The latter intervenes, reassuring the king about Viśvāmitra's mastery of supernatural weaponry and his consequent power to protect Rāma against even the most formidable foes. Comforted by his infallible guru, the king relents. He releases Rāma into the care of Viśvāmitra, and the prince sets forth on his adventurous career.[15]

Now one might well ask what the purpose of this episode is. What is the significance of Daśaratha's anguished retraction of his spoken word since, as it happens, he ultimately relents and accedes to the sage's request, as he had promised to do in the first place? After all, the king's histrionics and the sage's wrath appear to have absolutely no consequences for the continuing narrative. Rāma is not prevented from going forth on the critical quest that will gain him potent weaponry and culminate in his marriage to Sītā, nor is the king cursed for his recalcitrance. Still, it would be wrong to conclude that the passage is without significance. For it serves to reinforce the valuation of deference both to the brahman sage as a kind of earthly divinity and to the abstract concept of truth above the personal and the emotional. In this it foreshadows the aged king's future crisis and perhaps, most critically, establishes for the first time that Daśaratha, heretofore characterized as the ideal of Hindu kingship, has, in actuality, feet of clay. For he displays here a critical tendency to permit emotion to steer him away from the path of righteousness and sound policy. In this he is constructed as a significant contrast to Rāma, who, in almost all critical instances, will consistently place his sense of adherence to truth, dharma, and his public duty ahead of his emotions and personal concerns.

With this as a background, let me turn to some of the well-known debates in which Rāma engages which, even as they serve to reinforce the dominant ideologies of gender and class hierarchy, nonetheless, by the very fact of their being framed as debates, open up a window onto the universe of counter-discourse, social order, and resistance.

Surely the most complex and revealing debate around the issue of the potential conflict between personal loyalties and adherence to the abstract principles of truth and dharma is embodied in the series of emotionally wrought conversations involving Rāma, his brother Lakṣmaṇa, his mother Kausalyā, and his wife Sītā concerning whether Rāma should obey his father's order that he be banished and if so, who should accompany him into exile. These discussions, which in many ways lie close to the ethical, moral, social, and political core of the poem, occupy no fewer than twelve *sargas* (17–28) of the *Ayodhyākāṇḍa*.

The debates begin in earnest when Lakṣmaṇa, after hearing Kausalyā's lamentations at the news of her son's banishment, expresses his defiance of Daśaratha's edict and his intention to help his brother seize the throne by force. His motive is unambiguously that of personal loyalty to Rāma, but his argument is framed in terms of righteousness and political exigency.[16] He argues in essence that the king's order is illegitimate because Rāma, the presumptive heir to the throne, has committed no offense that would justify his being passed over for the succession. Moreover, he asserts, Daśaratha's rash and unrighteous command, issued to please a woman, is simply proof of his perversity, enslavement to sensuality, and senility. The king is thus unfit to rule, and his order should therefore be regarded as having no force.[17] Lakṣmaṇa proposes nothing short of a military coup, in the course of which he intends to slaughter any and all who might support the claim of Bharata. In brief, Lakṣmaṇa argues here for a higher order of dharma as well as for the realpolitik of the warrior ethos (*kṣatradharma*) in stark opposition to the imperatives of filial deference and adherence to truth that have governed Rāma's acquiescence in his dispossession.

The situation becomes more complex, however, when, before Rāma can respond to Lakṣmaṇa, his mother Kausalyā thrusts herself into the debate. She urges Rāma not to abandon her and to ignore the unrighteous (*adharmya*) orders of Kaikeyī.[18] She then seeks to wrest the dharmic high ground from Rāma by urging a version of filial piety gendered differently from the one that is motivating her son. She appeals to him in a verse noteworthy for its heavy iteration of the term *dharma*.

> *dharmajña yadi dharmiṣṭho dharmaṃ caritum icchasi /*
> *śuśrūṣa mām ihasthas tvaṃ cara dharmam anuttamam //*

> You understand dharma and if you wish to carry out dharma as someone well grounded in dharma, you must stay here and obey me. You must carry out the supreme dharma. (*VR* 2.18.19)

Kausalyā then puts the matter quite bluntly, opposing her authority as a mother to the paternal authority of Daśaratha. She cites the example (untraceable in the literature) of Kāśyapa, who, by obeying his mother's command (presumably to remain at home), nonetheless managed to acquire unequaled ascetic powers and attain the highest heaven.[19] She then makes the claim to equal authority with Daśaratha, laying it on the line in the form of an ultimatum.

> *yathaiva rājā pūjyas te gauraveṇa tathā hy aham /*
> *tvāṃ nānujānāmi na gantavyam ito vanam //*

> "I am just as much to be revered and respected by you as is the king. I do not give you leave. You may not go away to the forest." (*VR* 2.18.21)

In the end Kausalyā reinforces her refusal to let Rāma go with the time-honored threat of fasting herself to death should he disobey her, noting that if that were to happen, he like the divinity of the ocean through a similar but unexplained act of *adharma*, would incur the guilt of *brahmahatyā*. This last statement is particularly significant in its effort to force the issue by regendering the transgression, equating disobedience to the mother with the culture's ultimate and most unpardonable violation (*mahāpātaka*) of brahmanical patriarchy, the cardinal sin of killing the arch patriarch.[20]

In brahmanical culture, with its powerful valorization of maternal authority as shown by the equivalence of the injunctions *mātṛdevo bhava* (treat your mother like a god) and *pitṛdevo bhava* (treat your father like a god)[21] the *Mahābhārata*'s tale of the Pāṇḍavas' polyandrous marriage as a consequence of their mother's idle and unknowing remark,[22] and the story of Ādiśaṅkarācārya's inability to undertake renunciation *saṃnyāsa* without his mother's permission,[23] one might expect Rāma's dilemma to be a profound one. The literature is filled with numerous examples of people carrying out all manner of extreme and transgressive acts in blind obedience to the wishes of a father, mother, or guru. But rarely, as in the present case, are they faced with having to make a choice between the opposing orders of two such figures of authority.

Revealingly, however, the choice seems to present Rāma with little in the way of a real conflict. After hearing his mother's piteous words and her threat to end her life, the righteous (*dharmātman*) prince replies in words that the author signals in advance to be in keeping with dharma (*dharmasaṃhitam*) that there is really nothing to choose here, as regardless of what Kausalyā may do or say he is incapable of deviating from his father's instructions.[24] Significantly, he supports giving higher priority to a father's words than to those of mother by adducing not one but three exemplary tales from traditional lore in which sons obey transgressive orders from their fathers. In each of these cases, moreover, the paternal order is to destroy a mother or symbol of motherhood.

The first of these is that of the wise and dharma-knowing seer Kaṇḍu who, Rāma asserts, killed a cow on the instructions of his father.[25] The second is the story, told at length in the *Bālakāṇḍa*, of how Rāma's own ancestors, the sons of King Sagara, followed their father's orders to dig up the earth, though it cost them their lives.[26] These examples are pointed and saturated with cultural meaning. The thought of killing a cow is of course fraught with severe psychic trauma in the epics and the Hindu cultural formations they encode and support. The earth is a quintessentially maternal divinity, the "wife" of the king and, in the *Rāmāyaṇa* especially, the mother of Sītā. Then too, the adduction of the second story drawn from his own family history (*asmākaṃ ca kule pūrvam*) literally moves the matter closer to home. Rāma's third and final example is more immediate still, and is utterly stripped of even the thin veil of symbolism that slightly softens the earlier two. For this is the terrifying tale, narrated in full in the *Mahābhārata*, of how Rāma Jāmadagnya, the avataric precursor of Rāma, obeyed his father's dreadful command to slaughter his own mother with an axe.[27]

The message here is unambiguously clear, and Rāma reinforces it in his summation, telling Kausalyā that his inescapable duty on this earth, like that of the illustrious predecessors he has mentioned, is to obey the commands of his father above all.

Having thus disposed of his mother's objections, Rāma returns to those of his brother. He reverts to the central issue of dharma, equating it in this case with obedience to what he characterizes as the dharmic instructions of Daśaratha. Once again the emphasis on dharma and the iteration of the term are noteworthy.

> *dharmo hi paramo loke dharme satyaṃ pratiṣṭhitam /*
> *dharmasaṃśritam etac ca pitur vacanam uttamam //*

> Dharma is paramount in the world and on dharma is truth founded. This command of Father's is based on dharma and is absolute. (*VR* 2.18.33)

Having thus authoritatively settled this potentially thorny ethical dilemma, at least for the purposes of the present context, Rāma is free to revert to a more general śāstraic rule in which such a conflict is not anticipated. He tells Lakṣmaṇa,

> Having once heard a father's command, a mother's, or a brahman's, one must not disregard it, my mighty brother, if one would hold to dharma. (*VR* 2.18.34)

Once Rāma has settled this debate on the relative status of matriarchal and patriarchal authority in favor of the latter, he can turn his attention to the issue raised by Lakṣmaṇa, to wit, the conflict between the imperatives of filial deference on the one hand and that of the warrior code on the other. This too is not a trivial debate, nor is its resolution always as clear as Vālmīki tries to make it. It constitutes, after all, in many ways the narrative and emotional core of the *Mahābhārata* where, in its most critical tests—the battle between Arjuna and his surrogate father Bhīṣma and that between the same hero and his son Babhruvāhana—it is always resolved in favor of the warrior code and through the violence of parricide.[28] Rāma concludes his argument with Lakṣmaṇa here by contrasting the dharma of deference and filial subordination with the aggressive and unyielding code of the warrior.

> *tad enāṃ visrjānāryāṃ kṣatradharmāśritāṃ matim /*
> *dharmam āśraya mā taikṣṇyaṃ madbuddhir anugamyatām //*

> So give up this ignoble notion that is based on the dharma of the kshatriyas; be of like mind with me and base your actions on dharma not violence. (*VR* 2.18.30–31)

This idea of giving social or filial dharma precedence over the violent code of the warrior is central to the *Rāmāyaṇa's* construction of the ideal dharmic man and monarch,[29] and is in radical opposition to Kṛṣṇa's famous exhortation of Arjuna in the *Gītā* to place *svadharma*, in this case the very same *kṣatra-*

dharma mentioned by Rāma, above the compulsions of filial duty and deference.

Rāma's powerful arguments are critical to our understanding of Vālmīki's vision of social and political dharma. They are, however, not yet conclusive. There remain some additional issues that must be explored in debate with both Lakṣmaṇa and Kausalyā.

Rāma urges his brother to act at once to call off his own planned consecration so that the anxieties of Kaikeyī and Daśaratha can be speedily allayed.[30] He then turns to a secondary line of argument, stating that Kaikeyī's perverse actions and his own sudden reversal of fortune can only have resulted from the workings of fate (*kṛtānta, daiva*) which, he asserts, all men are powerless to resist.[31] In this way he seeks both to dissuade Lakṣmaṇa from any rash action and to relieve Kaikeyī of the onus of responsibility for her actions.

But Rāma's suggestion that one should submit meekly to one's fate only serves to inflame once more the manly wrath of Lakṣmaṇa. He denounces such submission as a sign of fear and cowardice, arguing that a real man must attempt to counter fate with his own virile action (*puruṣakāra*). He expresses only contempt for Rāma's conception of a dharma that can permit so wrongful a thing as his exile to take place. Finally, he once again takes recourse to the code of the warrior, vowing to massacre single-handedly any and all who might stand in the way of his brother's consecration.[32] But this outburst merely presents Rāma with yet one more opportunity to remind his brother (and us) that he is unalterably resolved to follow his father's orders. For only such deference to patriarchal authority, he asserts, constitutes the path of the virtuous (*satpathaḥ*).[33] This response is—at least for the time being—sufficient to silence Lakṣmaṇa's angry objections and reconcile him to his brother's unshakable resolve.[34]

In the meanwhile, Kausalyā, having failed in her efforts to prevent her son from leaving the city, attempts another line of argument. She proposes that if he will not stay with her, she will go with him, accompanying him into exile. This argument enables Rāma to steer the debate away from the issue of generational deference to patriarchal authority to that of the gendered deference of a wife to her husband.

Rāma rejects Kausalyā's plea to be permitted to accompany him on grounds that are interesting in the light of his extensive debate with Sītā on this very subject, to which the present one serves as a preamble. He argues that Kausalyā cannot accompany him because it is under no circumstances permissible for a woman to leave her husband.

> For a woman to desert her husband is wickedness (*nṛśaṃsaḥ*) pure and simple. You must not do so despicable a thing, not even think it. As long as my father and lord of the world, Kākutstha, lives, he must be shown obedience, for that is the eternal way of righteousness (*sa hi dharmaḥ sanātanaḥ*). (*VR* 2.21.9–10)

Thus reminded of her wifely dharma, Kausalyā sorrowfully accedes. The question, however, lies far too close to the heart of the poem's social message to be put to rest so easily. As Rāma goes on to reiterate the absolute imperative of obedience to the patriarchal power as it is manifested in all of its various manifestations—father, husband, ultimate guru, master, and king—and to speak of his own impending fourteen years of separation from his mother, Kausalyā once more loses her composure and presses him to take her with him to the wilderness.[35]

This presents Rāma with yet another opportunity to reiterate the necessity of a wife's complete subordination to her husband, which is parallel to the subordination of son to father. He pronounces this subordination to be infallibly enjoined, since it is part of the ancient and eternal dharma revealed in the Veda itself.

> *jīvantyā hi striyā bhartā daivataṃ prabhur eva ca /*
> *bhavatyā mama caivādya rājā prabhavati prabhuḥ // . . .*
> *vratopavāsaniratā yā nārī paramottamā /*
> *bhartāraṃ nānuvarteta sā ca pāpagatir bhavet //*
> *śuśrūśām eva kurvīta bhartuḥ priyahite ratā /*
> *eṣa dharmaḥ purā dṛṣṭo loke vede śrutaḥ smṛtaḥ //*

> So long as she lives, a woman's one deity and master is her husband. And today the king our master is exercising his mastery over you and me. . . . Even the most excellent of women, one who earnestly undertakes vows and fasts, will come to an evil end if she does not respect her husband's wishes. A woman must show her husband obedience and earnestly strive to please and benefit him. Such is the dharma discovered long ago, revealed in the Veda and handed down in the world. (*VR* 2.21.17; 20–21)

This argument at last succeeds in reconciling the grief-stricken queen to her son's fate; and she tearfully gives him her blessings and her permission to depart.[36]

This three-way debate with its complex dialectics is central to the construction of the poem and to the characterization of its hero. It also serves as an appropriate context for and transition to Rāma's next debate on social dharma, his lengthy and well-known argument with Sītā over whether she will be permitted to accompany him into exile or be forced to remain behind at the Kosalan court.

After calming his grieving mother, Rāma leaves her apartments and proceeds directly to those of his wife. There he tells her the terrible news of his exile, informing her that she is to remain behind in Ayodhyā. He then gives her detailed instructions as to how she is to comport herself under the rule of Bharata, always effacing herself, never boasting of Rāma's virtues, always showing respect and affection to the elders of the family including Kaikeyī, and treating Bharata and Śatrughna, respectively, as a brother and a son.[37]

Rāma's command that Sītā remain at home during his years of exile provokes an interesting and unexpected clash between the two absolute wifely obligations enunciated in his debate with Kausalyā. For there he had argued first that a wife must unhesitatingly and absolutely submit to her husband's will, and second that she must never, on the risk of incurring the vilest sin, leave his side. But now what in Kausalyā's case were complementary rules emerge in the case of Sītā as in irreconcilable conflict. The issue is a complex and provocative one, and the poet allows no fewer than five full *sargas* consisting (in the critical edition) of 123 verses in which it can be fully debated.[38]

Rāma's announcement that he proposes to leave Sītā behind prompts an unexpectedly powerful and angry response. She argues passionately and articulately for the special character of the husband-wife relationship that sets it apart from all other family ties, no matter how close. For, she claims, all other relatives are karmically independent agents, each experiencing the effects of his or her own past actions, while in contrast a wife is existentially bound to her husband, sharing in his karmic destiny. She thus insists that Daśaratha's order of banishment must apply to her as well as to Rāma, and she is therefore in fact obligated to accompany him to the forest.[39] She repeats Rāma's earlier argument that a wife's place is always at her husband's side, expressing only eagerness to enjoy life with him in what she imagines to be a romantic sylvan idyll.[40]

Rāma, however, although he had sternly rebuffed Kausalyā's request to accompany him on the basis of precisely this logic, now rejects this argument, telling Sītā that she must stay behind in Ayodhyā. In this he places wifely duty (*svadharma*) ahead of what he regards as mere personal desire. As in many of these debates in which Rāma attempts to seize the moral high ground, the poet signals this by clothing him in epithets incorporating the term *dharma*.[41]

evaṃ bruvatīṃ sītāṃ dharmajño dharmavatsalaḥ /
nivartanārthe dharmātmā vākyam etad uvāca ha //

> As Sītā was speaking in this fashion the dharmic prince, who understood dharma and cherished dharma, said the following in order to dissuade her. (*VR* 2.25.1)

In a further effort to persuade her to stay behind in the comfort and safety of the capital, Rāma launches upon an elaborate and detailed account of the many hardships, discomforts, and dangers of life in the wilderness.[42] Sītā, however, is not to be easily put off by Rāma's words. Instead she responds with a variety of rhetorical strategies of her own. She argues that the hardships he describes would seem like luxuries to her if only she could share them with him. She reiterates her claim that she is as fully constrained by Daśaratha and Kaikeyī's orders as he. She maintains that with him to protect her she could come to no harm. She threatens that she will commit suicide if she is abandoned. She tells him that her sojourn in the forest is preordained, having been foretold long ago, in her youth, by the brahmans at her father's court, and that she has in fact always longed for the simple life of a forest dweller. She even cites scriptural authority to the effect that death itself cannot part a woman from the man to whom she has been duly given in marriage.[43]

But all of Sītā's varied and impassioned rhetoric is in vain. Rāma once more refuses his consent.[44] Still Sītā will not accept her husband's command. She responds in a manner far more forceful than that of her earlier sorrowful entreaty. She lashes out angrily at her husband, reviling him with a vehemence more fitting to the sharp-tongued Draupadī than to that of the unusually deferential and submissive Sītā.[45] Her attack clearly foregrounds the issue of gender that lies at the heart of these debates. For not only does she assume here a "masculine" stance in outspokenly rebuking and criticizing her husband, she also explicitly characterizes Rāma's hesitation to take her with him as evidence of a distinctly feminine timidity.

kiṃ tv āmanyata vaidehaḥ pitā me mithilādhipaḥ /
rāma jāmātaraṃ prapya striyaṃ puruṣavigraham //
anṛtaṃ bata loko 'yam ajñānād yad dhi vakṣyati /
tejo nāsti paraṃ rāme tapatīva divākare //
kiṃ hi kṛtvā viṣaṇṇas tvaṃ kuto vā bhayam asti te /
yat parityaktukāmas tvaṃ mām ananyaparāyaṇām //

> What could my father Vaideha, the lord of Mithilā, have had in mind when he took you for a son-in-law, Rāma, a woman with the body of a man? How the people lie in their ignorance. Rāma's "great power" is not at all like the power of the blazing sun that brings the day. On what grounds are you so reluctant, what are you afraid of that you are ready to desert me, who has no other refuge? (*VR* 2.27.3–5)

Note how, in these sharp words, Sītā manages to conjure up in contrast to Rāma the figure of an idealized patriarch, a real man, as it were, in the person of her own father, King Janaka of Videha who, like the people of Ayodhyā themselves, she portrays as having been misled in his thinking of Rāma as a man of valor.

Sītā has thus knocked Rāma off balance, as it were, by appearing to dislocate the gendering of character that is so central to the poets' social vision. She has placed Rāma in a defensive posture with regard to his own courage and manliness and his ability to protect his wife. At this moment in the forensic battle of the sexes, Sītā is able cleverly to address the core gender concern that will emerge as critical to the poem and the culture that it has served. This is the sexual purity of women of the upper classes and the preservation of their male kinsmen's honor, which depends absolutely upon the perception of this purity.[46]

As an aristocratic woman in the patriarchal culture of the epic period, Sītā would have been rigorously sequestered in the private quarters (*antaḥpuras*) first of her father and then of her husband, guarded from even the sight of all but a small circle of male relatives. That this is in fact the case is made clear a few chapters later on, when the townspeople of Ayodhyā, watching Rāma, Lakṣmaṇa, and Sītā proceed on foot along the public highway to take their final leave of Daśaratha, cry out wonderingly:

> People on the royal highway can now look at Sītā, a woman whom even the creatures of the sky have never had a glimpse of before. (*VR* 2.30.8)

This is pointedly reinforced later on in the *Yuddhakāṇḍa*, when Rāma has Sītā, her reputation for chastity and fidelity now tarnished by her captivity in the hands of Rāvaṇa, marched through the streets of Laṅkā before the eyes of the assembled monkeys and *rākṣasas*.[47]

Sītā approaches the delicate matter of sexual purity obliquely and, in the normal epic fashion, through a reference to an exemplary figure from the past. In this case it is through an allusion to the culture's greatest paragon of wifely fidelity, the legendary Sāvitrī, to whom she compares herself in her devotion to her husband. She then swears that if she is permitted to accompany Rāma she will, unlike the sort of woman who brings dishonor upon her family (*kulapāṃsanī*), not so much as *think* of looking at another man. She even lashes out provocatively at Rāma, accusing him, in proposing to leave her in the city, of acting like a pimp (*śailuṣa*) eager to hand over to other men the chaste woman he had married as a virgin.[48]

After this brief but significant outburst, Sītā reverts to the more normative passive mode of feminine persuasion as it is represented in the epics. She declares her unconditional devotion to Rāma, remarking that even the hardships of exile will seem delightful to her so long as she can experience them with her lord and master at her side. Predictably, she threatens to commit suicide if she is left behind; and, at the last, she dissolves in a flood of helpless tears.[49]

These strands of argumentation, which touch, in turn, on a number of critical issues in the relationship between the genders, at last produce its desired effect. Rāma embraces Sītā, who is by now nearly unconscious with grief, and comforts her by announcing that his refusal to allow her to accompany him was merely a ruse, a rhetorical stratagem intended to elicit her true feelings. He tells her that although he is well able to protect her in the wilderness, he could not consent to take her to the forest there without knowing her "true feelings."[50]

In effect, Rāma is making a test here of the intensity of Sītā's devotion and the strength of her adherence to the cultural ideal of wifely behavior. His statement is, moreover, somewhat ironic as Rāma will, in the end, prove unable to protect Sītā in the forest. It also interestingly foreshadows the far more severe tests of her chastity to which Rāma will subject her in Laṅkā and in Ayodhyā. This issue will be discussed further below.

The courtly, poetic indirection of epic discourse cannot, however, conceal what is fundamentally at issue here and throughout the remainder of the poem: the sexual purity of women and the reputation, honor, and status of their men, of which it is perhaps the most significant index. Rāma's final acceptance of Sītā's request is expressed as follows:

> *yat sṛṣṭāsi mayā sārdhaṃ vanavāsāya maithili /*
> *na vihātuṃ mayā śakyā kīrtir ātmavatā yathā //*

> Since you are determined to live with me in the forest, Maithilī, I could no sooner abandon you than a self-respecting man his reputation. (*VR* 2.27.27)

Although the simile strives to distance the *upameya* from the *upamāna*, the virtuous Sītā from the abstract noun "reputation," there is no mistaking that the poet's choice of the former is dictated by his need to connect a woman's sexual propriety with the critical matter of male honor. For it is precisely the calling into question of Rāma's honor (*kīrti*), intimately tied to the public's perception of Sītā as a chaste wife, that will lead to the final tragedy of the poem, the very abandonment of Sītā that Rāma describes here, ironically enough, as an impossibility.

Rāma's forensic strategy of "testing" is in fact central to the structure of the *Rāmāyaṇa*'s debates on gender. For it serves to resolve the seeming contradiction between Rāma's position in his debate with Kausalyā, where he argues that a woman may never leave her husband for any reason, and the opposite position that he initially articulates here. It serves, therefore, as a kind of straw argument, a *pūrvapakṣa*, as it were, which forces Sītā to lay bare her soul in providing and performing the *siddhānta* in the form of the patriarchy's dominant discourse on gender, according to which male honor is indexed to and equated with the rigid control of female sexuality.

The issues raised in the preceding debates are in many respects the central concerns of the poet and therefore, although he has treated them exhaustively, he will return to them more than once throughout the remainder of the poem. Perhaps the most extensive such recurrence of the theme is to be found in the complex set of arguments between Rāma and Bharata, which also involve the brahman Jābāli and the seer Vasiṣṭha, the *purohita* and preceptor of the House of Ikṣvāku. This protracted conversation, which occupies fully ten chapters, 2.95–104, is an interesting one. As it serves principally as a vehicle to enable Rāma to reiterate his valuation of filial devotion and his insistence on the importance of maintaining the truth of his father's word, however, I will not examine the passage in any detail here. Many of the previous arguments concerning the gendered priority of a mother's versus a father's wishes and the generational pecking order (now largely focused on the relationship between older and younger brothers) are repeated here with variations. From the perspective of the conduct of these debates, however, there is one point of interest that may be noted in the present context.

Rāma does add some critical new information to the discussion of the nature of and the necessity for maintaining Daśaratha's reputation for absolute truthfulness. Up until this point in the narrative, the explanation of the precise nature of Kaikeyī's power over the aged king has been, it seems, both incomplete and confused. In the first instance we are told of the two famous boons that Daśaratha is said to have once granted to his wife in compensation for her help on the battlefield, but the fulfillment of which she has never, until now, demanded.[51] It is this device that the queen, under the influence of her politically savvy maidservant, uses to bring about the exile of Rāma and the succession of her own son Bharata. In fact, however, she coerces the infatuated king initially by sulking and withholding her sexual favors, bending him to her will and extorting his compliance before even referring to the two earlier boons.[52]

But now, some ninety chapters later, Rāma suddenly changes the basis for the debate on truthfulness. He informs Bharata that prior to granting the battlefield boons, indeed at the very time of the marriage arrangements between Daśaratha and Kaikeyī's father, the former had entered into a prenuptial bride-price agreement that guaranteed succession to the throne to Kaikeyī's son (*rājyaśulkam anuttamam*).[53]

This new information sends the *Rāmāyaṇa* commentators into a flurry of explanations of why the violation of such a seemingly solemn pledge is not contrary to dharma.[54] For it now places Rāma in the difficult position of holding his father true to a vow that he himself appears to have violated in deciding to consecrate Rāma and not the younger Bharata. By this logic, Kaikeyī is using her two battlefield boons only to recover what she had been promised and now stands on the brink of losing through her husband's fraud. In this the passage may serve to shed some light on at least some early stratum of the Rāmakathā and provide an all but silent gloss on the theme of Rāma's hyper-dharmic character as contrasted with Daśaratha's more flexible and situational approach to what is proper.

A second debate between Rāma and Sītā with implications for the discussion of dharma, gender, and hierarchy takes place near the beginning of the *Araṇyakāṇḍa*. This conversation, which has an interesting resonance with contemporary and often gendered debates over gun control,[55] arises when Sītā, noting that her husband and brother-in-law are entering the forest heavily armed, lectures him on the evils of unprovoked violence. She observes that of the three kinds of misbehavior born of desire—lying, adultery, and unprovoked violence (*vinā vairaṃ ca raudratā*)—Rāma is susceptible only to the last. She notes that he has promised the forest sages to kill the predatory *rākṣasas* for them, and expresses her fear that the mere presence of his weapons might incite him and Lakṣmaṇa to acts of wanton violence against those forest dwellers.[56] She makes the interesting point that the availability and the handling of weapons in and of themselves provoke violence, supporting her argument with an anecdote about a peaceful forest ascetic who having been given a sword to guard by Indra, who wished to obstruct his religious practices, became obsessed with it and turned into a violent criminal.[57] She urges Rāma to put aside his warrior nature and take fully to the peaceful life of the forest-dwelling sages, noting clearly that she speaks in this fashion from a particularly feminine sensibility (*strīcāpalād*), which has given her the temerity to lecture him—of all people—about dharma.[58]

Although Rāma expresses his pleasure at Sītā's gentle and tenderhearted admonition, he rejects its premise on two grounds. The first is that as a prince he is obligated to exercise the protective function of the warrior class in defending the virtuous sages from the violent depredations of the *rākṣasas*. The second is his unvarying adherence to the truth of his given word, in the form of his earlier vow to defend the forest sages against the predatory *rākṣasas*.[59] He concludes by stating that he values a promise, particularly a promise made to brahmans, above his own life, his brother, and even Sītā herself.[60] As always in the poem, solidarity with the representatives of the patriarchy and adherence to its contractual code are valorized above loyalties to generational and gender subordinates.[61]

One of the epic's most protracted and unsettling debates about dharma, and the one in which resistance to Rāma is most forcefully articulated, does not involve any other member of the royal family but is carried on between the hero and a monkey, the monkey (*vānara*) chieftain Vāli. It takes place between the hero and the dying *vānara* chieftan after the former has struck down the latter from ambush even while he was engaged in single combat with his brother and rival Sugrīva.

This is one of Rāma's most controversial and widely debated actions. Criticism of this act, frequently represented as a noteworthy departure from the kṣatriya code of battle and from Rāma's otherwise perfect adherence to dharma, is diverse and persistent in a variety of literary and didactic texts, and has been discussed by numerous scholars.[62] Its ethical propriety is first raised, however, by Vāli himself and forms the subject of a lively debate between him and Rāma.

In this well-known passage, the stricken monkey king rebukes Rāma for having shot him while he was engaged in battle with a third party. His reproach is a harsh one and includes a number of arguments. Vāli argues that Rāma has violated the rules of ethical behavior in killing someone who has done him no harm, an offence compounded further by his having done so when his victim was off guard. The monkey further argues that even if Rāma's action were to be regarded as falling under the rubric of hunting rather than of combat, it would still be wrongful since the skin, bones, flesh, and so on of monkeys is forbidden to people of high caste. He also implies that Rāma is cowardly, boasting that he himself would have proved victorious in a fair fight. Moreover he claims that Rāma is not merely unjust but foolish as well, since had he, Vāli, been asked, he could have easily defeated Rāvaṇa and recovered Sītā for him.[63]

Although Vāli's denunciation of Rāma for what he portrays as vicious and violent conduct is harsh and unsparing, the poet repeatedly describes his speech as "civil and consistent with righteousness."[64] Despite this, Rāma dismisses Vāli's seemingly reasoned reproaches, engaging the monkey's arguments in a lengthy rebuttal.[65] His defense, like the accusation of Vāli, rests on a number of grounds. His basic argument, stated briefly, is that the normal rules of chivalric combat do not apply in the case of Vāli since he, Rāma, in killing him as the agent of the rightful authority, Bharata, is executing an adulterer, not fighting an honorable enemy. His supplemental arguments, however, are somewhat less convincing and some of them even appear to contradict his principal line of reasoning. Thus, he argues that he had to kill Vāli since he had promised to do so as part of his agreement with Sugrīva, and to fail to follow through would be to commit the cardinal ethical sin of violating one's given word.[66] This is of course the principal leitmotif running through the ethical debates that lie at the heart of the poem. Still, it can at best be a subordinate argument in the present context, as it utterly evades the question of the morality of the act itself. Promising to do a wrongful act, one might well argue, would itself be wrong.

Rāma further dismisses Vāli's grievance on the grounds that the latter is a mere beast to be slain by a hunting king at his pleasure and is therefore not entitled to the benefit of the chivalrous treatment owed to a high-born warrior foe.[67] But this line of argumentation appears to be incompatible with the theme of crime and punishment that forms the substance of Rāma's principal justification of his actions. Clearly Vāli should either be held to the strict standards of sexual, social, and legal propriety enunciated by Rāma, and thus subject to punishment for violating them, or he is to be treated as a wild animal, utterly outside the range of human morality, to be killed at the whim of a hunter. The two perceptions cannot coexist. Finally, Rāma attempts to stifle even the possibility of debate on the ethical quality of his actions by invoking the divinity of kings and their immunity from censure.[68]

Surely, this whole episode, including Rāma's response to Vāli's indictment, raises a number of ethical questions, several of which are not addressed either in the text or in the commentaries.[69] Nonetheless, it is equally clear that, at least for those who brought the poem to the stage in which it has come down to us, the questions raised by Vāli are adequately answered by Rāma. This is demonstrated by the monkey king's wholehearted acceptance of Rāma's actions, his acknowledgment of his transgression, and his apology for his lèse-majesté.[70] In the end, the exoneration of Rāma and testimony to his unwaveringly dharmic nature are placed in the mouth of his victim, while the challenge to the hero's monopoly on righteousness is decisively rejected. Notice how, once again, when Vālmīki wishes to stress some aspect of a disputed area of dharma, he signals this through heavy iteration of the term. "You understand dharma. Therefore, with words consonant with dharma, comfort even me, known to be a flagrant violator of dharma."[71]

But the exoneration of Rāma in this case has not been accomplished so easily. Much of the resolution of the ethical dilemma depends not so much on reason and righteousness as on naked assertion of hierarchy, status, and privilege. Vāli, in his pain and shock, has literally spoken out of turn and, after hearing Rāma's calm reassertion of the preeminence of social hierarchy, he speaks for the epic, the culture, and himself in stating penitently:

> *yat tvam āttha naraśreṣṭha tad evaṃ nātra saṃśayaḥ* /
> *prativaktuṃ prakṛṣṭe hi nāpakṛṣṭas tu śaknuyāt* //

> Best of men, there is no doubt but that what you have said is true. Indeed, a lowly person must never contradict an exalted one. (*VR* 4.18.41)

Thus we see, as before and as in the Dharmaśāstras, that dharma is rarely if ever absolute, and the determination of what is right can often depend on the class, status, gender, or even species of the parties to an ethical debate.[72]

Let me close this brief survey of the often heated debates on dharma between Rāma and other characters in the *Rāmāyaṇa* with a discussion of what I regard as a potentially critical but stifled debate, the last one in the poem and one that—had it been permitted to take place—would have been perhaps the most interesting and controversial of them all. This would have been a discussion between Rāma and his brothers over his decision to repudiate Sītā, whom he knows to be innocent of any wrongdoing, and abandon her to her fate in the wilderness.

Few episodes in the Rāma story are as deeply controversial, and there are clear reasons for the depth of feeling it evokes. For here is an acknowledged injustice perpetrated by the hero against a character who is not merely of high status but is his own beloved wife, the long-suffering heroine of the poem. Moreover, it is a wrong inflicted on her purely for reasons of political expediency, and with Rāma's full awareness that she has done nothing to deserve it. Indications of this controversy or at least of an ambivalence of feeling regarding it are—as in the case of the *Vālivadha*—to be found in the epic itself. In contrast with the case of Vālī, however, no one, least of all Sītā herself, is given the opportunity to directly challenge Rāma's actions here. There are, however, some hints that resistance is, if imperiously suppressed, at least imaginable.

In deciding to renounce Sītā, Rāma makes it quite clear that he is certain of her innocence.[73] Nonetheless, he resolves to repudiate her rather than face the scandal that, as he has now learned through his spies, his taking her back has occasioned.[74] In instructing Lakṣmaṇa that it is he who is to undertake the actual task of deceiving the pregnant queen with the ruse of a pleasant outing to the countryside, only to cruelly abandon her in the wilderness, it would appear that Rāma anticipates some resistance on the part of his brothers. For he forbids Lakṣmaṇa and his two other brothers even to question his decision, warning them that any attempt to argue with him will incur his most severe displeasure.[75]

Suddenly Rāma, who has permitted and even praised debate, even angry debate, of his most critical ethical decisions, declares his ethically most questionable choice to be beyond discussion and silences any criticism with a thinly veiled threat of violence. This is no doubt because the issue at hand is none other than the very deeply imbedded one of female sexuality and male honor that lies at the heart of the patriarchal culture of the epic and its audiences. The stern imperatives surrounding this matter, however, run counter to the nascent humanism that is generally characteristic of the poem's ethos. This is not to say that Rāma's abandonment of Sītā has not been contested in a variety of ways from fairly early times. Indeed, a study of other versions of the Rāma story from at least the early medieval period to the present day shows that other significant authors' reactions have ranged from outright criticism, as in Bhavabhūti, through reimagination, as in Sagar's TV serialization; to outright suppression, as in Tulsīdās's *Rāmcaritmānas*.[76] In the case of the repudiation of Sītā, it would appear that two of the central thrusts of Vālmīki's *Rāmāyaṇa*—the reinforcement of the system of male honor, here closely tied up with the construction of *kṣatriyadharma*, and the emerging Vaiṣṇava characterization of

Rāma as a new kind of god-king, a compassionate savior and redeemer who subsumes "his caste-specific dharma under a larger, superordinate dharma"—have come into irreducible conflict.[77]

In Rāma's other, earlier debates discussed above, such as those with Lakṣmaṇa, Kausalyā, and Vāli, Rāma has either argued for the inviolability of the rules of generational, gender, and class hierarchy associated with the culture of *varṇāśramadharma* or, as in his debate with Sītā over the propriety of her accompanying him into exile, he has articulated a *pūrvapakṣa* position contrary to those values in order to "test" his opponent's true feelings. In either case, the debates serve the poet as didactic opportunities though which he can forcefully represent the epic's social ideology. Even Rāma's disputed slaying of Vāli, which has disturbed commentators and readers of the poem to this day, is put to rest, so far as the epic text itself is concerned, by Rāma's culturally syntonic assertions of his royal juridical function and the absolute deference due a king. In the end, in these matters debate is tolerated and even encouraged as it permits the poet and his hero to forcefully assert the governing principles of the brahmanical social order.

The unjust banishment of Sītā, however, seems to present Rāma with a genuine dilemma that neither he nor Vālmīki can confidently resolve. For the *Vālmīki Rāmāyaṇa* as it has come down to us is a complex document, part Dharmaśāstra, part Vaiṣṇava tract, part poetic romance, three genres that co-exist only up to a certain point.[78] That point seems to have been reached with the repudiation of Sītā. These three streams of the epic narrative appear to come into irreconcilable conflict here, in its closing scenes.

As an exemplary text on dharma, the poem gives Rāma every justification for his harsh treatment of his wife. In the stern culture of masculine honor out of which the poem emerges and for which it is surely the most frequently cited authority, Sītā's abduction and imprisonment at the hands of the notoriously libidinous Rāvaṇa is ample justification for treating her as sexually defiled and putting her aside. Moreover, the ability of a king to retain the respect of his people, so critical to the construction of kingship in ancient India, in many ways forces his hand here. Then, too, if Rāma is to be portrayed as the ideal self-controlled and perfectly dharmic sovereign, that portrayal must be made by the use of significant and recurrent counterexamples of monarchs who subordinate *rājadharma* to the emotional and sensual power of women and so come to grief. Rāma has always before him the fatal flaw of his own father, who allows himself to fall under the power of Kaikeyī, while the figures of the sybaritic Sugrīva and doomed, lascivious Rāvaṇa dominate the central portions of the narrative. So in making the personally devastating decision to banish Sītā, Rāma is, on this level at least, only acting out, vaingloriously perhaps, his vision of the perfect king who sacrifices all for the sake of dharma and the stern demands of righteous kingship. Moreover, at the juridical level, Rāma seems to be acting within the limits of the social code that holds the wife to be a kind of property of the husband which may legitimately be disposed of at his discretion.[79]

Nonetheless, on the theological and literary levels Rāma's decision is troubling. Throughout the poem, repeated stress has been placed upon Rāma's role as a compassionate savior of the troubled, the lowly, and the oppressed. Indeed, the very raison d'être of this or any avatar is the salvation of the suffering. Moreover, Rāma is constantly represented as quintessentially compassionate and forgiving even to those who have offended him and dharma. Thus, he liberates and purifies the adulterous Ahalyā, reuniting her with her estranged husband.[80] He offers refuge to the fugitive Vibhīṣaṇa against the counsel of his own military advisers.[81] And he is even frequently said to be ready to forgive his demonic enemies and even Rāvaṇa himself, should they come to him for refuge.[82] It is this characterization of the divine hero that lends the Rāma story its power as the foundational text for Śrivaiṣṇavism, with its profound emphasis on the Lord's compassion to those who seek refuge (*śaraṇa*) at his feet, and indeed for the general portrayal of Rāma as a quintessentially merciful savior throughout Hindu India.[83]

Thus even had Sītā been guilty of some infidelity, the soteriological logic of the text should have provided the means for her rehabilitation. But in fact, as Rāma knows very well, Sītā has been unwaveringly faithful to him in word, thought, and deed. This has been publicly demonstrated through her fire ordeal in Laṅkā when, after recovering her, Rāma abuses her and expresses a desire to be rid of her.[84] But now, back in Ayodhyā, Rāma is willing to deceive and abandon her cruelly without a word, merely on the strength of malicious gossip that he knows to be false. It is here that the question of the poem as a kind of romance arises, as well. For throughout the long epic, from the very first book, the tale has been constructed as one of the world's great love stories. The blossoming of Rāma and Sītā's love is touchingly described, as is their delight in each other's company during their long exile, and Rāma's nearly apocalyptic fury and affecting desolation when she is taken from him. How jarring, then, is his harsh repudiation of her not once but twice in the closing books of the poem.

What, finally, are we to make of this? For although a final separation of the lovers in this world may be dictated by a higher-order aesthetic-emotive logic in the form of the *karuṇarasa* in which the poem and, according to the *upodghāta*, all poetry is rooted,[85] the fact of the separation that proceeds from Rāma's harsh and questionable sense of political duty goes a long way toward vitiating the mood.

This final and most disturbing act of Rāma's cannot serve, like his others, as a basis for edifying debate precisely because of its failure to meet the criteria for a fully resolvable question within the limits of the *Rāmāyaṇa*'s discourse on gender, sexuality, and honor. In other words, the "argument" posed by Rāma's abandonment of Sītā meets with a sufficient degree of implicit structural resistance within the complex edifice of the text that it cannot invite or sustain an explicit critique from any quarter among the epic drama's cast of characters. Thus, although Vālmīki and Rāma clearly understand the controversial nature of the act and its vulnerability to contestation, resistance—even token resistance—is sternly silenced before it can be articulated.

It is this inherently self-contradictory quality of Sītā's abandonment in the light of the divergent purposes of Vālmīki's poem that, I would argue, accounts for the peculiar wavering of Rāma with regard to his acceptance of his long-suffering wife. At first he is desolate at her loss, vowing not to rest until her has recovered her. But once he has found her and freed her from her cruel captivity he repudiates her, claiming that he had fought to regain only his honor.[86] Once Sītā is proven through supernatural means to have been chaste, he announces that his sharp verbal abuse was merely for show and necessary in order to establish objective proof of her innocence.[87] Then, for a second time he repudiates her, this time actually banishing her purely as a political expedient. Still, even here, at the very end of the epic narrative he will try to reclaim her yet again on the strength of the infallible testimony of the sage Vālmīki himself[88]. The situation, tragic as it is, has become almost comical in its dramatic reversals, which end only when Rāma summons Sītā yet again for yet one more test of her devotion. This time, however, Sītā seizes the initiative through a final act of truth in order to return to the breast of her mother the earth, leaving Rāma a grief stricken victim of his own vacillation.[89]

So it appears that in the *Vālmīki Rāmāyaṇa* the most central and emotionally harrowing of the conflicts between patriarchal/political dharma and the inner world of the emotions, between the public and the private spheres, proves to be the only one that is resistant to a satisfactory resolution. For neither the narrative itself nor the medium of dharmic debate that the poet has used so successfully elsewhere is able to resolve the internal contradictions implicit in the construction of Rāma as, on the one hand, an inflexible executor of stern *kṣatriyadharma* and, on the other, a compassionate savior and a loving husband.

Through the above analysis of selected passages in the *Vālmīki Rāmāyaṇa*, I have attempted to demonstrate that in addition to its well-known role as an exemplary narrative, the poem employs a series of complex and carefully structured forensic encounters among its major characters to define and reinforce its vision of the hierarchies of gender, class, and authority. In these debates Rāma plays a decisive role in two ways. He entertains and then refutes arguments that question or resist the normative social dharma of generational, gender, and class hierarchy and/or articulates such resistance himself as a way of "testing" the firmness of his opponent's adherence to the dominant position. Using the medium of such debates, the poet is able to lend much greater subtlety and depth to an ideology of social order—largely through the instrumentality of the poem in turning to traditional South Asia's hegemonic discourse on gender and power.

Interestingly, however, the one rift in the otherwise seamless fabric of this discourse occurs at precisely the point at which its implications become clearest. In all instances of the conflict between the public and the private, the exemplary hero can effortlessly subordinate the latter to the former and triumph in the debates that bring the issues to the fore. However, when the contradictions between the imperatives of the *kṣatriyadharma* and the patriarchal culture of male honor, on the one hand, and those of truth and compassion, on the other, become truly irreconcilable, as in the case of the abandonment of Sītā, the narrative momentum of the poem begins to falter as its forensic exuberance is ruthlessly suppressed.

It appears then that Vālmīki, who is generally regarded as the virtual poet laureate of brahmanical patriarchy, may have had his own hesitations over an incident that has generated resistance in the literary and social realms from ancient times to the contemporary period. Although both he and Rāma come down nominally on the side of the patriarchy, sacrificing the subordinate feminine to the demands of male honor and political expediency, nonetheless the decision has rested uneasily with the poet, his characters, and his audiences. The very existence of the debates I have examined points to areas of resistance to the dominance of the social vision of the poem, even while these debates try to shore up the foundations of this vision. In the case of the abandonment of Sītā, however, the author's narrative fumbling and the hero's preemption of debate point to interesting leakages in the otherwise airtight system of brahmanical class, generation, and gender ordination.

Although we have long known that the *Vālmīki Rāmāyaṇa* is one of traditional South Asia's premier instruments for the formation and dissemination of transregional norms of social practice, the precise ways in which the text accomplishes this function certainly invite further investigation. A close reading of the forensic strategies of the poet and his characters, taking them as more than mere set pieces in the narrative flow such as has been attempted here, constitutes one element in this ongoing investigation.

NOTES

1. Just the past decade and a half, for example, has seen the publication of many works such as J. Brockington's substantial study of both poems, a new translation of the *Vālmīki Rāmāyaṇa* under the direction of Biardeau et al., an annotated translation of the critical edition of the *Sundara Kāṇḍa* of the *Vālmīki Rāmāyaṇa*, an edited collection of J. Brockington's papers on the epics, Narang's edited volume of studies of the *Mahābhārata*, two volumes of essays on *Rāmāyaṇa*s edited by Richman, Bose's collection of *Rāmāyaṇa* studies, M. Brockingon and Schreiner's collection of papers, and Hiltebeitel's large study of non-Sanskritic *Mahābhārata*s to name but a few.

2. For an illuminating recent discussion of this concept in connection with early Sanskrit literature, see Bailey 2000.

3. Obeyesekere 1990.

4. So important, evidently, is Vālmīki's need to describe minutely the hero as an ego ideal that he places other, similarly detailed catalogues of Rāma's physical and moral virtues at various points throughout the epic. Cf. *VR* 2.1.10–29, 2.2.18–34, and *VR* 5.33.7–20. Unless otherwise indicated, all citations from the *VR* are from the critical edition (Bhatt and Shah 1960–1977), and all translations are based closely on Goldman et al., in the Princeton edition (1984–).

5. *VR* 1.1 8–18.

6. *VR* 1. 1.18–77.

7. *VR* 1. 2.1–41. See the introduction to Goldman 1984, pp. 71–72.

8. *VR* 1.17.24–1.21.3.

9. *VR* 1.17.33–34.

10. *VR* 1.17.38.
11. *VR* 1.18.3–20.18.
12. *VR* 1.19.1–25.
13. *VR* 1.20.2–3.
14. *VR* 1.20.4.
15. *VR* 1.20.1–21.6.
16. *VR* 2.18.13–14.

anurakto' smi bhāvena bhrātaraṃ devi tattvataḥ /
satyena dhanuṣā caiva datteneṣṭena te śape //
dīptam agnim araṇyaṃ vā yadi Rāmah praveksyati /
praviṣṭaṃ tatra māṃ devi tvaṃ pur̄vam avadhāraya //

17. *VR* 2.18.3–7.
18. *VR* 2.18.18.
19. *VR* 2.18.20.
20. See Goldman 1978, pp. 325–92.
21. *Taittirāya Upaniṣad* 1.11.
22. *Mahabharata* (hereafter *Mbh*) 1.12.182.1–2.
23. *Śaṃkaradigvijayam* 5.56–68.
24. *VR* 2.18.26.
25. *VR* 2.18.27. On the culture's use of the cow as a symbol of motherhood, see Goldman 1978, pp. 340, 364–365.
26. *VR* 1.38–39.
27. *Mbh* 3.116.1–19; *VR* 2.18.29. On this last story, see Goldman 1977, pp. 22, 76, 80, 85; Goldman 1978, p. 343; Goldman 1982, p. 118.
28. See Goldman 1978.
29. See Pollock 1986, pp. 15–22.
30. *VR* 2.19.3–12. See Pollock 1986 on the *Rāmāyaṇa*'s discussion of fate and human action (*puruṣakāra*).
31. *VR* 2.19.13–22.
32. *VR* 2.20.1–35.
33. VR 2.20.36.
34. Lakṣmaṇa will raise similar arguments and threats at 2.90, when he sees Bharata and his army approaching Rāma's sylvan retreat. Here too he is chastened by his brother for his expression of belligerence (2.91).
35. *VR* 2.21.13–14.
36. *VR* 2.21.24–2.22.20.
37. *VR* 2.23.
38. *VR* 2.23–27.
39. *VR* 2.24.1–4.
40. *VR* 2.24.5–18.
41. *VR* 2.25.1–3.
42. *VR* 2.25.3–14.
43. *VR* 2.26.2–19.
44. *VR* 2.26.20.
45. *VR* 2.27.1–2. For a detailed and groundbreaking contrastive analysis of the characters of these epic heroines regarding their adherence to and divergence from literary and śāstric norms of female conduct, see Sutherland-Goldman 1989, pp. 63–79.
46. See note on purdah culture, *asūryaṃpaśyā* of king's wife *Mahābhāṣya* on Patañjali, 3.2.36.

47. *VR* 6.102.
48. *VR* 2.27.6–8.
49. *VR* 2.27.9–24.
50. *VR* 2.27.26.
51. *VR* 2.9.9–15. For a discussion of the problems raised by the clumsy introduction of the boon motif, see Pollock 1986, pp. 25–32.
52. *VR* 2.10.9.46–10.25.
53. *VR* 2.99.3–7
54. See Pollock 1986, pp. 27–28, 507.
55. Cf. the recent "Million Moms March" and the prominence of female legislators in the debate over gun control in America.
56. *VR* 3.8.
57. *VR* 3.8.12–19.
58. *VR* 3.8.29.
59. *VR* 3.9.17; see VR 3.5.
60. *VR* 3.9.18:

> *apy ahaṃ jīvitaṃ jahyāṃ tvāṃ vā sīte salakṣmaṇāṃ /*
> *na tu pratijñāṃ saṃśrutya brāhmaṇebhyo viśeṣataḥ //*

61. Goldman 1980, pp. 160–161.
62. URC V.34. See Masson 1975; and 1980, pp. 95–75. Masson (1980, p. 95) cites a verse found in the vulgate version of the *Mahābhārata* [equals critical edition 7.1375*] which compares the infamy of the slaying of Droṇa by Arjuna to that of Vālī's by Rāma:

> *ciraṃ sthāsyati cākīrtis trailokye sacarācare /*
> *rāme vālivadhād yadvad evaṃ droṇe nipātite //*

> From the killing of Droṇa will arise the same infamy that Rāma gained from the murder of Vālī: an infamy that will long endure in the triple world with its moving and unmoving contents.

For a thorough discussion of the various moral issues raised by the episode and the various justifications offered by commentators and scholars for Rāma's actions, see Lefeber 1994, pp. 45–50.

63. *VR* 4.17.12–45.
64. *VR* 4.17, 12; 18.1 (*praśritam, dharmasamhitam*).
65. *VR* 4.18.2–39.
66. *VR* 4.18.27.
67. *VR* 4.18.34–36.
68. *VR* 4.18.37–39.
69. One such question involves the fairness of the judicial procedure through which Rāma finds Vālī guilty, condemns him, and puts him to death. In the event, Rāma, purporting to act in the juridical role of the king, executes Vālī after hearing only the unsubstantiated charges of a clearly interested party. He makes no effort to determine the facts of the affair, and he permits Vālī no opportunity to present his side of the dispute. Sugrīva's story, it should be noted, has a number of inconsistencies, while his own action in usurping Vālī's wife and kingdom without making any attempt to verify his suspicion of Vālī's death has drawn scholarly attention. See Masson 1975.
70. *VR* 4.18.40–44.

71. *VR* 4.18.44:

> *mām apy avagataṃ dharmād vyatikrāntapuraskṛtam /*
> *dharmasaṃhitayā vācā dharmajña paripālaya //*

72. For a fuller discussion of such ethical dilemmas in the epics, see Goldman 1997.

73. At *VR* 7.44.6–8, he recounts Sītā's vindication by Agni and the other gods in the presence of the *ṛṣis*, going on to state at *VR* 7.44.9ab:

> *antarātmā ca me vetti sītāṃ śuddhāṃ yaśasvinām /*

> Moreover my own heart knows that glorious Sītā is pure.

74. Addressing his brothers, he states at *VR* 7.44.13:

> *apy ahaṃ jīvitaṃ jahyāṃ yuṣmān vā puruṣarṣabhāḥ /*
> *apavādabhayād bhītaḥ kiṃ punar janakātmajām //*

> For fear of a scandal I would renounce you and even my life itself. How much more easily would I give up the daughter of Janaka.

75. *VR* 7.44.18:

> *na cāsmi prativaktavyaḥ sītāṃ prati kathaṃcana /*
> *aprītāḥ paramā mahyam bhavet tu prativārite //*

> And you must not talk back to me regarding Sītā under any circumstances. For, any attempt to dissuade me would incur my most severe displeasure.

It is interesting to note that the commentator Śivasahāya, in his *Rāmāyaṇaśiromaṇi*, makes a considerable effort to put Rāma's warning to Lakṣmaṇa in a gentler light, even suggesting that Rāma precludes debate on the grounds that such a discussion would lead to an excess of grief on Lakṣmaṇa's part. This, the commentator claims, makes clear Rāma's inability to bear his brother's sorrow.

76. For a discussion of these forms of criticism of Rāma's treatment of Sītā, see Goldman 1997, pp. 199–207.

77. Pollock 1986, p. 69. For a discussion of these issues, see Pollock 1986, pp. 64–73 and 1991, pp. 43–54.

78. On the *Rāmāyaṇa* as a kind of romance, see Pollock 1991, pp. 10–14.

79. Cf. Meyer 1971, Hiltebeitel 1999 among others.

80. *VR* 1.47.30–31; 48.17–21.

81. *VR* 6.11–13.

82. *VR* 5.19.18; 6.16, for example.

83. Cf. his typical devotional epithets such as *karuṇāmaya, patitapāvana*, etc.

84. *VR* 6.103–104.

85. *VR* 1.2.14–39.

86. *VR* 6.103.15–25.

87. This is, of course, a strategy similar to that employed by Duḥśanta in the *Mahābhārata*'s *Śakuntalopākhyāna* (*Mbh* 1.68–69) to bring about the public acceptance of Śakuntalā and her child. There, however, one instance of divine testimony is sufficient.

88. *VR* 7.87.14–20.

89. *VR* 7.86–89.

REFERENCES

Ācārya, Nārāyaṇa Rām, ed. 1948. *Uttararāmacarita of Bhavabhūti*. Bombay: Nirṇayasāgar Press.

Bailey, Greg, and Mary Brockington, eds. 2000. *Epic Threads: John Brockington on the Sanskrit Epics*. New Delhi: Oxford University Press.

Bhatt, G. H., and U. P. Shah, eds. 1960–1975. *The Vālmīki Rāmāyaṇa: Critical Edition*. 7 vols. Baroda: Oriental Institute, University of Baroda.

Biardeau, Madeleine et al., ed. 1999. *Le Rāmāyaṇa de Vālimīki*. Paris: Gallimard.

Bose, Mandakranta, ed. 2000. *A Varied Optic: Contemporary Studies in the Rāmāyaṇa*. Vancouver: Institute of Asian Research, University of British Columbia, Vancouver.

Brockington, John. 1998. *The Sanskrit Epics, Handbuch der Orientalistik*. Leiden: E. J. Brill.

Brockington, Mary, and Peter Schreiner, eds. 1999. *Composing a Tradition: Concepts, Techniques, and Relationship*. Delhi: Munshiram Manoharlal.

Goldman, Robert P. 1977. *Gods, Priests, and Warriors: The Bhārgavas of the Mahābhārata*. New York: Columbia University Press.

———. 1978. "Fathers, Sons, and Gurus: Oedipal Conflict in the Sanskrit Epics." *Journal of Indian Philosophy*, no. 6: 325–392.

———. 1980. "Rāmaḥ Sahalakṣmaṇaḥ: Psychological and Literary Aspects of the Composite Hero of Vālmīki's *Rāmāyaṇa*." *Journal of Indian Philosophy*, no. 8: 11–51.

———. 1982. "Matricide, Renunciation, and Compensation in the Legends of the Two Warrior Heroes of the Sanskrit Epics." *Indologica Taurinensia*, 117–31.

———. 1984. *The Rāmāyaṇa of Vālmīki: An Epic of Ancient India*. Vol. 1, *Bālakāṇḍa*. Introduction and translation by Robert P. Goldman. Annotation by Robert P. Goldman and Sally J. Sutherland. Princeton: Princeton University Press.

———. 1997. "Eṣa Dharmaḥ Sanātanaḥ: Situational Ethics in the Epic Age." In *Relativism, Suffering, and Beyond: Essays in Memory of Bimal K. Matilal*, edited by P. Billimoria and J. N. Mohanty. New Delhi: Oxford University Press.

Goldman, Robert P., and Sally J. Sutherland Goldman. 1996. *The Rāmāyaṇa of Vālmīki: An Epic of Ancient India*. Vol. 5, *Sundarakāṇḍa*. Introduction by Robert P. Goldman. Annotation and translation by Robert P. Goldman and Sally J. Sutherland Goldman. Edited by Robert P. Goldman. Princeton: Princeton University Press.

Hiltebeitel, Alf. 1999. *Rethinking India's Oral and Classical Epics: Draupadi among Rajputs, Muslims, and Dalits*. Chicago: University of Chicago Press.

Keilhorn, F., ed. 1994. *The Vyākaraṇa Mahābhāṣya of Patañjali* 3rd ed. revised by K. V. Abhayankar. Pune: Bhandarkar Oriental Research Institute.

Lefeber, Rosalind. 1994. *The Rāmāyaṇa of Vālmīki: An Epic of Ancient India*. Vol. 4, *Kiṣkindhyākāṇḍa*. Introduction, annotation, and translation by Rosalind Lefeber. Edited by Robert P. Goldman. Princeton: Princeton University Press.

Mādhava. *Śrimad Śaṃkara Digvijayam*. 1985. Translated by K. Padmanabhan. Vol. 1, Viswesvarpuram Alwarpet.

Masson, J. L. (Moussaieff). 1975. "Fratricide among the Monkeys: Pschoanalytic Observations on an Episode in the Vālmīki Rāmāyaṇa." *Journal of the American Oriental Society*, 95: 672–78.

———. 1980. *The Oceanic Feeling: The Origins of Religious Sentiment in Ancient India*. Studies of Classical India, vol. 3. Dordrecht: Reidel.

Meyer, John. 1971. *Sexual Life in Ancient India*. Delhi: Motilal Banarsidass.
Narang, S. P., ed. 1995. *Modern Evaluation of the Mahābhārata*. Prof. S. K. Sharma Felicitation Volume. Delhi: Nag Publishers.
Obeyesekere, Gananath. 1990. *The Work of Culture: Symbolic Transformation in Psychoanalysis and Anthropology*. Chicago: Chicago University Press.
Pollock, Sheldon. 1986. *The Rāmāyaṇa of Vālmīki: An Epic of Ancient India*. Vol. 2, *Ayodhyākāṇḍa*. Introduction, annotation, and translation by Sheldon Pollock. Edited by Robert P. Goldman. Princeton: Princeton University Press.
———. 1991. *The Rāmāyaṇa of Vālmīki: An Epic of Ancient India*. Vol. 3, *Araṇyakāṇḍa*. Introduction, annotation, and translation by Sheldon Pollock. Edited by Robert P. Goldman. Princeton: Princeton University Press.
Richman, Paula, ed. 1991. *Many Rāmāyaṇas: The Diversity of a Narrative Tradition in South Asia*. Berkeley and Los Angeles: University of California Press.
———, ed. 2001. *Questioning Rāmāyaṇas: A South Asian Tradition*. Berkeley and Los Angeles: University of California Press.
Smith, W.L. 1988. *Rāmāyaṇa Traditions in Eastern India: Assam, Bengal, Orissa*. Stockholm: Department of Indology, University of Stockholm.
Sukthankar, V. S., et. al. ed. 1933–1970. *Mahābhārata: Critical Edition*. 24 vols. Poona: Bhandarkar Oriental Research Institute.
Sutherland-Goldman, Sally J. 1989. "Sītā and Draupadī: Aggressive Behavior and Female Role-Models in the Sanskrit Epics." *Journal of the American Oriental Society* 109.1: 63–79.
Thiel-Horstmann, M., ed. 1991. *Rāmāyaṇa and Rāmāyaṇas*. Wiesbaden: Otto Harrasowitz.
Vadekar, Ācārya, V. P. Limaye, and R. D. Vadekar, eds. 1958. *The Eighteen Principal Upanishads*. Poona: Vaidika Samshodhana Mandala.

2

Gendered Narratives: Gender, Space, and Narrative Structures in Vālmīki's *Bālakāṇḍa*

Sally J. Sutherland Goldman

The *Bālakāṇḍa* is generally considered a late addition to Vālmīki's poem. From the earliest scholarship, the book was considered inferior and filled with contradictions.[1] This opinion is still held by many scholars and can be seen in Brockington's own recent discussion on the *Bālakāṇḍa*:

> The basic purpose for the addition of the *Bālakāṇḍa* is to provide a curious audience with information on Rāma's birth, youthful exploits and marriage, while at the same time giving to Rāma the enhanced status that was by then being assigned to him. Some of its incidents are clearly elaborated out of suggestions in the main narrative, while others are purely fanciful, and others again are peripheral to the main story and are closer to Purāṇic than epic narrative. The *Bālakāṇḍa* has grown from a number of virtually independent episodes over a considerable period of time.[2]

Brockington is correct in his notion that the *Bālakāṇḍa* provides the audience with the details of Rāma's "birth, youthful exploits, and marriage." He understands that the book is late, and his use of the word "curious" implies that the audience, already familiar with the "central Rāma story," desires background information. Whether or not Vālmīki's audience was ever curious is impossible to tell. The issue, of course, is whether or not the *Bālakāṇḍa* was only added "later" to fill in the gaps, or whether it is integral to the main story. Moreover, Brockington sees many of the episodes as at best tenuously connected to the main narrative, calling them "Purāṇic" in style. This term in and of itself is somewhat pejorative here in that the *purāṇas* are not uncommonly considered to be late and "inferior" collections of heterogeneous matter. The attitude expressed here concerning the *Bālakāṇḍa* is often repeated for the *Uttarakāṇḍa*, the last book of the epic, whereas the remaining books are normally considered the "main" or "central" books.

This paper looks once again at the *Bālakāṇḍa* and parts of the *Uttarakāṇḍa*, but from a different perspective, one that will attempt to determine some underlying narrative logic(s) for the *kāṇḍa*. Rather than assume that the *Bālakāṇḍa* is late and made up of only loosely connected stories, the paper will attempt to demonstrate how other considerations, specifically those of gender and space, can be used to examine and understand narrative structure. I will argue that within the books' narrative, gender and space appear as organizing principals. This logic allows that both the physical space and narrative location in which the various episodes of the book occur are marked by considerations of gender. This marking of space is systematic, intentional, and necessary for the internal logic of the narrative. Moreover, I hope to use these considerations of structure, space, and gender to explain what have been considered narrative "gaps" in the story. The epic of Vālmīki, I maintain, is a coherent narrative, carefully structured and rarely allowing a "nod" on the part of the author/composer.

Although the focus of the paper is the *Bālakāṇḍa*, the opening sections of the book are part of a larger frame narrative, one that is reintroduced in the closing sections of the last book of the epic, the *Uttarakāṇḍa*. Thus, in order to understand the structural rationale of the entire *Bālakāṇḍa*, these sections of the *Uttarakāṇḍa* must be looked at, as well. The *Bālakāṇḍa* and the *Uttarakāṇḍa* are tied to the larger narrative of the *aśvamedha* sacrifice of Rāma and to the epic's own tale of its creation and first recitation.[3] The narrative that frames the entire epic, found in *sargas* 1–4, is that of the creation of the poem by the poet-seer Vālmīki. The epic is composed and then taught by the sage to two young men, "sons of kings" who were "in the guise of bards," named Kuśa and Lava (*kuśīlavau* 1.4.3–4). Later, at the close of the epic in the *Uttarakāṇḍa*, the boys will be explicitly identified as the sons of Rāma (7.58.9).[4] In the fourth *sarga* of the *Bālakāṇḍa*, these young men are depicted as recounting the tale of Rāma as Vālmīki has taught it to them, and are brought by Rāma to "his own dwelling" (1.4.22), where he declares:

śrūyatām idam ākhyānam anayor devavarcasoḥ /
vicitrārthapadaṃ samyaggāyator madhurasvaram //

imau munī pārthivalakṣaṇānvitau
kuśilavau caiva mahātapasvinau /
mamāpi tadbhūtikaraṃ pracakṣate
mahānubhāvaṃ caritaṃ nibodhata //

Let us listen to this tale, whose words and meaning alike are wonderful, as it is sweetly sung by these two godlike men.

> For although these two sages, Kuśa and Lava, are great ascetics, they bear all the marks of kings. Moreover, it is said that the profound tale they tell is highly beneficial, even for me. Listen to it. (1.4.25–26)

The frame then fades into the main story as a story within the story telling the tale of King Daśaratha of Ayodhyā (1.5).

This framing narrative reemerges in the *Uttarakāṇḍa*, starting with Rāma's ordering of the preparations for the *aśvamedha* sacrifice at 7.82, and finally fully completing its narrative cycle at sarga 7.85 with Rāma listening, as in the *Bālakāṇḍa*, to his own story as recited by his sons, Lava and Kuśa. At 7.85.11ab, the text clearly completes the circle, telling us that the boys recited the story "as it happened, from the beginning, from the *sarga* in which Nārada appears (*pravṛttam āditaḥ pūrvaṃ sargān nāradadarśanāt*)" (7.85.11ab).

Thus my examination of the *Bālakāṇḍa* will consist of two parts. In the first I will discuss its frame story, along with parts of the *Uttarakāṇḍa*. In the second, I will treat narrative elements and the remaining parts of the *Bālakāṇḍa*, up through Rāma's encounter with Rāma Jāmadagnya (1.72).

Engendering the Frame

The frame itself is inhabited by the masculine; it begins with Vālmīki questioning Nārada (1.1.1) about a hero—and the subsequent description of the hero—proceeds to the sage's sight of the Niṣāda killing the male of a pair of mating *krauñcas*, and ends with Rāma's *aśvamedha* sacrifice and the events leading to the end of the epic (the division of the kingdom, the visit of Kāla, the final journey to the Sarayū River, and the ascension to heaven). The sites and actions of these events can also be marked as masculine: the ashram, the sacrifice, battle, and even the forest.[5] However, the feminine inserts itself into the frame in at least two crucial places.

During the *krauñcavadha* of the second *sarga* of the *Bālakāṇḍa*, Vālmīki watches as the Niṣāda shoots the male of a pair of mating *krauñcas*. The male of the pair is slain, and the sage utters his famous curse:

> *mā niṣāda pratiṣṭhāṃ tvam agamaḥ śāvśatīḥ samāḥ /*
> *yat kruañcamithunād ekam avadhīḥ kāmamohitam //*

> Since, Niṣāda, you killed one [i.e., the male] of the pair of *krauñcas*, distracted at the height of passion, you shall not live very long. (1.2.14)

The verse has been a focus of scholarly attention, in that it is considered the first poetic utterance, a fact commonly commented upon and discussed by scholars.[6] The verse proves quite problematic, however. Since these words set in motion one of the tradition's most famous religious and literary works, the fact that they are inauspicious is disturbing. Moreover, the words do not, as the commentarial tradition would like, seem to reflect the central theme of the larger story, where Rāma is bereft of Sītā. For here the female is left deprived of her husband in the midst of sexual activity.

bhāryā tu nihatam dṛṣṭvā rurāva karuṇāṃ giram /

> Seeing him struck down and writhing on the ground, his wife uttered a piteous cry. (1.2.11cd)

The female *krauñca* is left crying piteously and sexually unfulfilled as the lovemaking has been broken off.[7]

It is the killing of the male rather than the female that has caused considerable debate among traditional scholars. These scholars are largely in agreement that the passage is symbolic and that the verse's emotional tenor of pity (*karuṇarasa*) goes beyond this one event, suggesting instead the theme of the entire poem. For this interpretation to work, some of these scholars have interpreted the text so that the female is the one killed.[8] In order to accomplish this, convoluted explanations are contrived. This, according to Masson, is the reason for the silent "correction" of Ānandavardhana and Abhinavagupta, who, without comment, interpret the verse in this way.[9]

Yet it is clearly and unquestionably the female who is left mourning in Vālmīki's text. The manuscript evidence is incontrovertible. The commentator Govindarāja, followed by Kataka, goes against the trend and provides a particularly creative understanding of the verse.[10] Like other traditional scholars, he understands the verse to be a *kāvyārthasūcaka*, a verse that hints at the longer poem, suggesting the events of all seven *kāṇḍas*. For him, the *mā* of the verse, normally the negative injunctive "don't," refers to Mā, or the goddess Lakṣmī, and is to be read in compound with *niṣāda*, and understood as Śrīnivāsa, that is, Rāma (the abode of Śrī) and the *krauñcamithunāt* refers to *rākṣasamithunāt*, that is the lovemaking of the *rākṣasas* (Rāvaṇa and Mandodarī). The verse then is reconfigured to mean, "O Rāma (Mānišāda) since you have killed the male (Rāvaṇa) of a pair of mating *krauñcas*, (that is, *rākṣasas*, i.e., Rāvaṇa and Mandodarī) you shall live for a long time!" This interpretation changes the verse from a curse to a benediction, thus allying concerns about the tenor of the utterance.

Govindarāja continues to explain the verse. Here his reading is telling, for he understands that the curse is not for killing an animal (*nanu mṛgapakṣyādivadhasya vyākuladharmatvāt katham anuparādhinam enaṃ muniḥ śaptum arhati*), which is well within the dharma of a hunter, but for killing somebody in the act of making love (*ratiparavaśatādaśāyāṃ tad vadho doṣa eveti*). Govindarāja then cites a verse from the *Mahābhārata* (1.109.21cd, 12.93.12cd) that asks the rhetorical question:

ko hi vidvān mṛgaṃ hanyāc carantaṃ maithunaṃ vane

> What wise man would kill an animal making love in the forest?

This is, of course, a reference to Pāṇḍu, who has slain a male deer in the act of lovemaking and is cursed for it. My mention of Govindarāja's reading here is not a digression. It is true that he has gone to great lengths to reinterpret the text in a manner that is syntonic with his cultural view. He has done so by maintaining that which is essential, and probably most disturbing about the original—the presence of a sexually active (and unfulfilled) female—while at the same time distancing that very sexuality from the epic's hero and heroine. Govindarāja understands that sexuality is a key component of the text. But, if one understands the *krauñcas* as a symbolic of Rāma and Sītā, as do Abhinavagupta and Ānandavardhana, that leaves Sītā bereft—a solution unsatisfactory for several reasons.

The mere fact that the verse is so disturbing, a fact reflected in the tremendous intellectual energy spent on its reinterpretation, is critical, and that the source of that anxiety is sexuality is telling. For the verse symbolically lets loose upon the epic story, as it were, an uncontrolled—therefore dangerous—sexual female. The female *krauñca* is, I argue, a harbinger of the sexual threat to be loosed upon the males of the Ikṣvāku lineage by various females, particularly Sītā.[11]

The second insertion of the feminine into the frame occurs in the *Uttarakāṇḍa*. Here the epic story merges with the frame story as Rāma decides to conduct an *aśvamedha* sacrifice. Hearing that the two young reciters of the epic tale, Lava and Kuśa, are the sons of Sītā and himself, Rāma decides to call Sītā back so that she might (again) declare her innocence. Rāma announces:

> *śvaḥ prabhāte tu śapathaṃ maithilī janakātmajā /*
> *karotu pariṣanmadhye śodhanārthaṃ mameha ca //*

> Tomorrow, in the morning, let the lady from Mithilā, the daughter of Janaka, in the midst of the assembly, take an oath as to her purity, and of mine as well.[12] (7.86.6)

Sītā has already undertaken one vow and test of her purity and devotion to her lord at the end of the *Yuddhakāṇḍa*. There, in the presence of the gods, we see her enter the fire. Since Sītā's purity was demonstrated by the trial by fire, the *agniparīkṣā*, then why must it be demonstrated again? A closer look at the passage in its larger structural context will help us understand this second oath of Sītā.

A messenger is sent off to summon Vālmīki and Sītā; and the sages, citizens of all types, even the *rākṣasas* and *vānaras*, assemble to observe. Note that the *Yuddhakāṇḍa*'s trial is carried out primarily before the gods, whereas the *Uttarakāṇḍa*'s is carried out primarily before creatures of the earth. At 7.86.12–13, Rāma extends an open-ended invitation:

> *tataḥ prahṛṣṭaḥ kākutsthaḥ śrutvā vākyaṃ mahātmanaḥ /*
> *ṛṣīṃs tatra sametāṃś ca rājñaś caivābhyabhāṣata //*
>
> *bhagavantaḥ saśiṣyā vai sānugāś ca narādhipaḥ /*
> *paśyantu sītāśapathaṃ yaś caivānyo 'bhikāṇkṣate //*

> Then Kākutstha, having heard those words of the magnanimous one, spoke in delight to the *ṛṣis* and kings gathered there:

> Let you, blessed ones, with your disciples, and you kings with your attendants, witness the oath of Sītā, as well as anyone else who so desires. (7.86.12–13)

The difference in audience is again crucial in our understanding of the structural logic of having both passages. The *Yuddhakāṇḍa* episode provides a nonhuman audience of gods, monkeys, and *rākṣasas*, whereas the *Uttarakāṇḍa* admits humans. It is important to note that at critical edition 7.87.7 even shudras are included in the list of those who come to witness the event. Moreover, we see the test of Sītā's purity carried out for the "common" man. The change of audience marks the change in location and time. We are back in the frame story, in the world of the audience, rather than in Laṅkā. What happens here is what happens to real people, not to those of the mythic past.

At *Uttarakāṇḍa* 87, as Sītā follows Vālmīki into the assembly, the poet says:

> *tāṃ dṛṣṭvā śrutim ivāyāntīṃ brahmāṇam anugāminīm /*
> *vālmīkeḥ pṛṣṭhataḥ sītāṃ sādhuvādo mahān abhūt //*

> Having seen Sītā following behind Vālmīki, like the Veda (*śruti*)[13] following behind Brahmā, a great cry of "Excellent!" arose. (7.87.10)

The description of Sītā is reminiscent of those found in the *Sundarakāṇḍa*, and here her association with the Veda is significant.[14] For Sītā will shortly utter her vow of truth and devotion to Rāma, wherein the power of language is understood as all-pervasive. In addition, the passage brings the audience's attention to focus once again upon the spoken word.

But before Sītā is allowed a voice, her purity and devotion to her husband must once again be demonstrated, here by the composer of the epic itself, who reinserts himself into the narrative to declare that his heroine has done no wrong. Vālmīki again, as in the *krauñcavadha* episode, is the agency through which the feminine voice is mediated. Unlike the *Yuddhakāṇḍa*, here it is first and foremost the word of the sage Vālmīki that allows the words of Sītā to be considered sufficient testimony of her purity. This is made clear as Rāma addresses Vālmīki:

> *evam etan mahābhāga yathā vadasi dharmavit /*
> *pratyayo hi mama brahmaṃs tava vākyair akalmaṣaiḥ //*

> O fortunate one who knows dharma, it is as you say. I have faith in (*pratyayaḥ*) (I am convinced by) your faultless words, O brahman. (7.88.2)

Although similar in seeming intent, the contrast between the *agniparīkṣā* at the end of the *Yuddhakāṇḍa* and the *Uttarakāṇḍa* oath most sharply focuses on audience and the mechanism under which the oath is taken. If we look more closely at these differences, their significance will become more apparent.

Both episodes center on feminine purity, a purity that can never be assumed nor over-challenged.

pratyayo hi purā datto vaidehyā surasaṃnidhau /
seyaṃ lokabhayād brahmann apāpety abhijānatā /
parityaktā mayā sītā tad bhavān kṣantum arhati. //

> In the past, an oath (*pratyayaḥ*) was given (taken) by Vaidehī in the presence of the gods. She, O brahman, was acknowledged by me as sinless; but from fear of the citizens, I abandoned Sītā. So please forgive me. (7.82.3)

The *agniparīkṣā* is certainly the more dramatic and decisive of the two ways of proving one's virtue. There, after all, the vow was taken in the presence of the gods and validated by Agni himself. The oath, moreover, was accompanied by an act few would be willing to undertake.[15] At the end of the trial, however, Sītā remains a sexually viable character, as is demonstrated by her pregnancy in the final *kāṇḍa.* What then is the significance of the oath of purity, first uttered by Vālmīki and then by Sītā, here in the *Uttarakāṇḍa*? For one, the *agniparīkṣā* belongs to the *Yuddhakāṇḍa,* and serves to demonstrate Sītā's purity within the main epic narrative. In the *Uttarakāṇḍa,* on the other hand, the attestation and vow of purity are directed toward the validation of the legitimacy of Lava and Kuśa. This is, of course, intimately linked to the demonstration of Sītā's sexual purity.

A dramatic shift is evidenced, however, in the mechanism of the oath. The burden of proof is placed on the validity of Vālmīki's word rather than on the purifying power of divine intervention. As Vālmīki utters his oath:

na smarāmy anṛtaṃ vākyam imau tu tava putrakau (GPP 7.96.18cd–20=CE 7.87.17cd)
bahuvarṣasahasrāṇi tapaścaryā mayā kṛtā
nopāśrīyāṃ phalaṃ tasyā duṣṭeyaṃ yadi maithilī / (=1358*)
manasā karmaṇā vācā bhūtapūrvaṃ na kilbiṣam (=1359*)
tasyāhaṃ phalam aśṇāmi apāpā maithilī yadi // (=CE7.87.1ab)

> I do not remember a false word (of mine): these two boys are yours. For many thousands of years, I have practiced austerities. Let me not acquire the fruits of that if Maithilī is tainted. In thought, word, or deed, I have never before sinned. If Maithilī is free from sin, I will obtain the fruits of that.

The audience hears first of all Vālmīki's attestation of his own inability to speak a falsehood, then of the male (*tava* = *rāmasya*) parentage of the twins. Note the structure of Vālmīki's oath as he denies himself the fruits of his ascetic labors if Maithilī is tainted, first as a negative, then as a positive statement. Validation of the reciters of the epic, and their lineage, allows the validation of that which they recite, the epic itself. Thus the scene can be understood within the narrative frame to mark the truth of Vālmīki's own epic as chanted by the young boys.

That Vālmīki reemerges for his final appearance in the epic at this juncture can be understood as the completed symbolic transformation of speech into poetry and of the epic narrative into poetic expression, a process that was initiated within the narrative frame with the *krauñcavadha* and the curse of Vālmīki.

At this point, Sītā utters her poignant vow of devotion to her husband:

yathāhaṃ rāghavād anyaṃ manasāpi na cintaye /
tathā me mādhavī devī vivaraṃ dātum arhati //
manasā karmaṇā vācā yathā rāmaṃ samarcaye /
tathā me mādhavī devī vivaraṃ dātum arhati //
yathāitat satyam uktaṃ me vedmi rāmāt paraṃ na ca /
tathā me mādhavī devī vivaraṃ dātum arhati //

> As I have never thought of a man other than Rāghava, may the earth goddess Mādhavī give me passage (*vivaraṃ dātuṃ*). As I have focussed on Rāma in thought, word, and deed, may the earth goddess Mādhavī give me passage. As what I have spoken here is the truth, and I have known no man other than Rāma, may the earth goddess Mādhavī give me passage. (GPP 97.14–16; CE 7.88.10, 1372*)

Although the powerful oath and subsequent events are open to numerous readings, for the purposes of this discussion issues of gender and voice are most relevant. The tragic irony of the passage is not lost on the audience. Once again, Sītā passes her test but this time, rather than reunion with her husband, she is reunited with her mother, Mādhavī, whom she has called upon. The result then is the end of her own earthly existence (7.88.11–14). Unlike the *agniparīkṣā* episode, where Sītā is permitted to emerge from the fire (in a symbolic sequence of death, rebirth, and purity), here the sexualized feminine is reabsorbed into the archaic mother, the earth, from which she emerged in the *Bālakāṇḍa* (1.65.14–15). Thus she no longer poses threat to Rāma or the patriarchy for which he stands. With that threat dissipated, the epic can come to an end. In this respect it is probably no accident that Rāma subsequently undertakes his sacrifices with a golden Sītā (7.89.4), a woman completely molded and controlled, and of absolutely no threat to the male in her absolute incorruptibility. Once Sītā is taken away by her mother, we have closure of the feminine rupture in the text. Note how the symbolism reflects the rupture and its final closure. For we are told of the Goddess Earth emerging from the earth, seated on a throne, borne on the heads of great *nāgas* (7.88.11–12). Taking up her daughter in her arms, she retreats to the lower regions (*rasātala*) (7.88.13–14). This closure, like the rupture at the opening of the epic, begins with the voice of the female calling out and ends with the suppression, the literal burying, of the feminine voice. Throughout the story the feminine voice is mediated by the masculine (here, Vālmīki), and these two episodes provide a symmetry of structure that holds the narrative frame together.

Voice and gender thus haunt the frame of the narrative story, providing a cohesiveness and structural unity to the epic story. The two framing episodes of the narrative use the voice of the female to rupture the narrative, mark decisive and structurally related events, and finally provide a space, an opening, symbolic as well as literal, in which the rupture can have closure. It is with this understanding of how space, gender, voice, and rupture function as a carefully constructed matrix in the narrative that we can turn to the events of *Bālakāṇḍa* proper.

The Feminine Face of the *Bālakāṇḍa*

Given the understanding that the *sarga*s that precede this are integral to the narrative structure of the larger epic, the *Bālakāṇḍa* narrative proper can be said to begin at *sarga* 5 with the description of Ayodhyā and the story of Daśaratha's *putreṣṭi* (rite for bringing forth a son) and *aśvamedha* (horse sacrifice). The epic itself provides a clear indication that this is a transition, one that functions much like the fade-out and fade-in of the modern cinema (1.4.27).

As Jacobi notes, the story begins within the confines of the city of Ayodhyā (*sargas* 5–20), the locus of civilization, moves to the forest (21–48), and then at its conclusion returns to the city, first Mithilā (49–72), and then once again Ayodhyā (76).[16] At both the opening and conclusion, the locus of action occurs within the confines of the city. At both junctures we have rites of passages wherein a female is an essential component—birth and marriage, respectively. In addition to the hero, these rites also include two additional figures of importance: a powerful sage and a dominant male, here a king. Although these figures may appear to be backgrounded at times, they are nevertheless key figures. Thus during the opening segment of the epic we have an *aśvamedha* cum *putreṣṭi*, the two sacrifices employed to provide the impotent or infertile Daśaratha with a long-desired son; whereas at the end of the *Bāla* we have the wedding ceremony in which all four of his sons take wives.

The events in both Ayodhyā and Mithilā have a significant priest or sage associated with them; moreover, the histories of these figures are told within the epic narrative. The son-producing sacrifices of Daśaratha are conducted by the young sage Ṛśyaśṛnga, whose own tale is interwoven with and reconfigured to reflect issues central to the larger epic, while the later section relates the well-known struggle of the sage Viśvāmitra to become a brahman. The stories or histories of both Ṛśyaśṛṅga and Viśvāmitra are often considered to be but loosely connected to the main narrative.[17] If, however, we look at the narrative structure of the *kāṇḍa* with an eye to issues of gender and sexuality, we can understand that their inclusion is not just logical but even necessary.

The story of Ṛśyaśṛṅga is widespread and certainly not original either to the epic or to the solar lineage of the epic's hero.[18] However, the choice of the figure of Ṛśyaśṛṅga is significant, and his character integral to the *kāṇḍa*'s development. At *Bālakāṇḍa* 8 and 9, the story tells of the kingdom Aṅga, whose king was Romapāda. The kingdom, because of a transgression on the part of the king, is suffering from a terrible drought. The king is advised by his ministers that in order to bring an end to the drought the son of Vibhāṇḍaka must be brought from the forest. The counselors are uncertain as to how to accomplish this at first, but then come upon a plan by which prostitutes are to be sent to the forest to seduce Ṛśyaśṛṅga. The scene of the seduction is sweet, and in the *Bāla* somewhat bowdlerized compared to other versions. The young sage is seduced and the rains come. He is brought back to Romapāda's kingdom and marries his daughter Śāntā.[19] It is this sage whom Daśaratha brings to Ayodhyā to perform his sacrifice.

The scene of the seduction of the sage appears at first to be only tenuously connected with the remainder of the *kāṇḍa*. As we will see in the discussion that follows, however, the story is important in a number of ways. After first hearing a brief account of Romapāda and Ṛśyaśṛṅga, Daśaratha's advisors repeat the story in greater detail[20] Romapāda's advisors counsel him to bring the young sage by sending out prostitutes to seduce him. They tell the king:

> *ṛśyaśṛṅgo vanacaras tapaḥsvādhyāyne rataḥ /*
> *anabhijñaḥ sa nārīṇāṃ viṣayāṇāṃ sukhasya ca //*
> *indriyārthair abhimatair naracittapramāthibhiḥ /*
> *puram ānāyayaiṣyāmaḥ kṣipraṃ cādhyavasīyatām //*

> Ṛśyaśṛṅga is a forest-dweller devoted to austerity and study. He is wholly unacquainted with women and the pleasures of the senses. So we shall bring him to the city with pleasant objects of the senses that agitate the thoughts of men. Let it be arranged at once. (1.9.3–4)

The women enter the forest and stay near the ashram:

> *vāramukhyās tu tacchrutvā vanaṃ praviviśur mahat /*
> *āśramasyāvidūre 'smin yatnaṃ kurvanti darśane //*
> *ṛṣiputrasya dhīrasya nityam āśramavāsinaḥ /*
> *pituḥ sa nityasaṃtuṣṭo nāticakrāma cāśramāt //*

> Upon hearing their instructions, the finest courtesans entered the great forest and stayed near the ashram trying to catch a glimpse of the seer's steadfast son who always stayed within it. Wholly content with just his father, he had never ventured outside the ashram. (1.9.7–8)

Once, however, when the boy's father left the ashram, the boy came out and the women saw him. Wearing beautiful clothes and singing with sweet voices, all those beautiful young women approached the seer's son and said these words:

> *kas tvaṃ kiṃ vartase brahmañ jñātum icchāmahe vayam /*
> *ekas tvaṃ vijane ghore vane carasi śaṃsa naḥ //*

> Who are you? How do you live? Brahman, we wish to know. Tell us, why do you wander alone in this dreadful and deserted forest? (1.9.12)

The boy feels "a sudden feeling of love for these women with their desirable bodies and their looks such as he had never before seen (*adṛṣṭarūpās tena kāmyarūpāḥ . . . striyaḥ / hārdāt tasya matir jātā*)" (13); and responds by telling them about his father and offering them hospitality in his ashram. The women accept and "are filled with longing" (18), but are afraid of Vibhāṇḍaka. They offer him fruits and sweets:

> *asmākam api mukhyāni phalānīmāni vai dvija /*
> *gṛhāṇa prati bhadraṃ te bhakṣayasva ca mā ciram //*
> *tatas tās taṃ samāliṅgya sarvā harṣasamanvitāḥ /*
> *modakān pradadus tasmai bhakṣyāṃś ca vividhāñ śubhān //*

> We too have excellent fruits, brahman. Bless you. Take some and eat them now. Then they all embraced him joyfully, offering him sweets and various other good things to eat. (1.19.19–20)

The next day, the boy again comes to where the woman had been, and meets them. They ask that he accompany them to their ashram, and he agrees. On the way the rain begins to fall.

Structurally, we have a number of issues here. The episode is the first time in the story, outside of the *krauñca*'s cry, that the feminine voice is heard in the text. That this voice is that of courtesans, pleasant and seductive, is notable and, as I hope to demonstrate, no accident on the part of the composer. The women are overtly sexualized figures—professionals, as it were. The story is of the initiation of a young boy into the sexual world. Their presence sets the tone for the remaining encounters with the feminine that the *kāṇḍa* will recount.

Before the sage can participate in the main story, his own history must be told, and that history is his own encounter with the sexual world. Thus this history of this sage, with its focus on symbolic and real potency and fertility, reflects, I would argue, the larger concerns of the *kāṇḍa* and even the main epic story. Romapāda, like Daśaratha, is, in effect, impotent or infertile. Romapāda's impotence is marked by the drought his kingdom was suffering, and by the fact that he had only a daughter. Romapāda's impotency/infertility is highlighted in some recensions where Śāntā is said to be an adopted daughter whose biological father is Daśaratha.[21] In order for King Romapāda to become fertile, his daughter must be given to the sage. That the issue is sexual potency is made explicit in the text by the fact that Ṛśyaśṛṅga's potency is marked conspicuously with a phallic displacement, the small erect horn on his head. Thus, when it is clear that the old, impotent Daśaratha needs assistance to help procure a son, the logical choice is the young, virile, ithyphaliic sage Ṛśyaśṛṅga. Although the potent male is a brahman and the impotent male is a kshatriya, issues of *varṇa* are not foregrounded in the episode.

What's in a Rite

It is only after Ṛśyaśṛṅga is brought to the kingdom of Ayodhyā (1.10) and after he had dwelt there for some time that the *aśvamedha* (1.13) and the *putreṣṭi* (1.14) are performed. The question now arises, why the two rites?

Unlike the *aśvamedha* of Rāma, which is employed for the traditional rationale of securing and demonstrating hegemony over a territory, the *aśvamedha* of Daśaratha is used at least in part to obtain a son. The use of this sacrifice, normally a sacrifice to sanctify a king's hegemony, in this context is unusual, and has been commented upon by modern scholars and as well as traditional scholiasts.[22] According to P. V. Kane, the rite can function in a variety of ways, including an expiation for the sacrificer of a *mahāpātaka*, or major sin, such as *brahmahatyā*, "murder of a brahman."[23] This is the very purpose that Bhatt assigns to it.[24]

What is additionally clear, however, is that the sacrifice has a strong fertility element to it.[25] After the horse has roamed for a year, the final stages of the sacrifice begin. On the second of the three pressing days, the horse is sacrificed. The animal is bathed and anointed by the chief queen with clarified butter. The horse is ritually slaughtered amid proper recitations, and so on. The wives of the king then circumambulate the horse three times, carrying out a number of ritual actions, including the beating of their left thighs.[26] Then the chief queen lies down next to the dead horse and has intercourse with it.[27] This is the very act that Kausalyā is said to have done at *Rāmāyaṇa* 1.13.27. The *Rāmāyaṇa* also has the other wives of Daśaratha "unite" with the horse (1.13.28). In the descriptions of the *aśvamedha*, the priest (the *hotṛ*) abuses the queen with obscene language, and she responds in kind.[28] The actions here are important, since the aspects of sexuality and fertility clearly are foregrounded in the ritual, and it is these very elements that tie the use of the *aśvamedha* to the concerns of the *Bālakāṇḍḍa*.

The second ritual, the *putreṣṭi*, comes in *sarga* 14, at verse 2, where the text tells us that "In order to procure sons for you, I shall perform the son-producing sacrifice (*Iṣṭiṃ te 'haṃ kariṣyāmi putrīyaṃ putrakāraṇāt*)." This rite is smaller and less imposing than the first, but nevertheless has the same basic function, the procuring of a son. In contrast to the *aśvamedha* with its thick description, the *putreṣṭi* is only mentioned. No performance details are given. We are told only that Ṛyaśṛṅga announces to Daśaratha that in order to procure a son, he must carry out a *putreṣṭi* and that it must be done "in accordance with the injunctions of the ritual texts and rendered efficacious by potent verses set down in the *Artharva Veda*" (1.14.2). The *putreṣṭi* is mentioned again at 1.15.8. Here we are told that that Viṣṇu chose King Daśaratha to be his father (1.15.7) at the very moment that Daśaratha was performing the rite (1.15.8).

Striking, too, is the nature of the texts used for legitimization of each rite. The *aśvamedha* draws upon the ritual tradition of the *Veda*, whereas the *putreṣṭi* specifically calls upon the *Atharvaveda*, a tradition understood to be later and held in somewhat less esteem than those of the *Ṛg*, *Sāma*, and *Yajur* traditions. The texts, as do the rituals they support, have different audiences and functions. The *aśvamedha* harks to the high brahmanic world of the formal and elaborate sacrifice, whereas the *putreṣṭi* clearly functions as a domestic, practical rite for obtaining a son.

Bulcke understands that the *putreṣṭi* is "superfluous," whereas R. Goldman argues that it is the *aśvamedha* that is "redundant" and included to demonstrate the "splendor and might of the Kosalan monarchy."[29] In reexamining the structure of the book for issues of gender, however, the rationale for the text's inclusion of both rites becomes apparent. The *aśvamedha* sacrifice of Daśaratha is linked to the larger epic frame story of Rāma's own *aśvamedha*, and also serves, as R. Goldman has suggested, to solidify and legitimize the Kosalan monarchy. However, the minute, and for the most part accurate, detail of the description of the sacrifice is somewhat unusual, especially the three verses dedicated to the role of the wives (1.13.26–28). I would argue that it is this clearly sexual component that makes the *aśvamedha* sacrifice of particular interest to the author of the *Bālakāṇḍa*, although the other issues are not necessarily unimportant. The *aśvamedha*, like so many other elements of the text, can be read on various levels. Both rites then must be seen as primarily directed toward the acquisition of a son.

Once we can understand the multivalent nature of the *aśvamedha* in the context of the *Bālakāṇḍa*, we can understand why there were two rites. The *putreṣṭi* is the expected domestic rite, but does little to function in terms of the larger narrative of either the *kāṇḍa* or the epic. The *aśvamedha*, as Goldman argues, links us to the larger tradition as well as to the frame narrative. It serves to glorify the brahmanic tradition and firmly establish the Kosalan monarchy among its most ardent defenders. At the same time, the detailed description of the sacrifice brings to the forefront the very sexual world to which the Ṛyaśṛṅga episode introduced us and on which the *kāṇḍa* will focus. That the sexual activity is legitimized through vedic ritual is perhaps a mechanism that permits larger investigation of the subject.

Beyond the City

The two sacrifices have one purpose, to ensure the birth of the epic's hero. His birth sets in motion the entire epic and sets the stage for the main narrative. The book itself is bracketed by two major life events of the hero: birth and marriage. The *kāṇḍa* is called the *bāla*, or "child(hood)." The book, however, spends virtually no time on the actual childhood of Rāma, and rather focuses on the adolescence of the young hero.

Unlike the Kṛṣṇa myth, Vālmīki's narrative allows us scant access to the early childhood of Rāma. Moreover, unlike Sagar, who inserts in his Doordarshan production a charming and, at least in reference to the Vālmīki legend, utterly spurious childhood sequence, Vālmīki is silent. In his telling, immediately after the birth of the boys and the rites accompanying their birth (17.6–12), the four boys appear as young men, over whose marriage Daśaratha is pondering (17 13–22).

Just at this juncture, the second important sage figure of the *Bālakāṇḍa* is introduced. Viśvāmitra suddenly arrives at Daśaratha's court to seek the king's aid, or more precisely, his sons' aid, in fighting *rākṣasas* (1.17.23–1.18.18). From this point until the marriage of the sons of Daśaratha at *sarga* 72, Viśvāmitra becomes the central paternal figure in the *kāṇḍa*. Daśaratha and the city of Ayodhyā are left behind. And for the next fifty-five *sargas* (approximately 70 percent of the book), the figure of Viśvāmitra dominates. Immediately following the marriage, however, Viśvāmitra departs and vanishes from the epic narrative for good (1.73) as the book comes to an end. The timing recalls traditional brahmanic period of studentship, or *brahmācarya*, with its required *guru/śiṣya* relationship. The difficulty with this interpretation is the timing. Normally, studentship starts at an earlier age.[30] Moreover, Viśvāmitra is to take the brothers for only a short period of time (1.19.17). What then is the purpose of Viśvāmitra's temporary guardianship of Rāma? The pretext of the journey is to defend Viśvāmitra's sacrifice from the depredations of the *rākṣasas*. But the journey is, in fact, haunted by a series of figures and episodes that have been considered by many scholars to be only loosely tied to the larger structure. That the stories, such as that of the sons of Sagara and others, reflect larger epic concerns has been discussed elsewhere.[31] But here I would propose that beyond reflecting the epic's themes, they are integral to the development of the character of both the hero and the epic story itself.

Within the Viśvāmitra narrative, as I will call it here, perhaps the most central event is the *Tāṭakāvadha*. Again, as in the frame story, what is striking here is the eruption of the feminine into narrative. Up until the appearance of Tāṭakā and the story of her killing at *sargas* 23–24, the feminine has been admitted to the text but has been minimized and controlled. The *aśvamedha* sacrifice (1.13.26–27), the drinking of the *pāyasa* (1.16.18–28), and even the birth of the boys 1.17.6–9) downplay the participation of the mothers. Thus, in the *Bālakāṇḍa*, the women of Ayodhyā (and for that matter Mithilā) are never given a voice, and references to them are sparse.[32] Only the seductive courtesans of the Ṛyaśṛṅga episode have been permitted to speak.

But with the appearance of Tāṭakā, the ugly, fearsome, and uncontrollably sexualized feminine appears at its most horrific.[33] That a demonic threat exists we have already been told. At 1.18.5, Viśvāmitra tells Daśaratha of the demons Mārīca and Subāhu. He makes no mention of Tāṭakā, however. Why is this? Western scholars tend to cite inconsistency and inadequacy of the text. But I have found that Vālmīki rarely truly nods.[34]

Before we can adequately address the question of why Tāṭakā is not mentioned, we need to step back and ask why the author introduces the sage Viśvāmitra. After all, Ayodhyā is filled with eminent sages, including the family *purohita*, who is no less a figure than Vasiṣṭha (1.7.3). What makes this sage narratively so important to the epic at this juncture? In order to understand this we need to look at the history of Viśvāmitra, an elaborate version of which is provided in the *Bālakāṇḍa* itself. This history, like that of the sage Ṛyaśṛṅga, is told in a number of places other than the *Rāmāyaṇa*, and is certainly not original to the *Bālakāṇḍa*.[35] The choice of Viśvāmitra here then is clearly intentional on the part of Vālmīki. The story has as its central focus King Viśvāmitra's hostility toward the brahman sage Vasiṣṭha over the wish-fulfilling cow Śabalā (1.52–64) and the frustrated king's struggles to become a brahman.[36] The cow, the symbol of all nurturing mothers, is in the possession of Vasiṣṭha. As a king, Viśvāmitra covets the cow and tries to take it away from Vasiṣṭha, only to discover that the power of the *daṇḍa*-wielding (phallus possessing) brahman is far greater than that of an ordinary weapon-wielding kshatriya. Viśvāmitra as the impotent kshatriya in his struggle against Vasiṣṭha the hyperphallic male brahman recalls the configuration at the outset of the epic with Ṛyaśṛṅga and Romapāda/Daśaratha. Viśvāmitra undertakes severe austerities in order to gain especially potent (in fact Śaivite) weapons (the phallus), only to discover that the power of even those weapons is not sufficient to gain the cow/mother.[37]

Viśvāmitra then undertakes still more severe penances in order to become a brahman, the equal of Vasiṣṭha. The sage undergoes a number of tests and adventures until at last he is forced to undergo two final trials. Both these tests focus on sexual seduction. First is the story of Menakā (1.62). The *apsaras* Menakā, sent by the gods, seduces Viśvāmitra and distracts him from his austerities. Realizing that his austerities have been compromised, he is filled with regret (62.12). Next is the story of Rambhā (1.63). Again the sage undertakes severe austerities. Once again the gods are threatened and send an *apsaras* (Rambhā) to seduce him. This time, however, the sage is filled with anger and curses the hapless woman. But despite the control of his sexual desire, the sage's austerities are compromised since he has not been able to overcome his wrath.

The focus of scholarship on this story of Viśvāmitra's history has been normally on the brahman/kshatriya struggle and the changing of one's class, a feat rarely accomplished elsewhere in the literature.[38] These issues are certainly present in the text, but are not, I would argue, central to it in this context. Rather, I suggest that it is Viśvāmitra's struggles with his oedipal anxiety and his own sexuality, and his final victory over them, that tie the story to the *Bālakāṇḍa*. Viśvāmitra's well-known sexual exploits make him an ideal choice to indoctrinate the epic's hero into the world outside of Ayodhyā, a world fraught with dangers, most importantly sexual threats. Notice that Viśvāmitra is a liminal brahman and is treated as such by the "true" brahman, Vasiṣṭha; Viśvāmitra's status is conferred by his ability to overcome his sensual desires rather than by birth or entitlement. His exploits (like those of Ṛyaśṛṅga), tell of his own coming of age, his own change of "sexual" or phallic status.

Rāma, too, is at a transitional place in his life, neither boy nor man; he is on the cusp of manhood. Daśaratha says of him: "my lotus-eyed Rāma . . . [is] not yet sixteen years of age" (1.19.2). Thus Viśvāmitra, a figure who has successfully encountered and overcome his own sexual demons, is a fitting choice to help Rāma conquer his. From the outset of the journey, the audience is left in little doubt that the adventure at hand has sexual underpinnings.

As the boys and Viśvāmitra leave Ayodhyā, they cross the Sarayū River, and come upon a holy ashram, the very place where Kāma, the god of love, shot Śiva (Sthāṇu) with his arrow and was burned by the great god's third eye (1.22.11–12). Inhabited now by ascetics of only the fiercest vows, it is marked as a contested locus of sexual activity (1.22.11).[39] This is the location where sexuality, personified as the god of love, Kāma, contests asceticism, as practiced by the archetypal ascetic, Maheśvara. The story is much abbreviated, telling us only that Kāma was burned by the wrath of Śiva (1.22.13). Of Pārvatī we hear nothing in the critical edition. The northern variant only mentions her in the context of her husband's name, that is, Umāpati. Clearly the mention of the incident is not to tell us the story—one that must have been well known to the audience—but to let the reference to the story serve as a symbol. The site marks the exit of the boys from the world of their childhood into the sexual world. Once they pass through the ashram, they are vulnerable to attack from this sexual world.

It is at this very juncture that we find the story of the *Tāṭakāvadha*. Who is Tāṭakā, and why does she appear at this point in the Rāma story? Tāṭakā is a figure known only to the *Rāmāyaṇa* tradition. The critical edition version of the story provides a brief history of her and her son Mārīca. We are told only this: There was a *yakṣa* named Suketu who had a beautiful daughter named Tāṭakā. She was given to Sunda in marriage. Tāṭakā gave birth to a son named Mārīca (1.24.4–8). The text is somewhat vague at this point. It says:

> *sunde tu nihate rāma agastyam ṛṣisattamam /*
> *tāṭakā saha putreṇa pradharṣayitum icchati //*
> *rākṣasatvaṃ bhajasveti mārīcaṃ vyājahāra saḥ /*
> *agastyaḥ paramakruddhas tāṭakām api śaptavān //*
> *puruṣādī mahāyakṣī virūpā vikṛtānanā /*
> *idaṃ rūpam apāhāya dāruṇaṃ rūpam astu te //*

> After Sunda had been killed, Rāma, Tāṭakā and her son tried to attack Agastya, greatest of seers. But Agastya cursed Mārīca, saying, "May you become a rākṣasa!" and in his towering rage, he cursed Tāṭakā as well: "You are now a great *yakṣa* woman, but you shall be a repulsive man-eater with a hideous face. May you lose your present form and take on a truly dreadful one." (1.24.9–11)

But why did Tāṭakā attack Agastya and why did Agastya curse her to be a man-eating *rākṣasī*? The critical edition of the *Vālmīki Rāmāyaṇa* has little to say.[40] That she becomes a "man-eater" (*puruṣādī*) provides a clue. The commentators of the vulgate (1.25.13) understand "man-eater" (*puruṣādi*) to refer to Tāṭakā after she has become a *rākṣasī*. Thus one commentator, Siromaṇi, glosses, "be a *rākṣasī* whose nature is to be an eater of men, a *puruṣādi* (*puruṣādīpuruṣabhakṣaṇasīlā rākṣasī bhava*)." Govindarāja, another commentator, glosses "be one endowed with the characteristics of a man-eater, etc. (*puruṣādyādiviśeṣaṇayuktā bhava*)." Elsewhere, I have discussed the connection between the eating of men by *rākṣasīs* and libidinal drive, and I would suggest here too that the libidinal underlies the gustatory.[41] This is further supported by manuscript evidence from the *Rāmāyaṇa* itself. In our notes to the *Bālakāṇḍa* on this passage, we provide a version of this episode that would lend support to the idea that the attack on Agastya by Tāṭakā has a sexual motivation, and that it is for this sexual transgression that Tāṭakā is cursed.[42] A number of southern manuscripts hint at it, but in one case, the sexual component is explicit, reading:

> *āyāntī saha putreṇa sakāśaṃ sā mahāmuneḥ* /
> *rūpaṃ dṛṣṭvā punas tasya manmathasya vaśaṃ gatā* /
> *tāḍitā kāmabāṇaughaiḥ yuvatī sā digambarā* /
> *ratyartham kṛtasaṃrambhā gāyantī sābhyadhāvata* /

> When she [Tāṭakā] drew closer to the sage with her son and saw how handsome he was, she was completely overpowered by the god of love. Smitten by swarms of the love-god's arrows, the young woman took off all her clothes and, wildly eager to make love with him, she ran toward him singing.[43]

It is with this in mind that Viśvāmitra's insistence that Tāṭakā be killed, not just maimed, becomes logical. She is a sexual threat to the brahmanic, and by extension the entire Aryan, world. She is the manifestation of the phallic, archaic mother and must be destroyed.[44] Her size, demeanor, and locus all speak to this.[45] The story of Tāṭakā is of matricide and speaks to the Oedipal fears of the young Rāma. This reading of the episode has been fully discussed by R. Goldman and need not be elaborated here.[46] What becomes apparent in light of this discussion is just how the figure of Viśvāmitra and his story as well as the episode of the destruction of Tāṭakā are integrated, logical components of the epic narrative.

The Journey

Once Tāṭakā is slain and Viśvāmitra has conferred the magical weapons upon Rāma—clear symbols of phallic compensation—Viśvāmitra takes the two boys to his ashram, where he performs his sacrifice (1.28–29). During the sacrifice the two sons of Tāṭakā, Subāhu and Mārīca, come to harass the sage. Subāhu is killed and Mārīca, who will figure significantly in the *Araṇyakāṇḍa*, is stunned (1.29.14–19). This, of course, is the purpose for which Viśvāmitra originally comes to Ayodhyā. However, the episode only takes up two of the *kāṇḍa*'s seventy-six *sargas*, suggesting that it is more of an excuse than a reason. Rather than returning the boys to their father, their mission accomplished, Viśvāmtira tells the boys that they will now all go to Mithilā to attend the sacrifice of Janaka and see his "jewel of a bow" (1.30.7). Like the episode of the demoness Tāṭakā, the journey to Mithilā is nowhere mentioned by Viśvāmtira when he comes to Ayodhyā. Here again, Viśvāmitra leaves out an important piece of information. He makes no mention of Sītā or marriage, or for that matter of any self-choice or bride contest that will eventually take place when he tells the boys of Janaka's bow and sacrifice.

As they travel along, Viśvāmitra tells the boys the history of various places, or family lineages, or in some case both. Again these stories appear to be only loosely tied to the epic story with respect to their narrative, but by changing our focus from issues like the brahman/kshatriya struggle to issues of sexuality and gender, we can see how the episodes become logical thematic sequences in the *kāṇḍa*.

On the first night of their journey to Mithilā, the party spends the night on the banks of the river Śoṇā, where Rāma asks the history of the region (1.30.18, 22). Viśvāmitra then tells the story of the daughters of Kuśanābha. The story's patriarch Kuśanābha is the grandfather of Viśvāmitra.[47] The story tells of his one hundred daughters, who were cursed by the wind god Vāyu.

The story is a fascinating one, especially in light of the journey to Mithilā that the boys are making. One day these young women, who like all epic unmarried heroines, were "youthful, beautiful, and richly ornamented," resembled lightning in the rains as they went to the park (*yauvanaśālinyo rūpavatyaḥ sālaṃkṛtāḥ / udyānabhūmim āgamya prāvṛṣīva śatahradāḥ*)" (1.31.10).

> *gāyanto nṛtyamāṇāś ca vādayantyaś ca rāghava /*
> *āmodaṃ paramaṃ jagmur varābharaṇabhūṣitāḥ //*
> *atha tāś cārusarvāṅgyo rūpeṇāpratimā bhūmi /*
> *udyānabhūmim āgamya tārā iva ghanāntare //*

> Adorned with the most exquisite ornaments, singing, dancing, and playing musical instruments, they enjoyed themselves immensely, Rāghava. Their every limb was beautiful, and indeed, there was no one on earth whose loveliness was like theirs. There in the park they looked like stars shining among the clouds. (1.31.11–12)

Vāyu, the wind god, "who lives in every one" (1.31.1) spies them and desires them. The young women spurn his advances, and mock him, replying:

> *antaścarasi bhūtānāṃ sarveṣāṃ tvaṃ surottama /*
> *prabhāvajñāś ca te sarvāḥ kim asmāṇ avamanyse //*
> *kuśanābhasutāḥ sarvāḥ samarthās tvāṃ surottama /*
> *sthānāc cyāvayitum devaṃ rakṣām astu tapo vayam //*
> *mā bhūtsa kālo durmedhaḥ pitaraṃ satyavādinam /*
> *nāvamanyasva dharmeṇa svayaṃvaram upāsmahe //*
> *pitā hi prabhur asmākaṃ daivataṃ paramaṇ hi saḥ /*
> *yasya no dāsyati pitā sa no bhartā bhaviṣyati //*

> Best of gods, you move inside all creatures and know their various powers. How dare you then treat us with disrespect? Best of gods, we are the daughters of Kuśanābha. Any of us could send you top-

> pling from your lofty state, god though you be, did we not prefer to keep the power of our austerities. Fool! May such a thing never happen! We shall never disregard the wishes of our truthful father and choose a husband for ourselves on our own account. For our father is our lord and our supreme divinity. That man alone will be our husband to whom our father gives us! (1.31.16–19)

Vāyu is enraged at the girls' response, and enters "into everyone of their limbs," and twists them (1.31.20). Deformed, they returned to their father, who says,

> *kim idaṃ kathyatāḥ putryaḥ ko dharmam avamanyate /*
> *kubjāḥ kena kṛtāḥ sarvā veṣṭantyo nābhibhāṣatha //*

> What is this? Speak, my daughters. Who has dared to so violate the laws of propriety? Who has turned all of you into hunchbacks? Though you all gesticulate wildly, you do not speak. (1.31.22)

Kuśanābha praises his daughters' forbearance and turns his mind to providing them (still deformed) with a suitable husband. He finds one in the mind-born son of the sage Cūlin named Brahmadatta. As soon as Brahmadatta takes the hands of his brides, "all the hundred maidens became radiant with great beauty, free from crookedness, and free from sorrow (*vikubjā vigatajvarāḥ / yuktāḥ parmayā lakṣmyā babhuḥ kanyā śataḥ tadā*)" (32.23).

The story explains both the history of a place and, as we find out in the following *sarga*, the lineage of Viśvāmitra. But the tale is unusual, and clearly speaks to the power of the patriarchy. The episode, it might be argued, is a story of seduction and rape, but such a reading does not conform to the typical scenario of other seduction and rape stories such, for example, as one would see in the rape of Vedavatī, who, ruined, commits suicide by immolating herself (7.17). Perhaps the tale can be most simply read as a coming-of-age story. Vāyu is not only determined to possess the girls but does so despite their protestations. Vāyu enters the girls and causes their bodies to be abnormal. But his actions do not make the young women ineligible for marriage—anything but. Once the girls have been entered, they become deformed. Deformity, especially possession of a hunchback, marks a phallic transference, and is considered a sign of impurity or evil.[48] Finally, when the girls explain what happened to their father, they say:

> *tena pāpānubandhena vacanaṃ na pratīcchatā /*
> *. . .vāyunā nihatā bhṛśam //*

> we were sorely afflicted by Vāyu, who meant us no good and would not heed our words. (1.32.4)

As soon as the girls are deformed, Kuśanābha begins to consider a suitable husband for the girls. Once they are given in marriage, their affliction ceases. The appropriate male (note that he is a brahman) functions as a restorative, and the girls once again become whole. Moreover, once in the possession of a suitable male/husband, their sexuality is no longer a threat. The story has a strong sexual undercurrent, and the encounter with Vāyu brings to mind sexual seduction. However, sexual seduction usually does not result in deformity, whereas uncontrolled sexuality is associated with such deformity. Additionally, sexual seduction precludes marriage. Once we understand Vāyu's "affliction" to be the onset of sexual viability, that is menarche, which leaves the girls under no male control, the restorative power of Brahmadatta becomes comprehensible.[49]

But why include a story of marriage and the onset of female sexual viability at this juncture in the narrative? If we understand that Viśvāmitra's intention is to go to Mithilā to bring about marriage between Rāma and Sītā, and that the journey is to prepare Rāma for his adulthood, then the story no longer seems incongruous in the context of the *Bālakāṇḍa* but becomes integral to its larger purpose.

Following upon this story, the seer and the boys travel for another day and come to the banks of the Ganges. There they camp for the night, and Rāma asks Viśvāmitra for the history of the river (1.34). Viśvāmitra begins by telling of the origin and greatness of the Ganges. Her father was Himālaya, who had two daughters, Gaṅgā and Umā. In succession we are then told the story of the two daughters of the mountain. Once again, we see the emergence of the feminine into the text. Rāma twice asks about the history of the river Jāhnavī (Ganges) (1.35.10, 1.36.2–4), but instead Viśvāmitra tells first the story of her younger sister, Pārvatī. The story of Umā, or Pārvatī, is well known from a variety of sources outside of the *Rāmāyaṇa*,[50] and in all likelihood the version here is early, but not original. But why here? Earlier, at *sarga* 22, the text told us of a holy ashram, the site where Śiva practiced austerities and burned up Kāmadeva (1.22.15).[51] There the episode scrupulously omits any mention of Pārvatī. Here, on the other hand, we expect the story of the Ganges, but are told instead a story that is at best only remotely connected to the history of the sacred river and is told in a somewhat selective manner.

The story opens with the marriage completed:

> *purā rāma kṛtodvāhaḥ śitikaṇṭho mahātapāḥ /*
> *dṛṣṭvā ca spṛhayā devīṃ maithunāyopacakrame //*

> Long ago, Rāma, when the great ascetic, black-throated Śiva, had gotten married, he looked with desire upon the goddess and began to make love to her. (1.35.6)

It goes on to tell of the intense lovemaking of the two and the fear born in the gods of the child that would be born from this union. The gods prostrate themselves before Śiva and beg:

> *na lokā dhārayiṣyanti tava tejaḥ surottama /*
> *brāhmeṇa tapasā yukto devyā saha tapaścara //*
> *trailokyahitakāmārthaṃ tejastejasi dhāraya /*
> *rakṣa sarvān imāṃl lokāṇ nālokaṃ kartum arhasi //*

> Best of gods, the worlds cannot contain your semen. You should, instead, perform with the goddess the austerities prescribed in the Vedas. For the sake of the three worlds, you must retain your semen in your body. You should protect all these worlds, not destroy them. (1.35.10–11)

Śiva agrees to the gods' request but asks what is to be done with the semen that "has already been dislodged from its place" (1.46.14). The semen is deposited on the earth, whereupon Vāyu and Agni enter and transform it into a white mountain with a thicket of white reeds.[52] It was from here that Kārttikeya comes forth. Pārvatī, enraged at being thwarted in her desire to bear a son, curses the gods that they too would be deprived of children.

Once again, if we look at the larger narrative structure of the *Bālakāṇḍa* and the "Viśvāmitra narrative," the reason for the inclusion and positioning of this episode becomes clear. The story begins after the marriage of the god and goddess, skipping completely their courtship and the burning of Kāmadeva, briefly alluded to in *sarga* 22, and instead takes up its narrative with the lovemaking of the divine couple and the birth of Kārttikeya. The omission of the earlier segments of the story is not surprising, if we examine the surrounding context. The story is placed immediately after that of the daughters of Kuśanābha. That episode ended with marriage. Now this next episode begins with marriage and takes up lovemaking, the power of semen, and the theme of birth.[53] Note how the birth is abnormal; the child is produced from only the male semen.[54] That these stories follow the *Tāṭakāvadha* supports the theory that the *Tāṭakāvadha* marks a rite of passage that allows Rāma to enter the sexualized world. For prior to Rāma's entry into this world, women and sexual issues concerning him are omitted, whereas afterward, the world of feminine sexuality is made manifest.

It is only upon the completion of this narrative sequence that the story of the descent of the Ganges is told, an episode that relates to the history of Rāma's own family. Note that after the story of Kuśanābha's daughters we had the history of Viśvāmitra's family. Again, the longer narrative combines the history of the place, the Ganges, with the lineage, this time of the Ikṣvāku dynasts, beginning with Sagara (1.37–43).

The second night of the journey is passed hearing this sequence of episodes. The party sets out the next morning and crosses the Ganges in a boat (1.44.6–8) near the city of Viśālā. Rāma once again asks about the history of the region. Viśvāmitra then responds with yet another story, that of Diti and Indra. This story, like the earlier ones, is difficult to place within the epic unless one understands that, like those of Kuśanābha and Śiva and Pārvatī, the story is included as part of the narrative of Rāma's coming of age.

The story takes us back to the *Kṛtayuga*, when the mighty sons of Diti and Aditi were engaged in an ongoing conflict. They decide to churn the ocean of milk for *amṛta*, the drink of immortality. The gods and demons churned the ocean, from which arose the *apsaras*es, Vārūṇī Surā, the horse Uccaiḥśravas, the gem Kaustubha, and finally the *amṛta*, nectar. In the course of the battle that ensued over the nectar, the sons of Diti were slain. The story of the *Amṛtamanthana* in the *Bālakāṇḍa* is quite short, taking up only fourteen *ślokas*.[55] At this point the story takes a twist and again moves in a direction that is understandable only in the context of the theme of the larger narrative that I have been attempting to trace here.

We are told of Diti's grief upon the death of her sons, and how she undertakes severe austerities in order to gain a son who can destroy Indra in retribution.[56] The story is, in a manner of speaking, the inverse of the story of the birth of Kārttikeya. There the role of the mother was omitted; the semen of Śiva alone is the source of the child.[57] The story here does not acknowledge sexual intercourse at all.

Her husband Mārīca Kāśyapa says:

> *evaṃ bhavatu bhadraṃ te śucir bhava tapodhane /*
> *janayiṣyasi putraṃ tvaṃ śakrahantāram āhave //*
> *pūrṇe varṣasahasre tu śucir yadi bhaviṣyasi /*
> *putraṃ trailokyahantāraṃ mattas tvaṃ janayiṣyasi /*
> *evaṃ uktvā mahātejāḥ pāṇinā sa mamārja tām /*
> *samālabhya tataḥ svastīty uktvā sa tapase yayau /*

> "Bless you, ascetic woman. Make yourself pure for you shall give birth to a son who can slay Śakra in battle. If you remain pure, then, when a full one thousand years have elapsed, you shall through me give birth to a son capable of destroying the three worlds." Speaking in this fashion, the mighty man stroked her with his hand. Then, having touched her in this way, he said, "Farewell," and went off to practice austerities. (1.45.5–7)

Diti is to get her son only if she is pure and undertakes austerities for one thousand years. The only physical contact comes with a touch of the hand. In this story, the father and his role is backgrounded.

The episode becomes more complex as it locates the site of the action within the womb itself. As Diti is undertaking severe austerities, none other than Indra, a figure known for his amorous adventures, as well as her enemy, attends upon her.[58]

> *tapas tasyāṃ hi kurvantyāṃ paricāryāṃ cakāra ha /*
> *sahasrākṣo naraśreṣṭha parayā guṇasampadā //*
> *agniḥ kuśān kāṣṭham apaḥ phalaṃ mūlaṃ tathaiva ca /*
> *nyavedayat sahasrākṣo yac cānyad api kāṅkṣitam //*
> *gātrasavāhanaiś caiva śramāpanayanais tathā /*
> *śakraḥ sarveṣu kāleṣu ditiṃ paricacāra ha //*

> But, best of men, while she was practicing these austerities, thousand-eyed Indra served her most virtuously. For thousand-eyed Indra brought her fire, kuśa grass, firewood, water, fruit, roots, and whatever else she desired. In this way, Śakra served Diti unceasingly, massaging her limbs to lessen her weariness. (1.45.9–11)

When only ten years remain of the vow, Diti, won over by Indra's faithful service, tells him not to worry and promises that she will appease her son. She vows that the two will together rule over the three worlds (13–14). Just as she utters this promise, the sun is at its peak and sleep overcomes her. She falls asleep with her head where her feet should be. Indra immediately understands the significance of this: Diti is in an impure state. He takes advantage of the situation:

> *tasyāḥ śarīravivaraṃ viveśa ca puraṃdaraḥ /*
> *garbhaṃ ca saptadhā rāma bibhedha paramātmavān //*

> Then Indra, that smasher of citadels, entered the opening in her body and, with complete self-possession, smashed her fetus into seven pieces. (1.45.17)

The weapon with which Indra destroys the fetus is the *vajra*, the symbolic phallus. The fetus cries so loudly that Diti wakes up, and begs Indra not to slay him. "In deference to a mother's words, Śakra came forth" (20). Indra explains that she had fallen asleep in the wrong position and made herself impure, thereby providing him the opportunity to destroy the fetus who was to destroy him. Diti understands that it was her fault, but wishes that some good might come of the tragedy, and requests, "Let the seven fragments become the guardians of the regions of the seven winds (*māruts*)" (1.46.3).

Though different in mechanism, the theme of the story is similar to that of the tale of the birth of Kārttikeya: the danger of a too powerful fetus/son. Note that the son of the god Śiva, the child born of the male, is a god himself. If left whole, the son of the female would cause destruction to the gods. The fact that Diti is the mother reinforces this. Note that when her power is diffused, her offspring are no longer a threat, and they too become "gods" (1.46.8), but minor ones, in fact attendants of Indra.

The sexual nature of the story makes it ripe for a myriad readings and possible interpretations.[59] For the purposes of this discussion, I am most concerned with the fact that it is a story that has sexual context. One can hardly escape the overt sexual nature of Indra's entry into the womb of Diti at verse 17. All commentators understand *śariravivaram*, "opening in the body" to mean *yonivivaram*, "vagina."[60] Somewhat more problematic here is the word *paramātmavān*, translated in its common meaning of "self-possessed" following Govindarāja, who glosses *dhairyavān*. The intent here, it would seem, is that although the entry was through the sexual organ, the god was in control of his (sexual) emotions. However, other commentators on the vulgate understand the word differently. Siromaṇi glosses *atiprayatnaśīlaḥ*, "with a very energetic nature *or* with great effort," and Tilaka understands *sāvadhānaḥ*, "with caution, cautiously." Govindarāja, it would seem, is eager to distance the sexual impropriety of Indra, whereas neither Tilaka nor Siromaṇi feels the need to do so. Regardless of the emotional state of the god, there is little doubt that he penetrates the pregnant womb of Diti.

The story of Diti and Indra, although known elsewhere, is not typically part of the *Amṛtamanthana* narrative.[61] The story would appear to have little if any connection with the *Bālakāṇḍa*, unless we place it within the larger narrative as part of the series of tales told by Viśvāmitra to prepare Rāma for his marriage. In this light, the story takes on a structural significance, and its connection with the stories of Kuśanābha's daughters and of the birth of Kārttikeya is strengthened.

That these stories are linked together is further shown by the repetition of the theme—particularly the threat of undesirable or prohibited (sexual) penetration of the female. Thus the daughters of Kuśanābha are propositioned by Vāyu inappropriately and against their will. Pārvatī is penetrated, but the penetration is interrupted as it poses too great a threat; and Diti is penetrated not by her husband but by Indra, who later in the story is identified as her son—presumably because he has waited upon her as student to a teacher and because he eventually emerges from her womb.[62] The sexual aggressor in each story—seducer, husband, student/son—differs in each story, as does intent, but it is clear that the stories are designed to relate to one another through their concern with issues of sexual penetration.

Another striking feature of the three stories is the presence of the figure of Vāyu. In the episode of Kuśanābha's daughters he is, of course, a major figure, in fact the ultimate "insider." In both of the other episodes, however, Vāyu shows up as a figure on the periphery. Thus in the story of the birth of Kārttikeya, we are told, "Then the gods spoke to Agni the eater of oblations, 'You and Vāyu must enter Rudra's abundant semen' " (1.35.17). Other versions of the story do not admit to Vāyu's participation in the creation of the prince.[63] Again, in the story of Diti Vāyu is mentioned as one of the sons of Diti (1.46.5) who will travel through the sky (the Maruts). And of course, the words Marut and Māruta are names of Vāyu. Vāyu's exact connection here is one that needs to be examined in greater detail, but his appearance is, it appears, intentional, especially in light of the story of the birth of Kārttikeya.

Viśvāmitra finishes the story of Diti and explains that this spot where Diti performed her austerities is where King Viśāla, an ancestor of Rāma, founded the city of Viśālā. In this fashion, Viśvāmitra ties the episode back to the journey. The trio spends the night there and one night with King Sumati, who rules in Viśālā. They then journey to Mithilā. On the outskirts of Mithilā, Rāma once again spies an empty ashram and asks to know its history. As before, Viśvāmitra narrates a story: the famous and widespread cautionary tale of Gautama and his wife Ahalyā, a tale of sexual crime and its punishment.[64] Once, Viśvāmitra tells Rāma, in Gautama's absence, Indra took his form and seduced Ahalyā, telling her:

> *ṛtukālaḥ pratīkṣante nārthinaḥ susamāhite /*
> *saṃgamaṃ tv aham icchāmi tvayā saha sumadhyame //*

> Shapely woman, men filled with desire do not wait for a woman's fertile period. Fair-waisted woman, I want to make love to you. (1.47.18)

Ahalyā is aware that it is Indra in disguise, but "in her lust" consents to making love with the king of the gods. Satisfied from lovemaking, she urges Indra to leave, and begs him to protect her and himself. Indra departs, but is fearful of Gautama. As Indra is leaving, he encounters Gautama on the path, and the sage, seeing Indra in disguise as himself, curses him:

> *mama rūpaṃ samāsthāya kṛtavān asi durmate /*
> *akartavyam idaṃ yasmād viphalas tvaṃ bhaviṣyasi //*

> Fool, taking on my form and doing this thing that is not to be done, you shall lose your testicles.[65] (1.47.26)

After cursing Indra, he then curses his wife as well:

> *vāyubhakṣā nirāhārā tapyantī bhasmaśāyinī /*
> *adṛṣyā sarvabhūtānām āśrame 'smin nivatsyasi //*

> You shall dwell in this ashram with nothing to eat, air your only food (*vāyubhakṣā*), suffering, lying on ashes, and invisible to all creatures. (1.47.29)

She is to remain thus until Rāma arrives to free her from the curse. Indra then addresses Agni (1.48.1), telling him that since he has done the gods a service by robbing Gautama of his ascetic power, the gods should restore his testicles. This they do by substituting a ram's testicles for the god's. Here the story ends, and Rāma, following Viśvāmitra into the ashram, sees Ahalyā and releases her from her curse.

The story is linked to the others through similar thematic concerns. Again it is tale of a sexual encounter, here an illicit one. The consequences for such transgressions are dramatic and clearly serve as a warning. The story, however, differs from those more commonly known from the purāṇic tradition, wherein Gautama curses Ahalyā to "be without flesh and bones" (*Padmapurāṇa* 54.33–34), or to be ugly (*Rām* 7.30), or turn to stone (*Adhyātmarāmāyaṇa* 1.6.14). As in the stories discussed above, there is penetration, here in the form of normal, if adulterous, sexual penetration. As in the story of Diti, the penetration is illicit and carried out by Indra.[66] Moreover as in the other stories, the figure of Vāyu appears on the periphery of the episode, for Ahalyā is cursed to be *vāyubhakṣā*, "one [feminine] who eats only *vāyu*." The ingestion of *vāyu* harks back to the story of Kuśanābha's daughters.

Additionally, the episodes all reinforce the dangerous and threatening nature of women. The phallic, uncontrolled woman like Tāṭakā is to be destroyed, but what of the others—those that live within our own walls, as it were, the young maid, the married woman, the pregnant mother, the adulterous wife? The message is clear: sexuality is pervasive in the adult world, in the control of women, and a threat to the male. Marriage is the culturally normative way to control women, but even within it women pose danger to the male, especially when pregnant or adulterous.

The story of Ahalyā marks the final element of the quartet of tales that Viśvāmitra tells to Rāma. Several narrative features mark this episode as the end of the sage's lessons to Rāma on sexuality. First, of course, is that the trio has now reached the outskirts of Mithilā, where the contest and marriage are actually to take place. Second, we see that the last ashram through which they travel is that of Gautama. As Viśvāmitra and the boys leave Ayodhyā, the first place they encounter is the ashram of Śiva (*kāmāśrama*) (1.22). Now as they end their journey, the last place they encounter before they arrive in Mithilā is also an ashram. This ashram is different in that it is deserted. It is deserted because it has been the site of illicit sexual activity. Only through Rāma's newly acquired mastery of sexual knowledge can Ahalyā be restored to her normal state. It thus makes sense that Rāma, now a fully phallicized male, has sight (*rāmasya darśanam*) (1.48.16) and that Ahalyā is once more visible to the world. The male gaze as a marker of the phallus has been discussed in great detail and I need not develop it here.[67] The Ahalyā episode is the point of transition wherein the narratives told by Viśvāmitra and the story of Rāma merge. It is Rāma's gaze that saves Ahalyā from her sexual lapse, and so marks his own passage to manhood. The trio has arrived at Mithilā and the wedding of Rāma and Sītā can take place, not without first, of course, giving the history of the sage that brought them there, Viśvāmitra. Once this sequence of stories has finished, Rāma can now master the feminine world. Thus when Viśvāmitra next discusses the bow of Śiva, the real purpose of the journey can be voiced.

The story of Ahalyā also serves as a cautionary tale and harbinger of the larger epic narrative. For, after all, the very crime that Ahalyā commits is the one for which Sītā will be falsely accused of and finally, like Ahalyā, punished.

If this is the case, then we can understand why, when Viśvāmitra first came to visit Daśaratha, neither the *svayaṃvara* nor Tāṭakā was mentioned. Rāma first needed to undergo an initiation into the sexualized world. Once that is completed, Rāma can break Śiva's primally phallic bow and thus lay sexual claim to Sītā.

In this way the middle section of the *Bālakāṇḍa*, *sarga*s 22–48—the section that I have called the Viśvāmitra narrative—is a clearly and logically developed episode, wherein the sage takes the young boy Rāma, and by default Lakṣmaṇa, on a "coming-of-age-tour." It is during this tour or initiation that the boys are exposed to the sexualized world. Rāma encounters and defeats the sexualized archaic mother, Tāṭakā, and then encounters through Viśvāmitra's storytelling a myriad destructive, threatening, and dangerous females. From the potential danger of uncontrolled sexuality of the daughters of Kuśanābha to the story of the unfaithful Ahalyā, an episode that has strong resonances with the epic narrative, the complexities and dangers of the sexual world are made all too clear to the young boy.

With the end of Rāma's journey, the two final events of the *Bālakāṇḍa*, the marriage and Rāma Dāśarathi's encounter with Bhārgava Rāma, fall into place. Prior to the actual events of the marriage, we have the story of Viśvāmitra's adventures and his own transformation discussed above. That this narrative occurs after the party arrives at Mithilā (1.49) and before a major rite (1.65) structurally places it in a parallel position to that of the story of Ṛśyaśṛṅga. The trio has come to the outskirts of Mithilā, the sacrificial grounds of King Janaka (1.49.2–3), where many thousands of brahmans are staying (49.3). Immediately upon their arrival, Śatānanda—the son of Ahalyā and Gautama and the family priest of Janaka—and the king welcome them. The sacrifice of Janaka will continue for twelve days (49.15), on one night of which Śatānanda tells the legend of Viśvāmitra (1.50.16–1.64.20) to King Janaka, Rāma and Lakṣmaṇa, and the assembled crowd (including Viśvāmitra).

Before the marriage is even mentioned, we have the story of the bow of Śiva. Viśvāmitra makes no mention of Sītā, only that the young men have come to see the bow of Śiva and, having seen it will return home. Janaka, too, in the course of telling the history of the bow, only briefly mentions Sītā, her birth, and how previous kings had tried to win her by lifting the bow (1.65).

Even after the history of the bow has been told, there is no mention of Rāma attempting to lift it; he is only to look at it. Here too there is no talk of other kings present; only Janaka's ministers and the five thousand men required to haul the bow in are mentioned. Rāma, of course, lifts, strings, and breaks the bow,

> *tasya śabdo mahān āsīn nirghātasamaniḥsvanaḥ /*
> *bhūmikampaś ca sumahān parvatasyeva dīryataḥ //*
> *nipetuś ca narāḥ sarve tena śabdena mohitāḥ /*
> *varjayitvā munivaraṃ rājānaṃ tau ca rāghavau //*

> There was a tremendous noise loud as of a thunderclap, and a mighty trembling shook the earth, as if a mountain had been torn asunder. Of all those men, only the great sage, the king and the two Rāghavas remained standing; the rest fell, stunned by the noise. (1.66.18–19)

Rāma, as is well known, then marries Sītā, and his brothers marry her sister Ūrmilā and two cousins, respectively. Two issues are of interest in terms of the present discussion. The first is the story of Sītā's birth and the second is that of the bow. The episode of the breaking of the bow has been subject to discussion in both the traditional commentaries and in more modern contexts. Such discussion has tended to focus on the religious and ethical aspects of the feat, for example the symbolism of breaking the bow of Śiva or the ethics of letting something left in trust be destroyed.[68]

Once Rāma has undergone his "initiation" aided by Viśvāmitra, he must prove his manhood. This he does by breaking the bow. The bow is a phallic projection of the father; its destruction, a symbol of his overcoming the father. In this context, we must look at the following episode of Rāma Jāmadagnya, where once again Rāma is challenged to lift and string a bow. This bow is in the possession of the irascible sage Rāma Jāmadagnya, also an avatar of Viṣṇu. This episode is seemingly unconnected with the remainder of the epic, and has been criticized as such.[69] That the battle is one between the two avatars—a transfer of power, as it were—is a probable interpretation, but does not help us understand the episode's narrative location.[70]

After the wedding, on the return to Ayodhyā, Rāma and the entire wedding party, including Daśaratha, Sītā, and the rest, observe inauspicious omens. The entire party falls unconscious except for Vasiṣṭha and the other seers, the king, and his sons. They then spy Rāma Jāmadagnya, also known as Paraśurāma, that is, Rāma with an axe. He approaches Rāma Dāśarathi and tells him that he has heard about his wonderful deed of breaking the bow. He challenges Rāma:

> *tad ahaṃ te balaṃ dṛṣtvā dhanuṣo 'sya prapūraṇe /*
> *dvandvayuddhaṃ pradāsyāmi vīryaślāghyam idaṃ tava //*

> If I see that you have strength enough to put an arrow to this bow, then I shall challenge you to single combat, which is praised by men of might. (1.74.4)

Daśaratha tries to intercede for his son:

> *kṣatraroṣāt praśāntas tvaṃ brāhmaṇaś ca mahāyaśāḥ /*
> *bālānāṃ mama putrāṇām abhayaṃ dātum arhasi //*

> Your wrath against the kshatriyas has now subsided, and you are a brahman of great renown. Please grant safe passage to my sons, for they are mere boys. (1.74.6)

However,

> *bruvaty evaṃ daśarathe jāmadagnyaḥ pratāpavān /*
> *anādṛtyaiva tad vākyaṃ rāma evābhyabhāṣata //*

> Despite the fact that Daśaratha was speaking in this fashion, the valiant Jāmadagnya paid no heed to his words, but spoke directly to Rāma. (1.74.10)

Rāma Jāmadagnya then tells of the history of the bows: how Viṣṇu in a fight with Śiva had unstrung and immobilized the latter's bow, and how the now impotent bow had been deposited in the care of King Janaka. Rāma Jāmadagnya then explains the history of the bow of Viṣṇu and how it came into his possession. Once again he challenges Rāma Dāśarathi to single combat (1.74.28).

Rāma, "tempering his response out of respect for his father (*gauravād yantritakathaḥ pituḥ*)" (1.75.1), is incensed and says:

> *vīryahīnam ivāśaktaṃ kṣatradharmeṇa bhārgava /*
> *avajānāsi me tejaḥ paśya me 'dya parākramam //*

> But, Bhārgava, you regard me as if I were some weakling, incapable of discharging the duty of a kshatriya. Now you shall witness my strength and valor for yourself. (1.75.3)

Rāma then snatches up the bow, strings it, and fixes an arrow to it. Once strung, however, Rāma "for the sake of Viśvāmitra," cannot harm Rāma Jāmadagnya, because he is a brahman. The arrow, however, must be loosed. He gives the brahman warrior a choice: either his retreat or his worlds, won through austerities, must be destroyed.

> *jaḍīkṛte tadā loke rāme varadhanurdhare /*
> *nirvīryo jāmadagnyo 'sya 'sau rāmo rāmam uddaikṣata //*

> Then as the world stood stunned and Rāma held the great bow,
> Rāma Jāmdagnya, robbed of his strength, stared at Rāma. (1.75.11)

Rāma Jāmdagnya then begs that Rāma destroy his worlds rather than his retreat. Rāma Jāmdagnya returns to his retreat, and the remaining party regains consciousness. Then, with bow in hand, Rāma enters Ayodhyā along with the rest, and the *kāṇḍa* comes to an end.

The episode is a variant of the preceding one, and some of the similarities are striking. Earlier, when Rāma breaks the bow of Śiva the force of the sound of the break stunned all, leaving only the king, the sage, and the two Rāghavas standing (1.66.18–19). In the Rāma Jāmdagnya story, only the sages, the king, and the sons remain conscious. During the lifting of the bow of Śiva, Daśaratha was absent; here Daśaratha is literally ignored, and not for the first time.

In both episodes, the bow is a phallic projection of a father figure. In the wedding episode the phallic symbol is destroyed. In the Rāma Jāmdagnya confrontation, the Oedipal nature of the struggle is more pronounced. The single-handed combat elsewhere is marked as Oedipal struggle over phallic possessions.[71] The bow, however, is not destroyed, but the male figure that possesses it is. Rāma Jāmdagnya is now described as *nirvīryaḥ*, "deprived of his virility" (1.75.11). Since his virility was destroyed (*hatavīryatvāt* 1.75.12), like the remainder of the world he becomes subject to the conditions of the world, and is becomes *jaḍīkṛtaḥ*, "stunned,"[72] as was the entire world at verse 11 above. The younger male comes into possession of the phallic symbol, gaining his newly discovered virility and depriving the older male of his.

It is clear that the two passages mark a transition. In the first, however, the phallic image itself is broken. Here the action occurs in the context of the marriage, and the phallus is in possession of the father of the bride. In order for the male to take possession of the woman, he must first render impotent the male who protects her. The second episode symbolically renders impotent Rāma's *own* father figure (and namesake). Here, Daśaratha has from the beginning of the *kāṇḍa* been marked as impotent; his phallus has been represented in turn by Ṛśyaśṛṅga, Viśvāmitra, and Rāma Jāmadagnya.

As we asked above concerning Ṛśyaśṛṅga and Viśvāmitra, we can now ask, "Why Rāma Jāmadagnya?" The story of Rāma Jāmadagnya is never told in the

Rāmāyaṇa; however, he is mentioned several times.[73] Viśvāmitra and Rāma Jāmadagnya are distantly related, and that they are both used in this *Bālakāṇḍa* is probably not accidental.[74] Rāma Jāmadagnya is known for two feats: that of killing all of the kshatriyas twenty-one times,[75] and for the absolute subservience that he showed his father, to the extent of chopping off his own mother's head for a sexual transgression. This last act, the one of more relevance for the present discussion, is narrated in the *Mahābhārata* and is known to the *Ayodhyākāṇḍa* (2.18.29).[76] The sexual transgression of Reṇukā, Jāmadagnya's mother, is described in the *Mahābhārata* as gazing upon another male with desire:

> *krīḍanataṃ salile dr̥ṣṭvā sabhāraṃ padmamālinam /*
> *r̥ddhimantam tatas tasya spr̥hayāmāsa reṇukā //*

> Gazing at him, richly endowed and lotus-garlanded, sporting with his wife in the water, Reṇukā desired him. (3.116.7)

Now this is significant, for it is Reṇukā's transgression, like Ahaylā's, that is the impropriety of which Sītā will be accused.[77] Reṇukā's punishment is swift and dramatic. Her husband orders her head chopped off. Now the fact that Rāma Jāmadagnya is the one who carries out that punishment, in absolute adherence to his father's words, ties him to Rāma Dāśarathi in a profound manner. For the incorporation of this figure at this point in the epic serves to reinforce one of the epic's most fundamental ethical and social codes and to prepare the audience for what is to come. In just a few *sarga*'s, Rāma Dāśarathi, too, will face his own challenges to do, unquestionably and unhesitatingly, the bidding of his father and ultimately to cope with the question of sexual infidelity. The encounter then serves, among other things, to highlight once again the impotence of Daśaratha, to demonstrate the newly gained manhood of Rāma Dāśarathi, and to remind the audience of the cultural imperatives to which our hero must conform.

The *Bālakāṇḍa*'s narrative is dominated by the phallic male, represented primarily by the sages R̥śyaśr̥ṅga, Viśvāmitra, and Bhārgava Rāma. The narrative is framed, however, by the two rites, birth and marriage, both of which are associated with the world of women. Nevertheless the feminine in the text is tightly emboxed within the masculine. Thus at both the birth and the marriage the woman is given no voice. Once outside the city, once outside of Daśaratha's impotent world, Rāma encounters the feminine, but only under the tutelage of the sage Viśvāmitra. The women are only given voice when they are represented as sexually unrestrained or dangerous. Ultimately that voice is destroyed or controlled. Thus figures such as Tāṭakā, the daughters of Kuśanābha, Diti, Ahalyā all have a voice, but are all defeated, contained, or silenced.

The narrative function of the final encounter between Paraśurāma and Rāma Dāśarathi serves as a transition, allowing our hero to return home a man, ready to undertake his duties as the prince regent. He returns in possession not only of a wife—who is still denied a voice—but also of powerful phallic weaponry, which he has mastered.

Conclusion

Both the framing narrative and the *Bālakāṇḍa* have in common their masculine landscape. It is a story told of males by males. But the feminine inhabits the text, encased, as it were, by the masculine. Wherever woman is allowed into the narrative, she serves as point of textual rupture, disrupting the narrative, challenging the order. The challenge is, for the *Bālakāṇḍa*, primarily a sexual one. Each female that is allowed a voice articulates a sexual threat to the male. The differing placement of the ruptures—the frame, the story of Ṛśyaśṛṅga, the Viśvāmitra episode, the narrative told to Rāma by Viśvāmitra—each presents the sexually threatening female in different guises. But she is always sexual and she is always dangerous. Those women who are appropriately contained within the masculine world, for example, Sītā (in the *Bālakāṇḍa* but not in the *Uttara*), Kausalyā, and so forth, are not given voice in the *Bālakāṇḍa*. This appears not to be exclusively the case for the other *kāṇḍas*, and thus marks the use of the feminine voice as significant to the *kāṇḍa*. Thus, here the feminine voice marks male confrontation with the sexual world. These confrontations are intentional, well developed, and interdependent.

Far from being a haphazard collection of disjointed episodes and myths, the *Bālakāṇḍa* can thus be understood as a carefully constructed and narrated work. Vālmīki, as I noted, rarely nods, nor is the popularity of the work among the traditional audiences difficult to understand. It provides an entertaining and yet instructive adventure from adolescence to manhood, and at the same time provides a means for a patriarchal society to articulate a negotiation of sexual anxiety.

NOTES

1. R. Goldman 1984, pp. 60–61; Holtzmann 1841, pp. 36–38.

2. Brockington 1998, pp. 380–381; see also R. Goldman 1984, p. 77.

3. For a detailed and insightful discussion on the prefatory materials of the *Bālakāṇḍa*, see R. Goldman 1984, pp. 60–81.

4. All references are taken from the critical edition of the *Vālmīki Rāmāyaṇa* except those marked GPP, that is, the *Rāmāyan of Vālmīki* published by the Gujarati Printing Press. Translations are based on the critical edition (CE) unless otherwise noted, and are generally taken from the Princeton translation (Goldman 1984).

5. See too, S. Goldman 2001. The gender of the forest is much more nuanced than that of the other sites of actions, for the tradition depicts multiple types of forest: the forest as a locus of sensuality, austerities, dread, delights, and so on. Here we see an intersection of multiple actions. The forest is the locus of both the hunter and the sage, marking it as male. However, the fact that it is the site of the sexual union of the birds marks it as a locus of sexual activity as well. The gendering of sites is also made more complex by the fact that the very gendering of a space allows it to be used as a location in which that very gendering can be contested. For example, in the Brāhmaṇas (see for example, *Śatapathabrāhmaṇa* 3.2.1.18–27), the sacrifice, which I would mark as masculine, is the very location marked as the masculine god Yajña, "sacrifice," where Vāc, the feminine goddess of speech, is seduced; yet in the *Upaniṣads*,

the female sexual organ(s) are mapped onto the sacrifice itself. For example, the sexual nature of the ritual sacrifice is reinforced at *Bṛhadāraṇyaka Upaniṣad* 6.2.13, where a striking comparison between woman and the *soma* sacrifice is made. The passage rather explicitly compares a man experiencing a sexual orgasm with the *soma* sacrifice. The woman's body, specifically her sexual organs, is mapped onto various aspects of the sacrifice:

> *yoṣā vā agnir gautama. tasyā upastha eva samit. lomāni dhūmaḥ. yonir arciḥ. yad antaḥ karoti te 'ṅgārāḥ. abhinandā visphuliṅgāḥ. tasminn etasminn agnau devā reto juhvati. tasyā āhutyai puruṣaḥ sambhavanti. sa jīvati yāvaj jīvati. atha yadā mriyate. . . .*
>
> The young woman (*yoṣā*), Gautama, is the fire. Her sexual organ is the fire stick; her hair, the smoke; her womb (*yoni*), the flame; when one goes inside, the coals; the excitement, the sparks. Into this fire the gods offer their semen. From this offering, a man comes into being. He lives as long as he lives, and then, when he dies. . . .

See also S. Goldman 2001.

6. For example, Bhatt 1959, Masson 1969, Vaudeville 1961–1962, R. Goldman 2000b.

7. The scene is voyeuristic, as the sage and presumably the Niṣāda observe the mating *krauñcas*.

8. Thus Ānandavardhana in his vṛtti on kāraka V, as well as Abhinavagupta in his comments (in the *Locana*) understand that it is the female, not the male, that has been killed. See also Masson 1969, p. 209. The *Tilakaṭīkā*, a commentary on the *Rāmāyaṇa* composed by Nāgojibhaṭṭa, understands the *krauñca* to be a demon, and thus the "curse" of Vālmīki is symbolic: "When he said, you killed one (i.e., the male), he meant his word to terminate with this idea 'just as you caused him to be without his wife, and made his wife be without her lover (*nāyaka*) so may you be separated from your beloved wife and may she be separated from you' " (*Tilakaṭīkā* on *Rām.* 1.2.14 GPP).

9. Masson 1969, p. 215.

10. Kataka understands the verse symbolically: "The meaning [of the verse] in the form of the curse uttered by Vālmīki to the hunter who killed the bird before his eyes, is quite clear. The deeper [or symbolic] meaning of the verse is this: Vālmīki addresses the stanza to Rāvaṇa calling him a *niṣāda* because he excessively tormented, i.e., troubled, all the three worlds with their hosts of gods and sages. . . . O tormentor of the three worlds (*niṣāda*), i.e., O Rāvaṇa! Since from a pair of *krauñca* birds, i.e., the pair of Rāma and Sītā, which had been very reduced, i.e., extremely emaciated, because they had been experiencing the sorrows of the loss of their kingdom, banishment to the forest, etc., you killed one in the form of [Sītā], that has plunged her into grief greater than the pain of death itself by kidnapping her and imprisoning her in Laṅkā. Therefore you will not any longer enjoy in the city of Laṅkā that stability, i.e., peace and happiness, which had been vouchsafed to you in the company of your sons and grandsons and servants, etc., by Brahmā himself. Thus the stanza hints at the main episode of the *Rāmāyaṇa*, namely, the abduction of Sītā by Rāvaṇa and his eventual destruction. And so this stanza, the first verse in Sanskrit, which is the most auspicious thing in all the three worlds, was first (*purastāt*) revealed by the true Goddess Sarasvatī" (*Śrīmadvālmīkirāmāyaṇam* 1965–1975).

Govindarāja, too, provides a long, and somewhat tortuous explanation of the passages. Like Kataka, he understands Rāvaṇa to be symbolized by the *Niṣāda,* and Rāma and Sītā the pair of *krauñcas.* "wherein out of the couple of Rāma and Sītā, Rāvaṇa killed, i.e., extremely tormented one member, namely Sītā, by subjecting her to the excessive pangs of separation and thereby causing them both to become emaciated" (*Śrīmadvālmīkirāmāyaṇam* 1953).

11. The feminine voice is, however, quickly taken and controlled by the masculine. The feminine voice, the piteous cry, *karuṇāṃ giram*—gendered feminine in the original—is heard, and then transformed by Vālmīki, the male agent, into *śloka,* also gendered male in the language, much as the feminine speech, *vāc,* of the vedic seers is revealed to and controlled by the vedic seers (S. Goldman 2001).

12. Tilakaṭikā understands that Rāma's purity refers to the fact that there might be a stain in reference to that purity, in that he might only have a desire for a beautiful woman.

13. Here, I am reading with the vulgate, which understands *śrutim iva,* "like *śruti.*" The critical edition reads instead *śrīm iva,* "like *śrī,*" even so, in this context *śrī* must be read as Veda or Sarasvatī. Śrī is not normally associated with Brahmā, whereas speech, the Vedas, and Sarasvatī are. The word *śrī* can mean the three Vedas, speech, and is a name for Sarasvatī (Apte 1957–1959, sv).

14. See S. Goldman 2000a; *Sundarakāṇḍa* 5.13.15–36, esp. 30–36; Goldman and Goldman 1996, pp. 154–155.

15. S. Goldman 1997a, 1997b.

16. Jacobi 1893, pp. 74–75; see also R. Goldman 1984, p. 73.

17. Jacobi 1893; Bulcke 1952–1953; R. Goldman 1984.

18. R. Goldman 1984, p. 75. See *Mahābhārata* 3.110–113; *Padmapurāṇa Pātālakhaṇḍa* 13; *Bhāratamañjarī* 3.758–795; *Bhadrakalāvadāna* 33; *Avadānakalpalatā* 65; *Alambusā* and *Naḷanikā Jātakas,* etc. See note on *Rāmāyana* 1.8.7 (R. Goldman 1984, pp. 292–293).

19. Śāntā in some editions is said to be Daśaratha's daughter. See R. Goldman 1984, p. 75. See, too, Chatterji 1954.

20. Compare the story and discussion on Umā and Gaṅgā below.

21. Chatterji 1954; R. Goldman 1984, p. 294.

22. R. Goldman 1984, p. 74; Bulcke 1952–1953; Govindaraja on 1.11.12.

23. Kane 1962–1975, 4:91–92.

24. See Bhatt 1960, pp. 331, 334, who argues that the *aśvamedha* here is merely a means to remove obstacles that were preventing the king from obtaining a son, a notion that the text itself supports (1.13.30).

25. See Jamison 1996, pp. 65–72. It is interesting to note that the wives of the king are allocated to different locations around the horse. The crowned queen is in the front, the favorite queen in the middle, and the discarded queen at the back of the horse; Kane 1962–1975, 2:1,234].

26. Kane 1962–1975, 2:1,234. The symbolism of the left thigh is meaningful in the sexual context, in that it represents the sexual side. See Sutherland 1989.

27. *Āpastamba Śatapathabrāhmaṇa* 22.18, 3–4, *Kātyāyana śrautasūtram* 20.15–16.

28. Kane 1962–1975, 2:1,234–1,235.

29. Bulcke 1952–1953, p. 331. R. Goldman 1984, p. 74.

30. According to Kane 1962–1975 2:276, the ideal age for the thread ceremony (*upanayana*) of a kshatriya is eleven years, with the secondary times being from the ninth to the sixteenth years. The standard period of studentship is thought is have been twelve years (p. 349).

31. Sutherland 1991; R. Goldman 1982.

32. 1.9.90–27 gives some voice to the courtesans that seduce Ṛśyaśṛṅga.

33. S. Goldman 2000b.

34. S. Goldman 2000a.

35. See note to *sarga* 52 in R. Goldman 1984. The story is also told at *Mahābhārata* 1.164–165.

36. Brown 1964, S. Goldman 2001, R. Goldman 1978.

37. R. Goldman 1978.

38. R. Goldman 1977, 1978; Sukthankar 1937.

39. See R. Goldman 1984, p. 332, for a discussion on the term *kṛtodvāham* "prior to his marriage." The northern rendering of the story makes it clear that the term is used for the marriage of Pārvatī and Śiva (*[kāmaḥ] āveṣṭum abhyayāt tūrṇaṃ kṛtodvāham umāpatim*).

40. See R. Goldman 1984, p. 336.

41. S. Goldman 2000b; see also R. Goldman 2000a.

42. *Rāmāyaṇa* 1.24.11.

43. See R. Goldman 1984, p. 336.

44. The term "archaic mother" is understood on the basis of Kristeva's expanded construction of the Freudian oedipal mother—sometimes referred to as the "archaic mother"—as the "fecund mother and the phantasmatic mother who constitutes the abyss which is so crucial in the formation of subjectivity" (Creed 1993 p. 25). It is this abyss that is the "cannibalizing black hole from which all life comes and to which all life returns" and is represented as a source of "deepest terror."

45. S. Goldman 2000b.

46. R. Goldman 1982.

47. At 1.33.6 we are given the lineage: Kuśanābha, Gādhi, Viśvāmitra.

48. Sutherland 1992; Masson 1980, pp. 110–124.

49. The story, it seems to me, is really a story of the onset of menstruation. When Vāyu enters them, their periods start and the young women are polluted and polluting and considered impure and deformed until the time that they are suitably married, this reflects traditional attitudes toward unmarried girls who have reached puberty. See Jamison 1996, pp. 237–240, on the haste needed in securing husbands for postpubescent females. The connection is further substantiated by the Āyurvedic tradition. There wind is said to be of four types: *prāṇa* (fore-breath), *udāna* (up-breath), *vyāna* (intra-breath), and *apāna* (down-breath). This last type is understood to be the force that causes urine, feces, semen, fetus, and menstrual blood to flow downward; see Wujastyk [1998] 2001, p. 165. For additional connections between wind [*vāyu*] and menarche, see *Carakasaṃhitā* 1.12.8, 1.1.59, 62; *Śārṅgadharasaṃhitā* 1.5.25; cf. *Suśrutasaṃhitā, Nidāna* 1.1–30. Furthermore, wind in the body is associated with countless illnesses and defects; Wujastyk [1998] 2001, pp. 166–173, esp. R. 171. I would like to acknowledge my deep gratitude to Professor R. K. Sharma for these references and his help in establishing these relationships.

50. For example, *Śivapurāṇa* (*Rudrasaṃhitā*) 4.1–2; *Mahābhārata* 3.213–216; *Matsyapurāṇa* 146; *Vāmanapurāṇa* 28; *Varāhapurāṇa* 25; *Kumārasambhava* 9–11, etc. See O'Flaherty 1973, pp. 161–168.

51. Note to 1.22.15 (Goldman 1984, p. 332).

52. See too, *Śivapurāṇa* 2.3.23,12; *Skandapurāṇa* 1.1.25.155 (where Vāyu ignites Agni, who sets the seed on fire).

53. The frame motif of interrupted lovemaking comes back to haunt us here, and that in both the frame and, here, the interrupter(s) are cursed: the Niṣāda and the

gods. There, however, the voice of the female is inarticulate, whereas here the curse is voiced by the female.

54. S. Goldman 1996.

55. See *Mahābhārata* 1.15ff.; *Bhāgavatapurāṇa* 8.6–9; *Matsyapurāṇa* 249.51; *Viṣṇupurāṇa* 1.9, etc. See Bedekar 1967, pp. 7–61, and Dange 1969, pp. 239–80.

56. *Skandapurāṇa* 1.1.35.27–34.

57. Symbolically, of course, the "earth" Pṛthivī, substitutes for the mother.

58. See the discussion of the story of Ahalyā below.

59. Psychoanalytic/feminist readings of this jump to mind, especially as we are told at 1.46.9 that Indra is Diti's son.

60. GPP 1.46.18.

61. See Bhatt 1960, p. 453, critical note to *sarga* 45. See too Kirfel 1947, where he has compared *sarga* 45 and verses 1–18 of *sarga* 46 with the *Vāyupurāṇa* passage at 91.68.

62. "Mother and son" (*mātāputrau*) return to heaven (1.46.9). Also note the Śukra story where he enters Śiva and emerges as his son, and the Kaca story where a similar theme, with a gender twist, occurs (*Mahabharata* 12.278.1–38: Śukra and Śiva; *Mahabharata* 1.71.1–58: Kaca and Śukra). See too R. Goldman 1977, pp. 1–27, 60–66; 90–92; 124–127; Sutherland 1979.

63. See *Śivapurāṇa* 2.4.1.44–63.

64. *Rāmāyaṇa* 7.30; *Mahābhārata* 12.329.14; *Śatapatha Brāhmaṇa* 3.3.4.18; 5.2.3.8, 12.7.1.10; *Brahmapurāṇa* 87; *Brahmavaivarta* 4.47; 61; *Padma purāna* 1.56.15–33; 5.51; *Skanda purāna* 5.3.136–138; 6.207–208; *Viṣṇudharmottara purāṇa* 1.128.7.30.

65. Tilakaṭīkā and Govindarāja gloss *viphalaḥu* as *vigatavṛṣaṇaḥ*, "of departed testicles"; Siromaṇi, *vṛṣaṇarahitaḥ*, "without testicles" (GPP 1.48.29).

66. R. Goldman 1978.

67. S. Goldman 1997b.

68. Schoebel 1888; R. Goldman 1982; Gail 1977, pp. 48–56.

69. Sukthankar 1937, p. 20; R. Goldman 1977, p. 115.

70. R. Goldman 1977, 1982.

71. S. Goldman 2000b.

72. Literally, "made cold *or* frigid," but also, "dull, paralyzed, motionless, benumbed. stupid, irrational, not able to learn the Vedas, senseless, etc." See Apte 1957–1959, s.v.

73. R. Goldman 1977, 1982.

74. R. Goldman 1977, 1982.

75. Sukthankar 1937; R. Goldman 1977.

76. *Mahābhārata* 3.115–117. See R. Goldman 1977 pp. 18–25.

77. *Mahābhārata* 3.1161–1129; see also R. Goldman 1978.

REFERENCES

Adhyātma-Rāmāyaṇa. 1884. With commentary of Ramavarman. Edited by Pandit Jibananda Vidyasagara. Calcutta: Valmiki Press.

Agnipurāṇam. [1900] 1957. Ānandāśrama Sanskrit Series no. 41. Poona: Ānandāśrama Press.

Āpastambaśrautasūtra. 1955, 1963. With Dhūrtasvāmibhāṣya. Edited by Paṇḍita Āchinnaswāmī Śāstrī. 2 vols. Baroda: Oriental Institute.

Apte, V. S. 1957–1959. *The Practical Sanskrit-English Dictionary*. 3 vols. Poona: Prasad Prakashan.

Aryan, K. C. 1975. *Hanuman*. n.p.

Bedekar, V. M. 1967. "The Legend of the Churning of the Ocean in the Epics and Purāṇas." *Purāṇam* 9.1: 7–61.

Bhāgavatapurāṇam. 1965. With thirteen commentaries. Edited by Kṛṣṇa Śaṅkara Śāstrī. Nadiyad: Kṛṣṇa Śaṅkara Śāstrī et al.

Bhāgavatapurāṇam. [1983] 1988. With the commentary *Bhāvārthabodhinī* of Srīdhara Svāmin. Delhi: Motilal Banarsidass.

The Bharatamañjari of Kṣemendra. 1989. Edited by Sivadatta and Kāsīnātha Pāṇḍurang Parab. Kāvyamāla 65. Bombay: Tukaram Javaji.

Bhatt, G. H. 1959. "Krauñcavadha in Dhvanyāloka and Kāvyamīmāṃsā." *Journal of the Oriental Institute* [Baroda] 9: 148–151.

Bhatt, G. H., ed. 1960. *The Bālakāṇḍa: The First Book of the Vālmīki Rāmāyaṅa: The National Epic of India*. Baroda: Oriental Institute.

Brahmāṇḍapurāṇam. 1973. Edited by J. L. Shastri. Delhi: Motilal Banarsidass.

Brahmapurāṇam. 1895. Ānandāśrama Sanskrit Series no. 28. Poona: Ānandāśrama Press.

Brahmapurāṇam. 1987. See *Sanskrit Indices and Text of the Brahmapurāṇa*.

Brahmavaivarta. 1935. Ānandāśrama Sanskrit Series no. 102. 4 vols. Poona: Ānandāśrama Press.

Brockington, John. 1984. *Righteous Rāma: The Evolution of an Epic*. Delhi: Oxford University Press.

———. 1998. *The Sanskrit Epics*. Leiden: E. J. Brill.

Brown, W. Norman. 1964. "The Sanctity of the Cow in Hinduism." *Economic Weekly* (February), pp. 245–255).

Bulcke, Camille. 1952–1953. "The Genesis of the Bālakāṇḍa." *Journal of the Oriental Institute* [Baroda] 2: 327–331.

Carakasaṃhitā. 1976. Text with translation and critical exposition based on Cakrapāṇi's *Āyurvedadīpikā*. Vol. 1. Edited and translated by R. K. Sharma and B. Dash. Varanasi: Chowkhamba Sanskrit Series Office.

Chatterjee, Ashoke. 1954. "The Problem of Śantā's Parentage as Affecting the Text of the *Rāmāyaṇa*." *Our Heritage*, 2.2: 353–374.

Creed, Barbara. 1993. *The Monstrous Feminine: Film, Feminism, Psychoanalysis*. New York: Routledge.

Dange, S. A. 1969. *Legends in the Mahābhārata*. Delhi: Motilal Banarsidass.

Dhvanyāloka of Ānandavardhana. 1891. With the *Locana* commentary of Abhinavagupta. Edited by Durgāprasād and Kāśināth Pāṇḍurang Parab. Bombay: Nirṇayasāgar Press.

Gail, Adalbert. 1977. *Paraśurāma: Brahmane und Krieger*. Wiesbaden: Otto Harrassowitz.

The Garuḍamahāpurāṇam. 1984. Delhi: Nag Publishers.

Goldman, Robert P. 1977. *Gods, Priests, and Warriors: The Bhṛgus of the Mahābhārata*. New York: Columbia University Press.

———. 1978. "Fathers, Sons, and Gurus: Oedipal Conflict in the Sanskrit Epics." *Journal of Indian Philosophy* 6: 325–392.

———. 1980. "Rāmaḥ Sahalakṣmaṇaḥ: Psychological and Literary Aspects of the Composite Hero of Vālmīki's *Rāmāyaṇa*." *Journal of Indian Philosophy* 8: 149–189.

———. 1982. "Matricide, Renunciation, and Compensation in the Legends of Two Warrior Heroes of the Sanskrit Epics." *Proceedings of the Stockholm Conference Seminar in Indological Studies. Indologica Taurinensia* 10: 117–131.

———. 1984. *The Rāmāyaṇa of Vālmīki: An Epic of Ancient India.* Vol. 1. *Bālakāṇḍa.* Translation and introduction by Robert P. Goldman. Annotation by Robert P. Goldman and Sally J. Sutherland. Princeton: Princeton University Press.

———. 2000a. "Rāvaṇa's Kitchen: A Testimony of Desire and the Other." In *Questioning Rāmāyaṇas,* edited by Paula Richman. Berkley and Los Angeles: University of California Press, pp. 105–116, 374–376.

———. 2000b. "The Ghost from the Anthill: Vālmīki and the Destiny of the Rāmakathā in South and Southeast Asia." In *A Varied Optic: Contemporary Studies in the Rāmāyaṇa,* edited by Mandakranta Bose. Vancouver: Institute of Asian Research, University of British Columbia, pp. 11–30.

Goldman, Robert P., and Sally J. Sutherland Goldman, eds. and trans. 1996. *The Rāmāyaṇa of Vālmīki: An Epic of Ancient India.* Vol. 5. *Sundarakāṇḍa.* Introduction and annotation by Robert P. Goldman and Sally J. Sutherland Goldman. Princeton: Princeton University Press.

Goldman, Sally J. Sutherland. 1996. "Soul Food: Eating, Conception, and Gender in the Literature of Premodern India." Paper delivered at annual meeting of the Association of Asian Studies, Honolulu, Hawaii, April; a revised version was presented at the annual Conference on South Asia, Madison, Wisconsin, October.

———. 1997a. "Suttee, Satī, and Sahagamana: An Epic Misunderstanding." In *Women, Power, and Cultural Difference: Negotiating Gender in South Asia,* edited by R. Sharma. Delhi: Indian Books Centre.

———. 1997b. "The Power of the Gaze: Scopophilic Behavior in Sanskrit Narrative." Paper delivered at "Re-Presenting Women: Workshop on Women in the Literary, Performing, and Visual Arts of India," University of California at Berkeley, April 25–27.

———. 2000a. "Anklets Away: The Symbolism of Jewelry and Ornamentation in *Vālmīki's Rāmāyaṇa.*" In *A Varied Optic: Contemprary Studies in the Rāmāyaṇa,* edited by Mandakranta Bose, Vancouver: Institute of Asian Research, University of British Columbia, pp. 125–153.

———. 2000b. "Rākṣasīs and Other Others: The Archaic Mother in Bhāsa's *Madhyama-vyāyoga.*" Paper delivered at the eleventh World Sanskrit Conference, Turin Italy, April 3–8.

———. 2001. "Speaking Gender: Vāc and the Vedic Construction of the Feminine." In *Gender, Religion, and Social Definition,* edited by Julia Leslie. Delhi: Oxford University Press, pp. 1–27.

Holtzmann, Adolf. 1841. *Uber den griechischen ursprung des indischen Thierkreises.* Karlsruhe: George Holtzmann.

Jacobi, Hermann. 1893. *Das Rāmāyaṇa: Geschichte und Inhalt, nebst Concordanz der gedruckten Recensionen.* Bonn: Friedrich Cohen.

Jamison, Stephanie, W. 1996. *Sacrificed Wife, Sacrificer's Wife: Women, Ritual, and Hospitality in Ancient India.* New York: Oxford University Press.

Jātakas with Commentary. 1877–1897. Edited by, V. Fausboll. 7 vols. London: Trübner Reprint London: Pali Text Society, 1962–1965.

Kane, Pandurang V. 1941–1975. *History of Dharmaśāstra.* 8 vols. Poona: Bhandarkar Oriental Research Institute.

Kātyāyanaśrautasūtram. 1990. Śulbasūtravṛttiḥ sahitam Kātyāyana-praṇītam; Vidyādharaśarmaṇā viracitayā. Vol. 46. Delhi: Caukhamba Saṃskṛta Pratiṣṭhāna.

Kirfel, Willibald. 1947. "*Rāmāyaṇa* Bālakāṇḍa und Purāṇa: Ein Beitrag zur chronologischen Fixierung des ersten Buches." *Die Welt des Orients,* 1: 113–118.

The Kumārasambhava of Kālidāsa. 1886. With the commentary (the *Sañjīvinī*) of Mallinātha (1–8 *sargas*) and of Sītārāma (8–17 *sargas*). Edited by Nārāyaṇa Bhaṭṭa Parvaṇīkara and Kāśīnātha Pāṇḍurang Parab. Bombay: Nirṇayasāgara Press.

Mahābhārata. 1929. With the commentary of Nīlakaṇṭha. 6 vols. Poona: Chitrashala Press.

Mahābhārata: Critical Edition. 1933–1970. With *Harivaṃśa* (1969–1971). Critically edited by V. S. Sukthankar et al. 24 vols. Poona: Bhandarkar Oriental Research Institute.

Masson, Jeffrey. 1969. "Who Killed Cock Krauñca? Abhinavagupta's Reflections on the Origin of Aesthetic Experience." *Journal of the Oriental Institute* [Baroda] 18: 207–224.

———. 1980. *The Oceanic Feeling: The Origins of Religious Sentiment in Ancient India.* Studies of Classical India 3. Dordrecht: Reidel.

Matsyapurāṇam. 1907. Edited by Hari Narayana Apte. Ānandāśrama Sanskrit Series, 54. Poona: Ānandāśrama Press.

O'Flaherty, Wendy Doniger. 1973. *Śiva: The Erotic Ascetic.* London: Oxford University Press.

Padmapurāṇam. 1893–1894. Edited by Viśvanātha Nārāyaṇa Maṇḍalik. Ānandāśrama Sanskrit Series 131. 4 vols. Poona: Ānandāśrama Press.

Rāmāyaṇa. 1928–1947. Northwestern recension critically edited for the first time from original manuscripts by Vishva Bandhu. 7 vols. D.A.V. College Sanskrit Series 7, 12, 14, 17–20. Lahore: D.A.V. College.

Rāmāyaṇ of Vālmīki. 1914–1920. With three commentaries called Tilaka, Shiromani, and Bhooshana. Edited by Shastri Shrinivasa Katti Mudholkar. 7 vols. Bombay: Gujarati Printing Press.

Sanskrit Indices and Text of the Brahmapurāṇa. 1987. Edited by Peter Schreiner and Renate Söhnen. Wiesbaden: Otto Harrassowitz.

Śārṅgadharasaṃhitā. 1983. Edited by Paṇdit Paraśurāma Śāstrī. Varanasi: Chaukhamba Orientalia.

Śatapatha Brāhmaṇam. 1940. With Sāyaṇa's commentary. 5 vols. Bombay: Laxmi Venkateshwar Steam Press.

Schoebel, Charles. 1888. *Le Rāmayaṇa au point du vu religieux, philosphique et moral.* Paris: Guimet.

Śivapurāṇam. 1906. Bombay: Veṅkaṭeśvara Press.

Śrīmadvālmīkirāmāyaṇam. 1953. Edited by Gaṅgāviṣṇu Śrīkṛṣṇadāsa. With the commentaries of Govindarāja, Rāmānuja, and Maheśvaratīrtha and the commentary known as Taṇiślokī. 3 vols. Bombay: Lakṣmīveṅkaṭeśvara Mudraṇālaya.

Śrīmadvālmīkirāmāyaṇam. 1965–1975. Edited by K. S. Varadacharya, et al. With Amṛtakataka of Mādhavayogi. 5 vols. Mysore: University of Mysore.

Skandapurāṇa Sūtasaṃhitā. 1954. Madras: Balamanorama Press.

Sukthankar, V. S. 1937. "The Bhṛgus and the Bharata: A Text-Historical Study." *Annals of the Bhandarkar Oriental Research Institute* 18: 1–76.

Suśrutasaṃhitā. 1963. Vols. 1 and 2. Chowkhamba Sanskrit Studies, 30. Edited and translated by Kavirāja Kunjalal Bhiṣgaaratna. Varanasi: Chowkhamba Sanskrit Series Office.

Suśrutasaṃhitā. 1980. Varanasi: Caukhambha Oriyantaliya. Anya Prāptisthāna, Caukhambha Saṃskṛta Saṃsthāna Series, Jayakṛṣṇadāsa Āyurveda Granthamālā 34.
The Suśrutasaṃhitā of Suśruta with various readings, notes and appendix, etc. 1945. Edited by Narayan Ram Acharya, with Vaidya. Bombay: Nirnaya Sagar Press.
Suśrutasaṃhitā Nidānasthānam. 1977. New Delhi: Meharacandra Lachamandas.
Sutherland, Sally J. 1979. "Śukrācārya: The Demons' Priest: Aspects of Character Development in Sanskrit Mythological Literature. Ph.D. dissertation, University of California, Berkeley.
———. 1989. "Draupadī and Sītā: Aggressive Behavior and Female Role-Models." *Journal of the American Oriental Society* 109.1: 63–79.
———. 1991. "The Bad Seed: Senior Wives and Elder Sons." In *Bridging Worlds: Studies on Women in South Asia*, edited by S. J. Sutherland. Berkeley: Centers for South and Southeast Asia Studies, International and Area Studies. pp. 24–52.
———. 1992. "Seduction and Counter-Seduction: Bedroom Politics in the Ancient Epics." *Journal of Indian Philosophy* 20: 243–251.
The Vālmīki Rāmāyaṇa: Critical Edition. 1960–1975. General editors, G. H. Bhatt and U. P. Shah. 7 vols. Baroda: Oriental Institute.
Vāmanapurāṇam. 1967. Edited by Anand Swarup Gupta. Varanasi: All-India Kashiraj Trust.
Varāhapurāṇam. 1973. Edited by V. Gautama. 2 vols. Bareli, University Press, India: Saṃskṛti-Saṃsthāna.
Vaudville, Charlotte. 1961–1962. "A Further Note on Krauñcavadha in *Dhvanyāloka* and *Kāvyamīmāmsa*." *Journal of the Oriental Institute* [Baroda] 11: 122–126.
Vāyupurāṇam. 1959. Gurumandal Series 19. 2 vols. Calcutta: Gurumandal Press.
Viṣṇudharmottarapurāṇa. 1971. Edited by Ashoka Chaterji Sastri. Gaṅgānatha-Jhā-granthamālā. Varanasi: Saṃskṛta Viśvavidyālaya Research Institute.
Viṣṇupurāṇa. 1972. With the commentary of Śrīdhara. Edited by Sītārāmadās Oṃkāranātha. Calcutta: n.p.
Wujastyk, Dominik. [1998] 2001. *The Roots of Ayurveda: Selections from Sanskrit Medical Writings*. New Delhi: Penguin Books India.

3

Rāmāyaṇa Textual Traditions in Eastern India

William L. Smith

Writing *Rāmāyaṇas*

How did one set about writing a *Rāmāyaṇa*? It had once been assumed that the medieval poets composed their versions of the epic with a manuscript of Vālmīki propped up in front of them; after all, histories of literature refer to this genre as *anuvāda sāhitya*, translation literature. However, many of the stories in these works are not found in Vālmīki, so the process cannot have been so straightforward. To gain a better notion of the way in which vernacular *Rāmāyaṇas* were constructed, we can look to the rich Rāma literature in the three eastern New Indo-Aryan (NIA) languages—Assamese, Bengali, and Oriya—that possess a wide range of Rāma works written over the span of many centuries, which makes it possible for us to study in detail the development of the theme and the various influences that transformed it.

It is difficult to say exactly how many premodern versions of the *Rāmāyaṇa* were composed in northeastern India, since many still remain in manuscript, but it is possible that more versions of the epic are found here than in comparable regions. The majority of these poems are popular works intended for a mass audience, and for this reason, snobbish (in the linguistic sense) brahmans often had little respect for them—an attitude that persists to a certain extent today. Poets elsewhere in India, such as some writing in Marathi and Brajbhāṣā, produced sophisticated versions of the Rāma story in strict conformance to Sanskrit rhetorical conventions. Although no similar works appeared in either Assamese or Bengali, several Oriya poets successfully emulated classical models. The most admired of them was eighteenth-century poet Upendra Bhanja, who composed a Rāma work entitled *Vaidehi Vilāsa*, a long poem, every line of which begins with the consonant V. This exercise in rhetoric can only be understood, if at all, with the help of an extensive commentary. Despite (or because of) the extreme difficulty of his style, Upendra Bhanja is considered the greatest medieval Oriya poet.

On the other end of the scale we have works like the Bengali *Rāmāyaṇa* of Candrāvatī. It circulated orally for three centuries before finally being written down around a century ago. It was, like many popular *Rāmāyaṇas*, composed in rhyming couplets called *payār* in Bengali, *pada* in Assamese, and *daṇḍa* in Oriya. These simple meters, which have been called rhymed prose, made both composition and improvisation easier. Most *Rāmāyaṇas* were semi-oral in the sense that they were not read but performed, that is, sung or recited, often by professional singers called (in Bengali) *gāyak* or *gāyen*, and a number of them were composed by such professionals. Durgāvara, author of the sixteenth-century *Gīti Rāmāyaṇa* in Assamese, for example, was a professional singer or *ojā* who also produced a song on the myth of the snake goddess Manasā. Only part of it has survived, and that part comprises songs composed in twenty different ragas, thus justifying the title of the poem. Other versions were designed for other purposes. In Assamese we have the *Śrīrāmakīrttana* of Ananta Ṭhākur Ātā, which was designed to be used in religious services; it was recited by the leader of the group while the members of the group repeated the refrain as they clapped their hands. In other words, it was performed in the same way as a *kīrtana*.

In terms of treatment, Rāma poems can be divided into two categories: full *Rāmāyaṇas* that relate the entire story, and episodic *Rāmāyaṇas* that concern themselves with a single episode or a few related episodes. Interesting examples of the latter are found in Assam in the form of unique prequels and sequels to the Rāma story. The *Śatruñjaya* of Raghunātha Mahānta tells the tale of the digvijaya (march of conquest) of the monkey king Vālī conducted by Hanumān. The *Adbhuta Rāmāyaṇa* (which has nothing to do with the Sanskrit work of the same name) of the same poet, as well as the *Pātālī Kāṇḍa* of Dvija Pañcānana, continue the story of Sītā after she has returned to the bosom of her mother, the earth, though one might have thought that Sītā's story had definitely ended there. These two works tell how Sītā, sitting in the underworld, misses her two sons Kuśa and Lava and sends a *nāga* to bring them back to her. The poems are largely concerned with Hanumān's pursuit of the boys and his battles with the *nāgas*. In Bengal there are a large number of such episodic poems, including the *Taraṇisena Yuddha*, the *Śiva Rāmera Yuddha*, the slaying of the hundred-headed Rāvaṇa, the *Aṅgada Rāybāra*, and various others. Sometimes they were inserted into complete versions of the *Rāmāyaṇa*. Even full versions of the epic often did not always circulate as complete manuscripts but as individual *kāṇḍas*. Since manuscripts underwent changes over the centuries, independently circulating versions of the same *kāṇḍa* often became increasingly divergent, and if they were reassembled into complete versions of the epic, these could differ markedly from one another. Similarly, sometimes "new" *Rāmāyaṇas* were composed by assembling episodes or *kāṇḍas* from different sources, the contributions usually still bearing the *bhaṇitās*, that is, signatures of their authors. This process almost seems like shuffling a deck of cards, each shuffle producing a more or less different *Rāmāyaṇa*.

There are also dramatic versions of episodes from the epic. The most important of them are the *aṅkīyā nāṭ* plays of Assam, a dramatic form devised by the reformer Śaṅkaradeva; many *aṅkīyā nāṭ*s are on Rāma themes, and they continued to be written until the nineteenth-century. In Orissa the best known of the dramatic versions of the Rāma theme are the *Vicitra Rāmāyaṇa* of Viśvānātha Khuṇṭīa (early eighteenth century) and the *Śrīrāmalīlā* of Vikrama Narendra, who wrote a century later. These dance dramas were performed outside in the open air during the Durgā Pūjā festival in October or on Rāmanavamī in April, the verses being sung by choruses while boys danced to the music.

Vālmīki

Though the regional *Rāmāyaṇas* may not be translations of Vālmīki, they do rely on him—more specifically, the eastern or Gaudian recension of Vālmīki—for the basic story line, and even though some poets include a great deal of non-Vālmīkian material, this original outline is left intact. There is no reason to suppose that this proves firsthand familiarity with the Sanskrit original, since the knowledge of Vālmīki's work could have been acquired in other ways. The first and final *kāṇḍas* are exceptions. The first or *Ādikāṇḍa*, as it is known in eastern India, differs in that it often becomes a repository for a considerable number of non-Vālmīkian (though not necessarily non-Sanskritic) stories. The seventy-six *adhyāyas* of the *Ādikāṇḍa* of the seventeenth-century Bengali poet Adbhutācāryya, for example, contain accounts of Viṣṇu's battle with Madhu Kaiṭabha, the story of Garuḍa, of the marriage of Śiva and Pārvatī, the birth of Kārttikeya; the fight of the forty-nine winds with Sumeru, Śiva's victory over Tripurāsura, the story of Dhruva, and of Indra's defeat of Vṛtra, as well as stories featuring Bali, Dilīpa, and other purāṇic figures.[1] The *Uttarakāṇḍa*, on the other hand, is sometimes radically abridged or simply omitted; some poets felt that the epic ended on a more satisfactory note with Rāma's triumphant return to Ayodhyā and his coronation. When speaking of Vālmīki, it should be kept in mind that in the opinion of the medieval poets he was not only the *ādi kavi*, the "original poet," and author of the original *Rāmāyaṇa* but also the author of many other Sanskrit *Rāmāyaṇas*, including the *Adhyātma Rāmāyaṇa, Adbhūta Rāmāyaṇa*, and *Ānanda Rāmāyaṇa*, in the same way that it was assumed that Vyāsa had composed the *Mahābhārata* along with all eighteen Purāṇas and eighteen Upapurāṇas.

The Other *Ādi Kavis*

The regional poets picked up their Rāma lore in various ways. A potential poet would most likely hear his first version of the story of Rāma sitting on grandmother's knee and then, as he progressed through life, would come into contact with it in other forms: folktales, dramatic performances, paintings, and sculpture, as well as written versions in his own language, and, if well educated, Sanskrit and even perhaps versions in other languages. We can feel sure that the first full version of the *Rāmāyaṇa* that any poet heard or read was one in his own language. Each of our three languages possesses a written version of the epic that has dominated the local tradition from the time it first appeared until today; these three renderings also happen to be the first full versions written in the respective languages. Because of their later influence, any stories selected by the three earliest Rāma poets tended to be included in the *Rāmāyaṇas* of their successors. The oldest of them is the fourteenth-century Assamese rendering of Mādhava Kandalī.[2] His version, which is unusually faithful to Vālmīki, lacks a first as well as a final *kāṇḍa*, and it is not known whether they have been lost or were never written. Around 150 years after Mādhava Kandalī's *Rāmāyaṇa* appeared, the devotional movement was introduced into Assam by the reforming poet-saint Śaṅkaradeva. Some of the Vaiṣṇava reformers were critical of the lack of the devotional spirit in Mādhava Kandalī's poem, and one of them, Ananta Kandalī, announced that he would rewrite the poem in conformance with bhakti ideas. According to later hagiographers, the long-deceased Mādhava Kandalī was so upset at the prospect of his *Rāmāyaṇa* being superseded by a new version that he appeared in a dream to Śaṅkaradeva and asked him to save it from oblivion. Śaṅkaradeva heeded his plea and "devotionalized" the poem with the help of his disciple Mādhavadeva by the simple expedient of inserting exhortations built up around phrases like *bolo rāma rāma* in the colophons, such as *palāuk pātaka bolo rāma rāma*, "let sin flee, say Rāma Rāma!" They did not apparently make any alterations in the narrative itself. These superficial alterations were deemed sufficient to make the work devotionally acceptable, and Kandalī's poem remained dominant in Assam. Śaṅkaradeva and Mādhavadeva also added the two missing *kāṇḍas*. Despite the fact that both reformers were excellent Sanskrit scholars, they chose not to rely upon Vālmīki, as Mādhava Kandalī had. Mādhavadeva's *Ādikāṇḍa* is rich in non-Vālmīkian stories, and in the *Uttarakāṇḍa* Śaṅkardeva concentrates on the story of Rāma's repudiation of Sītā and omits most else. His treatment of the story is remarkable for his strong sympathy with Sītā.[3] Despite this, Ananta Kandalī did carry out his plan: his revised version of Mādhava Kandalī's poem is distinguished by its homiletic asides and the thorough bowdlerization of all mention of deities other than Viṣṇu. His version of the epic never approached the original in popularity, and his approach probably had much to do with this.

The late fifteenth-century poet Kṛttivāsa dominates the *Rāmāyaṇa* tradition in Bengal in a very different way. Kṛttivāsa's original *Rāmāyaṇa* garnered so much prestige that before long other poets began writing new material under his name, and as a consequence eventually a number of diverse *Rāmāyaṇas* bearing the signature of Kṛttivāsa were in circulation. The seventeenth-century manuscript of his *Uttarakāṇḍa* edited by Hirendranāth Datta,[4] for example, is almost as long as a complete version of the *Kṛttivāsī Rāmāyaṇa* based on two eighteenth-century manuscripts edited by Sukhamaya Mukhopādhyāya.[5] Over fifteen hundred manuscripts bearing the signature of Kṛttivāsa are extant, including many episodic *Rāmāyaṇas* on diverse themes ranging from the war between Rāma and Śiva to the slaying of the hundred-headed Rāvaṇa.[6] This state of affairs did not come to an end with the introduction of printing. The first printed version of Krttivāsa, one of the first Bengali books to use the new (for India) technology, came out in 1803. Thirty years later it was decided to bring out a new edition, and a Sanskrit scholar named Jayagopāl was given the task of editing it. Jayagopāl found the first edition full of what he considered vulgarisms, inconsistencies, and linguistic impurities, so he revised it. After him, the process was repeated as new editors altered the text, changing the language and sometimes adding new materials much in the same way as their predecessors had been doing in pre-printing days.[7] As a result, there exist a number of *Rāmāyaṇas* that are only nominally by Kṛttivāsa, although they appear under his name. Many such editions have been printed, and when scholars refer to Kṛttivāsa, they often mean one or another of them. Because of this, when speaking of Kṛttivāsa it should be made clear which particular Kṛttivāsa is meant.

The dominant version of the *Rāmāyaṇa* in Orissa, that of Balarāmadāsa, which appeared at the beginning of the fifteenth-century, is known as *Daṇḍī Rāmāyaṇa* after the meter used in it, as well as the *Jagamohan Rāmāyaṇa*, "the world enchanter." It is a lengthy work and a need came to be felt for abbreviated versions; several with the title *Ṭīkā Rāmāyaṇa* were written. In the *Ṭīkā Rāmāyaṇa* of Maheśvara Dāsa, Balarāma's substantial poem is reduced to around forty printed pages.[8] Since Balarāmadāsa, like Kṛttivāsa, was extremely popular, later poets contributed new material to his manuscripts and signed his name to their versions. In Orissa, however, the process took a different course from that in Bengal. The version of Balarāma that circulated in southern Orissa steadily absorbed new, very diverse material in this way, and eventually assumed an encyclopedic character, growing to almost three thousand pages in its printed version, seventy times the size of the *Ṭīkā Rāmāyaṇa*. This version of the poem became known as the *Dakṣiṇī Rāmāyaṇa*, since it developed in southern Orissa. A great range of Rāma stories found a home in it. For example, not only do we find here the original villain, the ten-headed Rāvaṇa, but also Mahīrāvaṇa, the hundred-headed Rāvaṇa, and the thousand-headed Rāvaṇa; what is remarkable is not the fact that these stories are included but that the different Rāvaṇas are integrated into the plot, and regularly confer, plot and act in concert.[9]

Oral Traditions

Rāma literature in various oral forms had always been circulating in India; it was, after all, from such material that the original Vālmīki fashioned the original *Rāmāyaṇa*. Like Vālmīki, the vernacular poets made use of this rich literature, though it is not always easy to say whether a story that appears for the first time in a certain version of the *Rāmāyaṇa* was adopted from an oral tradition by its author or was the product of that author's imagination. The geographical range of such orally circulating stories varied. Some were restricted to a single region or subregion, whereas others seem to be found everywhere in India. Each of our three *Rāmāyaṇa* traditions possesses stories that are apparently not found in other language areas.[10] An example of Bengali Rāma lore is the story of the birth of Rāma's ancestor Bhagīratha, which first appears in the eastern recension of the *Svargakhaṇḍa* of the *Padma Purāṇa* no later than the fourteenth century.[11] According to it, after King Dilīpa died childless, his two wives, fearing the extinction of his line, went to the sage Vasiṣṭha for advice. He gave them a sacrificial oblation (*caru*) to share and said that the two should make love, with one of them playing the male role. The two queens followed his advice, and one became pregnant and gave birth to Bhagīratha. However, because he was fathered by a woman, he was born without bones. This handicap was remedied by a convenient curse from the sage Aṣṭāvakra. This story made its way into the *Rāmāyaṇas* of Kṛttivāsa[12] and Adbhūtācāryya,[13] and can also be found in the seventeenth century *Caṇḍī Maṅgala* of Mukundarāma, Bhavānanda's Bengali translation of the *Harivaṁśa*, (also of the seventeenth century), as well as in a unique manuscript of the *Vāsiṣṭha Rāmāyaṇa* preserved in the manuscript library of Dhaka University.[14]

Similarly, stories that were uniquely Orissan found their place in the *Daṇḍī Rāmāyaṇa*. One such tale tells how Rāma and Lakṣmaṇa were wandering through the forest in search of Sītā and began to suffer from hunger. They noticed a cow pen and Rāma suggested that they purchase some milk from the cowherds. The proud Lakṣmaṇa, however, was loath to beg and suggested that they instead kill the cowherds, take the cows as an ambulatory food supply, and give them away to brahmans when they eventually returned to Ayodhyā. Rāma told him to buy the milk instead, but when a reluctant Lakṣmaṇa offered the cowherds jewels in payment, they mistook the jewels for berries, and suspecting that Rāma and Lakṣmaṇa were trying to trick them, they showered Lakṣmaṇa with insults. Enraged, Lakṣmaṇa uttered a curse, and as a consequence the cows started giving blood instead of milk. This made the cowherds realize their mistake.[15]

Other stories circulated over a wider area. Both Kṛttivāsa and Mādhavdeva, for example, tell the story of how Daśaratha became infatuated with his many wives and spent his days amusing himself in his harem rather then administering his kingdom; as a result it was stricken by a terrible drought. One day while Daśaratha was out hunting, he happened to seat himself beneath a tree in which a pair of birds were discussing their decision to leave his unhappy kingdom and find refuge in a better-governed one. This made Daśaratha realize his mistake.

Some oral stories seem to be found in many regions of India. For example, the story of Mahīrāvaṇa was originally a Tamil folktale,[16] which eventually came to be found everywhere from Tamilnadu to Nepal and was so popular that it even made its way into printed editions of Tulsīdās. It is found in a number of variants: in some versions of the story there is one demon, Mahīrāvaṇa (or

Mairāvaṇa); in others two, Mahīrāvaṇa and Ahīrāvaṇa; and in versions current in Bengal and Assam, Ahirāvaṇa is the posthumous son of Mahīrāvaṇa.[17] It was very popular in eastern India. In Assam, the Mahīrāvaṇa tale was told at length in an episodic *Rāmāyaṇa*.[18] Kṛttivāsa includes it—all versions of Kṛttivāsa—and so do many of the later Bengali poets who follow him. Though not in Balarāmadāsa, it finds a place in the *Ṭīkā Rāmāyaṇa* of Maheśvaradāsa, and Mahīrāvaṇa plays an elaborate role in the *Dakṣiṇī Rāmāyaṇa*.

Vernacular *Rāmāyaṇas* both within and without India sometimes display common, non-Vālmīkian characteristics that are not the result of textual influence, whether of oral or written literature, but of coincidental efforts to improve upon Vālmīki. One notices, for example, that many poets prefer to tell the story of Rāvaṇa's birth and earlier career in the first *kāṇḍa* of the epic rather than in the last, as in Vālmīki. This seems far more sensible than telling it after the demon is dead and gone, or at least many poets thought so, including Kṛttivāsa, Balarāmadāsa, and others from other regions, including those from many Southeast Asian countries.

We can also speak of emphases, rather than innovations. Certain themes or stories enjoyed special popularity in certain areas. The story of the seduction of Ṛṣyaśriṅga, the sages's son with deer antlers, enjoyed a popularity in Orissa that was older than Oriya literature itself, since the story is illustrated in the temple sculptures of Bhuvaneśvara. A written version appears in the last quarter of the fifteenth century in the Rāmopakhyāna (or its equivalent) in the *vanaparva* of the *Mahābhārata* of Saralādāsa. Balarāmadāsa retells it at length, as do many of his successors, all of whom seem to be more interested in it than was Vālmīki. In Bengali a counterpart is the *Aṅgada Rāybāra*, (the embassy of Aṅgada), which describes the mission of Aṅgada to Rāvaṇa in an attempt to negotiate the return of Sītā before hostilities commence; what in Vālmīki is a minor episode is transformed here into a largely comic tale in which Aṅgada humiliates the demon king.[19]

Bhakti

The devotional movement was a major influence whose ideas chiefly made themselves felt through the medium of Sanskrit works such as the *Adhyātma Rāmāyaṇa*, the *Bhuśuṇḍi Rāmāyaṇa*, various Purāṇas, and other texts. As was noted, Mādhava Kandalī wrote his *Rāmāyaṇa* before the movement made an impression in Assam, and the *Gīti Rāmāyaṇa* of Durgāvara from early sixteenth century is equally unaffected by bhakti ideas, as was the original, unrecoverable, Kṛttivāsa, though some devotional themes were added to the Bengali poem later and are prominent in the popular printings. By the time of Balarāmadāsa, the situation had begun to change, and in his *Rāmāyaṇa* several of the most familiar devotional themes first appear in eastern India; later hagiographers describe Balarāmadāsa as a disciple of Caitanya, who spent the last period of his life in Puri. Thereafter the influence of devotionalism steadily grew, and generally speaking, the later a work was written, the more influenced it was by devotional ideas. Sometimes, as will be seen, these ideas were given remarkable expression.

The influence of the *Adhyātma Rāmāyaṇa* on the eastern NIA *Rāmāyaṇas* is less extensive than elsewhere in north India (as in Tulsīdās, for example), partially because some vernacular versions of the epic had already been written either before it made its influence felt, or perhaps before it had been written. The *Adhyātma Rāmāyaṇa* contains an abbreviated Vālmīkian account of events, which it reinterprets in a devotional light. Here Rāma is very much aware that he is the avatar of Viṣṇu, and this knowledge dictates the course of his and others' actions. Rāvaṇa only pretends to be Rāma's enemy because he knows that anyone who dies by the hand of Viṣṇu goes to his reward in Vaikuṇṭha. Mantharā and Kaikeyī are not moved by ill will either; the day before Rāma is to be crowned, the gods intervene in events by commanding Sarasvatī, the goddess of speech, to possess both of them, so that Kaikeyī will demand the fatal boon from Daśaratha, Rāma will be exiled, and Rāvaṇa killed.[20] This motif came to be frequently employed later, especially in Oriya *Rāmāyaṇas*. Its influence can already be seen in Balarāmadāsa, where the gods send down the celestial cow Surabhi to take the form of Mantharā and the celestial beings Khaḷa and Durbaḷa to possess Kaikeyī.[21] The influence of the *Adhyātma Rāmāyaṇa* continued to grow, and by the eighteenth century it had grown to be so popular in Orissa that it had appeared in two Oriya translations. We are speaking here of translation in the modern sense of the word, not free renderings, which are usually the case in older times.

Another very influential devotional theme (formally at least) was the story of Rāma's sons Kuśa and Lava, who unwittingly disrupt their father's horse sacrifice and become involved in a fierce battle with his brothers, friends, and allies. This theme was primarily transmitted through two Sanskrit texts, the *Rāmāśvamedha* of the *Pātālakhaṇḍa* of the *Padmapuraṇa*, and the *Kuśalavopākhyānā* of the *Jaimini Aśvamedhaparvan* or *Jaimini Bhārata*, as it is also known. The latter was the more popular of the two accounts in eastern India. This is an ancient theme; the earliest version appears in the *Paumacariyam*, a Jaina *Rāmāyaṇa* of Vimalasuri, which was the first complete version of the epic written after Vālmīki.[22] In Assam it was retold in the very early (fifteenth century?) *Lava Kuśara Yuddha* of Harivara Bipra and later in the *Sitāra Banabāsa* of Gaṇgādhara. In Bengal it is found in Kṛttivāsa and later versions.[23] It was not, however, popular in Orissa.

Many other devotional stories found a home in the eastern *Rāmāyaṇas*, though it is not always easy to ascertain the exact path they took to get there. One such story is Rāma's encounter with Śabarī (or Śavarī). In Vālmīki's *Rāmāyaṇa*, Śavarī is the pupil of the deceased sage Mataṅga and who offers Rāma and Lakṣmaṇa hospitality when they visit her ashram during their search for Sītā. After entertaining them, Śavarī immolates herself in order to join her guru.[24] The devotionalized version of this encounter first appears in a south Indian text, the *Divya Śrī Caritra*, and describes how Śavarī offers Rāma and Lakṣmaṇa fruit she has first tasted in order to test its sweetness. Since she is a member of the Śavara tribe, according to Hindu dietary rules this tasting polluted the fruit for all caste Hindus; despite that, Rāma deliberately selected the pieces of fruit with her tooth marks on them, thus illustrating his respect for her devotion and his indifference to such caste conventions. As one might expect, Mādhava Kandalī is not very interested in the story and doesn't even mention the name of Śavarī's mentor; some Kṛttivāsan manuscripts call her Śravaṇā Sundarī (in Vālmīki she's an old woman, *vṛddhā*) and a member of the Sarabha tribe.[25] In popular editions of the same poet, the story is glossed over and the fact that Śavarī gave Rāma and Lakṣmaṇa food is not even mentioned. Balarāmadāsa gives full play to the devotional version of the story, as do later poets such as the late-eighteenth-century Bengali poets Rāmaprasāda[26] and Raghunandana Gosvāmī. This tale, though originally first recorded in Sanskrit in the *Divya Srī Caritra*, which is a collection of hagiographies of Tamil saints, must have been transmitted to eastern India through some other medium, perhaps oral. Śavarī came to be considered a saint, and her story was widely told in north Indian hagiographical literature.[27] Many other Rāma devotional stories probably made their way east in a similar fashion.

Regional Devotional Innovations

The reformers preached that bhakti led to salvation for everyone, even sinners, including Rāma's demon foes. According to the *Adhyātma Rāmāyaṇa*, as we have seen, Rāvaṇa carried off Sītā—for whom he actually entertained only the noblest of feelings—for the sole purpose of ensuring his death by Rāma's hand. Later this idea was further developed: Not only is Rāvaṇa merely pretending to be the enemy of Rāma but Rāma, Sītā, and others are pretending as well, "for the sake of the *līlā* [play]." According to the *Rāmprasādī-Jagadrāmī Rāmāyaṇa*, during the siege of Laṅkā Rāvaṇa, a passionate devotee of Rāma, would meet secretly with his apparent opponent; Sītā would also be present, brought in a covered palanquin so no one could recognize her; at dawn they would separate and continue their official roles until, in order to ensure the success of Rāma's mission, Rāvaṇa officiated over a sacrifice intended to accomplish his own destruction.[28] A number of variants on a similar theme are found in Oriya and Bengali *Rāmāyaṇa*s where less prominent demons play the role of devotee. One such story makes an appearance in the *Daṇḍī Rāmāyaṇa*. Here the devout demon is Vīrabāhu, a son of Rāvaṇa, whose goal, like that of his father, is to be killed by Rāma on the battlefield. He, however, makes no secret of his devotion. Since his prowess is equal to his devotion, he wreaks havoc on Rāma's army before knocking Rāma himself unconscious, and when Rāma eventually recovers consciousness, he is surprised to see the demon groveling at his feet and is so impressed that he offers him a boon. The boon that Vīrabāhu asks for is that Rāma cut off his head. Rāma, of course, cannot kill a devotee and refuses, but the gods, who have been anxiously observing the course of the battle, worry that Rāma will give up the fight, and so they send Khaḷa and Sarasvatī to possess Vīrabāhu and speak in his voice in much the same way as they had done earlier. As a consequence, the demon begins taunting Rāma, who then changes his mind and obligingly kills him.[29] The motif turns up in Bengali Rāma literature a century or more later. There the best-known manifestation of the theme is the story of Taraṇīsena, which is most familiar from the versions in the popular editions of Kṛttivāsa; it is not, however, found in all the older manuscripts of Kṛttivāsa.[30] There are also versions of this story by Śaṇkara Kavicandra, Dvija Dayārāma, and other poets.[31] Taraṇīsena, the son of Vibhīṣaṇa, finally comes face to face with the object of his devotion, after defeating Aṅgada, Sugrīva, Hanumān, and Lakṣmaṇa. Here, too, Rāma refuses to kill his devotee, so Taraṇī finds himself obliged to feign hostility; this fools Rāma, who shoots off his head with an arrow.

Śākta Influences

Śākta influences, though less persuasive, are found in all three languages. The most common themes derive from, or are inspired by, stories from the *Śākta* purāṇas and the *Adbhuta Rāmāyaṇa*, which are intended to illustrate the superiority of the goddess to Rāma. They do this by showing that Rāma was only able to overcome Rāvaṇa because of the help of the goddess. The *Bṛhaddharma* and *Mahābhāgavata* purāṇas tell a story of how Hanumān convinces the goddess to withdraw her protection from Laṅkā on condition that Rāma offers her autumnal worship, that is, Dūrgā Pūjā, the most popular Hindu festival in much of eastern India.

The *Adbhuta Rāmāyaṇa* makes the same point in a much more dramatic fashion. It tells us how Sītā provokes Rāma into offering battle to the much mightier thousand-headed Rāvaṇa, who rules the island of Puṣkara. Rāma takes up the challenge only to be slain by the demon, whereupon Sītā transforms herself into Kālī and destroys Rāvaṇa and his army. In Assam we find the story of the slaying of this second Rāvaṇa in an unlikely place, an anonymous play entitled *Śataskandha Rāvaṇa Vadha* (the demon has only one hundred heads here); this seems odd, since the types of drama known as aṅkīya nāṭas otherwise only treated proper Vaiṣṇava subjects. In Bengal the story is retold in the *Rāmāyaṇa* of Adbhutācāryya as well as in episodic *Rāmāyaṇa*s bearing the signature of Kṛttivāsa.[32] It can also be found, perhaps somewhat incongruously, in the *Rāmprasādī-Jagadrāmī Rāmāyaṇa*. Most of the matter in the last work is taken from the *Adhyātma* and *Bhuśuṇḍī Rāmāyaṇa*s along with other devotional episodes, to which he adds an extra *kāṇḍa*, the *Puṣkarakāṇḍa* (after the island home of the demon), which is a lengthy retelling of the story of the *Adbhuta Rāmāyaṇa*. Then, after Sītā slays the demon, she returns to Ayodhyā with her husband, who not long afterward exiles her.

The oldest of the eastern versions of this theme is the Oriya *Bilaṅkā Rāmāyaṇa*, popularly attributed to the fifteenth-century *Mahābhārata* poet Saralādāsa. Here the action takes place in Bilaṅkā, or anti-Laṅkā, rather than Puṣkara, and Hanumān plays a much more important role. The work opens as Rāma, Sītā, and Lakṣmaṇa are returning to Ayodhyā in triumph. The citizens of the city are eager for their arrival, and a huge crowd headed by Bharata gathers to welcome them. When Lakṣmaṇa sees it, he immediately believes the worst, thinks it an army, and tells Rāma,

śuṇa sītānātha /
ayodhyāra thāṭa gheṇi āsanti bharata // . . .
niścaye karibe yuddha he raghunāyaka //
mote yebe ājñā debe prabhu raghunātha /
sainya baḷa sahite mũ māribi bharata // . . .
śuṇikari hasileka kauśalyā tanuja /
rajādele ghaüḍāi rājyare ki karyya /
se yebe nadeba mote rājye peśibāku /
kānakī gheniṇa puṇi yibi banasthaku //[33]

"Listen Lord of Sītā!
Bharata is coming along with the army of Ayodhyā. . . .
He certainly intends to give battle, Raghunāyaka!
If you give the order Lord,
I will kill Bharata along with his army." . . .
When he heard that, the son of Kauśalyā smiled and said,
"What's the use of a kingdom if they give it to you then drive you out?
If he doesn't allow me to enter the kingdom,
I will take Sītā and go back to the forest."

Their fears prove unjustified, though Bharata only manages to convince a very reluctant Rāma not to return to the forest after a long argument. Here, as so often in Oriya Rāma literature, the gods intervene in order to make sure that Rāma will slay the thousand-headed Rāvaṇa by having Khaḷa and Durbaḷa possess Sītā, who thereupon shames Rāma into facing the second Rāvaṇa. The *Bilaṅkā Rāmāyaṇa* proved to be so popular that a sequel with the name *Bilaṅkā Rāmāyaṇa Uttarakhaṇḍa,* in which the villain is a Rāvaṇa with a hundred thousand heads, was also written.

Popular editions of Kṛttivāsa contain a few *śākta* additions. One of the most original, which is not found in earlier manuscripts, tells how Rāvaṇa orders his court priest Bṛhaspati (all the gods are his slaves) to read the *Caṇḍī stava,* that is, the *Devī Mahātmya,* in order to stave off defeat; if he can recite it without error, the demon will be invincible. The gods, of course, take measures to prevent this and warn Rāma, who in his turn commands Hanumān to spoil the recitation. Hanumān then takes the form of a fly, lands on some of the letters of the book in Bṛhaspati's hand and licks them off; as a result, his pronunciation of the sacred text is incorrect.[34] The last obstacle to the killing of Rāvaṇa is thus removed.

One Culmination: The *Viṣṇupurī Rāmāyaṇa*

All these various influences helped determine the development of *Rāmāyaṇa* literature in eastern India over the course of the centuries, a development that culminated at the end of the eighteenth century, when British hegemony was established in eastern India. To get an idea of how of how these various influences ultimately made themselves felt, we can take a look at a *Rāmāyaṇa* from this period, the *Viṣṇupurī Rāmāyaṇa* of Śaṅkara Kavicandra. Śaṅkara was a learned poet and a professional singer who had also composed a *Śiva Maṇgala* as well as versions of the *Bhāgavata Purāṇa* and the *Mahābhārata*. Since this was the source of his livelihood, he must have been careful to give his audience what it wanted, and so he tends to include something for everyone. Naturally he includes many popular episodes, such as a lengthy account of the *Aṅgada Rāybāra*, the *Śiva-Rāmera Yuddha*, a tale which seems only to be found in Bengal,[35] and, inevitably, the story of Mahīrāvaṇa. Kavi Śaṅkara refers to his version of the epic as "spiritual" (*adhyātma*),[36] and he also includes many familiar devotional tales, such as that of Śavarī's fruit tasting and the story of the devout squirrels who help Rāma build the bridge to Laṅkā. Śaṅkara's treatment is especially fond of the demon devotee motif. First he tells the stories of Atikāya, Vīrabāhu, and Subāhu, all devotees whose only goal is death at Rāma's hands,[37] then goes on to the story of Taraṇīsena, which is the longest single episode in his poem. Not satisfied with that, he relates the tale, also at length, of Araṇisena or Araṇi, Taraṇī's younger brother. Araṇi, like the others, yearns to get *darśana* of Rāma and be slain by him. When Araṇi finally comes face to face with the object of his devotion on the battlefield, he delivers a *stuti*, a paean:

> *gale bastra puṭapāṇi, staba kare araṇi, tumi rāma akhilera bandhu . . .*
> *jagajīvana tumi, carācara cintāmaṇi, tumi brahmā visṇu bholānātha /*
> *indra varuṇa ādi, tomā bhaje paśupati, tumi yata brahmāṇḍera nātha //*
> *tarāite niśācara, āle nīla kalevara, janaka duhitā layyā /*[38]

> With scarf on neck, Araṇi folded his hands and said,
> "You, Rāma, are the friend of the universe. . . .
> You are the life of the world, the wishing jewel of creation,
> you are Brahmā, Viṣṇu, Indra, Varuṇa, and the other gods.
> Paśupati worships you, you are Lord of all the universes.
> With your dark blue body you came,
> bringing the daughter of Janaka with you, in order to grant salvation
> to demons."

He goes on with his encomium for another dozen verses before his wish is granted and Rāma's arrow cuts off his head. However, his devotion does not end with that, for his head rolls across the battlefield, singing Rāma's praises, and comes to a stop at Rāma's feet.

> *kāṭā muṇḍa uccasvare rāma rāma bale /*
> *dayāra ṭhākura tulya karilena kole //*
> *araṇira muṇḍa puna kahiche ḍākiyā /*
> *kothā pitā vibhīṣaṇa dekhaha āsiyā //*
> *eta śuniyā cetana pāila vibhīṣaṇa /*

dekhe kāṭā muṇḍa rāma bale ghane ghana /
ati bege dhāyyā vibhīṣaṇa gelā tathā /
araṇira muṇḍa bale dhanya tumi pitā //
sārthaka rāmera sevā kariyācha tumi //
tava puṇye rāmapada pāilām āmi //[39]

The severed head shouted out the name of Rāma in a loud voice
and the Lord of Mercy picked it up and embraced it.
Araṇi's head then shouted,
"Where is my father, come Vibhīṣaṇa and see!"
When he heard this Vibhīṣaṇa regained consciousness.
The head saw that and shouted "Rāma!" "Rāma!"
Vibhīṣaṇa ran swiftly to where it was.
"You are blessed, father," said Araṇi's head.
"You have served Rāma successfully
thanks to your merits I have gained His feet."

Then, with true Hindu catholicity, Śaṅkara Kavicandra adds the story of how Rāma placated the goddess. When Rāma confronts Rāvaṇa in the final battle, he shoots off the demon's heads one after the other, only to see them sprout back on. The gods then realize that Rāvaṇa is protected by a boon, and intervene. They send down Pavana, the wind god, from heaven to tell Rāma that the only way he can defeat Rāvaṇa is by placating the goddess. He then insures her favor with a *stuti* and the promise that he and his subject will give her autumnal worship, and that the three worlds will follow their example. She is finally moved to grant his wish when he tells her,

rāmanāma yāvada thākiva saṁsāre /
tāvata tomāra pūjā kariveka nare //[40]

Men will give you *pūjā*
as long as the name of Rāma remains in the world.

One of the most interesting features of the *Viṣṇupurī Rāmāyaṇa* is the contradictions that arise when different themes are juxtaposed. This is most obvious in the characterization of Rāma. There are at least three different Rāmas: first, underlying all others, we have the idealized heroic Rāma of Vālmīki, a noble but still recognizably human hero; second, we have the deified Rāma of devotional tradition, Rāma the God of the gods deliberately playing out his human role. Alongside these, we have a third Rāma, the village Rāma, a Rāma not so much humanized but banalized, for this Rāma often displays many less praiseworthy human qualities. Though Araṇi may praise the second Rāma as the Lord of the Universe, when Brahmā descends from heaven to congratulate him for his victory at Laṅkā, the third Rāma disagrees:

nara naha raghunātha trailokyera pati /
nara hena raghunātha taba kena mati //
rāma bale nara āmi narakule janma /

manuṣya haiyā kari manuṣyera karma /
brahmā bale nāhi jāna āpana avatāra /
anāthera nātha tumi saṁsārera sāra /
tomāra aṁśete janma yata devagaṇa /
lakṣmīdevī sītā āra tumi nārāyaṇa //[41]

"You are not a man" [said Brahmā], "you are the Lord of the Triple World.
Why Raghunātha, do you think you are human?"
Rāma said, "I am a man, born in a human family.
As a human, I performed a human deed."
Brahmā replied, "Don't you know that you are an avatar?
You are the Lord of the lordless, the essence of the world.
All the gods were born of parts of you.
The goddess Lakṣmī is Sītā and you are Nārāyaṇa."

Similar contradictions can be seen in Vāli's "deathbed" scene. Vāli has just been shot in the back by Rāma from his hiding place, and he bitterly upbraids his slayer. Vālmīki gives great attention to this scene, devoting one *sarga* to Vāli's accusations and another to Rāma's reply; Rāma's response is so convincing that Vāli clasps his hands together and forgives him.[42] Though the *Adhyātma Rāmāyaṇa* abbreviates this scene, it does include some of Vāli's bitter reproaches, and the discussion reaches an abrupt end when Rāma reveals his true identity to the monkey chieftain. Vāli is immediately overcome by fear (*bhayasantrasta*), and says,

rāma rāma mahābhāga jāne tvāṁ parameśvaram /
ajānatā mayā kiñcid uktaṁ kṣantum arhasi //[43]

O Rāma, O Rāma of great fortune! I know you are the supreme Lord.
Please forgive what I said to you in ignorance.

Vāli then delivers a paean praising Rāma as the highest god, and expressing his good fortune at having gotten *darśana* of him. Though Śaṅkara may call his poem an *Adhyātma Rāmalīlā*, things take a very different turn there:

rāma kahe Vālī rājā nindā kara more /
adhārmika duṣṭamati badhilām tore //
rājāra mṛgayā dharma likhita purāṇe /
śaśaka vānara vyāghra badhi mṛgagaṇe //
karaha parera hiṁsā nā jāni svadharma /
pakśa mṛga paśvādi jātira śuna karma //
brahmāra likhita sṛṣṭi sṛjila gosāñi /
tāhāra maithuna nīta paśupakṣera nāñi //
śrīrāma balen vālī śuna re durjana /
tore badhilām āmi pratijñā kāraṇa //
bujhyā dekha tomāra karinu upagāra /
svarga jāha vālī prīti haiyā āmāra //

rāma bale teja nāi jānilām tora /
kole kare bale rāma doṣa kṣema kara //[44]

Rāma said, "King Vāli, you're reproaching me.
I killed you because you are a violator of dharma and an evil-minded [one].
It's written in the Purāṇas that kings can hunt
and kill game like hares, monkeys, and tigers."
[Vāli replied], "You harm others. You don't know your own dharma.
Listen to the case for the behavior of birds and beasts!
Brahmā made laws when he created the world,
[but] his rules for sexual morality do not apply to birds and beasts!"
Rāma said, "Listen you villain,
I killed you because of my promise [to Sugrīva].
Try to comprehend that I have done you a favor.
Vāli, I am pleased with you, go to heaven!
I didn't recognize your dignity," said Rāma,
"forgive me!" he said, holding him in his arms.

Here, as he does in Vālmīki and the *Adhyātma Rāmāyaṇa*, Rāma accuses Vāli of sexual misconduct (he took his brother Sugrīva's wife), so he was fulfilling his kshatriya duty by killing a miscreant. But Vāli, quite logically it may seem, points out that these laws do not apply to animals, and he is clearly an animal. Exasperated, Rāma has to switch to his divine persona abruptly and inform the wounded monkey that he should actually be grateful (as Taraṇī and Araṇi would be), as he will go to heaven when he dies. But in the end, it is not Vāli who apologizes to Rāma, but Rāma who apologizes to Vāli. It does not end here. Guilt for the deed gnaws at Rāma and he repeatedly refers to it, up to the very climax of the poem at his coronation in Ayodhyā:[45]

sugrīve ḍākiyā rāma dila āliṅgana /
dilen kuṇḍala hāra mukuṭa vicikṣaṇa //
śrīrāma balen śuna parāṇera mitā /
vālīke māriyā kainu anucita //
trubhubane mājhe āmi baḍa pāi lāja /[46]

Rāma called out to Sugrīva and embraced him,
He presented him with earrings, necklaces, and a marvelous crown.
Rāma said, "Listen my dearest friend,
When I killed Vāli, I did something improper.
I was greatly shamed in all three worlds."

In these works Rāma can be suspicious, obstinate, guilt-ridden, and timid. The other characters, too, are less than ideal here. Daśaratha is portrayed as a weak, uxorious old man under the thumb of his young wife; Lakṣmaṇa, fanatically loyal to his brother, when faced by a problem always advocates the same solution—violence—whether dealing with demons, *gopas*, or his own brother Bharata. Other characters, too, readily resort to brutality. A good example of this can be seen in the meeting between Sītā and Hanumān after the fall of Laṅkā:

sītā bale śuna bāchā pabanandana /
tava upayukta dāna cinti mane mana // . . .
hanumān bale tājya nā cāi ṭhākurāṇi / . . .
eka dāna dibe more na karibe āna /
more dāna dile tuṣṭa haba bhagavān //
tomāra kāche āche yata rāvaṇera ceḍī // . . .
tomāra kāche prāṇa laba ei māgõ dāna //
danta upāḍiyā cula chiṇḍi goche goche /
āchāḍiyā praṇa laba baṛa baṛa gāche //[47]

Sītā said, "Listen dear Pavananandana,
I'm thinking of a reward appropriate for you." . . .
Hanumān replied, "I do not want a kingdom, O Queen,
Give me one thing, do but that.
If you give me that gift, God will be pleased.
All of Rāvaṇa's maidservants are with you. . . .
I ask the favor of killing all of them,
I want to yank out their teeth and rip out their hair in clumps,
I want to uproot a great big tree and beat them all to death."

Sītā is shocked at his request, and points out that he will be guilty of *strīvadha,* and manages to persuade him to ask a more appropriate boon.

Another quality one notices is what is called in Bengali *grāmyatā,* or "villageness," here understood as vulgarity. It is given its most vivid expression in passages of excretory humor featuring the monkey warriors, as in a scene that describes a fight between Nīla and Rāvaṇa. Nīla jumps up on the demon's head, and

mukuṭe bhramiyā bule dekhite nā pāy /
prasraba karile mukha buka bhāsyā yāy //
krodha karyyā daśānana mukha muche yata /
jharajhara karyyā nīla mute avirata //[48]

He ran round on his crowns and [Rāvaṇa] couldn't see him.
He urinated and it flowed all over his faces and chest.
Angrily Rāvaṇa wiped off all his faces,
Nīla went pissing torrents.

After Hanumān finds Sītā in Laṅkā, he takes the form of a sannyasi and urinates in a water pot (*kamaṇḍalu*) and tells the demons that it contains holy water that he has collected from the *pāñcatīrtha.* After the demons have drunk from it, he tells them what they really have done, and this results in the battle in which he is captured.[49]

It has sometimes been claimed that the humor in this literature is unintentional, the result of the authors having been half-educated rustic bumpkins.

Similar things have been said in regard to the depiction of Rāma and the other actors on the epic as pettily human. But this is a misapprehension. Being closer to the realities of everyday life, the folk poets were less liable to be overawed by the epic. Solemnity is not their style. One can see a similar approach in the treatment of biblical themes in the miracle plays of medieval Europe. In their earthiness, both traditions reflect the sensibility of common folk and the vigor of down-to-earth language.

Parochialization

The Rāma literature of eastern India was largely composed for a peasant audience, and so it naturally reflects the tastes and values of that audience. Of the three major poets, this is most obvious in the many poems attributed to Kṛttivāsa. This tendency toward parochialization seems the exact opposite of the devotionalization represented by works like the *Adhyātma Rāmāyaṇa* and the vernacular *Rāmāyaṇas* they influenced. In them the entire action of the epic becomes a passionless *līlā* in which Rāma and his fellow actors are fully aware that every one of their actions is intended to inspire, edify, and instruct devotees. The epic is transformed into a sermon. In parochialized treatments, the protagonists of the epic are not only prevented from being dehumanized but are even vulgarized, as are many of the other characters. Rāma's father is recharacterized as an old fool, who lets his wife boss him around, and a coward who hides in fear from Paraśurām. Rāma's courage often fails him, as well, as does his intelligence, which frequently leaves him facing dilemmas that his wiser companions have to help him out of. Hanumān becomes a comic figure, a role that is foreshadowed in Vālmīki. In the Mahīrāvaṇa tale, Hanumān knocks the goddess Kālī on the head, then impersonates her and greedily gobbles up all the food offerings. When the sun god refuses to obey him and delay setting, Hanumān tucks the god under his arm and goes on his way, making sure the sun will not set. Noble ṛṣis like Viśvāmitra tend to cut sorry figures, too, and though they can still hurl terrible curses, they are at the same time muddled and timid. This quality, although it is seen by some as detracting from the theme, is viewed by others as one of the more endearing features of the popular *Rāmāyaṇas*, lending them a lively and realistic flavor, which makes them much more than simply second-rate imitations of Sanskrit models.

NOTES

1. Chakravarti 1913.
2. Mādhava Kandalī 1972.
3. See Smith, 1994.
4. Kṛttivāsa 1900.
5. Kṛttivāsa 1981.
6. Many examples can be found in Ray and Bhattacharyya 1960; for example, mss. nos. 127–132 (*Labakuśara Yuddha*), 152–157 (*Śataskandha Rāvaṇera Vadha*), 159 (*Naramedhayajña*), and 159 (*Śiva-Rāmera Yuddha*).

7. For details, see Smith 1980.
8. Maheswar Das n.d.
9. Balarāmadāsa n.d.
10. Until Rāma lore in general is properly inventoried, one cannot speak with total confidence about the distribution of any element of it.
11. Chatterjee, 1972, 16. 1–22.
12. It is found in some modern editions of this poet; for the text and translation of such a version, see Bose 2000, "Introduction," pp. 4–5.
13. Chakravarti 1913, p. 169.
14. Ibid., p. 46.
15. Balarāmadāsa, 1912–1914, 4: 56–57.
16. See Zvelebil 1987.
17. See Smith, 1982, p. 10.
18. Śaṅkaradeva 1908.
19. See Ray and Bhattacaryya 1960 for examples.
20. Munilal 2001, 2.2.44–46.
21. Balarāmadāsa, 1912–1914, 2: 26–27.
22. For details see Smith 1999.
23. It is found in Hirendranath Datta's edition of the *Uttarakāṇḍa* and the popular printings, but not in Sukhamay Mukhopadhyaya's edition. It also occurs in episodic manuscripts; cf. note 6.
24. Vyas 1992, 4.70.
25. Sukhamay Mukhopadhyaya's edition, pp. 102–103
26. The *Rāmprasādī Jagadrāmī Rāmāyaṇa* was begun by Jagadrāma and continued after his death, which took place while he was working on the sixth *kāṇḍa*, by his son Rāmprasāda toward the end of the eighteenth century.
27. See Smith 2000, p. 207.
28. Bandyopadhyaya 1959, pp. 251–258.
29. Balarāmadāsa 1912–1914, vi 6: 254–270.
30. It is not found, for example, in Sukhamay Mukhopadhyaya's edition.
31. *Taraṇīsener Yuddha* by Dvija Dayārāma is found in Sen, 1914, pp. 540ff.
32. See note 6.
33. Saraladāsa n.d.
34. *makṣikāra rūpa dhare cāṭileka dvi-akṣare dekhite nā pāy bṛhaspati* Kṛttivāsa n.d., p. 453.
35. For this story, see Smith 1988, pp. 128–130.
36. *adhyātma rāmalīlā gāila śaṅkara*, Śaṅkara 1979, p. 8.
37. His account of Vīrabāhu differs from that in Balarāmadāsa.
38. Śaṅkaradeva 1908, pp. 153–154.
39. Ibid., p. 155.
40. Ibid., p. 175.
41. Ibid., p. 184.
42. Vyas 1992, 4.17–18.
43. Munilal 2001, 4.2.65.
44. Ibid., p. 67.
45. The *Viṣṇupurī Rāmāyaṇa*, like many other *Rāmāyaṇas*, omits the *Uttarakāṇḍa*.
46. Śaṅkaradeva 1908, p. 193.
47. Ibid., p. 181.

48. Ibid., p. 120.
49. Ibid., p. 79.

REFERENCES

Balarāmadāsa. 1912–1914. *Bṛhat o Sacitra Daṇḍī Rāmāyaṇa*. Edited by Gobinda Ratha. 2nd ed. Cuttack, n.p.

———. n.d. *Jagamohana Rāmāyaṇa bā Daṇḍī Rāmāyaṇa*. Cuttack: Dharma Grantha Store.

Bandyopadhyaya, Ajit Kumar, ed. 1959 [*baṅgābda* 1366]. *Rāmprasādī Jagadrāmī Rāmāyaṇa*. 3rd ed. Calcutta.

Bose, Mandakranta, ed. 2000. *A Varied Optic: Contemporary Studies in the Rāmāyaṇa*. Vancouver: Institute of Asian Research, University of British Columbia.

Chakravarti, Rajanikanta, ed. 1913 [*baṅgābda* 1320]. *Adbhutāchāryera Rāmāyaṇa ādyakāṇḍa*, Calcutta: Rangpur Parishat Granthamala.

Chatterjee, Asoke. 1972. *The Svargakhaṇḍa of Padma Purāṇa*. Varanasi: All India Kashiraj Trust.

Das, Maheshwar. n.d. *Ṭīkā Rāmāyaṇa*. Katak: Dharma Grantha Store.

Kṛttivāsa. 1900 [*baṅgābda* 1307]. *Rāmāyaṇa Uttarakāṇḍa*. Edited by Hirendranath Datta. Calcutta: Bangiya Sahitya Parishad.

———. 1981. *Rāmāyaṇa: Kṛttivāsa Paṇḍita viracita*. Edited by Sukhamay Mukhopadhyaya. 2nd ed. Calcutta: Bharavi.

———. n.d. *Kṛttivāsī Rāmāyaṇa*. Edited by Ashutosh Bhattacharya. Calcutta: Akhil Bharat Janashiksha Prachar Samiti.

Mādhava Kandalī. 1972. *Saptakāṇḍa Rāmāyaṇa*. Edited by Haranarayan Dattabarua. 3rd ed. Guwahati: Dattabarua.

Munilal, ed. 2001. *Adhyātma Rāmāyaṇa*. Gorakhpur: Gita Press.

Ray, Basantaranjan, and Taraprasanna Bhattacharyya, comp. 1960 [*baṅgābda* 1367]. *Bāṅglā Puthira Vivaraṇa*. Pariṣat-Puthiśālāy saṁgṛhita. Calcutta: Bangiya Sahitya Parishad.

Śaṅkaradeva. 1908. *Mahirāvaṇa Badha āru Betālacaṇḍī Upākhyāna*. 3rd ed. Calcutta: Shri Shivnath Sharma Bhattacharya.

Śaṅkara Kavicandra. 1979 [*baṅgābda* 1386]. *Viṣṇupurī Rāmāyaṇa*. Edited by Chitra Deb. Calcutta.

Saraladāsa. n.d. *Śudramuni Sarala Dāsaṅka kṛta Vilaṅkārāmāyaṇa*. Cuttack: Orissa Kohinur Press.

Sen, Dinesh Chandra. 1914. *Vaṅga Sāhitya Paricaya, or, Selections from Bengali Literature*. Part I. Calcutta: University of Calcutta.

Smith, William. 1980. "Kṛttibāsa and the Paṇḍits: The Revision of the Bengali *Rāmāyaṇa*." *Studia Orientalia* (Helsinki) 50, p. 229 ff.

———. 1982. "Mahirāvaṇa and the Womb Demon." *Indologica Taurinensia* 10.

———. 1988. *Rāmāyaṇa Traditions in Eastern India: Assam, Bengal, Orissa*. Stockholm: Department of Indology, University of Stockholm.

———. 1994. "The Wrath of Sītā: Śaṅkaradeva's *Uttarakāṇḍa*." *Journal of Vaiṣṇava Studies* (New York) 2. 4:5–15.

———. 1999. "Variants of the Lavakuśopākhyāna." In *Categorization and Interpretation*, edited by Folke Josephson Meijerbergs Arkiv for Svensk Ordforskning. Goteborg: Styrelsen for Meijerbergs Institut vid Goteborgs Universitet 24, pp. 107–123.

———. 2000. *Patterns in North Indian Hagiography*. Stockholm Studies in Indian Languages and Culture 3. Stockholm: University of Stockholm.

Vyas, Ramkrishna T., ed. 1992. *Vālmīki Rāmāyaṇa*. Vadodara: Oriental Institute.

Zvelebil, Kamil V., trans. 1987. *Two Tamil Folktales: Matanakāma, The Story of Peacock Rāvaṇa*. Delhi: Motilal Banarsidass.

4

Reinventing the *Rāmāyaṇa* in Twentieth-Century Bengali Literature

Mandakranta Bose

The subject of this essay is the ambivalence—if not outright subversion—that has characterized the response to the *Rāmāyaṇa* in Bengal since the nineteenth century. To begin with, it is necessary to acknowledge that for centuries the *Rāmāyaṇa* enjoyed one of the widest, if not *the* widest, circulation in the Bengali-speaking regions of India, reaching both literate and sub-literate audiences. The version of the epic that Bengali audiences knew was Kṛttivāsa's fourteenth-century rendering of Vālmīki's original poem, and its popularity depended to a large extent on Kṛttivāsa's supple verse form, which was particularly suitable for recitation. It fitted into an existing powerful oral tradition and enhanced it so far that for centuries it remained the principal text for public readings and recitation in Bengal. Thereby it fostered a tradition of performance that was supple enough to bring together bhakti and wit within a framework of narrative, drama, and music in the immensely popular nineteenth-century retelling of the epic by Dasharathi (Dashu) Ray.

Although Kṛttivāsa's is the best known and fullest version of the epic in Bengali, the *Rāmāyaṇa* has been subject to several retellings from early to recent times, covering a wide range of narrative and sectarian choices from renditions of the entire plot to selected episodes, and even from Vaiṣṇava to Śākta celebrations. Although Kṛttivāsa consistently remolded Vālmīki's text to emphasize Rāma's divinity, he nonetheless followed the older story faithfully in its main lines and the overwhelming majority of details, thereby placing Rāma firmly at the center of devotional Hinduism. Kṛttivāsa's alterations to the Vālmīki plot are plainly designed to serve the cause of bhakti, although the lack of a definitive copy-text urges caution in making critical claims about Kṛttivāsa's authorial purpose. Close to fifteen hundred manuscripts are extant, most of them from the nineteenth century, and both they and printed editions often vary in their content.

The earliest dependable text of the Kṛttivāsī *Rāmāyaṇa* is the one published in 1803 from the Mission Press of Serampore, which was followed by others that rely largely upon it but sometimes contain changes or interpolations, especially the editions known as *baṭ-talā* editions, which were cheap productions brought out for the mass market by publishers in a neighborhood of that name. But the numerous editions agree as to the bulk of the departures from Vālmīki's original, and these fit the narrative scheme of the Kṛttivāsī *Rāmāyaṇa* so organically that it is hard to attribute these inventions to anything but a single authorial imagination. To take one example, we may cite the story of the supernatural birth of Bhagīratha, Rāma's ancestor, who is born out of the same-sex union between the two wives of his dead father.[1] Bhagīratha is born deformed, without bones, and gains proper human shape only after his mothers manage to get him blessed by the sage Aṣṭāvakra. This extraordinary event is projected as a direct initiative of the gods to keep the dynasty alive that will eventually produce Rāma, the slayer of Rāvaṇa, and thus as proof of the loving care with which the gods keep watch over human life, which can be recompensated only by human devotion.[2] This and all other deviations from Vālmīki's story seem invariably designed to orient the epic to a devotional matrix. This impulse is so strong that Kṛttivāsa invents wholesale episodes to show that within many a lawless *rākṣasa* breast beats a devotee's heart, as in the stories of Taraṇīsena, Vīrabāhu, and Mahīrāvaṇa. But all this is surpassed by Kṛttivāsa's astonishing revelation that as Rāvaṇa lies dying on the battlefield, he confesses his recognition of Rāma as the eternal Brahma (*Brahma sanātan*), at whose feet he seeks a place as a devotee (*ciradin āmi dāsa caraṇe tomār*).[3]

Despite such substantial inventions, the Kṛttivāsī *Rāmāyaṇa* remains true to the basic narrative and ethical pattern of Vālmīki's original. It is still centered on Rāma's exemplary dutifulness, his irresistible prowess, his absolute ascendancy over everything and everybody, and on the unquestioned justness of his victory over his adversaries. Like all early epics, it is a battle story told from the victor's point of view. These generic marks of the epic established by Vālmīki appear in Kṛttivāsa and the storytellers who came after him. In addition, these successors follow in general the pattern of bhakti imposed by Kṛttivāsa on the narrative, sometimes shifting the focus of devotion from Viṣṇu to Śakti. But an alternative strain, both narrative and ideological, also appears in the eighteenth century, which leads to a very different view of the events, characters, and morality of what might be called the master text. A brief overview of Bengali Rāma tales since the fifteenth century will set this alternative voice in context.

Among the translators and retellers of the *Rāmāyaṇa* who followed Kṛttivāsa up to the nineteenth century, particularly interesting are Jagadram Ray, his son Ramprasad Ray, Raghunandan Goswami, Sankara Kavichandra, Ramananda Ghosh, and Dasharathi (Dashu) Ray. Jagadram and his son Ramprasad Ray, devotees of Śakti, invent for their *Rāmāyaṇa* (completed about 1790) an entirely new eighth part, the *Puṣkarakāṇḍa*, which reveals that Sītā is Kālī, who saves Rāma by killing a thousand-headed Rāvaṇa, far more terrifying than the ten-headed demon Rāma had vanquished.[4] Raghunandan Gosvāmī was a highly learned man who based his *Śrī Rāmarasāyaṇa*, published in 1831, on a careful study both of Vālmīki and Tulsīdās, and his work continued to be published well into the nineteenth century. Śaṅkara Kavichandra invented several supplementary episodes that became inseparable parts of the later versions of Kṛttivāsa's *Rāmāyaṇa*, a good example being Aṅgada's comic visit to Rāvaṇa's court as ambassador. In addition to his rendition of the entire epic, Śaṅkara also wrote poems centered on particular episodes, such as *Laṅkā Kāṇḍa*, *Rāvaṇavadha*, *Aṅgada Rāybāra*, and *Lakṣmaṇer Śaktiśela*. The *Rāmalīlā* of Ramananda Ghosh, written in the eighteenth century, is a curious amalgam because it follows both the *Adbhuta Rāmāyaṇa* and the *Adhyatma Rāmāyaṇa*, and combines the Vaiṣṇava and Śākta treatments of the Rāma legend. Dasharathi (Dashu) Ray used the *pāñcālī* form to tailor the *Rāmāyaṇa* to the needs of oral performances, as indicated by his highly musical prosody, the concise presentation of exciting episodes, and their frequently humorous treatment. After Kṛttivāsa, it was perhaps Dashu Ray who enjoyed the greatest popularity, especially among the lower strata of Bengali society.

These retellings and a host of minor works were designed to celebrate the glories of Rāma, and continued the devotional tune sung by Kṛttivāsa. In these renditions the center stage is held by divine beings in their human incarnation, and the events of the tale are seen as parts of a vast divine scheme, to which human identities and relationships contribute only background texture. Right is whatever Rāma does, and he is exempt from human questioning. This aspect of Bengali *Rāmāyaṇas* deserves close study, but here I must pass on to a different part of literary history.

As I have noted above, side by side with these narratives of devotion there also exist others in which we see a decisive turn in the presentation of the story, in that they force human issues into the narrative, thereby shifting the focal point of the received story from the doings of godly beings to the lives of men and women. This shift is far more radical than a narrative reorganization or expansion, for it subjects the actions of the gods to human questioning and shakes the ethical foundation of the Rāma cult. In the simplest terms, these Rāma tales reduce Rāma from a superhuman personage to a fallible and tragic human being, while the story, instead of celebrating Rāma's virtue and victory, emphasizes their costs. Although the earlier of these types of Rāma tales do not deny the greatness of Rāma, they do raise questions about his actions and their impact on others, especially Sītā. Both Vālmīki and Kṛttivāsa record Rāma's harsh treatment of Sītā, and Kṛttivāsa in particular plays on the deep pathos of Sītā's fate, yet both poets find it a necessary if unpalatable condition for the higher good either of social organization or religious faith. For a very different point of view, we may look at the *Rāmāyaṇa* of Candrāvatī, a late sixteenth-century woman poet from eastern Bengal. Although she reproduces the substance of the traditional story, her narrative choices, such as compacting the battle scenes, on the one hand, and expanding, on the other hand, all episodes dealing with women's experiences, turns it into a sustained account

FIGURE 4.1. Kaikeyī's daughter Kukuyā tricks Sītā into painting Rāvaṇa's face, resulting in Rāma's jealous rage and exile of Sītā. Episode from the *Candrāvatī Rāmāyaṇa* painted as a rural storyteller's scroll by Nurjahan Citrakar of Midnapur, West Bengal. Author's private collection.

of the suffering inherent in being a woman. It is necessary to note that Candrāvatī does not make Sītā blame Rāma. On the contrary, her Sītā can think of no better life than being married to Rāma. But the issue here is not whether the poem is an indictment of patriarchy; rather, it is that the poem filters the events of the Rāma legend through female eyes, whether they be those of Daśaratha's queens, or Mandodarī, or Sītā, or even Sītā's evil sister-in-law Kukuyā, whose envious machinations lead to Sītā's downfall. The narrative authority of the female voice is even more decisively confirmed by the addition of the poet's own life story, which thereby serves to set this revision of the customary Rāmakathā within a discourse on women's self-perception. What was traditionally a celebration of manliness is thus turned into a depiction of women's inescapably tragic lives.[5]

To set the record straight, we must note that Candrāvatī was not the only early poet to call attention to the human cost of Rāma's decisions, the acknowledgment of which exists in several *Rāmāyaṇas* from eastern India. A highly critical look at moral and ethical issues appears as early as the eighteenth century in the Oriya *Rāmāyaṇas* of writers such as Śaṅkaradeva and Durgāvara. Both Śaṅkaradeva's and Durgāvara's Rāma is a mean-spirited man who casts doubt on Sītā's fidelity (*pātivratya*). Durgāvara's Rāma jumps to the conclusion that Sītā must have left him for another man when the brothers return to their hut after the hunt for the golden deer to find Sītā missing. Rāma says, "women are easily swayed from constancy" *sahaje cañcala tiri jāti*. Śaṅkaradeva is more directly critical of Rāma's mistreatment of Sītā in the *Uttarakāṇḍa*, and makes Sītā say,

sabe bole enuvā rāmaka bhāla bhāla /
maito jāno mora rāmese yamakāla //
svāmi hena nidāruṇa kaita āche suni/

> All speak well of Rāma but I know that for me he is like Death itself. Tell me where else is there so cruel a husband?[6]

This is not only a lament for wronged women but an indictment of the very masculinity that spells the conventional Rāma's heroic fame.

Works such as these reveal an altered consciousness at work, which signals the beginning of a tradition of looking at the epic from below, from the point of view of passive participants or even victims rather than that of the victor. In this sense, such treatments subvert the whole practice of the conventional epic. But the change in point of view is not only from a male to a female sensibility but also from the powerful to the powerless. Opening up issues of both gender and race, this altered perception strengthens as we move from the despondency of Candrāvatī to Michael Madhusudan Datta's outright indictment of Rāma in his *Meghanādavadha Kāvya*, published in 1861. Few of Datta's contemporaries or successors went to the length of actually saying, as he did, "I despise Rama and his rabble; but the idea of Ravan elevates and kindles my imagination; he was a grand fellow" (reported by Rajnarayan Basu),[7] or of militantly demanding a fair hearing for the *rākṣasas*, but by the nineteenth century the Bengali cultural scene had begun to register a deep discomfort with the moral compromises and violation of common justice that drive the story of Rāma's supremacy. Even Dashu Ray's conventional affirmation of devotion to Rāma occasionally surprises the reader by questioning Rāma's righteousness, as we shall see below.

Precisely because questions such as these arise from within the celebratory narrative tradition, they must be taken as the soundings of some deep disquiet. The history of Rāma tales in Bengal, especially from the nineteenth century onward, shows that three episodes in particular have continued to cause this discomfort. The first is Rāma's treacherous killing of Vāli as a favor to Sugrīva; the second, the advantage that Lakṣmaṇa takes of Vibhīṣaṇa's treachery to kill the unprepared Indrajit; and the third, of course, Rāma's repeated exposure of Sītā to ordeals and eventual banishment. The best-known revulsion to the rule of expediency by which Rāma triumphs is Madhusudan Datta's *Meghanādavadha Kāvya* with its sustained criticism of Rāma and Lakṣmaṇa, the transformation of Indrajit into a Greek hero on the model of Hector, and the humanizing of Rāvaṇa without condoning his pride and lust. That there were other writers, less outspoken but at least as troubled by Rāma's actions, most powerfully by the sufferings of Sītā, is attested by no less a cultural arbiter than Datta's benefactor Ishwarchandra Vidyasagar. In a striking move in his long tale "Sītāra Banabāsa," published in 1860—that is, a year before Datta's poem appeared—he transfers the responsibility for the final rejection of Sītā entirely to Rāma's subjects. It is not Rāma who commands Sītā to undergo the ordeal by fire and—indeed there is no such ordeal—nor does Sītā sink into the earth but dies of a broken heart when, despite Vālmīki's affirmation of her chastity, the public at large refuses to accept it.[8] Kṛttivāsa's Rāma is grieved that his subjects question Sītā's virtue, and even though he complies with their demand, he does so only because *rājadharma* requires him to do so. We may note a similar turn given to Rāma's mental state by Kṛttivāsa, but Vidyasagar intensifies that state by relating Rāma's anguish in relentless length. His Rāma is thus left free of guilt in Sītā's end and thus not undeserving of devotion. Could Vidyasagar have thought of this apologia if he had not found Rāma's conduct indefensible?

The discomfort that pervades Bengali literary responses to the *Rāmāyaṇa* finds strong and persistent expression in twentieth-century critical and political essays.[9] But for the present I would like to look rather at a very different kind of expression, though it is, I would argue, a sign of the same violated sensibility. In the works I deal with here, that sensibility acts through laughter, which deflects attention from the betrayals, cruelties, and injustices of the conventional narrative. The first instance of this trend is Dasharathi Ray's version in *pāñcālī* form, that is, in rhymed verse designed for musical recitation. His version is a selective one that highlights the main events of the story. In its broad approach it is a celebration of Rāma's divinity and very much in the bhakti mode, and like Kṛttivāsa's *Rāmāyaṇa* it turns some of the *rākṣasa*s into devout Vaiṣṇavas. For instance, on his foray into Laṅkā, Hanumān is struck with wonder at *rākṣasa*s chanting the name of Hari:

kī āścarya mari, mari!
rākṣasete bale hari,

How astonishing, upon my life,
Demons utter the name of the Lord![10]

But an altogether opposite feeling crops up at the most unexpected moments. In a farcical episode, Hanumān almost chokes on a mango he is given by Sītā for Rāma. Saved by abjectly asking the absent Rāma for forgiveness, Hanumān nonetheless wonders how much truth there might be in Rāma's much-advertised reputation for loving his *bhakta*s when he is so quick to punish so insignificant a transgression.[11] But a much darker doubt colors a question voiced by no less an authority figure than the god Agni. When commanded by Rāma to undergo an ordeal by fire to prove her chastity after her rescue, Sītā enters the burning pyre; Agni saves her from burning to death and declares her absolute purity. This is, of course, the standard outcome in all formulations of this episode. To this, however, Dashu Ray adds the astonishing aside by Agni as he lifts her from the pyre:

FIGURE 4.2. Sītā's fire ordeal, the *agniparikṣā*. Painted scroll by Nurjahan Citrakar of Midnapur, West Bengal. Author's private collection.

Dekhilām eito kārya,
Je din habe Rāmarājya,
Diner prati to emni bicār habe!

Now I see how it works:
The day Rāma's reign begins
This is the justice that the powerless will get![12]

Will this be the pattern of justice in Rāma's reign?

As in Dashu Ray's frequently comic rendition, in much of Bengali retellings of the *Rāmāyaṇa* grave questions underlie the comedy. These are not complete versions but treatments of particular *Rāmāyaṇa* episodes, and here I shall take two major examples of the type. These stories are far less well known, possibly entirely unknown outside a Bengali readership, and never critically considered even within that readership, no doubt because they offer comic treatments of aspects of the story and can therefore be dismissed as frivolous. As we have seen above, of the several renditions of the *Rāmāyaṇa* in Bengali, Datta's is clearly the most radical and qualifies as a complete reformulation of the received narrative. But at least two Bengali humorists of the twentieth century present significant episodes of the narrative in the mirror of comedy in a manner that forces a revaluation of major themes and characters. These are *Lakṣmaṇera Śaktiśela*, a short play by Sukumar Ray, and "Hanumāner Svapna," a short story by Rajshekhar Bose, also known by his pen name Parashuram.[13] Although both are light-hearted spin-offs from the traditional *Rāmāyaṇa* and designed primarily to make people laugh, both offer to different degrees alternative views of the understanding of heroic identity and gender relations in the *Rāmāyaṇa*.

Lakṣmaṇera Śaktiśela is a farce in four scenes by Sukumar Ray written for a family group and first performed in 1910; this was followed by another performance in Shantiniketan in 1911, under the title *Adbhuta Rāmāyaṇa*, to mark Tagore's fiftieth birthday; and a third time in the Ray family home at Giridih, Bihar, in 1913. Sukumar Ray, the first and perhaps the only writer of sophisticated nonsense verse and fiction in Bengali, was born in 1887, graduated B.Sc. from Presidency College, Calcutta, in 1906, went to England for training in photography and printing, and returned to Calcutta in 1913 to work in the large printing press founded by his father. The next ten years were immensely productive, marked especially by the composition of his best-known works, the nonsense story *HaJaBaRaLa*, and the volume of nonsense verse *Abol Tabol*. He died an untimely death in 1923, leaving behind his wife and only child, the filmmaker Satyajit Ray.

Lakṣmaṇera Śaktiśela is in the form of the traditional Bengali *yātrā*, with much of the dialogue in song. The play is nominally about the encounter between Lakṣmaṇa and Rāvaṇa after Indrajit's death, which ends with Lakṣmaṇa felled by Rāvaṇa's irresistible weapon, a *śaktiśela*, to be revived only by medicinal herbs growing on Gandhamādana Parvata, which is uprooted and brought in by Hanumān. Although this basic plot line of the episode in the source *Rāmāyaṇa* is maintained by Ray, it is turned into a hilarious confusion of trivialities, such as the messenger describing his midday meal instead of Rāvaṇa's march toward Rāma's camp, Rāma's boastful companions suddenly remembering pressing engagements away from the battlefield, Rāvaṇa picking the fallen Lakṣmaṇa's pocket, Yamadūtas shaking with fear on seeing a live human, and Hanumān malingering over traveling all the way to Gandhamādana Parvata until Rāma hands out some baksheesh. The setting is that of the typical Bengali zamindar court, with Rāma as the lord of the manor and his legendary lieutenants as petty functionaries and hangers-on. The play begins with Rāma telling his court about his dream that Rāvaṇa is dead, whereupon Jāmbuvān declares in true courtier fashion that a regal dream (*rājasvapna*) is never false, and the sycophantic audience repeat: "is not, will never be, cannot possibly be false" (*hoy nā, habe nā, hote pāre nā*).[14] Like other Bengali zamindars in Bengali humorous literature,[15] Rāma shows no inclination to action, and his satellites always try to get out of performing their duties. Jāmbuvān has to be cajoled to wake up from his nap to offer counsel, and Vibhīṣaṇa sleeps on guard duty. Heroic postures are struck only to dissolve into falls and fumbles. Hearing in the third scene that Rāvaṇa may be near, Vibhīṣaṇa frantically looks for his umbrella and his bag—well-known markers of the typical Bengali babu—while Jāmbuvān tries to get away by climbing on Vibhīṣaṇa's back. Later in the scene, as Rāma laments the apparent death of his brother, the monkeys echo his *Hāi, hāi, hāi, hāi—hāi ki holo, hāi ki holo,* but take time out to gulp down a few more bananas. The invincible Yama himself is knocked down and buried by Hanumān under Gandhamādana Parvata at the very moment he is announcing in solemn, alliterative verse the inevitability of his capture of Lakṣmaṇa's soul. Throughout the farce Ray uses the typical humorist's technique of upstaging grand gestures and speech by commonplace idiom. For example, when Rāma strikes a noble pose in the third scene to declaim,

Rāvaṇer keno balo eto bāḍābāḍi? /
Piṁpḍer pākhā uṭhe maribār tare //
Jonākī jemati hāi, agnipāne ruṣi //
sambare khadyot līlā—//

> Tell me, why has Rāvaṇa grown so vainglorious? Ants grow wings only to die—just as, alas, a firefly rushes toward fire to meet his end!

Jāmbubān caps the heroic style by parodying it, presumably unconsciously:

Rāghav boāl jabe labhe abasar /
biśrāmer tare—takhani to māthā tuli //
chaṅg puṭi jato kare mahā āṣphālan /

> When the royal fish retires to take rest—that's when the small fry raise their heads to prance about.

The humor here consists as much in the parody as in the play upon the word Rāghav, which denotes both Rāma and the largest freshwater fish known to Bengalis, and generally considered unclean.

How may we explain this trivialization of one of the most tense moments in the *Rāmāyaṇa*? Going far beyond merely humanizing the traditionally deified Rāma and his heroic endeavor, this burlesque scales down the heroic characters into clowns. The troubling aspects of the *śaktiśela* episode in both Vālmīki and Kṛttivāsa, such as the reason for Rāvaṇa's fury or Rāma's declaration that he would rather lose his kingdom and Sītā than lose Lakṣmaṇa,[16] are entirely concealed by the farce. This is of course only one episode, but Ray's treatment of it seems part of a common attempt to block out the relentlessly grim character of the *Rāmāyaṇa*. To contextualize this approach in personal history, I would point out that Ray very likely inherited this light touch from his father, Upendra Kishore Raychoudhury, whose *Rāmāyaṇa* for boys (*Cheleder Rāmāyaṇa*) injects a strain of laughter even in battlefield scenes and turns the conflict into a high-spirited boys' adventure. Laughter seems at once an interrogation and an escape, in that it undercuts the icons of nobility in the *Rāmāyaṇa* even as it sidesteps the verbal and visual imagery of death and dismemberment.

A more sophisticated use of humor appears in my second example, a short story published in 1933 by the Bengali satirist and essayist Rajshekhar Bose.

"Hanumāner Svapna" starts with a dream of Hanumān's, from which he comes to understand that his celibacy will leave his ancestors without anybody after him to provide them with ritual offerings. On hearing of this dream, Sītā urges Hanumān to look for a bride.[17]

As Hanumān sets out on this quest, he begins to wonder how he would deal with the female of the species, mysterious creatures who laugh and cry without reason, hoard jewels, and acquire useless things: "If she does what pleases me, shall I honor her by placing her on my head? If she disobeys me, shall I slap her into obedience?" As he contemplates this *ghora karma* (grave business) he has undertaken, he runs into the noble young king of Tumba, Cañcarīka, shortly followed by the revered *ṛṣi* Lomaśa. These two very different men compound Hanumān's confusion. For Cañcarīka, having just one wife means nonstop nagging, whereas for Lomaśa having a hundred means the same multiplied a hundred times. Finding neither man a useful guide, Hanumān seeks out the monkey king Sugrīva who, with his 18,000 wives, ought to know how to deal with females if any male does. And sure enough, he has the failproof method of simply keeping his wives' mouths always tied except for love-making. Turning down Sugrīva's offer of his aging wife Tārā, Hanumān follows instead his suggestion to seek the hand of the monkey princess Cilimpā in a neighboring kingdom. The princess has succeeded her late father to the throne, and in her arrogance she puts all her suitors to tests, failure in which carries the penalty of having one's tail cut off. Facing the same fate, Hanumān resorts to direct action and, grabbing her by her hair, he leaps into the sky to rush back to Ayodhyā. Smitten with Hanumān's masculine prowess, Cilimpā declares her love for him, but Hanumān tells her to shut her mouth and, disenchanted with romance, literally drops her into the lap of Sugrīva, at play with his 18,000 wives in the calm waters of the Tungabhadra River. Arriving wifeless in Ayodhyā, he confesses to Sītā that his heart is so full of love for Rāma and Sītā that it has no room for wife and child. But what of his starving ancestors? His solution is immortality for himself, which Sītā gives him as a boon.

On the surface, the story is funny because it explodes the conventional image of Rāma's commanders as noble and wise heroes, as in Ray's treatment of the *śaktiśela* episode, but enhanced by the mock-heroic blending of a grand style with colloquialisms. But looked at more closely, Bose's story is a disturbing exposition of racial and sexist conditions which, it seems to suggest, are inherent in the *Rāmāyaṇa*. Even Sītā, Hanumān's self-declared mother figure from whom he eventually receives the boon of immortality,[18] acknowledges his inferior racial status when she reassures him that on her command the sage Vasiṣṭha would raise him to the kshatriya caste. Distinctly more bigoted is Cañcarīka; when *ṛṣi* Lomaśa reports that he has had to leave his ashram, the noble young king jumps to the suspicion that Lomaśa has lost his wives to marauding *rākṣasas*. Stringing his bow, he exhorts Hanumān: "Mahāvīra, why do you sit in amazed thought? Arise, you will have to cross the ocean once more. You didn't do well to let Vibhīṣaṇa run loose." All males in the story confess themselves sick and tired of females, whether human or simian. The only male who handles females successfully is Sugrīva, a sexual glutton to whom a female's only value consists in her body, as we see in his lust for Cilimpā and his eagerness to offload the faithful but aging Queen Tārā onto Hanumān because, he says, "I don't need her any more." Sugrīva's brutal formula for dealing with females carries the simple lesson that the only thing females understand is force. In this view of gender, female individuality becomes utterly repugnant, and subduing the female takes on a special sexual excitement, which explains Sugrīva's equal desire and fury (*lōbha* and *ākrośa*) with respect to the untamed Cilimpā.

The Sugrīva gender philosophy is quickly proven right as the Hanumān-Cilimpā encounter reaches its climax. She smiles kindly at him, flutters her delicately held bunch of bananas at him teasingly, and in a sweet whisper dismisses him as a "uncultivated, dumb, senile infant" (*ore barbar, ore abodh, ore bṛddha vālaka*). The other side of her gender identity as implied in Sugrīva's formula is equally clear. Proving that females enjoy violation, Cilimpā melts with love for Hanumān when he treats her roughly. Given this evidence of female inferiority, Hanumān makes the only reasonable choice, that of throwing Cilimpā to the insatiable Sugrīva, thereby triumphing over the unmanly emotion of romance and keeping his manly celibacy eternally inviolate.

It is the crudeness of the sexism that, I suggest, should alert us to the satirical potentialities of the story, which extend beyond its immediate action. Many questions that compel a critical rethinking of the *Rāmāyaṇa* crowd in upon the reader. The story is initiated by the need to preserve lineage, surely a parody of Daśaratha's anxiety, which ends in the terror of an answered prayer. Are we looking at parody as a vehicle of criticizing the longing for sons imputed to the traditional Indian ethos that sets off the tragic course of the *Rāmāyaṇa*?

More insistent questions arise from the abduction of Cilimpā, which is such an obvious parody of Sītā's abduction by Rāvaṇa that it is impossible not to see authorial deliberation behind it. Continuing the persistent devaluation of females in the story, which is reinforced by Cilimpā's presumptuous vanity, Hanumān's action affirms the necessity for keeping females in their subordinate place, by force if need be. So smoothly is this thesis developed that it slips past our guard before we realize that it is poised to validate Rāvaṇa's abduction of Sītā and to confirm the status of females as property. This may well compel the reader to reevaluate the treatment of females in the *Rāmāyaṇa*, from the dismemberment of Śūrpanakhā by Lakṣmaṇa to the abandonment of Sītā by Rāma. The failure of males to connect with females is a necessary condition of "Hanumāner Svapna": Cañcarīka fails with his one wife, Lomaśa with his hundred, and Hanumān with Cilimpā. This brings us to the brink of the unstated question: is Rāma any better?

One of the ironies of the *Rāmāyaṇa* as an epic tale is that it is centered on the abduction and recovery of a woman but it is not a story about her as a person. It seems to me that this decentering of the female is the critical target of "Hanumāner Svapna," which gains in ironic strength by overlaying with humor the author's recognition of justice compromised in the *Rāmāyaṇa*. In this victor's narrative, the powerless and the vanquished do not get a fair deal, and this seems to be the burden of Bengali treatments of the *Rāmāyaṇa* in modern times. I am not suggesting that Bose sets out to dismiss the *Rāmāyaṇa* ethic wholesale. His respect for the epic was great, and one of his major works was in fact an abbreviated translation of the *Vālmīki Rāmāyaṇa* (1946). But even as he praises the moral impact of the *Rāmāyaṇa* in his preface, he reminds the reader that "critical judgment must not be entirely suppressed while one enjoys [its] essence." "Hanumaner Svapna" shows, I think, how he put some of the central ideas of the *Rāmāyaṇa* to the test of critical judgment.

To sum up, it seems to me that since the nineteenth century, Bengali approaches to the *Rāmāyaṇa* have shown a persistent ambivalence in viewing the ethical positions established within the narrative tradition, giving rise to an implicit questioning of the moral integrity of Rāma. Spilling over from the literary domain, this questioning has become entrenched in the Bengali social discourse to the extent that at least from the twentieth century onward, Rāma has ceased to enjoy the preeminence he has in much of the rest of India. Temples to Rāma are virtually nonexistent in West Bengal (the postindependence location of Bengali Hindu culture). The erosion of Rāma's stature is marked not only by critical comments in political and ethical debates on the idea of the Rāmarājya but perhaps more tellingly when the Rāma legend is turned into comedy or even farce. While "rām" is a common enough element of older Bengali personal names (such as, Rāmmohan, Rāmprasād), it is only among Bengali speakers that we find "rām" used as an intensifying suffix to pejorative adjectives, such as *bokā* (foolish) or *hāṁdā* (witless). The least one might say about the response to Rāma in Bengal has been summed up by Stewart and Dimock in commenting on the *Rāmāyaṇa* of Kṛttivāsa: "the image of Rāma that lingers is less than complimentary."[19] Rāma and his party are by no means rejected as villains, but neither are they unquestioningly glamorized in the modern Bengali milieu.[20]

This ambivalence is, of course, not unique to the Bengali *Rāmāyaṇa* tradition. In addition to documenting the diversity of narrative elements in regional retellings of the epic, recent scholarship has noted with particular interest the contestatory nature of alternative narratives. Paula Richman reflects this interest when she describes the orientation of her pioneering collection of essays entitled *Many Rāmāyaṇas* as "a study of tellings of the *Rāmāyaṇa* that refashion or contest Vālmīki's text."[21] Nor is it an accident that Richman's more recent collection of *Rāmāyaṇa* studies bears the title *Questioning Rāmāyaṇas*.[22] Bengali retellings clearly fall within this alternative tradition of Rāma tales, which students of the *Rāmāyaṇa* have come accept as a literary, ethical, and political reality of as much authority as the tradition that stems from Vālmīki, though not conventionally as valorized. If within this alternative tradition twentieth-century Bengali versions have a claim to uniqueness, it rests on the prevalence of a comic spirit that stretches from farce to irony and intimates an undermining of received wisdom that is not the less critical for being implied rather than frontal. Yet even here, as they refashion criticism as comedy, Bengali *Rāmāyaṇas* reveal their alignment with a particularly intriguing yet neglected feature of the cultural, and perhaps political, history of India, namely, laughter in the face of convention. Cows are sacred but they are also fodder for newspaper cartoonists. Bhakti of both the Vaiṣṇava and Śākta varieties has been the mainstay of Bengal's religious life and has vastly influenced Bengali literature, but Bengalis tell the most outrageous jokes about *bhaktas*, and even gods and goddesses are not spared by folk humor. This comic deflation of themes and icons of gravity is the not inconsiderable contribution of twentieth-century Bengali tellers of Rāma tales to the reception of the *Rāmāyaṇa* in modern times.

APPENDIX: THE *RĀMĀYAṆA* IN BENGALI LITERATURE

Rāmāyaṇas of Bengal

Date	Author	Title	Theme
14th c.	Kṛttivāsa	*Rāmāyaṇa*	bhakti
16th c.	Ṣaṣṭhivara	*Rāmāyaṇa*	bhakti
	Gaṅgādās Sen & Dvija Durgārām	*Rāmāyaṇa*	bhakti
	Madhusūdan Gosvāmī	*Rāmarasāyaṇa*	bhakti
16th c.	Candrāvatī	*Rāmāyaṇa*	bhakti/ women's fate
17th c.	Lakṣmaṇa Bandoypādhyāya	*Rāmāyaṇa*	bhakti
18th c.	Rāmmohan	*Rāmāyaṇa*	bhakti
18th c.	Jagadrāma & Rāmprasad	*Rāmāyaṇa*	bhakti
18th c.	Adbhutācārya	*Adbhuta Rāmāyaṇa*	bhakti
18th c.	Rāmānanda Ghosh	*Rāmlīlā*	bhakti
18th c.	Śaṅkara Kavicandra	*Viṣṇupurī Rāmāyaṇa*	bhakti
18th c.?	Rāmgovinda Dās	*Rāmāyaṇa*	bhakti
18–19th c.	Balarāma Bandoypādhyāya	*Rāmāyaṇa*	bhakti
19th c.	Raghunandan Gosvāmī	*Śrī Rāmarasāyaṇa*	bhakti

Note: For lists, surveys, and dates (some of them tentative), see Sen 1954, pp. 163–183, and Smith 1988, pp. 30–32.

Pāñcāli (Narrative Poems Recited Musically for Popular Entertainment)

Date	Author	Title
19th c.	Dasharathi Ray	*Śri Rāmacandrera Vivāha*
	Anonymous	*Rāmera Vanagamana o Sītāharaṇa*
	Anonymous	*Sītā Anveṣaṇa*
	Anonymous	*Taraṇīsena Vadha*
	Śaṅkaradeva	*Adhyātma Rāmāyaṇa*, and 6 narrative poems based on it, including *Lakṣmanera Śaktiśela* and *Rāvaṇavadha*

Note: D. C. Sen (1954, p. 183) reports finding "a large number" of narrative poems based on the *Rāmāyaṇa* popular in the villages of Bengal, and lists fifteen composed between the fourteenth and eighteenth centuries.

Nineteenth- and Twentieth-Century Bengali Fiction and Drama Based on the *Rāmāyaṇa*

Date	Author	Title	Theme
19th c.	Vidyasagar	*Sitāra Vanavāsa*	Sītā's exile to the forest; shifts blame from Rama
19th c.	Michael M. Datta	*Meghanādavadha Kāvya*	The slaying of Meghanāda; *rākṣasas* cast as heroes
		Virānganā Kāvya	The story of Pramīlā, Meghanāda's heroic wife
19–20th c.	Rabindranath Tagore	*Vālmīki Pratibhā*	Vālmīki's realization of his poetic powers; operatic form
		Kālmṛgayā	Daśaratha's hunting episode; operatic form
20th c.	Sukumar Roy	*Lakṣmaṇera Śaktiśela*	Lakṣmaṇa's near-death at Rāvaṇa's hand and his revival; mock-heroic play for children
20th c.	Parashuram	"Hanumānera Svapna"	Hanumān's attempt to find a wife; ironic view of heroism
		Smṛtikathā	Śūrpanakhā remembers the good times; humorous tale

The Candrāvatī *Rāmāyaṇa*

The story is divided into three parts, the first of which begins with an account in six sections of Sītā's birth in Rāvaṇa's household. Sītā is born to Rāvaṇa's queen Mandodarī when Mandodarī, horrified by Rāvaṇa's cruel ways, takes the blood drawn by Rāvaṇa from the sages he torments and drinks it, mistaking it for poison, and conceives Sītā. The poet describes the dissolute life of Rāvaṇa, who is made invincible to all except humans and monkeys by Brahmā's boon, and who tyrannizes the gods and sages. Sītā is born out of an egg that Mandodarī delivers, which eventually falls into the hands of a fisherman, whose wife, Satā, names her after herself and presents her to King Janaka. In the last two sections of the first part, Rāma's birth is described and also that of a new character called Kukuyā, Kaikeyī's daughter and Rāma's evil sister, who later engineers Rāma's harsh rejection of Sītā in the second part of the story. The responsibility for Rāma's action is thus passed on to Kukuyā, a character who seldom appears in Rāma stories from India but in many versions from Southeast Asia.

In the second and highly poetic part of the story, Sītā recounts, first in brief summary, then at length, her life in King Janaka's household, the events leading to her marriage with Rāma, and her early life in Ayodhyā, followed by a month-by-month description of the twelve months ("Sitāra Vāromāsī") of their exile, including their conjugal life, and then her abduction, the war, and her rescue.

The third part describes life within the inner, women's quarters, in the palace at Ayodhyā after the return of Rāma, Sītā, and Lakṣmaṇa from Laṅkā.

At first they live happily but, envious of their happiness, Kukuyā devises a way to trick Sītā into drawing a picture of Rāvaṇa even though she had never actually seen him. Kukuyā brings Rāma to see the drawing and arouses his suspicion that Sītā is still attached to Rāvaṇa. Rāma's fury robs him of judgment:

> *raktajabā ānkhi rāmera go śire rakta uṭhe /*
> *nāsikāy agnisvās go brahmarandhra phuṭe //*
>
> Rāma's eyes turned red and his blood went to his head /
> He breathed fire and his head was boiling //

He commands Lakṣmaṇa to convey Sītā into banishment, which stuns her into disbelief when she learns of it from Lakṣmaṇa. But she blames her own fate for her misfortune, which had also caused so many women to lose their husbands and sons in the war to rescue her from Rāvaṇa. She adds that the curse of these women is the cause of her suffering. Never blaming Rāma, she volunteers to enter the final fire ordeal. When no one else is ready to start the fire, Kukuyā tries to do so but burns herself, and Sītā tries to comfort her. Sītā finally enters the fire, only to be taken away by her true mother, the earth, and Rāma is left to lament his loss.

NOTES

1. Kṛttivāsa, 1954, p. 28. The episode occurs also in the Serampore edition of 1803, the first *Kṛttivāsī Rāmāyaṇa* to appear in print. It is omitted from the edition by Harekrishna Mukhopadhyaya (1958).

2. In introducing such an event, however, Kṛttivāsa followed an Āyurvedic belief, as mentioned in the *Carakasaṃhita*, which asserts that a child may be born out of a lesbian relationship but that the child would be deformed and boneless. I am grateful to Dr. Rahul Peter Das for drawing my attention to this information. Kṛttivāsa introduces the story to illustrate the miracles that can be wrought by the gods and thus to validate bhakti. At the same time, by showing how incomplete human reproduction is if it is effected through mere female agency and without male contribution, the story further affirms the patriarchal mode in which the epic unfolds. We may further note that Bhāgīratha's mothers have to rely upon male intervention for a cure of his deformity.

3. Kṛttivāsa, p. 344.

4. Ray and Ray 2001, pp. 401–475.

5. As Candrāvatī's *Rāmāyaṇa* is decidedly the most original retelling of the ancient story in Bengali, a summary is appended to this essay. The text I have followed is Candrāvatī 1975.

6. Śaṅkaradeva, quoted by Smith 1988, p. 99.

7. Datta, [1860] 1995, p. 33.

8. Vidyasagar, "Sītāra Vanavāsa," in *Śakuntalā o Sītāra Vanavāsa* [1860] 1970.

9. A gentle but uncompromising criticism of the virtual erasure of Ūrmilā, Lakṣmaṇa's wife, in the *Rāmāyaṇa* was made by Rabindranath Tagore in an essay written in 1900 and titled "Kāvyer Upekṣitā" (Tagore 1974, 5: 548–555). Tagore argues that her abandonment by her husband cannot be any less shocking than Sītā's fate, and that it

imputes an inhuman exaltation of a narrow understanding of duty above human sympathies at the same time as it suggests a failure of imagination on the part of the poet.

10. D. Ray 1997, p. 51, verse 137.

11. Ibid., p. 56, verse 219.

12. Ibid., p. 114, verse 194.

13. This pen name was not deliberately chosen to express an iconoclastic persona, as one might assume from Bose's frequently satirical writings, but was apparently borrowed from a fruitseller who happened to be present when Bose and a friend were casting about for a pseudonym.

14. This and all other references to the play are to Ray 1987.

15. A ready example comes from Ray's own work, a farce for children called *Jhalapala* (Cacophony). One of several parallels from popular literature is the bumbling zamindar hero of humorous stories by the mid-twentieth-century writer Shibram Chakravarty.

16. *na hi yuddhena me kāryaṁ naiva prāṇair ṇa sītayā / bhrātaraṁ nihataṁ lakṣmaṇaṁ raṇapāṁsuṣu //* Vālmīki, 1971, *sarga* 89, verse 7; *rājyadhane kārya nāi, nāhi cāi Sīte,* Kṛttivśa, 1957, *Laṅkākāṇḍa,* p. 352.

17. Rajshekhar Bose 1973b.

18. As he does in the Kṛttivāsī *Rāmāyaṇa* (1958), p. 422, though not for the same reason as in Bose's story. In the *Uttarakāṇḍa* of the Vālmīki *Rāmāyaṇa* (1975), he gets the boon from Rāma (*sarga* 39, verses 16–19).

19. Stewart and Dimock 2001.

20. For a tongue-in-cheek confirmation of the Bengali disregard for Rāma, we may look again at Rajshekhar Bose's essay, "Gandhamādan Baiṭhak" (1973a), in which seven legendary immortals, including Hanumān and Vibhīṣaṇa, meet on Gandhamādan mountain to review the current state of the world. Hanumān reports that Rāma is worshiped everywhere in India except Bengal.

21. Richman 1991, p. xi.

22. Richman 2001.

REFERENCES

Bose, Rajshekhar [Parashuram]. 1946 [1353 baṅgābda]. *Vālmīki Rāmāyaṇa.* Calcutta: M. C. Sarkar.

Bose, Rajshekhar [Parashuram]. 1973a [*baṅgābda* 1380]. "Gandhamādan Baiṭhak." In *Paraśurām Granthābalī.* Vol. 2. Calcutta: M. C. Sarkar.

———. 1973b [*baṅgābda* 1380]. "Hanumāner Svapna." In *Paraśurām Granthābalī.* Vol. 3. Calcutta: M. C. Sarkar.

Candrāvatī. 1975. *Rāmāyaṇa.* In *Prācīna Pūrvavaṅga Gītikā,* edited by Kshitish Chandra Moulik. Vol. 7. Calcutta: Firma K. L. Mukhopadhyaya.

Datta, Michael Madhusudan. [1860] 1965. *Madhusūdan Granthābalī,* edited by Khsetra Gupta. Calcutta: Sahitya Sansad.

Kṛttivāsa. 1954 [*baṅgābda* 1361]. *Saptakāṇḍa Rāmāyaṇa.* Edited by Benimadhab Sil. Calcutta: Akshay Library.

———. 1957. *Rāmāyaṇa.* Edited by Harekrishna Mukhopadhyaya, with an introduction by Sunitikumar Chattopadhyaya. Calcutta: Sahitya Samsad.

Nag, Sujitkumar, ed. 1987. [*baṅgābda* 1394]. *Sukumār Bicitrā.* Calcutta: New Book Supply Agency.

Parashuram. *See* Rajshekhar Bose.

Ray, Dasharathi. 1997. *Dāśarathī Rāyera Pāñcālī*. Edited by Ardhendushekhar Ray. Calcutta: Mahesh Library.

Ray, Jagadram, and Ramprasad Ray. 2001. *Rāmprasādī Jagadrāmī Rāmāyaṇa*. Edited by Nirmalendu Mukhopadhyaya. 3rd ed. Calcutta: Mahesh Library.

Ray, Sukumar. 1987 [*baṅgābda* 1394]. *Lakṣmaṇera Śaktiśela*. In *SukumārRāya Racanāsamagra*, edited by Shyamapada Sarkar. Calcutta: Kamini Prakasalaya, pp. 256–67.

Raychoudhury, Upendra Kishore. [c. 1894] 1995. *Cheleder Rāmāyaṇa*. Calcutta: Nirmal Book Agency.

Richman, Paula, ed. 1991. *Many Rāmāyaṇas*. Berkeley and Los Angeles: University of California Press.

———. 2001. *Questioning Rāmāyaṇas*. Berkeley and Los Angeles: University of California Press.

Sen, Dinesh Chandra. 1954. *History of Bengali Language and Literature*. Calcutta: University of Calcutta.

Sengupta, Subodhchandra. 1976 [*baṅgābda* 1383]. *Hāsyarasik Paraśurām*. Calcutta: A. Mukherjee.

Smith, William. 1988. *Rāmāyaṇa Traditions in Eastern India: Assam, Bengal, Orissa*. Stockholm: Department of Indology, University of Stockholm.

Stewart, Tony K., and Edward C. Dimock. 2001. "Kṛttibāsa's Apophatic Critique of Rāma's Kingship." In *Questioning Rāmāyaṇas*, edited by Paula Richman. Berkeley and Los Angeles: University of California Press, pp. 229–249.

Tagore, Rabindranath. 1974. *Rabindra Racanāvalī*. Vol. 5. Calcutta: Visva Bharati.

Vālmīki. 1960–1975. *Vālmīki Rāmāyaṇa: A Critical Edition*. 7 vols. Baroda: Oriental Institute. Vol. 6, *Yuddhakāṇḍa*, edited by P. L. Vaidya, 1971. Vol. 7, *Uttarakāṇḍa*, edited by U. P. Shah, 1975.

Vidyasagar, Ishwarchandra. [1860] 1970. *Śakuntalā o Sītāra Vanavāsa*, Edited by Ujjal Kumar Majumdar. Calcutta: Sanyal.

5

Why Can't a Shudra Perform Asceticism? Śambūka in Three Modern South Indian Plays

Paula Richman

Among the deeds for which Rāma has been most roundly condemned in south India, the beheading of Śambūka is preeminent.[1] The earliest recounting of the shudra's death at the hands of Rāma, as punishment for practicing asceticism, appears in the *Uttarakāṇḍa* (last book) of the *Rāmāyaṇa* attributed to Vālmīki. Most scholars view the final book as a later interpolation, but whether it dates from Vālmīki's time or somewhat later, it soon became part of the ongoing *Rāmāyaṇa* tradition.[2] Subsequent writers, most notably eighth-century playwright Bhavabhūti in his *Uttararāmacarita,* have expressed profound unease with Rāma's willingness—allegedly for the sake of upholding dharma—to take the life of a person whose only misdeed was performing religious austerities.[3]

This essay examines three twentieth-century plays about Śambūka from south India, in Telugu, Tamil, and Kannada, respectively. Each of the three playwrights "sets the record straight" about Śambūka's desire to perform asceticism, doing so in light of the beliefs that are central to his own experience. Although all three condemn the prohibition against a shudra performing asceticism, each author re-envisions the motivations of the story's characters in his own way.

The earliest version of Śambūka's story, in the *Uttarakāṇḍa* of the *Rāmāyaṇa* attributed to Vālmīki, is quite brief. It relates how a brahman comes to the court of Rāma carrying the body of his dead son, who expired without any apparent cause. The father protests that such an inauspicious event would never happen in a land where the king insures that each citizen performs *varṇāśrama-dharma* (duty enjoined according to one's social rank and stage of life). When Rāma consults his ministers about the matter, they identify a deviation from dharma: a shudra named Śambūka has been practicing *tapas,* a form of religious austerity reserved for members of the upper three *varṇas.* Immediately, Rāma mounts his celestial chariot, rushes to the forest where Śambūka dwells, and questions him. Upon learning that he is a shudra, Rāma draws his gleaming, stainless sword and cuts off his head. "Well done!" shout the gods in praise. The brahman's son returns to life, and fragrant flowers rain down in celebration, a sign of celestial approbation.[4]

Between 1920 and 1954, in sharp contrast, three influential south Indian playwrights analyzed below responded to Śambūka's beheading not with approval but with horror. Significantly, each of the three would be considered a "shudra" according to brahmanical classifications, and each wrote in his own regional language (rather than Sanskrit or English).[5] The three playwrights retold this tale from *Rāmāyaṇa* tradition to convey how they understood the story's main characters: Rāma, Śambūka, and the brahman whose son died. Although these writers entered into a relationship with the *Rāmāyaṇa* narrative, rather than abandoning it altogether, they insisted on renegotiating the framework within which the story should be understood. Each playwright envisioned the main characters differently, but all did so in a way that removed the stigma of *adharma* from Śambūka's shoulders.

The plays deserve our attention not only for the individual ways in which they rethink Śambūka's asceticism but also for the insights they reveal about oppositional strands within *Rāmāyaṇa* tradition.[6] The three Śambūka plays, and others of their type,[7] offer narrative alternatives to depictions of Śambūka found in dominant tellings of Rāmkathā that reinforce caste hierarchy. The playwrights examined here not only demonstrate how Rāmkathā continues to be recounted in the modern period in light of topical issues,[8] they also reflect vigorous protest against caste hierarchy in south India between 1920 and 1954.

I explore three questions in my analysis of these three south Indian plays. First, when writers grapple with Rāma's beheading of Śambūka, what options exist for them (within or outside of Hindu tradition) that enable them to reenvision the incident? Second, what stance does each playwright take toward authoritative Hindu texts? Third, why does each text critique brahmanical caste prescriptions but not asceticism?

Scholars often study the history of one regional literary tradition in India in isolation (such as Tamil literature separately from Kannada literature), and hence a text's broader significance may be overlooked. In contrast, when dramas about the same incident, written in bordering regional languages, are placed side by side, a broader pattern emerges. In the southern region of the Indian subcontinent, the Hindu majority of the population would be categorized as "shudra" according to brahmanical classifications. Juxtaposing plays in Telugu, Tamil, and Kannada suggests how troubling Rāma's beheading of a shudra proved in twentieth-century south India.[9] These plays also anticipate certain themes that have developed more fully in recent dalit literature.[10]

Equality in Ascetic Practice

The earliest of the three plays examined in this essay was written in Telugu by Tripuraneni Ramasvami Chaudari (1887–1943). Chaudari's writings are among the earliest that explicitly interrogate the history of brahmans and non-brahmans in the Andhra region. After Chaudari returned from higher studies in Ireland, where he trained as a barrister, he established himself as a journalist and social thinker. He wrote *Śambuka Vadha* [The slaying of Śambūka] between 1914 and 1917, but the play did not appear in print until 1920. Although it was performed a few times, the play was primarily meant to be read rather than viewed in performance.[11]

Chaudari's interpretation of Śambūka is based on the belief that all have the fundamental right to practice *tapas*, religious discipline that advances spiritual progress. Chaudari rejected Vedic rituals that necessitated brahman services in favor of religious practices such as asceticism, by which an individual could make spiritual progress through acts of self-discipline that included meditation and yoga. In fact, he eventually founded his own hermitage for the practice of asceticism.[12] In the 1920s and 1930s, Chaudari advocated what we might today call "equal-opportunity" asceticism.

Chaudari's play identifies the brahmans in Rāma's court as those directly responsible for Śambūka's death. In *Śambuka Vadha*, Vasiṣṭha and his fellow brahmans persuade the Aśvins, celestial physicians, to cause the temporary death of a young brahman boy in order to blame his death on Śambūka. By discrediting the shudra in this way, they seek to neutralize the threat his asceticism poses to brahmanical claims of religious superiority. The brahmanical conspiracy in Chaudari's play fits with his view that brahmans had written religious law books to legitimate their high position and justify the oppression of lower castes. A member of the (non-brahman) Kamma *jāti*, Chaudari spent much of his life attacking brahman privilege and stripping away what he considered brahmanical accretions to Hindu texts. Using notions of racial difference brought to India by colonial anthropologists, he argued that Dravidians originally ruled south India, which was wrested away from them by Aryans who invaded from the north and subjugated those whom they conquered. Teaching the indigenous people that they were low caste helped to brainwash them into accepting their degraded status.

Since brahmanical power rests on the authority vested in texts, *Śambuka Vadha* engages in explicit evaluation of the categories by which religious works are classified. When Rāma goes to the forest to investigate allegations against Śambūka, Rāma finds the ascetic to be quite learned, so he invites Śambūka to debate the brahmans in his court. Śambūka knows, however, that unless he receives clear agreement from the brahmans that they will only draw upon valid sources of religious authority to substantiate their points, the power differential would be deeply in their favor from the debate's beginning to end. So he makes acceptance of the offer contingent upon the condition that evidence be admissible only if drawn from *śruti* (not *smṛti*). Śambūka defines *śruti* as divinely inspired texts (such as the Vedas and Upaniṣads). He deauthorizes *smṛti*, since he claims that brahmans wrote Dharmaśāstras to legitimate caste hierarchy and glorify their privileged status. Naturally, the brahmans reject Śambūka's stipulation. Their refusal dramatizes Chaudari's view that brahmans distorted the teachings of early Hindu scriptures to exclude non-brahmans from religious equality.

Suggesting that Rāma is fallible and insecure, Chaudari portrays Rāma as killing Śambūka out of fear that he will lose his power. His brahman ministers threaten that if Rāma does not eliminate Śambūka, ordinary citizens will realize that people of any rank can attain the highest religious goals. If it becomes generally known that Śambūka has successfully challenged religious exclusivism, the power base of brahmans and kshatriyas will be destabilized, making it impossible for them to continue to dominate the social order.[13] The priests warn Rāma that even he depends upon brahmans to maintain his position because brahmans perpetuate the notion that Kingship is divinely sanctioned. Ultimately, Rāma slays Śambūka either out of fear or because he is politically sagacious enough not to risk undermining a brahman and kshatriya alignment that has maintained its power for centuries. Chaudari's interpretation of Rāma's motivation raises doubts about Rāma's status. If he were actually the epitome of dharma, Rāma would not have killed Śambūka, because a virtuous person would not murder to maintain his status. Also, if it is virtuous to perform *tapas*, Śambūka should not be barred from it simply because of his low-caste birth. Ultimately in *Śambuka Vadha*, Rāma appears weak and easily manipulated by brahmans.

Śambūka, on the other hand, dies a heroic death, a martyr to the struggle for universal access to asceticism. His commitment to religious austerities is impeccable. In addition, his dichotomy between *śruti* and *smṛti* is a longstanding and recognized distinction in Hindu religious discourse. In *Śambuka Vadha*, Śambūka's actions earn respect from other non-brahmans (Chaudari calls them Dravidians), whom he rallies to fight for the right to perform *tapas*. In Chaudari's portrayal, he idealizes the self-discipline and compassion shown by non-brahman Śambūka, contrasting it with the behavior of brahmans: intrigue, protection of privilege, and incitement to murder. As final proof of Śambūka's goodness, when Rāma does slay Śambūka, the ascetic ascends immediately to heaven.[14] Chaudari's play "corrects" Vālmīki's version, furnishing Śambūka with the reputation he should have earned: that of a great ascetic and a person knowledgeable in religious wisdom.

Śambuka Vadha prompted many to take a closer look at both Rāma's story and their own assumptions about Rāma's character. The beheading of Śambūka seemed to contradict the fundamental message of Rāma's love for all creatures. If Rāma were truly compassionate, Chaudari reasoned that Śambūka's story must have been added, or at least distorted at some point, by those who felt threatened by the desire of lower castes to appropriate religious practices of upper castes. Since Chaudari assumes that brahmans have tampered with the text, he imagines and portrays what he thinks Śambūka would have said and done if his voice and experience had not been removed from the story.

Śambuka Vadha proved so controversial that it became the object of discussion throughout Andhra Pradesh. Although many plays make little impact upon public life, Chaudari's drama provoked debate throughout the Telugu-speaking region. Many traditionally minded devotees of Rāma found Chaudari's play appalling. As Narayana Rao recounts, "For almost ten years this unconventional presentation faced stiff resistance. The author persisted, arguing in favor of his position in town after town." This was no mere "academic" argument, nor were the arguments limited to a few literary critics: "There were serious discussions in town halls, clubs and restaurants, bar-rooms of district courts, the press, and most importantly within literary gatherings."[15] These discussions helped to bring a relatively minor *Rāmāyaṇa* character into public consciousness. Those who might never have pondered Śambūka's fate in the past now heard arguments about him in every town. Chaudari's play brought a little-known character into the spotlight and convinced many people that he deserved sympathy as a noble ascetic slain to maintain caste privilege.

Śambūka as Rationalist

A more extreme attack on Rāma's treatment of Śambūka appears in the 1954 play titled *Rāmāyaṇa Nāṭakam* [*Rāmāyaṇa* drama] by Thiruvarur K. Thangaraju, a Tamil journalist, playwright, and actor. In the late 1940s, he left Congress to join E. V. Ramasami's social reform group, the Dravida Kazhagam (the Dravidian federation). Viewing a *Rāmāyaṇa* performance by a drama troupe in Madras in 1950, Thangaraju radically disagreed with their portrayal of Rāma's story and determined to write his own version of the play. After reading a number of books in Tamil on the subject, he composed *Rāmāyaṇa Nāṭakam*, which was performed both in Madras and on tour throughout Tamilnadu between 1954 and 1958.[16]

Thangaraju composed his play under the influence of his mentor, E. V. Ramasami. Throughout the 1940s and 1950s, Ramasami lectured across Tamilnadu, advocating proportional representation of non-brahman groups in government, abolition of caste hierarchy, and rejection of rituals based on purity and impurity. Along with atheism, he preached an ideology that (like Chaudari) identified brahmans as Aryans who, supported by kshatriya might, subjugated and mentally enslaved Dravidians. He condemned religion in general, which he viewed as a combination of superstition and priestly privilege, and urged his followers to embrace scientific thought and to cultivate egalitarianism and self-respect. He attacked the *Rāmāyaṇa* story specifically, claiming its account of Rāma's defeat of Rāvaṇa really portrayed the Aryan conquest of Dravidians. Ramasami endorsed Thangaraju's play, giving him a silver cup and Rs. 2000 at the play's debut and writing an appreciative preface to the published version.[17]

Much of Thangaraju's originality as a playwright lies in the creative ways he dramatizes Ramasami's critique of Rāma: Ramasami lambasted Rāma as a coward who appropriated the lands of Dravidians, and then humiliated the people he conquered. Such a critique poses a number of challenges for a dramaturge. Thangaraju re-envisions the whole epic in light of three actions performed by Rāma: slaying Vāli in the back while hiding behind a tree, directing Lakṣmaṇa to mutilate Śūrpanakhā when she expressed love for him, and beheading Śambūka. Thangaraju portrays Vāli, Śūrpanakhā, and Śambūka as Dravidians whom brahmanical tradition labeled "low caste" because they did not support Rāma's invasion of the Dravidian kingdom. Although Thangaraju's play deals with the full *Rāmāyaṇa* epic rather than just the Śambūka incident, my analysis below focuses on that incident.

Chaudari and Thangaraju represent Śambūka's asceticism so differently primarily because the two playwrights held radically differing assessments of the nature of religion. Thangaraju and Chaudari both share the Aryan vs. Dravidian view of south Indian history, and both depict Śambūka as intelligent, articulate, and self-assured. Chaudari, however, glorifies Śambūka's spiritual attainments in yogic discipline. As an atheist, Thangaraju did not possess the same admiration for Śambūka's achievements in bodily mortification. Whereas Chaudari's play lauds Śambūka's performance of *tapas*, Thangaraju instead organizes his depiction of the incident so that he can highlight the persuasive logic of Śambūka's reasoning as he explains to Rāma why one must reject the notion that "shudra" functions as a meaningful or valid form of classification. In Thangaraju's depiction of Śambūka, the playwright provides his shudra hero with speeches that sound remarkably like those of E. V. Ramasami. Both the real-life mentor and the fictional shudra ascetic suggest that one should look to education and design of the natural world, rather than brahmanically disseminated Dharmaśāstras, to determine the principles that govern existence.

Thangaraju makes it a point in his play to portray brahmans as using their scriptures to justify both their claim to exclusive power and their attack on anyone who questions their monopoly. When pressed to justify Śambūka's killing, the brahmans can only quote from the legal treatises on dharma, texts that fall under the category of *smṛti*. For example, in *Rāmāyaṇa Nāṭakam*, when Rāma hears complaints that Śambūka is performing asceticism, he asks, "Is it an error for a person to perform *tapas*?" The brahmans respond that such behavior is prohibited in religious texts:

> PRIEST 1 Shall our pure texts emerge from the mouth of a shudra? O Rāma! No wonder brahmans are in danger during your rule (*rāj*). Why do you just sit there staring?
>
> PRIEST 2 Lord! Our *smṛtis* warn that it is a sin (*pāpam*) if shudras hear our Vedic texts, so one must pour red hot melted lead in their ears.
>
> PRIEST 1 Lord, our Vedas say that if shudras learn Vedic *śāstras*, their tongues must be cut off. And it is said that Śambūka violated both rules. Alas for him![18]

In this quote, there is no argument that E. V. Ramasami would judge persuasive in defense of prohibiting a shudra from performing asceticism. Instead of providing any independent justification (that is, reasoning not dependent upon the status of authoritative texts) for the prohibition, the priests refer to what the "pure texts" say, or cite *śāstras*. The answer boils down to brahmans saying that brahmanical texts do not allow such behavior.

Furthermore, the scriptural passages to which the quote refers prescribe heinous punishments for those who do not act in conformity with *śāstras*. If a shudra hears brahmanical texts, his ears must be burned so that he can never hear again. Similarly, if he quotes from brahmanical texts, his tongue must be severed so he loses the ability to speak. In each case, the punishment insures that the shudra can never again disseminate knowledge to which he is forbidden access. By similar logic, Śambūka must be put to death because he studied scriptures on *tapas;* he must never do so again, nor must other shudras imitate him. When the brahmans, at Rāma's request, consult the constitutional palm leaves of *Rāmrāj*, they specify death as punishment for a shudra who transgresses textual prohibitions.[19] In such a situation, Śambūka has no recourse.

Thangaraju was born into the Vellala community, a prestigious *jāti* of dominant landholding non-brahmans whom brahmans nonetheless rank as "shudras." When the priest asks "Shall our pure texts emerge from the mouth of a shudra?"[20] the statement is self-reflexive: Thangaraju, whom brahmans would categorize as a shudra, has—as he emphasized in his 1992 interview with me—heard and studied Hindu scripture. In fact, in these very lines of his play, he has appropriated the privilege of quoting scripture, something that—according to the constitutional palm leaves—would earn him death.

Not surprisingly, in Thangaraju's play Śambūka gets all the best lines. When Rāma, accompanied by Lakṣmaṇa and a host of vicious brahmans, confronts Śambūka and accuses him of violating dharma, Śambūka is puzzled. The shudra ascetic replies in a calm, cogent, and persuasive manner, drawing upon scientific discourse to demonstrate that Rāma is acting upon erroneous assumptions:

> For the sake of whom was the law written and instituted, Lord? Did God create brahmans and shudras in his creation? Look at the animals that he created in nature. Whatever you do to change a dog, can you make it a lion? Can you make a tiger into a goat? The structures of differing body parts are elements of nature.
>
> Deceitful are those who have classified human beings, claiming similar differences in human *varṇas*. Are there any natural differences—that is, differing body parts—between the brahman and the shudra, like those between the goat and the tiger or the lion and the small dog?
>
> Lord, that is God's work. This is rogue's work. Which will you accept, Respected Sir? Just because a murderer, a drunkard, or a fool is born in the womb of a woman labeled a brahman, should he become a brahman? And only because a learned man, an exemplar, a highly cultivated man is born in the womb of a woman labeled a shudra, should he become a shudra?
>
> We are all born only as men. Eminence and lowliness are cre-

> ated through one's own actions. That is how things must occur. This is the only law of nature, the law that God instituted. How can you label as law the books and Vedas, written and instituted in opposition to God's law for the sake of dishonest people who have forgotten the nature of God's creation?[21]

Here Śambūka provides a short science lesson for the king, explicating the genetic basis for distinctions between species and, conversely, the lack of any scientific basis for the differentiation between castes. Note that Śambūka dismisses the religious prohibitions found in the Vedas and *śāstras* as written "for the sake of dishonest people" and recommends instead that people be guided by the laws one can see in nature.

Interrupting Śambūka's speech at this point, Rāma seems to concede that Śambūka's argument has some validity. He begins his response with, "However much truth there is in what you say"; he continues, nonetheless, "you have still broken the law and deserve punishment." As Rāma then beheads him, the brahmans cheer. The Śambūka episode in *Rāmāyaṇa Nāṭakam* is one of the most intense, disturbing, and effectively scripted incidents in the play. Although the early parts of *Rāmāyaṇa Nāṭakam* have many humorous moments, including scenes that mock Rāma by portraying him as addicted to celestial ambrosia (liquor) and so frightened of face-to-face battles that he hides behind a tree,[22] Rāma's interactions with the shudra ascetic take on a tragic tone as noble Śambūka is slain.

E. V. Ramasami once declaimed, in light of Śambūka's beheading, "If there were kings like Rāma now, what would be the fate of those people called shudras?"[23] The question has a particular edge in Tamilnadu because in many areas where Ramasami was active, the *varṇa* structure is far more attenuated than in other parts of India: in Tamilnadu, according to brahmanical reckoning, the major caste divisions are: brahmans, "clean" shudras, "unclean" shudras, and untouchables. So only brahmans fit the *śāstras*' category of "twice-born" *varṇas* who can perform asceticism, while a high percentage of the Tamil population (except in Tanjore District)[24] would be classified as shudras or lower, including the dominant landholding *jāti* of Vellalas. It is not surprising, then, that most of those who attended Thangaraju's play identified strongly with Śambūka and the tragedy of his death.

Rāmāyaṇa Nāṭakam received wide exposure throughout Tamilnadu. After its initial five-week run in Madras, the cast toured the state with several truckloads of theatrical props and costumes, performing in town theaters or thatched village huts between 1954 and 1958. As a result, both urban and rural audiences saw the play. Throughout the 1950s, Ramasami's Dravida Kazhagam held conferences, gave public lectures, released publications, and participated in public protests against caste hierarchy. Its activities provided Tamilians with an intellectual framework within which they could place Śambūka's death scene, while their own experiences of caste prejudice helped them empathize with Śambūka.

Historical evidence confirms that many considered the play offensive.

When it opened in Madurai, orthodox Hindus lodged complaints with the police. In Karur some "rowdies" interrupted the play and prevented it from continuing; when the case was subsequently taken up in the Madras court, the judge decreed that police should have arrested those who disrupted the play. In Tirucchirappali, the actor playing Rāma was forcibly dragged off the stage.[25] Atal Behari Vajpayee, the present prime minister of India, even complained about the production in parliament, but Jawaharlal Nehru responded to Vajpayee's outrage by answering that the treatment of Śambūka was an atrocity and should be presented as such. Politician and writer C. Rajagopalachari formed a "Rāmāyaṇa Protection Society" after reading the play.[26]

Nearly twenty years later, Thangaraju revived the play, playing Rāvaṇa himself in Tanjore for a Dravida Kazhagam conference that he estimates was attended by over ten thousand people. In 1971–1972, *The Organiser* condemned the play.[27] Because of these many performances, as well as the play's condemnation and involvement in litigation, the morality of Śambūka's beheading played a crucial role in the debate about brahman vs. non-brahman relations throughout Tamilnadu.

Transforming a Brahman

In the mid-1940s, *Śūdra Tapasvī* [The Shudra ascetic] was published in Kannada. Its author, K. V. "Kuvempu" Puttappa (1904–1994) enjoyed an extraordinarily successful career as a writer and public intellectual in Karnataka.[28] Padma Bhushana recipient and vice-chancellor of Mysore University, he was among the most successful, prominent, and respected "shudras" of his day and the first to rise so high in the university system of Karnataka. In stark contrast to both Chaudari and Thangaraju, Kuvempu was an ardent devotee of Rāma. His belief in Rāma's compassion informs both his lengthy poem on Rāmkathā and his short play on Śambūka, *Śūdra Tapasvī.*

Kuvempu states his perspective on innovation within *Rāmāyaṇa* tradition in his major work on Rāmkathā, a monumental lyric poem of 23,000 lines entitled *Śrī Rāmāyaṇa Darśanam.* Near the beginning of this poem, which won him a Sahitya Akademi award in 1955, Kuvempu explains how he situates himself in relation to *Rāmāyaṇa* tradition:

> It is not correct to say that Vālmīki is the only *Rāmāyaṇa* poet.
> There are thousands of *Rāmāyaṇa* poets.
> There is a *Rāmāyaṇa* poet in every village.[29]

His words indicate that Kuvempu did not feel compelled to be "faithful" to Vālmīki's text. Instead, Kuvempu sought to present Rāmkathā in a way faithful to his own vision of Rāma's goodness.

A deeply religious man, Kuvempu was influenced at an early age by the teachings of the Ramakrishna Mission and later became an adherent of Aurobindo's metaphysics. At the heart of his religious beliefs were commitment to ahimsā (nonviolence) and love of Lord Rāma. The combination of nonviolence and devotion accounts for several unusual features of Kuvempu's treatment of Rāmkathā. For example, in his lyric poem, he omits Hanumān's burning of Laṅkā because Kuvempu did not believe that Hanumān would cause the death of so many innocent people. Furthermore, Rāma not only admits that he was mistaken in killing Vāli but even undergoes the fire ordeal alongside Sītā. In a nutshell, Kuvempu's Rāma would not—could not—kill Śambūka.[30]

Instead, the rising action in *Śūdra Tapasvī* impels the play toward the moment when the brahman, who has accused Śambūka of deviating from dharma, undergoes a radical transformation. Fairly early in the play, Rāma realizes that the brahman is a "bigoted pedant."[31] In *Śūdra Tapasvī*, therefore, Rāma's problem lies not with Śambūka but with the brahman who demands Śambūka's execution. Rāma must find a way to help the brahman overcome his pride, freeing him then to appreciate the value of Śambūka's asceticism. Unlike the other two plays we have examined, which pit a stock brahman villain against a stock shudra hero, several of Kuvempu's main characters are not "stock" at all; over the course of the play, they learn and become transformed into different kinds of people. Most centrally, the brahman matures from an arrogant person enslaved by scripture into a balanced, thoughtful, and enlightened person.

Śūdra Tapasvī does not deal with caste issues in isolation. Instead, Kuvempu interrogates caste's foundation in the purity/impurity dichotomy, from which both caste and gender hierarchy derive. Among major sources of pollution that brahmanical texts list, interactions with two categories of people are prohibited. A high-born male can be sullied by certain exchanges with people not born into the top three castes (such as shudras and untouchables). Also polluting to him are interactions with a woman of any caste who is menstruating or having sexual relations with a man other than her husband.

Śūdra Tapasvī suggests links between these two sources of pollution through Rāma's reflections upon an anthill. When Rāma and the brahman arrive in the forest, the brahman points out Śambūka, who has remained motionless in deep meditation for such a long time that an anthill has grown up around him. Seeing it unleashes Rāma's remorse about Sītā. Rumors that she became impure during her imprisonment in Laṅkā led Rāma to rid his palace of even the slightest taint of impurity by banishing his pregnant wife to the forest. Rescued there by Vālmīki, the ascetic poet who composed the first full literary *Rāmāyaṇa* and provided her with shelter in his ashram, Sītā raises her twin sons within its precincts. In a soliloquy, Rama ponders the fact that the poet's name, Vālmīki, is said to derive from *valmīka* (anthill), a reference to the rigor of his austerities. Vālmīki was also a shudra, Rāma recalls:

> That reference to the anthill
> touches me to the quick
> by recalling the great poet

who is today sheltering Sītā.
That poet too is a shudra
like Śambūka.
Born a hunter, he too achieved
greatness through *tapas*.[32]

Rāma considers the ironic fact that, at the moment when the brahman seeks to deprive Śambūka of the chance to perform *tapas* because he is "impure," another shudra shelters the monarch's pure wife, because Rāma succumbed to fear that (unfounded) gossip would mar the reputation of his reign. Familiar with the circumstances of Sītā's banishment, Kuvempu's audience would see that Rāma's treatment of Sītā and the brahman's antagonism toward Śambūka both involve mistreatment of an innocent and virtuous person due to obsessive concern with purity.

Immediately after his soliloquy, Rāma begins a verbal duel with the brahman. Kuvempu's stage directions instruct Rāma to speak "ironically but seriously." The weapon of choice is the epithet, a phrase expressing some quality possessed by the person being addressed. Each man uses a carefully chosen epithet to warn that the other must act according to precedents that set the standard for approved behavior. For example, Rāma asks the brahman, "Isn't *tapas* a holy practice?" The brahman first addresses him with the epithet "King of the Raghu Lineage," thereby warning Rāma to maintain his lineage's unsullied prestige, before the brahman agrees that *tapas* is unequaled in virtue. Rāma calls the brahman "Eminent among the Enlightened Ones," emphasizing the priest's mastery through *tapas* of the religious knowledge that cuts off rebirth and leads to enlightenment. This epithet implies the brahman should practice detachment rather than seek the ascetic's death, since true enlightenment entails overcoming emotions such as hatred.

The duel soon ratchets up to a higher level of intensity. Addressing the brahman as "One Who Knows Wisdom" to imply that he needs to abandon ignorance, Rāma then inquires whether it would be a sin to kill a person who performs *tapas*. The brahman concedes that such a deed would be a sin but, in a surprising turn, addresses Rāma as "Killer of Vāli." Rāma deviated from the proper dharma of a warrior by shooting Vāli in the back while hiding behind a tree, an act that is generally viewed as a blot on Rāma's otherwise relatively stainless record of virtuous action.[33] Kuvempu portrays the brahman as implying, through his choice of this unexpected epithet, that to rid Rāma's kingdom of Śambūka Rāma must again stoop as low as he did when he murdered Vāli.

Rāma, barely suppressing his anger, demands to know whether it would be a sin to kill Śambūka. Addressing Rāma as "Disciple of Vasiṣṭha" to remind Rāma that his guru, Vasiṣṭha, taught strict adherence to caste hierarchy, the brahman responds that one must look not to logic (*tarka*) but to *śāstra*s for the answer to Rāma's question. He adds, definitively, "Milk is sacred and nourishes life. But that doesn't mean you can drink dog's milk. A shudra's *tapas* is like dog's milk."[34] With tongue in cheek, Rāma praises the brahman as "Great Teacher" and compliments him on his erudition, thereby implying that he is clever but lacks inner wisdom.

How then, asks Rāma, should he carry out the brahman's demand that he execute the shudra? An ordinary arrow cannot kill a person who performs *tapas,* because meditation generates special protective power. The brahman, addressing Rāma as "Subduer of Enemies," urges that he resort to the deadly *brahmāstra,* which he wielded when he fatally wounded Rāvaṇa. By offering this advice, the brahman implies that the devious, tyrannical, lustful demon king and the calmly meditating shudra deserve the same terrible fate. Rāma notes that once the *brahmāstra* is launched, it will not stop until its enemy is destroyed. Delighted, the brahman urges Rāma to string his bow with the deadly missile.

That a travesty of justice seems about to occur is signaled by the sudden arrival of an actor personifying Death. She demands to know why Rāma intends to unleash the *brahmāstra,* a terrible weapon of destruction. Rāma replies only that it is necessary for Death to carry out the task before her, since "No one is exempt from doing one's duty." Perceiving that she must submit to his order, Death prepares to follow the *brahmāstra*'s course. Rāma then commands his weapon: "Seek out the sinner and destroy him!"[35] Kuvempu's stage directions at this point call for thunder, lightning, a dust storm, and tree branches to creak in the wind as if crying in anguish—all omens of impending doom.

Yet the *brahmāstra* embarks on an unexpected course, whose outcome absolves Śambūka of wrongdoing. Released from Rāma's bow, the weapon heads toward Śambūka, while Death follows obediently, but then it falls at the ascetic's feet in respect. The bewildered brahman asks Rāma whether the weapon has failed, but Rāma assures him that it will soon find its mark. A moment later, the arrow turns and heads directly toward the brahman. In terror he seeks refuge from Rāma, who warns him that he cannot save himself unless he can "open the eye of intellect." The brahman rejects this call to use his power to reason, protesting that nothing that contravenes the *śāstras* can be dharmic. At that moment a voice from the celestial realm chants in Sanskrit:

> Recourse to scriptures alone
> will not help decide the right deed.
> A thoughtless act can
> only do harm to dharma.[36]

Realization now dawns upon the brahman as the play reaches its turning point. The astonished but enlightened brahman then acknowledges:

> I have been hidebound,
> warped by the texts,
> blinded by prejudice.
> Does fire worry about
> the caste of its fuel?
> A sage is to be honored

regardless of his birth.
Humility leads to grace
while scorn corrupts the soul.[37]

The power of these words brings the brahman's son back to life. As they both venerate Śambūka and the sage extends to them his blessing, flowers rain down from the sky.

Thus Śambūka does not die, nor does the brahman. The subjugation of the lethal weapon demonstrates the inarguable efficacy of Śambūka's *tapas*. It halts the unstoppable weapon of death, confirming physically what the brahman has realized intellectually: that a shudra who practices asceticism is virtuous, whatever ancient texts say. In addition, at the symbolic level, the *brahmāstra* did kill the sinner, because it destroyed the brahman's bigotry. The play ends auspiciously, with Śambūka blessing everyone, the brahman enlightened, the child healthy, and Rāma triumphant. Rāma emerges from his debate and his archery, having proven himself virtuous, nonviolent, and a successful teacher.

Not surprisingly, *Śūdra Tapasvī* drew criticism when it was performed in 1944. Staged only a few times for a limited audience, it prompted a closely followed exchange in print between Kuvempu (1904–1994) and "Masti" Venkatesha Iyengar (1891–1986). Although both men were lionized as pioneers of early Kannada modern literature, famed as the first playwrights to compose Kannada drama in blank verse,[38] and celebrated as Jnanpith Award winners, they could not have been more different in background and sensibility. Masti was a learned brahman, Kuvempu a learned shudra. Masti's manner was weighty and magisterial, Kuvempu's persevering and sincere.

Masti reviewed Kuvempu's play in the July 1944 issue of the literary journal he edited, *Jīvana*. Observing that Kuvempu introduced major changes into the story—especially its ending—Masti proclaims that, however we might judge Śambūka's beheading today, Rāma had fulfilled his dharma because he abided by the religious prescriptions of his time. With unmistakable defensiveness, Masti also blames Kuvempu for trying to rescue Rāma's reputation at the expense of denigrating a learned brahman. Cautioning Kuvempu to keep away from traditional mythological stories if he does not respect the behavior of virtuous people in ancient times, he declares that Kuvempu should use new genres if he wants to write about new ways. Masti expresses concern that the play might fuel animosity toward brahmans, thereby serving to widen the already existing gulf between brahmans and non-brahmans.

In entering into debate with Masti, Kuvempu shouldered a heavy burden as the only shudra among the established Kannada writers of his time. Years later, pondering the implications of Masti's critique in a 1991 article, Kannada novelist Poornachandra Tejasvi (Kuvempu's son) noted that writers of Kuvempu's generation viewed the composition of literature as an act of *tapas*.[39] If Kuvempu had accepted Rāma's killing of the shudra ascetic as virtuous, in a sense he would be capitulating to Masti's denial that Kuvempu had the right to perform a writer's asceticism (*tapas*). From the perspective of *Rāmāyaṇa* tradition, one can develop the critique by Tejasvi one step further. In effect, brahman Masti is warning shudra Kuvempu that Rāma's story is off limits to him if he is presumptuous enough to question the legitimation of caste hierarchy found in dominant tellings of Rāmkathā.

In fact, Kuvempu did not accept Masti's prohibition against his retelling of "traditional stories." Furthermore, Kuvempu explicitly rejected the notion that Vālmīki's *Rāmāyaṇa* was the only true one. Kuvempu viewed *Śūdra Tapasvī* as a telling with as much validity as those of Vālmīki and Bhavabhūti, whose texts he had studied before composing his play. In his letter responding to Masti's review, Kuvempu politely but firmly disagreed with Masti, countering that his play need not widen the gulf between high and low castes. Indeed, the play could foster greater awareness, enabling brahmans and non-brahmans to join together in creating a society in which scholarship, *tapas*, and education would receive the respect they deserved. In all subsequent editions of *Śūdra Tapasvī,* Kuvempu had the last word: he followed his play with Masti's review and Kuvempu's answer, allowing readers access to their debate.

To sum up, in *Śūdra Tapasvī*'s final scene, Kuvempu departs most radically from all previous renditions of Śambūka's story. Yet Kuvempu created an end to the play that he found true to his belief in Rāma's wisdom and compassion. On the one hand, the ending of *Śūdra Tapasvī* rescues Rāma from accusations that he killed Śambūka unjustly. On the other hand, the play offers an unprecedented ending. Kuvempu hoped to bring understanding to brahmans and new aspirations to shudras by depicting Rāma as educating the ignorant and fostering respect for all ascetics. His belief in the power of education to transform the minds of human beings resulted, at least partly, from his own rigorous and persevering efforts as student, teacher, administrator, and writer in a university setting.

Kuvempu's Story in Multiple Forms

In the play's preface, Kuvempu admits to dramatic shortcomings in *Śūdra Tapasvī,* stating that "the play is useless from the point of view of the theatre."[40] Several facts about the play support his assessment. The play consists of fairly long speeches uttered by a small set of all-male characters. Furthermore, it depicts the transformation of a character's mind—not promising material for an action-oriented medium such as the stage. Then, too, there are no comic interludes or grand scenes of battle to vary the play's texture. Nor does *Śūdra Tapasvī* contain the songs, dances, and complexity of plot that people attending Kannada dramatic performances in the 1940s would have expected—whether in ritual dramas at festivals, spectacles mounted by traveling professional companies, or newly emerging social dramas enacted by groups at colleges.[41] Finally, the play is shorter than most performances of its day.

The appeal of the play can also be limited by the register of its language and the many lengthy speeches it contains. Written in a grandiloquent style that features Sanskritized vocabulary, complex word play, and phrases chosen for their musicality and rhythm, the play assumes the audience's familiarity with high literary style. Kannada literary scholar and historian of theater G. Shivarudrappa considered *Śūdra Tapasvī* so crucial a play that, to ensure that those who found some of the language daunting would still have access to it, he translated Kuvempu's 1944 play into the form of Kannada used in ordinary speech. Aside from such an alternative, the consensus among most was that Kuvempu's script worked better for readers than actors. That Kuvempu saw the play's ideal audience as an extremely well-read person with the creativity to conjure up its incidents and characters in the mind's eye is indicated by what Kuvempu wrote in his preface: "It [*Śūdra Tapasvī*] therefore has to be imaginatively visualized on the screen of your mind." In sum, neither the register nor the long speeches made it a play that could be staged in a readily accessible way.

Little more than half a century after Kuvempu wrote his play, Basavalingaiah, director of the Rangayana theatrical troupe in Mysore, conceptualized a compelling and original way to stage *Śūdra Tapasvī*. His production earned acclaim locally in Karnataka and later at the National School of Drama in Delhi as part of an Indian Theater Festival in 2001.[42] His imaginative revisions made the play longer, involved a substantially larger cast than the original, and incorporated aspects of Kannada folk theater into the performance. Basavalingaiah, who was born into a dalit family, entered theater through—and became active in—the Kannada theater movement Samudaya, which used drama to spread messages about social change among the poor. His *Śūdra Tapasvī* formed part of his long-standing commitment to making modern theater accessible to nonelite as well as elite audiences. Basavalingaiah demonstrates a power and topicality in *Śūdra Tapasvī* that went largely unacknowledged when it was first performed in the forties.

Basavalingaiah's central innovation called for staging *Śūdra Tapasvī* so that the audience experienced Śambūka's story thrice in three different modes: as narrative recounted chorally, as song, and as enactment of Kuvempu's scripted dialogues. The prose and musical renditions, which tell and comment upon the story, provide a framework within which those unschooled in elevated poetry can experience the story. An audience of modern colloquial English speakers unfamiliar with Shakespearean diction and vocabulary might more effectively savor some aspects of *The Tempest*, for example, if before hearing Shakespeare's lines in a production they read a recounting of the play in today's English and then heard sections of the original sung to popular musical tunes. Basavalingaiah gave his audience something similar.[43] By recounting the story and commenting upon it in prose and song, the actors avoid excluding illiterate members of the audience from Kuvempu's play. At the same time, those schooled to appreciate Kuvempu's original dialogue can not only savor it but also reflect upon Kuvempu's comments in his preface and enjoy the songs, which transform an otherwise somewhat staid play into a lively and memorable piece of theater.

Basavalingaiah's introduction of this material did not threaten the textual integrity of the 1944 play. Respectful of the playwright, Basavalingaiah added virtually no words to the performance except Kuvempu's own.[44] From Kuvempu's preface, the director inserted Kuvempu's summary of the story as attributed to Vālmīki, his comments on how Bhavabhūti revised the story in *Uttararāmacarita*, and his explanation of why he told the story in a way that differed from both Vālmīki and Bhavabhūti. Basavalingaiah also drew upon extensive stage directions that Kuvempu placed at the beginning and end of scenes, as well as before certain speeches. The stage directions deal with topics such as the emotions felt by characters and the way certain props should appear.[45] Ultimately, there was more Kuvempu on stage in Basavalingaiah's 2001 production than in the 1944 version overseen by Kuvempu.

Incorporating Kuvempu's literary history of Śambūka's story into his production allows Basavalingaiah to build self-reflexivity about *Rāmāyaṇa* tradition into his production. In *Adhyātma Rāmāyaṇa*, Sītā asks Rāma, who has refused to let her accompany him to the forest, "Have you ever heard of a *Rāmāyaṇa* in which Sītā doesn't accompany Rāma to the forest?"[46] Basavalingaiah's incorporation of Kuvempu's thoughts on Vālmīki and Bhavabhūti too encourages reflection on alternate tellings of Rāmkathā while the audience is in the midst of Kuvempu's recounting. Including discussion of the two literary predecessors who greatly influenced Kuvempu also brings the production into compliance with Kuvempu's foundational principle that Vālmīki's telling is not the sole one that the audience should take into account. By giving the audience insights that otherwise would only be accessible to readers of Kuvempu's preface, the director allows others access to Kuvempu's metacommentary on the Śambūka incident in the *Rāmāyaṇa* tradition.

The play begins with sections of Kuvempu's preface spoken by a primarily female chorus. This chorus reflects Kuvempu's point that ranking people based on a dichotomy between purity and pollution oppressed both Sītā and Śambūka (see Rāma's soliloquy quoted above). By casting mostly women in the chorus, Basavalingaiah incorporates gender issues more visibly into the fabric of a play whose characters are all male.[47] As one member of the chorus recalls, "Basavalingaiah had told us often that the most suppressed people in our society are women, especially untouchable women. So it is appropriate that they should be part of the storytelling in this play."[48]

Basavalingaiah chose a performance style for the chorus that serves to intensify the exploration of the relationship between caste and asceticism so central to *Śūdra Tapasvī*. The costumes, song patterns, and gestures come from the Jogatis of Karnataka, a group composed mostly of women or *hijras* (eunuchs) who are staunch devotees of Yarlamma.[49] To incorporate just any chorus would be arbitrary. In contrast, Jogatis are shudra women who have renounced marriage or *hijras* who have renounced male sex roles. The renunciatory features that characterize this performance style make it particularly suited to the content and characters in *Śūdra Tapasvī*. Basavalingaiah's use of Jogati style reiterates the major theme of the play: the Jogatis are shudras, as Śambūka and Kuvempu were. In addition, both Śambūka and the devotees of Yarlamma practice *tapas*, the subject of the play.

Basavalingaiah weaves into *Śūdra Tapasvī* theatrical devices from two other folk traditions in Karnataka. He draws upon *somana kunita*, a performance style using oversize masks, in his costumes for the character of Death, as well as her chorus of minions. The huge, grotesque, and terrifying masks make visible the lethal risk that Śambūka has taken in performing *tapas*. Basavalingaiah also draws upon *yakshagana*, a form of dance drama that depicts fierce warriors fighting with deadly weapons. Basavalingaiah draws upon *yakshagana*'s sophisticated and intricate footwork and stylized whirling body movements to choreograph Rāma's actions, particularly as he prepares to launch his *brahmāstra*. In both cases, Basavalingaiah uses multiple staging styles judiciously to intensify or enrich what already exists in Kuvempu's script.

Analysis of a specific theatrical device drawn from *yakshagana* shows how Basavalingaiah's choice serves not as a gimmick or add-on but as a means to reveal a heretofore hidden aspect of characterization. From *yakshagana*, Basavalingaiah borrows a specific staging feature: a large piece of cloth that prevents an actor from being seen by the audience while on stage behind it. In *Śūdra Tapasvī*, the cloth works to separate from each other (in time and space) the two actors who play the brahman, so that only one of them can be seen by the audience at any given time. To bring the second person playing the brahman onto the stage, two men walk on stage at either side of a person-size piece of cloth, concealing an actor who walks behind it. When they reach the point where they want the hidden actor to appear, the men turn slightly parallel to the audience and begin to walk in a circle. Consequently, the actor who has played the brahman until this point eventually disappears behind the cloth and a new brahman becomes visible to the audience, seeming to emerge from behind the other side of the cloth.

What is the payoff of this theatrical device? The first brahman, who approached Rāma early in the play to have his son's death avenged, appears frail and anguished, his hair shaven and his body shrunken from fasting and mourning for his dead son. Because the brahman had experienced such devastating loss, the viewer occasionally felt sympathy for the father despite his ignorance and pride. In contrast, the brahman whom the cloth discloses is altogether different: tall, broad, and muscular with knee-length dark hair unbound and whirling about him like a vengeful demon. He appears menacing, arrogant, and brutal. As this brahman gleefully waits for the *brahmāstra* to end Śambūka's life, the whole apparatus of caste hierarchy is revealed—treachery and its power. Basavalingaiah represents brahmanism as an institution, one that insures that shudras who do not stay in their place die by the hand of the king. By having two actors on view at different times with the aid of the revolving cloth, the play impresses upon the viewer that brahmanism is both a collection of brahmans and a repressive institution of social discipline, whose values ordinary people internalize.

Śūdra Tapasvī's self-reflexivity appears most strikingly when the women's chorus at the beginning of the play refers directly to Basavalingaiah's innovative staging. There the chorus draws from Kuvempu's preface, in which he acknowledges that the play has certain shortcomings from the staging perspective, and the chorus members acknowledge that in 1944 modern Kannada theater did not possess the dramatic resources to do full justice to *Śūdra Tapasvī*. In contrast, the chorus proclaims that today modern Kannada theater can finally stage *Śūdra Tapasvī* in a way that brings out the subtleties of Kuvempu's work.

This feat is made possible because the play has been formed out of multiple dramatic styles from what the actors in Rangayana call "our own theatrical traditions of Karnataka." Instead of "dumbing down" a play that many found inaccessible, Basavalingaiah enriched it, using the cultural capital of Kannada folk tradition. He drew upon the regional dramatic tradition not like a tourist seeking local color but like Kuvempu's heir seeking a way to enhance the visibility of dramatic styles often marginalized by brahmanical hegemony in religious and cultural spheres. Basavalingaiah thereby enabled Kuvempu's spirit and script to reach a much wider audience in the early years of the new millennium than it had in 1944.

Conclusion

This essay has analyzed the cultural work performed by three plays about Śambūka in three south Indian languages. These plays have received limited scholarly attention individually, and none as a group. Yet each play's interpretation of Śambūka's death, as well as the controversies surrounding the play's reception, fostered striking public debate about caste and asceticism. The reception of these plays demonstrates how dramatically a particular *Rāmāyaṇa* incident carried deep political resonances and evoked strong responses from members of the audience who identified with or felt threatened by various characters in Rāmkathā during the period between 1920 and 1954.

During this historical period, when anti-brahman movements were gaining momentum, especially in Andhra and Tamilnadu but to a lesser extent in Karnataka too, all three plays see the attack on Śambūka as instigated, in some way or another, by brahmans. Even though the Śambūka episode is short, self-contained, and fairly incidental to the overall plot of Rāmkathā, between the 1920s and 1950s it was intensely scrutinized and debated in south India. At least part of this incident's notoriety stems from its seemingly irrefutable example of Rāma's perfidy; in pro-Dravidian discourse it functions to prove that Rāma murdered low-caste people and suppressed their rights. Two of the plays analyzed here were devoted entirely to the incident, and it played a major role in the third. As a result, Śambūka became a relatively well-known figure, mentioned in speeches, tracts, and other forms of public discourse during this period.

In addition to examining individual differences between the interpretations of Chaudari, Thangaraju, and Kuvempu, the essay also considers each playwright's view of Hindu traditions that shaped those interpretations. Although Kuvempu's plot differs most radically from Vālmīki's account of the incident, Kuvempu's religious stance is the most familiar: Kuvempu expresses his devotion (bhakti) to Rāma by depicting Rāma's justice, compassion, and wisdom. In *Śūdra Tapasvī*, Rāma's dedication to justice and compassion compels him to defend Śambūka from death, while his commitment to wisdom motivates Rāma to educate the narrow-minded brahman. At the opposite end of the spectrum lies Thangaraju's drama, in which Śambūka's religious achievements as an ascetic are virtually ignored. Instead, his knowledge of science and his ability to argue his case without succumbing to the authority of religious scriptures qualify him as a heroic man, in Thangaraju's eyes. Chaudari's view lies somewhere between these two poles on a continuum. He idealizes Śambūka's virtuosity in *tapas*, as did Kuvempu, while also completely rejecting the authority of brahmanical *śāstras*, as did Thangaraju.

Yet ultimately Kuvempu's devotion does not prevent him from developing a potentially subversive attitude toward religious texts. In his play a celestial voice from the sky proclaims that recourse to scriptures alone does not determine what constitutes virtuous action. Furthermore, Kuvempu claims that each *Rāmāyaṇa* poet has, as did Vālmīki, authority to tell the story in a distinctive way. While Thangaraju and Chaudari attribute to Rāma, the brahman, and Śambūka motives that differ from those that Vālmīki gives to each character, the Tamil and Telugu plays follow Vālmīki's plot quite closely, while Kuvempu departs from it without qualms.

Intriguingly, whatever each playwright thinks about brahmanical texts, each writer reveals admiration for the practice of *tapas*. Chaudari puts the right to perform *tapas* at the heart of the struggle that Śambūka leads. Kuvempu depicts Śambūka's ascetic attainments as so extraordinary that they provide him with the power to halt the *brahmāstra*. Even Thangaraju, a confirmed atheist, portrays Śambūka as a highly accomplished Śaivite ascetic, in a play whose audience would either be atheists or, if they had religious affiliations, align themselves with Śaivism. Asceticism in the forest, the religious path least connected to the social prescriptions of Hinduism, is the only aspect of Hindu tradition that all three writers depict as admirable.

Of the three texts examined in this chapter, the plays of Chaudari and Thangaraju function primarily as texts that carry political messages about high-caste oppression against members of low castes. In contrast, Kuvempu's play, though certainly political to its core, is a piece of drama whose subtlety and craftsmanship was and still is savored by literary connoisseurs, and it is taught in college courses on literature. Basavalingaiah's recent restaging of Kuvempu's play resituates Kuvempu's script in the context of shudra performance traditions and makes viewers see both shudras and *tapas* in a new light. All in all, a study of the treatment of Śambūka in three south Indian plays demonstrates not only multiple views of an individual *Rāmāyaṇa* character, but also how that multiplicity takes varied forms in theatrical productions.

NOTES

1. Due to the complexity of using diacritical marks not just for ancient Sanskrit texts but for three modern regional languages during the twentieth century (when Anglicized spellings of Indian words have shaped daily usage for decades), I have

adopted four special transliteration policies. First, the three playwrights studied here published in both English and their regional language, so in the body of this paper I have used the English spelling of their names that they preferred when they published in English. When citing their original work in Tamil, Telugu, or Kannada in the notes, however, I have used the transliteration of their name in their regional language. For example, Thangaraju's English publications bear the name Tiruvarur K. Thangaraju, while the name he gives in the title page of his play is Tiruvarur K. Tankarācu. Second, in order to avoid confusing the reader unnecessarily, I have kept the spelling of the main *Rāmāyaṇa* characters consistent throughout the paper. For example, I refer to Rāma, rather than Rāman, the Tamil usage. In the case of Śambūka, in Sanskrit, Tamil, and Kannada, the "u" in Śambūka is long. It is not long in Telugu, but I retain the long "u" everywhere except in the title of Chaudari's Telugu text, which I write *Śambuka Vadha*. Third, in referring to the forms of folk performance of Karnataka I use the terms by which they are Anglicized in the Bangalore/Mysore area. Finally, since *jāti* and *varṇa* terms in Anglicized form are part of everyday discourse in modern India, I have presented them without diacritics (e.g. brahman, shudra, Kamma).

2. Richman 1991: 8.

3. Shulman 2000: 54; Narayana Rao 2000: 160.

4. Raghunathan, v. 3, 1982: 574.

5. Playwrights often were not familiar with plays about Śambūka in other languages. Although Sanskrit acted as a link language for brahmans across linguistic boundaries, and English functioned for pan-Indian elites, regional languages remained a barrier for many writers working on similar themes in another regional language. This situation changed somewhat through national institutions such as the Sahitya Akademi and the National School of Drama in the middle 1950s.

6. Richman 2000: 6–12.

7. For example, Lutgendorf 2000 analyzes alternative narratives of the story of Śavarī in a number of texts.

8. Thapar 1989.

9. Although it lies beyond the scope of this paper, the Malayalam play *Kāñcana Sītā* by C. N. Sreekantan Nair (1928–1977), published in 1965, also contains a short section critiquing the treatment of Śambūka. There, Rāma's horse sacrifice is interrupted by Śambūka's wife when she appears at the edge of the sacrificial enclosure shouting, "I want to see King Rāma. Don't stand in my way. Isn't the sword with which he killed my husband in his hand? Let him slice off my neck as well." Later, prevented from confronting Rāma, she curses him before leaving, calling him "a Niṣāda" and "king who is a killer of husbands," referring to the killing of her husband as well as the husbands of the monkeys and bears lying dead on the battlefield in Laṅkā. See the translation of act 4 by Krishnankutty: forthcoming.

10. Although there are many places in this essay where I would have preferred to use the term dalit instead of shudra or untouchable, such a usage would be anachronistic for the period during which the three plays studied here were written and performed. Even Kuvempu uses the term "shudra" so I have done the same. Nonetheless, it is crucial to keep in mind that many of the literary explorations that Kuvempu undertook have played significant roles in current dalit discussions. Ekalavya and Śambūka have appeared in a number of recent literary works. For example, consider the first lines of Sivasagar's poem "On-going History": "Sambuka with a smile on his lips / is executing Rama / Ekalavya is chopping off Drona's thumb / with an axe."

11. Mehtha 1963: 250.

12. Chaudari called it "Suta Ashram" after the bards considered "low caste" in brahmanical tradition, who recounted epic and purāṇic tales. For more information on the life of Chaudari, see Narayana Rao 2000: 159–162, 173–177.

13. Here Chaudari espouses the specific pattern of power relations analyzed by historian Burton Stein, who wrote, long after Chaudari's time, about collusion between brahmans and kings in medieval south India. See Stein 1978.

14. In Bhavabhūti's *Uttarāmacaritam*, as well, Śambūka becomes a friend of Rāma and after his death attains an immortal form.

15. Narayana Rao 2000: 196.

16. In my 1992 interview with Tiruvarur K. Thangaraju, he provided a bibliography of sources upon which his interpretation of the Śambūka episode was based. They included *Rāvaṇa Kāppiyam*, Pandit Nehru's writings on *Rāmāyaṇa*, and Cēkarāppāvalar's *Irāmāyaṇattiṉ Āpācam*. The first work is a Tamil epic poem describing the greatness of Rāvaṇa, and the third is an attack on the values and characters of the Rāmāyaṇa written by a scholar in sympathy with the political views of the Dravidian Kazhagam.

17. Preface, Taṅkarācu [1954] 1976: 3–6.

18. Ibid.: 140–141 (my translation).

19. Ibid.: 142. By referring here to the constitution, Thangaraju makes snide reference to what he considers the failure of the Indian constitution to live up to the "secularism" of the Indian state. In Thangaraju's eyes, the constitution insures continuing brahmanical exploitation of shudras by guaranteeing brahmans the right to religious freedom and warning that the state should not interfere with their religious practices or wound their religious sensibilities. Since purity and pollution can be viewed as part of "religious practice," such a phrase can be used to prohibit interference with caste hierarchy.

20. Ibid.: 141.

21. Ibid.: 144.

22. A well-known Tamil comedian played Rāma as an—at times—humorously corrupt, inept, and unprincipled prince impelled by desire for power.

23. Rāmacāmi [1930] 1972: 41.

24. See Washbrook 1989: 223–238.

25. Interview with Thangaraju 1992.

26. Harrison 1960.

27. May 1, 1970. *The Organiser* is a weekly published from Delhi since 1947 by the Rashtriya Swayamsevak Sangh (RSS), a Hindu nationalist organization.

28. "Kuvempu" derives from the Kannada initials, Ku. Vem. Pu. of his full name conflated into a single word, used affectionately by his admirers.

29. Kuvempu 1990: xii.

30. I am indebted to the following people for long and insightful discussions with me about Kuvempu's literary works: K. Marula Siddappa, Girish Karnad, Prasanna, Gangadhar Swamy, G. Shivarudrappa, G. Venkata Subbiah, and Nandini K. R.

31. Kuvempu 1990: 12.

32. Karnad (forthcoming): 16.

33. At the time of Vāli's death, when Rāma was questioned about killing Vāli in such a cowardly way, Rāma justified his action in largely strategic terms: There was no other way to rid the monkey kingdom of Vāli. For analysis of this scene, see Shulman 1979.

34. Karnad (forthcoming): 17.

35. Ibid.: 19.
36. Ibid.: 20.
37. Ibid.
38. Ranganath 1982: 195.
39. Poornachandra Tejasvi's article in the Feburary 24, 1991, issue of *Lankesh Patrike* is quoted in Niranjana 1993: 147.
40. Note that this preface was also reproduced in Basavalingaiah's program that accompanied his performances. See Kuvempu 1977 for the Kannada preface and the program from the 2001 performance for an English translation.
41. Chandrasekhara 1960a; Ranganath 1982: 80–163.
42. National School of Drama 2002.
43. Lest the similarity to a Shakespearean play seem arbitrary, I should mention that Kuvempu wrote two plays inspired by Shakespeare's, adaptations of *Hamlet* and *The Tempest*. See Chandrasekhara 1960b.
44. Also added were various exclamations of agreement, surprise, and encouragement such as *Howda* (yes) and *Shiva, Shiva*, spoken by members of the chorus in response to words uttered in the play.
45. Examples of stage directions that reveal emotions include, in act 2, the brahman coming to tell Rāma of his son's death speaking "with anger and grief" and the description of Rāma from the same scene: "His face is melancholy. He looks around as though he is searching for something. He walks gently, seriously like hope, like grace itself."
46. Nath 1913: 39.
47. A repertory company's director usually seeks scripts that make resourceful use of talent in the troupe; the chorus gave Basvalingaiah the chance to include more actors in *Śūdra Tapasvī* than if the production contained only the characters in Kuvempu's script. Furthermore, since the script was filled entirely with male roles, the actresses in the company would otherwise have been excluded from the cast.
48. I am grateful to all the members of Rangayana in Mysore for inviting me to their rehearsal of the play and then discussing it as a group with me: Ramu S., Jagdesh Manevarte, Mahadev, Ramnath S., Manjunath Belekere, Halugappa Kattimani, Prashanth Hiremath, Santosh Kusunoor, Geetha M. S., Pramella Bengre, Shashikala B. N., Nandini K. R., Saroja Hegde, Vinayak Bhat, Noor Ahmed Shaikh, Krishnakumar, as well as Rangayana director Prasanna, designer Dwarakanath, costume designer Raghunandan, manager Gangadhar Swamy, music director Srinivas Bhat, and musician Anju Singh.
49. This is the local name for a goddess known elsewhere as Renukā. Her husband, the ascetic Jamadagni, ordered his son to kill her. When the son performed this painful duty and was granted a boon, he asked that his mother be returned to life. For one version of this story, see van Buitenen 1975:445–446.

REFERENCES

Aithal, Parameswara. 1987. "The *Rāmāyaṇa* in Kannada Literature." In *South Asian Digest of Regional Writing*. Vol. 12, *Mythology in Modern Indian Literature*. Heidelberg: South Asia Institute, University of Heidelberg, pp. 1–12.

Chandrasekhara, B. 1960a. "The Modern Kannada Theatre." *Literary Half-Yearly* 1.1 (January): 19–38.

______. 1960b. "The Plays of K. V. Puttappa." *Literary Half-Yearly* 1.2 (July): 24–42.

Chaudari, Tripurāṇeni Rāmasvāmi. 1966. *Śambuka Vadha.* Reprinted in vol. 2 of *Kavirāju Sāhitya Sarvasvam* [Complete works of Ramasvāmi Chaudari]. 2 vols. Gunturu: Kaviraju Sahita Samiti, 1–79.
Harrison, Selig. 1960. *India: The Most Dangerous Decades.* Princeton: Princeton University Press.
Interviews with Tiruvarur K. Thanagaraju, Raja Annamalaipuram, Chennai: January 13, 1992.
Karnad, Girish, trans. Forthcoming. "The Shudra Ascetic." In *Telling Ramayana Stories in Modern South Indian Literature,* edited by Paula Richman. Bloomington: Indiana University Press.
Krishnankutty, Gita, trans. Forthcoming. "The Golden Sita." In *Telling Ramayana Stories in Modern South Indian Literature,* edited by Paula Richman. Bloomington: Indiana University Press.
Kuvempu (K. V. Puttappa). [1944]. *Śūdra Tapasvī* [The Shudra ascetic]. 2nd ed. Mysore: Udayaravi, 1948; reprinted in *Kannada Nataka,* edited by K. Marulasiddappa. Bangalore: Bangalore University, 1977, 117–150.
———. 1990. *Śrī Rāmāyaṇa Darśanam.* Bangalore: I. M. Vittala Murthy, Directorate of Kannada Literature and Culture.
Lutgendorf, Philip. 2000. "Dining Out at Lake Pampa: The Shabari Episode in Multiple *Ramayanas.*" In *Questioning Ramayanas, a South Asian Tradition,* edited by Paula Richman. Berkeley and Los Angeles: University of California Press, 119–136.
Mehtha, C. C. 1963. *Bibliography of Stageable Plays in Indian Languages.* Baroda: M. S. University of Baroda and Bharatiya Natya Sangha.
Narayana Rao, Velcheru. 2000. "The Politics of Telugu *Ramayaṇas*: Colonialism, Print Culture, and Literary Movements." In *Questioning Ramayanas, A South Asian Tradition,* edited by Paula Richman. Berkeley and Los Angeles: University of California Press, 159–185.
Nath, Lala Baij, trans. 1913. *The Adhyātma Rāmāyaṇa.* Allahabad: Panini Office.
National School of Drama. 2002. *Bharat Rang Mahotsav* [Indian theater festival]—An Overview. New Delhi: National School of Drama.
Niranjana, Tejaswini. 1993. "Whose Culture Is It? Contesting the Modern." *Journal of Arts and Ideas* 25–26 (December): 139–151.
The Organizer, May 1, 1970.
Puttappa, K.V., *see* Kuvempu.
Raghunathan, N. 1982. *Srimad Valmiki Ramayanam,* 3 vols. Madras: Vigneswara.
Rāmacāmi, I. Ve. [1930] 1972. *Irāmāyaṇappattiraṅkaḷ* [Characters in the *Rāmāyaṇa*]. Tricchy: Periyar Self-Respect Publishers.
Ranganath, H. K. 1982. *The Karnatak Theatre.* Dharwad: Karnatak University.
Richman, Paula. 1991. "E. V. Rāmasāmi's Reading of the *Rāmāyaṇa.*" In *Many Rāmāyaṇas: The Diversity of a Narrative Tradition in South Asia,* edited by Paula Richman. Berkeley and Los Angeles: University of California Press, 175–201.
———. 2000. "Questioning and Multiplicity within the *Rāmāyaṇa* Tradition." In *Questioning Ramayanas, a South Asian Tradition,* edited by Paula Richman. Berkeley and Los Angeles: University of California Press, 1–21.
Shulman, David. 1979. "Divine Order and Divine Evil in the Tamil Tale of *Rāmāyaṇa.*" *Journal of Asian Studies* 38.4, (August): 651–69.
———. 2000. "Bhavabhūti on Cruelty and Compassion." In *Questioning Ramayanas, a South Asian Tradition,* edited by Paula Richman. Berkeley and Los Angeles: University of California Press, pp. 49–82.

Sivasagar. 2000. "On-going History." Translated by Archana Chowhan. *Indian Literature* 200 (November–December), 108.
Stein, Burton. 1978. "All the King's *Mana*: Perspectives on Kingship in Medieval South India." In *Kingship and Authority in South Asia,* edited by John F. Richards. Madison: University of Wisconsin Press, 115–167.
Śūdra Tapasvī. Program for 2001 performance, Rangayana, Mysore.
Tankarācu, Tiruvarur K. [1954] 1976. *Rāmāyaṇa Nāṭakam* [*Rāmāyaṇa* play]. Madras: the author.
Thapar, Romila. 1989. "The *Ramayana* Syndrome." *Seminar* 353 (January): 72–83.
van Buitenen, J. A. B., transl. 1975. *The Mahābhārata.* Vol. 2. Chicago: University of Chicago Press.
Washbrook, David A. 1989. "Caste, Class and Dominance in Modern Tamil Nadu: Non-Brahmanism, Dravidianism and Tamil Nationalism." In *Dominance and State Power in Modern India: Decline of a Social Order,* edited by Francine Frankel and M. S. A. Rao. Delhi: Oxford University Press, 204–264.

6

Hanumān's Adventures Underground: The Narrative Logic of a *Rāmāyaṇa* "Interpolation"

Philip Lutgendorf

Roots and Crystals

Broadly speaking, *Rāmāyaṇa* scholarship during the second half of the twentieth century has moved in two divergent directions; on the one hand, toward the analysis of classical texts and the preparation of critical editions that seek to identify the "root" or *ur* version (*mūla pāṭha*) and to purge it of subsequent accretions; and on the other hand, toward a broad and inclusive view of the tradition as multivocal and subject to constant reinterpretation. The former tendency, drawing on the legacy of nineteenth-century text criticism and classical Indology, is epitomized by the seven-volume Baroda Critical Edition of the Vālmīki epic (1960–1975), which despite its editors' challenged methodology and assumptions inevitably casts a long shadow over Sanskrit *Rāmāyaṇa* scholarship and is the basis for what will undoubtedly stand for a long time as the most influential complete English translation (Goldman et al., 1984–). One may also mention the diligent if sometimes less rigorous editing of some of the great regional *Rāmāyaṇas*—texts that Indologists once tended to characterize incorrectly as "translations and adaptations" of a Vālmīkian archetype—such as the *Irāmāvatāram* of Kampaṉ and the *Rāmcaritmānas* of Tulsīdās, created by collating early manuscripts and by expunging *kṣepak* or "interpolations" (for example, the Kashiraj edition of the *Rāmcaritmānas*, edited by Viśvanāth Prasād Miśra, 1962).

The other tendency, inspired by the activities of folklorists and ethnographers and especially by the expansion of scholarly interest in oral traditions since the 1960s, is represented by a series of books that survey the geographical extent and narrative diversity of the *Rāmāyaṇa*, often downplay the centrality of the Vālmīki (or any other) literary archetype, assemble unusual or idiosyncratic variants, and stress the multivocal, performative, and even contested nature of the story. For such scholars, it is less important to dig up the "root" of the *Rāmāyaṇa* than to study it as (in a metaphor sometimes used by A. K. Ramanujan) a crystal: multifaceted and possessing (as in crystallography) inherent stress points or "flaws" that become nodes for the growth of new crystalline branches. To the latter approach belongs the groundbreaking research of Bulcke (1950), who offered the Hindi term *Rāmakathā* rather than *Rāmāyaṇa* for this composite tradition, and the volumes edited by Iyengar (1983), Raghavan (1980), Richman (1991 and 2001), and Thiel-Horstmann (1991).

Which is the more useful view of the *Rāmāyaṇa*—as a widely acknowledged narrative archetype that undergoes a series of extensive but historically explainable permutations, or as a far vaster but more amorphous cultural entity? Whereas text-critical studies may tend to buttress the former view (and one may also note repeated twentieth-century efforts to historicize and concretize the story, often motivated by nationalist and communal sentiments, as well as recent "Hindu fundamentalist" assertions of a unitary "correct" interpretation), the proliferating assemblage of variants—regional and folk *Rāmāyaṇas*, tribal *Rāmāyaṇas*, Southeast Asian *Rāmāyaṇas*, women's *Rāmāyaṇas*, esoteric-erotic *Rāmāyaṇas*, and Jain, Buddhist, and Tamil-separatist counter-*Rāmāyaṇas*—may challenge even the most "basic" elements of the story. In his 1991 essay "Three Hundred *Rāmāyaṇas*," Ramanujan variously termed the tradition of Rāma stories and performances a "pool of signifiers," "a common code," and "a narrative language," and spoke of a "meta-*Rāmāyaṇa*" that includes all possible variants, but he also offered the more extreme view that the core of the epic is merely a "skeletal set of relations" and that its various recastings may have no more in common than "a collection of people with the same proper name . . . a class in name alone" (Richman 1991, 44–46).

Although I too have emphasized the diversity of *Rāmāyaṇa* performance and storytelling traditions, and have even asserted that the epic functions within its culture area as "more a medium than a message," (Lutgendorf 1991: 170), I am uncomfortable with the last position stated above, on the grounds that it is too radical and tends to erode the usefulness of the category of *Rāmāyaṇa* and may discourage analysis of the admittedly contested but nonetheless identifiable meanings of the story.[1] For epic transmutations are not, in my view, random or arbitrary and (to return to Ramanujan's own metaphors), "signifiers" undoubtedly have significance, a "code" conveys a message, and a "language" is governed by a system of grammatical rules (even though all of these may be susceptible to modification and disputation). Moreover, one may ask, if the *Rāmāyaṇa* tradition is so flexible and open-ended, why are some elaborations much more successful than others, spreading across regions and sectarian divisions?

My own reflections on these questions lead me to suggest three principal ways in which the Rāma tale has historically undergone transformation. The first is through expansion or contraction at what I term (following Ramanujan) narrative "stress points." These are important episodes in the Vālmīkian master narrative that have, over time, proven troubling to audiences and have generated much questioning and debate. Later storytellers participate in this debate by either greatly expanding certain scenes—altering events, providing clarification of the motives of key characters, and offering additional rationalization for their behavior—or conversely by compressing the story to abridge or even eliminate the troubling episode. Thus Rāma and Lakṣmaṇa's encounter with the demoness Śūrpaṇakhā in Pañcavatī—which results in her mutilation at their hands and leads to their encounter with her brother Rāvaṇa—is treated only briefly in Vālmīki, who shows the brothers "jesting" with the ugly, lovesick woman in a way that some listeners have found duplicitous and cruel. This episode is greatly expanded by the Tamil poet Kampaṉ, who has Sūrpaṇakhā assume a lovely form before approaching Rāma (thus showing duplicity on her part); he depicts her subsequent lovesickness in detail and with a certain sympathy, reveals Rāma's own inner deliberations over how to handle her, and eliminates the deceitful jest of having him direct her to the allegedly "unmarried" Lakṣmaṇa (3.5; Hart and Heifetz 1988: 84–116).[2] On the other hand, Vālmīki's long and painful exchange between Rāma and Sītā when they are reunited after Rāvaṇa's death, precipitated by Rāma's venting his doubts regarding Sītā's chastity, is reduced to a single half-verse in Tulsīdās's version (" . . . the Compassionate One spoke some harsh words," 6.108; Sītā says nothing in reply), and the same poet entirely eliminates, from his seventh book, the controversial story of Sītā's second banishment from Ayodhya.

A second type of modification may be termed the counter-narrative or "anti-*Rāmāyaṇa*"—a full-scale retelling of the story that challenges the authority of the Vālmīkian model. Such works have a long history, perhaps dating back to the third-century B.C.E. Buddhist *Dasaratha jātaka* (though scholars debate its chronology relative to Vālmīki's work) and certainly including such influential Jain retellings as the *Paumacariya*. Although both these works exercise considerable freedom in adapting the basic story to a different sectarian worldview, they present less extreme transformations than the twentieth-century Tamil nationalist retelling popularized by E. V. Ramasami, which entirely subverts the traditional narrative by making Rāvaṇa, rather than Rāma, its hero, depicting Sītā as a wanton woman, and so forth (Richman 1991: 175–201). Specific episodes in these counter-narratives have sometimes acquired regional popularity and become influential (for example, the Jain tale that makes Sītā the daughter of Rāvaṇa and Mandodarī, abandoned at birth due to a prophecy that she will be responsible for her father's death, which has come to be widely circulated, especially in southern India), yet, to my knowledge, no narrative that drastically challenges the broad Vālmīkian archetype has ever achieved widespread popularity or authority within South Asia.

The third type of transformation is what I will term "organic" or "characterological" expansion. By this I refer to the elaboration of characters or episodes that have proven especially popular with audiences and concerning which they want to know more. Such elaboration need not directly address a narrative "problem" (as in the first type), nor does it deliberately subvert the main story (as in the second), although it may subtly have both these effects. There are a great many examples of such "organic" expansion, and these can sometimes be traced to particular regions, communities, or vernacular poets. Yet because they do not appear to directly challenge the master narrative, some of these expansions have achieved extremely wide circulation and evident popularity, as evidenced by their appearance in multiple texts as well as in visual art and folk performance. One example is a cluster of tales that elaborate on Rāma's establishment and consecration of a Śiva liṇgam at Rameshwaram (itself originally a non-Vālmīkian episode) prior to crossing the monkey-built causeway to Laṅkā; these include stories of Hanumān's being sent to Varanasi or Mount Kailasa to fetch a lingam and his ensuing adventures, and a rarer variant in which the Śaiva brahman Rāvaṇa is summoned from Laṅkā (sometimes accompanied by Sītā) to officiate as priest in the *sthāpanā* ritual. Other widespread "characterological" expansions include tales that give an enhanced role to female figures who appear only marginally (or not at all) in the master narrative, such as Lakṣmaṇa's wife Urmilā and Meghanāda's wife Sulocanā. Certain of these tales have inspired ambitious literary works, such as the nineteenth-century Bengali poet Michael Madhusudan Datta's tragic epic on the death of Rāvaṇa's heroic eldest son, *Meghanādavadha kāvya* (Seeley 2004). Although none of these examples systematically contradicts the master narrative of the *Rāmāyaṇa*, their introduction of such elements as Śaiva devotional themes, the highlighting of women, and the sympathetic portrayal of Rāma's "demonic" adversaries can all be seen as responses to perceptions of gaps or imbalances in the main story and hence as subtle forms of resistance to its dominant ideologies.

In the remainder of this chapter, I will examine what I consider to be one of the most widespread and popular examples of this third type of "organic" expansion: the saga of a second and more menacing Rāvaṇa against whom the primary heroes of the epic find themselves powerless, so that they must be rescued by their simian subordinate Hanumān. The success of this innovation, I will argue, exemplifies the tension between the process of narrative creativity and expansion on the one hand, and an underlying and conservative "narrative logic" on the other; or (to use another of Ramanujan's metaphors) between the relative freedom of individual "speech acts" and the underlying constraints of a grammatical code. Ultimately, I will offer another metaphor: of the *Rāmāyaṇa* as a musical raga, susceptible to almost infinite (but not unrestricted) variation.

Magicians and Monkeys

Although some modifications of the Rāma story are idiosyncratic or restricted to a single region or sect, others have gained such widespread acceptance that many people would not regard them as "interpolations" at all. The story with which I am concerned here belongs to the latter category, and although its oldest literary versions do not appear until the late-medieval period (that is, twelfth to fourteenth centuries C.E.), its subsequent spread is remarkable. As noted by W. L. Smith, it is found in Sanskrit, Gujarati, Marathi, Malayalam, Kannada, Tamil, Oriya, Bengali, Assamese, Hindi, and Nepali, as well as in Thai, Lao, Cambodian, Malay, and Burmese versions (Smith 1988: 145)—in short, in most of the South and Southeast Asian languages in which *Rāmāyaṇa* tales are told.[3] It appears in the form of independent poetic works and plays such as the Sanskrit *Mairāvaṇacarita* and *Mahīrāvaṇavadha nāṭaka*, the Tamil *Mayilirāvaṇan katai*, and the Assamese *Mahīrāvaṇa vadha*, as well as in the form of episodes included in late *Rāmāyaṇa* texts such as the Sanskrit *Anandarāmāyaṇa* and the Bengali *Rāmāyaṇa* of Kṛttivāsa (Smith 1988: 145–151; Zvelebil 1987: xi). Although Kamil Zvelebil speculates that it originated in the Tamil country, where it remains popular to this day (note that it was the subject of one of the first feature-length Tamil films; Zvelebil 1987: xlvi), its current popularity in north India may be gauged from the fact that, although Tulsīdās neither included nor alluded to it in his Avadhī epic (nor in any other of his generally accepted writings on the Rāma theme), popular editions of the *Rāmcaritmānas* often include a substantial version of it; thus the Veṇkaṭeśvar Press edition with *ṭīkā* by Pandit Jvālāprasād Miśra of Muradabad (first published in about 1889 and constantly reprinted as well as pirated in diverse formats) includes an artfully written version in twenty-one *caupāī-dohā* stanzas, inserted into the latter portion of *Laṅkākāṇḍa*. (Miśra 1982: 1032–1050). Although the more "critical" Gita Press edition omits it, the story remains, in my experience, extremely popular in Hindi-speaking regions. It appears in bazaar chapbooks and comics, is sometimes performed in Rāmlīlā plays, and is often represented in poster art and in temple icons of Hanumān (for example, the recumbent image on the riverbank adjacent to the Mughal fort at Prayāg/Allahabad).[4] Although pandits and Rāmāyaṇīs may be careful to label it an "interpolation" (*kṣepak*), the average north Indian undoubtedly thinks of it as just another *prasaṅg* or episode in the *Rāmāyaṇa*.

The villain of the episode is known by various names: Ahirāvaṇa or Mahi(Mahī)rāvaṇa ("snake-Rāvaṇa" or "earth-Rāvaṇa"), or the variants Airāvaṇa and Mairāvaṇa, in most of northern and eastern India; and as Mayilirāvaṇa ("peacock Rāvaṇa") in Dravidian sources; one scholar has suggested that all these names may ultimately derive from the Tamil *mai*, connoting "collyrium" or "blackness" (Dieter Kapp, cited in Smith 1988: 146). Such a derivation accords well with the cthonic and serpentine associations of the Sanskritized variants, since all the stories agree in making the villain a master of sorcery, who places spells of darkness and sleep over his victims, and all situate him in Pātāla Loka, a shadowy but prosperous netherworld often mentioned in the Purāṇas and in folktales, and thought to be inhabited by various ranks of *asuras* and *nāgas*, the latter sometimes under the overlordship of the serpent kings Vāsuki, Śeṣa, or Takṣaka, who reign from the opulent subterranean city of Bhogavatī. In some versions Ahirāvaṇa and Mahirāvaṇa are separate demons, father and son or brothers; in others they are collapsed into a single figure who in turn is said to be related to Rāvaṇa, the king of Laṅkā, either as a brother or a son. Since the story in its major eastern and southern variants has been ably recounted by Smith (1988: 146–152) and Zvelebil (1987: 173–219), I will only briefly summarize it here, and will base my summary on Hindi versions they do not discuss, of which I possess half a dozen modern examples showing only relatively minor variation.[5]

Following many days of heavy losses in the battle with Rāma's monkey army and the slaying of Rāvaṇa's supposedly invincible eldest son Meghanāda (a.k.a. Indrajīt), the demon king of Laṅkā becomes deeply depressed. He remembers, or is reminded of, his relative Ahirāvaṇa ("serpent Rāvaṇa," the name favored in Hindi sources) who reigns in distant Pātāla Loka and is a powerful sorcerer; Rāvaṇa then summons him, either by mental concentration or through the invocation of Śiva or Bhavānī. Although Ahirāvaṇa scolds his kinsman for foolishly kidnapping Sītā, he promises to secure his victory by spiriting away Rāma and Lakṣmaṇa to Pātāla Loka, where he will offer them as human sacrifices to his fierce patron goddess. Pandit Jvālāprasād Miśra and some other narrators add, in the characteristic fashion of epic bards, a subsidiary story-behind-the-story, explaining Ahi's birth and present situation: a son of Rāvaṇa's wife Mandodarī, his terrible appearance—"with twenty snakes"—frightens his father, who casts him into the ocean or buries him in the earth, and he is eventually adopted by the snake-demoness Siṁhikā, and makes his way to the serpent world, located in the third nether region. Here he performs intense *tapasyā* to please the local Devī and so acquires supernatural powers and nearly perfect invulnerability, and also the boon that Rāvaṇa, who insulted and abandoned him, will one day call on him for help; he then compels the king of Pātāla to give him his daughter in marriage and to establish him in his own realm.

Now called on to save embattled Laṅkā, Ahirāvaṇa tells Rāvaṇa to watch for a bright light in the sky. He then casts a spell of dense darkness over Rāma's army, which reacts by retreating into a huge fortress formed by Hanumān's expanded and coiled tail, at the only entrance to which the monkey champion stands guard. Ahi tricks him, however, by taking the form of Vibhīṣaṇa, and so gains entrance. Casting a sleep-spell over everyone, he spirits away the two princes, signaling to Rāvaṇa through a brilliant flash in the night sky. Awakening to find their leaders gone, Rāma's troops are distraught, but Vibhīṣaṇa quickly divines the identity of his mysterious double (since no one but Ahi possesses the skill to impersonate him) and dispatches Hanumān to Pātāla Loka. Here the great monkey assumes various disguises, and overhears a vulture couple discussing the fresh meat they will devour after the two princes are sacrificed. But when he tries to gain entrance to Ahirāvaṇa's citadel, his way is blocked by a huge monkey gatekeeper who looks exactly like himself, and who indeed identifies himself as the "fish-bannered" (Makaradhvaja) son of Hanumān, conceived by a fish who swallowed sea water containing drops of Hanumān's sweat following his burning of Laṅkā. The fish was later caught and brought to the royal kitchens of the netherworld. When its belly was cut open, a small but powerful monkey emerged, who was subsequently adopted by Ahirāvaṇa. Hanumān is both surprised and delighted to meet this immaculately conceived son, who reverently touches his feet. He is even pleased by the youth's fidelity to his demon-master—for Makaradhvaja is under strict orders to admit no one to the city—although this leads to a father-son battle, at the end of which Makaradhvaja is subdued and bound in his own tail so that Hanumān can get on with his mission.

Hanumān proceeds to the Devī temple, which he enters disguised as an insect on a flower garland, but quickly swells to enormous size, pressing the goddess's image into the floor (in a few versions she actively assists him in the plot) and assuming her form. Ahirāvaṇa arrives with his victims and begins an elaborate tantric *pūjā* ritual, first offering a huge feast to the goddess; when Hanumān greedily devours everything, the king and his forces are thrilled, supposing the Devī to be especially pleased with them (in some accounts the monkey demands additional food until the royal kitchens are emptied), but their delight turns to terror when "she" roars menacingly, places the captive princes on "her" shoulders, and begins slaughtering the demons, casting their bodies into the ritual fire-pit. After a brief battle, Ahirāvaṇa meets the same fate, whereupon Hanumān retraces his route, frees Makaradhvaja, whom Rāma appoints the new ruler of Pātāla, and then returns with the princes to Laṅkā, to the relief of the monkey forces and to the terrestrial Rāvaṇa's despair.

It may be noted, for the sake of completeness, that several elements common to many southern and eastern versions are missing from this account: notably, the demon's life-force being externalized in a group of bees or beetles, whom Hanumān must locate and destroy in order to kill him—the "life index" motif well known to folklorists; the monkey is sometimes aided in this task by the demon's *nāga* mistress, who demands the reward of marrying Rāma, which Hanumān cleverly manages to withhold. Another common folkloric element is the "show me" motif: prompted by Hanumān, Rāma tells his captor that, being a king's son, he doesn't know how to bow (before the goddess, prior to being decapitated) and politely requests that the demon demonstrate how it is done; when Ahirāvaṇa obliges, Hanumān seizes his sword and kills him. Several versions omit the presence of Hanumān's "fishy" offspring, and the Tamil *Mayilirāvaṇan katai* adds an elaborate subplot concerning the demon's sister and her son, who have been unjustly persecuted and whose cause Hanumān champions, so that he eventually establishes the nephew on the throne, with Hanumān's son Makaradhvaja (here called Maccavallapaṇ, the "fish hero") as guardian. It may also be noted that the behavior of Rāma and Lakṣmaṇa varies among the different accounts—from utterly passive in the Tamil version translated by Zvelebil (they are asleep in a wooden box most of the time), to somewhat more active in Jvālāprasād's artful addendum to Tulsīdās, wherein Rāma sees through Hanumān's disguise as the raging "Devī" and, asked by Ahirāvaṇa (prior to the sacrifice) to call upon his "savior," invokes the monkey's name. In some modern Hindi versions, Lakṣmaṇa then asks, "Is Hanumān here?" to which Rāma replies, "Where is he not present? Today I am having his *darśana* in the form of the Devī" (Gita Press 1975: 320). In any case, as Smith (1988: 153) and Zvelebil (1987: xxxviii, xlii–xliii) have stressed, it is the son of the wind who occupies center stage and is the real hero of the tale:

FIGURE 6.1. Hanumān rescuing Rāma and Lakṣmaṇa.

soaring and swooping between earth and Pātāla Loka (sometimes making the descent via tunnel or through the stalk of an immense lotus in the midst of the ocean), slaughtering crores of *rākṣasas* with his teeth and claws, and standing rampant and defiant with the two diminutive princes perched on his shoulders and the demon king or his patron Devī crushed under his heel—the latter a common tableau in pan-Indian poster art.

Snakes and Langurs

The explanations commonly offered for the expansion and proliferation of *Rāmāyaṇa* tellings—that they reflect diverse reinterpretations, such as, brahmanical, devotional, or regional—make sense with regard to certain episodes; thus Kampaṉ's elaboration of the Śūrpaṇakhā story can be shown to reflect both Tamil poetic conventions and bhakti sensibilities, and the motif of the *māyā* Sītā (common to both the Sanskrit *Adhyātma Rāmāyaṇa* and the Tulsīdās Hindi epic) may reflect the changing social role of women as well as the influence of

Advaitin-influenced Vaiṣṇava metaphysics. The great geographical spread and historical vitality of the (not especially Sanskritic or brahmanical) Ahirāvaṇa story would seem to require another explanation, and to conclude that its appeal rests on "folk" or "popular" elements is (like these terms themselves) too vague; moreover it has generated literary works of considerable craft, including a number in Sanskrit.

As Zvelebil has observed (echoing David Shulman), the cosmic conflict between *devas* and *asuras* that forms the essential plot of the vast *itihāsa-purāṇa* narrative tradition is implicitly understood to be endless and unresolvable (Zvelebil 1987: xxxvi). Purāṇic *daityas, asuras,* and *rākṣasas* are notably reproducible; indeed, their persistent but futile efforts at recapturing (through austerities and divine boons as well as through cosmic warfare) the immortality stolen from them by their junior cousins the *devas* often result in a kind of malignant corporeality—demons who sprout new heads when decapitated, reassemble severed limbs, or clone themselves from drops of spilled blood—which requires much divine ingenuity to finally defeat. So it should be no surprise to find, in an elaboration on the *Rāmāyaṇa,* another Rāvaṇa. Actually there are more, for the Śākta-influenced retellings of northeastern India sport hundred-, thousand-, and hundred-thousand-headed Rāvaṇas, each exponentially more terrible. Yet why not allow the same principal hero—Rāma—to slay each one in single combat, as he does so many other demon champions during the battle of Laṅkā? Instead, these elaborations implicitly play on a central element in the core narrative; for just as the ten-headed Rāvaṇa can only be slain by an incarnate god-man, so his cthonic and hydra-headed doubles can only be slain by some other composite being—goddess-mother or god-monkey.[6]

Both Smith and Zvelebil see the Ahirāvaṇa/Mayilirāvaṇa stories as fundamentally about Hanumān and their proliferation as linked to his own growing cult during the past millennium, concerning which I have written elsewhere (Lutgendorf 1994, 1998). This might seem "logical" enough to dictate their inclusion in the epic cycle, but I believe that there are other structural elements to the tale that warrant analysis. Certainly I would question Zvelebil's generalization that Hanumān's growing stature simply or even primarily reflects "the last and deadly struggle of Hindu India against Islam in the South" and that his trickster personality reveals "the valour, skills, and shrewdness of the medieval South Indian warrior class who have to keep up the struggle against a terrible foe—the Muslim invader" (1987: xli). This analysis of a pervasive twelfth- to-eighteenth-century story cycle strikes me as facile and tainted by twentieth-century communal hindsight.

In analyzing the northeastern versions of the Mahīrāvaṇa tale, Smith rightly critiques D. C. Sen's earlier argument that the story is "tantric in inspiration" (1988: 152), since the story's tantric trappings (evil red-clad sorcerer, blood-soaked altar, trembling human victims, and menacing but ineffectual and finally humiliated goddess) obviously show Vaiṣṇava-flavored parody—indeed, Jvālāprasād's lurid setting of the climactic scene (complete with booming kettledrums and massed ranks of *rākṣasa* priests around a huge fire-pit) might be entitled "Indiana-Hanumān in the Temple of Doom." Beyond this, however, Smith merely invokes Hanumān's proverbial "folk" appeal to explain the fascination of these "popular apocryphal tales" (1988: 153).

Zvelebil is correct, I think, when he speculates on the Rāma/Lakṣmaṇa dyad as an increasingly "distant divine entity" in Tamil medieval devotional *Rāmāyaṇas*, and suggests that there was a felt need for "a hero who would be *active*, have even 'human' follies and weaknesses, and yet be invincible" (1987: xl; italics in original). The process by which gods become otiose is well known to historians of religion and historically well attested in India: the gradual replacement of Dyaus-pitṛ by Indra, of Indra by Viṣṇu and Śiva, and of the once "wide-striding" Viṣṇu himself (increasingly found reclining on the Ocean of Milk) by his more active human avatārs. Rāma and Kṛṣṇa certainly have their legions of votaries, but both have also shown signs, in their theologies, of becoming otiose: receding (for *rasika* devotees) behind *hlādinī śaktis* (feminine powers) and (for common folk) approachable intercessors. Rāma in particular has always faced certain problems as a personal deity (*iṣṭadeva*); the fact of his being an elder son and a king, though important to his authority, does not render him especially approachable or sympathetic (although other elements in his story do stress his compassion toward the weak and lowly), nor does his (some say) excessive dedication to *maryādā* or "decorum" that permits his often-criticized treatment of Sītā and others. Historically, Rāma's theological elevation corresponded to his increasing abstraction—eventually to the two syllables *rā-ma* which largely replaced, in popular usage, the Vedic *oṁkāra* and were readily embraced by *nirguṇa* traditions. Although Tulsīdās toned down the excessive Advaitin discourse that characterized the *Adhyātma Rāmāyaṇa* and managed a better balance between Rāma's human and transcendent aspects, he too contributed to the proliferating cult of the impersonal *Rām-nām*. In approaching such a deity, intercession is essential, and while Śāktas and *rasikas* opted for Sītā, other Vaiṣṇavas and mainstream *sanātanī* Hindus have often preferred Hanumān.

The Ahirāvaṇa tale belongs to the genre of heroic quest that involves the overcoming of fantastic obstacles. This has its prototype within the classical *Rāmāyaṇa* in the encapsulated quest-within-a-quest that is *Sundarakāṇḍa*, as well as in the episode of Hanumān's journey to the mountains to fetch the miraculous *sañjīvanī* herb. Both these stories cast Rāma in a passive role—pining for Sītā atop Mount Prasravaṇa, or weeping over the mortally wounded Lakṣmaṇa—and give the spotlight to Hanumān, and significantly, both have come to enjoy a special popularity within the broader framework of the epic. The *Sundara* episode (with its odd and much-discussed name), which highlights Hanumān's power of flight and mastery of magical disguises, and shows him triumphing over a series of initiatory trials that involve the slaying of *nāga*-like marine demonesses (Surasā and Siṁhikā—the latter linked to Ahirāvaṇa, according to Miśra, as a foster mother), has long enjoyed "a significance and a popularity greater than that of the other books" of the Sanskrit epic (Goldman and Goldman 1996: 5). The *sañjīvanī* story, which like the Ahirāvaṇa tale occurs during a hiatus in the battle in Laṅkā, adds the additional theme of rescue and healing, and eventually acquires significant elaborations of its own—the story of Kālanemi, another powerful sorcerer sent to obstruct Hanumān's journey (assisted by a demonic *makarī* (female sea monster) whom the monkey also slays), as well as an emotional meeting with Rāma's brother Bharata and his family in Ayodhyā. Though absent from most recensions of Vālmīki, this episode is found in the (c. fifteenth-century) *Adhyātma Rāmāyaṇa* (6.6.35–63; 6.7.1–33), in the *Rāmcaritmānas* (6.56.2–6.60), and in many modern Hindi retellings of Hanumān's *carit* or memorable acts.

Whereas both of these adventures transpire within the normal mythical geography of Bhāratavarṣa, the Ahirāvaṇa story adds the element of an "otherworld" journey, involving a shamanlike descent to nether regions to recover demon-possessed souls. Several observations may be offered to underscore the elemental appeal of this scenario, and the ease with which it accommodates itself to the wider scope of the *Rāmāyaṇa* narrative. It too has generic precursors in the other great epic of ancient India, the *Mahābhārata*, in which the more "energetic" members of a heroic brotherhood—Arjuna and Bhīma—depart on personal quests that carry them to fabulous landscapes wherein they overcome extraordinary trials, while their senior brother and leader waits passively at home. These scenarios have themselves become loci for significant "crystalline growth" in the *Mahābhārata* tradition, and the Arjuna cycle has been embellished with a long episode, popular in Tamil regions, involving a descent to Pātāla Loka and a marriage with a *nāga* princess (Hiltebeitel 1988: 217, 225). The theme of an otherworld journey, coupled with the magical and illusory elements in the Ahirāvaṇa story, suggest other popular South Asian oral tale-cycles that assumed literary form in the nineteenth century, such as the Urdu *Dāstān-e amīr Ḥamzah* (which under the sponsorship of the redoubtable Naval Kishore of Lucknow eventually grew into a *Mahābhārata*-dwarfing opus of forty-six volumes of roughly nine hundred pages each; Pritchett 1991: 25) and the likewise expanding folk epic *Ālhākhaṇḍ*, both of which abound in episodes featuring evil sorcerers who inhabit magical fortresses (*tilasmī gaṛh*) and who specialize in illusions and abductions. The Ahirāvaṇa tale has provided an opportunity to introduce this kind of staple action-adventure material into the *Rāmāyaṇa* cycle, but it should be noted that its theme of netherworld descent and rescue also resonates with Hanumān's cultic role as an exorcist-healer, able to overpower and expel the possessing demons who induce mental illness (Kakar 1982: 53–88).

Here I must say more about the snake motifs in the story, particularly in the Hindi verse version by Miśra. In telling the story of "snake-Rāvaṇa" whose birth appendage of twenty snakes terrifies even his demon father, and who is adopted by the serpentine sea monster Siṁhikā, this pandit has artfully introduced an array of snaky images that suggest the ambivalent status of these semidivine beings: Hanumān standing guard over the protective fortress formed by his tail is compared to "the king of snakes who had formed a coil" (Miśra: 1,037), the sleeping Rāma's hand resting on Lakṣmaṇa's chest is likened to "a serpent on a lotus" (1,038), and throughout the episode Lakṣmaṇa is referred to by epithets—as he is not generally in the root (*mūla*) text of the *Rāmcaritmānas*—meaning "serpent king" (*phaṇināhu, phaṇipati*) that allude to his being the incarnation of the cosmic snake Śeṣa. Hanumān's iconic connection with *nāgas* is both pervasive and complex: like Garuḍa (with whom he is often paired as Viṣṇu's theriomorphic servitor and to whom Vālmīki sometimes metaphorically likens him), he can be an adversary of serpents, but as an illusion-creating *kāmarūpin* and *mahāyogin* he has snakelike qualities of his own, and he is the patron deity of wrestlers, who also worship *nāgas* as emblems of male power and whose principal holiday is Nāga-pañcamī (Alter 1992: 136–66, 198–213). "Crookedness" (*ṭeṛhāpan* in Hindi), which is a quality of wiliness and moral ambiguity as well as a physical attribute of snakes and of langur's tails, is not one of Rāma's strong suits, for he is the avatar of the straight and narrow path of dharma, and in the classical *Rāmāyaṇa* he runs into problems with Indrajīt's "snake noose" (*nāgapāśa*), becoming helplessly bound until Garuḍa arrives to free him, which poses an embarrassment to later bhakti-oriented retellers. Small wonder that he is so helpless in the clutches of the "snake-Rāvaṇa," and must await rescue by a more "crooked" hero who can beat the demon sorcerer at his own devious game.

Snakes, the netherworld, and illusion/magic represent a constellation of motifs in South Asian popular narrative, and the story of "snake-Rāvaṇa" abounds in motifs of doubling and disguise. Ahirāvaṇa himself is Rāvaṇa's darker double, literally a Rāvaṇa-from-hell who spreads impenetrable darkness over Rāma's army and begins an elaborate series of impersonations; in Kṛttivāsa's Bengali version of the story, which calls the character Mahīrāvaṇa, he assumes the forms of Vasiṣṭha, Kauśalyā, Kaikeyī, and Viśvāmitra, and tries to enter Hanumān's tail-fort before finally succeeding in the guise of Vibhīṣaṇa (Smith 1988: 151). Again, it is difficult to imagine the straightforward Rāma assuming a disguise for any purpose, but Hanumān easily matches the demon's moves. In the Assamese tale by Candra Bhāratī, the monkey successively transforms himself into a crow, a kingfisher, a fly, an aged brahman, a crow again, a second fly, and the goddess Vetālacaṇḍī in the course of his mission (Smith 1988: 149–50). This is not the end of the doubling, however, for at the gates of the demon city Hanumān encounters his own double in the form of Makaradhvaja, precipitating a charming father-son reunion scene that emphasizes both Hanumān's sexual potency (the procreative power of even his perspiration, saliva, or phlegm) and his strict celibacy. But despite this bit of male bonding (and bondage, since Makaradhvaja ends up secured by his own tail) the Ahirāvaṇa story has little to say about dharma, family values, kingship, or the importance of keeping one's word—themes that figure prominently in the classical *Rāmāyaṇas*. Instead it has everything to do with deception, resourcefulness, and power. In Pātāla Loka we expect the unexpected and are not disappointed: forms change with bewildering swiftness, divine champions prove helpless, and lifelong bachelors turn out to have children. The message—apart from sheer entertainment—seems to be that (as in the Purāṇas) demonic illusions will proliferate and may stupefy even the dharma-protecting gods, yet we need not despair because help is available in the form of a plucky superhero with talents as devious as his trademark appendage. Hanumān's traits in this tale suggest his appeal to socioeconomically weaker segments of the population, and to the aspiring middle classes of contemporary India, a phenomenon of which I have written elsewhere (Lutgendorf 1998: 325–327).

Although the Ahirāvaṇa story is, for all the reasons I have already suggested, widely acceptable to audiences as an "organic" expansion of the master narrative, it may (like several other expansions I cited earlier in this essay) also be seen as a subtle critique of that narative's implicit championing of hierarchical subordination to various regimes of authority—patriarchal and familial, ideological and political. Indeed, like the tale of the hundred-headed Rāvaṇa, it challenges what has sometimes been cited as one of the basic rules of the epic's "grammar": namely, that a *Rāmāyaṇa* is a story in which "Rāma kills Rāvaṇa"—for here that heroic task must be undertaken by Rāma's subaltern. Significantly, the Ahirāvaṇa story figures prominently in a series of recent Hindi "biographies" of the divine monkey; elaborate narrative cycles that place him at center stage, and which I collectively characterize (only half in jest) as an emerging *Hanumāyana* (cf. Miśra 1987; Prem n.d.; Śarmā 1987; Siṁha 1984). In this multiform and still proliferating epic cycle, as in Hanumān's widespread worship, I find subordination subtly yielding to subversion and de facto theological substitution.

To return to my opening question of how best to conceptualize the *Rāmāyaṇa* tradition—as a root or as a crystal—I would like to propose a metaphor from classical Indian music. For a rāga is, so to speak, both at once: in its essence, it is a minimal sequence of notes corresponding to Ramanujan's "skeletal set of relations" (though we observe that even in this form it is considered to possess distinctive qualities of atmosphere and emotion). In its development and realization in musical performance, a rāga is capable of extraordinarily wide variation, but always within limits set by formal criteria, as well as by the training of the performer and the expectations of the audience. Great innovation is possible, but if it violates certain limits the performance may fail to evoke the desired mood. History and geography play a role here as well, for they can give rise to different musical schools—such as Hindustani and Carnatic—within which the same rāga will come to be shaped by different rules and expectations. In my analysis of the Ahirāvaṇa story—which we might compare to a particularly satisfying and much-imitated melodic composition or *gat* introduced into the latter portion of a Hindustani rāga by a talented performer—its success derives from the fact that its narrative innovations are presented through structural features that both echo and complement older and more essential elements in the story. Thus the Ahirāvaṇa tale permits luxuriant crystalline growth without sacrificing a sense of rootedness; both of these qualities are highly prized within that creative yet essentially conserving worldview that is generically labeled "Hinduism."

NOTES

1. It should be noted that Ramanujan himself backed away from the last assertion, suggesting (in the next paragraph) that it "may be too extreme a way of putting it"; Richman 1991:44.

2. The treatment of the wounding and death of the monkey-king Vāli by Kampaṉ and other vernacular poets offers another good example of such a narrative "stress point."

3. To my knowledge, Smith is the only Western *Rāmāyaṇa* scholar to have given serious attention to this tale-cycle. In addition to the discussion of the subject in his comprehensive 1988 book on eastern Indian Rāma traditions, see his 1982 and 1996 articles, each of which deals with a specific textual retelling.

4. This is a famous temple visited by virtually all pilgrims to the *Triveṇī saṇgam*. It features a gargantuan sandstone Hanumān with a diminutive Rāma and Lakṣmaṇa sitting on his shoulders. One of his feet crushes a female figure, whom the *pūjārī* identifies as Pātāla Devī (Ahirāvaṇa's patroness), and he is flanked by a small monkey holding a flag; this is said to be Hanumān's son Makaradhvaja. See my précis of the story below for an explanation of these elements.

5. Dīkṣit 1978; Gita Press 1975; Gupta 1980; Miśra [1933] 1982; Pārāśara 1979; Śarmā 1987. Throughout this précis, I spell proper nouns according to Hindi pronunciation, omitting the unpronounced vowel *a*.

6. On the former scenario, see Coburn 1995. Miśra's rendering of the Ahirāvaṇa story (summarized above) is quite explicit about the terms of the Devī's boon to "serpent-Rāvaṇa": he cannot be slain by anyone except "a certain monkey" (Miśra [1933] 1982: 1,036).

REFERENCES

Alter, Joseph S. 1992. *The Wrestler's Body*. Berkeley and Los Angeles: University of California Press.

Bulcke, Camille. 1950. *Rāmkathā: Utpatti aur Vikās* (The Rāma story: origin and development) Prayag: Hindi Pariṣad Prakāśan, 1950; in Hindi.

Coburn, Thomas B. 1995. "Sita Fights while Ram Swoons." *Manushi* 90: 5–16.

Dīkṣit, Rājeś. 1978. *Hanumān upāsnā*. Delhi: Dehātī Pustak Bhāṇḍār.

Gita Press. 1975. *Kalyāṇ, Śrī Hanumān aṇk*. Gorakhpur: Gita Press.

Goldman, Robert P. et al. 1984–. *The Rāmāyaṇa of Vālmīki*. Princeton: Princeton University Press.

Goldman, Robert P., and Sally J. Sutherland Goldman, trans. 1996. *The Rāmāyaṇa of Vālmīki*. Vol. 5, *Sundarakāṇḍa* Princeton: Princeton University Press.

Gupta, Dīndayāl. 1980. *Hanumān mahimā*. Delhi: Pustak Mahal.

Hart, George, and Hank Heifetz, trans. 1988. *The Forest Book of the Rāmāyaṇa of Kampaṉ*. Berkeley and Los Angeles: University of California Press.

Hiltebeitel, Alf. 1988. *The Cult of Draupadī*. Vol. 1. Chicago: University of Chicago Press.

Iyengar, K. R. Srinivasa, 1983. *Asian Variations in Ramayana*. Delhi: Sahitya Akademi.

Kakar, Sudhir. 1982. *Shamans, Mystics, and Doctors*. Delhi: Oxford University Press.

Lutgendorf, Philip. 1990. "Ramayan: The Video." *The Drama Review*. T126: 127–176.

———. 1994. "My Hanumān Is Bigger Than Yours." *History of Religions* 33.3: 211–245.

———. 1998. "Monkey in the Middle." *Religion* 27: 311–332.

Miśra, Bhagavatī Śaran. 1987. *Pavanputra, ātmakathātmak śreṣṭh upanyās*. Delhi: Rajpal and Sons.

Miśra, Jvālāprasād. [1933] 1982. *Śrīmad Gosvāmī Tulsīdās-jī viracit Rāmāyaṇa*. Bombay: Śri Veṇkaṭeśvar Press.

Parāśara, Jvālāprasād. 1979. *Rāmāyaṇa āṭhoṁ kāṇḍ*. 13th ed. Mathura: Ramayana Press.

Prem, Sri Swami. n.d. *The Story of a Lovetrance Being*. Harbor City, Cal.: Aum Namo Bhagavate Vasudevay Foundation.

Pritchett, Frances. W. 1991. *The Romance Tradition in Urdu*. New York: Columbia University Press.

Raghavan, V., ed. 1980. *The Ramayana Tradition in Asia*. Delhi: Sahitya Akademi.

Richman, Paula, ed. 1991. *Many Rāmāyaṇas*. Berkeley and Los Angeles: University of California Press.

———. 2001. *Questioning Rāmāyaṇas*. Berkeley and Los Angeles: University of California Press.

Śarmā, Narendra. 1987. *Śrī Hanumān Rāmāyaṇa*. Ayodhya: Shri Hanuman Ramayana Mandir.

Seeley, Clinton B., trans. 2004. *The Slaying of Meghanada*. New York: Oxford University Press.

Siṁha, Sudarśan. 1984. *Hanumān kī ātmakathā*. Hardwar: Randhir Book Sales.

Smith, W. L., 1982. "Mahīrāvaṇa and the Womb Demon." *Indologica Taurinensia*, 10: 215–225.

———. 1988. *Rāmāyaṇa Traditions in Eastern India*. Stockholm: Department of Indology, University of Stockholm.

———. 1996. "Two Nepalese Versions of the Mahirāvaṇa Tale." In *Change and Continuity: Studies in the Nepalese Culture of the Kathmandu Valley*, edited by Siegfried Lienhard. Collana di Studi Orientali del CESMEO diretta da Irma Piovano 7 Turin: Orientalia.

Thiel-Horstmann, Monika, ed. 1991. *Rāmāyaṇa and Rāmāyaṇas*. Wiesbaden: Otto Harrasowitz.

Zvelebil, Kamil V. 1987. *Two Tamil Folktales*. Delhi: Motilal Banarsidass.

7

"Only You": The Wedding of Rāma and Sītā, Past and Present

Heidi Pauwels

In this essay I compare three different versions of the episode of the wedding of Sītā and Rāma, namely, the episode in the *Vālmīki Rāmāyaṇa*, in Tulsīdās's *Rāmcaritmānas*, and in the TV version by Rāmānand Sāgar. I will analyze how the classical, medieval, and contemporary portrayals differ from each other and speculate on the relevance of the differences in the contemporary context. An interesting "innovation" in the TV version, for example, appears to be the setting of the first wedding night for an explicit "vow of monogamy" or *ekapatnīvrata* of Rāma, where he promises Sītā to remain faithful to her alone.

Say the word *Rāmāyaṇa*, and immediately normative values come to mind. Often the epic is treated as a blueprint for Hindu ethics. In particular, the construction of gender roles in the *Rāmāyaṇa* has been the subject of much interest. Most obviously, the divine pair Sītā and Rāma is widely regarded as the ideal Hindu couple.[1] Their mutual love is a rare example of happy monogamy in the epic universe. Too often, though, the relationship of Sītā and Rāma is treated like a static, unchanging given, without provision for the fact that its portrayal differs in different versions of the *Rāmāyaṇa* story. It is imperative to reach a more nuanced view. A comparative study of different versions can reveal a lot about the historical evolution of gender relational ideals in different times and places.

In this essay I propose to concentrate on the construction of Sītā and Rāma's ideal love, as expressed in the episode of their wedding. The wedding ceremony is of particular interest in that it is a public ritual in which values are articulated and tradition is constructed in a way meaningful for the participants. I am mostly interested in what the contemporary depiction of Sītā and Rāma's ideal wedding tells us about constructions of gender relationships. The wedding episode immediately follows that scene, and represents the culmination of this privately blossoming love into a public ritual sanctioned by society.

The main focus of this paper is on a contemporary version of the *Rāmāyaṇa*, the immensely popular TV *Rāmāyaṇa* (*TVR*), directed by Rāmānand Sāgar (Ramchand Chopra), which was first shown on the official channel Doordarshan from January 25, 1987, until July 31, 1988.[2] As is well known, the series became a major hit and had incredibly high viewer rates at the time it was first aired. Its continued popularity is obvious from the fact that its video version is still a hot item in many "Indian" grocery stores, even in the United States and Canada. Clearly, the series carried a message that struck a chord with a large and varied public. Whether it was in itself normative or reflective of current norms, or a combination of the two, is difficult to say, but it is a message that is well worth analyzing in detail. The wedding episode itself has been very influential. Anecdotal evidence suggests that the TV wedding of Sītā and Rāma has set a precedent for actual wedding ceremonies. It seems that, at least in the Delhi region, it has become fashionable to hire wedding consultants who advertise a designer *Sītā-Rāma Vivāha*, a lavish style of public ritual.[3]

The remarkable influence that the TV *Rāmāyaṇa* has come to exert demands close attention to its message, and here I propose to attempt to decode it by carefully analyzing "what is old, what is new," by paying particular attention not only to the innovations by Sāgar, significant as they are, but also to what exactly he quotes from, and by noting what he leaves out from these sources and at which places. I believe this is a necessary critical task, for otherwise we end up ascribing to Sāgar's *Rāmāyaṇa* elements that are much older, and missing elements that are truly innovative in the *TVR*.[4]

Given the focus of this chapter, I will compare *TVR* with the two versions Sāgar, by his own admission, uses most extensively (at the beginning of each episode this is confirmed in the credits). First, he acknowledges as his source the Sanskrit *Rāmāyaṇa* attributed to the legendary sage Vālmīki (*VR*), the *ur*-text, too well known to warrant an introduction.[5] But it is his second acknowledged source that Sāgar uses most extensively, namely, the version from medieval times, Tulsīdās's vastly influential old Hindī (Avadhī) *Rāmcaritmānas* (*RCM*).[6] This work dates from the last quarter of the sixteenth century and was created in eastern Uttar Pradesh, in the cities of Benares and Ayodhyā. These are the two main "texts" I mine for similarities and differences, but I will occasionally refer to other, less well-known versions of the *Rāmāyaṇa* story, which will be introduced when referred to.[7]

Since my particular interest is in textual studies, it is to this discipline that I have oriented this essay. Textual analysis has been in discredit in some quarters, which is unfortunate because it has much to offer. I would argue that if we want to take the popular TV *Rāmāyaṇa* seriously, if we want to understand it fully, beyond easy clichés and sweeping generalizations, a close comparative reading is indispensable. This does not mean that I think other approaches are not valid. Rather, I welcome and have benefited from studies from other perspectives. It has been suggested that a study from the perspective of visual arts, in particular a comparative study with visual images and earlier films, would be revealing.[8] Another angle should be provided from an anthropological study of viewers' reactions (along the lines of Poornima Mankekar's 1999 study). The latter is important because it is commonly assumed that the *Mānas*, which is quoted so extensively by Sāgar, is not easily understood any more. In course of my close reading, I came to suspect more and more strongly that Sāgar's use of the *Mānas* was deliberate and that he targeted connoisseurs of the *Mānas*. Still, his audience was much broader, and many of the nuances that I note in this paper might well have escaped the "average viewer." It would be interesting to see how much of Sāgar's carefully crafted message came across in different milieus, but obviously that is a different study and one that requires a different expertise.

The story of the wedding of Rāma and Sītā can be subdivided into four major episodes, three of which are directly relevant to the construction of gender relationships. The first is the so-called *svayaṁvara* episode, where Rāma lifts Śiva's bow in the possession of the king of Mithila, Janaka, and thereby wins the hand of the princess, Sītā. This episode could be said to correspond to any ordinary wedding's first step, sometimes called *vadhūvara-guṇaparīkṣā* or examination of the qualities of bride and groom (Kane 1974, 531). In the case of Rāma and Sītā, however, it is the groom who is on the spot, not the bride. In the modern context, this episode raises issues related to partner choice and what constitutes "a suitable boy," or how "a proper match" is made.

The second part comprises the wedding ceremonies proper. This episode is of particular interest for the construction of the hierarchical relationship between the bride-givers (*kanyāpakṣa*) and bride-takers (*varapakṣa*), and can be read as a dramatic enactment of gender ideologies. Third is the episode of leave-taking and departure of the newly wedded parties to Ayodhyā. This raises the issue of the adjustment of new brides (*bahūs*) in the joint family of their in-laws (*sasurāl*). In this context the TV version adds an episode that features the beginning of Sītā and Rāma's wedding night as the setting for Rāma's vow of monogamy or *ekapatnīvrata*. There is no exact equivalent for this scene in any of the other *Rāmāyaṇas* considered here. In addition to these three episodes, all three versions also feature the incident of the challenge to Rāma by Paraśurāma (Bhārgava Rāma or Rāma Jāmadagnya), which I am not treating in this essay (for the Vālmīki version of this episode, see Sally Goldman's paper in this volume).

At first glance, the TV version follows closely the older accounts for all three episodes. It features frequent quotes from the medieval text, and occasionally also from the authoritative Sanskrit *ur*-text. It is important, though, to keep in mind that the contemporary retelling of these traditional episodes takes place against a changed backdrop of "modernity." The very medium through which the TV *Rāmāyaṇa* is disseminated puts it in the context of current debates about the advantages and disadvantages of traditional "arranged marriages" and "joint-family living," which are the subject of other more or less contemporary soap series on TV (such as *Ham Log* and *Buniyād*; see Mankekar 1999, 110–113). Issues of dowry (Mankekar 1999, 115–116) and "bride burning," which are in the media all the time, also constitute the semantic universe in which the *TVR* partakes. Whereas the traditional subject of the series does not leave much room to discuss these issues explicitly, they still loom large in the background. They constitute, so to speak, the unspoken *pūrvapakṣa* or "problematization" to which the actual portrayal in the series can be read as an answer. It is helpful to keep this in mind to understand some of the emphases of *TVR*.

I will proceed to the analysis of each of the episodes separately, and draw general conclusions for the construction of gender in the TV series. In an appendix, I provide a fully detailed comparative overview in which I map the three versions (*VR, RCM, TVR*) of the wedding of Sītā and Rāma. By doing this in an abbreviated chart form, I seek to provide a tool to facilitate an overview of the differences and similarities at a glance, and a quick reference for the reader.

Sītā's *Svayaṁvara*: Why a Contest?

It always comes as a shock to realize how much of what is commonly regarded as integral to the meta-*Rāmāyaṇa* is non-Vālmīkian. Calling this episode Sītā's *svayaṁvara* (self-choice of a groom) or even *dhanuryajña* (bow sacrifice) does not apply very well to the Vālmīki version of Rāma's stringing Śiva's bow in *Bālakāṇḍa* (*VR* 1.66). For one, no *dhanuryajña* or *svayaṁvara* is held in Mithilā when Rāma arrives. Rather, Janaka is performing a nonspecified Vedic sacrifice when Viśvāmitra and his two wards drop by and happen to ask to see the famous bow. There is no question of Rāma's having any competition from other kings at this occasion. The *svayaṁvara* proper seems to have taken place long ago, well before Rāma arrived on the stage. Janaka relates in the past tense to the sage and his two wards how the disappointed kings after their failure to string the bow laid siege to Mithilā but were eventually expelled (*VR* 1.66.16–25). There is no question of Sītā "choosing" Rāma. It is not even clear whether she witnesses his feat, and she certainly does not get to lay a "victory garland" or *jayamālā* on his shoulders. It is her father who "chooses" for her by simply declaring that Rāma is now entitled to his daughter's hand (*VR* 1.66.21–23).[9]

I hasten to add that things are, as usual, a bit more complicated than they seem at first glance. *VR* in fact contains a second, slightly different and shorter version of the *svayaṁvara* story at the end of the *Ayodhyākāṇḍa*. It is an important one, however, because it is put in the mouth of none other than the bride herself. The episode, then, provides a version of the *svayaṁvara* from Sītā's perspective. It occurs in the context of the meeting of Sītā with Anasūyā, Atri's wife.[10] After exchanging pleasantries and making sure they are on the same wavelength with regard to women's dharma (*VR* 2.117.17–29 and 118.1–22), Anasūyā requests Sītā to entertain her by telling the story of her *svayaṁvara*. Sītā starts with the story of her "birth" and adoption at Janaka's court (*VR* 2.118.27–33). Then she dwells on Janaka's worries when she came of age (*VR* 2.118.34–37). According to Sītā, these worries made Janaka decide to hold a *svayaṁvara* and set the test of the bow as the condition for Sītā's marriage (*VR* 2.118.38–42). Many kings failed, but "after a good long time" Rāma appeared and succeeded (*VR* 2.118.43–49). So, Vālmīki's "take two" of the episode allows for the possibility that Rāma was present at the *svayaṁvara* ceremony proper, and that the "sacrifice" he came to see was indeed the *dhanuryajña*.

The *svayaṁvara* setting and the competition element are a given for the TV version. Sāgar follows very closely the lead of Tulsīdās, who had already used the competition setting in his *Mānas*. Tulsī in turn seemed to have borrowed it from the Sanskrit dramatic tradition (Vaudeville 1955, 108–109). One minor difference between *TVR* and *RCM* is that in *TVR* the arrival of Viśvāmitra is no mere coincidence. In an earlier episode (*TVR* 5.77), we learn that Janaka had sent an invitation to the sage for the event and that he is pleased to learn that Viśvāmitra has come.

Tulsī had fully exploited the background of competition to demonstrate the greatness of Rāma, and Sāgar follows suit. The appearance of Rāma in this public setting becomes a major occasion for *darśana*. When Rāma enters the hall where the contest is to take place, Tulsī makes this explicit in his famous line "Everyone saw the Lord's image in the light of the emotion they felt" (*jinha keṁ rahī bhāvanā jaisī, prabhu mūrati tinha dekhī taisī; RCM* 1.241.2b). In *TVR* this very line is quoted, and the camera registers the reactions of the different parties present. Tulsī goes on to describe several *rasas* in which Rāma was seen by different groups of spectators, to create, one could say, a case of multidimensional *darśana*. Tulsī then provides a *nakha-śikha* (toe-to-head) description of the two brothers (*RCM* 1.242 *dohā*–244.1). Sāgar's camera lingers on the image of the brothers to provide a *darśana*, but there are no further quotes from *RCM*.

Notwithstanding the background of the contest, in Tulsī's *RCM* there is never any real doubt that Rāma will win.[11] On the morning of the contest, Tulsī's Lakṣmaṇa predicts that "someone on whom Viśvāmitra's grace (*kṛpā*) rests" will be the winner (*RCM* 1.240.1b). Sāgar reworks this incident in modern Hindī, and adds a short scene before it, where Lakṣmaṇa expresses to Rāma how eager he is to attend the *svayaṁvara*. Rāma, however keeps his cool and teaches a *Gītā*-esque lesson of detachment to his brother, saying "At the time of a test one should not be excited, one should only concentrate on one's action" (*parīkṣā ke samay uttejit nahīṁ honā cāhie; keval apne karm par dhyān rakhnā cāhie*; *TVR* 7.93). By doing so, Sāgar has reinforced the sense of predestination, as well as set up Rāma as a model for disciplined human behavior. The contest is not a real test but rather a blueprint, an occasion to set an example.

Exemplary disciplined behavior is also displayed by Sītā. We should recall that in *VR*, Sītā is nowhere on the scene; she does not even seem to merit a description of her beauty. Only the miraculous story of her "birth" is recounted by Janaka (*VR* 1.66.13–14), and that in one breath with the history of the bow (*VR* 1.66.8–12). In contrast, Tulsīdās provides a full *darśana*. Although he spends many more words on the beauty of Rāma than of Sītā, Sītā is very much on the scene. Tulsī gallantly spends a whole *kaṛavak* 1.247 to say there is no comparison for her, and calls her World Mother, or *Jagadambikā* (*RCM*

1.247.1a) and *Jagata Jananī* (*RCM* 1.248.1b). Notwithstanding these exalted titles, Sītā is a character of flesh and blood. Whereas Rāma does not lose his cool, Sītā definitely does. After all, she is the ideal bhakta or devotee. Tulsī describes how her agitated eyes scan the room for Rāma (*RCM* 1.248.4). Tulsī hastens to stress her self-control, however; out of respect to her elders (*gurujana lāja*), she turns her eyes to her friends, while keeping Rāma's image locked in her heart (*RCM* 1.248 *dohā*). Sāgar does not miss this occasion to make the heroine conform to conventional morality (*maryādā*). His Sītā enacts this scenario while these very lines from *RCM* are cited (*TVR* 7.95).

In case the message had not gotten across clearly, Sāgar seems to have felt the need to appear on the screen in person to explicitly address the issue of appropriate behavior. After the ninth episode, there is an appearance of the director on the video; he comments on the events he has portrayed (this is not transcribed in the edition by Mizokami). He does not quite apologize for the preceding episode with the *phūlvārī* or "flower garden" episode, where Rāma and Sītā are portrayed as falling in love, but apparently feels compelled to clarify some issues. He stresses first that the love of the divine couple is eternal, and that this was just their first meeting since they had descended on earth. Moreover, he stresses that although they feel romantic love, their behavior remains fully within conventional morality (*maryādā kā pūrṇa ācaraṇ*). He stresses that at every step *Rāmāyaṇa* teaches conventional morality and discipline (*maryādā* and *saṁyam*).[12] What is going on, I think, is that Sāgar tries to warn the young and eager that Sītā and Rāma's courtship is no justification for "love marriages."

Feelings

Tulsī uses the *svayaṁvara* contest to create dramatic tension.[13] He fully exploits the irony of the avatar, who acts like a human but is in fact God himself. Whereas Tulsī's audience was, of course, aware of Rāma's divinity, most of his characters act as if they are unaware of it, including Sītā. Tulsī provides a window into the minds of all present at the contest, and their own personal worries and desires about the outcome. This outpouring of emotions works well within *RCM*'s general agenda of promoting emotional devotion or bhakti. Sāgar pretty much follows suit, but there are some interesting differences.

First, when the kings see handsome Rāma, they figure that Sītā will choose him even if he does not break the bow (*RCM* 1.245.2). In *TVR* they even consider the test to be foul play on behalf of Janaka, and they voice the opinion that the match is pre-fixed (*TVR* 7.94). This is doubly ironic, of course, given that the match was indeed made in heaven, so to speak. To some extent this is underscored by an implicit equation of the bow with Sītā. The bow will not yield to anyone except Sītā's rightful husband. Tulsīdās had suggested as much in the scene where all the kings try but the bow refuses to budge, by likening the bow to a *satī*, or virtuous woman who does not give in to a suitor's pleas (*ḍagai na saṁbhu sarāsanu kaiseṁ, kāmī bacana satī manu jaiseṁ; RCM* 251.1b).

Significantly, in *TVR* this line is recited (*TVR* 7.97). Sāgar must have been aware of the implications of the comparison, and, as we shall see, they suit his purpose of legitimizing further Sītā's love for Rāma.

In *RCM*, when all the kings are defeated, Janaka expresses his despair at ever finding a real male (*vīra*) who can lift the bow and be a true match for his daughter (*RCM* 1.251.3b–252.3). There is irony here too, in that the audience knows he is about to obtain the best match of all. Sāgar follows Tulsī, and stresses even more explicitly Janaka's moral quandary. Either he is to break his vow or not marry off his daughter: "If I break my word, I'll be called a blot on my family name and I'll destroy all the good deeds of my ancestors. If I keep my word, my daughter will remain a virgin for this whole life, and the sin of rendering her life useless will be on my head" (*agar maiṁ yah praitjṇā toḍ dūṁ to kul kākalank kahlāū, pūrvajoṁ ke sukṛt naēṭ karūṁ aur maiṁ apnā prāṇ rakhūṁ to merī putrī ājanma kuṁvārī rahegī uskā jīvan viphal karne kā pāp mere sir caṛhegā; TVR* 7.98). Sāgar's Janaka is concerned with the wider repercussions, not just for himself, but for his whole lineage.

By comparison, no such despair is voiced in the *Bālakāṇḍa* by Vālmīki's Janaka. It merely seems that Janaka was pressured by the other kings into organizing a *svayaṁvara* (which predated Rāma's visit) (*VR* 1.66.17–18). In the fourteenth-century source text of Tulsī, the *Adhyātma Rāmāyaṇa* (*AR*), Janaka is not worried at all, which he himself explains later, after the wedding. Long ago Nārada had disclosed to him that Sītā, who is really Lakṣmī, was only to be married to Rāma, who is really Viṣṇu. This very disclosure was the reason for his strict condition on Sītā's marriage (*AR* 1.6.58–75).

The contrast of these relatively unworried Janakas with Sāgar's Janaka is striking. One might speculate that the stress on a girl's father's plight in the *TVR* strikes a chord in a contemporary situation where the requirement of a high dowry makes it problematic to marry off daughters to truly "suitable boys." Ironically, in the real-life situation, the frustration of the father with finding the right match for his daughter is caused not by any inability on the part of the groom but rather the inability of the bride's family to meet the groom's party's financial demands.

To return to the story, in both *RCM* and *TVR*, Lakṣmaṇa takes strong offense to Janaka's words, especially his claim that there seem to be no true men or heroes left on earth. However, he is calmed down by his brother and his guru. Eventually, Viśvāmitra urges Rāma to lift (or rather break) the bow. In *RCM*, when Rāma "steps up to the plate" to lift the bow, Sītā's mother vents her worry about this tender boy being able to pull off such a task (*RCM* 1.255 *dohā*–256.3a), which in turn provides the occasion for one of the ladies-in-waiting to reflect on deceiving appearances with several examples from mythology (*RCM* 256.3b–257.2a).

Sāgar seems to have particularly liked the perspective of the girl's mother, because he has Sunayanā vent her worries twice, once during the futile operations of the kings (*TVR* 7.97), and later, as in *RCM*, when Rāma takes his turn (*TVR* 7.99). The second occasion is modeled after *RCM*, with the difference that it is her sister-in-law, Kuśadhvaja's wife, who tries to comfort Sunayanā with the platitude that whatever is to be will come true. In Sāgar's version, Sunayanā is not happy with that answer, musing that the king seems to have gone mad to let such a young boy try and lift the bow. For more ironic effect, Sāgar also has the other assembled kings ridicule Rāma for his apparent immaturity. Finally, Sāgar has heightened the dramatical tension by breaking off the episode just before its climax. Doordarshan spectators had to wait a week before the tension would be relieved by Rāma's actually lifting the bow.

RCM and *TVR* also provide a window into Sītā's thoughts at the moment of Rāma's test. Sītā is prey to serious doubts, apparently having forgotten all about the divinity of her partner-to-be. Tulsī provides a touching episode where Sītā ardently beseeches the gods that they may lift the heaviness of the bow so that Rāma can lift it and she can become his (*RCM* 1.257.3–4). *TVR* quotes these same lines while the camera focuses on Sītā, interspersing her worried face with pictures of Śiva-Pārvatī and Gaṇeśa, as appropriate (*TVR* 8.100).

Then the *TVR* singers jump ahead a few verses in RCM to Sītā's humble voicing of her desire: "If in body, mind, and words, my vow is true, that my soul is attracted to the dust of Raghupati's feet; then, Lord, you who dwell in everyone's heart, make me the maid-servant of Raghuvara" (*tana mana vacana mora panu sācā, raghupati pada saroja citu rācā; tau bhagavānu sakala ura bāsī, karahi mohi raghubara kai dāsī; RCM* 1.259.2b–3a). Special stress is placed on these lines by singling out the first and last half-verse for repetition (*TVR* 8.100). The last line is further stressed in that it is delivered in declamation, not sung, as the rest is. Such humble desires may seem out of place in a contemporary context, and a priori one might have expected these lines to be dropped. Still, Sāgar chose to quote them rather emphatically. This is no coincidence. As we shall see, Sāgar later explicitly "updates" the traditional view of wife as servant (*dāsī*) of the husband, yet even on that occasion, he in effect portrays Sītā as ready to play the subservient role. In *TVR*, the ideal woman sees herself as subservient to her husband, her lord.

These lines are explicitly set up as having general relevance; the next verse in Tulsī reads, "Who truly loves, will get his true love, there is no doubt about it" (*jehi keṁ jehi para satya sanehū, so tehi milai na kachu saṁdehū; RCM* 1.259.3b). The catch here, of course, is the stipulation "a love that is true" (*satya sanehū*). Sītā's submissive attitude is generalized, and the message is that this will be the one that is rewarded in the end. We should remember here too how the bow was earlier compared to a *satī*, unyielding to anyone except her righteous husband. The image of the *satī* merges with the idea of true love, or *satya sanehū*. Sāgar adds at this point flashback images of the goddess Pārvatī, who granted Sītā the boon of the groom of her choice in the previous episode (see Pauwels 2000). These images reinforce the legitimacy of her desire, in view of the previously obtained divine sanction.

Having paid close attention to what Sāgar quotes from *RCM*, we should also note what Sāgar leaves out. In the ardor of the moment, Tulsī allows Sītā in her thoughts a split second of rebellion against her father's harsh condition for her marriage: "Alas, what terrible insistence of my father, he does not understand at all what brings benefit, what harm" (*ahaha tāta dāruni haṭha ṭhānī, samujhata nahiṁ kachu lābhu na hānī; RCM* 1.258.1b). She goes on to criticize, as her mother did out loud, the ministers and learned men present for not stopping such a tender boy from taking on such a big task. She thinks to herself that the bow should have become light for Rāma to lift, now that its obtuseness (*jaṛatā,* lifelessness or stupidity) seems to have been transferred on everyone present (*RCM* 1.258.4a). She does not shy away from criticizing the whole gathering of venerable elders as dull-witted (*sakala sabhā kai mati bhai bhorī; RCM* 1.258.3b). Sāgar does not allow his Sītā even that much loss of decorum in her thoughts, and leaves out these verses altogether. Whatever Sītā's private wish in favor of Rāma, in *TVR* she submits fully to parental authority. Far from getting to speak out about her private preferences to her confidantes, the very thoughts are suppressed.

Finally, in both *TVR* and *RCM,* we also get a window into Rāma's feelings and an interesting perspective on what prompts him to action. In the *Vālmīki Rāmāyaṇa,* there was not much psychological background. Significantly, though, it was Rāma himself who took the initiative to lift the bow and string it (though he proceeded to do so only after having received the permission of his guru and the king). Tulsī's and Sāgar's Rāma is much less keen to act. He waits for and then rather meekly follows the command of his guru. Again, the irony of the incarnation is central: God the almighty defers to mere mortals. To top off the irony, Tulsī's Rāma prays to Gaṇeśa before lifting the bow (*RCM* 1.255.4). Sāgar leaves out this line, but shows Rāma as bowing his head respectfully as he prepares for the task.

In both *TVR* and *RCM* the scene is stretched out to build tension, but ultimately it becomes clear that what prompts Rāma to lift the bow is compassion for Sītā. He acts really to save Sītā from the horrible tension she is going through (*RCM* 1.259.3–4 and *RCM* 260 *dohā*–261.2; the latter are quoted in *TVR*). Tulsī's bhakti agenda is to highlight Rāma's compassion as the motivation for his actions, notwithstanding his total self-sufficiency as supreme God. Central to the episode is the irony that this all-powerful God has to go through the motions of proving himself. In that limited sense, the scene could be seen as a counterpart to Sītā's *agniparīkṣā* or fire ordeal. Here Rām is on trial and has to prove himself publicly worthy of Sītā, although we know all along that there is no doubt he is.[14] The main point, though, is that Rāma acts for the sake of his devotees.

Sītā may prompt Rāma into action, but it would be a mistake to interpret that as a move to turn Sītā into Śakti, the female empowering principle. True, Sītā is called "Mother of the World" at several occasions, yet it is not Sītā's power that empowers Rāma but rather her powerlessness. The thoughts that flash through Rāma's head just before he lifts the bow are not flattering; there is even a comparison with a corpse: "When a thirsting man, for want of water, has left his body, what use is a lake of nectar for his corpse? What's rain when all crops have dried up? Why let the moment pass and be sorry afterward?" (*tṛṣita bāri binu jo tanu tyāgā, mueṁ karai kā sudhā taṛāgā; kā baraṣā saba kṛṣī sukhāneṁ, samaya cukeṁ puni kā pachitāneṁ; RCM* 1.261.1b–2a). Although these lines have strong dramatic force, they may seem a bit matter-of-fact for romantic love. Still, Sāgar singles out these verses for quotation in his *TVR* (8.100), but he does something interesting with them. He succeeds in making the reference of these lines less pointedly to Sītā, by focusing the camera alternately on her, her father, and her mother. In this way, Sāgar manages to suggest that Rāma acted out of grace for the whole Mithilā family, without ever changing an *akṣara* in Tulsī's work.

In his editorial comment, Sāgar voices an emphasis that is in fact opposite to Tulsī's version. Tulsī wanted to highlight Rāma's compassion, and consequently he stressed that Rāma's action was inspired by Sītā's despair. Sāgar, in his editorial comment, stresses that Rāma acts only on his guru's command, although he knew very well about Sītā's state of mind (*hālāṁki Sītājī kī adhīratā aur vivaltā ko acchī tarah se dekh rahe haiṁ, aur samajh rahe haiṁ*; not in the Mizokami transcription). Sāgar clearly is not so interested in Rāma's compassion as in his obedience to elders.

Once the bow is broken, Tulsī describes the reactions of all present, and Sāgar's camera registers the joy on all the faces, though without quoting *RCM* this time. Tulsī then lovingly describes how Sītā honors Rāma with the *jayamāla* or "garland of victory"—an element, we remember, that was totally absent from *VR*. Obviously, this moment lends itself well to a tableau-like scene (*jhāṇkī*), of which the *TVR* director makes full use. The camera moves from Sītā to Rāma and back again. We behold them beholding: *darśana* all around. Surprisingly, Sāgar does not orchestrate the scene with any of Tulsī's lovely phrases, such as "Outwardly hesitant, but inwardly ecstatic, no one can see such deep love" (*tana sakocu mana parama uchāhū, gūṛha premu lakhi parai na kāhū; RCM* 1.264.2a). Instead, he inserts a "women's song": "Put on the Victory Garland" (*pahanāo jayamālā, TVR* 8.101), probably following Tulsī's suggestion, "The clever girls instructed her, seeing [her being lost]: put on the beautiful Victory Garland" (*catura sakhīṁ lakhi kahā bujhāī, pahirāvahu jayamāla suhāī; RCM* 1.264.3a).

The instances where Sāgar chooses to deviate from Tulsī's lead are few, but usually significant. Here is an important one. Tulsī's Sītā does not touch Rāma's feet, even when reminded to do so by her girlfriends (*RCM* 1.265.4b). The reason for this, Tulsī says, is that Sītā knows what happened to Ahalyā when she came in contact with Rāma's feet and shrinks in fear from such powerful feet. Tulsī adds that Rāma understood and just smiled at Sītā's extraordinary love (*gautama tiya gati surati kari, nahiṁ parasati paga pāni, mana bihase raghubaṁsamani, prīti alaukika jāni; RCM* 1.265 *dohā*). Sāgar's Sītā, however, does not suffer from such subtle qualms. She can't help but touch her husband-to-be's feet. During the episode, Sāgar instead concentrates on showing Sītā's feet, and stresses how shyly and reluctantly they move (as noted by Dalmia-Lüderitz 1991, 218–219). The breach of decorum of Tulsī's Sītā did not find favor with Sāgar. Sāgar keeps his Sītā neatly within the boundaries of traditional *maryādā*.

Finally, let us return to *VR*'s second version of the *svayaṁvara* story. In her summary line of her story to Anasūyā, *VR*'s Sītā sums up: "Thus I was given away to Rāma there at the self-choice ritual" (*evaṁ dattāsmi Rāmāya tathā tasmin svayaṁvare; VR* 2.118.54a) and, she adds, "I am devoted to the best of the brave, my husband by dharma (*anuraktāsmi dharmeṇa patiṁ vīryavatāṁ varam; VR* 2.118.54b). This may seem to be a contradiction to a modern audience. Contemporary discussions tend to pit "love marriages" against "arranged marriages," yet, Sītā has the magical combination: a self-choice ritual in which her father sets the terms and gives her away, and a lawful husband to whom she is genuinely devoted. Interestingly, Vālmīki's Sītā has provided here a neat summary of what Sāgar's series promotes. It was all already in Vālmīki, after all.

Wedding Ceremonies: Preliminary Rituals

Initiating the Negotiations: Message to Ayodhyā

The wedding ceremonies in all three versions start with the message to Ayodhyā. This subepisode could be said to correspond with an ordinary wedding's phase of the "suing," or *varapreṣaṇa* in the classical jargon, although that usually means the suing by the groom's party for the bride (Kane 1974, 531–532). In contrast, here we have the party of the bride bringing the proposal to the groom's family.

In *VR,* the king, Janaka, takes the initiative to send a message to Daśaratha, but he makes sure to procure the blessing of Viśvāmitra (*VR* 67.24–25). This does not totally square with *VR*'s second description of the *svayaṁvara,* at the end of the *Ayodhyākāṇḍa*. Here Sītā says that Janaka was ready to give her away to Rāma on the spot, and had even a vessel of water (*jalabhājana*) handy for the ritual transaction, but that Rāma insisted on first securing the permission of his father (*VR* 2.118.50–51). This alternative reading, highlighting the respect of Rāma for his father, is not taken up by either *RCM* or *TVR,* at least not at this point. In *RCM* and *TVR,* neither Rāma nor Janaka takes the initiative. Instead, Janaka asks Viśvāmitra what to do next, and it is the sage who suggests sending messengers to Daśaratha (*RCM* 1.286.3–287.1; *TVR* 8.108). Still, Sāgar takes up Rāma's insistence that he ensure his father's permission a bit later in the story, at the beginning of the wedding negotiations between Janaka and Daśaratha. When Śatānanda formally proclaims the wedding proposal, he states that Rāma did not wish to marry without having secured his father's permission (*pitā kī ājñā milne par hī sītā kā pāṇi-grahaṇ karūṁgā; TVR* 9.120). The incident obviously fits well with Sāgar's agenda: his general stress on obedience for elders, and his insistence on making love marriages conditional upon parental approval.

The reception of the message in Ayodhyā is related in a straightforward way in *VR* (1.68; the chapter is only 19 *ślokas* long). Tulsī "devotionalizes" the passage by turning the message into a hymn of praise to Rāma (*RCM* 1.291 *dohā*–293.3). He also adds an interesting incident. When Daśaratha seeks to reward the messengers bringing the good news, they refuse, on the basis that accepting a gift is "improper" or *anīti* (*RCM* 1.293.4b). Everyone approves of the messengers' sense of propriety. Sāgar duly follows Tulsī's example, but makes it more explicit that the gift is inappropriate because the messenger cannot accept anything from his "daughter's" *sasurāl* (*TVR* 9.114).

In *VR*, Daśaratha is pleased with the message, but turns immediately to his counselors, so we get no hint of his personal feelings for his sons. By contrast, in Tulsī's version, Daśaratha's feelings are highlighted. In keeping with the mood of parental emotion or *vātsalya bhāva*, he gets tears in his eyes and can't utter a word when he first receives the message (*RCM* 1.290.2–3a). Later, he inquires in a fatherly way about the well-being of his sons (*RCM* 1.291.2–4). This prompts the messengers to confirm the king in his paternal pride about his two sons (*RCM* 1.291 *dohā*). The two brothers, Bharata and Śatrughna, also have a chance to demonstrate their brotherly love for Rāma (*RCM* 1.290.4–291.1). In *TVR*, Bharata and Śatrughna are also pleased with the news, and Daśaratha sends a touching message back for his sons, at which point the messenger comments that Daśaratha has the nerve to call these heroes his "kids" (*bāl*) whereas the whole world is in awe of them. Here the irony of the incarnation has resurfaced again.

What is radically different in the TV version is the setting in which the message is received. In *VR* and *RCM*, the scene is in public court and all the counsellors are present, whereas in *TVR*, it is in the king's private quarters, in an intimate family setting.[15] One may see a precedent in *RCM*, where Daśaratha reports to his queens (*RCM* 1.295.1–3), but that scene occurs only after the message has first been received and answered in court.

In *TVR*, the news is first broken to Daśaratha while he is relaxing in the company of Kaikeyī. There are no official messengers, but instead the two brothers Bharata and Śatrughna report the news (*TVR* 9.109). They tell the story of their brother's feat with much stress on Rāma's *vīrya* or bravery and a fair dose of good-humored family banter (*TVR* 9.109–111). Early in the story Kauśalyā comes in too, but Sāgar has taken good care to suppress any hint of rivarly between co-wives. One could say he hypercorrects with a display of female solidarity: both women rave over becoming mother-in-law (*sās*) and in the not too distant future grandma (*dādī*) (*TVR* 9.111–112). Poor Daśaratha hardly gets the chance to revel in his future grandfatherhood, as Kaikeyī informs him she will be much too busy to pay any attention to him (*TVR* 9.112). In their joy and rosy dreams, as Kauśalyā puts it, they nearly forget about the official messenger. Sāgar has succeeded in transforming the rather official episode into one of private family affairs.

In all versions, of course, Janaka's proposal is happily accepted. In *VR*, the king suggests immediately that the proposal should be accepted, if his counselors (that is, Vasiṣṭha, Vāmadeva, and the other ministers) approve of the appropriateness of the match (*VR* 1.68.14). Tulsī's Daśaratha humbly seeks his guru Vasiṣṭha's advice, but there is hardly any doubt about the verdict. Vasiṣṭha elegantly says that the king naturally deserves the good luck that he gets, given his extensive service to guru, brahmans, cows, and gods (*RCM* 1.294). Sāgar too is careful to have Daśaratha properly consult Vasiṣṭha first (*gurudev apnā nirṇay pradān kareṁ. Usī ke anusār kārya kiyā jāe; TVR* 9.113). Sāgar's Vasiṣṭha immediately uses the situation to put a megapolitical spin to the matter, describing the match as an appropriate alliance between two major Aryan political forces (*Mithilā aur Ayodhyā kā yah sambandha baṛā hī śubh hai. Is sambandh ke dvārā āryāvart kī do mahān śaktiyoṁ kā milan hogā; TVR* 9.113). Finally, preparations are made for the *barāt,* or what is classically termed the *vadhū-gṛhagamana* or procession to the bride's house (Kane 1974, 532).

In *VR* we are never informed about the reaction of the queens of Ayodhyā, but Tulsī describes their joy at the news and how they immediately proceed to do charity for brahmans (*RCM* 1.295.4)—a typical combination of bhakti and caste dharma. Sāgar duly includes an episode where Kauśalyā reports on her gift giving. What is new is that she gives a rationale for her actions by saying that a king cannot celebrate any private festival if even one of the subjects in his kingdom is in pain (*jis rājā ke rāj meṁ prajā kā ek bhī prāṇī dukhī rah jāe, unheṁ apnā koī utsav manāne kā adhikār nahīṁ hotā; TVR* 9.115). Another innovation of Sāgar's here is that Kauśalyā sends a message to Sunayanā, Sītā's mother. She gives her assurance that Sītā will be treated like a daughter (*beṭī*) rather than a daughter-in-law (*bahū*), and will be taken under Kauśalyā's wings (*Kauśalyā kī mamatā ke āṁcal meṁ saṁtān ke samān hī sthān pāegī; TVR* 9.). Kauśalyā's message sets the tone for the wedding scenes proper, where sympathy of the groom's party (*varapakṣa*) with the plight of the bride's party (*kanyāpakṣa*) is a major concern.

The Barāt's Arrival in Mithilā: Exemplary In-Laws

Throughout the whole of the following episode the groom's party (*varapakṣa*) is painstakingly concerned with treating the bride's party (*kanyāpakṣa*) as not inferior and with sympathizing with their plight. This preoccupation implies two things: on the one hand that this is exceptional and opposite to what normally would be the case, and on the other that the bride's party has something to worry about. Interestingly, one can trace this aspect all the way back to *VR*.

There is nothing explicit about the bride's family's worries in the version of the wedding as related in *VR*'s *Bālakaṇḍa.* Still, we find out about Janaka's worries when Sītā tells her story to Anasūyā in the *Ayodhyākāṇḍa.* One of the most striking aspects of her story is that Sītā lovingly portrays Janaka's worries when she comes of age, and sympathizes with his fears of losing prestige in having to look for a groom. Apparently it was already then a well-known truth that "In the world, the father of a girl experiences ill-treatment from equals and inferiors, be he similar to Śakra on earth" (*sadṛśāccāpakṛṣṭācca loke kanyāpiā janāt, pradharṣaṇam avāpnoti śakreṇāpi samo bhuvi; VR* 2.118.35).

Through this little "lapse" of Sītā in the *Ayodhyākāṇḍa,* the story as related in *Bālakāṇḍa* takes on a new meaning. Sītā's lapse can be interpreted as setting up a *pūrvapakṣa* or problem, namely, the inequality of bride-givers and bride-takers. The stress on Daśaratha's generosity in treating Janaka as an equal in *Bālakāṇḍa* can be read as a solution to this implicit problem. This is apparent in the exchange between Janaka and Daśaratha upon first meeting one another when the *barāt* arrives in Mithilā. The episode corresponds to the traditional *madhuparka* or lavish reception of the bridegroom's party at the bride's house (Kane 1974, 532). As behooves the father of a bride, Janaka goes out of his way to welcome Daśaratha respectfully in his hometown. What is surprising is that Daśaratha reciprocates in kind. He humbly answers with a proverb "The receiver [16] is in the power of the granter" (*pratigraho dātṛvaśaḥ; VR* 1.69.14), specifying, "We shall do as you will say, O wise man" (*yathā vakṣyasi dharmajña tat kariṣyāmahe; VR* 1.69.15). Though the proverb is a formula of politeness, meaning that one does not refuse a gift (Goldman 1984, 387), still the answer is considered surprisingly humble for the father of the groom. *VR* itself refers to this answer as surprising (*vismayam; VR* 1.69.1).

The proverb, interestingly, is one of the few literal quotes from *VR* that Sāgar introduces in his version (*TVR* 9.116). The quotation occurs in a longer passage of niceties interchanged by the two rulers on their first meeting. Janaka welcomes Daśaratha humbly, and expresses his joy at this match with the prestigious Raghukula. Daśaratha says that he is tied by the strings of love (*prem kī ḍor meṁ baṁdhe*). Vasiṣṭha specifies that the match and alliance between Mithilā and Ayodhyā is all God's wish (*parameśvar kī icchā*). When he calls this connection one of equals (*barābar ke saṁbaṁdhī*), Janaka feels compelled to protest that he, as father of the bride, is the subordinate (*dās*) of Daśaratha. Daśaratha then turns the tables and insists that he is like a beggar who has come to Janaka's door to ask for alms (*ek yācak, ek bhikhārī—jo āpke dvār par āpkī kanyā kā dān māṁgne āyā hai*). He quotes the Sanskrit proverb from *VR* (*pratigraho dātṛvaśa*) to prove the point that it is the giver who is in charge, and he humbly offers to carry out Janaka's wishes (*āp jo ājñā kareṁge, vah hameṁ śirodhārya hogī*).[17]

The solemn tone of these declarations is strikingly different from Tulsī's version, where spontaneous joy is the order of the day. Tulsī takes delight in describing the richness of the welcoming party (*agavāna*) and the delicacies and presents it brings to the *barāt* (*RCM* 1.304 *dohā*–305.3 and 306.2–3). A nice detail is that Sītā herself calls attention to her power by sending the *siddhis* (spirits who bring success) to welcome the guests (*RCM* 1.306.4–*dohā*). When the two parties catch a glance of one another, they cannot contain themselves any more and run into each other's arms (*RCM* 1.305.4–*dohā*).[18] All this abundance of emotions fits well with Tulsī's bhakti agenda, but creates a strikingly different atmosphere from the exalted seriousness of Sāgar and *VR*.

Still, Tulsī too is preoccupied with the exceptional situation where the inlaws (*samadhī*) are treating each other as equals. He expresses this most clearly of all three versions. When Janaka and Daśaratha first meet at their children's wedding altar (*maṇḍapa*), Tulsī has the gods comment that "Since the creation of the world, we have seen many weddings; but such preparations and attendance, equal in all ways, such balance of in-law parties, we've seen only today" (*jagu biraṁci upajāvā jaba teṁ, dekhe sune byāha bahu taba teṁ; sakala bhāṁti sama sāju samājū, sama samadhī dekhe hama ājū; RCM* 1.320.3). It appears that even the gods are surprised when the girl's party is treated on equal terms.

Finally, let us return to the TV series, where this anomaly is set up as an example. Sāgar expresses his own comment in the same "editorial appearance" at the end of the ninth episode I have already referred to above. He quotes the full *śloka* from Vālmīki where Daśaratha expresses his eagerness to carry out Janaka's command. Sāgar singles out Daśaratha's not insisting upon the prerogatives of the *vara-pakṣa* as exemplary for today's society, and reflects on how, if that behavior found imitators nowadays, many tensions would disappear from Indian society, how an environment of love would come about, and the *Rāmāyaṇa* story would come true (*Rāmāyaṇ kī kathā sārthik ho jātī*). Interestingly, the tense he uses is the "irrealis" or counterfactual, implying impossibility of the condition being fulfilled.

Family Reunion: Authority of the Elder Male

The next scene in the story is the reunion of the father Daśaratha and his sons Rāma and Lakṣmaṇa. This is dealt with in *VR* in just two *ślokas*. Vālmīki says that the two brothers touched their father's feet after having duly let the sage Viśvāmitra proceed (*viśvāmitraṁ puraskṛtya; VR* 1.69.18). Tulsī adds a little dramatic action: he has the two brothers hesitate to express their eagerness to see their father. Viśvāmitra, however, is pleased with their humbleness and takes them to see Daśaratha (*RCM* 1.307.2–4). Agency is transferred to the sage. The king then first does a full prostration (*ḍaṁḍavata*) for the holy man, and embraces his sons only after the sage gives his blessing (*RCM* 1.308.1). It wouldn't be Tulsī's work, however, if all this decorum were not balanced by ecstasy of emotion. True to form, he adds a comparison of the king's joy with a dead man coming to life again (*mṛtaka sarīra prāna janu bheṁṭe; RCM* 1.308.2b).

Sāgar clearly liked Tulsī's version, but goes a step further by splitting up the characters of Rāma and Lakṣmaṇa in a "good cop, bad cop" routine. The latter, in his youthful enthusiasm, is all set to go and meet with his father, but Rāma points out that they should not act on their own account and suggests that they wait until their guru brings up the matter himself, on grounds that they are dependent on Viśvāmitra's command (*Guru Viśvāmitra kī ājñā ke adhīn haiṁ; TVR* 9.117). Viśvāmitra then praises Rāma's savoir faire (*śiṣṭācār*) and takes them to see their father. The reunion is perfect for a *jhāṇkī*, and Sāgar exploits this fully. In the background, the verses from *RCM* about Daśaratha's prostration to the guru and embrace of his sons are quoted, while the characters enact Tulsī's lines. This stress on deference for elder males is reinforced by the next scene, an innovation in Sāgar's *TVR*. We have an intimate scene of father and son "getting caught up," while Rāma is massaging his father's feet (*TVR* 9.118–119). The docile subservience of the son is underlined by the conversation. When Daśaratha compliments him on his exemplary behavior, Rāma protests that it was really his father who was the source of inspiration (*preraṇā-srota*) of all he has done. He also says his father's example provided him guidance (*mārga-darśana*) even when he was far away. Daśaratha insists that Rāma's behavior is superior to his own in that Rāma did not act for self-glorification. Rāma smilingly comments that each father lovingly sings the praise of his own son. He attributes all his own actions to the duty (*kartavya*) of carrying out his father's wishes, even the unspoken ones. Daśaratha then pseudo-teasingly asks him to whose inspiration the lifting of the bow is to be attributed. At this point some romantic music is heard, suggesting the obvious answer, namely Sītā's inspiration. This undermines to some extent the total obedience of Rāma. However, this is just one little "rupture" in the otherwise perfectly tied-up text of Sāgar. Rāma's father then dismisses his son lovingly, without uttering any word of disapproval and thus implicitly approving of the romantic liaison.

The Nuptial Rituals

The Nature of Wedlock: Private and Public Perspectives

Sāgar's next scene is again an innovation (*TVR* 9.119–120). We catch Lakṣmaṇa in the middle of a passionate report to Bharata and Śatrughna about Rāma's state of mind after the first meeting with Sītā. Rāma arrives unexpectedly, and Lakṣmaṇa sheepishly admits what he was talking about (*bhābhī ke pahle darśan kaise hue*). Śatrughna then teasingly asks Rāma where he got this love-education (*prem kī śikṣā*), given that gurus don't teach *prem-śāstra*. Rāma's answer is dead serious. He lectures about "primordial love" (*pahle se hī nirdhārit*), saying that cannot be forced by man (*jo manuṣya ke banāne se nahīṁ bantā*). Rāma insists that his love for Sītā came about in the same way that nature (*prakṛti*) teaches mothers to love childeren, brothers to love brothers, and the waves of the ocean to be attracted by the moon. Love for a spouse is preordained by God (*vidhātā*). So when man meets his mate, all he has to do is to put full trust and love in her, so that afterward his attention will not even turn elsewhere (*manuṣya ko cāhie ki jab usse bheṁṭ ho to apnā sampūrṇa viśvās, sampūrṇa prem use sauṁp de jis se uske paścāt jīvan meṁ kisī dūsrī or dhyān hī na jāe*).

In this scene, Sāgar is again working hard to come to terms with the "problem" raised by the flower garden scene. He is addressing a possible objection (*pūrvapakṣa*) that the marriage of Rāma and Sītā is really a love marriage that just happens to be sanctioned by the elders. By giving Rāma's private perspective, Sāgar manages to stress that the match was "made in heaven," that it was not a matter of the girl or the boy's initiative, and that the wedding is arranged, even preordained after all.

The same concern is highlighted from a public angle in the next scene, showing a full court meeting of Janaka and Daśaratha with their counselors (*TVR* 9.120–121). Vasiṣṭha gets the floor for a longish lecture on the meaning of marriage. He starts out by saying that a wedding is not a personal affair but a social sacrament (*vivāh vyaktigat kārya nahīṁ hai, yah ek sāmājik saṁskār hai*). It is not just a matter of a man and a woman tying the knot, but together with them are joined their societies, their families, and their religions (*keval ek strī aur ek puruṣ ke gaṭh-baṁdhan ko hī vivāh nahīṁ kah sakte kyoṁki un donoṁ vyaktiyoṁ ke sāth unkā samāj unkā kul, unkā dharm juṛā hotā hai*). One could say that, according to Vasiṣṭha, rather than a meeting of hearts it is a meeting of families (*do kuloṁ kā saṁgam*).

Clearly, Sāgar has worked hard to transmit his message to the younger generation. This is no love marriage, but, as Janaka's guru, Śatānanda, had put it, a "gift of a bride" according to custom and religion (*vidhipūrvak aur dharmpūrvak kanyādān*). In case anyone would miss this point, Sāgar, in his "editorial appearance," elaborates the point that a wedding is not a personal affair but societal and familial. As indicated above, he connects this issue with the romantic flower garden (*phūlvārī*) episode in the same speech.

Prepatory Arrangements: Settling of Parties and Date, and Material Preparations

The public meeting that takes place to determine the specifics could be said to correspond to the classical "settling the marriage" known as *vāgdāna* or *vāṇiniścaya* (Kane 1974, 532). First to be determined are the parties that will be wedded. Up till now that seemed to be only Rāma and Sītā. In *VR*, it seems to be understood that Lakṣmaṇa is to marry Janaka's other daughter, Ūrmilā, because Janaka does preparatory rituals for both his daughters (*VR* 1.69.19). However, it is not till the public meeting in Mithilā that Vasiṣṭha sues for both Janaka's daughters (*VR* 1.70.45), and Viśvāmitra then proposes a fourfold wedding, in which Bharata and Śatrughna are also to marry the daughters of Kuśadhvaja (*VR* 1.72.1–8). Sāgar follows Vālmīki (*TVR* 9.121–122), though he does not forget to let his camera roam to the women's quarter to register surprise and happiness at the expansion of the matches. Kuśadhvaja and Lakṣmaṇa are shown to be happy with the proposals in a dignified way. The reasons given for the fourfold wedding are slightly different in *TVR*: Vālmīki's Viśvāmitra seeks to strengthen the alliance between the two houses, whereas Sāgar's Viśvāmitra judges that it is not proper that two of the four brothers should remain bachelors.[19] Sāgar not only registers the joy of Sunayanā and Kuśadhvaja's wife when they hear the news up in the balcony, but also adds a scene where the girls themselves are informed about the news. There is much joy upon hearing that the four "sisters" will go to the same *sasurāl*. Interestingly, in Tulsī's version, the suggestion of the fourfold wedding comes first from the women of Mithilā, when they behold the arrival of the *barāt* (*RCM* 1.311 *chand*). One could say that in *RCM* the wedding parties are expanded on popular demand. It is significant that Tulsī gives so much airtime to the people of Mithilā, and stresses their comments approving of the match (*RCM* 1.309.4–311).

Next, the date of the wedding is fixed. Sītā and Rāma's wedding is to take place at an auspicious moment, of course, as determined by astrologers. Vālmīki has it fixed for the second day (*uttara*) of the two *phalgunīs* (a particular astrological alignment) in which Prajāpati Bhaga presides (*VR* 1.72.13, also *VR* 1.71.24; in both cases it is Janaka who suggests this date). The *phalgunīs* seem to have been recognized as auspicious dates from a very early point, even in the Vedic tradition (Kane 1974, 512). In Tulsī's version, the auspicious moment (*lagna*) is in the winter month of *Agahan*. He is not more specific, but assures us that the precise astrological conjunction (*nakṣatra*) is super-auspicious in all respects. Eager to establish the credentials of his deviating date, he claims that the creator himself had researched it, and sent it to Janaka via Nārada. As it turned out, Janaka's astrologers had calculated the very same day (*maṁgala mūla lagana dinu āvā, hima ritu agahanu māsu suhāvā; graha tithi nakhatu jogu bara bārū, lagana sodhi bidhi kīnha bicārū; paṭhai dīnhi nārada sana soī, ganī janaka ke ganakanha joī; RCM* 1.312.3–4a). Sāgar apparently did not buy this, and chose to follow *VR*. In *TVR*, Śatānanda suggests *uttarā phālgunī* (the second day of the conjunction) as the *nakṣatra,* thus sticking with a spring wedding around Holī (*TVR* 9.122).

As regards the material preparations for the wedding, Tulsī's version is replete with loving descriptions, whereas there is much less of the kind in Vālmīki's text. *VR* has a short description of the preparation of the wedding altar or *vedi* (*VR* 1.73.20–24, a passage that is not retained in the critical edition), which is brimming with Vedic sacrificial references. Tulsī, on the other hand, has an elaborate description of the *maṇḍapa*'s beauty, which has little to do with sacrificial sites (*RCM* 1.287.2–89 and 320 *chand*), though it is one of the classical steps in a wedding, called *maṇḍapakaraṇa* (Kane 1974, 532). Interestingly, Sāgar first shows the *maṇḍapa* while the priests are busy purifying the site, engaged in sacrificial prepatory activities, and reciting Sanskrit mantras from the *Yajurveda* (*TVR* 10.130). Sāgar thus hearkens back to Vālmīki's Vedic sacrificial stress. With regard to the *barāt,* Vālmīki again uses only a few *ślokas* on the topic (*VR* 1.69.1–6), which are hardly worth mentioning compared to Tulsī's wealth of physical details about horses, chariots, and even amphibi-cars that can traverse water and land (*RCM* 1.298–302).[20] Interestingly, Sāgar does not portray the *barāt* with horses and chariots, but shows the grooms and their party only when they arrive in the palace halls on foot. Limitations on the budget may have played a role here. Still, in general, *TVR* has recourse to its extra visual dimension. Without having to quote Tulsī, Sāgar has provided a lavish, though by Bollywood standards low-budget, set for the wedding scenes.

Tradition, Great and Little

The ceremonies preceding the wedding day in *VR* focus on the recitation of the lineages of the parties to be married by Vasiṣṭha and Janaka. The better part of two chapters (*VR* 1.70.19–45 and 71.1–15) are devoted to the topic. Janaka adds to his family history a "disclosure" about the particular geopolitical situation of his kingdom (*VR* 1.71.16–19). It sounds like an oral legal contract, a model document for kings who wish to intermarry their offspring.

Sāgar too accommodates some recitation of the ancient genealogy of the Raghukula in his version. It fits in well after Vasiṣṭha's sermon on marriage as in essence a union of two families. Naturally, then, the family tree of Rāma is relevant. This stands in contrast to Tulsī, who cuts out such dry parts to make room for more bhakti moments. Tulsī prefers to focus on different auspicious moments of high emotional content, which he underlines by switching to a different meter (*chand*). Much later, in the midst of the actual nuptial rituals, Tulsī simply remarks in passing that the gurus recite the lineages (*sākhocāru dou kulagura karaiṁ; RCM* 1.324 *chand* 3.a).

Vālmīki also highlights among the activities prior to the wedding certain traditional ceremonies that have a Vedic ring, in particular Daśaratha's sons' ceremony of "the gift of cows" (*godāna*) and the rite to the ancestors (*pitṛkārya*), which are (in the Gītā Press translation) interpreted as the Vedic rites *samāvartana*, the ceremony ending study with guru, and *nāndīśrāddha*, a rite for deceased ancestors preceding wedding (*VR* 1.71.23; see also Kane 1974, 405–411 and 532). The cows are described in much detail (*VR* 1.72.21–24).[21] Tulsī also describes Daśaratha's big *godāna*, presided over by Vasiṣṭha, but this takes place only after the wedding proper is over and is combined with other gift giving to beggars (*RCM* 1.330.4–331). Sāgar follows his sources to some extent. Here too, Daśaratha is urged at the end of the meeting to settle the wedding details, to have a *godāna* and *nāndīmukha śrīkārya* (*TVR* 9.122). However, in Sāgar's version it is the guru, Vasiṣṭha, who commands him to do so. Sāgar had also mentioned a *godāna* as a preliminary ceremony in Ayodhyā: it is mentioned in Kauśalyā's list of preparations for the wedding referred to above (*TVR* 9.115). Sāgar does not show any *godāna*, maybe because of budget limitations or because it is not really part of popular living tradition, the cow being substituted mostly by monetary gifts and presents of sweets.

Tulsī follows *VR* in portraying the wedding as exemplary, but in addition to Vedic ceremonies we get also more folksy ones. This is, of course, a familiar aspect of the bhakti tradition, as is well exemplified by the projection of folk rites onto the Kṛṣṇa mythology (Entwistle 1987, 46). Tulsī seeks to balance the two; there is a lot of stress of everything being carried out according to both great and little tradition. "Everything was done according to Veda and popular rites": variants of these phrases return again and again (just some examples are: *kari kula rīti beda bidhi rāū*, *RCM* 1.302.1; *beda bihita aru kula ācārū, kīnha bhalī bidhi saba byavahārū*, *RCM* 1.319.1b; *kari baidika laukika saba rītiṁ*, 1.320.1a). Tulsī lovingly describes the rituals conducted by women, such as the *pūjā* of the groom (*parachani*) (*RCM* 1.318–319.2), singing of *maṅgala gīta* at the *maṇḍapa* (*RCM* 1.323.4), and so on[22] Often he mentions both in one breath, such as "Auspiciously married women sing their songs, holy brahmans recite the Vedas" (*subhaga suāsini gāvahiṁ gītā, karahiṁ beda dhuni bipra punītā; RCM* 1.313.2b).

We find the same concern with balancing Vedic and family rites in Sāgar, who features a combination of Sanskrit recitation (from Vedic texts, as well as *Durgāśaptaśati* and so on)[23] and women's songs (*maṅgala gīta*), together with, visually, close-ups of sacrificial activity by brahmans as well as of women's rites. At the beginning of the wedding rites proper, for instance, Sāgar shows the brahmans busying themselves with preparing the site while reciting Sanskrit (*TVR* 10.130), and in the next shot we see Sītā and the other brides being adorned (*śṛṅgār*) and having their hands decorated (*mehndī*) by their girlfriends. The latter part may also be interpreted as following the traditional steps of the classical marriage, as it corresponds to *paridhāpana* and *samañjana* (the dressing and anointing of the bride; see Kane 1974, 532–533).

It needs to be pointed out that whenever women's songs are sung, these follow the traditional performance pattern of having a line sung by one singer and then repeated by the chorus. The songs differ from real-life wedding songs, however, in that they are neatly sanitized. Tulsī had still made references to the practice of singing insulting songs (*gārī*) by the bride's party's women during the *jevanār* or feast for the *barāt* (*RCM* 1.329.1a). He even specified that these were "personalized" (*jevata dehiṁ madhura dhuni gārī, lai lai nāma puruṣa aru nārī*; *RCM* 1.329.3b). The same practice is depicted, and relished by the audience, at the Rāmnagar Rāmlīlā (Kapur 1990, 72). Similarly, when describing the happiness in Ayodhyā upon the return of the *barāt,* Tulsīdās mentions that the women of the city sing auspicious *gārī* (*RCM* 1.358.1b). Sāgar, however, does not feature any such songs. He may be catering to the sensitivities of "reformed" Hindu tastes. A more explicit rejection of the practice can be found in the so-called *Rādheśyām Rāmāyaṇa* (*RR* 1.4.19–20). As we shall see, Sāgar's portrayal of the rites conducted by women to break the ice between bride and groom also seem sanitized.

Another striking general feature of the wedding rite is the prominent role that the gurus play. We have already noted that in both *RCM* and *TVR* the gurus have taken over much of the agency of the kings in the initial negotiations, and we will see that this trend continues during the ceremonies proper. At every step, they take the initiative, and the kings merely carry out their commands. The kings show great respect to their gurus. We saw that Daśaratha greeted Viśvāmitra respectfully before he embraced his sons. At every turn of the action there is room for a guru *pūjā*. Janaka, for instance, thus honors Vasiṣṭha and Viśvāmitra and all *ṛṣis* starting with Vāmadeva when they arrive at the wedding *maṇḍapa* (*RCM* 1.320 *dohā*). Daśaratha extends the greatest honor to the gurus in his own house after the return of the *barāt* (*RCM* 1.352).

Sanction from gurus seems not to be enough for Tulsī, who introduces divine sanction for the wedding. In contrast to Vālmīki, who is much more restrained,[24] Tulsī intersperses the events at regular intervals with vistas of the gods in heaven raining down flowers. The density grows during the actual wedding rites. The gods are described to shower flowers, for example, on Sītā's arrival (*RCM* 1.323.3a), on Sītā's mother's arrival (*RCM* 1.324.4a), when Rāma's feet are washed (*RCM* 1.324 *chand* 1b), on the ceremony of *bhāṁvarī* (*RCM* 1.324 *dohā*), and when the *barāt* leaves the altar (*RCM* 1.326 *chand* 4)

In Tulsī's version, the gods' wives actually participate in the wedding ceremonies disguised as happily married mortal women (*RCM* 1.318.3a–*chand*), who are called to sing for Sītā on her wedding day (*RCM* 1.322.3–4). The gods follow their wives and join the *barāt* disguised as brahmans (*RCM* 1.321.3b–4). Neither is recognized in the general joy, except by Rāma, who honors the gods with a seat in his heart (*sura lakhe rāma sujāna pūje mānasika āsana dae; RCM* 1.321 *chand* c). Sāgar follows Tulsī's lead, but he has Śiva and Brahmā descend before the ladies do so. Rāma nods smilingly to the gods disguised as brahmans, while they pay their obeisance with folded hands.

In *RCM,* when Sītā arrives, the gurus have her do a pūjā of Gaurī, Gaṇapati, and the brahmans. The gods reward her by manifesting themselves to give their blessing in person (*sura pragaṭi pūjā lehiṁ dehiṁ asīsa ati sukhu pāvahīṁ, RCM* 1.323 *chand*). Tulsī continues in this vein to illustrate the perfection of the wedding ceremonies. Ravi himself, the dynastic patron, instucts the ritual agents about what do do (*RCM* 323 *chand*). At the time of the libations in the fire, the god of fire becomes manifest and the Vedas themselves take the form of brahmans to give correct ritual advice (*RCM* 1.323 *dohā*). Sāgar does not follow Tulsī here, but later on, when the newlyweds go to pay their respects to the divinity or *kuladevatā,* the accompanying song stipulates that everything was approved (*siddha*) by her (*TVR* 10.137).

Nuptial Ceremonies

In *VR* the actual nuptial ritual is dispatched rather quickly, among rhetorical flourishes and courtesies of the groom's and bride's parties. We have a quick description of Daśaratha and his sons arriving in festive attire at the sacrificial enclosure or *yājñavāṭa,* where the *kautukamaṅgala* or ceremony of tying a thread around the wrist of the grooms takes place (*VR* 1.73.7–9; for references about the ceremony, see Goldman 1984, 391). Vasiṣṭha then goes to see Janaka and announces very humbly and politely that the groom's party is ready, again using a variant of the previously mentioned politeness formula that stresses the equivalence of donor and receiver (*dātṛpratigrahītṛbhyāṁ sarvārthā sambhavanti hi*; *VR* 1.73.12a). Janaka answers with much courtesy that his kingdom is theirs, so they can command when to start. His daughters too have undergone the *kautukamaṅgala* and are ready, standing near the altar as shining flames of fire (*dīptā vahnerivārcia*; *VR* 1.73.15b).

In Tulsī's version, by contrast, when the auspicious moment (late afternoon or *dhenudhūri*) has arrived, it is the bride's party that takes the initiative. More precisely, the brahmans exhort Janaka to fetch the *barāt* from its quarters (*janavāsa*). Before leaving, Daśaratha consults with his guru (*RCM* 1.313). More than Vālmīki, Tulsī keeps the girl's party in the humble position here, although, as described above, he goes out of his way to describe the amazing equality of both parties later, when they have arrived at the *maṇḍapa* (*RCM* 1.320). Sāgar does not follow either version here. At the beginning of the wedding proper, the groom's party is shown to arrive and enter the palace; it is not clear on whose initiative this occurs. Whereas in *VR* the brides are already present when the grooms arrive, in *RCM* they are summoned (again on the gurus' initiative: Vasiṣṭha asks Śatānanda to do so, and Sītā's mother gets the hint) after all the others are seated (*RCM* 1.322). Here, Sāgar follows *RCM* quite closely (*TVR* 10.132).

A more important contrast is that although Vālmīki devotes only a few descriptive *ślokas* to the matter, Tulsī and Sāgar have turned the event into an occasion of mega-*darśana.* Tulsī takes his audience along to the wedding in the company of none other than the gods themselves, providing a doubly divine *darśana:* of God through the eyes of the gods. Tulsī gives a full report on the reaction of the gods upon beholding the wedding (*RCM* 1.313 *dohā*–317.4). Interestingly, they are portrayed as country bumpkins arriving in the big city from their own regions or *lokas.* Brahmā himself does not recognize his creation (*RCM* 1.314.4b). Śiva is described as something of a rural tour guide, who exhorts his ox to move on, after he has explained to his bewildered "co-villagers" that this society wedding is a major cosmic event (*RCM* 1.314 *dohā*–315.2a).[25] In tune with the bhakti agenda, Śiva's speech is really a hymn glorifying Rāma.

Sāgar's gods, too, to some extent fit the second-rate participant status that Tulsī's gods have. This is clear from their speech, which is remarkably different from the *atiśuddha* Hindī the noble human characters speak. When the gods perceive that preparations for the wedding are taking place, Brahmā mentions what is going on, and Śiva says rather rustically "I've been keen on seeing it since ages. So, goddess, let's go?" (*ham to kab se utāvale ho rahe haiṁ, kyoṁ devī, caleṁ?* not transcribed in *TVR*). The contrast is all the more remarkable because this scene is preceded by the lofty Sanskrit recitation of the *Yajurveda* by Janaka's brahmans.

In Tulsī's version, when the gods arrive at the scene they are thrilled at having a *darśana* of Daśaratha and his party, moved with love when they see the young couples, and they get tears in their eyes when beholding Rāma as groom (*RCM* 1.315.2b–*dohā*). There follows a full description of Rāma mounted on his horse, which includes a lyrical interlude (*chand, RCM* 1.316). The gods are all eyes, and Tulsī exploits this masterfully by having them be thankful for their multiple eyes that afford them a better *darśana* of Rāma (*RCM* 1.317.1–3a). Even Indra praises himself lucky for Gautama's curse (*RCM* 1.317.3b), which had left him with "thousand" eyes. More than that, he becomes the envy of all others (*RCM* 1.317.4a). This is ironical since, of course, the curse was the result of his undharmic seduction of Ahalyā, who had only just before been set free from her curse by Rāma. In a way, Rāma here does the same for Indra by turning the curse into a blessing. Surprisingly, Sāgar does not even show Rāma on a horse: the groom's party is shown entering the palace on foot, presumably just after having dismounted. Sāgar again leaves out the hymns of praise to Rāma. In *VR*, after the grooms arrive, the sacrificial site is prepared under the direction of Vasiṣṭha (*VR* 1.73.20–24; this passage is not in the critical edition). The first view we have of the wedding altar in Sāgar's *TVR* is also one where brahmans are preparing the sacrificial site while reciting Sanskrit mantras. In contrast to this Vedic ritual atmosphere, Tulsī puts more stress on loving devotion. We have already mentioned the welcome ceremony (*parachani*) by the women (*RCM* 1.318–319.1), which is occasion for much display of emotion. Sāgar also shows the welcome ceremony. He exploits the cinematic possibilities by showing close-ups of the women with tears in their eyes, and the grooms in their serious anticipation of what is to come.

However, it is not only the women who display bhakti in Tulsī's version. Loving devotion prevails also when Janaka with his own hands prepares seats for his guests on the *maṇḍapa*. He performs *pūjā* of the gurus of the groom's party (*RCM* 1.320 *chand*–321.1), and welcomes everyone humbly. In Sāgar's version, while Janaka's welcome is enacted, Sanskrit recitation is interspersed with a "vernacular" song (*lagana maṇḍapa meṁ padhāro, kuṁvar jī*; *TVR* 10.131–132). Further, the attempt to reconcile bhakti and *maryādā* is well exemplified by the two first lines of the vernacular singers: the men sing: "Follow the custom of receiving guests" (*mela milāpa kī rīti nibhāo; TVR* 10.131), which is repeated by the women, who then add: "Let the mutual love of relatives grow (*sajana paraspara prīta baṛhāo; TVR* 10.132). Sāgar thus works on keeping in Tulsī's loving aspect, while making clear that everything is carried out according to tradition.

The climax of the wedding is quickly reached and is very short and simple in VR. Sītā was already standing near the altar when Rāma arrived, and Vālmīki simply says that Janaka placed Sītā opposite Rāma and gave her away with the words: "This, my daughter Sītā, is your partner in dharma. Accept her, bless you. Take her hand in yours. She has great fortune, is devoted to her husband, and will always follow you like a shadow" (*iyaṁ sītā mama sutā sahadharmacarī tava; pratīccha caināṁ bhadraṁ te pāṇiṁ gṛhīṣva pāṇinā, pativratā mahābhāgā chāyevānugatā sadā; VR* 1.73.26b–27b). The same formula is repeated for the other couples. The grooms then take the hands of the brides, and circumambulate with them the fire, the altar, and Janaka and the sages. This is the only occasion on which Vālmīki seems eager to hold the action for a moment of intensification of emotion: the gods rain down flowers, heavenly nymphs dance, and so on (*VR* 1.73.37–39).

By contrast, Tulsī and Sāgar have a much more elaborate lead-up to the final event, turning each aspect of the ritual into a major occasion for *darśana*. In *RCM*, this is underscored by a plethora of lyrical meters (*chand*), one of which is quoted in *TVR* (10.132).[26] First we get a glimpse of Sītā's procession approaching the *maṇḍapa*, and of the rites she carries out upon arriving (*RCM* 1.322–323). Tulsī describes how Sītā and Rāma behold one another (*siya rāma avalokani parasapara premu kāhuṁ na lakhi parai*; *RCM* 1.323 *chand* 2c). This may be seen as a reference to the rite *parasparasamīkṣaṇa* (Kane 1974, 533). Significantly, Sāgar does not quote this verse, and with the exception of one glance that Sītā seems to cast on her groom-to-be upon arrival, the two do not behold one another at any point during the whole ceremony. There are, though, many close-ups, suggesting that everyone else is beholding the couple with much tender love.

After this, in *RCM*, the arrival of Sītā's mother in the *maṇḍapa* is described (*RCM* 1.324). This is not shown by Sāgar. Tulsī then lovingly describes how Sītā's parents wash the feet of the groom (*RCM* 1.324.4b *chand* 2), again using the occasion to turn this into a hymn of praise to Rāma. Sāgar also dwells lovingly and extraordinarily long on the feet-washing episode.[27] It is actually Janaka who washes the groom's feet, while Sunayanā pours the water. Again, Sāgar's *darśana* is underlined with parts from Tulsī's *chand*s. Sāgar's camera underscores Tulsī's words. While reciting that Janaka washes those lotus feet, the pollen of "which sages and yogīs served, their minds turning into bees, to attain the salvation they desired" (*kari madhupa mana muni jogijana je sei abhimata gati lahaiṁ; TVR* 10.133), the camera registers the beatifically smiling faces of the gurus of Ayodhyā.

Then comes the climax, the actual nuptial rituals. The ceremonies of "taking the hand" (*pānigahanu*), "walking around the fire" (*bhāṁvarī*), and "filling the parting of the hair" (*seṁdura*) are described in Tulsī as taking place among general rejoicing (*RCM* 1.324 *chand* 3–325.5). Sāgar shows the ceremonies, with much recitation from Tulsī, stressing again that the ceremony is all in accordance with both the Veda and local practice (*RCM* 1.324 *chand* 3d). Sāgar also singles out for recitation Tulsī's verses that make comparisons with the weddings of the goddesses Pārvatī and Śrī (*RCM* 1.324 *chand* 4a–b). Interestingly, while Sītā's hands are daubed with paste by her mother, the Sanskrit recitation is in praise of Nārāyaṇa from the *Durgāsaptaśatī* (*TVR* 10.134), as if to acknowledge Sītā's divinity.

The *pāṇigraha* ceremony is again one of the rare occasions on which Sāgar quotes directly from Vālmīki. He has his Janaka solemnly and theatrically recite the Sanskrit *ślokas* to the effect that Rāma is to take Sītā's hand, and thereby accept her as his *sahadharmacarī*, and that she is a very fortunate *pativratā* (wife devoted to her husband) and will follow him like a shadow. By choosing to quote Vālmīki, Sāgar is extra conservative. He chose not to use the classical formula that reportedly is used even today in wedding ceremonies. That formula is an interrogation of the groom by the father of the bride, urging him not to be false to the bride in *dharma*, *artha*, and *kāma* (*dharme cārthe ca kāme ca nāticaritavya*, Kane 1974, 519 n. 1209), and the groom has to respond that he will not (Kane 1974, 533).

More Sanskrit is to come with recitation from the *Yajurveda* during the tying of the knot, from *Viṣṇu Sahasranāma Stotra* while Sītā adorns Rāma with the *mālā*, and recites *Durgāsaptaśatī* when he garlands her. Sāgar's intention is to have his audience realize that this is a divine affair. Interestingly, the exchange of the *mālā*s is not mentioned by Tulsī, and seems, surprisingly, not to be part of the classical wedding ceremony descriptions (not in Kane 1974, 533–534). The scene is also interspersed with shots of brahmans reciting, performing sacrifices in the fire, and blessing the couple. On the other hand, the actual *agnipariṇayana* or *pherā* (circling of the fire) and *māṁg bharnā* (adorning of the parting of the woman's hair) is accompanied by a folk song that describes the general joy, and is performed by young women (*siyā raghuvara jī ke saṁga parana lāgīṁ; TVR* 10.135). At the appropriate moments, there are shots of all happy parties involved, including the gods Śiva and Brahmā disguised as brahmans. Incorporated in the song are again quotes from *RCM*.

Finally, Tulsī says that on Vasiṣṭha's bidding, the newlyweds sit next to one another, which provides another wonderful occasion for *darśana*, this time by Daśaratha, who rejoices at the sight (*RCM* 1.325 *chand* 1). Sāgar shows Sītā and Rāma paying obeisance to the gurus and their parents before sitting down again to give *darśana*. The wedding of the other three couples is much less elaborately described, but essentially similar. It is described lyrically in *chands* by Tulsī. Sāgar quotes a verse (in *caupāī*, which sounds like *RCM*, but is not in the Gītā Press edition) that stipulates that it is on Vasiṣṭha's command that these couples are married.

Whereas Vālmīki and Sāgar give the actual wedding formulae, Tulsī stresses more the feelings of the fathers, in particular Daśaratha (*RCM* 1.325 *dohā*), but also Janaka (*RCM* 1.326). The latter humbly addresses Daśaratha and, concerned for the welfare of his daughters in the new house, asks for his patience: "Make these girls your servants, and cherish them with ever-new forgiveness" (*e dārikā paricārikā kari pālibīṁ karunā naī; RCM* 1.326 *chand* 3a). He also asks for forgiveness for his own obstinacy in establishing the match (*aparādhu chamibo boli paṭhae bahuta hauṁ ḍītyo kaī; RCM* 1.326 *chand* 2b). Daśaratha returns the politenesses. Sāgar follows suit (*TVR* 10.136), and as we shall see, he has Janaka apologize for possible mistakes, and takes this paternal concern up again later, in the leave-taking rituals (see 2.3.3). The scene ends with an embrace of the in-laws.

Retreat for the Night

At the end of the ceremonies, Vālmīki simply says that the newly wedded couples return to the guest quarters (*VR* 1.73.40). In Tulsī's version, the festivities are not quite finished. There is first a visit to the site of the divinity presiding over the wedding (*kohabara*). Sāgar shows the procession, while a rather pedestrian folk song is heard in the background, which ends by quoting one *dohā* from *RCM* (1.327 *dohā*). He shows the couples striding solemnly, restrainedly smiling but not looking at each other. He misses a chance to quote Tulsī's beautiful description of Sītā's feelings: she acts shy, but feels eager: "Looking at Rāma again and again, Sītā withdraws, but her heart does not withdraw. Her eyes, thirsty for love, supersede the beauty of pretty fishes" (*puni puni rāmahi citava siya sakucati manu sakucai na, harata manohara mīna chabi prema piāse naina; RCM* 1.326 *dohā*).

Sāgar's folk song states that the *kuladevī* confirmed all ritual activity that had been going on (*sāre kāraja siddha bhae; TVR* 10.137), and we have a shot of all bowing to her image. Tulsī does not describe the deity. Instead, he gives a full description of Rāma, from top to toe (*nakha-śikha; RCM* 1.327.1–*chand* 1a). This might be interpreted as a view from Sītā's shy perspective, but it changes into a public view, with a description of the joy of all witnesses at the event. Tulsī has again managed to get maximal benefit from the opportunity to sing a hymn of praise to Rāma and to provide a reverential *darśana* for the devotee.

Upon arrival in the bridal apartment (*kohabara*), according to Tulsī, folk rituals or *laukika rīti* are carried out (*RCM* 1.327 *chand* 2b–4). This is probably a reference to pranks played by the bride's relatives, including games conducted by women that function as icebreakers between bride and groom. Sāgar does not break the solemn atmosphere at this point, and he treats these icebreakers later, so I will take them up there. Instead, Sāgar skips the whole *kaṛavāk* and ends the folk song with the last *dohā* from *RCM* on the topic (1.327 *dohā*), which states that the couples went to Daśaratha. Sāgar shows each couple respectfully greeting the father-in-law and receiving his blessings.

At this point, Sāgar ends the wedding ceremony proper, leaving the audience with a taste of grand style. In Tulsī's version, the folk rites are followed by the big feast (*jevanāra*) to which Janaka invites the *barāt*. Janaka again humbly washes the feet of the main guests, and treats them to a gourmet meal served swiftly on exquisite dishes and described in much culinary detail (*RCM* 1.328–329). The meal is topped off with *pān*. While they have dinner, the guests are entertained on the traditional "insult songs" (*gāri, RCM* 1.329.1a and 3b–4a), which they relish.[28] Tulsī ends the wedding day proper with a short description of the trip back to the guest quarters, and the joy in the city on the occasion (*RCM* 1.330.1–2a). None of this is shown in Sāgar's *TVR*.

Farewell Rituals

Paternal Gifts and Reluctance to Let the Bride Go

In Vālmīki, the leave-taking is described in just eight *ślokas*. First, Viśvāmitra leaves, an event that is not taken up by Tulsī nor Sāgar at this point (Sāgar spends more time on it in episode 12). Then, Daśaratha asks permission to leave, and Janaka sends him with a huge gift for his daughters (*kanyādhana*), which is described in detail. Tulsī too describes the gifts of Janaka in detail (*RCM* 1.326.1b–3), but he speaks of a dowry (*dāija; RCM* 1.326.1b and 1.333 *dohā*) instead of *kanyādhana*. The issue comes up twice, once just after the wedding ceremony proper and and again at the time of leaving. The first time, Daśaratha is said to accept everything but promptly divides it among the beggars (*RCM* 1.326.4).

Significantly, Sāgar dodges the dowry issue. The only reference is in passing. When Sunayanā offers her final advice to her daughters, she refers obliquely to a dowry. She says that although a father may give a lot of material wealth, which engenders surprise in the three worlds (this may be a reference to *RCM* 1.333 *dohā*), all a mother has to offer is advice on how a woman should behave (*Pitā ne tumheṁ itnā diyā hai ki tīnoṁ lok meṁ uskī śobhā ho rahī hai, par maiṁ to tumheṁ nārī-dharm kā jñān hī de saktī huṁ, jo jīvan ke har moṛ par tumheṁ karttavya aur dharm kā rāstā dikhāegā; TVR* 11.142).

It seems to me that Sāgar has dealt masterfully, or rather not dealt, with the issue of dowry. Sunayanā's passing remark acknowledges that there must have been a big dowry, without saying so explicitly or calling it by name. By placing it in the context of the leave-taking ceremonies (*vidā*), it is conflated with the more acceptable practice of sending away visitors with a gift. At the same time, Sāgar has downplayed the importance of the material dowry, privileging instead the mother's gift of "spiritual" advice. Given all the controversy regarding dowry, its condemnation in the media (and the constitution), yet its abiding—even expanding—prevalence in practice, it is not surprising that Sāgar avoids addressing the issue. It is surprising rather that he manages to let this much slip by without condemning the practice on an official government channel of communication.

Tulsī's Janaka had been reluctant to let the groom's party leave. Affectionately, he made Daśaratha stay (*dina uṭhi bidā avadhapati māgā, rākhahi janaku sahita anurāgā; RCM* 1.333.1b). It seems that love for the in-laws is at the root of this reluctance to send the groom's party away. This impression is reinforced during the actual leave-taking, where the majority of the verses are devoted to Janaka's leave-taking of Rāma and his brothers (*RCM* 1.341.1b–342), and Viśvāmitra (*RCM* 1.3431–3). In his eagerness to make the groom's party stay just a bit longer, Tulsī's king is acting by popular consent (*nita nava nagara anaṁda uchāhū, dasaratha gavanu sohāi na kāhū; RCM* 1.333.2b). It is not until Viśvāmitra and Śatānanda intercede that the *barāt* finally gets the go-ahead. The royal women share the king's feelings and are unhappy when they are informed that the *barāt* is about to leave. They entrust the girls to their husbands, taking the opportunity to praise Rāma (with a *chand, RCM* 1.336.4–337.1).

Sāgar follows Tulsī's main lead, and elaborates. His Janaka pleads very politely with Daśaratha that the *barāt* should stay on for some time. Sāgar's Janaka does not act out of love for the groom's party but rather for his beloved daughter, and he says as much. The groom's father understands the bride's father's plight and promises to wait till Janaka tells him to go (*TVR* 10.138–139),[29] and the two kings embrace. Sāgar thus dwells on the chivalries of the two parties and takes up again the issue of the exemplary gallantry of the groom's party (*varapakṣa*) toward the bride's party (*kanyāpakṣa*). To drive his point home, he adds a new scene. His camera shifts to the queens in Ayodhyā getting impatient when the *barāt* does not return (beginning of the next episode, *TVR* 11.140). While Kauśalyā is the voice of reason and understanding, the impatient Kaikeyī argues that after all the bride's party should respect the wishes of the groom's party (*ham varpakṣ vāle haiṁ, ham jaisā cāheṁge kanyāpakṣ vāloṁ ko vaisā hī karnā paṛegā; TVR* 11.140), and she sends a message to that effect to Daśaratha. The latter reacts very negatively to such reasoning, however, and refuses to force the bride's party to do anything against their wishes. Nevertheless, it is clear that Daśaratha must return home at some point. The scene ends with a realpolitik argument by his counselor that carries more weight: a king should not stay away from his responsibilities too long.

On the other side, Janaka is finally convinced to let the *barāt* go by Viśvāmitra and Śatānanda, just as in *RCM*. But in Sāgar's version, we get the full argumentation. Viśvāmitra points out that Janaka is setting a bad example by giving in to his emotions so much, and should rather pull himself together and help protect the ways of proper conduct (*nīti kī rakṣā; TVR* 11.142). Śatānanda tells Janaka that once the girl is given away, she belongs to someone else (*parāī*). This finally prompts Janaka into action.

Interestingly, Sāgar follows Tulsī in giving airtime to the popular view of the public of Mithilā. Tulsī's public, like its king, relished the presence of the *barāt*. Sāgar's focus is different. He has some "people" sympathize with Janaka's state of mind on the general human principle that it is difficult to send one's daughter away to her in-laws. The *dolī*-makers, while preparing the palanquin in which the brides are to be taken away, quite poignantly phrase the dilemma a girl's parents face: "Any father and mother wish not to send her, and yet, they cannot keep her" (*kauno bāp-mahtārī kā na bheje ko jī karat hai aur na rakh sakat haiṁ; TVR* 11.141). Following the tradition of the classical drama (and the Hindi film), the "people" speak a rustic language, not modern standard Hindi, but this does not impede at least one of them from getting quite philosophical: "A daughter is the true manifestation of what they call illusion" (*vah jise māyā kahte haiṁ na, uskā asalī rūp hī biṭiyā hai; TVR* 11.141). They add that even a king like Janaka will forget all his asceticism, which may be an echo of *RCM* (1.338.3a: *sīya biloki dhīratā bhāgī, rahe kahāvata parama birāgī*). Although the people's words capture well the king's emotional state and, for that matter, those of every parent, they constitute a different type of popular endorsement of the king's actions from that in *RCM*.

Touching Maternal Farewell

When describing the farewell in the women's quarters, Tulsī takes the opportunity to exploit fully the emotional depths of the sentiment of tragedy or *karuṇā rasa*, as he himself puts it: "All men and women, the queens and the girl friends, were overwhelmed with love. They seemed to have turned the city of Videha into a dwelling for pathos and farewell" (*premabibasa nara nāri saba sakhinha sahita ranivāsu, mānahuṁ kīnha bidehapura karunāṁ birahaṁ nivāsu; RCM* 1.337 *dohā*). Tulsī touchingly describes the goodbyes of the women: "Again and again, they embraced Sītā, blessed her and gave her advice" (*puni puni sīya goda kari lehīṁ, dei asīsa sikhāvanu dehīṁ RCM* 1.334.2a). The parting words of the queen mothers are first of all a blessing: "May you always remain your husband's darling, we bless you to live a long, happily married life" (*hoehu saṁtata piyahi piārī, ciru ahibāta asīsa hamārī; RCM* 1.334.2b). The advice proper is very short: "You should look after the needs of your mother- and father-in-law, and the guru. You should carry out all commands, but be sure to check your husband's facial expression" (*sāsu sasura gura sevā karehū, pati rukha lakhi āyasu anusarehu; RCM* 1.334.3a). Tulsī further describes the goodbye of the girlfriends: "Overwhelmed with extreme love, the clever girlfriends whisper instruction on women's matters (*ati saneha basa sakhīṁ sayānī, nāri dharama sikhavahiṁ mṛdu bānī; RCM* 1.344.3b). The next verse again returns to the goodbye of the mothers, who cannot get enough of embracing the girls. Interestingly, they curse the fate of women: "They said: 'why did the creator create women?' " (*kahahiṁ viraṁci racīṁ kata nārīṁ; RCM* 1.344.4b). Following the *kāvya* tradition, even the birds raised by Sītā share in the general outburst of tears: "The parrot and mynah that Sītā had helped hatch, kept in a golden cage, and taught [to speak]; desperately cried out: 'Where's Sītā.' When they heard this, no one could keep cool" (*suka sārikā jānakī jyāe, kanaka piṁjaranhi rākhi paṛhāe; byākula kahahiṁ kahāṁ baidehī, suni dhīraju pariharai na kehī; RCM* 338.1).

Sāgar too exploits the dramatic possibilities of the scene and its *karuṇ rasa*. Already in the previous episode, there was an innovation to allow for that effect. Sunayanā confided in the wife of the royal guru about her sadness at losing a daughter (*TVR* 10.137–138). She does not quite curse the fate of women, but her words are bitter nevertheless: "It seems like someone is getting away with wounding someone, and then plundering their all" (*jaise kisī ko ghāyal karke koī sab kuch lūṭ karke jā rahā hai; TVR* 10.137). She despairs at the charade a mother has to go through in blessing the groom, the very one who is taking away her dearest (*māṁ ke hṛday kī kaisī viḍambanā hai, jo uskā sab kuch chīn kar le jā rahā hai, use āśīrvād de rahī hai; TVR* 10.137).

Sāgar, however, feels compelled to temper these poignant feelings with the voice of reason, here in the person of the guru's wife. First, the guru's wife says that this is just the way of the world (*saṁsār kī yahī rīti hai; TVR* 10.137). Sunayanā protests: "What a way is that? That a mother and father have to bring up a daughter lovingly for so many years, and then send her off to a strange house, by their own doing?" (*kaisī hai yah rīti ki mātā-pitā itne baras pāl-pos kar beṭī ko baṛā karte haiṁ aur phir ek din use apne hāthoṁ parāe ghar bhej dete haiṁ? TVR* 10.137–138). The guru's wife then reminds Sunayanā that things won't be that bad, and that Sītā, after all, will have her husband to confide in, just as Sunayanā herself has now Janaka. Still, Sunayanā finds it hard for a mother to let go of her daughter: "A mother's heart does not understand the language of reason, it knows only the delusion of possessing love" (*mā kā hṛday jñān kī bhāṣā nahīṁ samajhtā, keval mamatā kā moh jāntā hai; TVR* 10.138). The guru's wife, then, points out that such concern with matters of the world is not fitting for a queen, especially one of the king of Videha. Here she is punning on the literal meaning of Videha, "detached from the body."[30] Sunayanā confesses that the king of Videha himself is caught in this web of affection; he too feels *mamatā* that is so strong, that he cannot let go of his daughter. To be sure, Sunayanā gets the last word, but still, in comparison with Tulsī's version, the atmosphere of *karuṇā* is tempered by words of wisdom. Sāgar seems eager to warn his public against the excesses of emotion.

Notwithstanding all Sunayanā's pathos in the scene with the guru's wife, her farewell of the young brides is remarkably restrained compared to Tulsī's version. Whereas Tulsī's queen mothers would embrace the girls over and over again, blessing them, and sending them off with just one line of instruction, Sāgar's Sunayanā gives a long Sanskritic sermon to instruct the girls, while she acts sternly like a schoolteacher and the young brides listen deferentially with bowed heads. She has prepared her speech well, and it bears a close look at what married women are supposed to do.

First, a woman's husband is her god, equal to no other. A woman does not need to worship (*pūjā*) anyone but him. A woman's first duty is to give up her own self-interest (*svārth*) and to be concerned only with what fosters her husband's welfare (*kalyāṇ*). That is the only self-denial (*tapasyā*) required of a woman. A woman who is fully, in thoughts, words, and deeds, devoted to her husband (*pativratā*) does not need anyone else's blessing, for even God himself is compelled to carry out her wishes (*uskī ājñā ke adhīn*). A woman should be her husband's moral partner (*sahadharminī*) in carrying out his duty. Her highest duty (*uttama dharma*) is to honor her husband's parents. She should only speak after having checked her husband's facial reactions, because even if her words would be true, she may be speaking at the wrong moment, with dire results. Finally, she should consider her in-laws' house (*sasurāl*) to be her home, she should never make her own paternal home (*maikā*) out to be better, and she should even try to forget it altogether (*TVR* 11.142–143).

This is a remarkably conservative view of women's duty for a popular series on contemporary TV. One can hardly imagine a more explicitly patriarchal statement, and that in the mouth of a woman, the bride's mother. It is apparent that Sāgar is keen to send an explicitly conservative message to mothers and young brides, especially if one considers that at this point there is nothing equivalent in the other texts discussed here. This stern speech is strikingly different from Tulsī's emotional farewells, and Vālmīki did not mention anything of the kind. Still, Sāgar can claim sanction from the *Mānas,* but from a later passage in that text, after the exile, where Sītā meets the venerable female ascetic Anasūyā. Much of Sāgar's sermon by Sunayanā is reminiscent of Tulsī's words of Anusūyā to Sītā (*RCM* 3.5).[31] To further beef up the *Mānas* credentials of the TV sermon, Sāgar throws in a quote from another later passage, namely, the scene where Rāma tries to dissuade Sītā from following him into exile, and says her duty is to serve her mother- and father-in-law (*RCM* 2.61.3a, quoted in *TVR* 11.143). In short, our comparison shows an important fact. Sunayanā's conservative sermon in Sāgar's TV version is deliberately constructed to look as if it was lifted straight out of the medieval text. Actually, it is based on a single line in Tulsī's corresponding version, which is expanded to the effect that it has become an innovation. Paradoxically, the most modern version here is the most conservative one.

Concerned Paternal Farewell

If women are urged to subordinate themselves completely to husband and in-laws, Sāgar does not forget to address the other side of the issue, and to stress that in-laws should treat young brides well, even with respect. That is the topic of the next scene, which focusses on Janaka's farewell. Janaka pleads with Daśaratha to be patient with the girls, who are after all very young and will need to adjust to the ways of their new environment. Sāgar may well be following Tulsī's lead here again, but Tulsī had this scene at the end of the nuptial ceremonies proper.

Janaka asks Daśaratha to treat the new brides generously, and to give these "servants" a place "at his feet" (*āpke caraṇoṁ meṁ sthān dījiegā TVR* 11.144). Daśaratha counters that his new daughters-in-law are goddesses of good luck (*ghar kī lakṣmī*), and that as such their place is rather at the head (*lakṣmī kā sthān caraṇoṁ meṁ nahīṁ, sir-māthe par hī hotā hai; TVR* 11.114); he promises to treat them as the future queens of Ayodhyā. Janaka fawns over this great generosity of the groom's father. As earlier, the stress here is on the graciousness of the groom's party and its lack of display of superiority. That was already apparent at the beginning of the scene, when Janaka wanted to touch Daśaratha's feet as a sign of subservience but the latter chided him gently about it.

Notwithstanding the plea for treating young brides well, the scene ends again on a note of female subjugation. Tulsī's Janaka had simply "instructed his daughter manifold, taught her about women's duty and family ways" (*bahubidhi bhūpa sutā samujhāīṁ, nāridharmu kularīti sikhāīṁ; RCM* 1.339.1a). Sāgar's Janaka's paternal farewell to Sītā is much shorter than Sunayanā's but highlights again the ultimate subordination to a patriarchal system: the bride's conduct is never to bring down the father's or in-laws' good name (*tumhāre kisī bhī ācaraṇ se tumhāre pitā kī lāj aur sasurāl kī kīrti ko dhakkā na lage; TVR* 11.144). Though Janaka showed concern for his daughters' welfare, the fear of dishonor due to female sexuality surfaces in these last moments of farewell. After her father's words, a close-up of Sītā's face suggests to the audience all that is to come, and how indeed Sītā will be accused of breaking these rules.

Finally, Sāgar returns to the sentiment of *karuṇā*; a proverb is quoted that sets the tone, and follows a wedding song of the type *bābul*. In this song, finally, we find an echo of Tulsī's queens' poignant lament of women's plight (*kahahiṁ viraṁci racīṁ kata nārīṁ; RCM* 1.344.4b): "Ruthless creator, explain just this: why did you create daughters?" (*niṭhura vidhātā itnā batā de kāhe ko biṭiyā kī jāta banāī; TVR* 11.145). Paradoxically, by narrowing the lament down to the fate of daughters, rather than women in general, the bitter statement in the song is actually opened up to incorporate not only the perspective of women but also that of the father, as is of course traditional in the north Indian wedding songs. This is reinforced by the camera showing at this moment Janaka addressing Daśaratha, the latter empathizing with Janaka's plight, and the two embracing.

Although the voices that sing are female, the song is not the sole domain of the women. During this song, the camera registers the pathos on the face of all participants, in particular a dignified type of sadness of Janaka, who alone follows the palanquins just a few steps farther and then returns despondently, to retreat in the inner quarters of the palace, followed by Sunayanā. Meanwhile a verse is quoted that voices the despondence of all participants but stresses Janaka's sadness, how all his happinesses now belong to another (*TVR* 11.145–146). Tulsī's Janaka too had followed the *barāt* back for a while. Tulsī too had highlighted the exemplary *samdhī* relations and extreme courtesy of both parties. His Daśaratha had to give permission for Janaka to go back repeatedly, before the latter took him up on it. Even then he did not leave until after elaborate farewells to each of the members of the *barāt*. When Janaka said goodbye to Rāma, Tulsī turned the farewell into a hymn of praise to Rāma (*RCM* 1.340.4b–342.3a). This was all in the spirit of bhakti.

The close comparison of the different versions of the same episodes in *TVR* and *RCM* bring out differences that are significant. Often, it is taken for granted that the *TVR* is a bhakti text, just like *RCM*, the main difference being that it is electronically mediated. I do not seek to downplay the differences in the media, and it is undeniable that Sāgar has exploited the medium of TV very well for the sake of providing maximum *darśana*. However, our comparison shows that he also left out crucial bhakti elements in favor of moral sermons that seek to reinforce unapologetically a patriarchal normativity, more than even his ancient and medieval sources.

Arrival in Ayodhyā

Auspiciousness and Women's Rites

Finally, after all the courtesies are played out, the *barāt* can leave for Ayodhyā. Tulsī describes the elaborate gift giving by Daśaratha, and continues on an auspicious note by describing the good omens that accompanied the *barāt*'s departure (*RCM* 1.339.4). This is an interesting contrast with Vālmīki, where inauspicious omens are observed as the procession leaves. The narrative rationale here is different, though. Vālmīki's omens announce the arrival of Bhārgava Rāma, but Tulsī had already dealt with the confrontation with Bhārgava Rāma, immediately after the *svayaṁvara*. Sāgar too had dealt with it before, and he entirely skips the good omens.

Sāgar, Tulsī, and Vālmīki catch up again when they describe the auspicious welcome Ayodhyā is preparing for the newly wedded couples (*VR* 1.77.6–9, *RCM* 1.344–345, *TVR* 11.146). Tulsī compulsively adds more gift giving to brahmans (*RCM* 1.345 *dohā*). Vālmīki simply mentions that the queens carry out the ritual reception of the new daughters-in-law (*vadhūs*) (*VR* 1.77.10–13). Tulsī elaborates, weaving in as much gift giving, devotion, and love as will fit in verse. He stresses the jubilant joy of the queens who are anticipating Rāma's *darśana* (*RCM* 1.346), and that of the citizens of Ayodhyā when enjoying *darśana* of Rāma (*RCM* 1.347–348). The climax in *RCM* is the queens' *parachani* or auspicious welcome ceremony (RCM 1.349). Sāgar has concentrated on this scene, quoting two *dohās* from *RCM*, and suggesting the happiness of everyone in the city in the accompanying song *Ayodhyā nagarī dhanya bhaī* (*TVR* 11.146).

Tulsī stresses again that the rites follow both great and little tradition (*nigama nīti kula rīti*; *RCM* 1.349 *dohā*), though he clearly seems to relish the women's rites. The queens then wash the feet of brides and grooms (*tinha para kuṁvari kuṁvara baiṭhāre, sādara pāya punīta pakhāre*; *RCM* 1.350.1b) and continue *pūjā* in great joy for the rest of the *kaṛāvak*. Sāgar quotes two *dohās* from *RCM*, including the one that stresses the ultraorthodoxy of the rites. Sāgar does not show any foot washing here, but he takes up the hint of Vālmīki, who had said the brides worshiped in local temples. In *TVR*, they are shown to join in a *pūjā* of Ayodhyā's royal family's *kuladevatā*, the sun god. Sāgar throws in some more Sanskrit mantras recited by Vasiṣṭha, who blesses all present.

Tulsī then briefly mentions that the royal women engage the newlyweds in more mundane folk praxes, probably a reference to games designed to break the ice between bride and groom and to determine who will be the dominant one in the relationship (this is usually called *juā khel*). He reports that all the young people act shyly, but that Rāma smiled secretly (*loka rīti jananīṁ karahiṁ bara dulahini sakucāhiṁ, modu binodu biloki baṛa rāmu manahiṁ musukāhiṁ*; RCM 1.350 *dohā* 2). Only after these rites does Tulsī mention worship of the gods and ancestors, which is instantly rewarded (*RCM* 1.351.1–2a).

Icebreakers and In-Laws' Care of Bahūs

Sāgar, on the other hand, concentrates on the icebreakers or *juā khel* (*TVR* 11.146–147). Following Tulsī's hint, the shyness of the participants is highlighted, but the voluptuous images in the background evoke an atmosphere of *śṛṅgāra*. Kauśalyā and Kaikeyī preside over a touching ceremony, called here *dūdh-bhāt*, where bride and groom feed each other. It is only at this point that Sītā and Rāma look at each other shyly. Kaikeyī whispers something in Sītā's ear, which is instantly understood by Bharata, who warns his brother that his new bride may well use the occasion to bite his finger. Sītā, though, just smiles blissfully and does not do any such thing. Sāgar may well have been inspired here by an earlier passage in Tulsī featuring *lahakaura* (ritual offering of food by the bridegroom and the bride to each other). Right after the nuptial ceremonies, Tulsī had described how the newlyweds went to the *kohabara* (apartment) for folk ceremonies. In *RCM*, no one less than Pārvatī was instructing Rāma, and Sarasvatī took Sītā's side (*RCM* 1.327 *chand* 2c). The most significant difference, though, is that Tulsī reports a lot of merrymaking and joking on the occasion (*hāsa vilāsa; RCM* 1.327 *chand* 2d; *vinoda pramoda; RCM* 1.327 *chand* 3c). In contrast, Sāgar features a rather solemn and serene atmosphere. This may be a consequence of his having chosen to concentrate on the games played at the groom's house rather than those at the bride's paternal home.

In *TVR*, then follows a contest for finding an object (it looks like a ring, but is called *kaṁganā*) in a bowl of liquid. Again, the participants smile beatifically, this time without looking at one another, while their hands search in the liquid. This is in contrast to Tulsī's early icebreaker, where Sītā was so eager to behold Rāma that she remained transfixed on her rings that reflected Rāma's face (*RCM* 1.327 *chand* 3a–b). Back to Sāgar's games: Neither of the two is engaged in the competitive element; they both have to be encouraged to start the game. Sītā wins, smiling shyly. Lakṣmaṇa, of course, true to character, cannot really keep himself from telling Rāma to let her win, but Bharata counters that it is not bad that at least at some point Rāma loses. Everyone savors the irony that Sītā wins over Rāma. Sāgar could be said to be merely elaborating on Tulsī's hint (*RCM* 1.350 *dohā* 2), since indeed the participants remain restrainted and shy. It should be said that Sāgar may here well draw his inspiration from the myriad folksongs for wedding rituals, some of which irreverently make fun of Rāma as a clumsy groom (unable, for instance to untie the wedding knot, whereas breaking Śiva's bow was easy for him). Sāgar has obviously transformed the situations sketched in such songs into more solemn occasions, while still allowing for the role reversal; his scene is not irreverent but merely ironic, reinforcing the irony of the incarnation.

There is something else going on in this episode of *TVR*, however. Throughout, the stress is on women's solidarity. The mothers-in-law take the side of the new brides against their sons. This is made explicit by the encouragements they give during the *kaṁganā ḍhūḍhnā*, commented on by Lakṣmaṇa, who says "Now the daughters-in-law are counting for more than the sons" (*Ab betoṁ se baṛhkar bahueṁ ho rahī haiṁ bhayyā!; TVR* 11.147). To this the reply is "What's that label 'daughter-in-law'? Rather, they are our daughters" (*Kyā bahū-bahū lagā rakhā hai? Are, hamārī beṭiyāṁ haiṁ; TVR* 11.147). Clearly, Sāgar is taking up the earlier message of the gracious behavior of the girls' in laws toward her. The mother-in-law, her traditional enemy, is here transformed into an ally. Lest we get carried away, it needs to be said that the women's solidarity is well entrenched within the patriarchal frame.

Meanwhile, in *RCM*, the *barāt* is dismissed with proper gift-giving (*RCM* 1.351.2 *dohā*). Again, in accordance with *loka beda bidhi* and following Vasiṣṭha's orders, brahmans are honored and fed (*RCM* 1.352.1–2). Everyone says good-night to the gurus Viśvāmitra and Vasiṣṭha, to whom great wealth is offered, but they only take their traditional fee or *nega* (*RCM* 1.352.3–353.2a). All guests are sent away with appropriate gifts (*RCM* 1.3532b *dohā*). The king then retires to the women's quarters for private celebrations of joy, hugging the newlywed brides and relating the full story of the wedding to his queens, as skilled as a bard (*bhāṭa jimi; RCM* 1.354). King and sons bathe, and together with gurus and brahmans take an elaborate meal. The joy of all this, Tulsī says, is too much to describe (*RCM* 1.355.1–3). That may have discouraged Sāgar, who, somewhat surprisingly, shows none of this, not even the honoring of the gurus.

Tulsī's next scene is taken up by Sāgar. In *RCM*, King Daśaratha, before retiring, urges his queens to take good care of their new daughters-in-law: "The brides are just girls arrived in a strange house. Take care of them like eyelids protecting the eye" (*badhū larikanīṁ para ghara āīṁ, rākhehu nayana palaka kī nāīṁ; RCM* 1.355.4b).

Sāgar transforms the scene into a private conversation between Daśaratha and Kauśalyā (who is engaged in sewing) (*TVR* 11.148–149). Daśaratha muses about Janaka's worry when he sent off his daughters. Kauśalyā points out that the mother must feel even worse. Daśaratha confirms that "Only a woman can understand a woman's pain" (*strī kī vedanā strī hī samajh saktī hai; TVR* 11.148). This nod to the women's perspective is typical for Sāgar, and is in line with the scene where Sunayanā stated her plight, an innovation compared to *RCM*.

In *TVR*, Daśaratha then tells Kauśalyā that he has promised Janaka that the girls will never be uncomfortable at their in-laws. It is, he says, Kauśalyā's task to help him keep his word (*TVR* 11.148). Kauśalyā, sincerely hurt, asks whether he seriously fears any less than good treatment. Daśaratha hastens to say that that's not the case but that they need special care, having arrived in a new environment, and that they need to be loved even more than they were at home. He echoes Tulsī: "Just like the apple of the eye is protected between the eyelids, take these four girls under your wings of love" (*Jaise palakoṁ ke bīc āṁkh kī putalī ko sambhālā jātā hai, usī tarah in cāroṁ ko apne pyār ke āṁcal meṁ lapeṭ ke rakhnā; TVR* 11.148). Kauśalyā assures him that this will be done and that within a few days the girls will have forgotten their old home. In this way, we have come full circle: Sītā's mother had instructed her that it is a woman's duty to forget her parental home. In the ideal scenario, that is indeed the case, by the extra love and care of the women in the husband's home. Sāgar's point is clearly that if everyone plays his or her part the way it is supposed to be, a woman's position is enviable indeed.

The Wedding Night

In contrast to some other versions,[32] Vālmīki does not report on the wedding night, but simply states that, after they had fulfilled all their obligations, the new brides got to enjoy themselves in private with their husbands (*VR* 1.77.13–14). Tulsī's version is surprisingly different. After Daśaratha retires, the queens spread a wonderful bed, described in loving detail (*RCM* 1.356.1–2), upon which they invite Rāma to sleep. Rāma has to insist repeatedly that all the brothers retire for the night, for they are keen to massage his feet. However, if we expected any hint at the first wedding night (*suhāg rāt*) once he enjoys privacy, we are disappointed. Instead, Tulsī does a great job of evoking the queen-mothers' emotions, which are convincingly those of typical mothers. We nearly hear them whisper while they glance at Rāma dozing off that they can't quite fathom how their tender boy could have done all they've heard tonight he did, such as kill the terrible demons, break the bow, and so on (*RCM* 356.4–357.4).[33] All they can think of is that this must be the guru's grace. The mothers stay with Rāma until he falls asleep, and Tulsī adds a loving description "In his sleep too his very handsome face looks like a golden lotus at dusk" (*Nīdaūṁ badana soha suṭhi lonā, manahuṁ sāṁjha sarasīruha sonā; RCM* 1.358.1a). In the background we hear the sound of songs coming from every house in Ayodhyā (*RCM* 1.358.1b). Finally the queens go to bed themselves, taking their *bahūs* with them.

What is going on is that Tulsī here radically avoids all hint of erotics (*śṛṇgāra rasa*) in favor of vivid motherly feelings (*vātsalya rasa*). The contrast with Kṛṣṇa bhakti is too obvious to miss. It seems that Tulsī quite consciously seeks to distance himself from the eroticism of the Braj poets. Still, he makes sure bhakti is central. The queens' motherly words form yet another hymn of praise to Rāma. Sāgar here chose to ignore Tulsī's *vātsalya* angle. The reason may be that there is a danger that such a portrayal would evoke a hint of child marriage (a much-debated issue with regard to *VR*; for references see Brockington 1998, 432). Next to dowry, this is another much-debated problem that forms an embarrassment to "reformed" Hindus. The discourse is that the practice is pretty much confined to unenlightened villagers, so it would not be fitting at all for a leading kshatriya family. That is probably why, instead of following Tulsī, Sāgar shows the beginning of Rāma and Sītā's wedding night (*TVR* 11.147–148).

We see Sītā, decked out in all her jewelry, seated on the wedding bed or *phūl-sej*, waiting for her groom to arrive, while a *dohā* from *RCM* is recited. The *dohā* in question contains Daśaratha's command before he retires: " 'The boys are tired, and overpowered by sleep, go and put them to bed.' Saying thus, the king retired to his bedroom, meditating on Rāma's feet" (*larikā śramita unīda basa sayana karāvahu jāi, asa kahi ge biśrāma gṛha, rāma carana citu lāi; RCM* 1.355 *dohā*). That is totally out of context in the bridal chamber, but Sāgar seems to bet in this case that his audience gets just enough of the *dohā*, thus taken out of context, that it might think that the meditation on Rāma's feet refers to Sītā. While the reference to Rāma's feet is made, Sītā's meditative face lights up as she apparently hears his footsteps.

When Rāma enters, they look at each other and smile. She gets up and ever so slowly walks to him and stoops to touch his feet. He stops her, and asks why she does so. Now Sītā gets to speak her very first words in his company. She speaks very emphatically, like a child eager to pronounce clearly. She says that her mother told her that he is her Lord (*parameśvar; TVR* 11.147). Rāma then teases her mildly: "Okay, so you have taken your mother's instruction to heart. Will you also listen to one of my instructions?" (*Māṁ kā upadeś to sun liyā, ab merā ek upadeś sunogī?; TVR* 11.148). Sītā demurely answers, bowing her head: "Please command me, because I am your slave-girl" (*Ājñā kījiye, maiṁ to āpkī dāsī hūṁ; TVR* 11.148).

The rest of the scene consists of a long sermon by Rāma. First, he redefines the meaning of what a wife should be: not a slave but a partner. He says: "In that case, my first command is that you should not remain my slave (*dāsī*). Be my better half (*arddhāṁginī*), my friend (*mitra*), my mate (*sakhā*), my companion (*sāthī*), walking by my side." Rāma's word choice is interesting in that, except for the first, all these epithets are masculine in gender. One might speculate that equalization entails a desexualization of the wife. Rāma goes on to explain what the woman's companionship involves: "Take part in every good work I carry out, and if you ever see me lose track of the right path, keep me from getting astray. That is the duty of a true friend or a real companion." There is some irony in Sāgar's putting these words in Rāma's mouth. After all, he is *maryādāpuruṣa,* a paragon of virtue, himself. Since Sāgar's Rāma is set up as an example, we should also consider the real-life implications of this statement. In effect, he is saying that women are to keep their men on the right track. This transfers the burden of responsibility for the man's moral character to the woman's care!

Rāma continues with a promise: "Mother Kaikeyī told me that I should make sure to give you a present to keep the memory of the first meeting alive. I have brought a gift. It is not one of pearls or diamonds. By way of gift, I give you today a promise. [You know that] kings have the custom to take many queens, but in Rāma's life there will never be anyone but you. This is Rāma's oath. Do you know when I first took this oath? When I saw you for the first time in the flower garden, just this way!" Sītā does not receive any spectacular diamond ring or set of pearls. Instead, she gets the most valuable thing for a woman, namely, a vow of faithfulness from her husband.

Sāgar's Rāma is quite in character here with his earlier statement of marital faithfulness in the company of his brothers. Of course, Rāma is popularly considered to have taken just one wife, as is expressed by the epithet "monogamous by vow" or *ekapatnīvratadhara*. Vālmīki does not really explicitly say so, though he says that Rāma did not take another wife after banishing Sītā, and of course throughout the epic Rāma and Sītā are very devoted to one another (Brockington 1998, 433). Still, there is some debate about whether there are hints at other wives of Rāma in *VR* (Brockington 1984, 173). Tulsī never uses the term *ekapatnīvratadhara* with reference to Rāma, either, which is surprising. He must have been aware of it, since it occurs at least in the *Bhāgavata Purāṇa* (9.10.55). One may infer that Tulsī did consider Rāma monogamous, because he says later that all males in Rāma's kingdom (*Rāmrājya*) had taken a vow of monogamy or *eka nārī vrata* (he hastens to add that the women too were devoted to their husbands in deed, word, and thought; *RCM* 7.22.4). However, nowhere in *RCM* is there a description of how Rāma took that vow, certainly not during the wedding night. In short, Sāgar manages to make his scene look traditional, but again this is an innovation.

At first sight, the scene seems to send a very positive message. Certainly,

Rāma's tenderness and wonderful tact on the first wedding night set a great example. Further, all that he says is politically correct. Woman is explicitly lifted in status from subordinate to being equal to man. Marriage is a bond between companions, rather than a subordinating relationship. To top it off, there is Rāma's promise of, if not quite explicitly faithfulness, at least monogamy. Women might rejoice about Sāgar's portrayal of this excellent example for mortal men.[34]

One might well argue, though, that the linking of woman's partnership and her custody of the man's morality with the man's faithfulness is in itself a tricky proposition. Does the first become a condition to be fulfilled before the last is imperative? If the final responsibility for the husband's morality is in the woman's, not the man's, hands, does that mean that he cannot be blamed? In other words, does she first have to deserve his faithfulness before it can be granted, and is she then the one who has to wakefully secure it? And has she only to blame herself if he goes astray?

It is also significant that the promise is prefaced very emphatically by Sītā's own attitude of self-subjugation. Implicitly, it seems, this is set up as a sine qua non. Deserving women, that is, women who are prepared to play the subordinate role, are promised marital fidelity. It does not take much imagination to see the other side of the coin: women who are not subordinate do not deserve such consideration. The way the episode is portrayed seems to reinforce the old stereotype, after all. One might, in other words, well ask whether only subordinate Sītās deserve monogamous Rāmas?

It is also striking that Rāma's lifting Sītā from a state of *dāsī* to that of *arddhāṁginī* explicitly takes the form of a command (*ājñā*). Isn't it a contradiction in terms that a man commands his wife to be his equal? Rāma's tone is paternalizing: he knows what is best (for them, if not for her). Sītā does not get to answer; she merely smiles, presumably overcome with happiness with everything he says. Obviously, it is not expected that she will reciprocate his promise. Such would be totally superfluous. If his monogamy is a gift, hers is a given.

Conclusions

What can we conclude from this detailed analysis? In which ways does the *TVR* follow and differ from its sources, and what does that tell us about its biases? Sāgar is well in tune with Tulsī in the main. Tulsī's version of the wedding is itself an attempt to "wed" dharma and bhakti. Hymns of praise and expressions of deep emotion are interspersed with references to obeisance to elders and gurus, gift giving to brahmans, zeal for ritual precision, and strict observation of caste dharma. Sāgar too tries to have it both ways. Many have remarked on Sāgar's bhakti agenda and the way he exploits the medium of TV to provide multiple occasions for *darśana*. What is less commonly realized, however, is that, in comparison to Tulsī's medieval version, the balance has shifted away from emotional bhakti toward strong endorsement of dharma.

Sāgar's privileging dharma over bhakti is clear from the many occasions where he turns down Tulsī's emotional pitch and gives more airtime to moralizing sermons. *Darśana* is balanced with *śravana* or moral instruction. This becomes very apparent if we take note of how many of Tulsī's hymns in praise of Rāma have been dropped and replaced with moral sermons. On several occasions Sāgar suppresses Tulsī's *darśana* verses in favor of reinforcing dharma. One example is the adoration of the *kuladevī* after the wedding ceremonies are over, where Sāgar substitutes Tulsī's *nakha-śikha* description of Rāma with a pedestrian song stressing the *dhārmika* nature of the event.

Sāgar's bhakti, in other words, has become suffused with dharma. Sāgar's message is that emotional devotion needs to be restrained and disciplined, and emotional excess is strongly discouraged. This is perhaps most strikingly seen on the occasion of the leave-taking of the *barāt,* where Tulsī's scenes are drenched in *karuṇa rasa,* and he indulges in a description of all Sītā's relatives crying their full. Sāgar instead uses the occasion to warn against excessive emotions. One example of an innovation to make that point is the scene where Sunayanā confesses her trepidations for her daughter to the *gurupatnī,* and is chided for not better restraining her emotions. A good example of change in focus is the scene of the farewell of the queen-mother to Sītā. Hardly any emotion is allowed to surface until after a long lecture on women's dharma.

Of all the classical types of bhakti, it seems that Sāgar has worked deliberately to stay safely away from the erotic or *śṛṅgāra* mode, and favors instead modes like serenity or *śānti,* and servitude or *dāsya.* The latter comes to the fore most strongly in the wedding scene, where Janaka washes Rāma's feet. Whereas Tulsī's text had several other occasions for foot washing, this is the only one that Sāgar chooses to depict. He dwells on the scene a comparatively long time, which seems significant in assessing his bhakti preferences.

Sāgar's privileging dharma over bhakti has also its repercussions in the way the character of Rāma is portrayed. Sāgar makes every little thing Rāma says or does exemplary for human moral conduct. As a result, Rāma becomes more and more remote, less a likely object for bhakti. He becomes so "sanitized," so disciplined and detached in everything he does, that there are hardly any emotions left to endear him to us. Sāgar's stress on the irony of the incarnation is such that we are never allowed to lose track of the fact that he is just "going through the motions." We cannot very well identify with him and sympathize during the "contest," because he himself is so aloof. Even when he is falling in love, winning Sītā's hand, and then marrying the woman of his choice, he is portrayed as perfectly equanimous. The irony is that the main object of Sāgar's bhakti, namely Rāma, has become devoid of emotion himself.

The whole point of his "going through the motions" once again, of his incarnation on TV, is to provide plenty of occasion for *darśana* and to inspire love. Here again Sāgar seems to be in agreement with Tulsī, but his emphasis is on love channeled within the boundaries of propriety. If Sītā is the ideal loving *bhakta,* he emphatically states that her love (and of course Rāma's) remains well within boundaries of *maryādā.* Their love is emphatically said to be preordained (by Rāma himself in his musings to his brothers), and of course it is sanctioned in Vedic and family traditional manner by a wedding. Even the gods explicitly approve. What is more important, at no point does Sītā give in to her emotions. Everything she does is always with due respect for elders and for her subordinate position to Rāma. It is even following his command that she gets to consider herself to be his partner rather than his slave. In Kṛṣṇa bhakti, the ideal loving devotee is God's beloved, yet Sītā's conjugal love seems light years away from Rādhā's *śṛṅgāra,* and shows more affinity with *dāsya bhakti.*

If one compares Sāgar to Vālmīki, it is apparent how much the latter focuses on women's rites and women's perspective. Again, he has this in common with Tulsī, but one should also refer to the context on Doordarshan, where several serials had women-oriented narratives (Mankekar 1999, 104). Interestingly, these serials were set in a joint-family context (Mankekar 1999, 110), and Sāgar's "soap opera of the gods" turns out to be also family-focused. This perspective is one that we do not find in Tulsī, and that seems to have inspired many of Sāgar's innovations. This is particularly clear from the reception of Janaka's message in Ayodhyā, which is depicted in a family rather than court context. It is also evident from the repeated stress that the wedding is a family affair, not one of individuals.

Sāgar's picture of the joint family is very rosy. In his ideal epic world, there is no tension between the bride's party and the groom's party, or between mother-in-law and daughter-in-law (nor, for that matter, between co-wives). Interestingly, stress on the unusual harmony of these traditional dyads is not new, but already present in *VR*. What is new is that in his editorial comments Sāgar explicitly recommends following the epic example. The message sent to the family of grooms is to treat the bride's family with respect, and the new brides, once they arrive, with love and understanding. In his editorial comments, Sāgar says that if people follow this example, a lot of tensions will disappear from "our society" and the *Rāmāyaṇa* story will come true. There is a hint here of a suggestion that the "tensions" are later accretions, whereas the pure Hindu ideal does not insist on the inequalities.

When Sāgar asks his audience to follow the royal house of Ayodhyā's example, he does not deal with the cause of many of the problems, namely dowry. He does not address the issue directly, just mentions Sītā's dowry in passing. In doing so, he seems to condone the practice, or at least, he does not condemn it and classifies it in the category of auspicious elements that constitute a successful wedding. This unwillingness to confront the issue directly is all the more suspect because Sāgar does show the problem of the plight of the father of the bride, by dwelling on Janaka's despair. He does so without ever touching on the issue of dowry, which hovers like a ghost in the background.

The way Sāgar portrays it, the secret of the happy joint family seems to be obedience to elders and male dominance. At every step, Sāgar is keen to highlight the submissive attitude of his characters, even of Rāma himself, to paternal and elder male authority. To some extent this was already the case in *VR*, and more so in *RCM*. However, Sāgar definitely goes farthest. His characters show impeccably respectful behavior and obedience to elders in word and deed.

Sāgar's innovation of the intimate conversation of father and son after their reunion in Mithilā seems to have for its raison d'être exactly driving home this point. During the whole scene, Rāma is seen busily massaging his father's feet, while repeatedly humbly ascribing his success to his father's inspiration, even in absentia. The importance of obedience to paternal authority is also clear from the passages of *RCM* that Sāgar chooses to leave out, such as Sītā's rebellious thoughts about her father's condition for her wedding. Sāgar also had Sītā touch Rāma's feet after the *svayaṁvara,* whereas Tulsī had said she refrained from doing so. Modesty in front of elders is another form of respectful behavior that Sāgar favors. He singles out for quotation verses from *RCM* that stress Sītā's modesty during the *svayaṁvara* ceremony. He goes further in this respect than Tulsī: during the whole wedding ceremony, Sāgar's Rāma and Sītā are not shown looking at each other, whereas Tulsī had explicitly added a verse to describe their beholding one another.

Sāgar's message to the young stresses the priority of the family above the individual. This is clear in several of his innovations, most explicitly in Vasiṣṭha's lecture about the social importance of a wedding. Sāgar is most explicit: a wedding is a meeting of families, not of hearts. If classically *svayaṁvara*s were seen as *gāndharva vivāha,* Sāgar is quick to subvert this. We have seen how in more than one way he does all he can to make it clear that though Sītā and Rāma may have fallen in love at first sight, theirs is no love marriage. Sāgar is very concerned to communicate clearly that in the ideal epic world love marriages are out. Parental approval, if not determination of the match, is central.

Sāgar also stresses the need for private desires to be submerged and made secondary to dharma and *maryādā.* He values positively the lack of agency of Rāma and Sītā in having their love sanctified in marriage. In his editorial comment, he stresses that Rāma makes no move to lift the bow until commanded to do so by his guru, although he understood Sītā's agony full well. Such self-effacing silence is typical for the idiom of the Hindi movie. Whereas the *Rāmāyaṇa* tradition is often blamed for such morality that glorifies the submergence of individual desires for the common good, paradoxically the contemporary *TVR* allows for much less agency than *VR* itself.[35]

The message sent to young women is remarkably conservative, notwithstanding all the stress on women's perspectives and the airtime given to women's rituals, which creates the illusion of empowerment of women. Sāgar's characters endorse unabashedly patriarchal values. Sunayanā's *upadeśa* to the young brides and Janaka's parting words to Sītā are explicit statements to that effect. Sāgar's stress is all the more remarkable because, contrary to what one might suspect, he is not basing these passages directly on his sources. Vālmīki had none of this *upadeśa* during the wedding, and Tulsīdās significantly less. Another example where Sāgar is more conservative than Tulsī is at the climax of the wedding. The actual formula spoken by Sītā's father in *TVR* is Vālmīki's. The father asks the groom to accept the bride as *sahadharmacarī* or partner in dharma. He calls her *pativratā* and says she will follow her husband like a shadow. This formula is significantly different from the classical formula according to the *dharmaśāstras* spoken at this point. Sāgar chose Vālmīki's formula, which solely refers to the bride's duties, whereas the classical one focused on the groom's duties not to transgress against his wife in *dharma, artha,* and *kāma.* Sāgar seems concerned to stress women's duties rather than women's rights. One could argue that Sāgar makes up for this in the wedding night scene, where Rāma makes his promise of monogamy. However, the husband's exclusive commitment to the woman is not presented as her right, but as a favor.

More than Vālmīki or Tulsī, Sāgar seems to promise that if (and only if) a young bride is ready to subjugate herself to her husband's family, she will encounter love and understanding. Ditto for the relationship between husband and wife. If she is prepared to obey him unconditionally, his command will be that she should be his equal, his partner rather than a *dāsī.* He may even promise to return her exclusive devotion. In both cases, the outcome for women seems liberating, but in both cases it is actually predicated on the condition of a woman's subjugation. A woman's subjugation is always a given, whereas anything she receives in return is portrayed as a gift.

We see very much the same phenomenon in popular recent Hindi hit movies. I have in mind particulary *Hum Aap ke Hain Koun,* the *Rāmāyaṇa* elements of which I have discussed elsewhere (Pauwels 2000). The heroines featured are Hindu women loved by their men and in-laws. They have a veneer of modernity, yet at the same time they are firmly rooted in dharma and in their joint family. The latter is portrayed as a happy harmonious group.

The current popularity of both TV *Rāmāyaṇa* and such movies—as opposed to the elite "feminist" movies—seems to indicate that this hits a nerve. There is a strong desire among women to have an identity that allows for both: a measure of Western-style "emancipation," yet also a strong family basis. Maybe we should also look at it from the other side, and say that men like to be seen as being "enlightened" toward their womenfolk, yet at the same time assured of their subservience? Clearly, the series answered a strong need, a yearning to overcome the dichotomy between modernity and tradition and to find a symbiosis of both in a hybrid identity to be proud of. In other words, like the *TVR,* the movies show how you can have your cake and eat it too.

The picture we get from the *TVR* also fits well with what has been said about the Hindu right's construction of Hindu women. On the one hand, the Hindu right offers an empowing self-image for women, yet this remains in service of the ultimate cause of the Hindu nation—in particular, the goal of instilling in their children obedience to authority.[36] This fits Sāgar's privileging societal and political welfare above individual happiness. The Hindu nation's supremacy comes true particularly in Vasiṣṭha's sanctioning of Sītā and Rāma's wedding as the union of two important Āryan powers. Further, as we have pointed out, even more than *RCM, TVR* stresses obedience to gurus, to the point that all agency seems to be transferred from the political rulers to holy men. This fits again well with the political agenda of the Hindu right.

I am not trying to make a case for blaming *TVR* for the rise of the Hindu right. Nor am I trying to make a statement about Sāgar's political sympathies.[37] All I have shown is that the "message" of the televized *Rāmāyaṇa* is considerably on the conservative side compared to its ancient and medieval "sources." This may not ring politically correct in a Western academic climate, yet the popularity of the series shows that its message struck a chord in India.

NOTES

1. Such is the common perception, though there are notable exceptions; see Kishwar 1997.

2. Throughout the paper I will refer to *TVR* by giving the episode as well as the page number in the extremely helpful (though sometimes incomplete) transcription of the text by Girish Bakhshi, as edited by Tomio Mizokami (1992).

3. I am grateful to Julie Mehta, a contributor to this volume, who shared with me her observations on this social innovation.

4. There is a tendency in contemporary research to dismiss several ideological aspects of Hinduism in general, and Sāgar's *Rāmāyaṇa* in particular, as originating in or in response to colonial discourse. Obviously the *Rāmāyaṇa* tradition is older than the much-studied nineteenth century, and many elements, including unflattering descriptions of "indiginous people," are much older. The fallacy is often that scholars conflate particular *Rāmāyaṇa* versions with meta-*Rāmāyaṇa* ideas. Even such a careful analyst as Purnima Mankekar conflates those (1999: 205–207). She traces the portrayal of Rāma as embodying both sannyāsi and kshatriya to Bankimcandra, whereas, of course, the combination is much older.

5. References in what follows will be to the vulgate edition of the Gītā Press, rather than to the critical edition, because of its widespread popularity and availability. The translations I have provided are intended to be functional and literal. I have much benefited and occasionally taken over phrases from the Gītā Press and Goldman translations.

6. References in what follows will be to the vulgate edition by Gītā Press rather than to the critical edition, again because of its popularity. Again, the translations are meant to be functional, and I have benefited much from the Hindi paraphrase published with the edition, and occasionally also from existing translations, in particular Vaudeville 1977.

7. For a comparison of Tulsī's *RCM* and *Jānakīmaṅgal* versions of the wedding, see Stasik 1995. I am grateful to the author for bringing this article to my attention; unfortunately I only found out about it after my paper was finalized.

8. Kapila Vatsyayan suggested this in response to my presentation at the "Mediating Culture" conference on the *Rāmāyaṇa* at the University of British Columbia in June 2000. Another participant, William Smith, also suggested comparison with Bengali portrayals of Sītā in film. A more visually oriented interpretation of part of the wedding scenes has been carried out by Dalmia-Lüderitz 1991.

9. Interestingly, the epic kshatriya *svayaṁvaras* deviate from what is outlined in the *śāstras*; see Kane 1974, pp. 523–524. The authors of the *śāstra*s apparently interpreted it as a form of *gāndharva vivāha*, which is exactly what Sāgar works hard to counter. This interpretation is already in Vālmīki, though some elements of the more prestigious *kanyādāna* type of marriage are present, and this is most explicit again in Sāgar's version. For a full discussion of the evolution of the *svayaṁvara* from the epics to the *śāstras*, see Brockington 2000.

10. The passage is of great interest because of its explicit instruction to women, and deserves to be examined in its own right. I plan to study it at a later date.

11. Tulsī is inspired by the *Adhyātma Rāmāyaṇa*, in which predestination is palpable in every line. This work is usually attributed to the fourteenth century and seen as one of the major sources of Tulsī's *Mānas*; see Vaudeville 1955. I have used for reference an edition by the Ramakrishna Math (*AR*). The wedding episode in *AR* starts out following *VR*: Viśvāmitra asks for Rāma to see the bow, which, it is well known, others have seen too. Still, there is a definite *svayaṁvara* flavor to the episode: Rāma is said to string the bow "in the assembly of the kings," and Sītā is present and "crowns" him with a *svarṇamayī mālā* (*AR* 1.6.29).

12. This has also been noted by Dalmia-Lüderitz 1991, p. 225.

13. This is in contrast to the *Adhyātma Rāmāyaṇa*. *RCM* also creates tension in its description of the reaction of the people once the Rāghava boys and Sītā have arrived in the public space of the contest. There is an element of predestination in that people know that Rāma is the right match for Sītā (1.249.1). On the other hand, they see Janaka's condition for winning Sītā's hand as an obstacle to the outcome (1.249.2–3). The TV version owes much in its dramatic treatment to the theatrical conventions of Hindi theater and movies, as noted by Dalmia-Lüderitz 1991, p. 211.

14. It is only in this limited sense that we can speak of a parallel. There are also many differences. For one, in *RCM*, Rāma's trial is "more real" than Sītā's, since the latter is undergone by a shadow-Sītā. Moreover, Sītā is supportive and concerned that Rāma may win his trial, whereas Rāma "speaks some harsh words" during Sītā's trial. In terms of audience reaction, also, as Vidyut Aklujkar has rightly pointed out in her response to this paper, Rāma's trial does not come even close to eliciting the same emotional response as Sītā's does.

15. This seems also to be in contrast with the traditional Rāmlīlā performances of Rāmnagar, as exemplified by the corresponding *līlā* performed on September 10, 1979 (Kapur 1990, p. 67).

16. Literally "receiving."

17. The stress on the relative status of bride-givers and bride-takers in this episode has also been noticed by Lutgendorf (1990, p. 150), who translated this passage.

18. The *barāt* also sings of the greatness of their host (*RCM* 1.307.1), a striking difference from current practice.

19. Goldman (1984, p. 390) notes that some commentators felt uncomfortable with the simultaneous wedding of the four brothers on one day.

20. Note also Tulsī's special stress on the good omens that accompany the *barāt* (*RCM* 1.298–300). This may be read as a counterpart to the bad omens in *VR* that announce the arrival of Paraśurām when the *barāt* is on its way back home (*VR* 1.74.6–14).

21. Vālmīki also describes Kaikeyī's brother Yudhājit's arrival during the *godāna* ceremonies (*VR* 1.73.1–6), but this is not taken up by *RCM*. In *TVR* there is a faint echo, in an episode that is an innovation. Here, upon hearing the news of Bharat's wedding, Mantharā encourages Kaikeyī to take the preparations for her son in hand and argues that as soon as he hears the news, her father will send her brother (*TVR* 10.130). Sāgar also uses this episode as an ironic foreshadowing of later happenings, when Mantharā will encourage Kaikeyī to have Rāma banned.

22. To some extent, one could argue that Tulsī strives for a popularization of the wedding with full participation not only of women but also of low castes. In one line, the presence of *nāīs*, *bārīs*, *bhāṭs*, and *naṭs* is mentioned (as recipients of money distributed by Rāma); see *RCM* 1.319 *dohā*.

23. The wedding ceremonies of the Rāmnagar Rāmlīlā too are reported to be conducted in Sanskrit, as exemplified in the *līlā* of September 10, 1979 (see Kapur 1990, p. 70).

24. Only during the actual circumambulation of the fire are the heavenly flowers said to rain down (*VR* 1.73.37). For text-critical remarks on the phenomenon, see Goldman 1984, p. 391.

25. This reduction of the other gods to second-balcony spectators has interesting parallels in vernacular descriptions of Kṛṣṇa's *rāslīlā* (see, for example, Harirām Vyās's version as analyzed in Pauwels 1996, p. 170).

26. Interestingly, Tulsī's text says "Hearing the melodious singing, holy men abandoned their asceticism, and Cupid and cuckoos were ashamed" (*kalagāna suni muni dhyāna tyāgahiṁ kāma kokila lājahiṁ; RCM* 1.322 *chand*). Although this verse is sung in *TVR*, the gurus present are shown with their back to the women, and they do not even so much as glance in their direction.

27. This episode is reportedly very popular with the audience of the Rāmnagar Rāmlīlā (see Kapur 1990, p. 72).

28. Both the meal and the *gārī* performance are highlights of the Rāmnagar *Rāmlīlā* (see ibid.).

29. Daśaratha says emphatically that this is "Daśaratha's word," an element of foreshadowing of later more dramatic happenings.

30. Sāgar may well have been inspired by Tulsī's pun to that effect in the context of the *pānigahanu* ceremony of Rāma: "How could Videha's king pay his respects, when the image of the dark one (Rāma) had made him bodiless (*bidehu*)" (*kyoṁ karai binaya bidehu kiyo bidehu mūrati sāvaṁrīṁ; RCM* 1.324 *chand* 3c).

31. There are some different emphases in Anasūyā's speech. Appropriately for the occasion, she also stresses that a woman should never leave her husband in bad days. She also colorfully describes the dire consequences of any tresspasses, including becoming a child widow in one's next birth (*vidhvā hoi pāi tarunāī*). As a true brahman, she gives a classification of the different types of wives, and she also stresses that though a woman may be impure (*apāvani*), she still can reach the highest good (*śubh gati*) through service of the husband.

32. I have in mind the *Mahānāṭaka*, the entire second act of which is devoted to the love-play of Sītā and Rāma.

33. This is also the scenario depicted in the Rāmnagar Rāmlīlā, see Kapur 1990, pp. 74–75.

34. Moving beyond gender issues, one could say that the scene also has an apologetic ring to it. Sāgar's linking of these issues is typical for a discourse of modernity: "In the old days, when women were regarded as slaves, polygamy was the norm. Now, women can become full partners, so monogamy prevails." At the same time it enforces a Hindu chauvinist discourse, that even in those unenlightened days Rāma got it right.

35. In *RCM* too, Rāma has less agency than in *VR*, but the stress here is on the irony of the avatar, a typical bhakti theme. In the *TVR*, by contrast, it is the exemplary function of Rāma that is explicitly stressed.

36. As Sarkar points out (Sarkar and Butalia 1995, p. 184), significantly, they are called "woman-servant of the nation" or *rāṣtrasevikā*, not "volunteer of the nation" or *rāṣṭrīya svayamsevak*.

37. It is interesting that Sāgar makes frequent use of the term *saṁskāra*, which is a key term for the Hindu right (Ibid., p. 189). However, Sāgar's political position seems quite ambiguous, as in 1987 he credited the go-ahead for his succesful TV se-

ries to Rajiv Gāndhi at a ceremony in his honor presided over by a stalwart of the Hindu right, Swāmī Viśveṣ Tīrth (Jaffrelot 1996, p. 390 n. 81).

REFERENCES

Primary Sources

AR Swāmī Tapasyānanda, ed. and trans. 1985. *Adhyātma Rāmāyaṇa: The Spiritual Version of the Rāma Saga. Original Sanskrit with English Translation.* Madras: Sri Ramakrishna Math.

RCM Poddār, Hanumānprasād, ed. and comm. [1942] 1990. *Śrīmadgosvāmī Tulsīdāsjīviracita Śrīrāmcaritmānas.* Gorakhpur: Gītā Press.

RR Kathāvācak Rādheśyām. 1971. *Rādheśyām Rāmāyaṇa.* 7th ed. Śrī Barelī: Rādheśyām Pustakālay.

TVR Sāgar, Rāmānand. 1987. *Rāmāyaṇa.* Video cassettes. Transcribed nearly completely in Girish Bakhshi and Tomio Mizokami, eds. *Ramayana: A TV serial by Ramanand Sagar.* Osaka: Osaka University of Foreign Studies, 1992.

VR Goswami, Chinmanlal, ed. 1969. *Śrīmad Vālmīki-Rāmāyaṇa, with Sanskrit Text and English Translation.* 3 vols. Gorakhpur: Gita Press.

Secondary Sources

Brockington, John L. 1984. *Righteous Rāma: The Evolution of an Epic.* Delhi: Oxford University Press.

______. 1998. *The Sanskrit Epics.* Leiden: Brill.

______. 2000. "Sanskrit Epic Tradition IV: *Svayaṁvaras.*" Paper delivered at the Eleventh World Sanskrit Conference, Torino, Italy, April 3–8, 2000.

Dalmia-Lüderitz, Vasudha. 1991. "Television and Tradition: Some Observations on the Serialization of the *Rāmāyaṇa.*" In *Rāmāyaṇa and Rāmāyaṇas,* edited by Monika Thiel-Horstmann. Wiesbaden: Otto Harrassowitz, pp. 207–228.

Entwistle, Alan W. 1987. *Braj: Centre of Krishna Pilgrimage.* Groningen: Egbert Forsten.

Goldman, Robert, ed. and trans. 1984. *The Rāmāyaṇa of Vālmīki: An Epic of Ancient India.* Vol. 1. Princeton: Princeton University Press.

Jaffrelot, Christophe. 1996. *The Hindu Nationalist Movement and Indian Politics: 1925 to the 1990s.* London: Hurst.

Kane, Pandurang Vaman. 1974. *History of Dharmaśāstra: Ancient and Medieval Civil Law in India.* Vol. 2.1. Poona: Bhandarkar Oriental Research Institute.

Kapur, Anuradha. 1990. *Actors, Pilgrims, Kings, and Gods: The Ramlila at Ramnagar.* Calcutta: Seagull.

Kishwar, Madhu. 1997. "Yes to Sītā, No to Rām." In *Manushi* 98: 20–31.

Lutgendorf, Philip. 1990. "Ramayan: The Video." In *Drama Review* 34.2: 127–176.

Mankekar, Purnima. 1999. *Screening Culture, Viewing Politics: An Ethnography of Television, Womanhood, and Nation in Postcolonial India.* Durham: Duke University Press.

Pauwels, Heidi R.M. 2000. "Three Ways of Falling in Love: Tulsīdās's Phulvārī Episode and the Way It Is Portrayed in Contemporary Electronic Media." In *A Varied Optic: Contemporary Studies in the Rāmāyaṇa,* edited by Mandakranta Bose. Vancouver: Institute of Asian Research, University of British Columbia, pp. 55–100.

______. 1996. *Kṛṣṇa's Round Dance Reconsidered: Harirām Vyās's Hindī Rāspañcādhyāyī.* London Studies on South Asia 12. Richmond: Curzon Press.

Sarkar, Tanika, and Urvashi Butalia. 1995. *Women and the Hindu Right: A Collection of Essays*. New Delhi: Kali for Women.

Stasik, Danuta. 1995. "The Divine Marriage: The Nuptials of Rām and Sītā as Seen by Tulsī." In *Proceedings of International Conference on Sanskrit and Related Studies (Cracow, September 23–26, 1993)*. Cracow Indological Studies, vol. 1. Cracow: Enigma Press.

Vaudeville, Charlotte. 1955. *Étude sur les sources et la composition du Rāmāyaṇa de Tulsī-Dās*. Paris: Adrien Maisonneuve.

———. trans. 1977. *Le Rāmāyaṇa de Tulsī-Dās, texte hindi traduit et commenté*. Paris: Société d'Edition "Les Belles Lettres."

APPENDIX. COMPARATIVE OVERVIEW OF THE WEDDING SCENE IN *VR, RCM, TVR*

The following abbreviations are used in this chart for the sake of brevity: R stands for Rāma, S for Sītā, L for Lakṣmaṇa, D for Daśaratha, J for Janaka, Vi for Viśvāmitra, Va for Vaśiṣṭha, Kai for Kaikeyī, Kau for Kauśalyā, Bh for Bharata, Ś for Śatrughna. I have used the sign ~ to indicate a comparison made by the poet. For *VR* and *RCM*, the numbers in parentheses indicate section and verse. For *TVR*, numbers indicate episodes and page numbers in the transcribed version.

VR	*RCM*	*TVR*
Breaking of Bow		
Context: J is performing a *yajña*	J performs *dhanuṣyagya/svayaṁvara*	J is performing *svayaṁvara* (*Śivadhanuṣpūjā*)
Vi comes on own initiative but is well received	Same as *VR* (214–5)	Vi had come on invitation of J (5)
	Morning: R & L do ablutions (239)	Morning: L excited, R "teaches the *Gītā*" (7)
	Śatānanda, sent by J to invite (239)	Vi announces invitation from J: "let's see who wins" (7)
	L: winner = Vi's *kṛpābhājan* (240)	L: winner = on whom you have *kṛpā*
		Prearrival conversation of kings (7)
Courtesy call of Vi on J (65)	On arrival: public *darśana* (240–3)	On arrival: *RCM* 241.1&2 (acc. to own *bhāvanā*) (7)
	Each beholds acc. to own *bhāvanā*	TABLEAU
	& *nakhaśikha*	
	& each own emotions (S, Rāṇī)	
Vi asks J to show boys the bow (65)	Special welcome by J (244)	J's welcome (7)
	Reaction of good & bad kings (244–6)	King's reaction: match has been predetermined (7)
Story of origin of bow & S (65)	Arrival of S (246–8) (*jagat jananī*, eager to see R, yet shy in front of elders)	Arrival of S: *RCM* 246 *dohā* & 248.1. 2b, 4 & *dohā* (7) (*jagatjananī*, eager to see R, yet shy in front of elders) (7)

VR	*RCM*	*TVR*
	Reaction of people to S's appearance (249)	TABLEAU
Vow: *vīraśulka* (S born from earth) (65)	Bards proclaim *paṇa* (249–50)	Bards: *RCM* 248 *dohā* (call *bandījan*) (7)
		Genealogy: Hindi pop song *Ham bandījan* (7)
	Rāvaṇa & Bāṇa could not lift (250)	*RCM* 249: *vrat* & *RCM* 250.1–2 (Rāvaṇa and Bāṇa)(7)
Story: failed suitors & ensuing siege (65)	Kings try to lift the bow (251)	Kuśadhvaja announces beginning (7)
		Kings try to lift the bow (7)
		S's mother Sunayanā tense, Kuśadhvaja's wife advises calm (7)
	Bow unmoved ~ *satī*; words of lecher	*RCM* 250.4 & *dohā* (all try) (7)
	Kings ridiculous ~ *sanyāsī* ~ *virāga*	*RCM* 251.1b (*satī* comparison) (7)
J proclaims: if R succeeds, is to marry S (65)	J's despair (251–2)	J's despair (7)
	Moral quandary	Moral quandary (7)
	Bīra bihīna mahī/binu bhata bhubi bhāī	*Āj yeh dhartī vīroṁse khāli ho gaī* (7)
	L's reaction (252–3)(eager to lift bow)	L's reaction (insulted on behalf of R) (7)
	All (also S & R) react to L's words (254)	J apologizes (7)
Bow publicly shown to Rāma (66)		
Vi commands R to behold bow (66)	Vi commands R to break bow (254)	Enacting: *RCM* 254.3 (Vi commands R) (7)
R does so	R on stage ~ sun, people's eyes ~ lotus	R gets up, bows to Vi: *RCM* 255.3 (7)
	R gets up, bows to Vi (255)	254 *dohā* (R on stage ~ sun, people's eyes ~ lotus) (7)
		Bad kings laugh & ridicule him (7)
R expresses intention to lift & string (66)	R's prayer (255)	
Permission of guru & king (66)	S's mother Sunayanā tense, yet comforted (255–7)	Sunayanā tense, not comforted by Kuśadhavaja's wife (7)
	S's prayer (257–9)	Enacting *RCM* 257b–4 (S's prayer) (8)
	Devoted *tana mana bacana*	*RCM* 259. 2b–3 (devoted *tana mana vacana*)
	Make me his *dāsī*	Make me his *dāsī*
	True love will find its true mate	True love will find its true mate (8)
	R knows S's worry (259)	*RCM* 260 *dohā* (R knows S's worry) (8)

(*continued*)

VR	*RCM*	*TVR*
	L: "earth should hold still" (260)	
	Everyone holds breath (260)	
Rāma breaks bow (66)	R breaks bow because S is dying (261)	R breaks bow: *RCM* 261.1b–3a (S is dying) (8)
Everyone falls down except king and R & L (66)	Reaction: guru & gods & people (262)	Sunayanā asks Sītā to put on *varamālā* (8)
J: "my daughter belongs to Rāma"(66)	Queen, king relieved, kings react (263)	TABLEAU
	Reaction of S & L (263)	Enacting *filmī* song: *pahanāo jayamālā*
	S brings *vijayamālā* (263–4)	
	General jubilation (264–5)	
	S does not touch his feet (265)	
	Reaction of good and bad kings (266–7)	
	Confusion: S back to mother (267)	
	Women of Mithila scold kings (268.1)	
	Paraśurām (268–285)	Paraśurām (8)
J sends messenger with Vi's permission (66)	J sends messenger on Vi's cue (286–7)	Vi urges J to send messenger to Ayodhyā (8)
	Further instructions wedding prep (287)	Wedding is fait accompli by breaking of bow (8)
	Construction of *maṇḍapa* (288–9)	
Message to Ayodhyā		
Messengers in Ayodhyā (67)	Messengers in Ayodhyā (290)	B & Ś tell news to D & Kai and Kau (*vīryatā* stressed) (9)
See godlike D (67)	Effect on D (290)	Effect on Kai and Kau (*sās* and *dādī* to be) (9)
	B & Ś arrive to hear (290)	Family banter (9)
	D asks how sons are doing (291)	
Message (courteous but short) (67)	Message (praise of R) (291–3)	D's private message for R & L (9)
D's approval with counselors (67)	D wants to give *nichāvar* (293)	Messenger notes irony (children to you, heroes to others) (9)
	Messengers reject: *anīti* (293)	Official message (cut short: already known) (9)
		D offers gift (pearls) (9)
		Messenger refuses (daughter's *sasurāl*) (9)
		Va approves (9)
		D first asks Va's opinion (9)
		(political overview: union of 2 major *āryāvarta śakti*s) (9)

VR	*RCM*	*TVR*
	Va's blessing (the good [D] will be happy) (294)	
	Report to queens, who honor brahmans & give other gifts (295)	Kau prepares for great gift giving (9)
	Avadh happy (women's songs) (296–7)	Kau sends message for S's mother: S is not *bahu* but *beṭī* (9)
Barāt		
Sumantra charged with *barāt* prep (69)	B (& Ś) arrange for *barāt* (298–300)	Va sets *muhurt* next morning (9) B & Ś to arrange for *barāt* (9)
Journey (4 days)	Journey: good *śakun* (303–4) & great	
Welcome Ceremonies		
D greeted by J (68)	Greeted by *agavān* party & gifts (304–6) Terrific *Janvās* (306) Special welcome from S (306) Reaction of *barāt*: praise of J (307)	In Mithila: Sanskrit recitation from *Yajurveda* (9) D greeted by J (*vinamratā*) (9) D: I've come tied by love (9) J marvels at his luck (9) D: it's all the work of *vidhātā: barābar ke saṁbandhī* (9) J: not equality (9)
D: "receiver dependent on giver" (14)		D: quotes *VR pratigraho dātṛvaśa* (9) More pleasantries (9) Śatānanda suggests guests rest (9)
	R & L eager to meet D, don't ask, but Vi understands (307)	L eager to meet D, R calm (9) Vi takes them to meet with father (9)
	When meeting, D pays respect to Vi, R & L to Va (307–8)	TABLEAU: meeting with father (9) *RCM* 307 *dohā* & 308.1–2 (D sees sons but greets Vi first) (9) Innovation: R massaging father's feet, D compliments him (9) R attributes all success to his father's example (9) D: I've acted for myself, R for others (9) R: son's duty is to carry out father's wishes even unspoken (9)

(*continued*)

VR	*RCM*	*TVR*
		D: but who inspired you to break the bow (music suggests Sītā) (9)
		Innovation:
		L tells B & Ś about R's meeting with S (*bhābi ke pahle darśan*) (9)
		R appears, Ś asks: *prem śāstra* in *guru aśram?*
		R: taught by nature (*prakṛti se*): match fixed by God, exclusive (9)
	General joy (309)	
	Videha women: fourfold wedding (310–1)	
	Kings go home happy (312)	
Janaka suggests next day for wedding (69)	Jyotiṣ set engagement time (312)	J's welcome, Śatānanda announces: *vidhipurvak aur dharm purvak kanyādān* (9)
	(*agahān* month, as fixed by Brahmā)	Set time on basis of *lagnapatrikā*(9)
	Everyone happy, esp. gods (313–5)	D: Va will show *mārgdarśan* (9)
	Darśana of R etc. as grooms (316–7)	
	(even gods praise their eyes)	
Bride's rites are done (69)		
Wedding Preparations		
Kuśadhvaja *yajñagoptā* (69)		
D is invited (69)	Meeting D & J *saṁdhi* equals (320)	
Va recites lineage & asks for 2 daughters (69)		Va recites lineage to indicate R is fully worthy (9)
		J agrees (9)
		Vi, with Va give permission, suggest fourfold wedding (9)
	pūjā of Va, Vi, D all brahmans (320–1)	
J recites his lineage (70)	Bards do *śākhoccār* (324)	
Urges D to do tonsure & ancestor worship (70)		
J suggests date: *uttaraphālgunī* (70)		J agrees (women happy); suggestion all in 1 day (*uttaraphālgunī*) (9)
Vi suggests fourfold wedding (71)		
Va confirms and also date		
J agrees (71)		
D retires & ceremonies (*godāna*) (71)		Va exhorts D to do *godān*, etc. (9)

VR	*RCM*	*TVR*
		Innovation 1: Girls' quarters: Sunandā relates news (9) Happiness about 4 sisters marrying 4 brothers (9) Innovation 2: Speech of director explaining supremacy of *maryādā* Innovation 3: Kai gets news about fourfold wedding, tells Kau & Su (10) Mantharā urges Kai to celebrate separately for B (ref. *maikā*) (10)
Kaikeyī's brother joins festivities (72) *kautukamaṅgala* (72) V reports to Janaka (72)		
Brides are ready too (72)	J calls *suhāginīs* for *parachan* (317)	Preparation for wedding fire, *munis* reciting from *Yajurveda* (10)
	Women (& goddesses) *maṅgalgīt* (318)	Gods decide to go & witness events (10)
	Esp. S's mother (318)	*Śṛṅgār* of brides & *mehndī*, but *sakhis* leave to see *barāt* (10) Folksy songs for *barāt* (*āī hai barāt jankajīke dvāre*) (10) *Pujā* by women led by Sunayanā (10)
Wedding Ceremony Proper		
Grooms enter (72)	Grooms enter *maṇḍapa* & get *ārati*(319)	Grooms enter *maṇḍapa* Songs for *maṇḍapa*: (*lagana maṇḍapa meṁ padhāro*) (10) Welcome *tilaka* (*Śaṅkaracārya stuti* & *Durgāsapataśatī*) & *ārati* by J (10)
	Gods unrecognized, except by R (321)	Śiva & Brahmā come down and are recognized by R (10) J welcomes & gives command to call for S (10)
	Arrival S & reactions (322–3)	Brides arrive: *RCM* 322 *chand* (beauty of S)(10)
	S's *pūjā*: Gaurī, Gaṇeśa, brahmans (323)	S does not look at R (10)
	S looks at R (323)	TABLEAU
	Pakhārnā of feet of R (324)	*Pakhārnā: RCM* 324 *chand* 1a–b & 324 *chand* 2c–d (10) *Hastalepa: Durgāsapataśatī* (10) *Paṇigraha:RCM* 324 *chand* 3 (10)

(continued)

VR	*RCM*	*TVR*
Janaka bestows hands of brides to grooms (72)	*kanyādān* (324)	J grants S's hand: *VR* 1.72.17, *GP* 73.27 *pativratā mahābhāgā chāyevānugatā sadā*(10)
	Comparison-wedding Śiva & Pārvatī	*RCM* 324 *chand* 4a–b (comparison with Girijā's wedding) (10) Knot & *Varamālā: Yajurveda, Viṣṇusahasranāmastotra,* Durgā seven hundred (10)
Circumambulation of fire, etc. (72)	*bhāṁvarī* (325) & *sindur*	Women's song (*baraṇa lāgī bhāṁvariyā*) & RCM 325.1 (10) R does *māṁgbharaṇ*: *RCM* 325.4 (*sindur*) & song (*maṅgal gāo rī*) (10)
	Other brides & grooms (325)	Marriage of others (recitation) (10) J & D vie in humbleness (10)
	Big dowry, most given away (326)	
Grooms return to camp with brides (72)	Brides and grooms to *kohabara* (326)	Procession brides & grooms, obeisance to *kuldevī* (folksy song) (10) Exit: *RCM* 327 *dohā* (10) Innovation 1: Sunayanā reflects on sadness of losing daughter (10) *Gurupatnī* comforts her (10)
	S shyly gazes at R (327) *Gahakaura* (327) Brides & grooms to D (328) & *jevanār* While eating hear *gārīs* (329) Big *godān*(330–1)	
Leaving Ceremonies		
Vi departs (73)		
D takes leave (73)	D doesn't get permission to leave (332)	J pleads with D not to go yet, D promises not to go till told to (10) Innovation 2: Kai & Kau & Su decide waiting too long (11) Kai sends message: *kanyāpakṣa* will have to do as *varapakṣa* pleases (11) D rejects message but Sumantra talks realpolitik (11) Innovation 3: Comments of people: daughter & *māyā* (11)

VR	*RCM*	*TVR*
	Vi & Śatānanda ask J, then leave (333)	Vi and Śatānanda convince J (*nītirakṣā* & girl = *parāyī*) (11)
		Va reports to D and calls for *bidāī* (11)
Many gifts to daughters *(kanyādhana)* (73)	J sends *barāt* back with big dowry (333)	Sunayanā hints that her husband gave big dowry (11)
	Reaction of queens & *upadeśa* (334)	Sunayanā *upadeśa* (gift of mother = *nārī dharm*) (11)
	People eager to see them (335)	
	Ceremonies by queens (336–7)	
	Tragic sentiment on *bidāī* (337–8)	She has to be reminded to do *bidāī* (11)
	J sends them off with tears (338)	
		D comes to get girls; stops J from touching his feet (11)
		J pleads with D to be gentle toward girls (11)
		D: "brides = *ghar kī* Lakṣmī" not at feet, at forehead (11)
		Girls are not servants, but *mahārāṇīs* (11)
	J gives *upadeśa* (339)	Śatānanda announces it's time (11)
		J gives *upadeśa*
Procession leaves (73)		Folksong (*jab doli meṁ baiṭhkar biṭiyā jāe bides*) (11)
Paraśurāma		
Ill omens: Rāma Jāmadagnya appears (73–5)	Good *śakuns* (340)	
	J accompanies for a while (341)	
	D asks him finally to leave (341)	
	J sings praise of R (342)	
R's obeisance to Va, etc. let's go home (76)	J takes leave from Vi (343)	
Arrival in Ayodhyā		
Beauty of Ayodhyā (76)	Welcome in Ayodhyā (344–5)	
Queens welcome brides (76)	Queens getting ready (345–6)	
	Va orders *barāt* to enter city (347)	
	People gaze (348)	
	Queens do *parachan* (348–9)	*RCM* 348–9 (mothers do *parachan* of grooms (11)
Princesses perform *pūjā*	Queens do *lokrīti* (350)	*RCM* 349 (all according to *nīti*, *rīti*, etc.) (11)

(*continued*)

VR	*RCM*	*TVR*
		Va recites Sanskrit *stotra* (11)
		Enactment: queens do *parachan*
		Brides & grooms do *pūjā* of Sun deity
		Kai suggest R does his *kautuk* (*negcār*) first, B agrees (11)
		First *dudh bhāt* (not *bahu*, but daughters) (11)
		Searching for *kaṁganā:* S wins (11)
	Barāt guests leave (351)	
	D & all honor Va (352)	
	Presents to women (353)	
	D in *Raṇīvās* & reports news (354)	
	Private meal (355)	*RCM* 355: all tired & retire (11)
	D asks queens to care of *bahus* (355)	D asks Kau to make *bahus* happy, Kau sees Sunayanā's plight (11)
	D retires (355)	
Duties fulfilled, couples make love (76)	Queens set up bedrooms (356)	
	Brothers muse: tender R = strong (357)	
	All brothers in own beds (357)	
	Queens lead *bahus* to bed (358)	
R devoted to S, he to her (76)		R & S's wedding night: *ekapatnīvrata* (11)

8

When Does Sītā Cease to Be Sītā? Notes toward a Cultural Grammar of Indian Narratives

Velcheru Narayana Rao

"Of all the *Rāmāyaṇa*s that have been told so far, is there any one in which Sītā does not go to the forest with Rāma?" asks Sītā when Rāma discourages her from following him to the forest, in one of the versions A. K. Ramanujan reports.

Anachronistic and even postmodern as it might sound, this question raises the more general issue—when does Sītā cease to be Sītā? Clearly, Ramanujan's Sītā knows that she must go to the forest because every Sītā in every version of the *Rāmāyaṇa* goes to the forest. If Sītā does not go to the forest, she is not Sītā, nor is the story a *Rāmāyaṇa* story. My question in this essay is simple: How many changes in the narrative does a Sītā character comfortably accept and at what point does a change trigger another character that is no longer Sītā? To use a linguistic analogy, the phoneme /p/ in English is a cluster of features of a particular sound value within which you may vary, but by the time you shift from the feature of voiced to unvoiced, you are no longer saying /p/. Now it is /b/. Is there a similar boundary for the features that make up the "phoneme" Sītā in the "language" of the *Rāmāyaṇa*?

Using Vālmīki's text for *Sundarakāṇḍa,* and several versions of the events of *Uttarakāṇḍa,* where Sītā's personality is on full display, I discuss this question, drawing upon several non-Vālmīki versions of the *Rāmāyaṇa* and some more recent "anti-*Rāmāyaṇa*" texts to illustrate this point further. Making a broad classification of narratives based on a tripartite cultural ideology of land, trade, and pastoralism, I suggest that the Sītā in Vālmīki and Vālmīki-based texts is a heroine of a land narrative, in contrast to the heroines of the trade and pastoral narratives. In conclusion, I suggest that the prominence of Sītā as a role model of Indian womanhood is the result both of the political dominance of the landed ideology at the expense of the other two and of a recent impulse to imagine the *Rāmāyaṇa* as a national epic. I will begin with a reading of Sītā in Vālmīki.

Vālmīki's name, if not his actual narrative, provides the infallible basis for all *Rāmāyaṇa* texts. What I intend to do here is something unconventional: I want to suspend all the religious and devotional layers tradition has invested in Vālmīki's name, which transform his text into a sacred utterance. I want to read Vālmīki's text for its human drama. Since my intention is to discuss gender and power relations in *Rāmāyaṇa* narratives, I hope to be forgiven for this somewhat literalist project.

Sītā in *Sundarakāṇḍa*

Let us begin with Sītā as Vālmīki presents her in *Sundarakāṇḍa*. Vālmīki gives a woman extraordinary passive power as long as she stays within the limits of the house, trusts in the strength of her husband to save her from all troubles, and does not sleep with any other man. A chaste woman, a *pativratā*, has a social and moral power that she can manipulate to her advantage. This is what Sītā does more intelligently than the bhakti readers of Vālmīki's text usually realize. *Sundarakāṇḍa* provides strong evidence of her manipulative skills.

In captivity Sītā is utterly helpless, with no apparent strategy to protect herself. Her total helplessness and her unshaken confidence in Rāma's ability to save her are the two inseparable qualities that endear her to her readers. In the face of death threats from the *rākṣasa* women who guard her, Sītā defiantly says she is ready for any physical suffering, including death, because life without her husband is worse than death.[1] She continues to reject the advances of Rāvaṇa, saying she would not touch such a despicable creature even with her left foot. Immediately after this, she goes into a soliloquy about Rāma's invincible strength. She wonders how this puny demon Rāvaṇa is able to imprison her while she has a mighty husband who can easily kill him in battle. However, she has one worry: perhaps Rāma has neglected her, forgotten her? Otherwise, why would he not come to save her? She consoles herself with the one comforting thought available to her: Rāma does not know that she is on this godforsaken island. To keep her sanity, she continues to remain confident that Rāma will come and save her. She imagines in graphic detail how totally and completely Rāma will destroy Laṅkā—and more particularly, how the women in Laṅkā will suffer widowhood when Rāma, along with Lakṣmaṇa, comes and kills their husbands in battle[2]

As is well known to every reader of *Sundarakāṇḍa*—in almost any telling—Hanumān offers to take her away from Laṅkā and solve the problem once and for all. Sītā can reunite with her husband, put an end to her own and every one else's suffering, and the story can end happily ever after. The arguments that Sītā gives against this solution demonstrate her manipulative intelligence at its perfect pitch. First, she compliments Hanumān for his strength and agrees he is capable of rescuing her.

> I know your strength and courage.
> You are the greatest among monkeys.
> You have the speed of wind and the strength of fire
> astonishingly blended in you.
>
> I know you are able to return home
> and take me with you, too.
> And the swift accomplishment of Rāma's mission
> is to be the goal in all our plans.[3]

Then a host of reasons follow why it would not be correct for Hanumān to rescue her. She could fall off Hanumān's shoulders and die. Or the demons could chase after Hanumān, and Hanumān could find the responsibility of protecting her an additional burden. Sītā could also fall out of fear, or even from an accidental push when Hanumān is involved in a fight. The demons would then get a second chance to imprison her, and this time they would hide her in a secret place, impossible for any one, even Hanumān, to find. They might even kill her. And then Rāma, Lakṣmaṇa, even Sugrīva and Aṅgada would die of grief. The inclusion in this list of Sugrīva and Aṅgada—total strangers to her until Hanumān had told her of them—is clearly to discourage Hanumān from any further interest in pressing his offer. Finally, the last argument is the real clincher: Hanumān himself might be killed; after all, success or failure in battle is never sure.

At this point, Sītā realizes that she is probably humiliating Hanumān by so graphically depicting his defeat in this imaginary battle with the demons. She quickly corrects herself by adding that she knows Hanumān could kill all the demons and more. But then, if Hanumān takes care of all those who deserve to be killed, what is left for Rāma to do? Rāma's fame as an incomparable warrior would be deflated. Hanumān should not show off his strength now; it would be a disservice to Rāma.

Sītā then offers a final argument that cannot fail. She, as a *pativratā,* will not touch another man and for this reason she cannot sit on Hanumān's shoulder. She immediately remembers that the demon Rāvaṇa did actually touch her; he lifted her with his hands on her buttocks and placed her on his chariot when he took her away to Laṅkā. But she excuses herself this lapse because she was helpless. She was utterly weak, unprotected, and was not in a position to resist or fight with Rāvaṇa. Touching Rāvaṇa was not her doing, whereas touching Hanumān would be her choice, and therefore very compromising.

This argument makes Hanumān feel guilty for having suggested that he take her on his shoulders, and he offers an apologetic explanation. Sītā now concludes her presentation with a request. She wants Hanumān to persuade Rāma to come and save her. She is absolutely confident of the invincible power of Rāma:

If Rāma kills Rāvaṇa, his family and his relatives,
takes me in pride and returns home, that's an action that befits him.

I know his strength and I have seen him fight.
He is powerful, a killer in battle.
Gods, demigods, dragons or demons—
no one equals him if he decides to fight.

Who can stand up to him in an open battle?
He holds no ordinary bow.
In his strength he equals the king of the gods.
Coupled with his brother, Rāma is invincible.
He is like fire ablaze, quickened by wind.

He is like the burning sun at the end of the world.
He is like an elephant guarding space.
He is a killer in battle. Who can stand up to him
if he comes with his brother, swift as an arrow?

So bring him here and make me happy
with his army, his commanders and his powerful brother.
I grieve without him, alone in this island.
Great monkey, do this for me.[4]

What Sītā wants is to make Rāma destroy Rāvaṇa, his family, his entire clan, and the city. Not until then is she willing to leave Laṅkā. She is willing to extend her personal suffering until that moment, until Hanumān convinces Rāma to go to Laṅkā to battle with Rāvaṇa.

Sītā relates an incident from her life to Hanumān that only she and Rāma know of. This would serve as proof to Rāma that Hanumān did actually find Sītā herself. The story she chooses is carefully calculated to appeal to Rāma's male pride by reminding him how he was provoked to valor when someone else tried to molest his wife. When a demon in the form of a crow attacked Sītā in the forest, tearing at her breasts, Rāma took a blade of grass and infused it with the power of *Brahmāstra,* the ultimate weapon of destruction, and sent it against the crow. Sītā concludes, addressing Rāma:

You know your weapons; they are the best.
You are strong and truthful, for certain, but
why not use these weapons on this demon,
if you really care for me? (36.36)

And why doesn't that brother of yours
take orders from you?
That scourge of his enemies doesn't help me.
What could the reason be? (36.39)

The two of you, strong as tigers
and equal to wind and fire.

Even gods can't face you, let alone demons.
Why are you so passive about me? (36.40)

You used the deadliest of your weapons
on a mere crow that hurt me.
Why do you then forgive the demon
who stole me away from you? (36.43)[5]

She continues her message to Rāma, complaining about his tardiness in rescuing her and questioning why his brother has not been helping him in this task. Sītā's competence as a skillful diplomat is not complete without her compliments to Lakṣmaṇa as part of her final message to the brothers. She praises Lakṣmaṇa's physical strength as a warrior with broad shoulders and long arms, and compliments him on his good heart. She acknowledges that Lakṣmaṇa respects his brother as a father and—what's more critical here—loves Sītā as his mother. She concludes by saying she is very fond of Lakṣmaṇa and knows he will skillfully complete any task given by his brother, no matter how difficult.[6] These words about Lakṣmaṇa appear on the surface to be good wishes sent by a sister-in-law to her brother-in-law. But they have a crucial significance for Lakṣmaṇa, who knows that Sītā had accused him of harboring a secret desire for her. Lakṣmaṇa had left Sītā alone against his brother's command precisely because of this terrible accusation. It was her adamant demand that Lakṣmaṇa leave her alone in the forest and go to help Rāma who had gone after the magic deer that precipitated matters in the first place and brought her to her present captivity. She remembers very poignantly that Lakṣmaṇa might feel justified in letting her suffer her fate for her willfulness and abusive temper. But now she needs Lakṣmaṇa's support to encourage his brother to invade Laṅkā. This message is carefully worded as a veiled apology for her past behavior and is a poignant appeal for help.

The Sītā of *Sundarakāṇḍa* is weak, unable to help herself, and by the very same token very skillful in prodding her man to become the hero he has to be in order to protect her. It is this Sītā who makes Rāma the warrior and punisher of demons. In other words, the hero we know Rāma to be is a male response to a weak and dependent Sītā, generated by the power relations in the gendered world of the *Vālmīki Rāmāyaṇa*.

Problematics of *Uttarakāṇḍa*

Now let us turn to *Uttarakāṇḍa*, the "later" *Rāmāyaṇa*, the more complicated part of the Rāma story that describes his abandoning the pregnant Sītā in the forest without even warning her. The details of the narrative are too well known to need repetition here. The narrative is beset with difficult and troubling events that have challenged the imagination of *Rāmāyaṇa* poets for ages. Some of them, such as Kampaṉ in Tamil and Viswanatha Satyanarayana in Telugu, have even rejected the entire later *Rāmāyaṇa* as an interpolation and saved themselves the trouble of answering uncomfortable questions. If Vālmīki did not write it, it has no validity. The easiest way of devaluing a text is to divest it of its original source of authority, its author. But then there are great writers such as Kālīdāsa, Bhavabhūti, and Diṅgnāga who took the narrative and presented it in brilliantly creative ways, interpreting Vālmīki without apologies. I will begin with a close reading of Vālmīki's text to argue that the Rāma created by the first part of the *Rāmāyaṇa* is obligated, in the second part, to behave the way he does toward Sītā, and that Sītā has no choice other than to accept Rāma's decision.

In *Uttarakāṇḍa,* Rāma is happy that his wife is pregnant, that she is going to give him a child, and so he lovingly asks her what she desires and what he may do to please her. She requests to see the forests on the shore of the river Ganges where sages practice their austerities. She even wants to spend one night there eating roots and berries among the trees. Eager to satisfy the craving of his pregnant wife, her loving husband Rāma is willing to give that gift to her. "You will definitely go to the forest tomorrow," he says, "trust me."[7] Rāma spends time with his friends, who banter and joke with him, when he casually asks one of them, "What are people saying about me and my wife and my brothers?"[8] Evidently, the friends come from among the ordinary folk of the city and they have access to people in all walks of life. The friend who was asked this question responds in the same friendly and intimate tone, "They say a lot of things about you, both good and bad (*śubhāśubham*)."[9] He describes how people praise Rāma for his extraordinary achievements, such as building a bridge across the ocean, something unheard of before, and killing the powerful demon Rāvaṇa, making friends with monkeys, bears, and even demons. They also say that Rāma has put his anger behind him, has brought Sītā back and taken her into his inner chamber. Now comes the criticism. His friend reports that people say:

> He [Rāma] must really love the sexual pleasure she gives to him (*sambhogajam sukham*). He is not disgusted that she sat in Rāvaṇa's lap when he dragged her to Laṅkā and later kept her in the Aśoka garden. That whole time she was under Rāvaṇa's control (*vaśam*). How could he take her back? From now on this behavior will be the law of the land because whatever the king does, the people also do (*yathā hi kurute rājā prajā tam anuvartate*). This is what people have been saying in the city and the countryside, all over.[10]

It is clear that Rāma does not suspect his wife himself, but feels he has to be a good king to his people, be a role model for them all. Clearly, the conflict is between his personal feelings and kingly responsibilities. He discusses the matter with his brothers Lakṣmaṇa, Bharata, Śatrughna, and tells them with tears in his eyes the problem that he faces. He describes how this slandering of Sītā pains him. He reminds them that Sītā was born into a noble family and points out that Lakṣmaṇa witnessed the events in the forest when Sītā was taken by force. Then he confesses that he did have questions in his mind about bringing Sītā back to Ayodhyā. Would his people accept her? He describes how Sītā entered the fire to prove her chastity and how, while Lakṣmaṇa and everyone else was looking on, the god of fire and the god of wind both testified that Sītā was pure. Even the sun and the moon gave the same testimony to a group of gods and sages. Sītā was unblemished.[11] He agonizes. "I know in my own mind that Sītā is unblemished. But people still speak ill of her. The good name (*kīrti*) of the royal family is important."[12] He therefore decides that he has no alternative but to banish Sītā.

A question arises from his decision: Could he not convince the people by properly informing them and educating them? Apparently he could not, because it would be self-serving to speak in favor of his own wife. Anything he does to prove her chastity would be suspect. But more important, the social norm that makes women responsible for showing evidence of their chastity and constantly suspects them is the very bedrock of this culture. It cannot be changed. It is this conviction that makes Rāma choose to behave like the king he is in preference to the husband he is—at the expense of his and Sītā's personal feelings.

What is significant is that Sītā understands this, too. She does not fight against the cultural values that cause this suspicion to begin with. She does not question the value of chastity. She is not even angry with Rāma for what he has done to her. She approves of his decision to discard her for fear of scandal and takes the responsibility upon herself to clear Rāma's name. She even rejects the idea of suicide because that would kill Rāma's children that she is carrying in her womb. If she blames anyone at all, she blames her own fate, the sins she may have committed in a past life. In effect, Sītā wants to continue to be a respected *pativratā* in this culture, and accepts all the pain and suffering that it brings, hoping that in the end she will be rewarded with the absolute approval of being a chaste wife.

Here Vālmīki enters the story to rescue Sītā. He does not suspect her because he has seen everything with his divine vision and therefore knows the truth. Toward the end of *Uttarakāṇḍa* we are reintroduced to the context that was first narrated in the beginning of the text, when Sītā's sons Kuśa and Lava sing the *Rāmāyaṇa* story as composed by Vālmīki to King Rāma. Realizing that Sītā is still alive and that Kuśa and Lava are none other than his sons, Rāma wants to know who is the author of the story and wants Sītā to be brought back to him. After being informed that Vālmīki, who incidentally is visiting the city, is the author, Rāma tells Vālmīki that he would accept Sītā back if she performs an act of truth (*śapatha*) to prove that she is chaste. By performing such an act of truth, Rāma hopes that her name will finally be cleared and with it his name as well (*śodhanārtham mamaiva ca*). Vālmīki approves of the idea and promises that Sītā will do as required. Rāma is happy that he will get his wife back because she will now have an occasion to prove her chastity in front of all the sages, citizens, and anybody else who wants to witness it. Sītā arrives with her head bent, walking behind Vālmīki. Putting his own reputation as a sage and the merit of all his austerities on the line, Vālmīki declares in the presence of everyone gathered that Sītā is pure, and that the twins are Rāma's sons. Sītā does perform an act of truth, asserting her absolute fidelity to Rāma, but not in a way Rāma would have expected. Sītā declares:

> I have never set my mind on any man other than Rāma, so may the goddess of the earth open up for me. I have served only Rāma in thought, word and deed, so may the goddess of the earth open up for me. If all that I have spoken is true, and if I do not know any man other than Rāma, may the goddess of the earth open up for me.[13]

At that moment, the earth breaks open and a golden throne rises from below with the goddess Earth seated on it. The goddess invites Sītā into her lap, and the throne disappears into the underworld as gods rain flowers from the sky. An amazed Rāma realizes what has happened and gets angry at Earth for taking his wife away from him. He demands the goddess return his wife to him or else he will destroy the entire earth with its mountains, forests, and all. He wants her back badly (*matta*). He is even willing to go and live in the underworld or anywhere else as long as he can have Sītā back. Once the good name of Sīta is reestablished to the satisfaction of his people, he is now free to admit that he loves her, and wants her back. But it is too late; Sītā is gone forever.

This is the most intriguing part of Vālmīki's text and one that is difficult to interpret definitively. Based on her behavior as an obedient and chaste wife, one would expect Sītā to ask Earth or some other god or goddess to clear her name for everyone to hear, so she could be taken back by her husband. In choosing to return to the earth, she has accomplished two things: she has proven her chastity and demonstrated her independence, as well. It is both a declaration of her integrity and a powerful indictment against a culture that suspects women. It is difficult not to interpret this as Sītā's protest against the way she was treated by her people and by her husband. She probably concluded that the people would never believe in her chastity, and Rāma would never be allowed to take her back with love and affection. The only course left for her was to leave the scene once and for all. Even with this, Sītā has not done anything that would compromise her status as a faithful wife. An expression of such independence is apparently acceptable as long as she has not touched another man.

Diṅgnāga in his *Kundamālā* and Bhavabhūti in his *Uttararāmacarita* revisit the story of Sītā's abandonment in the forest. Apparently, there is something ideologically unacceptable and emotionally unsatisfying for them when Sītā demonstrates her independence in rejecting Rāma as well as the people, albeit within her bounds. Both playwrights have expressed an intense need to reunite Rāma and Sītā as husband and wife separated by a third, inevitable force, whatever that might be. Both Diṅgnāga and Bhavabhūti repeat what we know from Vālmīki: that Rāma abandoned Sītā not because he suspects her but because the people in his kingdom suspect her. Lakṣmaṇa says to Sītā in the forest where he has taken her to be abandoned on his brother's orders, "The sages saw, as did the rulers of the world. Rāma himself was there and I watched too. You came out pure from the fire. The people still blame you and the people are powerful (*loko niraṅkuśaḥ*)."[14]

Both Bhavabhūti and Diṅgnāga take us through an elaborate and complex psychology, drawing a distinction between Rāma as a private person and Rāma as a player in the larger theater of the world. Both authors distinguish between being for oneself and being for others—the inevitable existential tragedy of a kings's life. Diṅgnāga does this with great sensitivity to Sītā. In his play, Sītā is intensely aware of the painful distinction between her role as a mother and carrier of the seed of the Raghu dynasty and her place in Rāma's heart as his beloved companion.

In a poignant scene, Vālmīki encounters the pregnant Sītā in the forest yet unaware of her identity. Vālmīki asks her if she has been exiled by King Rāma. When Sītā answers affirmatively, Vālmīki says: "If you are driven out by the king who is dedicated to establishing the rule of *varṇāśrama* social order, good luck to you. I am going (*yadi tvam varṇāśramavyavasthābhutena mahārājena nirvāsitāsi tat svasti bhavatyai gacchāmy aham*)." Sītā repeats her appeal for help—this time in a different tone: "If you cannot show compassion to me because Rāma threw me out, you should at least rescue me because I carry the seed of the family of Raghu, Dilīpa, Daśaratha and others in my womb." A curious Vālmīki asks if she is the daughter-in-law of Daśaratha and the daughter of Janaka. Sītā answers, "Yes." Vālmīki pursues further, "Are you then Sītā?" And Sītā says, "Not Sītā. I'm an unfortunate woman."[15]

It is very significant that Sītā disowns her own identity as Sītā when her faithfulness to Rāma is in question. She ceases to be Sītā when she is suspected of not being a faithful wife of Rāma. The distinction is important. Sītā as suspected wife has no status in this world. But as a mother she has all the power she would want to command, provided she uses it powerlessly, so to speak. She shows her personal anger against Rāma, but in a very controlled manner. When Lakṣmaṇa takes her to the forest to abandon her there on Rāma's orders, he asks if she has a message for Rāma. Sītā says: "If I am giving a message to that cruel man, it is because you asked and I can't say no to you. Tell him to take care of the kingdom and the rule of law, not to disregard his duties as king worrying about me. Ask him to take care of his health." The sarcasm is obvious. Then she collects herself and asks Lakṣmaṇa: "Am I being too harsh to the king?" To which Lakṣmaṇa responds, "You have the right to be, don't you?"[16] Sītā is acutely aware of her public status as a wife when she says: "People always mention—when they talk about ideal couples—Śiva and Pārvatī in heaven, and Sītā and Rāma on earth."[17] Despite all her anger, she is aware of her place in Rāma's heart—and does understand the difference between Rāma's action in his kingly role and his feelings toward her as loving husband.

Even after convincing herself that Rāma abandoned her to save the kingship from being tarnished, in her own mind Sītā continues to doubt if Rāma really loves her. In her conversation with her sons in Vālmīki's hermitage, she always refers to Rāma as "that merciless man," *niranukrośa* (giving the impression to the boys that that is actually their father's name).[18] Sītā never expresses her doubts to anyone, even her intimate friends. The conversation between Vedavatī and Sītā illustrates Sītā's public posture. Vedavatī asks "Why do you suffer for him? You are growing thin like the waning moon. He has no love for you. He doesn't want you back." Sītā immediately objects, and insists that Rāma loves her and has not really left her. He has only left her physically; not in his heart. She confidently says, "His heart is never far from me."[19]

The question still persists. *Loko niraṅkuśaḥ*, the people cannot be disciplined. Neither Diṅgnāga nor Bhavabhūti accept this as inevitable and refuse to live within the dictates of the people. They believe that people can be educated to examine the evidence and change their minds, and unlike Vālmīki, both authors want Sītā to reunite with Rāma. Both show in some detail that Rāma suffers for Sītā in her absence, as much as Sītā suffers the separation, clearly suggesting that he had to abandon her as king, but as husband her absence was unbearable for him. In the *Kundamālā*, the poet devises a strategy to make this happen. Through his ascetic power Vālmīki arranges it such that women become invisible to men when they walk around the river, so their freedom is not curtailed when Rāma and his retinue visit the hermitage on the invitation of the sage. This allows Sītā to walk invisibly close to Rāma, whom she can see but who in turn is unable to see her. Thus, an invisible Sītā overhears Rāma speaking to himself, expressing his feelings for her. A similar but more elaborate strategy is adopted by Bhavabhūti to let his audience know that Rāma has suffered quietly in agony because of Sītā's absence.[20] Clearly, both Diṅgnāga and Bhavabhūti show that in order for her to return to Rāma, Sītā needs the personal reassurance that Rāma really loves her, just about as much as Rāma needs a public testimony that Sītā has been faithful to him, so his people would be convinced of her chastity. There are incidents in both plays when Rāma is directly condemned by one of the characters; for instance, in *Kundamālā*, Vālmīki publicly rebukes Rāma for not respecting the testimony of Fire and for choosing to obey the slander of uneducated people. One wonders, listening to the harsh tone of the sage addressing Rāma, if Diṅgnāga is condemning Rāma much like an anti-*Rāmāyaṇa* author of modern times. Listen to Vālmīki's words in the play:

> Hey King, you think of yourself as a kindhearted man, a person of noble birth, wise and just. Is it proper for you to abandon your wife Sītā—a woman given by King Janaka, received by your father Daśaratha, recognized as auspicious by Arundhatī, declared chaste by sage Vālmīki, accepted as pure by Vibhāvasu, daughter of the goddess Earth, and mother of your sons, Kuśa and Lava—just because you happened to hear some people slander her?[21]

The interrogation continues, "After you killed the ten-headed antigod Rāvaṇa, when you took Sītā back, who vouched for her chastity?" Rāma meekly responds, "The god of Fire." Then Vālmīki asks, "What then made you disregard his testimony?" At this point, Sītā feels that she is to blame for the public condemnation her husband is being subjected to by Vālmīki. She covers her ears so as not to hear Vālmīki railing against her husband, calling him a dictator, *niraṅkuśa*. Soon, the goddess Earth appears with great fanfare and declares to all assembled there that Sītā is chaste, totally above blame. The people accept this declaration with approval and celebration. Rāma accepts Sītā, acknowledging her chastity.[22] On close reading of this section of the play, we realize that Vālmīki's angry words are not really aimed at Rāma but at the people who are assembled there and who have slandered Sītā unjustly. This is the education that Diṅgnāga believes the people in the story require, and which he provides through this incident. In the end, Rāma remains justified in his act of abandoning Sītā, as Sītā is honored in willingly going through the suffering without blaming Rāma.

To summarize, in the world of Vālmīki and his followers, women have to carry the seed of the family in its purity and therefore not only are they bound to be chaste, they also bear the responsibility to prove their chastity. A *pativratā* has to accept the burden of proof that she is a *pativratā*. In other words, she is guilty until proven innocent. Once the *pativratā* creates herself, she also creates her protector who by definition has to turn into her tormentor. If this man has to live up to what is expected of a *pativratā's* husband, he has no alternative except to abandon her when her *pātivratya* is suspected, giving her the opportunity to prove her innocence in public. In effect, Sītā creates Rāma, and Rāma creates Sītā. They mutually construct each other. You cannot have one without the other.

Sītā in Selected Non-Vālmīki Versions

Long before modern revisionist readings of the Rāma/Sītā relationship, there were several radical readings during the premodern period, some of which are well known, such as the Jaina versions of the *Rāmāyaṇa* and the version popularized by Kṛttivāsa in Bengal. Among them, the versions told by women in Telugu are quite striking. Telugu women's *Rāmāyaṇa* songs include a song entitled *Kuśalava-kuccala-kathā*.[23] In this story, Rāma's sons kill him without knowing who he is. The story begins when Rāma leaves a horse to roam the world unchecked as a part of the horse sacrifice he is performing, a ritual that allows him to declare himself a king of the whole world. Anyone who objects to this declaration would have to stop the horse from crossing their land. Rāma would then fight and defeat them and get the horse released. If he fails to do so, he would lose the title of king of the world. When Lava and Kuśa notice the horse where they live, they catch it as an expression of their strength. The guards following the horse go and report to Rāma that two young boys have captured the horse. Rāma sends his army to fight the boys, but the boys defeat the army. Puzzled and bewildered, Rāma sends Lakṣmaṇa to take care of the problem, but the boys kill Lakṣmaṇa, as well. Left with no other choice, Rāma himself goes to battle the boys. The boys kill Rāma, too, and quietly go to tell their mother that they have killed a couple of men who were pretending to be the kings of the world. Sītā wonders who they could be and goes to the battlefield to discover the dead heroes are Rāma and Lakṣmaṇa. A saddened Sītā tells the boys they have killed their father and uncle, and runs to Vālmīki for help. Vālmīki recognizes the tragedy and with his magical power brings the dead heroes and their army back to life. Rāma realizes that the heroic boys are his own sons and that Sītā is still alive. He wants the boys and Sītā to be reunited with him, but the boys adamantly refuse and declare that Sītā is not going either. They demand that Rāma apologize for his treatment of Sītā and bow down to them seeking forgiveness. Sītā and Vālmīki, and all those gathered, advise the boys to show respect for their father, but the boys do not listen. They reject the advice even of Vālmīki because, after all, he wrote the *Rāmāyana* favoring Rāma. The point of the story is clear. Sītā as a wife has no proper way of opposing her husband, whereas her sons can fight for her and can be as critical as necessary to condemn their father for all his faults while protecting their mother from being victimized. Sītā retains her status as a good wife by standing outside the conflict while her sons fight for her and say all the harsh words against Rāma—which Sītā may have wished to say herself, but could not as a proper wife.

Another story that comes from women's songs and represents Sītā in a different light is "Śūrpanakhā's Revenge."[24] Śūrpanakhā, angry that her brother Rāvaṇa died at Rāma's hands, wants to avenge his death. She goes to Sītā dressed as a religious mendicant and asks her to draw Rāvaṇa's picture. Sītā protests that she has never set eyes on that man's face; she has only seen his toes. Śūrpanakhā persuades Sītā to draw a picture of Rāvaṇa's big toe. Śūrpanakhā then completes the picture herself and gives life to the picture. She leaves the picture in Sītā's possession and abruptly leaves. Sītā, who is stuck with the picture, tries to get rid of it, by throwing it into the well behind her house, but the picture returns to her. She tries to destroy the picture, tear it, burn it, bury it. No matter what she does, the picture comes back to her. It just won't leave her. Desperate, Sītā hides the picture under her bed and lies on top of it. Rāma, who comes to bed at night, feels the pressure of the picture from under his side of the bed. Even before he begins to wonder what is pushing him, the picture pushes Rāma off the bed. Rāma is furious with Sītā for pushing him off, but when he sees the picture, he is firmly convinced that Sītā is in love with Rāvaṇa. This is the most innovative reason women's songs find for the banishment of Sītā to the forest. These songs mention neither the people's suspicion of Sītā's chastity due to her living in Rāvaṇa's Laṅkā nor the people's disapproval of Rāma's decision to accept her as his loyal wife. Such an emphasis on Rāma's suspicion of his wife rather than his sense of duty to his people clearly isolates Rāma as the person to be blamed. If the men's version saw Rāma as a tragic character, torn between his duties as king and his desires as a husband, this women's song views him as a suspicious husband and therefore a flawed man. Significantly, the song does not make any effort to hide the eroticism in the narration of the story. The big toe, the bed, lying right on top of Rāvaṇa's picture—the entire narrative texture of the song is quietly permeated with erotic suggestions that subvert the narrative structure, which ostensibly defends Sītā's *pātivrātya*. The images of the story playfully suggest a hidden sexual desire on the part of Sītā for Rāvaṇa, which, very much like the hidden picture under the bed, is never out in the open. The traditional representations of Sītā are rarely erotic—we hear of her chastity, nobility, her suffering, and her motherly love, but we usually do not hear much about her sexuality. The erotic descriptions in this song are mild, too, and that is as far as the singers of the song can go, while carefully protecting Sītā's honor as a chaste wife. Anything more radical would cause Sītā to lose her status as a *pativratā*, and as I suggest, her identity as Sītā.

There is a tradition at weddings in Andhra whereby the family of the bride praises the virtues of their daughter while putting down the groom. This discourse, popularized in women's wedding songs, takes the *Rāmāyaṇa* theme as a metaphor. In these songs, Rāma is depicted as a hard-hearted, tricky, and deceptive husband and Sītā is extolled as an innocent, trusting, and virtuous woman. During weddings, the bride's family often sings songs with this theme to celebrate the good qualities of the bride's family while playfully denigrating the negative qualities of the groom's family. The bride's family may even claim that whatever good fortune the groom has acquired is due to his luck in choosing their daughter as his wife. A popular song by Tyāgarāja uses this theme and suggests that Rāma would not have been so great a king, nor would he have been famous if he had not married Sītā:

> You chose our Sītā for your wife, and now you are king of kings
> And on top of that you have the fame of slaying the demon Rāvaṇa.
> Because you chose our Sītā for your wife
> She obediently followed you to the forest,
> took a false form, stayed by the fire for real,
> followed the demon, lived under the Aśoka tree in his garden.
> She was furious at his words, but did not kill him right away.
> She wanted *you* to get the fame of killing the mighty Rāvaṇa.
> Lord of Tyāgarāja,
> Because you chose our Sītā for your wife.[25]

Sītā in the Twentieth Century

The narrative changes even more radically in the hands of the authors of modern anti-*Rāmāyaṇas*. Gudipati Venkatachalam, popularly known as Chalam, is a great writer to whom Telugu literature owes a whole new language of sexuality, especially female sexuality. Among the several plays he wrote questioning religious/mythological narratives that preach female chastity, his *Sītā Agnipraveśam* (Sītā enters fire), is the most well known.[26] The play presents Rāma and Sītā for the first time as human beings similar to us, rather than as distant and divine characters beyond ordinary human accessibility. They speak ordinary spoken Telugu as opposed to the Sanskritized high literary style of classical texts. Hearing Rāma and Sītā speak like man and wife, like our next-door neighbors, brings them into an emotional world we all inhabit. The play focuses on the events in Laṅkā immediately after Rāvaṇa's defeat and death. A rejoicing Sītā welcomes Rāma and invites him to embrace her, but Rāma expresses his unwillingness to accept Sītā because she has lived in another man's house for many years. Sītā responds sharply that it was not her choice; she was in captivity. Rāma argues that it does not make a difference, and that as a heroic descendent of the Raghu family he fought to protect his honor and destroyed Rāvaṇa; he cannot bring dishonor to it by accepting a woman who was touched by another man. Sītā protests:

> Let me speak. Ravana loved me. Even your sharp arrows could not kill his love for me. Your love, it was gone the moment you suspected that another man might have loved me. . . . Did I love him in return? That's what you fear, don't you? If I had loved him, I would have covered his body with mine as a shield against your arrows. Did he molest me? No, he was too noble a person for that. He loved me, even when he knew I would never love him in return. . . . I feel sorry I did not return his love. I shall pay the price for it now. I shall purify my body, which was soiled when I uttered your wretched name, by the flames of fire which touched his blood-stained limbs. You, Rama, reject me because you fear that my body was defiled by his touch, though you know my heart is pure. This antigod wanted my heart, even though he knew my body was taken by you. Some day, intelligent people will know who was a nobler lover.[27]

Sītā then throws herself into the funeral pyre burning Rāvaṇa's body instead of walking through the fire Rāma has set for her to prove her chastity. The passage could be interpreted in two ways: Sītā performs a type of *satī* by throwing herself into Rāvaṇa's funeral pyre, which simultaneously marks her as his wife in death. Or, she regrets not having loved Rāvaṇa in return and wants to purify herself of that flaw by throwing herself into his funeral pyre.[28] In either case, the limits clearly are crossed. This character is not the chaste wife of Rāma anymore. The story of the *Rāmāyaṇa* is stretched beyond recognition.

The following poem by the Telugu modern poet Pathabhi, a contemporary of Chalam, and a rebel in modern poetry, is in the same vein.

> Sita was my classmate.
> She and I pored over
> that great new poem the *Ramayana*
> of Satyanarayana.
>
> When we were finished I asked her,
> looking at her thoughtful eyes:
>
> "You listened to the whole story.
> We followed Rama
> with the swiftness of poetry
> into the wilderness of ancient time.
> We met him, went to the forest with him; we saw him

kill Vali from behind the tree
and test his wife by fire.
Now tell me, do you really want to
live like Sita, the wife of the hero
Rama?"

When she heard me, she said:
"Hey, Pathabhi,
Sita is the very epitome of
Indian womanhood.
It's a dream, having
the good fortune
to live like her.

"But even if I should want to be Sita,
I would never want to be Rama's wife.
Tell me, would you ever want to be Rama
yourself?"

"Why would I, when you don't want
to be Rama's wife?
My desire, rather,
is to become Ravana.

"With all my ten mouths
I will kiss your lips, your face. I will bind you
with the gaze of my twenty eyes.
I will press you to my chest
with twenty strong arms
and make you one with me
in one embrace."

Now,
Sita is my wife.[29]

Breaking all taboos about Sītā being forever devoted to Rāma, the poem introduces new nuances in the imagined relationship between Sītā and Rāvaṇa. Sītā, in this poem, wants to be like the Sītā of the *Rāmāyaṇa* because of the latter's honesty and love for her husband. But the husband she wants is not Rāma. And the man in the poem also vehemently rejects identifying with Rāma, and chooses to be Rāvaṇa instead, with all the erotic excitement that comes with that choice. Both characters in this poem reject Rāma and, in effect, reject Sītā too, and create a new Sītā outside the parameters of Vālmīki's narrative. The new Sītā says:

Sita is the very epitome of
Indian womanhood.
It's a dream, having
the good fortune
to live like her.

Clearly, she is choosing the good name of Sītā and the honor that comes with the status of a *pativratā*. She follows this with a rejection of Rāma, meaning that she only wants the honor and not the suffering that goes with this choice. By definition, Sītā is Rāma's wife. She has no existence without Rāma in Vālmīki's world. Once Rāma is rejected, there can be no Sītā. Therefore, the new Sītā who marries Rāvaṇa is not a *pativratā*, even assuming that she is faithful to Rāvaṇa.

Chalam and Pathabhi were writing at a time when a modernist trend in Telugu literature created an atmosphere of a critical rejection of religion and tradition. This trend was, however, limited to the English-educated middle class, which enjoyed a certain degree of latitude and therefore freely exercised its liberal ideas in literature. At present, a conservative and revivalist movement is growing strong, with a goal to reverse the trend started in the early decades of the twentieth century of modernist anti-*Rāmāyaṇas*.

In January 2000, *Andhra Jyoti*, a popular Telugu weekly magazine, received a long story, *Rāvaṇa Josyam* (Rāvaṇa's prophesy) by D. R. Indra, a relatively unknown writer, and the journal decided to publish it in three parts. The first part of the story apparently angered some people. The magazine received a letter that threatened dire consequences should it continue publishing the story. Namini Subramanyam Naidu, the editor of the weekly magazine, refused to be intimidated, and went ahead with the publication of the second part of the story. In response, nearly a hundred men and women, all self-proclaimed members of the Rashtriya Swayamsevak Sangh (RSS), forced their way into Namini's office on the afternoon of January 25, showered him with obscenities, rampaged through his office, and threatened him with physical harm. A staff member who came to his rescue was reported to have been physically assaulted. Cowed by the threats and vandalism, the editorial management of *Andhra Jyoti* withdrew the publication of the third part of the story, and published an apology for "unintentionally hurting [readers'] sentiments."

I will not discuss the issues related to the freedom of the press and civil liberties that arise from this incident, which should be obvious and which in fact led to a wide-scale protest by intellectuals, poets, and writers against the perpetrators of this incident and against the magazine management, which had yielded to the pressure of the conservative thugs. My interest here is to focus on the representation of Sītā and Rāma in the story. To summarize the relevant portion of the story:

> Sītā and Rāvaṇa take long strolls in the Aśoka garden. They enjoy talking to each other; Sītā admits that while she was rattled when she was first kidnapped, she does not find Rāvaṇa half as demonic as people say he is. She listens to him boast of how he has seduced or raped hundreds of the most beautiful women of the gods. But in the case of Sītā, he has fallen in love and will patiently wait until she herself loves him in return. Sītā rejects him and spurns his vanity, but she also realizes that Rāma is no better; he is just as vain, boastful, and cruel, and is as lustful a womanizer as Rāvaṇa is. She finds

> no great choice between them. The only benefit she finds in her captivity is that ever since she has been brought to the Aśoka garden, she finds new freedom and peace—away from the pressures of the palace and the forest, released from the tensions of being a wife and the burden of having to be a *pativratā*. She finds this freedom to be herself more enjoyable than any glory or greatness in the world. Meanwhile, Rāma attacks Rāvaṇa. Mortally wounded in the battle, Rāvaṇa comes to Sītā with his last wish—to hear from Sītā's lips that she loves him. Sītā consoles him in her lap, and assures him that she loves him as her son. Rāvaṇa dies in her lap. Soon, Rāma arrives and expresses his suspicion of her chastity. Rāma asks her to prove herself by walking through fire. In front of her is a blazing fire ignited by Lakṣmaṇa for her to walk through to prove she is chaste. She approaches the fire, takes off her wedding necklace, *māngalya*, throws it into the fire and walks away.

A couple of decades ago, this story would probably have received critical acclaim from the modernist critics of the traditional *Rāmāyaṇa* narrative, and quiet disdain from the devotees of Rāma, as Chalam's play and Pathabhi's poem received in the 1930s. That it generated a more violent protest in 2000 is due to the activist nature of militant Hindu groups and the general deterioration of political discourse. The point, however, is clear. The Sītā represented in this story as well as in Chalam's play and in Pathabhi's poem is not the same character as is presented in Vālmīki's text and that of his followers. She is a distorted Sītā, an anti-Sītā. The crucial boundary that makes her Sītā is her loyalty to Rāma and the moral power that comes from it. Once she has crossed that boundary, even with the symbolic act of throwing her wedding necklace into the fire, she is no longer Sītā.

Why, then, have authors in the twentieth century deliberately changed the well-understood traits of a character so deeply embedded in the popular mind? Why do these authors feel the need to rewrite the *Rāmāyaṇa* by violating its narrative grammar? Part of the answer is in the obvious modernist artistic impulse of reworking classical themes with individual imagination unfettered by conventions. The answer to these questions perhaps also lies in the unprecedented importance the *Rāmāyaṇa* has received in the nationalistic imagination. The Gandhian use of *Rāmāyaṇa* metaphors such as Ramarajya for the ideal of independent India and the nationalist fervor of presenting Indian women as the symbol of purity and passive resistance, suffering for a noble cause, presented Sītā as the supreme role model for all Indian womanhood. Due to its vast popularity, the *Rāmāyaṇa* is mistaken for an epic that represents the entire range of value systems in India. An attempt to make the *Rāmāyaṇa* and its heroine Sītā stand for a variety of cultural role models apparently has not led to a uniformity of national values; on the contrary, it has led to a masking of complexity. We now have a superficial uniformity that hides the contours of this complexity. Sītā now appears in a variety of roles not available to her as the heroine of Vālmīki's text. In effect, a number of heroines are now called Sītā, while retaining at the same time the special features the heroines portray in the narratives of their particular culture. This, I would believe, partly explains the multiplicity of *Rāmāyaṇa* narratives that differ from the Vālmīki narrative among the modern *Rāmāyaṇa*s and the variety of comments on the role of Rāma and Sītā, such as the ones we encounter in Madhu Kishwar's study.[30]

An Ecology of Indian Narratives

This would lead us into a survey of the types of heroines in Indian narratives, a task too big to attempt in the space of this essay. I would still ask if there are compelling and significant representations of women other than Sītā, depicted positively in literature. At the expense of being simplistic, I want to place the major Sanskrit narratives in the context of the broad cultural systems of India: agricultural, pastoral, and mercantile. In this classification, the *Rāmāyaṇa* belongs to the agricultural, the *Mahābhārata* to the pastoral, and the narratives of the Kathā tradition to the mercantile cultures. I would suggest that each of these narratives reflects distinctly different types of value systems and different types of heroes and heroines.

Land is significantly different from other forms of property that are movable, such as gold, material goods, or marketable skills. In times of crisis, other kinds of property can be taken to a safer place. Land is immobile; you cannot put it in your pocket and walk away with it. The only way of protecting it is to fight for it. A hero in this value system is one who fights to protect the land and dies fighting. He does not negotiate a settlement, a compromise, or a politically acceptable deal; he wants all or nothing. Castes that primarily share the landed culture equate women with their land; own them as they own their land, restrict their movement, control their sexuality, and deny them remarriage. Loyalty to one man (*pātivrātya*), which is generally perceived as a value for all women in India, is primarily a landed-caste value. Landed culture values certain qualities in men, such as the willingness to protect their women. A woman herself is not allowed to fight for her own safety. She should wait for her man to save her. Indian history, literature, and folklore related to the landed castes are littered with stories of women who die voluntarily when their men are unable to save them. Death is preferable to falling in the hands of the enemy. A woman who falls into captivity is considered truly "fallen." A permanent stigma attaches to her character because people assume she may, either willingly or by force, have sexual relations with her captor. The biological and therefore uncontrollable condition of life that women become pregnant and give birth to children makes them vulnerable to conquest, just like the land, and for that reason, it makes their constancy a matter of anxiety and suspicion. Chaste women are given miraculous powers in legends and myths: men who threaten their chastity can be cursed to death by chaste women. The same women, however, cannot curse men who threaten their lives. Chastity for a woman in this culture is more important than life itself. In a landed culture, the inheritance of land is strictly limited to the authentic male heirs of the owner, and legitimacy of children is assured only by a strict control of women's sexual behavior. As might be seen in Diṅgnāga's narrative, Rāma declares his son Lava king as soon as it is made publicly clear that Sītā is chaste. The *Rāmāyaṇa* is a narrative that reflects the ideals and cultural ideologies of landed communities, but not all Indian communities.

Communities that live on trade and manufacturing skills, on the other hand, are not tied to the land and are generally mobile. People with such skills are capable of migration and of developing a new livelihood in a new place. Manufacturing is also very different from growing food. Craftsmen create a new reality different from the reality of nature. Food growers, who have a sense of dependence on nature to produce their world, often marvel at the skill of the "makers." At the same time, they are also suspicious of their craft, which they see as crafty, untrustworthy. The stories and epics of trading communities stand in sharp contrast to the landed-caste stories. In Sanskrit, there is a huge body of Kathā literature, from the legendary *Bṛhat-kathā* to the extant *Kathā-sarit-sāgara* and the *Bṛhat-kathā-śloka-saṁgraha*. The hundreds of such stories, generally interpreted as collections of erotic stories, reflect the cultural ideology of mercantile communities.

Women in these stories are intelligent, capable of protecting themselves, and have control of their lives without total dependence on their men. They are clever, cunning, and are celebrated not so much for their chastity as for their skill in having affairs without being caught. The theme of the clever adulteress in the narratives of the Kathā tradition, such as *Śuka-saptatī*, is too well known to need repetition. The ideal woman in this culture is the heroine of the "Red Lotus of Chastity," who cleverly protects herself from the mischievous advances of men in the absence of her husband while at the same time safeguarding her husband from the allure of other women. Chastity and fidelity to the husband are still important for a woman in this culture, but she is not bound to depend on her husband to save her, nor is she bound to prove that she is a *pativratā*. The heroine in this story takes initiative, plans her future, and manages to achieve a triumphant end to her plans. Furthermore, heroes in the narratives of the mercantile classes use cunning and trickery to achieve their goal—as opposed to the heroes in the narratives of landed culture, who prefer battle as their first choice. Heroism in the narratives of mercantile classes consists of gaining success and living happily afterward, rather than opting for a foolhardy rush to battle and death in order to gain *vīrasvarga*—the hero's heaven. A mercantile hero is intelligent, just, and capable of judiciously resolving conflicts, such as King Vikramāṅka in the *Vetāla-pañcaviṁśati* stories.[31]

A similar value system is found in the literatures of other Indian languages, which have a number of epic narratives that reflect the values of pastoral culture. Pastoral communities have a functional interest in land, which they need to graze their cattle. They do seek to control the land, but do not care who actually owns it. Pastoral stories celebrate heroism but do not value death on the battlefield as superior to success in gaining power over the enemy by cunning. The heroes and heroines of pastoral epics reflect characteristics very different from the epics of the land owning class. To represent the *Ma-*

hābhārata as a pastoral epic would drastically reduce its complexity, but it should be clear that none of the women in the *Mahābhārata* resembles Sītā in her relentless pursuit of fidelity to and dependence on her husband. Apart from the well-known Draupadī, who has five husbands and is an extremely strong woman who takes control of any situation she is in, women such as Damayantī and Sāvitrī demonstrate a characteristic agency, an ability to take initiative to resolve a problem, rather than wait for their husbands to come and save them. They are no less *pativratās* for the strength and independence they demonstrate, but they are not Sītās either. It is easier to see the features of a pastoral culture in oral epics such as *Cāndāinī, Devnārāyan,* and *Katamaraju kathā*.[32]

Since landed culture is socially dominant to the extent of projecting itself as the only culture of the country, nonlanded values get short shrift as low castes are treated as less respectable. Modern scholars tend to class these narratives as folklore, while in Sanskrit literary tradition themes borrowed from *Kathā sarit-sāgara* do not have the same high status as those borrowed from the *itihāsa*. Pressured by the dominant landed culture, nonlanded communities tend to borrow cultural practices from landed communities in order to present themselves as respectable. In south India, a large number of castes of nonlanded cultures are classified as left-hand castes, among whom women follow a lifestyle more relaxed than landed culture would sanction. Women of these communities remarry and maintain a certain degree of economic and personal independence. Such groups tend to be socially invisible, and their stories and cultural tradition is lost to scholarship.[33]

One significant feature of Indian narrative is retelling. Stories and themes from major narrative traditions have been told—again and again—for centuries. As a result, characters of these narratives take on a life of their own, away from authorial controls, and become as familiar as your next-door neighbors. Poets and writers and tellers and performers enjoy a wide degree of freedom in depicting these well-known characters. At the same time, there are restrictions to this freedom. We know a lot about the variations in the telling of these stories, and the freedom the tellers take. What is not well understood is that there are limits to this freedom. The limits, I suggest, are best understood by exploring the underlying cultural grammar of these narrative traditions.

NOTES

1.

> *bhidyatām bhakṣyatām vāpi śarīram visrjāmyaham /*
> *nacāpyaham ciram duḥkham sahyeam priyavarjitā //*
> *caraṇenāpi savyena na spṛseyam niśācaram /*
> *rāvaṇam kim punar aham kāmayeyam vigarhitam //*
>
> *chinnā bhinnā vibhaktā vā dīptevagnau pradipitā /*
> *rāvaṇam nopatiṣṭeyam kim pralāpena vas ciram //*
> (*Sundarakāṇḍa* 24.8, 9, 11)

2.

tato nihatanāthānām rakṣasīnām gṛhe gṛhe /
yathā'hamevam rudatī tathā bhuyo nasamśayaḥ /
anviṣya rakṣasām laṅkām kuryād rāmaḥ salakṣmaṇaḥ // (Ibid. 24.23)

3.

tava satvam balaṁcaiva vijānāmi mahākape /
vāyoriva gatiṁāpi tejascāgnerivādbhutam // (Ibid. 35.42)

jānāmi gamane śaktim nayane cāpi te mama /
avaśyam sampradharyāśu kāryasiddhir ihātmanaḥ // (Ibid. 35.42, 44)

4. Ibid. 35.64–68.
5. *Sundarakāṇḍa*, 36.36, 39, 40, 43.
6. Ibid. 36.45–46, 48.
7. *Uttarakāṇḍa* 41.26.
8. Ibid. 42.4–6.
9. Ibid. 42.13.
10. Ibid. 42.17–19.
11. Ibid. 44.5–9.
12. Ibid. 44.11–12.
13. Ibid. 88.10.
14. *Kundamālā*, act 1.
15. Ibid., act 2.
16. Ibid., act 1.
17. Ibid., act 2.
18. Ibid., act 5.
19. Ibid., act 2.

20. Bhavabhūti, *Uttararāmacarita*, Act 7. Bhavabhūti devises a play produced by Vālmīki within the play. Vālmīki invites all gods, antigods, animals, serpents, and all classes of human beings to his play, which presents Sītā's story following her abandonment, as follows. A distressed Sītā tries to kill herself by drowning in the Ganges River. The goddesses Gaṅgā and Earth dramatically rescue her and present her with the twins she has given birth to in the water. Following their birth, the Jṛmbhaka weapons manifest themselves to serve the boys. Earlier, when Sītā was pregnant and was still with Rāma in Ayodhyā, Rāma had declared that these weapons would one day belong to his sons. True to his utterance, the weapons promptly appear upon their birth. This act serves as a divine DNA test which proves that the twins are Rāma's legitimate sons. Toward the end of the play, Arundhatī testifies to the purity of Sītā in front all the people assembled, and thus Rāma and Sīta are reunited.

21. *Kundamālā*, act 6.

22. Ibid.

23. See Gopalakrishnamurti 1955, pp. 256–262. I discussed this story in my essay "A *Rāmāyaṇa* of Their Own: Women's Oral Tradition in Telugu" (1991). Here I extensively adopt from that discussion.

24. Narayana Rao 1991, pp. 126, 130.

25. Tyāgarāja, *Mā jānaki cēṭṭa baṭṭaga mahārājuvaitivi*. Rāga Kāmbhoji, *Ādi tāla*. Madhu Kishwar, in her article "Yes to Sita, No to Ram" (2001), argues that people believe that Rāma was wrong to abandon Sītā in the forest while she was

pregnant, whereas Sītā, on the other hand, lived up to the expectations of Indian womanhood suffering silently without saying one harsh word against Rāma. She presents evidence from her fieldwork among a number of people from different classes, castes, and occupations in favor of this position. But the value system of the *Rāmāyaṇa* is not that simple.

26. Venkata Chalam [1934] 1976.

27. Ibid. Following Telugu usage, diacritical marks have been omitted. The discussion here is adopted from my essay "The Politics of Telugu *Rāmāyaṇas*" (2001).

28. I am indebted to Paula Richman for this interpretation.

29. Pathabhi 2002.

30. See note 25.

31. J.A.B. van Buitenen drew our attention to these stories as early as 1959 in his introduction to *Tales of Ancient India*.

32. For summaries of these epics see Blackburn et al. 1989, and for a study of the Cāndāinī epic, see Flueckiger 1989.

33. See my "Tricking the Goddess" (1989), and "Epics and Ideologies (1986), where I discuss the narratives of left-hand castes.

REFERENCES

Bhavabhūti. 1990. *Uttararāmacarita*. Edited by R. S. Tripathi. Varanasi: Krishnadas Academy.

Blackburn, Stuart, et al. 1989. *Oral Epics in India*. Berkeley and Los Angeles: University of California Press.

Diṅgnāga. 1983. *Kundamālā*. Edited by Jagdish Lal Shastri. Delhi: Motilal Banarsidass.

Flueckiger, Joyce Burkhalter. 1989. "Caste and Regional Variants in an Oral Epic Tradition." In *Oral Epics in India*, edited by Stuart Blackburn et al. Berkeley and Los Angeles: University of California Press, pp. 33–54.

Gopalakrishnamurti, Sripada ("Krishna Sri"), ed. 1955. *Strīla Rāmāyaṇapu Pātalu*. Hyderabad: Andhra Sarsvata Parishattu.

Kishwar, Madhu. 2001. "Yes to Sita, No to Ram." In *Questioning Rāmāyaṇas: A South Asian Tradition*, edited by Paula Richman. Berkeley and Los Angeles: University of California Press, pp. 285–308.

Narayana Rao, Velcheru. 1986. "Epics and Ideologies: Six Telugu Folk Epics." In *Another Harmony: New Essays in the Folklore of India*, edited by Stuart Blackburn et al. Berkeley and Los Angeles: University of California Press.

———. 1989. "Tricking the Goddess: Cowherd Katamaraju and Goddess Ganga in the Telugu Folk Epic." In *Criminal Gods and Demon Devotees: Essays on the Guardians of Popular Hinduism*, edited by Alf, Hiltebeitel. Albany: State University of New York Press, pp. 131–164.

———. 1991. "A *Rāmāyaṇa* of Their Own: Women's Oral Tradition in Telugu." In *Many Ramayanas: The Diversity of a Narrative Tradition in South Asia*, edited by Paula Richman. Berkeley and Los Angeles: University of California Press, pp. 114–136.

———. 2001. "The Politics of Telugu *Rāmāyaṇas*: Colonialism, Print Culture, and Literary Movements." In *Questioning Rāmāyaṇas: A South Asian Tradition*, edited by Paula Richman. Berkeley and Los Angeles: University of California Press. pp. 159–185.

Pathabhi. 2002. "Sita." In *Twentieth Century Telugu Poetry: An Anthology*, edited by Velcheru Marayann Rao. Delhi: Oxford University Press, pp. 70–71.

Richman, Paula, ed. 1991. *Many Ramayanas: The Diversity of a Narrative Tradition in South Asia.* Berkeley and Los Angeles: University of California Press.

———. 2001. *Questioning Rāmāyaṇas: A South Asian Tradition.* Berkeley and Los Angeles: University of California Press.

Vālmīki *Rāmāyaṇa.* 1960–. Edited by J. M. Mehta et al. Critical ed. Baroda: Oriental Institute.

Van Buitenen, J.A.B. 1959. *Tales of Ancient India.* Chicago: University of Chicago Press.

Venkata Chalam, Gudipati. 1976. *Sita Agnipravesam.* 3rd ed. Vijayawada: Aruna Publishing House.

9

Representing the *Rāmāyaṇa* on the *Kūṭiyāṭṭam* Stage

Bruce M. Sullivan

In the state of Kerala, south India, dramas have been enacted for centuries in a style known as *kūṭiyāṭṭam*.[1] Composed in Sanskrit and related languages, and enacted by temple servants as a religious obligation, these dramas have traditionally been regarded as sacred by Hindus in Kerala.[2] Three of the dramas recount the well-known story of the *Rāmāyaṇa*, but in each case the playwright has conceived innovative ways of presenting the narrative. Performers have contributed additional material and significantly modify the texts of the dramas as they enact them. This essay examines these dramas and the *kūṭiyāṭṭam* tradition of enactment.

Two of the dramas were attributed by T. Ganapati Sastri to Bhāsa, *Pratimā Nāṭaka* and *Abhiṣeka Nāṭaka*, though neither drama cites an author's name.[3] The third drama is *Āścaryacūḍāmaṇi* by Śaktibhadra, a Kerala playwright, who wrote in the ninth century C.E. All three dramas present the *Rāmāyaṇa* story in full, though in different ways. As the story is well known, I shall emphasize the innovations of the playwrights rather than recounting the dramas in detail.

Pratimā (The Statue) begins with the failed consecration of Rāma. With Rāma, Sītā, and Lakṣmaṇa in exile, King Daśaratha dies of grief on stage (act 2). Bharata returns from a stay with his uncle, and stops at a temple with which he is unfamiliar on the outskirts of Ayodhyā. There he sees statues of his Ikṣvāku ancestors, including Daśaratha, thus realizing that his father has died, and hears from the caretaker what has happened (act 3). The drama also includes an interlude beginning act 6 in which the audience learns that Jaṭāyu has died, and an interlude beginning act 7 in which the audience learns that Rāvaṇa has died. The only suggestion of Sītā's trial is mentioned by the queens to Sītā of "the fulfillment of your vow." The seven-act drama ends with Rāma's consecration.

Abhiṣeka (The Consecration) is a drama in six acts, though performers have made it into seven by taking the interlude beginning act 6 as a separate act. The drama begins with Vāli dying on stage, shot by Rāma's arrow, and the alliance between Rāma and Sugrīva. In act 4, Rāma reaches the ocean, but rather than showing the building of a bridge so that Rāma and his army can reach Laṅkā, the play shows Varuṇa appearing and dividing the waters so that they can pass. Act 6 begins with an interlude that informs the audience that Rāvaṇa is dead. Rāma refuses to see Sītā, due to questions of her fidelity, so she undergoes trial by fire. The drama ends with Rāma's consecration.

One remarkable feature of these two dramas is that they include the deaths of characters on stage. In Sanskrit dramas deaths are customarily described after the fact, not shown on stage. There is no prohibition on doing this, because Bharata's *Nāṭyāśātra* specifies the means of depicting a character's death on stage (7.85–90 and 26.101–115), but custom dictates it. In these two dramas the playwright(s) chose to depict the deaths of Daśaratha and Vāli (though not Rāvaṇa) before the eyes of the audience. Another drama sometimes attributed to Bhāsa, *Ūrubhaṅga*, features Duryodhana dying on stage. *Ūrubhaṅga* is all the more remarkable for its radical transformation of Duryodhana into a noble and generous ruler beloved by those around him, one whom the gods convey to heaven in a divine chariot at his death. No such profound shift in a character's depiction is found in these two *Rāmāyaṇa* dramas, nor is either death scene itself a great departure from traditional accounts of the narrative. The playwright, however, has been innovative in *Pratimā* with regard to the statue gallery for which the drama is named. Construction of such a memorial hall is not a feature of Hindu religious traditions, and one can only wonder at the inspiration for it. Might Greek, Roman, or other (Kuṣāṇa?) practices have suggested it to the author?

Āścaryacūḍāmaṇi (The Wondrous Crest-Jewel) is a drama in seven acts by Śaktibhadra of Kerala. It is named for an ornament given to Sītā in the forest, later brought to Rāma as a token of her devotion to him while she is held captive. Rāma also received a ring in the forest, which was carried to her. Both ornaments in this drama have a special quality that the playwright has conceived: each enables the one who wears it, on touching a demon, to restore that demon to its original form so as not to be deceived by its capacity for illusion. In act 2, Rāma touches Mārīca and learns his true identity, then kills the demon. In act 4, Sītā has been taken into Rāvaṇa's chariot while he is disguised as Rāma, but when he touches her he reverts to his true form and is recognized as a demon. In act 7 of the drama, after the audience learns of the death of Rāvaṇa in an interlude, Lakṣmaṇa suggests that Sītā be tested to answer the questions that people have about her fidelity. Sītā enters the fire, but celestial voices announce that Rāma and Sītā are in reality Viṣṇu and Lakṣmī, and that Anasuyā's boon in the forest was that Sītā would appear ornamented by anything, even the dust covering her in captivity. In this fashion, all misgivings are put to rest, and the drama ends with Rāma's consecration. Both Anasuyā's boon and the powers of the ornaments are complications in the plot deployed by the playwright.

These dramas have had a number of functions in Kerala society. Obviously there is an entertainment function to such performances; there is also a religious function, as they are devotional offerings to the deity. In addition, there is also a political function that I shall briefly note before discussing the dramas in more detail. For many centuries, Hindu kings patronized theater construction and *kūṭiyāṭṭam* performances in Kerala, right up to the termination of the monarchy at independence in 1947. In fact, the Maharaja of Travancore (the southern half of Kerala) was traditionally crowned in conjunction with the dramatic representation of the coronation of Rāma on the stage of the capital's temple.[4] As indicated above, each of these three *Rāmāyaṇa* dramas ends with the coronation of Rāma, and the three were sometimes performed in succession as a year-long celebration of Rāma. *Abhiṣeka* seems to have been the drama of choice for this political function, as it ends with Rāma consecrated for kingship by Agni and acclaimed by all the gods. The *bharatavākya* or benediction at the drama's end is as follows:

> May the cattle be faultless,
> and may our lion-like king,
> subduing the sovereignty of his foes,
> rule over the earth in its entirety.

This auspicious proclamation by the playwright applies to both Rāma and his human counterpart who is being installed as the new maharaja. The enactment of Rāma's consecration for kingship actualizes the structural homology of king and deity. There is, of course, a long history of evoking imagery from the *Rāmāyaṇa* and the *Mahābhārata* to build a sense of community and national identity among Hindus. *Kūṭiyāṭṭam* is a tradition, from ancient times into the twentieth century, in which drama has promoted the sovereignty of kings who have claimed an affinity with God.

Kūṭiyāṭṭam is Sanskrit theater, that is, the texts of the dramas that serve as scripts are in Sanskrit and related Prakrit dialects. But performers also utilize other languages in representing on the stage the ancient stories they enact, including the vernacular Malayalam or a creole of Sanskrit and Malayalam (Maṇi-pravālam, "jewel and coral") in certain circumstances. In addition, an elaborate language of gesture, and of course music, are also used.[5] *Kūṭiyāṭṭam* is a distinctive adaptation of Sanskrit drama enactment to Kerala's environment; the very name of the tradition is not in Sanskrit but the local vernacular of Malayalam. *Kūṭiyāṭṭam* means "acting together." This is actually somewhat deceptive, as often there is only one performer on the stage, even if that person enacts multiple characters.

Performance time is greatly lengthened by a variety of means in *kūṭiyāṭṭam*. Interpolated commentary, particularly by the *viduṣaka* (jester), is a typical feature; as these three dramas do not have a *viduṣaka*, they do not provide an occasion for his discourse. In every drama, each line recited is repeated several times and enacted in pantomime in an intricate language of gesture. Hand positions and facial expressions, particularly eye movements, communicate the meaning of a line nonverbally. Another convention of performance that greatly lengthens the time needed is that the entrance of a character on stage is deemed to require a description of that character's prior deeds that bring him or her to this point. Accomplished via flashback (*nirvahaṇa*), the account usually takes hours, and is one of the primary vehicles for the introduction of verses composed by the performers or borrowed from other sources, these verses being either recited or gestured. The Sanskrit text is thus elaborated upon extensively for the purpose of bringing out the emotional quality (*rasa*) inherent in the situation and the words.

The tradition of enacting Sanskrit dramas in Kerala is ancient, with a history of a millennium or more in a form similar to what one sees now.[6] Chapter 28 of the Tamil classic *Cilappatikāram* (perhaps third century C.E.) makes reference to a performance at court by Parayur Kuttaccākkaiyan, in whom some see a *cākyār* performing drama.[7] *Kūṭiyāṭṭam* has not been static and unchanging but, as with any living tradition, has adapted to developments in its society. Although many such changes in the tradition can only be guessed at, some are known; for example, its shift from performing in the royal palace to a specially constructed theater building (*kūttambalam*) in each of Kerala's major Hindu temples, a transition effected by the fourteenth century.[8] Performers also made the transition to the temple setting, becoming a *jāti* or subcaste of temple servants. The actors, known as Cākyārs (males) and Naṅgyārs (females), had the exclusive right and religious duty to perform dramas within a temple compound in its theater building.[9] The Cākyārs are quasi-brahmans who ritually take the sacred thread (*upanayana*) to mark their status, but who learn the drama's texts instead of the Veda, and stage movements instead of the Vedic rites.[10] Cākyārs say that they are the descendants of the *suta*, famous in the *Mahābhārata* and *Purāṇa* literature as half-brahman royal bards. They insist that their performance of *kūṭiyāṭṭam* dramas is a religious act for them, comparable to doing yoga or praying. For centuries, performance of the dramas has been a regular feature of the ritual calendar at major Hindu temples in Kerala.

These dramas have been traditionally performed for an audience of high-caste Hindus, primarily brahmans, temple servants, and royalty.[11] Moreover, God is regarded as part of the audience, as well; the theater's stage faces the temple's main icon in its adjacent building, and the doors to both are left open during performances. The audience attends a *kūṭiyāṭṭam* performance in the hope of having an experience both aesthetic and religious, these not being regarded as separate categories. Dramatic enactment, witnessed by a spectator who by reason of his nature and experience is qualified to appreciate the performance, may result in the spectator relishing the *rasa* intended by the playwright and performers. In the *rasa* theory, effective enactment of a drama is a precondition that allows an audience member the opportunity to experience that blissful aesthetic appreciation that is *rasa*. Any one of the nine *rasa* states may predominate in a drama and be experienced, with other *rasa* states being present in a subordinate fashion. The *kūṭiyāṭṭam* performers are aware of the

FIGURE 9.1. Kuṭṭan Cākyār (as Hanumān) and Āmmānur Mādhava Cākyār (as Rāvaṇa) enact a scene from "Toraṇa Yuddham" (act 3 of *Abhiseka Nātaka*) in which Hanumān comes to Laṅkā with a message for Sītā and confronts Rāvaṇa.

rasa theory and its religious overtones.[12] Indeed, the religious significance of the dramas traditionally has been emphasized, with devotional moments highlighted in performances; the appearances on stage of deities, and even the mention of them, are occasions for extended enactment of their deeds and qualities.

Interestingly, despite the insistence of performers and supporters that *kūṭiyāṭṭam* complies with the ideals of Bharata's *Nāṭyāśātra*, providing audience members with an opportunity for a *rasa* experience seems not to be foremost in the minds of performers. In a series of interviews I have conducted with major figures in the tradition since 1992, *rasa* has usually gone unmentioned until I have brought up the issue. Several Cākyārs have told me that they perform for the oil lamp at the front of the stage that represents God, not for an audience, if any. They have even stated that if you try to please an audience or if you look at them as you perform, you lose concentration, become yourself again, and cease to be the character you are portraying. Guru Mulikulam Kochukūttan Cākyār, presiding teacher at the Margi center, told me that his aim in performing *kūṭiyāṭṭam* was to lead people onto the path of good conduct through enacting the stories, and to have personal satisfaction from a good performance.[13] He stated that at the moment an actor dons the red headband, he begins to transform himself into the character he is to perform hours later on stage, by concentrating and remembering the qualities and deeds of that character. The dressing room is often noisy, people such as myself taking photos and videos of the process, with interruptions for tea, so I asked how an actor could stay in character as, for example, Rāvaṇa. The guru smiled and said, "Even Rāvaṇa may take tea."

But clearly the *Nāṭyāśātra* envisions performance for an audience, the purpose being to provide an opportunity for audience members to attain the *rasa* experience. If a *kūṭiyāṭṭam* actor is performing for God rather than for an audience, what is the point of costume, make-up, and lighting? Or for that matter of the flashback sequences? Surely God does not need to be reminded of Rāma's prior deeds?

The fact that current performers and supporters do not refer often to the *rasa* theory when discussing their work is all the more surprising, given the recent changes that their tradition has experienced. The social upheaval occasioned by independence a half century ago included the replacement of Kerala's Hindu monarchy by a democratic government, and the repeated election to power of the Communist Party in Kerala. Their land reforms have eliminated the main source of financial support for Hindu temples in Kerala. Temples now have less ability to support temple servants, and the number of *kūṭiyāṭṭam* performances in temples has declined; there are more performances outside temples than within their precincts. Four centers of *kūṭiyāṭṭam* performance and instruction have arisen, including Margi in Kerala's capital Trivandrum, and in central Kerala the Chachu Cākyār Madhom and the state arts institute, Kerala Kalamandalam. These three centers cooperate and compete with one another in an effort to sustain the tradition, and each has received aid from the state and/or central governments for their training programs. Since 1995, a new center for the study and performance of *kūṭiyāṭṭam* has arisen: Śree Śaṅkarāchārya University of Sanskrit in Kalady, central Kerala. Vice Chancellor N. P. Unni has hired several performers of *kūṭiyāṭṭam* as instructors at the university. All these centers emphasize the aesthetic aspects of *kūṭiyāṭṭam* and its entertainment value much more than the religious. In light of the secular nature of most performances today, in auditoriums rather than temple theaters and without the ritual activities of temple priests, such an emphasis on the aesthetic dimension of theater rather than the religious is unavoidable. Guru Mulikulam said to me, "Once *kūṭiyāṭṭam* was done for the deity; now the people have become the deity, and we try to please the people." This statement highlights the extent to which the tradition is confronted with modernity and change. Performers struggle with making the transition from the ancient traditions of temple ritual (performing for God, not an audience) to the modern situation of entertaining audiences and patrons.

Performance style in *kūṭiyāṭṭam* is best understood through specific examples. The first act of *Abhiṣeka,* known in Kerala as *Bālivadham,* in which Rāma kills Bāli (Vāli) at the behest of his ally Sugrīva, includes the following verse from Sugrīva praising Rāma:

mukto deva tavādya bālihṛdayam bhettuṃ na me saṃśyaḥ
sālan sapta mahāvane himagireḥ śṛṅgopamān śrīdhara /
bhitvā vegavaśāt pravīśya dharaṇīm gatvā ca nāgālayaṃ
majjan vīra payonidhau punarayaṃ samprāptavān sāyakaḥ //

O Lord! You will shoot an arrow today to pierce Vāli's heart,
no doubt, for in the great forest it split seven *sāla* trees,
each a Himlayan peak, O hero, tore through earth and underworld,
and after immersing in the sea has returned, Śrīdhara.[14]

Performance of this verse is much more complex than translation of it would seem to indicate.[15]

Day one is taken up by the Sūtradhāra reciting the invocation and by Rāma's entrance. Rāma enacts through gesture and movement his meeting with Hanumān and Sugrīva, tossing the corpse of Dundubhi, entering Kiṣkindhā forest, Sugrīva's comments about seven big *sāla* trees, Rāma's act of shooting an arrow through all of them to fortify Sugrīva's resolve, then recitation of verse 4 of the drama (Rāma's lines on entrance). He enacts the meaning by gesture then again recites the lines, and ends the day's performance with a ritual dance sequence.

Day two of the performance is dedicated to Rāma's flashback. Through gesture and pantomime, while seated on the stage's wooden stool, he enacts in a retrospective fashion his prior deeds, that is, first the shooting of the arrow through the *sāla* trees, then flinging the body of Dundubhi, then entering into the alliance with Sugrīva, and so on. Then he begins to enact the story from the beginning of his exile, including the incidents with Śūrpaṇakhā, defeating the army of her brother Khara and killing him, Rāvaṇa's plot with Mārīca, the abduction of Sītā, wounding of Jaṭāyu and death of Mārīca, and the beginning of his search for Sītā. At this point the actor stands up and pantomimes the presence of Lakṣmaṇa as they search, and he has half a dozen verses (composed by Cākyārs, not the playwright) that he pantomimes, questioning where she could be, finally getting an answer from the dying Jaṭāyu. Rāma (and the imagined Lakṣmaṇa) cremate the body of the vulture. They hear a celestial voice telling them that the vulture has gone to heaven; this is enacted by facial expression and hand gestures, not by speaking. Hanumān is imagined to appear and introduce Rāma to Sugrīva, whose verse of praise for Rāma is sung on the stage by a seated female performer. A solemn pact of alliance is made, and Rāma and the imagined companions enter the forest, where he shoots his arrow through the seven *sāla* trees. Finally, Rāma enacts through gesture again the meaning of his entrance verse, then recites the verse accompanied by gestures, and ends the performance of some three hours.

Day three of the performance is dedicated to Sugrīva's entrance. Through gesture he enacts the appearance and qualities of Rāma, with emphasis on his act of shooting an arrow through the *sāla* trees. He then recites the lines just prior to the verse above, which state that with Rāma's help he could conquer heaven, so he is sure that the monkey kingdom will be his. He repeats the lines and enacts them by gesture, then brings out the meaning of his verse above, but without yet reciting it. With a ritual dance sequence his solo performance ends.

Day four is Sugrīva's flashback, which includes the birth of Brahmā and ultimately reaches the birth of the demons Mandodarī (who will be Rāvaṇa's wife) and Dundubhi (whom Rāma will kill despite a boon from Brahmā). Dundubhi challenges the gods, who send him off to the forest to challenge Bāli, who kills him. The seer Mataṅga curses Bāli for dropping some blood on him. The brother of Dundubhi comes to challenge Bāli, who enlists the aid of Sugrīva in fighting and they defeat the demon, though Sugrīva thought Bāli dead and assumed kingship. The two monkeys fight and Sugrīva flees in fear. His performance for the day ends.

Day five brings us at last to true *kūṭiyāṭṭam*, multiple actors on stage together. Sugrīva enters first and recapitulates through gesture and facial expression much of what happened on day four between himself and his brother Bāli, including an extensive flashback (*nirvahaṇa*) about Hanumān and his description of Rāma and Lakṣmaṇa, and the alliance. Seeing Rāma lift with one toe and fling the dead body of the demon Dundubhi a great distance, Sugrīva gains some confidence in Rāma, but has many doubts (for example, perhaps the demon's body had shrunk considerably after death). So he enacts showing the *sāla* trees to Rāma, and Sugrīva is now ready to progress with his role. He enacts through gesture his line about how with Rāma's help he can do it, and he recites the verse above. He enacts the meanings of the words by gesture, then recites the verse again, at which point he exits the stage. Actors portraying Rāma, Hanumān, Lakṣmaṇa, Bāli, and Aṅgada all come and go from the small stage in fairly rapid succession to bring to an end the action for the day and the act, with the death of Bāli as the climax. This day's action is fully five hours in its traditional format. It is popular, and has even been enacted on Doordarshan, India's national television network.

I have presented considerable detail for this act in an effort to indicate innovations by the actors to represent the text. Note that on day one Rāma enacts words and psychological states of Hanumān and Sugrīva; on day two Rāma conveys actions and words of various demons, a couple of celestial voices, and his brother, in solo performance. Day three includes Sugrīva enacting Rāma's appearance and qualities, while on day four he enacts the encounters of demons with gods and a brahman sage cursing Bāli. Day five features all the characters on stage as themselves, but also Sugrīva as Hanumān describing Rāma and Lakṣmaṇa, and so on. In short, attending a *kūṭiyāṭṭam* performance presents a challenge of keeping track of who is enacting whom at any given time.

Another example of enactment is drawn from act 1 of *Āścaryacūḍāmaṇi*, and features the encounter with Śūrpaṇakhā in her pleasant form as Lalitā.[16]

pratikūlamidamācaritam/yadeṣā
ācārānanucaratā tapodhanānāṃ
sāvajñaṃ paruṣataraṃ mayekṣitāpi /
savrīḍā vadanamadhaḥ karoti kampāt
uttaṃsapragalitaṣaṭpadena mūrdhnā //

Her behavior is contrary to our way of life, for . . .
Although I regard her very severely and with disdain,
observing the austere conduct of ascetics,

> she bashfully lowers her face, the trembling of her head
> dislodging the bees from the flowers in her hair.

Again, the performance is highly elaborate.[17]

After the invocation by the Sūtradhāra, the rest of the text's prologue is skipped and day one begins with Lakṣmaṇa's entrance and his communication through gesture that he is happy. By means of gesture and without reciting, he pantomimes the fifth verse of the drama, describing how he scatters wild animals, prepares the leafy hut, constructs a bed, and thereby has complied with Rāma's wishes. After some dance movements, the actor goes to the main shrine room of the temple and worships while still in costume, then returns to the dressing room.

Day two features Lakṣmaṇa's flashback, again going back in time to the foundation of Ayodhyā, then forward to the present situation, then he recites verse 5 for the first time while also showing its meaning through gestures. Then he recites the verse silently and enacts building the hut, including even rites for propitiating deities after house construction. He recites verse 6, and the Naṅgyārs recite an interpolated verse indicating entrance of the demoness as Lalitā. The actor pantomimes the effect of seeing her: he is struck by Kāma's arrows, trembles with delight, and recites verse 7. All this must occur during daytime. Lalitā's formal entrance takes place at night, and begins with her full description of Lakṣmaṇa by means of words and gestures.

The third day includes her flashback, which takes us all the way back to the origin of the demons and forward to her present situation.

On the fourth day Lakṣmaṇa and Lalitā interact on stage, beginning with his recitation of verse 8 (above). Lalitā imitates Lakṣmaṇa, showing the meaning of the phrase "very severely and with disdain" and then Lakṣmaṇa imitates her, using the phrase "bashfully lowers her face, the trembling of her head dislodging the bees from the flowers in her hair." They complete their prose lines back and forth and the day's performance ends.

The fifth and sixth days feature Rāma's entrance, interaction with his brother, and completion of the text through verse 12 and the end of the act. In act 2, Śūrpaṇakhā returns as Lalitā and in the *kūṭiyāṭṭam* tradition she again has a flashback, reminds the audience how she got to this point (act 1 may not have been enacted), and in the course of her flashback she pantomimes lines from the *Rāmāyaṇa* of Vālmīki (3.17 and 3.18) and *Raghuvaṃśa* of Kālidāsa (chapter 12), as well as verse 8 from act 1. In short, she recapitulates her performance in act 1, along the way performing Lakṣmaṇa's lines by gesture.

This segment is interesting for the way in which Lakṣmaṇa and Lalitā portray each other for the audience. She takes a portion of his line and enacts his manner of behaving toward her. Such a performance requires great skill, according to the Cākyārs, because the characters are so dissimilar, he being a great hero and she a demoness in disguise as a demure lady. With all such enactments by one character of the qualities and actions of some other character, no change of costume or makeup is included. The actor drops out of character and into another by signaling that shift. For example, when a male character is to portray a female, one end of a pleated cloth that is worn around the waist is tucked into the waistband; for a male to portray a demoness, both ends are tucked in. For the depiction of a low character, two ends of the cloth are tied together. Female characters portraying males achieve this effect by movement and stance rather than tucking up portions of their garments, since their costumes are quite different from those worn by males. A demoness such as Śūrpaṇakhā (when not disguised) is always enacted by male performers. This is due to the view that such roles are too demanding physically, and the evil depicted too intense, to be performed by women, and it may also show the influence of Kerala's many traditions of Kālī possession. Noteworthy too is the fact that *kūṭiyāṭṭam* does not put Sītā on stage in act 2, though she should be, according to the text; her lines in the drama's text are instead sung by the naṅgyārs.[18]

The Cākyārs have obviously added a great deal to the text composed by the playwright, and made other changes too, in their efforts to bring out the *rasa* fully. A single verse that can be recited in two minutes requires two hours for enactment in *kūṭiyāṭṭam* because of repetition, use of gesture, and the addition of imagined scenes that are not found in the drama's text. Yet the verses cited above are by no means unique. They are good examples of the Cākyār technique of elaboration and expansion of the received text. One sees a similar approach to every playwright's work in *kūṭiyāṭṭam*.[19] This mode of enactment, however, has been controversial for centuries.

Although those close to the *kūṭiyāṭṭam* tradition often state that this style of performance is in conformity with the dictates of the *Nāṭyaśātra* concerning dramaturgy, such an assertion has also been questioned. A critique of *kūṭiyāṭṭam* called *Naṭāṅkuśa* ("A goad on actors") was composed in perhaps the fifteenth century.[20] The author is unknown, but was intimately familar both with *kūṭiyāṭṭam* performances and Bharata's *Nāṭyaśātra*, and much preferred the latter style. The author criticizes the Cākyārs for adding ritual performances during the drama (chapters 1–3), and for other interpolations into the received text of the play that were not intended by the playwright, such as the *nirvahaṇa*, and the repetition of lines by the actors (chapter 4). All these are regarded as interruptions of the action that deviate from the intention of the playwright, and deviate from the guidelines of the *Nāṭyaśātra*. One of the most vehement attacks on *kūṭiyāṭṭam* practices concerns the depiction of one character in the costume and makeup of another, particularly such changes of identity as an actor portraying Hanumān who temporarily enacts Rāma. To the rejoinder that such an enactment shows the great skill of the actor, the critic answers that merely thinking "I am Rāma" on Hanumān's part does not make it so. To the argument that the gesture language effectively overcomes any perceived problem in the costume or makeup, the critic replies that curdled milk does not become milk again and that this poor design and execution destroys *rasa*. The convention of tucking part of the costume into the waistband, as is done by Hanumān when he imitates Sītā, is singled out for condemnation as an awkward device (chapter 4, part 7). Makeup is regarded as the first clue an audience member has regarding the identity of a character on stage, and to present one character imitating another without proper makeup and costume is a jarring deviation from the author's script, and an unwelcome invention of the actors. Moreover, certain features have been added that have no textual basis, such as in act 2 of *Āścaryacūḍāmaṇi*, where the *kūṭiyāṭṭam* actors cut the breasts as well as the ears and nose of Śūrpaṇakhā, something not found in the drama or in Vālmīki's text (4.12); this is regarded as mischief due to the imagination of the actors. The essence of acting, according to this critic, is for an actor to consistently depict the identity of one character. The realization of *rasa* by audience members is eclipsed by the addition of unconnected incidents, according to the author of *Naṭāṅkuśa*, and actors should perform the dramas as composed by playwrights.

An actor in any tradition, of course, is trained to adopt a variety of guises and to depict convincingly an array of identities. In the *kūṭiyāṭṭam* tradition, however, this ability is cultivated to a degree rarely if ever seen elsewhere. On any given night, an actor may transform himself from his own everyday identity to that of a mythic hero, then into the woman that hero loves, or perhaps the demon the hero fights, and someone else describing that action, then back to the hero; eventually the actor reverts to his own identity. The range of identities adopted on stage by the *kūṭiyāṭṭam* actor, and the ease with which the shift is accomplished, are astonishing. Only India's dance traditions such as odissi and bharatanāṭyam entail a similar approach to the enactment of multiple characters by a single performer without change of costume and makeup. *Kūṭiyāṭṭam*, however, takes the approach much farther.

In addition, *kūṭiyāṭṭam* systematically narrates a story in a nonlinear fashion, as demonstrated above. The *nirvahaṇa* interpolations in the dramas are somewhat similar to the *Rāmāyaṇa*'s and the *Mahābhārata*'s own flashback narratives, in which actions performed generations earlier are recounted for the audience. Often the text includes a listener who prompts the reciter to a detailed exposition, so that those hearing the story can appreciate fully the meaning of a character's actions. These texts have preserved in written form an aspect of their performed recitation before audiences. The technique of embedding a story within a larger narrative is a frequently encountered feature of India's literary texts, including the *Rāmāyaṇa* and the *Mahābhārata*. Such nonlinear and embedded narratives are thus not unique to *kūṭiyāṭṭam*, and occur in the texts for similar reasons, namely, that audiences want to appreciate fully the meaning of the action depicted.

The iconic status of *kūṭiyāṭṭam* as a theater tradition is paralleled by the iconic postures adopted by actors as they represent Rāma and other divine personages on the stage.[21] Traditionally, enactments have had religious purposes of profound importance both for audiences and performers.[22] *kūṭiyāṭṭam*'s proponents and performers now tend to see it as emblematic of India's great culture and a living link to a glorious past, its aesthetic and sociopolitical aspects taking center stage. As a living art form, *kūṭiyāṭṭam* must, as reflected in the techniques of its own actors, transform itself and reveal new identities. So long as the stories of Rāma and Sītā remain relevant to Kerala Hindus, *kūṭiyāṭṭam* may have a role to play.

NOTES

I am grateful to the Center for International Exchange of Scholars for a Fulbright grant on two occasions that allowed me to do research in Kerala. Thanks especially to N. P. Unni, L. S. Rajagopalan, and Rama Iyer for their help while I lived in Kerala. An earlier version of this essay was presented at the University of British Columbia in June 2001, and benefitted from seminar discussion.

1. Among the best short studies of *kūṭiyāṭṭam* are Richmond 1990; Tarlekar 1991, Venu 1989, Sullivan 1996 and 1997, and Unni and Sullivan 1995; Farley Richmond's CD-ROM *Kūṭiyāṭṭam* (2002) is also very useful.

2. In addition to the three dramas discussed in this essay, the *kūṭiyāṭṭam* tradition does or did include performance of the following dramas in their entirety or in part: *Tapatī-Saṃvaraṇa* and *Subhadrā-Dhanañjaya*, both by Kulaśekhara Varman, a king of Kerala, and based on *Mahābhārata* episodes (see Unni and Sullivan 1995; Unni and Sullivan 2001). Other dramas performed are all thirteen dramas sometimes attributed to Bhāsa (two of which are discussed in this essay), *Kalyāṇasaugandhika* by Nīlakaṇṭha, *Nāgānanda* by Harṣa, *Bhagavadajjukīya* by Bodhāyana, *Mattavilāsa* by Mahendravikrama Pallava, and *Abhijñānaśakuntalā* by Kālidāsa.

3. Evidence for authorship by Bhāsa is not convincing, nor does any of the dramas name him as author. Performers in the *kūṭiyāṭṭam* tradition apparently did not attribute them to Bhāsa prior to Ganapati Sastri's publication of them as such. I regard these dramas as anonymous, and the time of their composition as unknown. Among the many translations of the dramas attributed to Bhāsa, see Menon 1996 or Woolner and Sarup [1930] 1985; selected dramas have been translated by Haksar 1993, Gerow 1985, Jones 1984, and Miller 1985. See also the important study by Brückner (1999–2000) and her Web site: http://www.uni-wuerzburg.de/indologie/indologie.php?datei=projekte/trivandrumstuecke.

4. See Unni (1978, pp. 244–248) for more detailed discussion of the royal consecration tradition.

5. Hence I will not use the term "classical" in describing this tradition, for it contains elements that are not envisioned in Bharata's *Nāṭyāśātra*, and uses vernacular language as well as Sanskrit/Prakrit. As it involves both solo performance (usually a feature of "classical" traditions) and group performance (usually a feature of "folk" performances), *kūṭiyāṭṭam* does not fit either pattern; see Blackburn 1998, p. 7; see also de Bruin 1998, pp. 14–16, 34–35.

6. References in the *kūṭiyāṭṭam* tradition's performance manuals and commentaries on dramas indicate a long tradition of performance of these dramas. Unni discusses modifications made to certain plays for the Kerala stage; see Unni 1978 and 1992. A critique of the *kūṭiyāṭṭam* style of performance called *Naṭāṅkuśa* and composed in perhaps the fifteenth century gives many details of *kūṭiyāṭṭam* performance of that era; see Paulose 1993; and Kunjunni Raja 1987.

7. See Jones 1984, pp. ix–x); Panchal 1984, p. 17; Paulose 1993, p. xi; and Tarlekar 1991, pp. 247–48 and 324. Kunjunni Raja (1964), however, dismisses this as a dance performance that "has nothing to do with the staging of Sanskrit plays." As de Bruin has written (1998, p. 21), it is often "difficult to identify the genre or style of theatrical performances referred to in historical literature." Whether this ancient literary account describes drama or not, King Kulaśekhara Varman and his brahman minister Tolan are credited with reforming the practice of Sanskrit drama enactment in Kerala perhaps about 1100 C.E., not with introducing the practice, indicating that dramas were already being performed at that time.

8. Paulose 1993, p. xix.

9. Naṅgyārs and their performances are discussed by Daugherty 1996, Panikkar 1992, and Rajagopalan 1997. Cākyārs are more extensively discussed; see especially Menon 1996. On the theaters see Jones 1972, 1973, Rajagopalan 1987, and Panchal 1984.

10. Unni 1977 discusses the actors' rituals.

11. Outcastes, a substantial percentage of Kerala's population, were excluded from Kerala's temples for centuries.

12. The *rasa* concept as developed by the Gosvāmin theologians envisions Kṛṣṇa as the hero of the ongoing sacred drama and all devotees as performers in that drama. See Haberman 1988, Larson 1976, and Wulff 1986.

13. This and other reports cited are from personal communication in February 1999.

14. *Abhiṣekha Nāṭaka* 1.5. The verse can be heard recited by an actor from Kerala Kalāmaṇḍalam as track 9 on the following CD from Radio France: *Inde de Sud: Kutiyattam* (Paris: Ocora, 1999). This is a good example of *kūṭiyāṭṭam* recitation style. The verse is printed as in Venu 1989; the translation is mine. See also Bhāsa 1913, or Menon 1996, vol. 2.

15. The following summary of performance is from personal observation; see also Venu 1989 for translations of performance manuals on this act.

16. *Āścaryacūḍāmaṇi* 1.8. See Jones 1984 for the Sanskrit text; the translation is mine. The text as printed in Jones substitutes *ḷ* for *ḍ* in *savrīḍā*.

17. The following performance summary is largely drawn from translations of performance manuals on this act; see Jones 1984, pp. 104–108.

18. Rajagopalan 1997, p. 19.

19. The one exception is Kālidāsa; performers seem not to have interpolated ritual and commentary into their performance of *Abhijñānaśakuntalā*.

20. Paulose 1993 gives the text, translation, and introduction; Kunjunni Raja 1987 has a brief summary. The author of the *Naṭāṅkuśa* rightly points to ways in which the performance of drama in *kūṭiyāṭṭam* style deviates from the ideals of the *Nāṭyāśātra*. The deviations are in the elaboration, repetition, and interpolations in the texts, leading to the single act being the unit of performance rather than entire multi-act dramas. That authors intended for the drama as a whole to be enacted may be indicated by the fact that they did not name individual acts (as the Cākyārs have) and did not give any directions for how to begin enactment with a later act. Conformity with the ideals of the *Nāṭyāśātra* is primarily in regard to rituals consecrating the theater and the performance, patronage by the king, and the general (if vague) guidelines about costumes, makeup, music, and so on. Perhaps the performance of *kūṭiyāṭṭam* can best be understood as temple ritual.

21. Stuart Blackburn has written regarding various art forms of south India, "As artistic and religious expressions, these performances have become icons of south India" (1998, p. 1). Although he does not mention *kūṭiyāṭṭam* explicitly, his comment applies well to this drama tradition. *Kūṭiyāṭṭam*'s more famous offspring, the dance tradition of kathakali, is often featured in advertisements for Kerala tourism as representative of the region's culture.

22. See Sullivan 1997 for a detailed discussion.

REFERENCES

Bhāsa. 1913. *Abhiṣekha Nāṭaka*. Edited by T. G. Sastri. Trivandrum Sanskrit Series 26. Trivandrum: Kerala University Press.

———. 1924. *Pratimā Nāṭaka*. Edited by T. G. Sastri. Trivandrum: Sridhara Power Press.

Blackburn, Stuart. 1998. "Looking across the Contextual Divide: Studying Performance in South India." *South Asia Research* 18.1: 1–11.

Brückner, Heidrun. 1999–2000. "Manuscripts and Performance Traditions of the So-called 'Trivandrum Plays' Ascribed to Bhāsa: A Report on Work in Progress." *Bulletin d'Études Indiennes* 17–18: 499–549.

Daugherty, Diane. 1996. "The Naṅgyārs: Female Ritual Specialist of Kerala." *Asian Theatre Journal* 13.1 (Spring): 54–67.

de Bruin, Hanne M. 1998. "Studying Performance in South India: A Synthesis of Theories." *South Asia Research* 18.1: 12–38.

Gerow, Edwin, trans. 1985. "*Ūrubhaṅga*: The Breaking of the Thighs." *Journal of South Asian Literature,* 20.1: 57–70. Reprinted in *Essays on the Mahābhārata,* edited by A. Sharma, Leiden: E. J. Brill, 1990.

Haberman, David. 1988. *Acting as a Way of Salvation: A Study of Rāgānugā Bhakti Sādhana*. New York: Oxford University Press.

Haksar, A.N.D., trans. 1993. *The Shattered Thigh and the Other Mahābhārata Plays of Bhāsa*. New Delhi: Penguin Books.

Jones, Clifford Reis. 1972. "Temple Theatres and the Sanskrit Tradition in Kerala." *Saṃskrita Ranga Annual* 6: 101–12.

———. 1973. "Source Materials for the Construction of the Nāṭyamandapa in the *Śilparatna* and the *Tantrasamuccaya Śilpa Bhāgam*." *Journal of the American Oriental Society* 93.3 (July–September): 286–296.

———, ed. 1984. *The Wondrous Crest-Jewel in Performance*. Delhi: Oxford University Press.

Kunjunni Raja, K. 1964. *Kūṭiyāṭṭam: An Introduction*. New Delhi: Sangeet Natak Akademi.

——— 1987. "*Naṭāṅkuśa*: A Goad on Actors." *Saṃskrita Ranga Annual* 8:118–23.

Larson, Gerald James. 1976. "The Aesthetic (*rasāsvāda*) and the Religious (*brahmāsvāda*) in Abhinavagupta's Kashmir śaivism." *Philosophy East and West* 26.4: 371–387.

Menon, K. P., trans. 1996. *Complete Plays of Bhāsa*. 3 vols. Delhi: Nag Publishers.

Menon, K.P.S. 1995. "Major Kūṭiyāṭṭam Artists and Families." *Sangeet Natak* 111–14: 128–40.

Miller, Barbara Stoler, trans. 1985. "Karṇabhāra: The Trial of Karṇa." *Journal of South Asian Literature,* 20.1: 47–56. Reprinted in *Essays on the Mahābhārata,* edited by A. Sharma. Leiden: E. J. Brill, 1990.

Panchal, Goverdhan. 1984. *Kūttampalam and Kūṭiyāṭṭam: A Study of the Traditional Theatre for the Sanskrit Drama of Kerala*. New Delhi: Sangeet Natak Akademi.

Panikkar, Nirmala. 1992. *Nangiar Koothu*. Iriñjālakuḍa: Natana Kairali.

Paulose, K. G., ed. and trans. 1993. *Naṭāṅkuśa: A Critique on Dramaturgy*. Tripunithura: Government Sanskrit College.

Rajagopalan, L. S. 1987. "Consecration of the Kūttambalam Temple Theatres of Kerala." *Saṃskrita Ranga Annual* 8: 22–40.

———. *Women's Role in Kūḍiyāṭṭam*. 1997. Chennai: Kuppuswami Sastri Research Institute.

Richmond, Farley. 1990. "Kūṭiyāṭṭam." In *Indian Theater: Traditions of Performance,* edited by F. Richmond, D. Swann, and P. Zarrilli. Honolulu: University of Hawaii Press, pp. 87–117.

———. 2002. *Kūṭiyāṭṭam.* CD–ROM. Ann Arbor: University of Michigan Press.

Sullivan, Bruce M. 1996. "*Tapatī-Saṃvaraṇam*: A Kūṭiyāṭṭam Drama by Kulaśekhara Varman." *Asian Theatre Journal* 13.1 (Spring): 26–53.

———. 1997. "Temple Rites and Temple Servants: The Role of Religion in the Survival of Kerala's Kūṭiyāṭṭam Drama Tradition." *International Journal of Hindu Studies* 1.1: 97–115.

Tarlekar, G. H. 1991. *Studies in the Nāṭyāśātra, with Special Reference to the Sanskrit Drama in Performance.* 2nd ed. Delhi: Motilal Banarsidass.

Unni, N. P. 1977. "Consecration of the Actor in Kerala." *Journal of Kerala Studies* 4: 305–312.

———. 1978. *New Problems in Bhāsa Plays.* Trivandrum: College Book House.

———. 1992. *Some New Perspectives in Bhāsa Studies.* Dharwar: Karnatak University.

Unni, N. P., and Bruce M. Sullivan. 1995. *The Sun God's Daughter and King Saṃvaraṇa: "Tapatī-Saṃvaraṇam" and the Kūṭiyāṭṭam Drama Tradition.* Delhi: Nag Publishers.

———. 2001. *The Wedding of Arjuna and Subhadrā: The Kūṭiyāṭṭam Drama "Subhadrā-Dhanañjaya."* Delhi: Nag Publishers.

Venu, G. 1989. *Production of a Play in Kūṭiyāṭṭam.* Iriñjālakuḍa: Natana Kairali.

Woolner, A. C., and Lakshman Sarup, trans. [1930] 1985. *Thirteen Plays of Bhāsa.* Delhi: Motilal Banarsidass.

Wulff, Donna M. 1986. "Religion in a New Mode: The Convergence of the Aesthetic and the Religious in Medieval India." *Journal of the American Academy of Religion* 54.4: 673–688.

10

The "Radio-Active" *Gīta-Rāmāyaṇa*: Home and Abroad

Vidyut Aklujkar

The *Gīta-Rāmāyaṇa* of Maharashtra came into existence in the spring of 1955, four years before the advent of television in India, when radio was the major means of broadcasting in urban as well as rural India. Radio, with its power to broadcast across regions, had become the stationary substitute for the wandering minstrels of earlier times singing the epics from town to town. Since the radio recitals and dramas lacked a visual component, the radio performance narrative was entirely oral/aural. The newly coined word for radio drama was *śrutikā*, that is, the one that is heard, as it was only to be heard, and not seen. The *Gīta-Rāmāyaṇa* was a product of this era of orality/aurality. Even though it lacked the powerful visual component, it soon became extremely popular. Hence the adjective in the title of this chapter, the "radio-active" *Gīta-Rāmāyaṇa*. The samāsa (compound) therein is of the *tṛtīyā tatpuruṣa* class, as in "Radionā activitam," if I may indulge in a cross-lingual play on words. However, upon completion, this "radio-active" *Gīta-Rāmāyaṇa* did not join the ranks of hundreds of already available isotopes of the original *Vālmīki Rāmāyaṇa*, nor was there any sign of decay in decades to follow. Instead, the impact of the *Gīta-Rāmāyaṇa* was felt far and wide beyond the confines of the original medium of broadcasting, the original language, and the provincial borders. The *Gīta-Rāmāyaṇa* thrived, sending forth a steady stream of concerts and live performances by Marathi singers in Maharashtra and other provinces of India in the last four decades of the twentieth century. It is still flourishing in the twenty-first century. It has been carried around by millions of Marathi speakers wherever they have gone to reside, in Europe, North America, or Australia. Even the onset of the ubiquitous TV *Rāmāyaṇa* of Ramanand Sagar could not eclipse the hold of this popular oral *Rāmāyaṇa* on the minds of Maharashtrians. To this day, the Marathi-speaking people both at home and abroad fondly sing the songs of the *Gīta-Rāmāyaṇa*, listen to the audiocassettes on their car tape decks in transit, or on their audio systems at home, and attend its public performances by numerous artists, young and old. There are short concerts of select songs of the series or daylong performances covering all fifty-six songs. The *Gīta-Rāmāyaṇa* has become a living legend: it has already been translated into other modern Indian languages, including five translations in Hindi and at least one each in Gujarati, Bengali, Assamese, Kannada, Telugu, Konkani, English, and Sanskrit. In all these languages it was (and in some still is) being performed and lovingly enjoyed by people, both at home and abroad (see appendix 1).

In this essay, I propose to outline the manifold impact and enduring appeal of the oral rendition of the *Gīta-Rāmāyaṇa* on the Marathi-speaking community and on the larger, multilingual diasporic community of Indians. I shall argue that though it is composed in a provincial vernacular, the *Gīta-Rāmāyaṇa* has succeeded, mainly through its orality, in bringing together several linguistic communities of India, and has done similar service to the international communities of Indian diaspora. I shall further argue that the popularity of the *Gīta-Rāmāyaṇa* is not so much due to the religious significance of the Rāma epic in Maharashtra as to secular factors such as drama in its composition, extremely singable lyrics, and memorable musical melodies. We will experience the orality of the narrative being interactive with its textuality through the translations, and observe the continuity among its various modes of transmission such as radio (the original medium), live concerts, LPs, audiocassettes, videos, dances, and TV serials.

The Birth of the *Gīta-Rāmāyaṇa*

The *Gīta-Rāmāyaṇa* was a series of fifty-six songs composed by a renowned Marathi poet, Gajanan Digambar Madgulkar (1919–1977). It was created for the specific purpose of broadcasting on All-India Radio's newly started Pune Kendra, thus being composed and serially transmitted over a year in 1955–1956. The creation of the radio serial was an exceptionally unusual phenomenon in the history of the radio station, however, as it took place in the absence of bureaucratic red tape. The radio station was in its infancy, willing to try new schemes. Unlike serials that are aired on All-India Radio now, which must have fully written drafts and musical melodies and acting directions before they can be submitted, analyzed, and accepted or rejected, the idea of the *Gīta-Rāmāyaṇa* or the rendition of Rāmakathā in singable poems (the *Gīta-Rāmāyaṇa*) was suggested as a novelty in a friendly chat between the station director Sitakant Lad and the poet Madgulkar. It was accepted as a challenge by the poet and launched by the radio station with the minimum of conditions and specifications, even before the first song was written. The poet Madgulkar (fondly nicknamed Gadimā) and the music director Sudhir Phadke (often called Bābūjī) were long-time friends and knew how to work with each other. They were to be the constants in this scheme, and everyone else would be selected as needed. The poet had a free rein as to the choice of the meters, execution of the story line, and the message he could convey through it. Apart from the number of songs, everything else was left to spontaneity in order to anticipate and answer any suspicion of its being called a government production and propaganda. The series of songs was to be aired starting with Rāmanavamī, the traditional birth date of Rāma, and it was an ongoing process of creativity and live recording/performance, the outcome of which was as unknown to the composer and the music director as it was to the audience and the radio station authorities. Every week, Madgulkar used to compose and write a new song of the series, in pen and ink on foolscap paper, which would be set to music within hours by the noted singer and versatile music director Sudhir Phadke. Old and new singers selected by the music director sang the song, accompanied by an orchestra of radio artists, and the song was recorded and simultaneously broadcast in the newly built studio of Pune Radio Station. (Since Sudhir Phadke was a friend of my father, my family and I attended one such live recording session in that studio, where the song of the monkeys' building the bridge was coming alive.) Every song was aired first on a Sunday morning and then again that Tuesday night. We, the young school-going children and their music-loving parents in Pune, Mumbai, and nearby places in Maharashtra, never missed either one of those occasions. As the series became popular, the daily newspapers in Pune began to print the text of the new song every week after its first release. We, the school-going children, used to clip the column of the song with its introductory narration from these newspapers and paste it in a diary, thus creating our own copy of the yet-to-be-published text. The words that were sung and heard thus preceded those in public print, and the words in print served as a mnemonic tool in the retention and recall of the oral word. Before the next week's song appeared, the previous one was repeated and memorized in our household by my father, sung by us children, and discussed by everyone we knew at home, in school, and in friends' houses. I must observe at this point that the listening, repetition, and memorization was not done in our friend's circle from the religious attitude of gathering merit or *puṇya*. No one in my family was a temple-going or otherwise religious person. No one observed any rituals or *vratas*. Still, we were enchanted by the weekly serial. It was a natural outcome of being smitten by the charm of Madgulkar's poetic skills and Sudhir Phadke's singable melodies.

The Impact of the Text and the Performances

Since the *Gīta-Rāmāyaṇa* is a composite of textual recreation of Rāmakathā and oral radio performance that later snowballed into other performances, the total impact should be analyzed by outlining each of these aspects separately. In the following parts of this section, I shall delineate the historical and literary context of Rāmakathā in Maharashtra to situate the newly created text in it, and also place the multiple performances in the context of the musical milieu of Maharashtra and India.

Before I begin, I must clear a possible misunderstanding of the religious significance of Rāmakathā in Maharashtra. Although Rāma and Hānumān temples abound, and plenty of Rāmkathā texts have been written through the centuries, Rāma is not the central deity in Maharashtra. True, the story of Rāma has been fondly treasured, and there are even popular expressions that originate from the epic. A common greeting in villages for centuries has been "Rām Rām" instead of "namaskāra" or "namaste." In order to say, "There is no sense/no substance/no significance in it," a Marathi uses the expression, *tyānt rām rāhilā nāhī*" or "there is no Rām in it." However, although Rāmakathā has thus significantly colored the language, and Rāma is a significant deity, he is still not the central deity of the region. If social festivals are any indication of the centrality of deity, one has to say that the deities of major social importance are Viṭhobā (a pastoral representation of Kṛṣṇa/Viṣṇu) and Gaṇeśa (the latter assuming even political and socially progressive significance due to Lokamanya Bal Gangadhar Tilak's influence). The most prominent yearly pilgrimages are made to the temple of Viṭhobā in Pandharpur, and the most popular yearly festival for which a multitude of images is locally created, displayed in public places, worshiped, and ceremonially immersed in water is of Gaṇeśa. Even the festival of Diwali, which is celebrated in the north as the occasion of Rāma's return from Laṅkā after the rescue of Sītā, is not associated with Rāma in Maharashtra. Instead, we associate it with Kṛṣṇa's killing of Narakāsura and rescuing the divine damsels from captivity. There is no counterpart to the Rāmlīlā of the north in Maharashtra, nor is there anything that comes close to a mass-scale Rāma festival in Maharashtra, although the birth of Rāma (Rāmanavamī) is observed in smaller temples and in certain families by chanting and singing *bhajans*, by listening to the Purāṇa stories, and by distributing sweets. In spite of a steady stream of Rāma texts in all genres of Marathi, there is none that holds a place of religious sanctity similar to Tulsīdās's *Rāmacaritamānas* in the north. The attraction of Rāmakathā in Maharashtra remains on the level of poetry and drama, which generate from time to time heated debate regarding the social and personal dilemmas in the epic.

The Text

The *Gīta-Rāmāyaṇa* was not just a retelling of Vālmīki's *Rāmāyaṇa*; it was a composition in an established literary language, Marathi, which already had its share of eminently poetic recreations of the original. The *Bhāvārtha Rāmāyaṇa* of Eknāth's (1533–1599) was famous and popular among the temple-going public. Rāmdas (1608–1650) rendered portions of *Yuddhakāṇḍa* and some other portions of The *Rāmāyaṇa* in his inimitable terse and provocative style. The *Rāmavijaya* of Śrīdhara (1658–1729) was also popular and was being recited routinely until the early twentieth century in ladies' gatherings in middle-class households. Moropant (*paṇḍita kavi*), the erudite poet, had fulfilled a vow of composing 108 *Rāmāyaṇas* of every imaginable sort, including one without labial consonants, one in which every line included the word *parantu* (however), and so on. In short, there was no dearth of *Rāmāyaṇa* retellings in Marathi. Madgulkar's *Gīta-Rāmāyaṇa*, however, immediately caught on, partly because it was a re-creation suited to a modern technological medium, and partly because of the quality of the text and the music. Among many elements that combine to make it unique, the novelty of its songs sung by different singers to bring out the characters of the epic and retain the element of drama, coupled with its semiclassical music, proved to be immensely appealing to the contemporary audience of the fifties.

Unlike the other *Rāmāyaṇa* retellings in Marathi, the *Gīta-Rāmāyaṇa* was created in postindependence times, in a genre of *gīta* or lyrical song, while observing the limits of weekly deadlines and the arbitrary quantity of fifty-six songs. Chance and accidents had their share in the making of this series. Take, for example, the arbitrary number of fifty-six songs. This was an afterthought. The series was originally to have had only fifty-two songs, but since the year 1955 had an extra month, *adhika māsa*, in the Hindu calendar, four more songs were added to extend the series over the entire year, and thus it came to have fifty-six.[1] Vidya Madgulkar, the wife of the poet, mentions in her memoirs how, even though she prepared his seat, *baithak*, in his sitting room, Gadimā used to write the songs anywhere as they occured to him, and how he always was rushed and pressured by repeated phone calls from Sudhir Phadke inquiring about whether the song was ready.[2] In this context, she also mentions the incident of the loss and revival of the very first song. She says that when Gadimā wrote the first song and handed it to the music director and singer Sudhir Phadke just before the day of the recording, somehow Phadke lost the paper and could not find it. The date and the time of the recording/broadcasting were set and advertised. So Gadimā rewrote the first song from memory, within half an hour, and Sudhir Phadke hurriedly put it to music shortly before it was to be recorded at ten o'clock in the morning. Anxiety about the outcome and anticipation of the unknown were two constants of this weekly production of the epic.

After the text was assembled piecemeal by us listeners from newspaper clippings, the first official edition of the text of fifty-six poems and their prose narrations came out on the occasion of Vijayā Daśamī, October 3, 1957. This was published for Akashwani by the director of the Publications Division, Delhi, in pocketbook size. It was embellished with beautiful black-and-white drawings by Padma Sahasrabuddhe. Many more editions followed, and soon it was being translated in sister languages and also transliterated in braille. The lyricism of the original in its Sanskrit-based yet colloquial Marathi language yields easily to translation. One noteworthy feature of these translations is that most of them are equi-verse (*sama-ślokī*) translations and thus, are amenable to being sung in the original style. Since the melodies to which they were originally set by Sudhir Phadke were regarded as an integral part of their lyrics, each of the equi-verse translations uses the same rāgas and tunes as the original Marathi version. This brings us to the performance aspect of the phenomenon.

The Performances

The Original Performance

Ever since *Gīta-Rāmāyaṇa* was first heard on the occasion of Rāma-navamī in 1955, Maharashtrians and others have been smitten by its charm. After the first song was aired, the radio station received a shower of handwritten letters of praise, and the poet and the music director also got several such letters. The shower continued to grow as the series progressed. After it was over in March of 1956, listeners experienced a sense of loss. Again, requests of "encore" flooded the infant radio station. All-India Radio repeated the entire series of fifty-six weekly songs due to popular demand. In the history of Akashwani, or All-India Radio, this is a singularly ever-popular program written by a single poet over the duration of a whole year, and put to music by a single music director. Even when I visited India in April of 2001, I was told that the original series of fifty-six songs was being repeated in another *āvartana* or recycling by Sangli radio station in Maharashtra.[3]

Live Concerts by Sudhir Phadke

After the completion of the broadcasting of *Gīta-Rāmāyaṇa*, the music director and lead singer Sudhir Phadke started to give live public concerts of select songs. These were attended by an increasing number of fans. He would read the narrations and play the harmonium while singing the songs. In his lifetime, he gave hundreds of solo performances of the series, singing select songs to a record number of live audiences. One memorable occasion was the twenty-fifth anniversary of the *Gīta-Rāmāyaṇa*, when Sudhir Phadke sang the entire *Gīta-Rāmāyaṇa* of fifty-six songs. This silver anniversary celebration (*Rajata Mahotsava*) took place in the large open-air yard of the New English School on Tilak Road in Pune, and it went on for eight consecutive nights. Tickets were sold out as soon as it was announced. Political leaders such as Yashwantrao Chavhan, Atal Bihari Vajpayee, Vaasoo Bhattacharya, and Dada Kondke, and celebrated classical singers such as Bhimsen Joshi and Kishori Amonkar all attended the performances. By then the songs had been translated into nine other vernaculars such as Kannada, Hindi, Bengali, Gujarati, and Telugu. So every night, in addition to Sudhir Phadke's Marathi songs, another prominent singer would sing a few songs from another language. On the last day, or the *sāṅgatā samāroha*, when Sudhir Phadke was to bring the entire performance to its culmination, the pressure of well-meaning townspeople wanting to listen and participate in this joyous event was so great that the organizers had to take down the tin fences erected all around the schoolyard and open the last night's performance to everyone, ticket holder or not. The ticket holders did not object. They sat on their chairs while others perched on the branches of trees, stood on the balconies of nearby houses, or gathered in the alleys and side streets, and listened in perfect attention. In all, nearly fifty thousand people attended the entire performance, and went home feeling blessed.

Besides live concerts, other modes of technology have also been explored in the dissemination of the *Gīta-Rāmāyaṇa*. The HMV company brought out a ten-LP recording of all the songs in the voice of Sudhir Phadke, starting in 1965. It sold so well that a platinum record was cut by HMV and presented to Sudhir Phadke. Also, a set of ten audiocassette tapes comprising the entire *Gīta-Rāmāyaṇa* in the voice of Sudhir Phadke was released in 1968 by the Gramophone Company of India, and is still one of the bestselling items in the music markets of Mumbai.

Other Artists in India

In a recent attempt to present the *Gīta-Rāmāyaṇa* as a legacy of the twentieth century to the new generation of the twenty-first century, Anand Madgulkar, a son of the poet, produced a TV version of the *Gīta-Rāmāyaṇa* in twenty-eight episodes on the Alpha Marathi channel of Z TV. It started on September 27, 2000, went on into 2001, and was transmitted in fifty-four countries. He used the original tunes of Sudhir Phadke, but directed, choreographed, and dramatized some songs and sang them himself along with other singers. This has brought forth mixed reviews, as some felt that adding low-budget visual components to the splendidly aural *Gīta-Rāmāyaṇa* did nothing to enhance it, and others disliked the visual tampering with the old series of songs, but the producer reports a warm reception from younger audiences. He attributes the sustained popularity of the *Gīta-Rāmāyaṇa* to the very human characters created by the poet. "We Marathi people are practical, down-to-earth people, we felt that these were people like us, and so these characters as portrayed by Gadimā became our own," he said in a conversation with me during my recent trip to India. His analysis corroborated my argument that religiosity of the audience has very little to do with this living legend. Its lasting appeal is in its lifelike characters, along with its memorable music.

Singers Abroad

Other dedicated singers have popularized *Gīta-Rāmāyaṇa* in other provinces of India,[4] and also in several cities in North America. For example, from 1980 until now, 2003, Dr. Gopal Marathe of Los Angeles has performed the *Gīta-Rāmāyaṇa* every year in Los Angeles and on numerous occasions in other cities of North America. He has given concerts of the original *Gīta-Rāmāyaṇa* in New York, Philadelphia, Houston, Seattle, Portland, San Francisco, San Diego, San Jose, and Phoenix in the United States, and in Fredericton and other cities in Canada. On April 3, 1983, in Los Angeles, he gave a twelve-hour-long concert in which he sang the entire *Gīta-Rāmāyaṇa* of fifty-six songs all by himself. Since a tabla player competent enough to accompany him was hard to come by, he played the tabla for each song himself beforehand, recorded it on cassettes, and played those cassette tapes while he sang the songs for this program. In 1986, he gave one more day-long performance of the entire series, this time with another singer, Shobha Ambegaonkar. People flocked from as far as Seattle and Phoenix to Los Angeles to attend this program. Audio and video recordings of this event are available. His next year's concert for Rāma-navamī is already booked in Los Angeles, and another one is being planned in Australia for the following year. In 1990 he organized and produced a concert of the *Gīta-Rāmāyaṇa* in Los Angeles where the main performers were forty-five children under the age of twelve, all from the Marathi and Indian diaspora. All of them had received instruction in classical Indian music from Gopal Marathe, but on stage, on that day, the only performing artists were these children, who narrated, sang, and played the accompanying instruments such as tabla and harmonium.[5]

Another singer, Narendra Datar of Toronto, has also given many concerts of the original Marathi *Gīta-Rāmāyana* in North American cities, and now is giving concerts in Hindi of the same. I had the good fortune to attend the first Canadian Hindi concert in Toronto on March 31, 2001. In this concert, Datar sang eleven of the fifty-six songs translated in equi-verses, set to the exact tunes of the original rendering. This audience of five hundred people included Canadians, of Indian heritage and otherwise. Many of these concerts are given to aid local charities, and they are all attended not just by Marathi people but also by Gujarati, Hindi, Sindhi, Tamil, Telugu, and Kannada speakers and, of course, by Americans and Canadians of all kinds who do not speak any Indian language. Incompatibility of verbal language seems amply compensated by the universal language of music.

The *Gīta-Rāmāyaṇa* is by no means sacrosanct, and musical innovations are, of course, possible, as was witnessed on the University of British Columbia campus at the *Rāmāyaṇa* Conference in June 2000, where Sudnya Naik presented a bharatanatyam dance in the hall of the Museum of Anthropology. The dance was based on a song from the Marathi *Gīta-Rāmāyana*, on the episode of *kāñcana-mṛga*, the chase of the golden deer, and it was sung by a Telugu-speaking local singer, Sunita Bapuji, who had set it to rāga Revatī, a melody of the Karnataka style of Indian classical music.

In a May 5, 2002, concert program of semiclassical Indian music, the diasporic Marathi youth of Vancouver ended the concert by singing the last song of the *Gīta-Rāmāyaṇa, gā bāḷāñno śrī rāmāyaṇa* as it is in rāga Bhairavī, which traditionally ends music concerts. The fact is that due to its well-loved lyrics, the Marathi *Gīta-Rāmāyaṇa* is in a constant process of regeneration both at home and abroad.

The Appraisal

The blend of poetry and music that made the *Gīta-Rāmāyana* a resounding success was often described by fans and critics as the *maṇi-kāñcana-yoga* of the world of music. It was as if a precious gem were set in a genuine gold setting; each succeeded in enhancing the other. At this point, we can attempt to analyze these elements in detail by first examining the poem and then the music.

The Poem

The Opening and the End

Vālmīki was the main source and inspiration for the fifty-six songs, although Madgulkar was conversant with the *Rāmāyaṇa* retellings of Tulsīdās, Eknāth, Mukteshvar, and Moropant.[6] Where to begin, where to end? What to choose and what not? Here Madgulkar's past experience in the field of cinema was helpful. Although he could not complete his formal education due to poverty in his childhood, he had become an accomplished poet and short story writer. Many of his short stories were made into films. He had not only written songs for these films but he also had been a successful screenplay writer for years in the Marathi film industry, and he brought his astute sense of drama and visual imaging to the present task. He chose to open his *Rāmāyaṇa* at one of its most dramatic moments, focusing on the episode of the first public recital of the epic, with these words:

> *svaye śrī rāma prabhū aikatī / Kuśa lava rāmāyaṇa gātī //*
>
> Śrī Rāma, the Lord himself is listening / as Kuśa and Lava sing the *Rāmāyaṇa* //

The song reminded the audience of the original recitation of the *Rāmāyaṇa* with the Lord himself in attendence, and thereby situated the present performance on a divine plane. It also linked the present singers to the singing twins of ancient times, Kuśa and Lava, the progeny of Lord Rāma. The first song focused on the irony that the sons were singing the life of their father, even though all were unaware of the connection between them. It was as if the lamplight was worshiping the divine brilliance of which it partakes: *jyotine tejācī āratī*. The ignorance of one's real identity, one's lineage, one's heritage in that episode created the philosophical setting of the first song. The song ended just short of the epiphany, where Rāma leaves his throne and embraces the twins, without realizing that he is embracing his own children. This allowed the successive songs of *Gīta-Rāmāyana* to appear in the voice of the narrating twins overlaid by the voices of appropriate characters. The opening song was saturated in self-reflexivity. It described how the seven heavenly notes were reviving the thoughts of Vālmīki in a confluence of the nine *rasas* or sentiments. The scene that brought tears to the eyes of Rāma as he was listening to his own life through the song of the twins was described as *pratyakṣāhuni pratimā utkaṭa*, meaning "the image is more intense than the actual." Here, the poet had, in effect, offered a definition of poetry or art. That line reverberated in the minds of the listeners of the radio rendition for a long time, and was later used by many critics to admire Madgulkar's recreation of Vālmīki's poem.

Gadimā never took the position of excelling Vālmīki, as he was humble and felt great reverence for Vālmīki. In choosing the beginning and the end of his re-creation, however, Madgulkar had departed from Vālmīki. He did not simply end with the coronation and happy union of Rāma and Sītā, as some

Rāmakathā versions meant for children ended. He did include Sītā's abandonment by Rāma, and her giving birth to Lava and Kuśa, but he chose not to include the last episode of Sītā's final confrontation in Rāma's court and her entering the earth. Instead, in the last song of the *Gīta-Rāmāyana*, Vālmīki has the last word. In that song, Vālmīki tells his disciples, Lava and Kuśa, how they should go to the city of Raghu-rājā, and how they should present the songs of *Rāmāyaṇa* to the citizens and render them in the presence of Rāma himself. This ending achieved many things. It neatly completed the cycle of songs just where it had begun, with Lava and Kuśa in Rāma's court, but this time, the poet is paying homage to the first poet Vālmīki by bringing in his character alive. Again, this is a song full of self-reflexivity, where the sage instructs the young singers on the proper mode of singing and artistic behavior. Madgulkar's Vālmīki says to Lava and Kuśa, as the poet says to the future singers, "Pay attention to the order of the cantos. Make sure you evoke the emotions in your clear notes. Sing a little every day to complete the entire story. Stay within the limits of rhythm and pace. Keep the acting on your faces to a minimum when the king himself listens. And remember, this is not just a poem, this is a treasure of immortal nectar. Do not tell anyone your name or your city; call yourselves only my disciples. Do not accept money or gold, either as a donation, or again as *dakṣiṇā*, as wealth is of no value for the sages. Just make all your aspirations dedicated to Śrī Rāma."

The Format

For all of his songs Gadimā chose a simple format. Every song had a refrain and a flexible number of stanzas, anywhere from five to eleven stanzas of three to four lines of varying length. The meters he chose were simple singable meters of *pada* style popular in the Marathi *bhāvagīta* tradition, with roughly the same number of *mātrās* in each line, and not of the rigid syllabic (*akṣara-gaṇa-vṛtta*) style of Sanskrit. The meters were suited both to the episode and to the voice of the epic character who sings the song. An example is the song *Sāvaḷā ga rāmacandra*, in which Kausalyā sings the joys of raising the child Rāma to her co-wives. It was written in the four-quartered sonorous *ovī* meter used by rural women to sing their extemporized songs every morning while grinding grains on the grindstone. The choice of this popular meter and of the right words to illustrate Kausalyā's motherly pride, hope, and thankfulness for her good fortune made that song so memorable that it was heard at many women's ceremonies such as *ḍohāḷ-jevaṇ* (somewhat like the baby shower), *bārsa* (naming ceremony), and even the *haḷdī-kuṅku* ceremonies celebrating the blessed state of being married.

Madgulkar expertly utilized the power of refrain for his songs. Some of his refrains have become proverbial in present-day Marathi. An oft-quoted one is *ākāśāśī jaḍale nāte dharaṇī-mātece, svayaṁvara jhāle sītece*. It describes the occasion of Rāma and Sītā's wedding as the alliance between the sky and Mother Earth, since Rāma is divine as the incarnation of Viṣṇu, and Sītā is the daughter of Mother Earth. Another proverbial refrain comes from the song of

Rāma in which he rejects Bharata's passionate pleas to return to the throne of Ayodhyā, and advises Bharata on the nature of life, saying, "All sorrows are created by destiny, Bharata, no one is to blame. The son of man in this world is not independent" (*daiva-jāta dukhe bharatā, doṣa nā kuṇācā, parādhīna āhe jagatī putra mānavācā*). Many others were memorable; for example, when Sītā says to Rāma, "How can you bid me farewell? Where there is Rāma, there is Sītā" (*Niropa kasalā mājhā ghetā? Jethe rāghava, tethe sītā*).

The Content

The songs of the *Gīta-Rāmāyana* can be grouped in broad types in view of their content. They can be roughly grouped as narrative, descriptive, communal, and voiced. In each category, Madgulkar's poetic skills are notable. For example, the opening song that describes how the sons are singing the life of their father is acutely dramatic. Very few songs—about seven—are episodic narrations: the birth of Rāma, the wedding of Rāma and Sītā, Kuśa and Lava's two songs describing the airborne Hanumān setting fire to Laṅkā with his blazing tail and the famous battle of Rāma and Rāvaṇa in progress, the song of the *gandharvas* and *apsarās* on the occasion of the slaying of Rāvaṇa, and the song of the citizens of Ayodhyā when they sing victory chants upon Rāma's return to Ayodhyā. In these songs, listeners feel as if they are listening to a running commentary of live incidents. Only two songs are simple poetic descriptions: Kuśa and Lava's description of Ayodhyā, and Rāma's description of Citrakūṭa. In these Madgulkar has successfully portrayed pen-pictures of prominent places in the epic story.

A few songs are communal songs, or *saṅgha-gītas*: the song of Guha and his boatmen giving a ride to Rāma and his party (*jaya gaṅge jaya bhāgirathī*), and the song of the monkeys when they build the bridge across the ocean to Laṅkā. Both these songs became instantly popular. The boatmen's song was heard at many a school picnic, sung by the marching or traveling schoolchildren. Part of its popularity with schoolchildren was its lively tune, which made everyone hum the notes and tap the rhythm. But its popularity was also due to the humility, the devotion, and the ethic of doing the appointed task (dharma) that found expression in it. The monkey song, *setu bāndhā re*, was also a favorite of children due to its wonderful thoughts and lively imagery, and of course its inspiring vocal imitation of a monkey cry of victory. Both these were Madgulkar's original additions to the story line, and a certain departure from Vālmīki. Here he had his chance of giving voice to the lowliest characters in the epic.

The Characterization through Voiced Songs

The greatest number of songs were in the voices of major and minor characters. These were the songs that brought to life the characters of the *Rāmāyaṇa* and thus became the most memorable. In these, you could hear Kaikayī cajoling and conniving to secure her two boons, Bharata striking at his mother with words like arrows, and Daśaratha gasping for one last glimpse of Rāma. Here you could hear prince Rāma consoling Bharata, admonishing Sugrīva, ordering Aṅgada to go with an ultimatum to Rāvaṇa. You could witness Rāma uttering astonishingly cruel words to disown Sītā after having killed Rāvaṇa and rescued her, and then again, after Sītā's fire ordeal, swearing on oath that she is the only one in his heart and soul. In these voiced songs, the spotlight was mainly on Rāma and Sītā. Rāma had the most, that is, ten songs, closely followed by Sītā, who had six. Unlike Vālmīki's Sītā, who is known to speak little, Madgulkar's Sītā speaks her mind. She argues with Rāma and produces convincing reasons why he should take her into exile. She makes entreaties to Rāma to get her the golden deer, which she describes vividly. In a progressive episodic song, she talks to Rāvaṇa, telling him not to wait at her door, sensing his evil intentions and ordering him to leave. This song ends in her being terrified as she is forcefully abducted, and in her cry for help. In captivity, Sītā again talks to Rāvaṇa, sternly admonishing him and threatening him with reminders of her husband's valor and his imminent victory over her abductor. In another song, Sītā, as a mother-to-be, expresses to Rāma in most endearing terms her wishes to roam in the forest woods. In her last song, Sītā is shocked to realize that she is abandoned by her beloved without his even communicating with her. This is the most haunting song of the series, the only song sung in the original radio series by the phenomenal Lata Mangeshkar. In this song, Sītā's question "Tell me Lakṣmaṇa, where shall I go?" is repeated in the refrain and in the end, and remains painfully unanswered.

The greatest achievement of Gadimā was to regenerate vivid characters who were already living in the minds of the audience without sacrificing their authenticity, and yet to make them thoroughly relatable and appealing to a contemporary audience by using familiar idioms. He accepted the challenge and succeeded in it beyond expectation. His characters were close to the *Vālmīki Rāmāyaṇa* characters, and therefore appeared human to the practical-minded, not overly religious Maharashtrians. There was no attempt to disguise the original physical abduction of Sītā by a lame device of "shadow-Sītā" nor any attempt to whitewash the frailties of Kaikayī or Sītā, or even the shortcomings of Rāma. Sītā, in the *Gīta-Rāmāyaṇa,* was really tempted by the golden deer, and even believed that Kaikayī and Bharata would be jealous of her when they saw her with her pet. Lakṣmaṇa was impatient, quick to anger, and doubtful even of his younger brother, Bharata's motives. Bharata's wrath at his mother's foolish deed was felt in his angry words, just as much as his genuine sorrow was heard in the song in which he tells Rāma that he is an orphan without his father and mother, and then he reasons with Rāma to come back and accept the kingdom.[7] Rāma was a lovable human prince in the process of realizing his divinity. He could be very patient when trying to pacify angry Lakṣmaṇa, and philosophical when convincing Bharata why he could not come back to Ayodhyā. Patient with brothers and mothers, obedient of father and sages, heroic on the battlefield, and diplomatic when dealing with the monkey king, Rāma still had human weaknesses. He was really distraught at the loss of his beloved wife, and wailed in Lakṣmaṇa's presence. His song in which he uttered some heart-wrenching, cruel words in front of his army, and the next song, in which he explained his astonishing behavior with oaths and confessions of loyalty to Sītā, were both touching, and these were the favorites of audiences because they sensed here the inexplicable irony of the human situation in which there are no simple answers to pressing ethical dilemmas. Madgulkar's Rāma also confronted at least one other tough ethical question when he answered the dying Vāli, who asked him why he was killed by Rāma when Rāma was not wronged by him.[8] Rāma's duty as a kshatriya to protect the wronged Sugrīva and his promise to Sugrīva were given as reasons for the killing. Rāma was thus portrayed as a complex character full of emotions and passions, at times capable of questionable actions, yet bound by a constricting weight of traditional virtue and the sanctity of a promise. Just as his personal ethical dilemmas were voiced in these songs, his courage, stately diplomacy, and steadfastness under attack also found forceful expression.

Even minor characters became memorable through these eloquent songs. Women, monkeys, and demons had voices along with kings, princes, and sages. Kausalyā had three songs; Daśaratha, Viśvāmitra, Lakṣmaṇa, Bharata, Hanuman, and Śūrpaṇakhā each had two songs; Kaikayī, Ahalyā, Śabarī, Jaṭāyu, Sugrīva, and Jāmbavān each had one song. Although Kumbhakarṇa had a sobering song admonishing and reassuring Rāvaṇa, Rāvaṇa had none. Rāvaṇa's oppressive presence was only felt through prose narrations, poetic descriptions, and the words addressed to him by the others.

I could go on analyzing each song at length, but suffice it to say that through these voices Madgulkar succeeds in recreating Rāmakathā in a truly memorable form.

The Music

Dr. Sunanda Chavji, in a recent article entitled, "I, My Generation and Sudhir Phadke,"[9] says, "The wealth of Madgulkar's language in the *Gīta-Rāmāyaṇa* is indeed a topic fit for an article, but there is absolutely no doubt that it was the notes of Sudhir Phadke that conveyed it so masterfully to the audience, and that was itself a great service." She reminisces, "On every Rāmanavamī, in the courtyard of Nutan Marathi Vidyamandir, there was the concert of the *Gīta-Rāmāyaṇa* sung by Sudhir Phadke, and we would attend as many times as possible. No matter how many times we heard it, it would seem fresh every time, and never tire us. I don't believe that there was any other performance of its kind that stayed so fresh in the minds of the audience, not in Maharashtra, and most probably not even in all of India." She also asserts that the "*Gīta-Rāmāyaṇa* was a miracle, and our generation actually experienced it to the fullest." It is difficult to gauge the exact contribution of music to the success of the series since the words and the music behave like an ideal couple, each enhancing the other and presenting to the world a totally united front. Since I am not a connoisseur of music, my appraisal of the music will be rudimentary and mainly based on the comments of music teachers and singers such as Gopal Marathe (see appendix 2).

The original tunes under the music direction of Sudhir Phadke are all based on basic, commonly known ragas of the north Indian classical music tradition such as Yaman, Bhoopali, Sarang, Vasant, Bhimpalas, and Bhairavi. They are palatable to music lovers and connoisseurs alike, and easily accessible to the most elementary singer. The ragas and talas were selected to suit the time of the day of the incident and the mood of the song. The original choice of male and female singers was just right for the voice of the epic characters. All were singers well versed in classical Indian music, and knew how to sing in the popular *bhāvagīta* style of light music, paying close attention to the pronunciation of words and bringing out the emotions through their melodies. The most important factor in making the series a sustained succcess, however, was the choice of musical settings that evoked the right mood by the music director, Sudhir Phadke. The following songs give a few examples of his versatility as music director and as singer:

The joy at the occasion of the wedding of Rāma and Sītā. (*ākāśāśī jaḍale*)
Lakṣmaṇa's passionate anger at Rāma's banishment (*rāmāviṇa rājyapadī*)
Bharata's anguished outcry at Kaikayī's outrageous action (*mātā na tū, vairiṇī*)
Rāma's ultimatum to Rāvaṇa through Aṅgada (*jā jhaṇi jā rāvaṇāsa*)
Śūrpaṇakhā's flirtations (*koṇa tū kuṭhalā rājakumār*)
The outcry of mutilated Śūrpaṇakhā to Rāvaṇa for revenge (*sūḍa ghe*)
Rāma's soothing advice to Bharata (*parādhīna āhe jagatī putra mānavācā*)
The brotherly admonitions of Kumbhakarṇa to Rāvaṇa (*yogya samayi*)
The voice of the *ādikavi*, Vālmīki, to singers (*gā bāḷāñno śrī rāmāyaṇa*)

Conclusion

As I have shown above, the *Gīta-Rāmāyaṇa* was a spontaneous recreation of Vālmīki's Rāmakathā in sophisticated Marathi poetry through lyrical and dramatic songs, broadcast in radio serial and then through live concerts. The enduring appeal of the *Gīta-Rāmāyaṇa* as a radio serial, and in live performances, remains uneclipsed even after four decades, at home and abroad. The credit of its success and appeal can be attributed to a combination of many aspects, such as the poet's ability to bring to life the original characters in voiced songs without sacrificing authenticity, his ability to create an impeccably appealing idiom, and the music director's talent in popularizing the songs through the choice of the right rāga and endearing melodies. The happy combination of all these factors was perhaps a blessed coincidence in the history of performances of Rāmakathā. The Marathi *Gīta-Rāmāyaṇa* has indeed secured for itself a place of pride and pleasure in the hearts of music lovers.

APPENDIX I. TRANSLATIONS AND THEIR PERFORMERS

In a recent trip to India, on April 23, 2001, in Pune, I visited Anand Madgulkar, second son of the late poet Gadimā, and talked with him about the *Gīta-*

Rāmāyana. He knew of equi-verse translations in several languages, and had heard of several performances of the translations to the original melodies. Dr. Gopal Marathe also gave many details of translations and their performances. Based on my conversations with Anand Madgulkar and Narendra Datar of Toronto, and e-mail communications with Gopal Marathe, here is a partial list.

There are at least five translations in Hindi:

1. By Rudradatta Mishra from Gwalior, published by Nagesh Joshi, 27 Jayamangala, Shiva srishti, Chembur, Mumbai, in 1976. Sung by Vasant Ajgaonkar. The text used by Narendra Datar in his Hindi concert in Toronto.
2. By Hari Narayan Vyas, composed in the sixties. Sung by Bal Gokhle.
3. By Kusum Tambe of Mandla, Madhya Pradesh.
4. By a singer from Nagpur, in Avadhi (as recalled by Anand Madgulkar).
5. By Gokhale from Baroda.

In Kannada by Prof. B. H. Tofakhane. Sung by Upendra Bhat.

In Telugu by Vaman Mullai Varadacharya. Sung by Dhondushastri and Shyamala Satyanarayan Rao.

In Bengali by Kamala Bhagwat, who lived in Calcutta and also was a performer.

In Gujarati by the late Hansraj Thakkar, from Mumbai. Sung by Hansraj Thakkar and Kumud Bhagwat.

In Konkani by Mr. Kamath. Sung by Upendra Bhat.

In English by Mr. Ursekar, a retired judge, who rendered it in "Shakespearean"!

In Sindhi by Rita Shahani, poet and singer, who rendered the songs in classical ragas and created a ballet based on them. (*Stri*, Sept. 83, p. 39)

In Sanskrit by Vasant Gadgil. Sung by Malati Pande; Kamala Ketkar, who taught Sanskrit in Srimati Nathibai Damodar Thackersey Women's University, Mumbai, and perhaps also by Sanjay Upadhye, from Vile Parle.

Narendra Datar mentioned one Prof. Sitaram Datar, of Andheri/Thane, who has translated it back into Sanskrit.

Gopal Marathe said that he has on a cassette tape several *Gīta-Rāmāyana* songs sung in Kannada to the original melodies. Gopal Marathe also told me that in 1990 he met a blind singer in Mumbai who sang the *Gīta-Rāmāyana* with the help of a braille transliteration of the *Gīta-Rāmāyana*.

APPENDIX 2. MUSICAL FORM

Dr. Gopal Marathe sent me the following information on the musical setup of the *Gīta-Rāmāyaṇa*. He uses the song numbers from the published text of the *Gīta-Rāmāyaṇa*.

Tāla (beat). These songs are in the following tālas:

6 songs in Ektāl of 12 beats (8, 16, 24, 35, 39, 45)
1 song in Khemtā of 6 beats (47)
1 in Dādrā also of 6 beats (6)
1 in Jhaptāl of 10 beats (9)
3 in Tintāl of 16 beats (14, 23, 28)
1 in Rūpak of 7 beats (26)
12 songs in Bhajanī of 8 beats (1, 2, 4, 5, 10, 34, 37, 49, 51, 52, 53, 56)
The rest of the 31 songs are in Kehrwā, also of 8 beats.

Ragas: Bhūpalī, Kafī, Deś, Bhīmpalāś, Pilū, Vasant, Haṁsa-dhvani, Bibhās, Bahār, Madhuvantī, Toḍī, Bairāgī, Adāṇā, Kedār, Hamīr, Yaman, Pūriyā Dhanāśrī, Maru-bihāg, (Vṛndāvani) Sāraṅg, Multāni, Tilang, Asāvarī, Hindol, and Bhairavī.

In most case these ragas match the time when the incident in the story is possibly taking place. For example, song no. 10, *Calā Rāghavā calā*, is in raga Bihās (morning raga) and it is clear from the commentary that the incident is taking place in the morning. They also match the mood of the song. For example, song no. 22, *Dāṭalā cohikaḍe andhār* of Daśaratha, is in Bairagi to suit the dejected mood of the lamenting king.

NOTES

This essay was read at the workshop on "Performance, Gender, and the Narrative Design of the *Rāmāyaṇa*," at the University of British Columbia, June 15–16, 2001. Second reading at the Centre for India and South Asia Research, March 13, 2003.

1. "Mantarlele Divas, *Gīta-Rāmāyaṇāce*" by Vidya Madgulkar. From www.gadima.com, the Web site of Gadimā; the Web site was created in honor of the poet.

2. Ibid.

3. Information given to me by Sudhir Phadke in a conversation in April 2001.

4. For example, N. B. Datar of Toronto has given about 250 concerts of the *Gīta-Rāmāyaṇa* in and around Bombay in the sixties. Sudhakar Kawthalkar used to give several concerts of Marathi *Gīta-Rāmāyaṇa* in Ahmedabad, Gujarat, in the sixties and seventies.

5. Information collected in telephone conversation with Dr. Gopal Marathe on June 11, 2001. The events' news coverage also appears in the North American Marathi newsletter *Bṛhan Mahārāṣṭra Vṛtta*, issued on May 15, 1990. Available from BMM newsletter, Box 18154, Philadelphia.

6. Anand Madgulkar told me that after the death of his father, they donated fifteen different *Rāmāyaṇa*s in his father's collection to the Jaykar Library of Pune University.

7. Although alive, Kaikayī is mentioned as dead by Bharata, since he thinks she behaves unlike his kind mother that he used to know.

8. "I have only fulfilled my dharma, my duty. It is not just killing Vāli, it is eradicating evil" was the refrain of the thirty-sixth song.

9. Chavji, "Mī, āmacī piḍhī āṇi Sudhīra Phaḍke," *Sāptāhik Sakāḷ*, Pune, March 23, 2002, pp. 30–33.

11

Mysticism and Islam in Javanese *Rāmāyaṇa* Tales

Laurie J. Sears

Ki Cabolek said: "I first embraced mystical knowledge in Yemen, when I studied / under a teacher, whose name was Ki Shaikh Zain, / the doctrine he taught was similar to that of *Dewa Ruci* / that was the mystical knowledge passed on [to me] / which was similar to *Bhima Suci*."[1]

Yasadipura I

To hear mystical Islamic voices in Javanese *Rāmāyaṇa* tales, this essay focuses on several discursive moments in the web and flow of Javanese shadow play stories when particular densities of beliefs and symbols coalesce to reveal new textual authorities. The study of power within societal and historical narratives has been enriched over the past decades by Michel Foucault's interest in intellectual genealogies as points of analytical access to the discourses—what it was possible to think—in a certain age. Foucault was concerned with how different discourses came into being and the ways in which such discourses were appropriated for various purposes. Foucault's description of the movements of power in society is especially useful: "Power's condition of possibility . . . must not be sought in the primary existence of a central point, in a unique source of sovereignty from which secondary and descendent forms would emanate; it is the moving substrate of force relations which, by virtue of their inequality, constantly engender states of power, but the latter are always local and unstable."[2]

These continually unfolding local and unstable relations of power constitute narrative traditions like the shadow play tales as sites of contestation and accommodation in the search to hear new relations of power in specific story cycles. Exploring these local sites allows us to see the absorption and appropriation of imported religious, intellectual, or technological ideas as creative acts with unpredictable consequences. Rather than proposing that Javanese poets or performers were compelled by powerful patrons to incorporate new symbols and ideas into their stories, I suggest that they chose to adopt and adapt new concepts because these concepts allowed them to accrue cultural capital while introducing intellectual tensions that enhanced their art. In this essay, I trace the emergence of Islamic ideas in Javanese *Rāmāyaṇa* stories by examining several poetic and narrative texts from the late eighteenth and nineteenth centuries. I end with a focus on the adoption and adaptation of new ideas and technologies as the shadow theater and its stories became sites of interpretive struggles in colonial and postcolonial Javanese society.

History of the Story of Rahwana's Birth

It must have been during the seventeenth and eighteenth centuries—and possibly earlier—that older Saivite/Buddhist ideas of power and knowledge in the shadow theater traditions began to be expressed in Islamic terms. To explore the absorption of Islamic ideas and imagery into Javanese *Rāmāyaṇa* tales in the late eighteenth and nineteenth centuries, I investigate a particular story that has circulated through Javanese culture for over a thousand years to illuminate the workings of power that bring Islamic imagery into specific and localized sites. In the repertoire of the central Javanese shadow theater, the story is called "The Marriage of Sukesi" or *Alap-alapan Sukesi,* and the germ of the story, the birth of the demon-king Rahwana [Skt. Rāvaṇa], can be traced back to the Sanskrit *Rāmāyaṇa* attributed to Vālmīki. The story was first rendered into Old Javanese in the tenth century C.E.[3]

The permutations of the story of Rahwana's birth in the nineteenth century document a late stage in the history of Islamic penetration into the archipelago, when Javanist Sufi mystical traditions were making an accommodation to more orthodox interpretations of Islam. As part of this accommodation, Islam was molded to fit the shape of indigenous Javanese religious beliefs. Certain mystical practices that had flourished freely under the older Indic kingdoms were increasingly frowned upon in the central Javanese courts, where Islamic titles and rituals were increasingly adopted by Javanese rulers—new practices that both shored up the charisma of the courts and antagonized the Dutch trading company, or VOC, which was to collapse at the very end of the eighteenth century and give way to the imposition of Dutch colonial rule. These attitudes are reflected in the written texts of the story of Rahwana's birth produced by Javanese court poets in the late eighteenth and early nineteenth centuries. Although for several centuries Islamic ideas had grown together with *kejawen* or Javanist practices, Islamic and Javanist traditions began to fragment into separate domains demarcated across class and urban/rural lines in the latter part of the nineteenth century, due to pressures from Dutch administrators on local Javanese elites.

The earliest mention of the story of the birth of Rahwana occurs in the *Uttarakāṇḍa* of the Sanskrit *Rāmāyaṇa* attributed to Vālmīki. Although the Vālmīki *Rāmāyaṇa* is believed to date back to at least 200 B.C.E., the *Uttarakāṇḍa* is a later addition which assumed its present form by the second half of the second century C.E.[4] In the Sanskrit *Uttarakāṇḍa*, a *rākṣasa* (demon) named Sumāli emerged from the nether world with his beautiful daughter Kaikesī. Seeking to increase the power of the demons, he wished to marry his daughter to the sage Viśravas, so that she might beget sons equal to Vaiśrāvaṇa (Viśravas's son), also called the Lord of Wealth. On her father's instructions, Kaikesī went to Viśravas, but she inauspiciously interrupted him as he was engaged in the fire sacrifice. He replied thus to her brief admission of her name and that she had come at her father's request:

> I know well, O Fortunate One, what brings thee here, thou art desirous of having sons by me, thou whose gait is like unto an intoxicated elephant! But, having presented thyself at this hour, hear me, O Fortunate One, thou shalt bring forth offspring of a dark aspect delighting in the companionship of doers of evil deeds. O Lady of Lovely Form, thou shalt beget Rakshasas of cruel exploits.[5]

When Kaikesī bemoaned her fate, Viśravas relented and said that her last son would be virtuous, like him. Thus were the demons Rahwana (Rāvaṇa), Kumbakarna (Kumbhakarṇa), and Surpanaka (Śūrpaṇakhā), a daughter, born, as well as Wibisana (Vibhīṣaṇa), the promised son of virtue.

The Old Javanese *Uttara Kandha*, which Zoetmulder groups with the prose *parwa* literature recounting the episodes of the *Mahābhārata*, is believed to date back to the late tenth century C.E.[6] In the Old Javanese *Uttara Kandha*, the story of Rahwana's birth remains basically the same.[7] Sumali wishes his daughter to have children equal to Waisrawana (Vaiśrāvaṇa) in order to strengthen the power of the rakshasas. He thus manages to give his daughter to Wisrawa (Viśravas), and she begets Rahwana and his brothers and sister. The *Uttara Kandha* and the rest of the Old Javanese *parwa* do not have authors attributed to them.

The first Javanese author to be connected to the story of Wisrawa and Kaikesi is Mpu Tantular, who rendered a prose text of the early history of Rahwana, the *Arjunawijaya Kakawin*, into poetry. Scholars agree that it is most likely that Tantular used the Old Javanese *Uttara Kandha* as the basis for his story rather than a Sanskrit text, although Tantular may indeed have had a firsthand knowledge of Sanskrit. According to Balinese tradition, Tantular was supposedly a Buddhist in Kadhiri during the reign of Jayabhaya, but it is now accepted that he lived and wrote in the late fourteenth century, during the reign of Hayam Wuruk in the Majapahit kingdom.[8]

The telling of the story recounted in the *kakawin* of Tantular agrees with that of the Sanskrit and the Old Javanese *Uttara Kandha*, and again mentions that Wisrawa was engaged in devotions when Kaikesi came to him. In the *kakawin*, however, there is no mention of inauspiciousness, and Kaikesi is said to have been granted favors by the great sage as he answered her request for children. The *kakawin* also describes how Sumali's daughter Kaikesi "assumed a form unlike that of a descendant of the great demons; as a goddess in visible form descending into the world."[9] Supomo recounts that there are more than twenty manuscripts of the Old Javanese *Arjunawijaya Kakawin*, coming from Java, Bali, and Lombok, which were copied and recopied over the next few hundred years.[10]

Concerning the literature of the following centuries, the anonymous encyclopedic collections of eighteenth-century tales in which *Rāmāyaṇa* and *Mahābhārata* stories were enfolded and transformed, the *Serat Pakem Ringgit Purwa* or *Serat Kandhaning Ringgit Purwa*, include examples of how older Indic traditions were blended with Islamic stories. The *Serat Kandha*, for example, gave the Indic heroes genealogies that led them back to the Islamic Nabi Adam.[11] When Islam entered the archipelago, it had already been filtered through the fabric of Indian religious philosophy, which emphasized meditative practice in the effort to contact the divine. Traders, who were often connected with Sufi *tariqat* (paths or schools of esoteric teachings), brought their interpretations of Islam to the north-coast cities of Java where merchants, who perhaps had not been participants in the elite mystical Śaivite-Buddhist faith of the inland kingdoms, were quick to adopt the new religion, which required no priests or rituals other than the performance of the five pillars of the faith. The mythological carriers of Islam to Java were the nine *wali* or saints, some known for their spiritual and mystical powers and others known for their knowledge of Islamic textual traditions. In the ensuing centuries, Islamic stories and Indian legends were intertwined in the *Serat Kandha* texts as they were in the plays of the shadow puppet theater. *Serat Kandha* tellings of the Arjunawijaya story differ from the older texts; these renderings have more in common with storytelling traditions and shadow theater plays.[12]

Writing in the early years of the nineteenth century, the British administrator Sir Stamford Raffles recounted a story of Rahwana's birth, which he took from a *Serat Kandha* text extant at that time.[13] He says that it is to the *Serat Kandha* "that the modern Javans constantly refer for an explanation of their ancient mythology." He commented on the many passages in this work "otherwise written in a very correct style" which were "unfit for a chaste ear," and on his inability to entirely purge this quality from the work. He also mentioned that the word *Pepakem* was another name for the *Serat Kandha*. The word *pakem* is used in modern Javanese to refer to the most stable stories of the *wayang purwa* repertoire, as well as to written outlines of the stories. The rendering of the story of Rahwana's birth that Raffles recounts is quite different from the Old Javanese renditions as well as from the later renditions in modern Javanese:

> *Brama* then following the example of *Narada*, purifies himself, and at his desire, first there appears before him a boy of strong make, on whom he confers the name of *Brama Tama*: secondly, a boy, also of strong make, whom he names *Brama Sudarga*; and thirdly, a beautiful girl, on whom he confers the name of *Bramani Wati*.

The two boys, when they attained maturity, descended from *Suralaya*. *Brama Sudarga* united in marriage with a female from the earth: from them, in the third degree, were descended *Raja Sumali* and *Mangliawan*. In the reign of the latter of these a destructive war is stated to have taken place. *Mangliawan* laid waste *Suralaya* and slew *Sri Gati* [Wisnu's son], but afterwards, when he shewed a desire to possess *Sri* [Wisnu's wife], *Wisnu* exerted all his strength, and put him to death. As *Mangliawan* expired *Wisnu* heard a voice saying unto him, "The work is not yet complete; hereafter, when there shall be on the earth a man named *Rahwana*, who will be descended from *Brama Tama*, beware of him: in his time the peace of heaven will again be disturbed, and he will lay it waste." *Brama Tama* espoused a princess of *Champa*, named *S'rati Dewi*, by whom he had a son, named *Brama Raja*, who became *Raja* of *Indrapuri*, and had a son named *Chitra Bahar* or *Angsarwa*, to whom, when he became advanced in age, he delivered over charge of the country, proceeding himself into the forests as a devotee, and assuming the name of *Resi Tama*.

Sumali had a daughter named *Sukesi Dewi*. This prince, alarmed at the accounts of [his brother] *Mangliawan's* death, fled with her to *Chitra Bahar* [his generational uncle and third cousin], and requested him to protect her as a maiden, giving him authority to sanction her marriage on any proper occasion which might offer. He himself fearing the vengeance of *Sang yang Guru*, fled further into the woods for concealment, but died on the way. *Chitra Bahar*, forgetting the nature of his charge, became enamoured of the girl [who could have been his grandchild]. This happened when he was performing a penance; for he had two sons, named *Misra Warna* and *Bisa Warna*, to the former of whom he had entrusted the charge of his government. The girl resisted on account of his age, but he at last succeeded. During the first amour he received from her nine strokes on the head with a stone. In due time she became pregnant and was delivered of a boy, having nine marks or excrescences on his head, which added to his natural face, making as it were ten fronts to his head: he was thence called *Dasa muka* (ten-faced). In the second attempt she pulled the lobes of both his ears with great strength, and when delivered she produced a child in the form of a *Raksasa*, and having immense lobes to the ears: this child was named *Amba karna*, or long-eared. In the third she scratched him all over, and the fruit of it was a girl, born with long nails and claws at the end of each finger: she was named *Sarpa kanaka*, or serpent-nailed; the wounds inflicted by these nails are said to have been mortal. But the fourth being unresisted, she was delivered of a most beautiful boy, who, having a countenance and mouth beautiful like those of a girl, was named *Bibisana*.[14]

I have quoted this passage at length as it throws interesting light on the development of the story of Rahwana's birth as well as on the ways in which Indian stories become recontextualized in Java. Several themes and variations that will be stressed in the texts of the story produced in the eighteenth- and nineteenth-century courts already have surfaced in the *Serat Kandha* story. Rather than Sumali emerging from the netherworld as a demon, here Sumali's ancestor descends from Suralaya. Brama Raja turns his kingdom over to his son Chitra Bahar and retreats to the forest, where he becomes known as Resi Tama. Sumali, who is fleeing from the wrath of Batara Guru, gives his daughter to Chitra Bahar who is supposed to marry her off properly. Instead, Chitra Bahar marries the girl himself, even though he is much older than she. Chitra Bahar, who has turned his kingdom over to his son, falls in love with Sukesi while he is performing a penance or sacrifice. Then follows the explanations of the forms of the children of Chitra Bahar and Sukesi in accordance with the style of their lovemaking.

Although it is tempting to see in these folk etymologies indigenous Javanese interpretations, the theme echoes the Indian *Mahābhārata* stories of the births of Pāṇḍu, Dhṛtarāṣṭra, and Vidura, where the three sons acquire different characteristics according to the degree of revulsion that their various mothers felt for their father, the sage Vyāsa (Jv. Abiyasa), during the lovemaking act.[15] The Indian antecedents and Javanese explanations of the names of Rahwana and his brothers and sister show the recontextualizations of the stories that made them more understandable to their audiences and bring to mind the etymologies (*jarwa dhosok*) that all Javanese puppeteers create to explain the names of major characters in the *wayang* stories.[16] The importance of the interpretation lies not in an approximation of fact but rather in the ability of the puppeteer to draw together disparate images into a coherent whole. These stories that recount the early history of Rahwana are known as Arjunasasrabahu or Lokapala stories after King Arjunasasrabahu of Lokapala, who finally defeated the demon Rahwana. The Arjunasasrabahu cycle of stories is considered to be the earliest cycle of the Indian-inspired stories from which many Javanese oral and written traditions draw their repertoire. After the Arjunasasrabahu cycle comes the *Rāmāyaṇa* cycle and then the *Mahābhārata* cycle. The Javanese believe that the action of the earlier cycles took place in the distant past, before the action of the later cycles.

A Story of Rahwana's Birth in the Late Eighteenth Century

In the late eighteenth and early nineteenth centuries, a so-called renaissance of Javanese literary arts unfolded in the central Javanese courts, in particular in Surakarta, residence of the famous court poets (*pujangga*), the elder and younger Yasadipura and Ranggawarsita. Ricklefs suggests that this literary renaissance may have fitted into a cyclical pattern of Javanese history that saw an outpouring of literary works at the end of each hundred-year epoch in the

Javanese calendar.[17] The literary revival may have camouflaged not only the Javanese inability to remedy the political situation of the late eighteenth century, where the Dutch were assuming more and more political power, but also the Javanese prophetic tradition that called for a new dynasty to arise at the turn of each hundred-year cycle. I am suggesting that the interest in *Mahābhārata* and *Rāmāyaṇa* stories at the end of the eighteenth century was inspired by the ways in which those stories of an ancestral past served as allegories of the colonial present. Tales of the rival kingdoms of Ngastina and Ngamarta reflected the growing rivalry between the courts of Surakarta and Yogyakarta, and stories of wars between powerful foreign kings and noble princes served to mirror the expanding power of the Dutch foreigners over the noble princes of Java.

The next written text of the story of Rahwana's birth, although no longer extant, is attributed to this late-eighteenth-century revival. This was the *macapat* (sung poetry using indigenous Javanese meters) text of Yasadipura I (d. 1803), the famous court poet, which is mentioned in the later *macapat* text of his son Yasadipura II.[18] A text that has survived is the *tembang gede* (or *kawi miring*) telling of Yasadipura II, which rendered the Old Javanese *kakawin* into modern Javanese with metrical forms based on the Sanskrit-derived Old Javanese prosody. Sixteen years later, Yasadipura II wrote a *macapat* text of the *Arjunasasrabahu,* the larger work, also called the *Arjunawijaya* or the *Serat Lokapala,* which contains the story fragment of Rahwana's birth. It is the *macapat* text which Day believes most effectively translated the Old Javanese poetry into modern Javanese poetry, making it comprehensible to the audiences of the nineteenth century.[19] The tellings of the story of Rahwana's birth produced by Yasadipura I and Yasadipura II differ considerably from those recorded in earlier texts.

A Nineteenth-Century Telling of the Story of Rahwana's Birth

This text narrates the actions that take place in three countries: Lokapala, Ngayodya, and Mahispati. What is narrated first takes place in the kingdom of Lokapala. The king is named Wisrawa and he wishes to retire to the forest to undertake ascetic practices. He turns the kingdom over to his son, who is named Dhanapati or Wisrawana.

Then it is said that there is a king of the demons named Sumali, who holds his court in Ngalengka. He has one daughter named Sukesi of exceeding beauty. King Dhanapati hears of the beauty of Sukesi and asks his father to make the proposal for the hand of Sukesi. Wisrawa agrees to his son's wishes and quickly departs for the kingdom of Ngalengka to meet with King Sumali and make the necessary arrangements. Sumali says that he is willing to accede to Wisrawa's request, but before the marriage can take place he would like Wisrawa to give them mystical teachings that will bring well-being to body and soul in this life and the next. Wisrawa agrees, and Sumali is then given the teaching he has requested as well as other mystical teachings. Sukesi is sitting at the back of her father.

Batara Guru (Siwa) and his wife Betari Durga descend to the earth and head to the kingdom of Ngalengka, to the very place where the teaching is being given. Guru enters the body of Wisrawa, and Durga enters the body of Sukesi. At that moment, Wisrawa becomes fatally attracted to Sukesi and he asks Sumali if he might marry the girl himself. Sumali and Sukesi both agree, and soon Wisrawa and Sukesi are married.

King Dhanapati is waiting for his father's return when he hears the news that his father has married Sukesi himself. He becomes very angry and orders his soldiers to prepare to go to Ngalengka to fight with Wisrawa. They have not yet departed when the god Endra appears and informs Dhanapati that it is the will of the gods that Sukesi marry Wisrawa. Dhanapati is asked to give up his battle plans, and then he is given two celestial nymphs, Nawangsih and Sasmitaningsih. Dhanapati is satisfied and his anger toward his father disappears.[20]

In Yasadipura II's rendering, Waisrawana or Dhanapati, his more common Javanese name, hears of the beautiful Dewi Sukesi, the daughter of Sumali, the king of the ogres, and Dhanapati asks his father, Wisrawa, to arrange the marriage. Sumali is unwilling to give up his daughter unless the sage Wisrawa initiates him into certain esoteric mystical teachings. Wisrawa agrees, and Sumali is so pleased with his new knowledge that he asks if Wisrawa will initiate his daughter Sukesi also. When Wisrawa explains the *sastra harjendrayuningrat* (*sastrajendra*) to Sumali and Sukesi,[21] the gods in the heavens feel the heat and turmoil (*gara-gara*) that the unauthorized revelation of this mystical teaching has aroused. Batara Guru (Siwa) and his wife Durga, wishing to punish Wisrawa, descend to earth and incarnate into the bodies of Wisrawa and Sukesi, causing them to fall in love and marry. From this union the three *raksasas* (ogres), Rahwana, Kumbakarna, and Surpanaka, and the noble Wibisana are born. Dhanapati is enraged when he hears of his father's marriage. He plans to take up arms against his father until he is calmed by a visit from the god Indra, who offers him two beautiful celestial nymphs to compensate for the loss of Sukesi.[22]

The new elements in the story center on the conflict between Wisrawa and Dhanapati and the unauthorized expression of the mystical teaching *sastrajendra*. In speaking of Yasadipura II's *macapat* text of 1819, Poerbatjaraka says, "But here resi Wisrawa has already been made to carry out dishonorable actions. He was asked by his son King Dhanaraja to look for a wife; he proceeds to petition the prospective bride on his son's behalf, and then winds up marrying her himself. These happenings are not found at all in the kakawin rendering of the story. But how or why resi Wisrawa has been made to undertake these dishonorable actions has not yet been investigated."[23]

Several scholars give clues that help to explain this new turn of events in the story of Sukesi and Wisrawa. Since the first telling of the story connected with the elder and younger Yasadipura was the *macapat* text of Yasadipura I,[24] which is dated during the reign of Pakubuwana III (1749–1788), other writings by Yasadipura I might clarify Wisrawa's dishonorable actions. Soebardi argues that in the *Serat Cabolek,* Yasadipura I uses a motif that was common in the literary traditions of the period—the conflict between Javanist mysticism and orthodox, legalistic Islam.[25] Day says that both Yasadipura I and II were critical of "the sorts of heterodox, intuitive, anti-court and anti-Dutch mystical methods of acquiring knowledge and power."[26] In Day's opinion, Yasadipura I is a rationalist establishment figure worried about village-style magic and *kejawen* mysticism. Soebardi, however, presents Yasadipura I as a self-conscious continualist but also as a preserver of secret knowledge in this passage from the *Serat Suluk*: "The reason that Wisrawa, the *rsi,* incurred the wrath of God, was because he dared to lift the (Divine) veil, and claimed to be God: This happened a long time ago. Those who behaved in similar fashion were (as follows): during the period of the *wali* a man named Shaikh Siti Jenar; during the reign of the second ruler of Demak: Pangeran Panggung; and during the period of Mataram: Shaikh Among Raga."[27]

Soebardi contends that this passage was written by Yasadipura I for the purpose of establishing continuity between the traditions of the three periods mentioned above with the pre-Islamic period that Wisrawa represented. The characters mentioned above, well known in Javanese literary tradition, all shared the same fate of revealing mystical knowledge to the uninitiated and being put to death or otherwise suffering for their indiscretion. These figures suggest the life of Islamic saint al-Hallaj, who was put to death in Baghdad in the tenth century for the same reason.[28] Inappropriate revelation of mystical knowledge was a theme that appeared in many Javanese Islamic textual traditions of the eighteenth and nineteenth centuries. Wisrawa, in these particular nineteenth-century tellings of the story, suffers the anger and virulent curses of his own son, comes to actual battle with his son in several interpretations, and, through his marriage to Sukesi, causes the destruction of the *raksasa* race. Elements of the Yasadipura nineteenth-century rendering of the story of Rahwana's birth can be seen in the *Serat Kandha* story recounted by Raffles: an older man inappropriately marries a young maiden intended for someone else; the man falls in love with the younger woman in the course of a penance; Batara Guru takes revenge against the family of Sukesi.[29] What is lacking in the *Serat Kandha* telling of the story is the mystical teaching, which would be more likely to be preserved in an oral rather than written form.

The events of the story of Rahwana's birth that are highlighted in the nineteenth-century texts of Yasadipura II and Sindusastra indicate a preoccupation with problems of religious orthodoxy. Day comments on the number of renditions of the *Arjunasasrabahu* story that were commissioned by the Solonese kings in the late eighteenth and early nineteenth centuries, and he isolates Arjunasasrabahu's victory over Rahwana as the theme of the stories which the audiences of that day probably found most central.[30] The inappropriate revelation of mystical knowledge seems to have been an equally pressing subject, as this theme was also stressed in shadow theater tellings of the story.

Rahwana's Birth in Shadow Theater Traditions

Tracing the story of Rahwana's birth in shadow theater traditions presents problems, as the only extant sources in an oral tradition date from the present day. There are, however, testimonies from older puppeteers who remember the ways in which the story was handled in earlier times, as well as court summaries of the *wayang* stories.[31] The outstanding feature of this story in the shadow play tradition, or what is significant to the puppeteers about this story, is the mystical teaching, the *sastrajendra*. Drewes discusses a passage from the *Serat Dermagandul* that explains the meaning of the *sastrajendra*, called the *sastra rancan* in this passage.

The attendants give a symbolic interpretation of the different parts of the human body, adding from the *Tajussalatin* that it exists of 208 parts, 32 teeth, and 1993 veins. In connection with this they stress the importance of the *nelmu wirasat* (Arab. *ilmu 'l-firasa*), the knowledge of human character as derived from physical features. In former times this knowledge was kept a secret by the gods, but Resi Wisrawa divulged this secret knowledge to his prospective daughter-in-law, destined for his son Dasamuka (*sic*). Tempted by Hyang Girinata (Lord Siwa), he became enamored of her and eventually married her himself. Their children were monsters, by way of punishment for his disclosing this secret of the gods.[32]

This passage contains, perhaps, one of the more clearly Islamic explanations of the mystical teaching *sastrajendra*, which has become a blanket expression in Javanese mysticism for all types of esoteric and exorcist knowledge. The origin of the expression, which is not found in Old Javanese literature, has been explained in a somewhat orientalist way by Supomo as an example of cacography that arose in the process of rendering the Old Javanese tellings of the Indic stories into modern Javanese.[33] The expression *sang stryahajong* in the *kakawin* text of Mpu Tantular becomes *sastra harjeng* in the modern Javanese texts of the Yasadipuras and Sindusastra, and the meaning changes from "beautiful woman" to "auspicious writings." How and when this phrase became associated with the sorts of heterodox mystical knowledge with which it was associated in the nineteenth century, and with which it is still associated today, is an intriguing question.

Some answers to this question might be found in other stories from the *Serat Kandha* literature of the sixteenth century *pasisir* culture of the north-coast cities, as Islam was making its accommodation to the remnants of the Śaivite-Buddhist culture of the inland Majapahit kingdom. Certainly the mystical tradition that has survived under the rubric of the term *sastrajendra* was not brought to Java by the entry of Islam. Rather the term represents the blending of Śaivite-Buddhist and Islamic Sufi mysticism, which enabled Islam to be so easily overlaid on the Indic local traditions of sixteenth- and seventeenth-century central Java.[34] Johns argues that Sufism was an important category in Indonesian history and social life between the thirteenth and eighteenth centuries until the rise of Wahhabism (c. 1800). He believes that the Sufis were the ones who brought Islam to Java, and that their effectiveness lay in their ability and willingness to use elements of the non-Islamic culture in order to make Islam acceptable.[35] The shadow theater may well have served as a vehicle for this process. Pigeaud has commented on the present-day practice of devout Muslims staying away from *wayang* performances: "Earlier this must have been otherwise, for it is said that some of the walis, who brought Islam to Java, made *wayang* puppets and performed as puppeteers themselves."[36]

In the shadow puppet theater repertoire, the term *sastrajendra* has come to represent esoteric knowledge, and the characters Pandu and Bima of the later *Mahābhārata* cycle of stories also possess this secret doctrine in the *lakon* (story) *Sena Rodra* and *Pandu Papa*.[37] The meaning of the term, however, is far from clear. A teacher from the puppeteering section of the Fine Arts Academy in Solo admits, "Because there has never been a clarification about the contours or the contents of the *sastrajendra* in the *Lokapala* text, the result is the mushrooming of various interpretations among the Javanese people in the past and the reverberations of this can still be felt today."[38]

Puppeteers and scholars associate the interpretations of the *Arjunasasrabahu* story that are enacted in the shadow play tradition with the *Serat Lokapala* of the court poet Sindusastra, a *macapat* poem written in 1829. This telling of the story differs from the earlier texts of the Yasadipuras, and Poerbatjaraka contends that Sindusastra's work is based on the *Serat Kandha* traditions rather than on the *kakawin* tellings of the story.[39] Murtiyasa found that the puppeteers he interviewed in the areas around Solo all associate the *lakon, Alap-alapan Sukesi* (The marriage of Sukesi), with the *Sindusastra* text.[40] Javanese mystics today can still recite the verses from the Sindusastra text that are connected with the *sastrajendra*. The two most important verses can be translated very roughly as follows.

> The *sastrajendrayuningrat*
> Is able to liberate all beings
> Beyond that which can be spoken
> In knowledge there is no equal.
> Surrounded by this noble teaching,
> The end of knowledge,
> Demons, giants, and ogres,
> And the creatures in the mountain woods,
> If they know the meaning
> Of the *sastrajendra*
> They will be liberated by the gods.
> Reaching the perfect death,
> Their souls take on human qualities.
> Incomparable humans.
> If they know this teaching,
> They become one with the gods at death,
> The noble gods.
> Thus Prabu Sumali

When he heard his heart,
He searched for the meaning of this teaching.[41]

Although these are the passages from the *Sindusastra* text associated with the *sastrajendra*, they only describe the power of the mystical teaching. The knowledge contained in the teaching is not explained and remains open to interpretation. Herein lies the power and permeability of mystical teachings; they always remain open to new interpretations.

The shadow theater links poetry and performance and court and village traditions of the story of Rahwana's birth by its emphasis on the *sastrajendra*. Speaking of the mystical teaching *sastrajendra*, Murtiyasa says that he has never seen a puppeteer explain exactly what this teaching is.[42] Usually they describe the action of the story in rhythmic prose recitations set to music, and sometimes they use phrases from Sindusastra's Lokapala. Murtiyasa quotes a local authority on the Solonese shadow theater, Probohardjono, who explained that each puppeteer interprets the *sastrajendra* according to his or her own inner beliefs or mystical leanings. The village puppeteer Ki Gandawajiran from Boyolali defined the *sastrajendra* as a magical charm with the power "to exorcise all forms of defilement in the world" (*Sastrajendra punika lak saged nglebur sekathahing sukerta*).[43] In the Sindusastra tradition of the story of Sukesi and Wisrawa, Sumali actually wants to be taught the *sastrajendra* because he believes it will exorcise his demonic qualities and allow him to be reborn as a human instead of an ogre (raksasa). This interpretation of the *sastrajendra* as magical charm rather than mystical teaching is another connection between shadow play traditions and the textual traditions of the *Serat Lokapala* and the *Serat Kandha*.[44]

The courtly explication of the *sastrajendra* as an example of the inappropriate revelation of the oneness of man and god is found in the texts of the Yasadipuras, and represents one possible interpretation of the term held by the educated, court elites. And yet certain village puppeteers today, often those who had some association with the courts in their youth, share this court understanding of the term, and believe in the mystical tradition to which the term refers and which the Yasadipuras were trying to limit.[45]

The Islam Controversy in Javanese *Wayang*

Yasadipura I tried to limit the heterodox mystical tradition, which must have been widespread in the Javanese countryside of the late eighteenth century. Yet Yasadipura I is also the author of a text of the Dewaruci story, the quintessential text that promulgates the Javanese belief in the absolute identity of man and god.[46] Thus Yasadipura's identification of Wisrawa with such figures as Seh Siti Jenar indicates a belief in the heterodox traditions but an aversion toward the improper revelation of these beliefs. Yasadipura I, an Islamic force at the court, showed his identification with Islam while maintaining his belief in Javanist traditions. The improper revelation of mystical knowledge became associated with improper sex in the texts of the Yasadipuras, and both indiscretions became punishable. In their control over the meaning of the *sastrajendra*, the puppeteers were powerful figures whose performances could either support or subvert the position of the courts. In the nineteenth-century Javanese courts controlled by Dutch power, some Javanese rulers reflected the ambivalence of Yasadipura I. They believed in the power associated with mystical knowledge but they wanted to limit the power of rural Islamic teachers (*kyai*), who were anticourt although some may have supported those who were anti-Dutch.[47]

Although the *sastrajendra* could be interpreted in Islamic mystical terms, the ability of a *dhalang* (puppet master) in days past to convincingly explicate the *sastrajendra* according to his or her own mystical beliefs was a mark of power. *Dhalang* were respected and feared for their command of mystical knowledge. Training for aspiring puppeteers consisted mainly of mystical exercises assigned to them by their parents or other relatives. Although some modern writers insist that Islamic imagery and belief do pervade the *wayang* tradition, these Islamic elements are difficult to find.[48] In fact, older *dalang* today relate that the *wayang* is not an appropriate vehicle for sectarian religious teachings—possibly an idea they learned from Dutch scholars. Rather they stress Javanist mystical exercises that associate ascetic practices with the acquisition of power.

In this essay I have looked at the transmission of a *Rāmāyaṇa* tale in Java through an exploration of Javanese Islamic mystical teachings. The synthesis of Javanist mystical traditions and Islam discussed here was to prove less and less acceptable to those segments of the Javanese population most clearly under colonial control as time went on. For most Javanese, Islamic teachings remained a possible path to spiritual power that meshed well with their *kejawen* beliefs. In shadow play performances, each puppeteer could interpret the *sastrajendra* in his or her own way. Today in Java most puppeteers and mystics associate the *sastrajendra* with *kejawen* mysticism rather than Islamic traditions.[49] What was most Islamic about the nineteenth-century interpretations of the story of Rahwana's birth was the association of Wisrawa with figures like Seh Siti Jenar.[50] By distinguishing between belief in the mystical oneness of individual and god and public expression of that belief, the Javanese equated their understanding of *wadhah* (vessel) and *wiji* (seed) with Islamic distinctions between outward behavior and inward conviction. Thus in their acceptance of Islamic belief, Javanese literati molded Islam to suit their own purposes. Although Yasadipura I sided with the *ulama* (those learned in Islamic teachings) who believed that good external behavior was a necessary part of Islamic religious life, he maintained that the essence of Islam was contained in the Dewaruci story, one of the clearest statements of Javanist mystical teachings.[51] Some Javanese today discredit Yasadipura for undermining Javanist traditions.[52] By textually punishing Wisrawa for improper revelation of mystical knowledge, Yasadipura I symbolized the accommodation of Islamic authority to Javanist mystical beliefs.

By the end of the Java War in 1830, the Dutch had secured their control over Javanese rulers and realms. Although the nineteenth century was to see continued unrest in the Javanese countryside, ideas of progress, secular history, and scientific investigation filtered through the thought-worlds of the Dutch administrators whose control over Java penetrated to deeper levels throughout the century. These European ideas influenced the way the Dutch viewed this society so different from their own. In the latter part of the century, the influence of the Romantic movement was felt in Java as the Dutch scholars became fascinated with Java's ancient Indic heritage. The Dutch colonial government, however, continued to see Javanese Islam and the passions it could ignite as inimical to their rule. Reverberations of the Islamic Wahhabi movement from the Middle East and India, which called for a purification of Islam, had made the mystical doctrines of Sufi belief less acceptable among those who adhered to stricter Islamic beliefs by the second half of the nineteenth century. In the twentieth century, the Javanese Islamic Reform movement attempted to fill the place of mystical teachings with scriptural studies, reflecting the Islamic usages to which some Javanese put the new attitudes toward narrative traditions that they had adopted in their interactions with Dutch scholars and administrators. The coincidence of the Dutch scholarly fascination with the "Hindu-Javanese" heritage of *Rāmāyaṇa* and *Mahābhārata* traditions, and Dutch efforts to suppress and discredit Islam in central Java, led to the creation of new vehicles for the stories in the late nineteenth and early twentieth centuries.

NOTES

A different version of this essay was originally published as part of Chapter 1 of Laurie J. Sears, *Shadows of Empire: Colonial Discourse and Javanese Tales* (Durham: Duke University Press, 1996). I thank Duke University Press for allowing it to be included in this volume.

1. In Soebardi 1975. The Javanese stories *Dewaruci* and *Bhimasuci* tell of the mystical exploits of the *Mahābhārata* character Bhīma.

2. Foucault [1978] 1990, p. 93. Cf. ibid., pp. 92–96, and Anderson, "The Idea of Power in Javanese Culture" [1972], in Anderson 1990, pp. 21–23, for discussions of power and how it is conceptualized in both Javanese and European worldviews. See also Ricklefs's critique of American-based scholarship on ideas of power and kingship in precolonial Java (1992), pp. 61 and 62 n. 1). This critique loses much of its sharpness if one reads, for example, Ben Anderson's 1984 work "*Sembah-Sumpah*: The Politics of Language and Javanese Culture" republished in Anderson, 1990, p. 203.

3. Zoetmulder 1974, pp. 95–96.

4. Supomo 1977, p. 18.

5. Shastri 1959 vol. 3, pp. 398–399.

6. Zoetmulder 1974, pp. 96–97.

7. Supomo 1977, p. 28; Zoetmulder 1974, p. 83. In citing Javanese sources, I have followed the spelling and orthography in common use.

8. Supomo 1977, pp. 1–15.

9. Ibid., p. 183.

10. Ibid., p. 83.

11. Olthof 1941; Moertono 1981; Padmapuspita 1985.

12. Pigeaud 1938, vol. 1, p. 142; Brandes 1920, pp. 207–208.

13. For more information about Raffles and his brief time of jurisdiction (1811–

1816) over Java during the Napoleonic wars, see Sears 1996, pp. 13, 48n, 77; and Steenbrink 1993, pp. 73–74.

14. Raffles [1817] 1830, pp. 417–418; 424–426.

15. Cf. Narasimhan 1965, pp. 15–17.

16. Cf. Becker 1979, pp. 236–238.

17. Ricklefs 1974, pp. 187–88. See Florida's introduction to *Writing the Past* (c. 1993) for a fresh discussion of the birth of what came to be known as "traditional" Javanese literature.

18. Supomo 1977, p. 338; Day 1981, pp. 54–58.

19. Day 1981, pp. 60–77.

20. Winter 1845, pp. 152–153. Winter's text gave summaries of the *Rāmāyaṇa*, Bratayuda, and Arjunasasrabahu stories in Javanese script.

21. In her catalogue of the manuscripts held in the library of the Kraton Surakarta, Nancy Florida (c. 1933, pp. 317–319) includes a number of *sastrajendra* texts in a section entitled Javanese Mysticism or Kejawen. Most of the manuscripts use the name *sastraharjendra*. Florida describes these texts as Javano-Islamic mystical speculations, usually conversations by "Hindu" deities, and most of the texts she lists were inscribed during the reign of Paku Buwana X (1893–1939. She also includes two Bimasuci texts in this section (KS 577.4; KS 578.2).

22. Drewes 1966, p. 356 n. 52; cf. Winter 1845, pp. 152–53.

23. Poerbatjaraka 1952, p. 138.

24. Supomo 1977, p. 338.

25. Soebardi 1975 p. 43.

26. Day 1981, p. 56 n. 86.

27. Soebardi 1975, p. 38.

28. Johns 1961, pp. 46–48.

29. LOr 6379 as described in Pigeaud 1968, vol. 2, p. 356, in the library of the University of Leiden, records another version of the *Serat Kandha*. In this version Wisnu and his wife Sri take human shapes in order to resist Rahwana, which suggests the incarnating of Guru and Durga in the bodies of Wisrawa and Sukesi.

30. Day 1981, p. 54 n. 80.

31. Mangkunegara VII 1965. The compilers of this 1965 edition of the *lakon* collected under the auspices of K.G.P.A.A. Mangkunegara VII over a three-year period from 1930 until 1932, and published by Balai Pustaka, mention in their introduction that the *lakon* "Sastra Djendra Juningrat" (the story of Sukesi and Wisrawa) was among the three *lakon* that they added to the Mangkunegara's original 177. The version of the story that they present is credited to Kamadjaja and U. J. Katidja Wp. This version is very similar to the nineteenth-century version of the story, except for a reference to the relationship between the brothers Sumali and Mangliawan that was recorded in the *Serat Kandha*. Djambumangli is presented as Mangliawan's son who lost his chance to rule when the kingdom of Ngalengka went to Sumali, Mangliawan's brother. Thus Djambumangli wishes to marry Sukesi so he can get control over the kingdom.

32. Drewes 1966, p. 356.

33. Supomo 1964.

34. A Sufi is an Islamic mystic or holy man. Sufis taught a wide array of Islamic teachings as Islam spread east from Mecca, reaching even the southern Philippines, but Sufis are most commonly associated with the most esoteric doctrines of Islamic mysticism.

35. Johns 1961.

36. Pigeaud 1938, p. 103.

37. Drewes 1966, p. 335, n. 4; Kats 1923, p. 296.

38. B. Murtiyasa 1981, p. 34.

39. Poerbatjaraka 1952, p. 149. Cf. Sunardi 1982.

40. Murtiyasa 1981, p. 17. In *Het Javaansche Tooneel,* Kats (1923, p. 182) gives a summary of the story of Sukesi and Wisrawa. He then refers the reader who wishes further detail to the work of Sindusastra, "*waarmee de inhoud van de lakon's in hoofdzaak overeenstemt.*" (where the substance of the *lakon* is basically the same).

41. A slight variation of this text was recited to me by the Hindu teacher Bp. Hardjanta during the summer of 1990. The exact text in Sinom meter is taken from Sindusastra 1936, vol. 1, pp. 26–27.

42. Murtiyasa 1981, p. 39.

43. Interview with author, May 22, 1984.

44. The interpretation of *sastrajendra* as a magical charm brings to mind the performances that are held on Gunung Kawi in East Java by many Chinese-Indonesians seeking to increase their fortunes. These performances generally have no audiences, and the hosts are hoping to receive a boon or blessing for their sponsorship or are giving thanks for a boon they have already received. *Sastrajendra* interpreted as a boon also connects to the dispensing of *wahyu* or boons in many *wayang* stories. What these examples underscore is the plasticity of the *sastrajendra.*

45. In Solo in 1983, Nancy Florida had a storyteller perform the legend of Seh Siti Jenar, who had been put to death for revealing mystical knowledge to the uninitiated. A puppeteer whose family had strong connections with the Solonese courts in the past and present said that he thought Florida was *terlalu berani* or "too bold" in holding a performance for the purpose of bringing the Siti Jenar story to the public's attention. He said that he himself was a follower of Siti Jenar, but that he would not want to make that public, so he chose not to attend the event.

46. Johns 1966–1967, p. 48.

47. Although these literary and dramatic works document an early stage in the transfer of authority from Indic to Islamic models, Ricklefs commented on the literary texts produced in elite Javanese circles in the latter part of the nineteenth century that reject Islam as being a religious tradition foreign to Java. He then concludes: "Whether these texts from the earlier and later nineteenth century spring from two different groups among the elite, or whether (as this writer [Ricklefs] suspects) they reflect a positive growth of a commitment to Islam in elite circles which was stopped short and reversed by the more zealous Muslim proselytizing of the latter years of the century, cannot be known on present evidence." See Ricklefs 1979, p. 117. Elsewhere I discuss the argument that the Dutch distrust of Islam as a rallying point for anti-Dutch movements put pressures on Javanese elites to turn away from Islam (Sears 1996; chapter 2).

48. Zarkasi 1977; Mulyono 1975 and 1978.

49. Articles about the *sastrajendra* have continued to appear in Javanist publications since independence. See, for example, the articles on *sastrajendra* in the magazine *Pandjangmas* in 1955, p. 11, and 1958, p. 13. More recently, there was an article on *sastrajendra* in *Gatra,* a new name for the older publication called *Warta Wayang,* in issue No. 7 (1985): 15–23. Most of these publications associate the *sastrajendra* with Javanist mystical beliefs that relate sounds to mystical points within the body.

50. Although the view that the transmission of mystical teachings should be carefully controlled is found throughout the Islamic world, many Javanese of other religious persuasions as well as Balinese believe that the mystical path is fraught with

danger. The idea of the dangers of the left-handed path—the quick path to enlightenment in one lifetime—is also a common theme in tantric Buddhism and Hinduism.

51. Soebardi, 1975, pp. 42–43.

52. Oral communication from Pak Hardjanta, July 15, 1990.

REFERENCES

Anderson, Benedict R. O'G. 1990. *Language and Power: Exploring Political Cultures in Indonesia*. Ithaca: Cornell University Press.

Becker, A. L. 1979. "Text-Building, Epistemology, and Aesthetics in Javanese Shadow Theatre." In *The Imagination of Reality*, edited by A. L. Becker and A. A. Yengoyan. Norwood, N.J.: Ablex.

Brandes, J.L.A. 1920. "Pararaton (Ken Arok) Tweede druk bewerkt door N.J. Krom." *Verhandelingen van het Bataviaasch Genootschap van Kunsten en Wetenschappen* 62.

Day, J. A. 1981. "Meanings of Change in the Poetry of Nineteenth-Century Java." Ph.D. dissertation, Cornell University.

Drewes, G.W.J. 1966. "The Struggle between Javanism and Islam." *Bijdragen tot de Taal, Land- en Volkenkunde* 122.

Florida, Nancy. c1993. *Javanese Literature in Surakarta Manuscripts*. Vol. 1. Ithaca: Southeast Asia Program, Cornell University.

Foucault, M. [1978] 1990. *The History of Sexuality*. Vol. 1. *An Introduction*. New York: Vintage.

Johns, A. H. 1961. "Muslim Mystics and Historical Writing." In *Historians of Southeast Asia*, ed., D.G.E. Hall. London: Oxford University Press.

______. 1966–1967. "From Buddhism to Islam." *Comparative Studies in Society and History*, 9.1.

Kats, J. 1923. *Het Javaansche Tooneel, De Wajang Poerwa*. 2nd ed. Vol. 1. Weltevreden: Comissie voor de Volkslectuur.

K.G.P.A.A. Mangkunegara VII. [1930–2]. 1965. *Serat Padhalangan Ringgit Purwa* Jogjakarta: U. P. Indonesia.

Moertono, S. 1981. *State and Statecraft in Old Java*. New York: Cornell University Press.

Mulyono, I. S. 1975. *Asal-usul, Filsafat dan Masa Depannya*. Jakarta: Gunung Agung.

______. 1978. *Tripama, Watak Satria dan Sastra Jendra*. Jakarta: Gunung Agung.

Murtiyasa, B. 1981. "Tinjuan lakon Alap-alapan Sukeksi dalam pakeliran padat susunan Soemanto." Surakarta: Akademi Seni Karawitan Indonesia.

Narasimhan, C. V. 1965. *The Mahabharata*. New York: Columbia University Press.

Olthof, W. L., ed. 1941. *Poenika serat Babad Tanah Djawi wiwit saking Nabi Adam doemoegi ing tahoen 1647*. The Hague: Martinus Nijhoff.

Padmapuspita, J. 1985. *Serat Kandhaning Ringgit Purwa*. Jilid 2. Jakarta: Penerbit Djambatan dan KITLV.

Pandjangmas (journal). Tahun III/No. 10 (1955); and Tahun IV/No. 2 (1958).

Pigeaud, Theodore G. 1938. *Javaanse Volksvertoningen*. The Hague: Martinus Nijhoff.

______. 1968. *The Literature of Java*. The Hague: Martinus Nijhoff.

Poerbatjaraka, R. Ng. 1952. *Kapustakan Djawi*. Djakarta: Penerbit Djambatan.

Raffles, Sir Thomas S. [1817] 1830. *History of Java*. London: John Murray.

Ricklefs, M. C. 1974. *Jogjakarta under Sultan Mangkubumi, 1749–1792: A History of the Division of Java*. London: Oxford University Press.

______. 1979. "Six Centuries of Islamization in Java." In *Conversion to Islam*, edited by N. Levitzion. New York: Holmes & Meier.

———. 1992. "Unity and Disunity in Javanese Political and Religious Thought of the Eighteenth Century." In *Looking in Odd Mirrors: The Java Sea,* edited by V. J. H. Houben, H. M. J. Maier, and W. van der Molen. Leiden: Vakgroep Talen en Culturen van Zuidoost-Azie en Oceanie, Rijksuniversiteit te Leiden.

Sears, L. J. 1996. *Shadows of Empire.* Durham: Duke University Press.

Shastri, H. P. 1959. *The Ramayana of Valmiki.* London: Shanti Sadan.

Sindusastra, R. Ng. 1936. *Serat Lokapala.* 2nd ed. Batavia: Bale Pustaka.

Soebardi, S. 1975. *The Book of Cabolek.* The Hague: Martinus Nijhoff.

Steenbrink, K. A. 1993. *Dutch Colonialism and Indonesian Islam.* Amsterdam: Rodopi.

Sunardi, D. M. 1982. *Arjuna Sasrabahu.* Jakarti: Balai Pustaka.

Supomo, S. 1964. "Sastra Djendra: 'Ngelmu' yang timbul karena kakografi." *Majalah Ilmu-Ilmu Sastra Indonesia,* 2:177–86.

———. 1977. *Arjunawijaya: A Kakawin of Mpu Tantular.* The Hague: Martinus Nijhoff.

Warta Wayang (journal; formerly *Gatra*). 1985. No. 7: 15–23.

Winter, C. F. 1845. *De Brata-Joeda, de Rama en de Ardjoena-Sasra,* uitgegeven door T. Roorda. Amsterdam: Johannes Muller.

Zarkasi, H. E. 1977. *Unsur Islam dalam Pewayangan.* Bandung: P. T. Alma'arif.

Zoetmulder, P. J. 1974. *Kalangwan: A Survey of Old Javanese Literature.* The Hague: Martinus Nijhoff.

12

Chasing Sītā on a Global/ Local Interface: Where Cartographies Collide, Silent Vessels "Tell in Full"

Kaja M. McGowan

To become aware of it is to realize that the line between mode of representation and substantive content is as undrawable in cultural analysis as it is in painting; and that fact in turn seems to threaten the objective status of anthropological knowledge by suggesting that its source is not social reality but scholarly artifice.[1]

The focus is not just the visual appearance of the work of art, but also the relations between the describer and that work. In other words, an awareness of the scene and context and agent of the description is brought to our attention. An ekphrasis is thus to be both a clear representation of visible phenomena, and also, in Clifford Geertz's fine phrase, "thick description."[2]

On October 10, 1999, Indonesian troops opened fire on Australian troops at the border town of Motaain near the north coast of East Timor. The incident was later explained as only a confusion over maps. Whereas the Australians were consulting a 1992 map of Indonesia in general use by Interfet forces, the Indonesians were reportedly referring to a map drawn up by the Dutch in the 1930s.[3] This singular collision of cartographies, well publicized for political purposes though comparatively insignificant in terms of either destruction to property or number of casualties, would appear to trivialize or render invisible what has been a continuous and devastating bombardment of local East Timorese mapping systems since 1975.

One week later, on October 17, 1999, Nobel Peace Prize laureate Bishop Carlos Belo gave a speech in the yard of his burned-out home near the seafront capital of Dili, East Timor. Having returned just twelve days earlier from a brief forced exile, and standing before an elated crowd composed largely of nuns recently returned from refugee camps in West Timor, Belo remarked that soon priests would be returning to their parishes and teachers to their classrooms. Until then, he added, schooling in the Portuguese language would begin again in early November under the mango trees in the yard behind his home.[4]

Belo's forced exile resulted when his home and adjoining church (along with 75 percent of East Timor's buildings) were bombed, burned, and gutted by Indonesian army-backed militias. This wave of terror, murder, and destruction, leaving more than a thousand civilians dead (according to a recent United Nations estimate) and forcing hundreds of thousands of East Timorese to flee from their homes and into the forest, or to refugee camps in neighboring West Timor, came in direct response to the September 4, 1999, announcement of a 78.5 percent vote for independence on the August 30 ballot of a referendum, agreed to by interim president B. J. Habibie less than one year after Suharto's forced resignation in May of 1998. Though memories of the atrocities have reportedly faded, after three long years of delay by successive Indonesian governments in bringing the military to account, finally March 19, 2002, marked the official beginning of courtroom proceedings in Jakarta for the first four accused military officers to be tried for their crimes in East Timor. Opening the trials has been interpreted in large part as an attempt to placate demands in the United States Congress that Indonesia indict those in the military responsible for human rights violations in East Timor before the nation can receive renewed American military aid. With the Jakarta spotlight, however selectively applied, back on the murder and destruction committed in the days following the referendum, and with renewed promises to Indonesia of U.S. military aid hanging in the balance, it is imperative to return to the site of Bishop Belo's home as a conscious act of remembering and of bearing witness.

Whether Portuguese, Indonesian, English, or Tetum is ultimately taught under the shady trees in the yard behind Bishop Belo's house, new maps must be drawn up by the East Timorese themselves. How will the language(s) chosen for the new republic, Timor Loro Sa'e, ultimately shape these emerging cartographies? Just last year, President Megawati Sukarnoputri signed a decree that the court would have to restrict itself to only a partial mapping of the atrocities perpetrated during two months in 1999, April and September, and could deal only with the violence in three localities, even though it had engulfed the entire territory. Will East Timorese be able to critically expand these cartographic boundaries circumscribed by the Indonesian government in order that their personal, unabridged accounts can be told and heard more effectively? Where both the real and imagined cartographies collide, can the marked preference for envoicing silent objects in Southeast Asian personal narratives, whether orally or textually transmitted, help us to understand the salvaged and recycled testimonies that are emerging?

E. V. Walter has remarked that by grasping a sense of place, feeling it on our skin, and carrying its confluence of forces in our memory, we are better prepared to understand who we are and where we are going.[5] When viewed in this way, can objects become "seats of experience," fully activated "artifacts" capable of generating and regenerating compelling cross-cultural biographies of their own?[6] The social lives of the artifacts, once mapped, reveal the dynamic force of what Thongchai Winichakul has called a "global/local interface."[7] These potentially far-flung topistic connections are not always evident in an object's original design and construction, but may be seen to accrue in their ultimate consumption, destruction, and reconstitution. For the purposes of this article, two divergent streams of object-oriented narrative will be investigated, forcing the imagined visual ambivalence of both East Timorese survivors and Indonesian (chiefly Javanese) military elite a chance to approach some kind of convergence through the disparately salvaged detritus of war. The houses of East Timor, reduced to rubble, will serve as sites to be mapped. What will be saved, and what will be relegated to oblivion? Who will be entitled to make these choices? It is the reconstitutions and recontextualizations of objects from out of the wreckage, their curiously entangled, tragic, playful, and even promiscuous transformations from instrument of war to commemorative trophy in Bali's bustling entrepôt or from burned-out rubble to successful eatery in Dili, which will be explored here. Where cartographies collide, can silent vessels be made to bear witness? From the *Rāmāyaṇa*, the theme of Sītā's abduction by Rāvaṇa, intricately embossed on shell-casings, will serve as an interpretive framework for these observations.

East Timorese Heirlooms as Substitutes for Genealogical Reckoning: Who Will Replenish Our Sacred Pitchers?

John Taylor has argued convincingly that, contrary to colonialist assumptions, the secret to the resistance of East Timorese over four and a half centuries can be found in part in the rich oral histories supplied in ethnographic and anthropological accounts.[8] He suggests that it is the resilient systems of exchange, stimulated by goods, persons, and sacred objects, and not the colonial narratives that will equip us today with a more adequate means for understanding twentieth-century developments. Though it is ill-advised to think of any one ethnography as being indicative of beliefs held by all of East Timor's various ethnic groups, there does emerge a pervasive theme in the literature whereby the idea of history as a product of genealogical memory is more often mapped on objects than on persons or texts. Elizabeth Traube provides a vivid example in her study of the Mambai of East Timor. She writes, "just as houses do, heirlooms have their own names, personalities, and histories, and the memorizing of their movement from house to house (called 'the walk of sacred objects') is frequently used as a substitute for genealogical reckoning."[9]

From gathered testimonies, Traube discerns a pattern for determining ancestral authority, whereby junior informants, speaking of their own heirlooms, describe them as first "going out" of a designated senior house. Elsewhere, she recounts how certain heirlooms had the power to return to their place of origin on auspicious days, often literally "dragging their owners behind them."[10] The cyclicity of these object-oriented narratives forces us to reexamine the observation made by anthropologist Janet Hoskins on the Kodi of Sumba, an eastern Indonesian society similarly steeped in exchange. Hoskins questions whether a " 'person-centered' ethnography has to be rethought as one that uses objects as metaphors to elicit an indirect account of personal experience."[11] The image of the Mambai being guided by their ancestral heirlooms can perhaps enhance our perceptions of the repeated pronouncements made by journalists surrounding the August 30 referendum, namely, that East Timorese were said to "vote with their feet," descending from the hills in record numbers, and braving the ruthless militias, as if propelled by some unexplainable force.

During the violent outbursts following East Timor's vote for self-determination, serious violations of human rights occurred. These included widespread intimidation, brutal massacres, rape, humiliation, and torture. Due to the overwhelming destruction of property and the large-scale displacement of persons, not only was the basic infrastructure demolished but the very spirit of the people, so traumatized by violence and destruction, has yet to experience an effective and sensitively attuned process for healing, one that respects the rights of East Timorese to speak and to know the truth, and, in time, to achieve some semblance of restitution. What will be the role of objects in mapping these emerging testimonies, particularly in cases concerning sexual abuse, where victims are too intimidated to speak for fear of continuing social stigmatization? How will the new language(s) chosen determine which cultural artifacts will emerge to speak out about the gross injustices that have occurred? How can teachers help the younger generation, many of whom do not remember a time before Indonesia's violent annexation, to come to terms with their painful pasts in order to make the most of newly promised opportunities for the future? Objects will arguably play an important role in the healing process; where cartographies collide, can these silent vessels be relied upon to "tell in full" under the mango trees?

Much like Bishop Belo's backyard, the historical model for Plato's Academy, founded in 338 B.C.E., required that disciples live and learn under the trees in a garden with adjoining huts, a shrine to the Muses, and lecture halls. It was Plato's disciple Horace who expressed the ideal of "searching after truth in the groves of Hekademos." Hekademos was reputed to be the first ancestor or founding hero, later known as Academus (from whom is derived the word "academe"). E. V. Walter describes how the site of the first academy acquired its earliest identity, meaning, and feeling from prehistoric tradition through the legend of a mythical person. His bones in the soil grounded the spirit of the hero as lord of the place and guardian of the mortals who dwelt there.[12]

In many East Timorese myths, fruit-bearing trees likewise come to symbolize the sacred world of knowledge—the origin house—composed from the body of the first ancestor and, therefore, the symbolic womblike vessel for the accretion of exchange valuables. In a Carabaulo Tetum origin myth, for example, a prince steals his intended bride, Bui Lailua, daughter of a buffalo. Offended, the mother buffalo pursues the couple, reducing their first house to rubble in her rage. Then she enters a sacred tree. When this "tree of many fruits" is cut down, it blossoms again four days later—its sprouting horns, leafy hide, and bark-covered limbs transformed into a powerful object-oriented portrait of the progenitor, an interior map of sacred heirlooms intended for the new house of the conjugal pair. According to the story, "the trunk had become a pregnant stone, the buffalo's horns were now made of gold, her hide was a magnificent piece of cloth, and her bones made of gold and silver. They carried their treasures home."[13]

The symbolic classification of many societies equates "home" with rooms, wombs, and tombs.[14] In the English language, the resemblance is only phonetically apparent, but in Tetum the correlation is so complete that the same word, *lolon*, signals all three types of container. According to Tetum beliefs, the back of the house is perceived, symbolically, as the wife's womb (*uma lolon*). Every living member of a household owns a small sacred water vessel, red in color, and made of local clay and sand, called *u'e lolo oan* (or "little womb"). Soon after birth a mother fills a vessel with cool water taken from one of the large pitchers standing in the *uma lolon*. When a child leaves for more than a month, his mother replenishes the child's sacred pitcher and keeps water in it until he returns. When someone born into the household marries outside, the bride or groom, as the case may be, takes the sacred pitcher from the original ritual shelf to his or her new home. The vessels of a married couple are later joined by the pitchers of their children. If the most desirable arrangements of postmarital residence and inheritance are fulfilled, a younger son's sacred vessel stays in the same room from birth to death.[15] These vessels are included among one's possessions in death. Normal deaths take place in the womb-chamber of the house. The pitcher is smashed one year later as part of the postmortem ritual called *keta-mate* (meaning "destroyed"), a symbolic act that emphasizes final severance, which consists of shattering and mutilating the heirlooms of the deceased (the pitcher, sleeping mat, and clothing). The destroyed remains are then thrown into the jungle to be reintegrated into the sacred womb of the earth. Both the myth of the origin house and the necessary rites of severance require a systematic shattering of the map of genealogical memory en route to reintegration into the sacred world.

But what happens when the cartographic strategies of more powerful nations collide irreversibly with the various local mapping systems of the East Timorese, resulting in the splitting and felling of the island's proverbial trees: the raping, looting, and annihilation of ancestral homes, schools, and churches? What happens to the bodies of those who died abnormal deaths? When houses are reduced to rubble, what happens to the "walk of sacred objects" within? Who will replenish the proverbial pitchers for the departed East Timorese, both for those who have died and for the countless still in refugee camps in West Timor? According to Jose "Xanana" Gusmao, once popular leader of the resistance and soon-to-be-elected president of Timor Loro Sa'e, these self-same houses/trees will bear fruit again as the fledgling nation begins to engage in international exchange, not only importing goods from overseas and developing tourism at home, but through the exportation of coffee, vanilla, sandalwood products, oil, and gas. At the moment, however, East Timor's only real income is limited to the export of coffee. Food, clothing, construction materials, and other basic necessities must still be imported from neighboring countries at a far greater cost. If the current gulf between the income of UNTAET (United Nations Transitional Administration in East Timor) personnel continues to widen in marked contrast to the abject poverty and prevalent unemployment of the majority of East Timorese, the seeds for more destruction and devastation are inevitably being sown. Surely the recent tragic experiences of the East Timorese, both on the land and in the surrounding sea that currently holds so many scattered bones of innocent victims, can become a place for learning, a border seen as a bridge not only on a local but on a global scale where all countries involved must address their respective roles and continued responsibilities in what should be remembered as one of the worst crimes of the twentieth century.[16]

From Sacred Bowls to Shell Casings: Indonesian Commemorative Vessels for a Military Elite

One afternoon in 1991, I first visited the artist, I Made Sekar, at his home and workshop in Kamasan, Klungkung, Bali. I had arrived to begin my research in Indonesia at the height of the Persian Gulf crisis. Each evening, I would sit with Balinese friends who were engrossed in watching the media's role in the war, especially the nightly pyrotechnic displays of lights in the Gulf skies and the spectacle of laser-guided glider bombs, and Tomahawk missiles piloted by Digital Scene Matching Area Correlation technologies that were explicitly seductive advertisements for the power of the media commodity itself. ("Rudal Scuds," the Balinese diminutively called these tomahawk missiles, as if they were toys. That year "Rudal Scuds" were deployed in silver foil on giant floats, replacing the traditional Balinese demons [*rākṣasa*] and, from the year before, cinematically inspired Native American war chiefs, in the Balinese equivalent of a New Year's celebration in March surrounding Hari Nyepi, when giant floats of monstrous creatures [*ogoh-ogoh*] are paraded about in the streets near the central square in Denpasar and then destroyed as the New Year begins on a symbolically clean slate.)[17]

I was first led to Sekar, and other artists like him, when reading the *Bali Post* one day. A cartoon caught my eye, depicting the drama of the war in the Persian Gulf with missiles flying over a desert landscape (see figure 12.1). Beneath the missiles, a man is seated. Dressed in a deftly folded cloth hat and white ceremonial attire, he appears unaffected by the chaos surrounding him. Seated on a woven mat with a stack of large shell casings beside him, he resembles a salesman bartering his wares in a bustling market. A sign over his head describes this man as a shell-case artisan (*pengrajin selongsong*) in the somewhat precarious process of collecting his materials for his trade. The war in the Persian Gulf represented a war openly fought for control over dwindling oil resources; it is perhaps interesting to compare what was clearly the intense

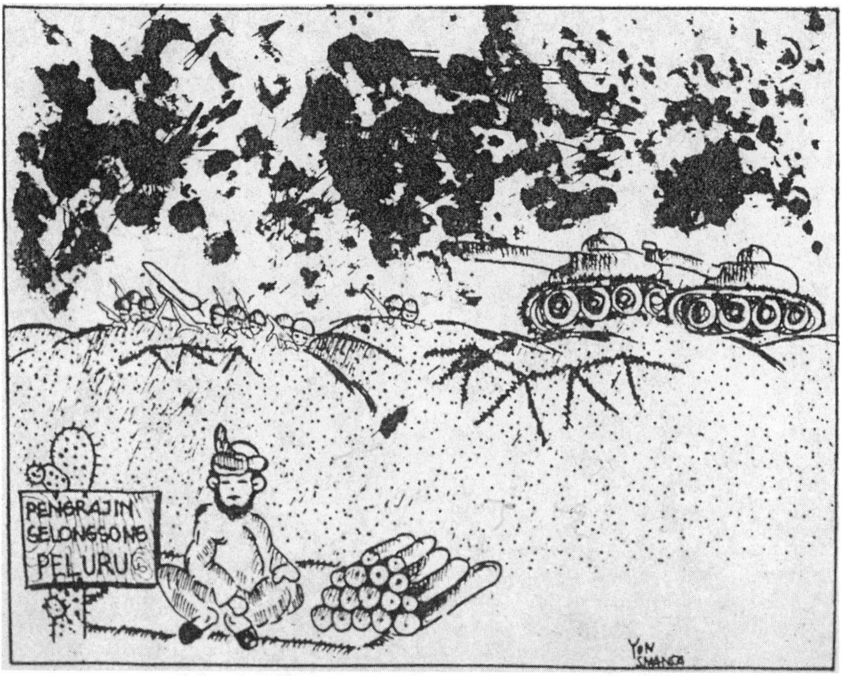

FIGURE 12.1. Cartoon in the *Bali Post,* January 1991, in response to the Gulf War, with the caption "Pengrajin Selongsong Peluru" (shell-casing artisan).

media footage on the Gulf War with the relative invisibility of the war in East Timor, where potential oil and gas resources are also politically and economically at stake for global investors.

When asked, Sekar describes his carved shell casings as transforming "the detritus of war to decorate a peaceful situation" (*sisa sisa perang untuk menghiasi suasana perdamaian*). Using a hammer and a punch with a rounded edge, Sekar outlines figures in a stylized landscape with a series of overlapping indentations. Then with a variety of handmade tools, he fills in and shades the design. Employing a technique called "chasing" on this highly polished covered vessel, Sekar reveals how each implement leaves its mark, from a profusion of tiny pinpricks to deeper impressions (see figures 12.2 and 12.3). After heating sheets of brass until they are pliable, one of Sekar's young apprentices can be seen shaping a series of conoids on a special anvil. These lids are uniquely fabricated for the purpose of returning the already spent casings to the "ghosts" (*hantu*) of their formerly lethal incarnations, quite literally "chasing them back" with petalled incisions into tight lotus buds. Sekar's name, by the way, means "flower" in high Balinese.

Originally trained as a silversmith to carve ceremonial bowls in Kamasan, Sekar embarked on his comparatively lucrative shell-casing industry in 1977, when the wife of the national hero, Josaphat Sudarso, brought a previously fired naval shell casing to his workshop. (Born in Salatiga in 1925, Sudarso

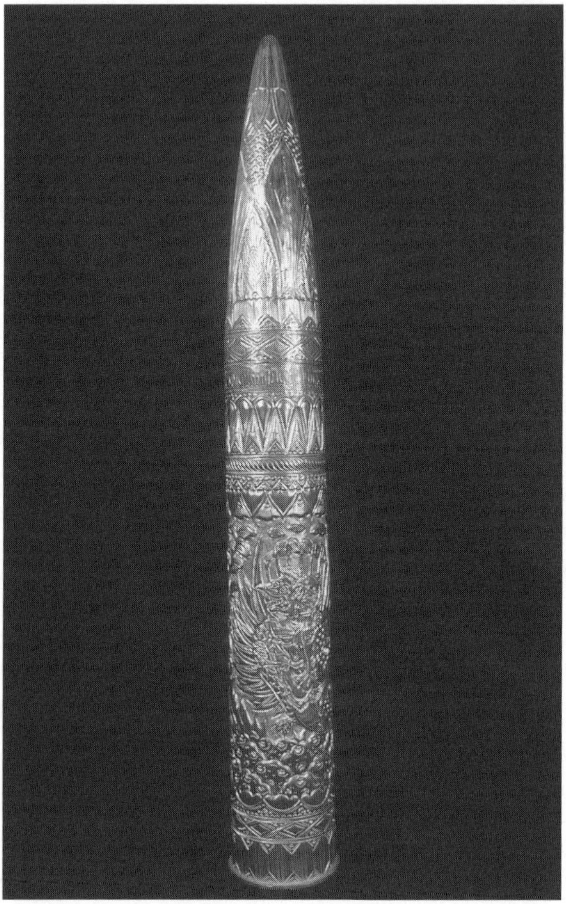

FIGURE 12.2. A brass vessel depicting "The Abduction of Sītā by the Demon-King Rāvaṇa," inspired by the *Rāmāyaṇa*, by I Made Sekar, Banjar Kamasan, Klungkung, Bali, Indonesia, 1995. Embossed and chased shell casing for a U.S.-manufactured M48 B-1 76mm recoilless rifle. Height, 64.5 cm; diameter at the base, 4.5 cm. Author's private collection. Photograph by Bill Staffeld.

was commemorated by Suharto's New Order regime in 1973 for his involvement in the campaign to seize Irian Jaya from the Dutch in 1962.) Accompanied by a lieutenant colonel of the Indonesian armed forces, Mrs. Sudarso commissioned Sekar to carve the story of her husband's heroism in the face of adversity, when he and his crew on the naval frigate known as *KRI Macan Tutul* were fired upon by Dutch planes. Moments later, the ship foundered and sank beneath the waves in the Aru Sea. Finding himself unable to compose a more contemporary battle, Sekar turned to what he knew best, a scene from the Bharatayudha War in the *Mahābhārata*.

During the year, I visited Sekar a few times at his home and workshop in

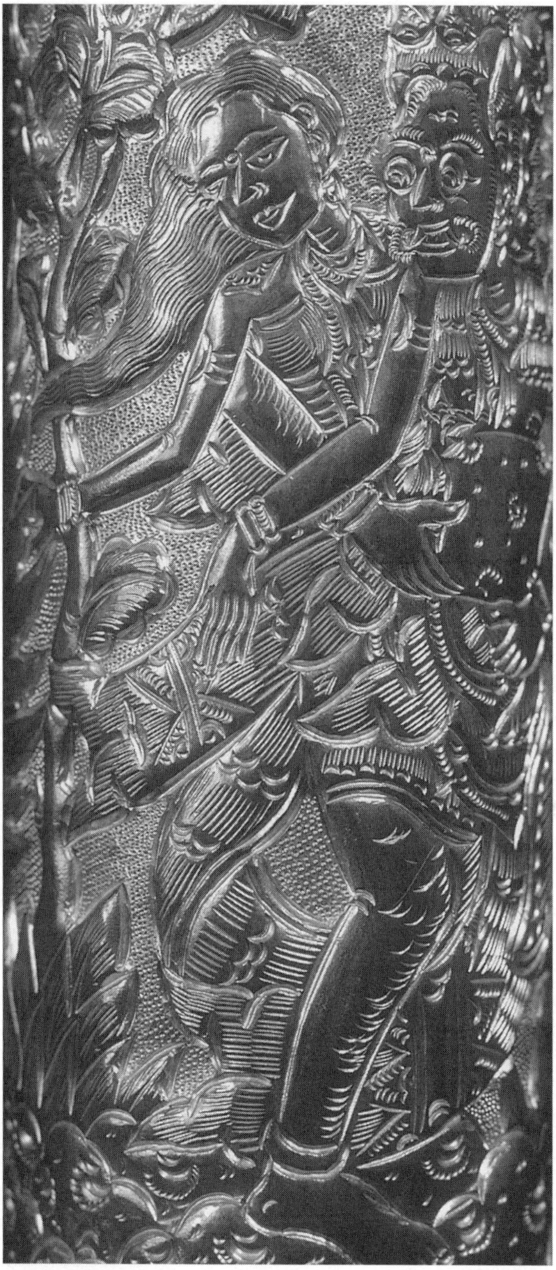

FIGURE 12.3. Detail of Sītā's abduction from Figure 12.2. Photograph by Bill Staffeld.

FIGURE 12.4. I Made Sekar seated on the front step of his home. Photograph by Kaja M. McGowan.

Kamasan (see figure 12.4). He spoke repeatedly of Jakarta as the source of his good fortune (*rejeki*), in the guise first of Mrs. Sudarso and then of General M. Jusuf. In the 1980s, Jusuf began inviting many of his elite military cronies to see Sekar at work, and to commission a flurry of commemorative shells. Sekar described how frequently these military officials would bring boxes of shell casings in a variety of sizes for Sekar's use, as part of the payment. He reported that one naval shell had not been fired prior to its arrival in Kamasan. Sekar's older apprentice pointed to the extensive scars on his torso and neck as a consequence of being the one to first apply heat to the still-loaded cartridge. Sekar recalled how the roof of the workshop had been entirely removed by the explosion. When asked if the vast majority of spent shells, stockpiled in a back room, probably came from the ongoing war in East Timor, Sekar maintained that the generals had always assured him that these shells were left over from military exercises (*latihan militer saja*).[18] A flurry of commemorative shells were commissioned in the 1980s and early 1990s. Sekar remarked with a wistful smile that suddenly it was "raining bullets" (*dihujani peluru*). He immediately began to renovate his house. He then resurrected and expanded his workshop, hiring more local apprentices to help him carry out his commissions. Sekar insisted that part of what made these vessels so desirable to his Jakarta clientele was their limited supply.

With new orders streaming in, Sekar was inspired to extend his repertoire to include scenes not only from the *Mahābhārata* but from the *Rāmāyaṇa*, as well. One image frequently incised on traditional Balinese offering bowls and painted on Hindu ancestral seats, shaped much like miniature palanquin (*jem-*

FIGURE 12.5. Painting depicting Sītā's abduction by Rāvaṇa on the back of a Balinese portable shrine (*jempana*). Photograph from F. A. Wagner, *Indonesia: The Art of an Island Group* (London: Baden Baden, 1959).

pana), is that of Sītā being abducted by Rāvaṇa, the demon-king of Laṅkā (see figure 12.5). As the story goes, while exiled to the Daṇḍaka forest, Rāma, accompanied by his brother Lakṣmaṇa and his beloved bride Sītā, takes up residence in a house adjoining a hermitage. Charmed by a golden deer, Sītā encourages first Rāma and then Lakṣmaṇa, to follow the creature into the forest. Once they are away from the house, Rāvaṇa, disguised as a wandering brahman priest, gains admittance. When Sītā spurns his advances, Rāvaṇa changes back into his demonic form and overpowers Sītā, who bravely resists. Sītā is abducted and carried off to Rāvaṇa's island kingdom of Laṅkā. As they fly away, Jaṭāyu, the faithful Garuḍa bird, flies after Rāvaṇa to defend Sītā's honor to the end. Jaṭāyu is mortally wounded, and Sītā, in final desperation, drops a clue that is picked up by some monkeys. This information is presented later to Rāma, who then prepares with simian forces to build a causeway of stone and storm the ramparts of Rāvaṇa's mighty fortress.[19]

Why did Sekar select this image for depiction on the shell casing? Does the narrative of Rāvaṇa's flight over the ocean to Laṅkā, with Sītā as helpless victim in tow, confer symbolic movement upon this recycled bullet, which, once discharged from a recoilless rifle either positioned on the deck of a naval frigate in Dili's harbor or deployed, one round at a time, from the back of a military jeep, likewise whizzed through the air taking out unsuspecting victims in its wake?[20] A single bullet from a 76-millimeter M48 B–1 U.S. naval gun, shot from a recoilless rifle at close range, can knock out an entire building or level a bunker. As these bullets strike the walls of houses in Dili, for example, their projectiles disengage, resulting in an explosion capable of shattering homes beyond recognition. The spent casings, collected by the army, are then immediately removed from the crime scene before they can be evaluated as potential forensic evidence. Brought to Bali by the boxful, these casings are physically modified as trophies of war, souvenirs that not only commemorate the making of generals (many Indonesian military careers were established on East Timor), but also renew their sense of fraternity with American military might and power.[21] The capacities for objects to serve as traces of authentic experience is, in fact, exemplified here by what is salvaged and reconstituted for the sake of nationalist memory.

As the tragic testimonies of East Timorese begin to emerge in print without the immediate fear of reprisals, the possibility of a culturally comparative approach emerges, whereby the perverse recontextualizations of the shattered life of war-torn things can be forced to partake in a dialogue. Oliver Wolters has encouraged a process for "restoring the effects of foreign fragments when they retreat into local cultural ambiences," arguing that the term "localization" has the merit of calling our attention to something else outside the foreign materials.[22] His is a language in which foreign elements are seemingly fickle, forever "retreating" or "advancing" in intractable ways into local statements. Alien materials either "enhance," "amplify," "intensify," or have the opposite effect of "shrinking" to the status of the purely decorative. I would like to expand Wolter's idea to explore a veritable collision of cartographies, where the foreign element—in this case, a 76-millimeter U.S.-manufactured bullet—explodes on the local scene, annihilating itself as it pulverizes its surroundings, reducing the immediate global/local interface to scattered fragments that must be salvaged forensically in parts and pieces in order to be understood. In any collision, one strikes while the other is stricken. What of the detritus of war remains profoundly foreign, and what is localized? What fragments are retrieved, recycled, and what is discarded, deemed disposable? Who makes these decisions? What parts and pieces are inscribed with epic narratives, transformed into monumental trophies that honor military service and are placed proudly on pedestals for visual consumption; while other fragments, accommodating local accounts, dissolve, like the sacred clay pitchers, into ephemera with the coming of the rainy season, or are hastily buried in shallow graves or wells? Whose bruised bodies are exonerated, while the wounds of others are concealed? Whose battered house walls are left in ruins, while others are swiftly spackled, puttied, and repainted? Can the monumental and ephemeral, the visible and invisible, the foreign as "global," and the ever-shifting and multiplying sites called "local" secure common ground for their mutually emerging narratives? And finally, can such an artificially reconstituted juxtaposition help to encourage a shared sense of responsibility?

While charting these shattered cartographies, I would like to render problematic the tendency for theoretically oriented scholars either to read a work of literature spatially, as one might view the bas-reliefs depicting the *Rāmāyaṇa* at Angkor Vat, for example; or to decode this Angkorian relief semiotically, as if it were a text. Both of these adventures in close reading tend to limit and level the playing field to a clever textual exegesis that looks for possible localized variants, oral and/or literary, carefully attempting to analyze those points where perhaps a later rendition of a text either departs or converges with, in the case of the *Rāmāyaṇa*, Vālmīki's original. [23]

More promising from the perspective of a potentially gendered reading is an ekphrastic approach, which explores the dynamic struggle between text and image. James Heffernan offers an invaluable discussion of the development in the West of *ekphrasis* (from the Greek *ek-phrassein*: "to speak out," and "to tell in full"), originally one of the more advanced rhetorical exercises in a Sophist handbook of style entitled the *Progymnasmata*.[24] From Homer's *Iliad* to John Ashbery's 1974 poem "Self Portrait in a Convex Mirror," Heffernan reveals how ekphrasis continually stages what he refers to as "a contest between rival modes of representation: between the driving force of the narrating word and the stubborn resistance of the fixed image."[25] The earliest classical examples of ekphrasis describe shields from epic literature: Homer's shield of Achilles in book 18 of the *Iliad*; the Hesiodic fragment entitled "Shield of Herakles," and, of course, Virgil's description of Aeneas's shield in book 8 of the *Aeneid*. What is most persuasive about these early descriptions of objects is that they are not nominally works of art but more often utilitarian things, simultaneously biographical and portable—shields, cups, cloaks, and woven tapestries.[26] Ekphrasis is intertextual. To borrow W. J. T. Mitchell's pun, it is as much about "citing" artworks as it is about "sighting" them. I would add a third element to the wordplay here, by suggesting the importance of grasping a sense of place, thereby "siting" the object as well within its various cartographic domain(s) of desire. Most conducive for a cross-cultural comparative approach is Heffernan's discussion of the struggle between text and image as a "duel between male and female gazes." He describes the ambivalence of the gendered contest of power as one where the voice of male speech is "striving to control a female image that is both alluring and threatening, of male narrative striving to overcome the fixating impact of beauty poised in space."[27]

In *The Shadow of Mount Ramelau: The Impact of the Occupation of East Timor*, George J. Aditjondro likens the relationship of East Timor to Indonesia as "the gagged and bound victim of a rape" who is "deemed to have enjoyed its own violation."[28] The symbolic meaning of rape in this context is as powerful as the act itself. Sekar's image of Sītā on the shell casing comes to mind. There is little trauma in Sītā's facial expression as depicted by Sekar. She does not seem to struggle, or even break a sweat. In fact, she almost appears to be smiling as Rāvaṇa sweeps her off her feet en route to Laṇkā. As Virginia Sapiro has pointed out, "The control over women's sexuality has often been played out in intergroup conflict through the dynamics of rape. . . . What we might call 'the politics of honor' [is] played out between groups through the medium of women's sexuality. The assault on the enemy involves a wide range of physical and psychological tactics, but one of the most notable means of assaulting the honor or pride of a nation or community is to assault the honor of its women through rape."[29]

It is in the ambiguities of this global/local interface, the junctures between the iconophobic and the iconophilic aspects of rape as either referencing Indonesia's male honor and virility or East Timor's loss thereof through the victimization of her women—the diluting or derailing of genealogical memory, comparable perhaps to the shattering of Carabaulo Tetum clay pitchers—that Sekar's chased shell casing can be read in multiple ways. But who and what are being glorified in Sekar's brass vessel? If we call on it as an object to "tell in full," how many versions of the story can it communicate? As we literally chase the images around and around with our eyes; who is being honored here, and what are we being asked to remember? Sekar assured me repeatedly that it was he alone, and not his wealthy Javanese patrons, who chose which themes to depict on these brass vessels. If so, I ask again, why did Sekar choose this particular image? Can his thematic choice be interpreted either as direct complicity with his patrons or as a subtly scathing critique (albeit unintended) of the Indonesian military in their treatment of women?[30] Sekar would emphatically deny either interpretation. His repeated statements to me when I suggested the possibility of such diverse readings was that he was only attempting to turn something lethal and violent into something peaceful and beautiful. In his search for inspiration, Sekar turned to what he knew best, namely, to his training as a carver of sacred bowls for Balinese ceremonies. In order to understand Sekar's provocative choice of subject matter, we must try to divine what Sītā's abduction might mean within the sacred domain of Balinese ritual.

Beyond the earlier symbolic connection made between Rāvaṇa's urgent flight and the movement of a speeding bullet, traditional Balinese ceremonial bowls and sacred ancestral seats are likewise transported through the air, carried in rituals where circumambulation often occurs as a patterned response to group prayer. Like the body of Sītā, the sacred bowl and/or ancestral seat is repeatedly lifted and carried across the landscape. On ceremonial occasions, these containers for ancestral forces may be transported from the comfort of a house to a new landscape, the sea for example, where the figures can be cleansed and purified before they are returned to their ritual domain in the house or village temple. One side of a ninth- to tenth-century ornately carved gold bowl, uncovered along with a hoard of other ceremonial objects near the village of Plosokuning, Wonoboyo, central Java, and now at the Jakarta National Museum, prominently depicts Sītā's abduction by Rāvaṇa.

More interesting to reconsider is the choice of theme, where Sītā's abduction (or rape [*perkosaan*], as it is often referred to in Indonesia), as depicted on the vessel, is juxtaposed with themes related to the harvesting of certain crops, rice in particular. Rice in Bali is connected symbolically to the goddess Sri; it is also indirectly tied to Sītā through her connection with agriculture. The Balinese terms for the maturation of a rice crop are synonymous with the development of a child in the womb. When Dewi Sri, personified in the rice plant, is ready to be harvested (or "pregnant") in Bali, she is said to be at her most vulnerable. It is then that interlocking rhythms (*oncangan*) are sometimes played. These resonating sounds are thought to exorcise the demons, like Rāvaṇa, who lie in wait to attack the fertile crop. The terminology used is often sexually explicit, even violent in its connotations. When the rice is ready to be harvested in Bali, the knife (*anggapan*) must be concealed in the right hand so that the ripe plants will not be afraid as they are cut and harvested in tied bundles. As I mentioned earlier, within many epic traditions, the theme of rape is frequently associated symbolically with the harvest. The image of the fertile woman's body as "harvested" refers not only to the land through the various sacrificial myths of the rice maiden, or the suffering nation as an allegorical symbol but, in the case of Bali, perhaps can also be seen to allude to the land being owned not by the living but by the ancestral gods, who when invited to descend into offerings in sacred bowls are said to "beg for rice" (*nunas nasi*).

On the shell casing, the symbolic meaning of rape and abduction in this, Sekar's simultaneous production and staging of metal, text, and world, can be seen to be as powerful as the act itself. And yet, when I asked Sekar, it was clear that the generals from Jakarta had not commissioned or requested this theme as indicative of male honor or bravery. Sekar alone had selected it because it was a traditionally depicted segment from the *Rāmāyaṇa*, one he knew well and had embossed many times on sacred offering bowls. When asked, Sekar appeared ill-informed or even ignorant of any relationship to the abusive activities of soldiers stationed in East Timor. His sole desire was to "decorate" (*menghiasi*) something lethal into something peaceful, a lotus bud. By turning to his repertoire of themes from sacred vessels, Sekar in part unwittingly sets into motion a powerfully ambiguous message, which can be read in its cyclicity as either an exoneration of Indonesian male virility or as evidence of a brutal pattern of sexual practice, damning in its confessional seriality. The image can also be read as one of ultimate victory or a return to safety for East Timorese victims in that, as Sekar repeatedly pointed out, the form of the bullet will never allow Sītā to experience the complete brutality of Rāvaṇa's abduction because the narrative is incessantly vanquished by the bullet's return to the lotus. In the virtual multiplicity of possible readings, depending entirely upon who is witness to the cyclic patterns of intended or aborted flight, Sekar's brass vessel reveals a complex interface of global and local encounters in a proliferation of possible places.

Can Sekar's lidded vessel, once opened (see figure 12.6), speak out for East Timorese concerns? In the emerging testimonies from East Timor, there appears to be a direct correlation between the threats to women's bodies and their houses. In the workshops arranged by UNTAET and East Timor's Jurists Association (ANMEFTIL) after the post-ballot rampage, many East Timorese women are now coming forward to relate how, in the hours prior to the August 30 referendum, they were threatened with rape and the loss of their identity cards if they voted for independence. These threats were similarly directed toward the house as a symbolically female domain. An American Associated Press correspondent in Dili wrote: "In a hopeless gesture of home-making,

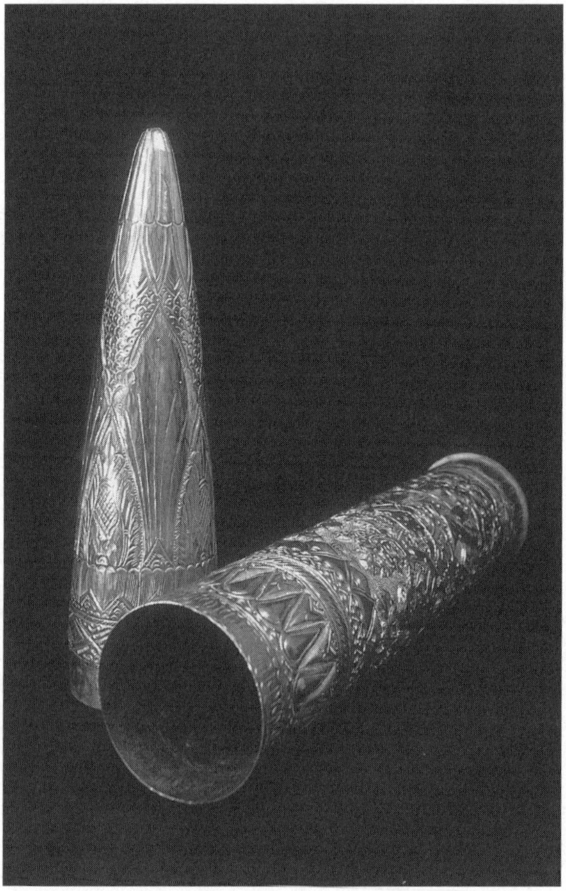

FIGURE 12.6. "Open Vessel." Photograph by Bill Staffeld.

Nica Sousa has pinned a magazine image of Diana, Princess of Wales, to the wall of her former living room in suburban Dili. . . . Apart from the picture, debris is all the house contains. . . . In 23 year old Ms. Sousa's former bedroom, the militia who destroyed her house left a message in red chalk: "If you [had not] voted for autonomy, we would not have destroyed your house."[31]

Here the body of the woman mapped on the house, as in the Carabaulo Tetum origin myth collected by Hicks, encourages a reexamination of Sekar's narrative selection. Sītā's abduction from her home at the hands of Rāvaṇa, when read and reread in its abrupt and abortive cyclicity, suggests the repeated threats and intimidation tactics of the Indonesian army-backed militias. Jaṭāyu, on the other hand, barely lifting a feather to assist Sītā in her terror, can perhaps be interpreted as Indonesia, whose symbol is the Garuḍa bird, here revealing its full complicity with the activities of the Rāvaṇa-like militias. And, finally, where content encounters material form, Jaṭāyu, with pinfeathers raised like a quiver of arrows, can be seen literally to be armed and financed by the United

States, as evidenced by the very reflective surface in which he is chased. Note the ekphrastic quality of Nica Sousa's testimony as construed by the Associated Press correspondent. It is as if the photograph of Diana, Princess of Wales, serves as the visual mooring (according to Heffernan, a female image in confrontation with a male narrative gaze): the moment of stasis in an otherwise chaotic description of an interior. Many of the house narratives emerging from East Timor seem to utilize the ekphrastic device of describing a single object—a photograph, a crucifix, a statue of the Virgin, a candle that has been blessed, an overturned child's tub—as a mooring around which to visualize the indeterminate rubble and debris.

Whereas the profits from Sekar's new patronage led to his renovation and expansion of his house, the bullets, once deployed, resulted in the shattering of East Timorese homes. These demolished-house narratives can be read in relation to Sekar's success, both reflecting "localizations" that have been altered significantly by their encounter with Indonesian military greed and ambition. Since I began this discussion of "collision of cartographies" with Bishop Belo's October 17, 1999, address, given in the yard of his burned-out home, I will now return momentarily to the following detailed testimony offered by a witness who had sought refuge in Belo's compound on Saturday, September 4. The witness describes how the Aitarak militia arrived two days later, aided by police and Indonesian military. He relates how the bishop's compound was razed, utilizing a mixture of automatic weapons and homemade water-bottle bombs filled with gasoline. Ordered to vacate the bishop's premises, the refugees were forced to sit directly under the sun as they watched the unfolding events:

> Next to be attacked was the Sister of Canosian's house. The militia began to shoot in front of the sister's house while screaming that if all of you (sisters) don't get out of the house we will burn all of your houses along with you. Hearing this the sisters ran outside carrying objects used for mass such as chalices, etc. . . . Those sisters joined us. After making us sit in the sun for two hours, they ordered us to take our things inside. After taking our things inside, they threatened us to leave the bishop's residence because if we didn't leave, they would attack all of us later at 5:00 in the evening (17:00). We ran outside carrying as much of our things as we could.

Here the chalice in the arms of a Sister of Canosian, being carried in and out of the sacred house as the militias repeatedly threaten, reveals a cyclical pattern, simultaneously indeterminate and terrifying in its ambiguity. The brave Canosian Sister carrying the receptacle for the symbolic blood of Christ (perceived perhaps by some as a Catholic variant on the Carabaulo Tetum family pitchers) when viewed in relation to Sekar's vessel depicting Sītā's abduction—both descriptive portrayals of symbolic sacrifice, involving women transporting and being transported by vessels (active and being acted upon)—argues for the relevance of looking to the ekphrastic power of objects in the healing process. If East Timor's current vulnerability as a fledgling nation can be better understood historically in relation to Aditjondro's previous comparison of East Timor to Indonesia as the victim of a rape who has been deemed to have enjoyed its violation—the voice of male speech, according to Heffernan, "striving to control a female image"—then Sītā's plight, chased on Sekar's shell casing, argues forcefully for our immediate consideration of the role of epic as a genre that stages a continual struggle to narrate the stories of things past in such a way as to make them resonate with the present. Each object retrieved and reconstituted from the wreckage can perhaps be construed as a step toward partial restitution for East Timor's suffering. As the personal object-oriented testimonies accumulate, if epic serves, then the very process of healing itself, leading both to Sītā's recovery and the problematic reclaiming of her honor, can be compared to the rocks and boulders cast into the sea by Sugrīva's monkey armies who rally with Rāma to build the bridge to Laṅkā.

Following Rāvaṇa's abduction of Sītā, the building of the causeway, and the great battle that Rāma incites to reclaim his beloved, it is public scandal concerning Sītā's virtue during her forced captivity on Laṅkā that ultimately drives Rāma to abandon her in the forest. Maintaining her innocence, Sītā consents to a trial by fire, from which she emerges unscathed, only, in some versions of the epic, to be banished again. In a cover story for *Time Asia*, entitled "Starting Over," Terry McCarthy writes: "The walls are blackened by fire and graffiti. The windows and doors are gone; a lone crucifix hangs undamaged on the wall. Welcome to Dili's best restaurant, 'Uma Mutuk'—the Burned House. At night, oil lamps and candles flicker off the walls as dinner is prepared over open fires in the rear. The food is simple, but the atmosphere is what draws customers. Guests feel ever-so-slightly uneasy, as if they were eating in a church—a feeling the owners do not attempt to dispel."[32]

Libania Borges, thirty-eight, and her sister Manuela opened this successful eatery in Dili in January of 2000. Most nights the nine tables are booked solid. Even United Nations Secretary-General Kofi Annan has partaken of the fare. Since the Indonesians invaded East Timor in 1975, the two siblings have been living in Darwin, Australia. When they returned in October 1999 in search of surviving relatives after the army-backed militias had carried out their scorched earth campaign, they found only one family member, their aunt Maria, hiding in fear in the debris that was her home. The two sisters decided to use their savings to transform the house into a restaurant as a way of helping their aunt recover from the trauma of the attack. After four weeks of grueling work clearing the debris, a local carpenter was called in to build a new roof for the structure. "My aunt wanted to clean the walls and paint them," said Libania, "but we said no—we wanted to leave it the way it [was] to remind the people of what the militias did. What happened here makes me very angry." Now Libania's and Manuela's aunt is alleged to be smiling again. On busy nights, she helps her nieces serve the guests. While much of Dili awaits reconstruction, "Uma Mutuk," like Sītā, has risen from its ashes, both to bear witness and to choose again a new life.

Building Bridges to the Battles of Laṅkā Sites as Monuments to Memory or Oblivion?

It is precisely epic's subscription to the challenge of contemporaneity that makes it such a dynamic and powerful art form for us to wrestle with today. It has a role like that of ekphrastic description; we not only come to understand more fully but are ourselves also caught within the social, political, and cultural forces that at once inspire the production of epics and are shaped and directed by them. In the case of the "Battle of Laṅkā" panel at Angkor, Eleanor Mannika has attempted to interpret some of the possible contemporary twelfth-century references to the commissioning and carving of the bas-relief that bears the name. From 1128 to 1133, King Suryavarman II enlisted the Chams as allies in waging war against the Dai Viet in northern Vietnam.[33] But by 1135, the Chams refused to uphold their compact with the Khmer, and, several years later, would in turn be invaded unsuccessfully by Suryavarman. In the "Battle of Laṅkā" Sugrīva's simian troops are allied with Rāma to help him overthrow Rāvaṇa and his army. Did the artists working at Angkor intend to depict a striking visual corollary between the alliance of the Khmers and Chams against the Dai Viet? If so, according to Mannikka, the artists have judiciously refrained from depicting the outcome of the battle by carefully suspending the action at a series of duels between the protagonists, Rāma and Rāvaṇa, whose bodies, enlarged and centrally located, stand prominently poised and isolated in space. If the scene of the "Battle of Laṅkā" at Angkor does indeed refer to King Suryavarman's affiliation with the Chams, this reflects a shrewd compositional strategy on the part of the artist(s) who were forced to address what Heffernan has called an ekphrastic "duel between text and image." Their choice reflects considerable cunning, precisely because the Khmer alliance with the Chams and the attacks against the Dai Viet ultimately failed.[34]

Similarly, on Sekar's shell casing, two opposing trees can be seen to arrest Rāvaṇa's abduction of Sītā from the seemingly apathetic presence of Jaṭāyu. Where Sītā faces Jaṭāyu, her flowing hair, outstretched hand, and billowing sash are embossed evenly, like furrows in a field over the tree's barklike surface, each extension touching the tips of the bird's feathers (see figure 12.7). On the other tree, it is Sītā's foot alone that stretches beyond the trunk, her toes trailing behind, suspended, indeed lost in Jaṭāyu's ineffectual tail (see figure 12.8). When the shell casing is set in motion, Sītā's bodily extensions and the two trees can be seen to weave together visually. Sītā, whose name means "furrow," is related to the archetypal prehistoric tree and fertility goddess. The image of the brass cylindrical shell casing entwined with the trunk and branches of Sītā as a living ancestral tree would seem to echo visually one of the principal independence monuments soon to be unveiled on the evening of May 19, 2002, accompanying the eight-hour program of festivities to mark East Timor's transition to formal independence. The monument, a massive flagpole entwined with the trunk and branches of a symbolic banyan tree forged in steel,

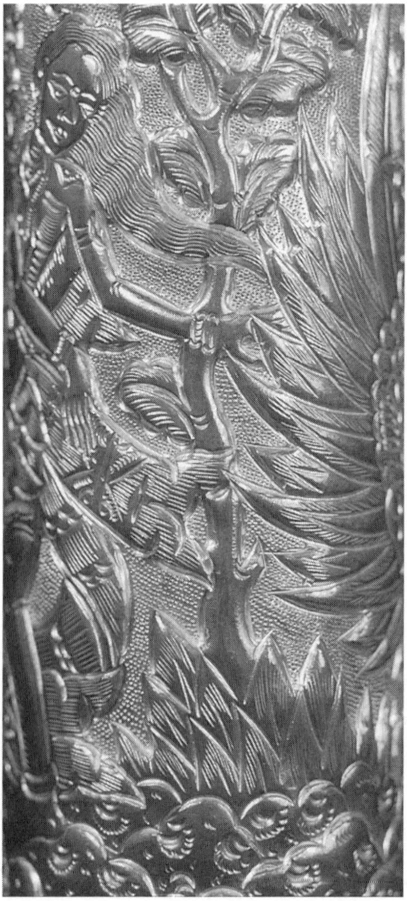

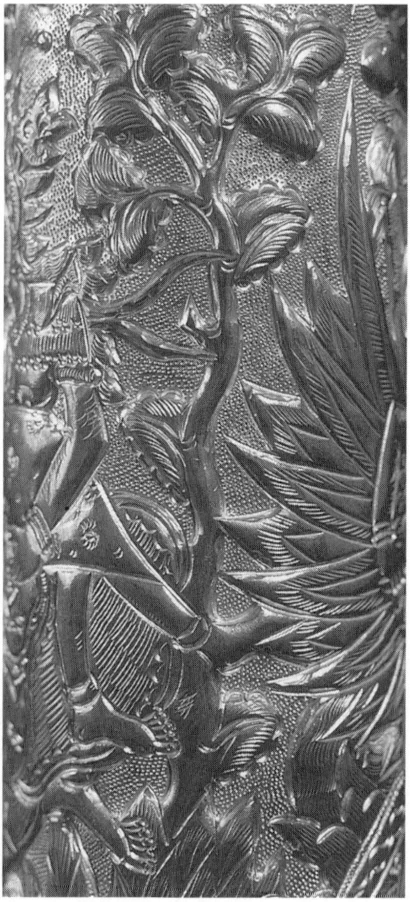

FIGURES 12.7 AND 12.8. Close-ups from the shell casing in Figure 12.2. Seen side by side, the composite image revealing Sītā touching the two trees as the shell casing is visually set in motion, as described in the essay. Photographs by Bill Staffeld.

will stand on a hill overlooking Dili, the capital of newly independent Timor Loro S'ae.

It will be a momentous occasion when East Timorese finally govern themselves after four centuries of Portuguese rule, twenty-four years of Indonesian occupation, and most recently a two-year stint for the United Nations interim administration (UNTAET). In the last two years, UNTAET's activities have frequently been compared to the earlier hegemonic regimes, whose seaside haciendas they continue to inhabit, and whose lavish lifestyles and floating hotels (miniature islands of Laṅkā in the making, complete with their captive women) speak of the gross disparity between the internationals and the locals, and the unwillingness yet again on the part of those in power to relinquish their hold on the untapped potential resources of East Timor. Remembering the ordered rows of Cham soldiers embarking with Khmer troops on Angkor's bas-relief, we might stop to ask who are the new corporate sponsors lining up to secure their affiliation with Timor Loro S'ae? Which companies are offering to help finance the upcoming events and, especially, to sponsor the various monuments being unveiled? Oklahoma-based Phillips Petroleum, an oil company active in the Timor Sea, is vying for position, along with one of Australia's major banks; and first to respond, although cordially bumped to tertiary status as having the wrong image for the new, devoutly Catholic, nation is Aristocrat, an Australian company specializing in poker and gaming machines. Surprisingly enough, with regard to the independence monument—the flagpole entwined with a banyan tree—there has not been a rush to sponsorship. Hamish McDonald, a reporter for the *Sydney Morning Herald*, writes: "On a plaque at the base of this $200,000 independence monument will be words of thanks to its corporate sponsor: a generous Australian company, it is hoped. . . . Australia's top executives may admire the spirit. But how many would put their company's logo on a monument to 24 years of guerilla resistance or be otherwise associated with a nation whose emergence was so long opposed in many of Asia's lucrative markets?"[35]

The immediate hybrid transformations implied as commemorative monuments move along perilous trajectories from zones of danger to relative comfort (or in Sekar's own words, from the "detritus of war to decorate a peaceful situation") would appear to resonate in reverse with a compelling short story by the Indonesian author Putu Wijaya, entitled "If He Could Choose Again." In the story, the main character, Oki, wakes up one morning to find himself hugging a bomb and not his familiar pillow. Quite naturally, he is overcome by a sense of helplessness. Wanting to spare his immediate family and the world, he wanders out into the street, clutching his ticking terror. At a loss to know what to do with the bomb, at last he climbs a flagpole, where he proceeds to wrap his heavy burden, significantly, in the flag. The drama is punctuated by the pillow's metamorphoses from something comfortable and familiar to something deadly, the wrapped object becoming a trope capable of playing upon the insecurities of the audience, who are, similarly, in rapt attendance beneath the flag. When Oki's wife finally arrives, she is convinced that the bundle in her husband's arms is their baby. In a clumsy attempt to save the infant, a misinformed policeman shoots Oki, and the bomb falls with its devastating consequences. Within an instant, the image of a peaceful community with hands outstretched becomes a gruesome scene of chaotic dismemberment. What is more, in a shockingly radical shift of time frame, Putu includes us beneath the flagpole. As witnesses, we are confronted by the gut-wrenching question: "Who is really responsible?"[36]

Charles Armstrong has recently asked himself a similar question with regard to the tragedy of September 11, 2001. Within the globalizing rhetoric, there has been a tendency to imagine that social science methods are universally applicable, and the dominance of America and the pervasiveness of the English language make the knowledge of other cultures and languages seem almost irrelevant. He urges us to reconsider the importance of place, culture, and war. "It is hard to imagine," Armstrong remarks, "how one can explain recent events with a 'view from nowhere.' The study of specific places, histories, cultures and languages is suddenly in vogue once again, and probably will be for some time to come." Advocating a return to the importance of Asian studies, he argues that "it is precisely those of us who are aware of the complexity and variety of 'non-western' cultures who can offer more nuanced interpretations against the simplistic division of humankind into immutable and mutually hostile cultural identities." Finally, for Armstrong, the study of war seems too important to be left to those with a vested interest in it: the foreign policy think tanks, the intelligence and national security apparatuses, the military academies. It is important to apply a wide range of scholarly methods and resources in attempting to explain how we got to this point of conflict, and where we go from here.[37]

Armstrong's thoughts from "Ground Zero" can easily be applied to the events unfolding in East Timor since 1974. Building such comparative bridges to the sites of the various "Battles of Laṅkā" reveals forcefully the epic importance of chasing Sītā on a global/local interface, if only to ensure that all parties involved accept responsibility. Certainly Sekar's shell casing can be made to bear witness not just to the ongoing trial of the Indonesian military but to America as well: to Ford, Kissinger, and all the presidential players who have been in office since, who continued to sell arms and to train the Indonesian military, right up until the post-ballot atrocities.

Set on separate bluffs looking down on Dili's harbor, two commemorative monuments now stand poised in space as silent witnesses: Christo Rei, a twenty-seven-meter statue of Christ given to East Timor by Indonesia's former President Suharto, and East Timor's new Independence Monument, secured at the base of the flagpole/banyan with Australia's hoped-for sponsorship. Suspended in Dili's landscape, their conspicuous forms can be seen to echo symbolically an earlier alliance forged between Indonesia and Australia in September of 1974, just prior to Indonesia's 1975 illegal invasion of East Timor. President Suharto traveled to Yogya to meet with Australia's then prime minister, Gough Whitlam. As a result of Suharto's briefing of Whitlam on the question of whether or not to grant self-determination to the East Timorese, Whitlam's response to Suharto was supposedly immediate: "An independent East Timor would be an unviable state, and a potential threat to the area."[38]

While floating hotels, monuments to oblivion, flooded with lights festoon Dili's harbor below, these two commanding and isolated images, observed in tandem, can be seen to represent an important site of memory. Forging their alliance visually in the mind allows us to locate Christ on the banyan tree of life and of death. His crucifixion on the mound at Golgotha, sacrificing his life so that all humanity may be spared, resonates hauntingly not only with the Carabaulo Tetum origin myth of the mother buffalo described earlier but also with Sītā's ancestral roots. These comparative instances point to ritually ordained sacrificial deaths, leading, respectively, to eternal life, ancestral heirlooms, or a fertile harvest; but what of the bodies of East Timorese who died abnormally in the wake of the August 30 referendum? Still in living memory for many East Timorese, and set in the self-same coves where a whole flotilla of hotels float luxuriantly today, under the watchful eye of the Indonesian security forces the militias allegedly executed hundreds of people and dumped their bodies in the water in the fortnight after the results of East Timor's ballot was announced. Witnesses described huge sharks accustomed to the taste of human flesh circling in the shallows. This frightening image is, perhaps, one to bear in mind as sponsors currently compete for their place in the profits.

Ultimately, the sponsorship of commemorative monuments to Timor Loro S'ae's independence must be seen in light of the current need to prosecute those guilty of violations against humanity going back to 1975. Clearly, there is a growing necessity for an effective international intervention mechanism, coupled with real accountability. Few Timorese expect anything from Indonesian justice. Many speak of the gross imbalance of bringing only the Indonesian military and their militias to trial when, arguably, their actions were spurred on in large part by the interests of other countries in the global community. Had the United States and other influential countries pushed for such a tribunal and been willing to admit their role in the carnage, and had they not allowed Jakarta to pursue the charade of investigating and prosecuting its own, we would not find today the culture of impunity that permits the Indonesian military and the militias to succeed, a culture that will only continue. Commemorative monuments can help us to locate ourselves within such an international arena, a global/local interface—one in which all players must account for their activities. An art object like Sekar's shell casing depicting "Sītā's abduction" or Angkor's "Battle of Laṅkā" can allow us to suspend our actions momentarily, to rethink our impetus for involvement with certain countries, and perhaps to choose again. Are we being motivated by humanitarian concerns or pure greed? Are we really trying to help another nation succeed, or are our gestures only fanning the flames of discontent, leading to the building of future bridges to echo the epic Battle of Laṅkā from contemporary moment to moment?

Homi Bhabha has urged us to "acknowledge the force of writing, its metaphoricity and its rhetorical discourse, as a productive matrix which defines the 'social' and makes it available as an objective of/for action."[39] In this essay, I have tried to locate a space at the intersection of text and image, from which to observe moments of struggle or political change in all its hybridity. Meditation on Sekar's shell casing, for example, allows us to posit a space where cartographies have collided, a dialogical realm something like the "Third Space of enunciation" that Bhabha has described. It represents a suspended moment, if you will, between ourselves and others, a global/local interface where potential understandings can emerge without fear of reprisals. In this process, however, both textual and visual space can also converge on difference, disaffection, fragmentation, and dispersion at the heart of knowledge. This presupposes that, as surely as there exists our sovereign space, a space of the other will always prove inaccessible to our understanding.

Finally, what kind of audience does ekphrasis encourage us to be? The writer's responses to visual objects can be seen to become a model for the audience's response. It is important to stress that these "thick" descriptions should serve as reminders to those in attendance that they are witnessing a human response, one of many possible responses, to depicted phenomena, and not the phenomena themselves. Since this battle is fought on the field of language, it would be mismatched save for one thing: Ekphrasis exposes a profound ambivalence toward the visual image, a concurrent feeling of adoration and anxiety. To try to comprehend the shattered world of the East Timorese through words is to try to come to terms with the images selected for personal narratives, the power for objects as sites—Christo Rei, East Timor's Independence Monument, the Burned House, Christ's chalice in the arms of the Canosian Sister, and/or Sītā's abduction chased in brass—to fix, astonish, excite, disgust, devastate, or regenerate the viewer. In closing, we may recall Kenneth Gross's comment: "Ekphrasis would entail not just translating a statue's language into our own, finding a place for its imagined words in the given world. It would also involve letting the words which the statue speaks unsettle or recreate the words we already seem to know."[40]

NOTES

About the photographer: Bill Staffeld is the photographer for the College of Architecture, Art, and Planning and the Department of the History of Art in the College of Arts and Sciences at Cornell University. Besides his duties at the university, Staffeld is a documentary photographer who works in upstate New York.

1. Geertz 1973, p. 16.

2. Becker 1995, p. 29.

3. A preoccupation of mapmakers for centuries, Timor's forests of white sandalwood (*santalum album L.*) lured traders en route to western Indonesia and India from as early as the second or third centuries ce. (Wolters 1967, p. 65). It was China's source for the aromatic wood during the Sung (Wheatley 1959: 203–4); Timor was later selected by the Portuguese, who, joining an already profitable Asian trade network, determined to settle on the island in the sixteenth century. In 1656, a well-armed Dutch fleet landed on the western coast of Timor. When Indonesia achieved independence in 1945, all Dutch holdings, including West Timor, were surrendered to Sukarno's New Republic (Taylor 1991, pp. 1–5). With the illegal invasion of East Timor in 1975, Batara Indra, an Indonesian conglomerate backed by retired generals Moerdani and Kalbuadi, seized control of East Timor's sandalwood production, exporting not only oil but also Buddhist statues to Taiwan and Catholic statues to Italy (Aditjondro 1999).

4. As East Timorese have slowly begun the process of rebuilding their independent nation under United Nations supervision, the question of which language to adopt has been controversial. Whereas East Timor's independence leaders have advocated a return to Portuguese, a legacy from more than four hundred years of colonial rule, members of the Renetil Youth Congress—many graduates of Indonesian universities and fluent in Bahasa-Indonesia—have argued the merits of selecting a new language, not reflective of either Portuguese or unauthorized Indonesian domination. Almost 95 percent of Timorese speak either the lingua franca, Tetum, or Indonesian, the teaching of Portuguese having been banned by the New Order regime. More recently, Tetum has been designated as the language of church; Indonesian, the market-

place; while English and Portuguese are employed for more formal negotiations surrounding the politics of nation building.

5. See Welty, 1957; and Walter 1988, pp. 132–145, for an integrated discussion of what it is like to "grasp a sense of place." By "grasping," both authors mean a more full-bodied response than can be experienced with the hands alone.

6. Walter, 1988, p. 130. Referring to Plato's *Timaeus,* Walter asserts that metaphors represent place as a "seat of experience." Igor Kopytoff's "cultural biographical" method argues for a processual approach to studying objects. Charting a biography entails observing an object's transmutations from, for example, sacred status to commodity and back again, a fluid trajectory that often reveals dynamic fluctuations in value and a variety of encounters, simultaneously global and local, that attend and transform an object over time. See Kopytoff 1986.

7. Winichakul 1997, p. 12.

8. Taylor, 1991, pp. 1–3.

9. Traube 1986, pp. 75–76.

10. Ibid.

11. Hoskins 1995, p. 1.

12. See Walter 1988, p. 193.

13. See Hicks 1976, p. 66.

14. For a discussion of East Timorese houses as symbolic wombs, see Waterson 1990, pp. 196–198.

15. According to villagers, the pig supplied to the wife-givers by their wife-takers in the marriage ritual is given "to replace the sacred pitcher the bride brings with her to her husband's house." For a detailed discussion of these symbolic connections, see Hicks, 1976, pp. 23, 63–65.

16. Since Ford and Kissinger gave Suharto the go-ahead to invade East Timor in 1975, the United States has sold to Jakarta about 1 billion dollars worth of military equipment. Not only did 90 percent of the weaponry utilized in East Timor since 1975 come from the United States, but America is also responsible for granting diplomatic support and military training for Indonesia's special forces, many of whom claim to have made their careers in East Timor. Given Indonesia's weakened economy, if U.S. funds had simply been withheld, Indonesian troops would have been forced to evacuate, and much of the bloodshed and property damage could have been avoided. The prospect of off-shore oil has prompted more powerful countries to ally with Indonesia at the expense of East Timor. The insidious presence of foreign investors can be described as arriving first in the guise of ballistic calling cards, sold to the Indonesian military and deployed so that their projectiles will dislodge on contact, shattering everything in their wake. In the aftermath, powerful countries like Australia, Britain, and the United States can move in, and by offering a hand in the recovery efforts of a fledgling nation, attempt to corner some of her potentially abundant resources. East Timor Questions and Answers. Stephen R. Shalom, Noam Chomsky, and Michael Albert. Z Magazine, September 15, 1999. Consulted at www.chomsky.info/articles/199910–02.htm.

17. During the Persian Gulf Crisis, CNN was observed to come into its own as a global network, eradicating the word "foreign" from all its broadcasts; at one point Saddam Hussein admitted to the press that "we are getting our news from CNN just like everyone else." Aside from the fact that TV networks like NBC were owned by parent companies that were and are major defense contractors in their own right, we must stop to ask what the relationship is between this economy of the media spectacle and the economy of war and oil consumption that provides the political context for the war.

18. I was struck in 1991 by how little Sekar, or any Balinese I asked for that matter, seemed to know about what had been going on in East Timor since 1975. Misinformation abounded, particularly regarding the exaggerated importance of Indonesia's sustained military presence and the supposedly heroic attempts at containment of this so-called "newest and most antagonistic addition to the nation." Around the military barracks in Denpasar, stereotypes proliferated of the relentless East Timorese guerrilla fighters, whose unpredictable pugnacity and whose ability to evaporate as if into thin air in their mountain settings was almost legendary.

19. The Balinese *Rāmāyaṇa* is not derived directly from Vālmīki's version, but rather by way of an Old Javanese *Rāmāyaṇa* cycle from the ninth or tenth century, written by Yogiswara in accordance with a later, abbreviated Indian version. See Robson 1980.

20. From discussions with naval personnel at Cornell's ROTC, it transpires that the United States sold off their outdated recoilless rifles from World War II to many Asian countries, including Korea and Indonesia. The Indonesian military purchased these rifles and their corresponding bullets in the late 1960s and early 1970s. Recoilless rifles were intended for antiaircraft defense, most often blasting away from the decks of ships, targeting planes overhead or strategic buildings on land. General Moerdani's account of the "liberation" of Dili in 1975 includes a description of the deployment of special forces (*Kostrad*) on land, fortified from the sea by the navy *Marinir* brigades, blasting buildings in Dili from the harbor. On land, recoilless rifles are easily loaded onto the backs of military vehicles, with one soldier operating the gun off the back while the other drives.

21. Nicholas Thomas describes a similar process of appropriation in the Western Solomons during the nineteenth century, where the decoration of imported U.S. guns and hatchets with ornate shell inlay reveals, through physical modification, distinctive processes of assimilation. A highly embellished gun, for example, might no longer be prized by Western Solomon islanders for its functional capabilities alone but also for its commemorative potential, that is, as a symbol of their alliance with the U.S. Navy, made historically manifest through the biographical connection with a certain Captain David Porter. (See Thomas 1991, pp. 100, 101, 105–106.)

22. See Wolters [1982] 1999, pp. 65, 57.

23. For more in-depth discussions of origins of the Indonesian *Rāmāyaṇa*, see Holt 1967 and Fontein 1990.

24. Heffernan, 1993, p. 1. I would like to acknowledge my gratitude to Stanley J. O'Connor for suggesting this reference.

25. Ibid., pp. 1–8. Aside from Heffernan's invaluable discussion of ekphrasis, I have also relied on two other important sources: Becker 1995 and Scott, 1994.

26. It is only much later in Philostratus's *Imagines* in the second century and Callistratus's description of fourteen statues in the fourth century that ekphrasis narrows its focus to become a specialized genre devoted to objets d'art. For this essay, however, I choose to observe ekphrasis in its original trappings as describing functional objects, aesthetically pleasing, perhaps, but not viewed as Fine Art. Ekphrasis has the potential to resurface more significantly now in the wake of postmodernist critiques, particularly in the emerging field of visual studies, with its renewed focus on reception theory and the problems of representation.

27. Heffernan makes the following observations with regard to this gendered struggle in Western literature: "In the Aeneid," he writes, "the fixating power of the image that threatens the forward progress of the hero is decisively linked to *pulcherrima Dido*, queen of picture-perfect beauty and—like Cleopatra later—a threat to male

authority. In Keats' 'Ode to a Grecian Urn,' the figures sculpted on the womb-like urn that is called an unravished bride of quietness refuse to cooperate with a male narrative of desire and consummation. And in the Ovidian myth of Philomela, which begets a remarkable series of variations culminating in Shakespeare's *Rape of Lucrece*, a picture of rape woven by a mutilated woman unweaves the story told by a man." Philomela, whose tongue has been cut out, finds the power to speak through a woven textile, which allows her to "unweave the false story told by her male offender." The power of the woven designs allows her to break through the silence in which women are inextricably and traditionally bound. Heffernan 1993, pp. 1, 6.

28. Aditjondro 1994, pp. 21, 83.

29. See Sapiro 1993, p. 40. This remains a significant aspect of nationalist politics in the Balkans. Margaret Beissinger has remarked that "rape is (and has been throughout the ethnic conflicts in the former Yugoslavia) a powerful 'mode of warfare,' because it not only assaults its female victims' sense of self-respect, but it also shames and thus dishonors their husbands, fathers, brothers, and sons." See M. Beissinger, "Epic, Gender, and Nationalism: The Development of Nineteenth-Century Balkan Literature," in Beissinger, Tylus, and Wofford 1999, p. 78.

30. Rape has been used as a tool of intimidation and torture in E. Timor and in other areas in Indonesia where conflicts have arisen. Recently, Dr. Radhika Coomaraswamy, U.N. special rapporteur on violence against women, remarked that during the Suharto regime military personnel frequently raped women in East Timor, Aceh, and Irian Jaya. She also confirmed the mass rape of women from Jakarta's minority Chinese community during riots in May of 1998.

31. *The Australian*, November 6, 1999, "Despair as Families Face Dili Destruction" (from an AP correspondent in Dili). Consulted at www.theaustralian.news.com.

32. "Cover Story: Starting Over," by Terry McCarthy in *Time Asia*, March 20, 2000. Consulted at www.timeasia.com.

33. Maspero 1928, p. 155.

34. Mannikka 1994, p. 135.

35. Hamish McDonald, *Sydney Morning Herald*, April 4, 2002. Consulted at www.smh.com.au.

36. Putu's story can be compared to Mikhail Bakhtin's theory of narrative as an attempt to transform the relationship between performer and crowd in dialogic rituals so that spectators acquire the active role of participants in collective processes that are sometimes cathartic and that may symbolize or even create a community. Wijaya has remarked that short stories are like mental time bombs. Drawing upon traditional material as an impetus for addressing current issues and problems, Putu's stories are intended to make his readers think. However humorous or illogical, he provokes his readers to question values and common assumptions in their lives and in society. See Wijaya 1988.

37. Armstrong 2002.

38. *Sydney Morning Herald*, November 19, 1974. Also, see Taylor, 1991, p. 32.

39. Bhabha 1989, p. 115.

40. Gross 1989, p. 24.

REFERENCES

Aditjondro, George J. 1994. *In the Shadow of Mount Ramelau: The Impact of the Occupation of East Timor.* Leiden: INDOC.

———. 1999. "ABRI Inc." *Sydney Morning Herald*, August 5.

Armstrong, Charles. 2002. "Viewpoints." *AAS Newsletter,* 47. 1: 10–11.
Bakhtin, Mikhail Mikhailovich. 1981. *The Dialogical Imagination: Four Essays.* Edited and translated by Michael Holquist and Caryl Emerson. Austin: University of Texas Press.
Becker, Andrew S. 1995. *The Shield of Achilles and the Poetics of Ekphrasis.* London: Rowman and Littlefield.
Beissinger, M., J. Tylus, and S. Wofford. 1999. *Epic Traditions in the Contemporary World.* Berkeley and Los Angeles: University of California Press.
Bhabha, Homi K. 1989. "The Commitment to Theory." In *Questions of Third Cinema,* edited by Jim Pines and Paul Willemen. London: British Film Institute Publishing, pp. 111–132.
Fontein, J. ed. 1990. *The Sculpture of Indonesia.* Washington and New York: National Gallery of Art/Harry N. Abrams.
Geertz, Clifford. 1973. "Thick Description: Toward an Interpretive Theory of Culture." In Geertz, *The Interpretation of Cultures.* New York: Basic Books.
Gross, Kenneth. 1989. "Moving Statues, Talking Statues." *Raritan,* 9.2: 1–25.
Heffernan, James A. W. 1993. *Museum of Words: The Poetics of Ekphrasis from Homer to Ashbery.* Chicago: University of Chicago Press.
Hicks, David. 1976. *Tetum Ghosts and Kin.* Palo Alto: Mayfield.
Holt, Claire. 1967. *Art in Indonesia: Continuities and Change.* Ithaca: Cornell University Press.
Hoskins, Janet. 1998. *Biographical Objects: How Things Tell the Stories of People's Lives.* New York: Routledge.
Kopytoff, Igor. 1986. "The Cultural Biography of Things: Commoditization as Process." In *The Social Life of Things: Commodities in Cultural Perspective,* edited by Arjun Appadurai. Cambridge: Cambridge University Press, pp. 64–91.
Mannikka, Eleanor. 1994. "The Battle of Lanka at Angkor Wat: A Visual Metaphor." In *The Legend of Rama: Artistic Visions,* edited by Vidya Dehejia. Bombay: Marg Publications, p. 135.
Maspero, Georges. 1928. *Le royaume de Champa.* Paris: G. van Oest.
McGowan, Kaja M. 1995. "Balancing on Bamboo: Women in Balinese Art." *Asian Art and Culture* 8. 1: 75–95.
Ramseyer, Urs. 1977. *The Art and Culture of Bali.* New York: Oxford University Press.
Robson, O. 1980. "The *Rāmāyṇa* in Early Java." *Southeast Asian Review* 5.2:5–17.
Sapiro, V. 1993. "Engendering Cultural Differences." In *the Rising Tide of Cultural Pluralism,* edited by C. Young. Madison: University of Wisconsin Press.
Scott, Grant F. 1994. *The Sculpted Word: Keats, Ekphrasis, and the Visual Arts.* Hanover, N. H.: University Press of New England.
Taylor, John G. 1991. *Indonesia's Forgotten War: The Hidden History of East Timor.* London: Pluto Press.
Thomas, N. 1991. *Entangled Objects: Exchange, Material Culture, and Colonialism in the Pacific.* Cambridge: Harvard University Press.
Traube, Elizabeth. 1986. *Cosmology and Social Life: Ritual Exchange among the Mambai of East Timor.* Chicago: University of Chicago Press.
Walter, E. V. 1988. *Placeways: A Theory of the Human Environment.* Chapel Hill: University of North Carolina Press.
Waterson, Roxana. [1990] 1997. *The Living House: An Anthropology of Architecture in Southeast Asia.* Singapore and New York: Oxford University Press.
Welty, Eudora. 1957. *Place in Fiction.* New York: House of Books.

Wheatley, Paul. 1959. "Geographical Notes on Some Commodities Involved in Sung Maritime Trade." *Journal of the Malayan Branch of the Royal Asiatic Society* 32.

Wijaya, Putu. 1988. "If He Could Choose Again." In *Bomb: Indonesian Short Stories by Putu Wijaya,* edited by Ellen Rafferty and Laurie J. Sears. Madison: University of Wisconsin Center for Southeast Asian Studies, pp. 32–43.

Winichakul, Thongchai. 1997. "Viewpoints." *AAS Newsletter* (Summer).

Wolters, O. W. 1967. *Early Indonesian Commerce.* Ithaca: Cornell University Press.

———. [1982] 1999. *History, Culture, and Region in Southeast Asian Prespectives.* Ithaca: Cornell Southeast Asia Program Publications.

13

The *Rāmāyaṇa* in the Arts of Thailand and Cambodia

Julie B. Mehta

When traders from India began to bring their goods to Southeast Asia in the early sixth century C.E., the article of the most enduring value they brought was the *Rāmāyaṇa.* The ancient Champa, located in what is now southern Vietnam, had a temple dedicated to the sage Vālmīki, composer of the *Rāmāyaṇa*, with an inscription that mentions both the epic and the avatars or incarnations of Viṣṇu, of which Rāma was the seventh. Evidently, Khmer sculptors knew the epic as far back as the Sambor Prei Kuk period during the eighth century. Through a millennium and a half, the epic has come to be woven into the very fabric of life in the varied though related cultures of the region, despite political turmoil and wide-ranging social change. Especially in Thailand and Cambodia, countries that share both a history of serious dispute and a rich cultural heritage, the *Rāmāyaṇa* has provided much of the energy of artistic production, particularly in the visual and performing arts. As recently as 1998, the story was commemorated in a set of postage stamps depicting large Nang Yai figures.[1] Performances of the *Rāmākien* in Thailand and *Reamker* in Cambodia continue to precede religious practices conducted by resident brahman priests in Thailand and Cambodia. Episodes are also performed at ceremonies at the royal court and royal chapel.

The high points of Thai and Cambodian history show the Rāma theme running as a common thread. For example, the first Thai ruler to consolidate an absolute monarchy was the legendary Rāmāthibodhi I, the founder of Ayutthya (1351–1369), who set himself up in the style of the Khmer god-kings or *devarājas*. Not only did his name align him with Rāma, he deliberately sought to validate his rule by calling his capital city after Rāma's own capital. That this association was a successful political move is evident in that his reign is referred to as *Rāma rājya,* and that this mode of validation is still considered necessary is attested by the continued assumption of the name Rāma by modern Thai kings.

The links especially between Thai rulers and the *Rāmāyaṇa* are many. The scholarly interest that the Thai royal family has taken in the *Rāmāyaṇa* is one of the principal reasons why it has remained so much at the center of Thai public life. In the late 1700s the great King Rāma I (1782–1809) composed the *Rāmākien* as the quintessential Thai epic romance familiar to us. His descendants in the royal line, notably Prince Damrong Rajanubhav, Prince Kittiyakara Krommaphra Chandavurinarunath, and Prince Bidyalongkorn, carried on the patronage of *Rāmāyaṇa* scholarship. Thai royalty, culture, and society have always revered the great king Rāma as an integral part of their heritage. The legendary kings of the Chakri Dynasty were named after the epic hero, believed to be the seventh incarnation of Phra Narai or Phitsanu (Lord Viṣṇu). King Rāma I created the first local version of the *Rāmākien* with a distinctly Thai twist in 1807. At Wat Phra Keo, in Bangkok, scenes consisting of a complete series of illustrations from the Thai *Rāmākien* inspired by the text of King Rāma I, line the walls of the temple cloisters, with some of the first paintings dating back to the reign of King Rāma III (1824–1851). In modern times, King Rāma VI (1910–1925) traced the sources of the *Rāmākien* to the *Viṣṇu Purāṇa,* the *Hanumān Nāṭaka,* and a number of other ancient Sanskrit texts, some of them obscure. The tradition continues to this day. It was only a few years ago that Her Royal Highness, Princess Maha Chakri Sirinidhorn, brought out a translation and scholarly study of the lengthy Sanskrit inscription at Prasat Phanom Rung.

In Thailand, the legend of Rāma is so much a part of life that one encounters it on a daily basis. One may detect its presence even at unexpected places and on unexpected occasions, if one is aware of the deep-rooted presence of the Lord Phra Rām (Rāma) in the richly wrought tapestry of Thai life. In my first week in Bangkok I was pleasantly surprised to find certain food items named after the leading characters of the *Rāmāyaṇa. Phra ram long srong* is a curry concocted out of the leafy morning glory with a sprinkling of meat on top. Another dish is called *sida lue fai,* also known as *pak boong fai deng,* made with morning glory and other vegetables tossed into smoking hot oil, which causes a flare that is supposed to resemble the fire ordeal of Sītā.

The pervasiveness of the *Rāmāyaṇa* in Thailand and Cambodia is particularly interesting because it demonstrates the union of diversities on many levels, including the religious and political. The long history of conflict between the two peoples is also a history of social and cultural development, which can be traced back to the common Hindu heritage of ancient times. It is marked by the similarity of art forms, such as Thai classical dance and shadow theater, and the classical *khon* performance of Cambodia. Again, although both are Theravada Buddhist nations, they have a deep-rooted affinity for the Hindu pantheon, as we see in the simultaneous veneration of the Buddha side by side with Brahmā, Viṣṇu, Śiva, and Indra. The Hindu Buddhist syncretism presents an exceedingly complex, multitextured phenomenon that continues to be nurtured and passed on from generation to next generation of teacher and pupil. This culture of *guru-śiṣya paraṁparā* relates not only to religious life but also to cultural practice, as I have discovered in course of numerous visits to the Cambodian capital Phnom Penh and to Siem Reap. It has also been essential to the conservation and development of the *Rāmāyaṇa* tradition in the arts of these cultures.

Although the survival of the *Rāmāyaṇa* tradition has depended largely upon the ancient practice of oral transmission, the vigor of performance modes is not to be underestimated. The master musicians, choreographers, and dance teachers who survived the Khmer Rouge genocide in Cambodia continue to teach *Reamker* performances to small but dedicated bands of students, making Cambodia a particularly fruitful field for the study of the *Rāmāyaṇa* in its performance modes. More than any other parts of the transplanted Hindu culture, the story of Rāma seems to have captured the Thai and Khmer imagination. In Thailand and Cambodia, the performing and visual arts are often exclusively woven around the *Rāmākien* and *Reamker*. Performances range from the esoteric and highly complex *khon* mask-dance dramas and Khmer royal classical ballet in Cambodia to the widely attended and dexterous shadow puppetry of Nang Yai and Nang Talung throughout Thailand.

In terms of visual representation, the finest example in Thailand is the set of murals on the cloister walls of Wat Phra Keo, the Temple of the Emerald Buddha. The paintings were originally done in the reign of King Rāma III, but because of climatic conditions they have to be redone periodically. They present the key scenes of the *Rāmāyaṇa* in a linear fashion, and in their selectivity and organization we may see a directing principle in common with the *Rāmākien* as a dance narrative. A different kind of visual aesthetic exists in both Thailand and Cambodia in the form of fabric and furniture design drawn from the *Rāmāyaṇa*. Scenes from the epic are vividly portrayed on wood panels in gilt-on-lacquer work in emulation of models from the Rattanakosin or Bangkok period in Thailand, while less complicated but equally brilliant images are woven into the brocade for the sarong-like garments known as *pha sins* and *sampots* worn by *Rāmākien* and *Reamker* performers. In sculpture, we find the delicately wrought lintels of the Banteay Seri Śaivaite shrine, with their dramatic depiction of Rāvaṇa shaking Mount Kailasa. Cambodia boasts the vast temple complex at Angkor Vat, built by Suryavarman II, where the stone galleries and bas-reliefs show not only divinities in stylized postures but also battle scenes of monkey and demon armies carved in all their dramatic intensity of arrested motion.

Notwithstanding the construction of the *Rāmākien* and *Reamker* on the foundation of the *Rāmāyaṇa* narrative, it is necessary to note that these performance forms are expressions of their distinctive national origins. Historically, the *Rāmākien* and *Reamker* have evolved through so dynamic an exchange between imitation and invention that in order to understand these forms, their similarity with and departure from the Indian originals, must be noted.[2]

Two major points of deviation from the original *Rāmāyaṇa* plot draw our

FIGURE 13.1. Hanumān capturing Tosakanth's heart. Temple of the Emerald Buddha, Bangkok. Photo by Julie Mehta.

immediate attention. Although both Thai and Cambodian adaptations follow the broad outline of the narrative derived from India, they often deviate dramatically from it to produce considerable differences in detail that arise out of their particular worldviews. Not only are the names of the characters modified but also the dress, customs, way of life, and even the flora are given local flavors. At the same time, both Thai and Cambodian versions follow the general plot line centering on the descent of the Hindu preserver god of the universe, Lord Viṣṇu, to the human realm at a critical time in the history of the world, incarnate as Lord Rāma. His purpose is to rid the world of evil as symbolized by the arrogance and lust of the demon King Rāvaṇa, who forcefully abducts Rāma's wife Sītā. Rāvaṇa pays an enormous price for it, first with his kingdom, then with the death of his family and, finally, with his life. To this point the Thai versions follow the Indian. It is in the sufferings of Sītā that the *Rāmākien* and the *Reamker* differ vastly from the Indian *Rāmāyaṇas*.

The first major difference is seen in the order of Sītā's "murder" by Rāma, which calls for at least a quick look. The very idea that Rāma ordered Lakṣmaṇa to arrange the killing of his *sahadharminī* (partner sharing one's dharma equally) seems hardly credible in any version of the *Rāmāyaṇa* from India. The Rāma of India is not only unquestionably an avatar of Lord Visṇu, the preserver god, whose nature cannot tolerate the murder of an innocent person. Perhaps more important from a secular point of view, the Indian Rāma is known for his love for his wife. However, in the Thai and Khmer psyche, the image of Rāma appears to be somewhat different. Phra (Lord) Rāma is not quite the Lord as worshiped by Indians. No doubt he is revered and offered oblations

FIGURE 13.2. Rāma riding into battle on Hanumān's back holding his mighty bow. Angkor Vat. Photo by Julie Mehta.

and prayers, and occasionally commands his own shrine, but in a somewhat muted manner. The *Rāmākien* and *Reamker* are more about human desires, daily conflicts, jealousy, and marital tension, that is to say, the causes of human actions that make the hero of both the *Rāmākien* and the *Reamker* go to war, which is not understood as a divine mission. This difference is clearly reflected in the titles that the story has in its Thai and Khmer forms: *Rāmākien* means the memorable deeds of Rāma, and *Reamker* the glory of Rāma, the emphasis being on the human acts rather than the divine personhood of Rāma. True, like the Indian Rāma, Phra Rām represents all the kingly virtues imaginable; he is a courageous warrior, righteous prince, and faithful husband. Again, as in the Indian tradition, Phra Rām's brother Phra Lak acts as his shadow. But this does not stop them from acting quite differently at times. Exchanges between Rāma and Sītā are often distinctly rancorous, and Lord Śiva intervenes to admonish Rāma for his unjust treatment of his consort. Apart from being refreshing departures, such inventions considerably change the denouement and add a new spin to an old tale.

The second point of difference is the influence of the *śakti* cult or the veneration of Mahādevī, the great Goddess, and the Daśamahāvidyās, who are aspects of the Goddess. These conceptions are essential to the Indian pantheon and are specially powerful presences in the eastern *Rāmāyaṇas*. The idea of *śakti* seemed not to have been understood or adapted in either the Thai or Khmer milieu. Images of Mahiṣāsuramardinī do surface, as at Banteay Seri, but are very rare. Because of the absence of the *śakti* cult, Sītā is perceived more as an ideal wife with the necessary virtue of faithfulness and patience and complete obedience to her husband than as a powerful goddess who is a manifestation of Mahādevī and hence cannot be annihilated.

Perhaps less profound but certainly not less striking a departure from Sanskrit and other Indian *Rāmāyaṇa*s is the portrayal of Hanumān, the monkey warrior who is revered in India, particularly in north India, as a god. His reputation there is as a fearsome warrior whose prowess is closely associated with his celibacy. But to Thai and Cambodian audiences he appears quite different. At the touch of the Thai scribe's brush he becomes a Casanova of the east, seducing women every minute. In the Khmer version, he is portrayed as a monkey, literally, with an embarrassing itch that might amaze an Indian audience that sees Hanumān as nothing less than a god, as Saṅkaṭamocan, the remover of obstacle and danger. In both Thai and Cambodian versions he acts as a foil to the high-mindedness of Rāma while retaining his chief distinction as Rāma's devoted servant. He is loyal and brave and always full of good ideas about solving problems. But he is also associated with magic and has much of it at his command. He also lightens the story's mood. Even when he is engaged in battles and business on Phra Rām's behalf, his playful monkey nature shows through, and he is always ready to woo a beautiful lady of almost any ancestry, and he rarely fails. Even after singeing Benjakai, his advances are not spurned, and the fishy Princess Suppanamacha, despite being thwarted when Hanumān stops her bridge-destruction efforts, succumbs to his charms. The Thai or Cambodian Hanumān is certainly not the chaste and proper monkey that one meets in India or Indonesia.

Despite these differences, the two major elements of the original narrative, the heroic resolve of Rāma and the sufferings of Sītā, continue to capture the mind of the people. Rāma's greatness—physical, moral, and spiritual—makes him the ideal man and the model ruler. Dynasties have been named after him, shrines have been built for him, roads have been inaugurated in his honor, and battles have been waged in his name all through the region. In fact the very idea of kingship in Thailand was founded on the idealized Rāma. Though primarily Buddhist, countries like Thailand and Cambodia have been led by individuals who have worn the mantle of Rāma with pride, weaving the god-king's legend smoothly into their cultural fabric. These countries were already familiar with the worship of the Hindu gods Śiva or Viṣṇu as *devarāja* (king of gods) as far back as the early year of Angkorean splendor during the reign of Khmer king Jayavarman II. This familiarity is sometimes expressed in unexpected intersections of Hindu and Buddhist practices. A striking example occurs in the Silver Pagoda in the Royal Palace in Phnom Penh. At the foot of the altar stands a gold statue of Buddha, studded with diamonds. To the unknowing visitor, it looks like any of the many statues of the Buddha, though perhaps costlier. But its history lends it a distinct ambivalence. It was made from the melted jewelry of King Norodom, and its measurements are exactly the same as that of the deceased ruler; this relates it to the statues of Viṣṇu (or Rāma) or Śivaliṅgas in the ancient temples of Angkor. Here, then, we have an icon that is Buddhist in form but resonant with Hindu associations. Similarly, in the currency of the *Rāmāyaṇa* we see the meeting of traditions—religious, social, and literary.

Whether in the visual or the performing arts, the story is rendered in typical Thai style, using established conventions of colors and attributes that denote specific characters. Thus, the *Rāmākien* is presented through an artistic code that the audience readily recognizes. The Cambodian *Reamker* similarly follows a recognizable code. Hanumān is always the white monkey, Sugrīva red, Laksṃaṇa golden white, and Sītā white. Rāma appears in green, mostly in a special mask and with his bow, while Rāvaṇa always appears in black.

In the performing arts arena, the Nang shadow play with *Rāmākien* characters as cutout buffalo-hide figures held high on two sticks and held against a lighted screen as a silhouette originated in India and found its way through Java to Thailand. The first recorded mention of this Nang style appears in the Palatine Law by King Borom Trailokanath of Ayutthaya in 1458. Samples of the Nang Yai figures can still be seen at the National Museum of Bangkok dating from the era of King Rāma II (1809–1824). Like shadow theater, *khon* consists of episodes from the *Rāmākien*, and all the characters of the *khon* dances don opulent costumes glittering with gold braid and sequins and jewels (Fig. 13.3 & Fig. 13.4). Glitter likewise characterizes the papier maché masks that denote particular characters by brilliantly painted expressions. Phra Rām in the Thai version of the *Rāmākien* is colored green, and this is because he is a reincarnation of the god Phra Narai. His brother Lakṣmaṇa is indicated by the color gold, and their monkey companion Hanumān is always in white, so the association between character and appearance is firmly entrenched in the mind of the average Thai spectator at a *Rāmākien* performance.

In Cambodia we find a similar pervasiveness of the *Rāmāyaṇa*, known in Khmer as *Reamker*, that is, the Glory of Rāma. Like the Thai *Rāmākien*, the *Reamker* differs both in narrative detail and in conceptual orientation from the *Rāmāyaṇa*, but remains true to its essential plot line. The *Reamker* is composed of three parts and an epilogue, as compared to the seven books of the Indian original, and instead of emphasizing the hero's divine mission, it plays upon the *ker* or glory of Rāma, or Preah Ream, as the Khmers know him. His wife is Neang Seta (Sītā) and his brother is Preah Lak (Laksṃaṇa). They fight the demon Rab (Rāvaṇa) with the help of the monkey Hanumān and win back Neang Seta. They are substantially more humanized than their Indian coun-

FIGURE 13.3. Sītā and Hanumān in a *khon* mask performance. Photo by Julie Mehta.

terparts, and their stories illustrate human problems and desires, especially the personal relationship between Preah Ram and Neang Seta, rather than some divine plan for saving the world.

Of the many arts of Cambodia that have flourished around this saga, dance and dance drama have perhaps the most enduring presence. The roots of Cambodian dance are believed to lie in ancient indigenous ritual, such as funerary ceremonies or rites connected with ancestor worship within the framework of an animistic religion. Cambodian scholar and former minister of culture Nouth Narang says, "the Cambodian version of the *Rāmāyaṇa* dance drama and all other Khmer dances are based on the movement of the *nāga*, the snake, because we believe that our grandparents are the *nāga* king's stock. So our dance follows the movements of the *nāga* or snake, which are graceful loops or spirals. It is very important to remember this because whether it is the Apsarā dance, the dance by the heavenly court dancers, or the dances depicting scenes from the Indian epic, the *Rāmāyaṇa,* the movements are basically of the loops and spirals that embody the movement of the snake."[3] Cambodian scholars trace the snake king legend to Kambu, a legendary ancestor of the Cambodian people from Āryadeśa in ancient India. In this legend, Kambu Svayambhuva, a king from Āryadeśa, on his wanderings found himself in a grotto in the arid Cambodian wilderness, where he met a *nāga* or snake king. The *nāga* king invited him to stay in the land and offered his daughter's hand in marriage. Kambu accepted, and the *nāga* king used his magic powers to turn the desert land into a lush and fertile paradise. Kambu ruled over the kingdom, which came to be called Kambuja or modern-day Cambodia.

FIGURE 13.4. A masked *khon* performance of the four-hour-long Thai *Rāmākien*. Temple of the Emerald Buddha, Bangkok. Photo by Julie Mehta.

The animistic belief system and its artistic forms predate the emergence of Funan (100–500 C.E.), the first Indianized kingdom in the present area of Cambodia, which signals a decisive turn toward the Indian material that began to appear. Early documentary sources clearly indicate strong Indian influences. One such source is a sixth-century inscription describing arrangements for the daily recitation of holy texts of Indian origin, such as the *Rāmāyaṇa*, the *Mahābhārata*, and the Purāṇas. They were adopted from India along with the Sanskrit language and brahmanical Hinduism in its Śaivaite form, with Lord Śiva as its central deity. Later, the Hindu god Viṣṇu took precedence, as Angkor Vat shows. But although the dance was introduced by Indian traders, it flowered as a courtly art only after the Khmer god-kings retained temple dancers as a part of royal ritual. Numerous records from the sixth century onward mention dances performed within temple precincts as offerings by female dancers, who were donated or belonged to the temple as "slaves of the gods."

There is an obvious similarity here with the Indian custom of *devadāsīs* that began in the early medieval period and continued until the twentieth century, which again suggests the influence of India.[4]

In the days of the Angkor empire, dance was a holy offering made to the Hindu deities each night, especially during the full moon. Inscriptions from the tenth-century temple of Banteay Seri, the citadel of women, mention rituals that included offerings by temple dancers to the gods. Royal patronage was crucial in creating these conditions. When Jayavarman II acceded to the throne, he made Khmer dance an integral part of the royal Cambodian milieu. Later, with the fall of Angkor to the Thai army in 1431, Thai artistic practice began to shape Khmer art form. Legend has it that when the traditional Khmer dance was first performed at the Thai court by captive, bare-breasted Khmer dancers, the Thais were horrified and gave strict orders to "clothe" the innocent Khmers.

Khmer dance reached its peak during the "golden age of Cambodian history" from the ninth to the fourteenth centuries, and played a prominent role in Khmer society. The dance tradition developed around the *Reamker*, which was linked to the royal court where the king dwelt, surrounded by female dancers, and also to the temples where large female corps de ballet were responsible for ceremonial dance offerings. For instance, over three thousand dancers are known to have been installed in the main state temples in the reign of Jayavarman VII who, though himself a Buddhist, allowed the *Reamker* to be performed at his court. The court dance, supported by an elaborate *pinpeat*, or orchestra, incorporated tales from the *Reamker*, which the common folk used to come to watch on special festive occasions. Thereby the *Reamker* gained a permanent place in Khmer culture, both aristocratic and popular, in much the same way that the *Rāmākien* did in Thailand.

The *Reamker* dance tradition is a vastly complex social undertaking, each of its constituent practices having developed as an art in itself. Costumes, for example, are of immense importance, and the dancer waits patiently for up to two hours while her costume is literally "stitched on" to her body by a couturier. A variety of belts and motifs are manufactured by silversmiths, as are the rich *sampots* or skirts woven out of gold and silver thread. *Reamker* characters often wear elaborately ornamented headdresses, whose motifs are reminiscent of the patterns of architecture decoration, as we may see in the threefold arrangement of the ornaments and the pyramidlike forms on the crown.

The Cambodian dance tradition gained such vigor that it survived through centuries of struggle for national survival, and that vigor may be attributed to the appeal of its narrative base, the *Rāmāyaṇa*. The Royal Cambodian Ballet, known as Lakhon Lueng, or the King's Dancers, were supported by the royal household till 1970 and staged spectacular shows of the *Reamker* (Fig. 13.5). The gravest threat to the *Reamker* performance occurred in modern times, during the Pol Pot regime in the 1970s. Along with the monarchy, the Royal Ballet dance was abolished. The dancers were lured or forced into private troupes and other professions. Most ancient costumes and jewelry housed in the royal palace were destroyed. In recent years, however, the Royal Khmer Ballet has experienced a spirited revival through the unflagging enthusiasm of

FIGURE 13.5. Kuśa fights in the Khmer Lakhon Leung court dance. Photo by Julie Mehta.

a handful of committed artists, such as the choreographer Proeung Chheng, the famous teacher Madam Em Theay—now in her seventies—and Princess Buppha Devi. Their goal of opening the classical performance form to mass audiences has led to the creation of hybrid forms by combining the traditional Thai style of movements with poses, costume, and jewelry copied from ancient Khmer bas-reliefs. Revival has been made difficult by the loss of much of the written notations of classical Khmer dance as far back as the fifteenth and sixteenth centuries during Siamese and Vietnamese invasions, and more extensively in the 1970s. That present initiatives are gaining success owes more than a little to the appeal of the *Rāmāyaṇa* story that has been so intrinsic a part of the Cambodian national psyche.

On looking at the arts of Thailand and Cambodia, one is struck by the pervasiveness, durability, and vitality of the *Rāmāyaṇa* theme. Introduced into these domains almost two thousand years ago, the story and the character archetypes it has engendered continue to command both scholarly interest and the entertainment market, and to influence the ethical and political belief systems of these cultures.

NOTES

1. Nang Yais are large leather figures of the characters from the *Rāmāyaṇa*.

2. The Indian originals I have in mind are the *Rāmāyaṇas* of Vālmīki and Tulsīdās, as well as eastern *Rāmāyaṇas*.

3. Private communication to the author.

4. Bose 2001, pp. 111, 113; Orr 2000.

REFERENCES

Bose, Mandakranta. 2001. *Speaking of Dance: The Indian Critique*. New Delhi: D. K. Printworld.

Mehta, Julie. 2001. *Dance of Life*. Singapore: Graham Brash.

Orr, Leslie. 2000. "Women's Wealth and Worship." In *Faces of the Feminine in Ancient, Medieval and Modern India*, edited by Mandakranta Bose. New York: Oxford University Press.

14

The *Rāmāyaṇa* Theme in the Visual Arts of South and Southeast Asia

Kapila Vatsyayan

To speak about any perennial theme and its permeation, percolation, diffusion, and transformation would be like an attempt to measure the tidal oceanic waters of the Pacific and Atlantic. Both the tides and the waters change and yet they remain the body of the ocean. This phenomenon of a constant movement within and change from without is perhaps nowhere as evident as in the case of the *Rāmāyaṇa* theme spatially and temporally. Whenever the kernel of the theme originated, from the first moment to this day, the theme has captivated the mind and imagination of people across a vast geographical area extending from West Asia to Southeast Asia and East Asia. To capture that kernel and trace its transformations through time and space, it is necessary to bring within a unified scholarly view the entirety of the representational modes, all the artistic and literary genres in which the *Rāmāyaṇa* continues to flourish. Although such an effort is clearly not within the capacity of an attempt such as the present one, this essay will attempt to present an overview of available material and identify some of the aesthetic principles on which they may be approached.

In a short monograph written some decades ago, published ironically in Iran and now totally out of print, I made an attempt to identify the principal sites of monuments and list sculptural reliefs and miniature sets. This was a bare draft outline presenting a rough mapping. This data was then collated with the "textual" and known verbal oral versions in different regions, as also the inscriptional evidence. A similar exercise was done with respect to the history of the performance of the *Rāmāyaṇa* theme from primary and secondary sources. Finally, there was an overview of contemporary performance, theater, dance drama, ballad, solo narration, puppet masks, and much else. Even from this preliminary survey, the interpenetration and mutual dependence of the verbal, visual, and kinetic arts could be realized, leading to a clear sense of the interrelationship among regions and artistic genres and styles. It was also obvious that as in the eternal ocean, here too we could see constant movement and change. The processes of interpretation, reversal, and even wholesale metamorphoses of themes, characters, episodes, and values were evident, and yet each version was nevertheless the *Rāmāyaṇa,* unique and perennial. Here is a dynamic relationship between what we might call the core and its offshoots that I find particularly worth studying.

Before we go on to that relationship, it will be useful to take brief stock of the development of the textual narrative and the inscriptional and sculptural material from the period when the *Rāmāyaṇa* began to spread across cultural boundaries. Without pausing to address the knotty question of the presence of the Rāma theme in the *Ṛg Veda* or to mention the appearance of King Janaka in the *Taittirīya Brāhmaṇa* and of Sītā in the *Kṛṣṇa Yajurveda,* we may start by acknowledging that Vālmīki's *Rāmāyaṇa* is indeed the *ādikāvya,* the fountainhead of the countless versions of the *Rāmāyaṇa.* Although there is yet no consensus on the dating of the *Vālmīki Rāmāyaṇa,* or even on whether the *Mahābhārata* preceded or succeeded it, it would not be incorrect to place the work in the pre-Buddha and Mahāvīra period and roughly between the sixth to fifth centuries B.C.E. It is also obvious that one should not be overexercised over the historicity of Rāma. The power of the theme lay, as it does today, in its potential to energize and elevate the self-reflection of communities coalescing around a heroic archetype to create a mythical contest of good and evil. It is also obvious that changes could be possible only because of the inherent potential for interpretation and remodeling, in short, because of its fluidity.

The post-Vālmīki period shows that the theme was just as popular in later literature, in Pali, Prakrit, and Sanskrit. This is evident from the *Jātakas*, particularly the *Daśaratha Jātaka* and the Jain *Rāmāyaṇa* (*Paumacariyam*) of Vimala Sūri (third century C.E.), and from the works of Bhāsa, Kālidāsa, Bhavabhūti, and numerous other Sanskrit poets and dramatists. From the internal evidence of the *Uttararāmacarita* of Bhavabhūti, it is clear that the painted versions of the *Rāmāyaṇa* were almost contemporaneous with the composition of the literary version.

From the second century onward, there is a fair amount of inscriptional evidence that testifies to the deep respect for Vālmīki and his *Rāmāyaṇa.* The Girnar inscription from Gujarat (about 130 C.E.) of Mahākṣatrapa Rudradaman acknowledges his indebtedness to Vālmīki,[1] and so also does its near contemporary, the inscription of Balasiri in the Nasik cave. Of a later period, the inscription on the rock of Girnar from 457 C.E. also echoes lines from the *Rāmāyaṇa,* as does an important inscription from Champa from the same period.

These textual outcroppings of the *Rāmāyaṇa* are important not only as verbal representations, brief though they are, but equally as visual signs in their materiality. In looking at inscriptions one is also looking at pictorial and

FIGURE 14.1. Rāma, Sītā, and Lakṣmaṇa. Viṭṭhala temple, Hampi (old Vijayanagar). Photo by Michael Dowad.

sculptural embodiments. Sculpture is, of course, one of the richest media through which the *Rāmāyaṇa* has been propagated. The earliest sculptural evidence of the Rāma theme can be traced to the depiction of the *Daśaratha Jātaka* in the reliefs of Bharhut, dating from the second century B.C.E. There are two beautiful medallions in Bharhut, a short time later to be emulated by those in Nagarjunakonda. A similar depiction of the *Daśaratha Jātaka* is seen in Sanchi (first century B.C.E.–first century C.E.). But the most important and sustained visual narrative occurs for the first time during the Gupta period in the Viṣṇu temple in Deogarh, constructed in 425 C.E., and at Nachna. Although both sites are virtually ruins, the fragments are impressive and important. The Deogarh panels depicting the salvation of Ahalyā by Rāma is a magnificent example, as is the dramatic scene of Lakṣmaṇa cutting off Śūrpanakhā's nose. If one is tender and gentle, the other is full of dramatic power. In limited space, the artist compresses a tumultuous drama of the advent of Śūrpanakhā and her confrontation with Lakṣmaṇa. In another panel, Rāma, Sītā, and Lakṣmaṇa proceed to the Daṇḍaka forest. In yet another, royal visitors enter the hermitage of Atri and his wife Anasūyā. Yet another dramatic fragment depicts the death of Vāli on the lap of Tārā.

In Nachna there are reliefs of Rāvaṇa begging alms from Sītā, Lakṣmaṇa putting his hand on his ears when Sītā rebukes him, Rāma hesitating to shoot heroic Vāli when both Vāli and Sugrīva look alike to him, and the adoration of Rāma by Vāli, Sugrīva, and Hanumān. Other Gupta sites have yielded similar narratives on carved panels, such as a striking scene of the building of the bridge of rocks to Laṅkā (now in the collections of the Bharat Kala Bhavan). There is a beautiful panel of Sītā in the Aśoka grove in the National Museum of India, and the famous panels from Nachna. Particularly memorable is an amusing panel on terra-cotta, in the National Museum, in which Rāvaṇa is shown with a donkey's head. One of the notable aspects of these panels from the Deogarh temple, consecrated to Viṣṇu as Śeṣaśāyī, is that whereas in many of them Viṣṇu is depicted as a god appearing as Nara-Nārāyaṇa, in the panels where he appears as Rāma he is treated as a human being, two-armed and participating in ordinary human activities. In these panels Rāma does not appear as a cult image, nor does he have a divine aura, as one might expect of an incarnation of Viṣṇu. Although by the fifth century the story of Rāma has obviously reached legendary status, his cult images are largely a medieval phenomenon, which suggests that his deification is yet to come.

The monuments erected by another early dynasty, the Western and Eastern Chalukyas (fifth to eighth centuries) reverberate with the echoes of the *Rāmāyaṇa.* Already a change takes place. Kings subsume themselves and their royalty under the character, mythical or historical, of Rāma. The textual renarration of the story of Rāma moves concurrently on the planes of the primal myth and contemporary history. Royalty begins to identify itself with Rāma the character, and the wars of conquest are legitimized as the fight of good over evil. The inscriptions emulate Vālmikī's verses and the reliefs attempt to contain the dual identity of Rāma and the king. In a famous inscription of Pulakeśī, a Western Chalukyan king, at Aihole, there is the graphic description of the battle:

> *jalanidhi iva vyoma vyoṁnah samo bhaved aṁbudhi*
>
> the sky resembled the ocean and the ocean the sky,[2]

which is an unambiguous echo of Vālmīki's verse:

> *gaganaṁ gaganakāra sāgaraḥ sāgaropamaḥ rāmarāvaṇeyor yuddhaṁ rāmaorāvaṇayoriva*
>
> the sky resembled the ocean and the ocean the sky as the battle between Rāma and Rāvaṇa[3]

Pulakeśī, we know, considered himself an upholder of the moral order. Pampā and other poets of Kannada eulogized him. The sons of Pulakeśī, the Western and Eastern Chalukyans, identified themselves with Rāma. Consequently, the temples of Dūrgā, Pāpanātha, and Virupākṣa are crowded with scene after scene from the *Rāmāyaṇa.* Some episodes follow Vālmīki, others not. The visit of Tāṭakā to Visvāmitra's *ashram,* the journey to Daṇḍaka, the abduction of Sītā, the fight with Jaṭāyu, the fight between Vāli and Sugrīva, Rāma piercing a tree to aim an arrow at Vāli, Tārā's mourning, and the final battle, as also the first coronation of Rāma (which does not feature in earlier sculptures) are popular. There is the magnificent sculpture of Rāvaṇa shaking Kailasa. These themes are repeated with slight modifications in the different temples mentioned above. Although some studies have been undertaken of

FIGURE 14.2. Rāma, Lakṣmaṇa, and Sage Viśvāmitra, and the liberation of Ahalyā. Hazara Rāma temple, Hampi (old Vijaynagar). Photo by Michael Dowad.

these panels, a fuller and more detailed work on these panels and their literary base would be welcome.

Like the Western and Eastern Chalukyans, the neighboring Pallavas and later the Cholas also extolled Rāma but often fought one another in the name of Rāma, each claiming his authority. Narasiṁharāman, the Pallava king, uses epithets in his inscription picked from Vālmīki's *Rāmāyaṇa,* appropriating all the qualities attributed to Rāma.[4] Again, in the early-eighth-century Kailāsanātha temple at Kanchipuram erected by the Pallavas, there are panels depicting scenes from the *Rāmāyaṇa.*

A particularly impressive batch of illustrations of themes from the *Rāmāyaṇa* appears in the grand edifice of the Kailasa temple in Ellora Cave XVI. This late-eighth-century temple, carved from a single rock in the reign of the Rastrakuta Dynasty, replicates a natural mountain, which the visitor metaphorically circumambulates through its double quadrangles. While Gaṅgā and Yamunā guard the entrance, riding the crocodile and tortoise, respectively, and the *devī* sits on the lotus, on the walls are the flying *gandharvas* in breathtaking pulsating movements. In the niches, Śiva dances dynamically, to be juxtaposed with the immutable stateliness of the lingam in the *garbhagṛha.* And on this monumental mountain is played out in sculptural relief the story of the *Rāmāyaṇa,* panel by panel, on one side, and that of the *Mahābhārata* on the other. It is to be noted that at many sites initiated by the Rastrakutas, the *Rāmāyaṇa* panels appear in both Śiva and Viṣṇu temples. A clear distinction has to be made between Rāma conceived only as an incarnation of Viṣṇu, as in the Daśāvatara, and the subsequent expansion of his representation as the divine

FIGURE 14.3. Rāma, killing the golden deer Mārīca. Viṭṭhala temple, Hampi (old Vijaynagar). Photo by Michael Dowad.

hero of the *Rāmāyaṇa*. In Ellora, the panels are sequential, with the episodes selected carefully. There is no rescue of Ahalayā, no visit to Atri's ashram, but there is the depiction of Rāma and Sīta in Viśvāmitra's ashram and the journey to the Daṇḍaka forest. Most dramatic and dynamic among these, not as low bas-relief but as sculpture almost in the round, jutting out from the walls, is the episode of Rāvaṇa's abduction of Sītā and the fight with the mythical bird Jaṭāyu. The artist's skill in collapsing the tumultuous moment of abduction, of seating Sītā in the chariot, and the subsequent fight with Jaṭāyu, is remarkable for its comprehension of the theme and ability to translate it into stone with powerful intensity.

Another sculpture captures the previous life of Rāvaṇa. We are reminded that Rāvaṇa was a devotee of Śiva. He had once cut off his heads and had offered them to Maheśvara. The relief portrays this powerfully—reminding the visitor of Rāvaṇa's life of penance, which was the source of his power. Drawn

FIGURE 14.4. Rāvaṇa, lifting Mount Kailasa with Śiva and Pārvatī. Virūpākṣa temple, Pattadakal. Photo by Michael Dowad.

from purāṇic sources is the other story of Rāvaṇa's attempt at a forced entry into Kailasa, where Śiva and Pārvatī are engaged in playing dice. Kuvera tries to stop Rāvaṇa and forbids him to disturb the couple. Rāvaṇa does not listen; forbidden from entry, he shakes the mountain with all his might—though Śiva and Pārvatī are unruffled. A mighty sculptural relief relives the cosmic drama. Through the techniques of enlarging and foreshortening, of deep and shallow incisions, the major and minor characters are brought alive. It is noteworthy that in the earlier depictions of Rāvaṇa, his previous life of penance and his devotion to Śiva are given importance. In this depiction, he is not the stock villain presented in the black hue of later times. Also from the eighth century, and one of the most extensive depictions of the saga in sculpture, are the diminutive panels on the *Rāmāyaṇa* at the Nāgeśvara temple in Kumbhakonam. The set of panels begins with the sacrifice by Daśaratha for a son and proceeds panel by panel to the last battle.

Even so cursory an overview as the above shows how solid yet varied is the tradition that has developed over the centuries around the core narrative of Rāma in literature and the arts. The same dynamic of a central theme continually refashioned through many retellings characterizes the *Rāmāyaṇa* elsewhere in Asia, although the situation there is more complex insofar as the dynamic includes as well the relationship between India, the country of origin, and other Asian cultures that drew upon that fountainhead. The interplay between a cultural constant and its variants becomes in itself a perennial experience located in the *Rāmāyaṇa*.

It was toward the end of the first millennium that the *Rāmāyaṇa* began its journey across the waters to Southeast Asia. In Cambodia, Indonesia, and Thailand the Indian epic took deep root. The depiction of the saga at Angkor Vat and Banteay Seri show its travels across regions, as does the fact that the Khmer and Thai *Rāmāyaṇas* (the *Rāmākien*) are related. The *Rāmāyaṇa* reliefs at Prambanan and Panataran in Java, created during the rule of the Majapahit Dynasty, rely heavily on the *Kakawin Rāmāyaṇa*. The *Kakawin* itself is related to *Bhaṭṭi Kāvya* and even the *Hanumān Nāṭaka* and the *Bhuśuṇḍi Rāmāyaṇa*, although there are significant departures. In 1925, Willem Stutterheim made a full and comprehensive study of the Indonesian monument and its reliefs. Soewito Santoso has dealt at some length with the text of the *Kakawin*. The Malaysian *Hikyat Seri Rāmāyaṇa* is distinct but has affinity with the Indonesian *Rāmāyaṇa*. The work of the late H. B. Sarkar and the more recent work of Ameen Sweeny and Mohammed Yosuf from Malaysia are relevant for a comparative study of the texts, the visual narration in reliefs, and the treatment of the narrative in *Wayang Kulit*. A further comparison with the contemporary reliefs in the temples of Kumbhakonam in Tamilnadu shows how the artists of Indonesia (Lara Jongreng-Prambanan) and those of India differed in their selection of themes and episodes. Whereas the early history of Rāma fascinates the Indian artist, the Indonesians focus on the episodes relating to the Demon Crow and elaborate on the episode relating to the Demon King Kabandha. The latter episode is altogether omitted by the Indian artist.

Such differences in choice and emphasis are common. Although the monuments of East Java at Panataran and the Hāzāra Rāma temple at Hampi (Vijayanagar) are almost contemporary (13th to 14th centuries C.E.), they reveal the different character of the traditions in the two countries. Although the East Javanese monument selects incidents that are reminiscent of the *Kakawin Rāmāyaṇa*, the formal treatment is altogether different, for the Panataran reliefs are inspired by *Wayang* and its particular aesthetic. In contrast, the reliefs that depict the enactment of the Rāma story on the throne platform at Hampi are based on the royal spectacle of the enactment of the Rāma story in Karnataka. A shift of emphasis characterizes the recreation of the *Rāmāyaṇa* by the Khmer kings of Cambodia. The grand temples of Angkor, especially Prasant Au, and those at Banteay Seri and Baphoun (eleventh to thirteenth centuries C.E.) are crowded with reliefs in which battles and combats dominate. In a most impressive scene at Baphoun there is the famous, much reproduced, scene of the battle of Rāvaṇa and Hanumān spread over four panels. In the first there is

FIGURE 14.5. Rāma killing Tāṭakā. Hazara Rāma temple, Hampi (old Vijayanagar). Photo by Michael Dowad.

Rāvaṇa with his ten heads and twenty arms riding a chariot; in the next, Hanumān grapples with the horse; in the third, Hanumān is on top of the horse; and in the fourth, Rāma is seen victorious, riding a horse.

After the thirteenth century, the Rāma theme dispersed even more extensively over all parts of Asia. Highly detailed depictions in reliefs were carried out at the Wat Po and Emerald Buddha temples in Thailand, followed by a still later series of panels in Burma. The murals from Cambodia and Thailand are cognate with those found in the temples of Kerala and in Tamilnadu in the Naik period. The numerous Kerala murals based on the *Rāmāyaṇa* encapsulate local versions of the epic and are closely related with the performance traditions (*Rāmanāṭṭam*) of Kerala.[5]

From the fifteenth century onward, the *Rāmāyaṇa* began to attract artistic work in an altogether new form, that of miniature painting, which often appears as part of manuscript versions of the *Rāmāyaṇa*. There are several sets of miniature paintings, both on palm leaf and paper in India, Indonesia, and Thailand. Outstanding among these is the Mughal *Rāmāyaṇa* in Persian, fully illustrated, commissioned by Akbar, in which the 156 paintings are remarkable for their artistic skill and grandeur.[6]

Among the products of the popular Mughal school, two other sets of *Rāmāyaṇas* are important for their textual base and also as indicators of the fusion of the Mughal and Rajasthani styles. In the seventeenth and early eighteenth centuries appear many fully illustrated *Rāmāyaṇas* in the diverse schools of Rajasthan, such as Mewari and Kotah. One of these is by the famous Sahibadin,

FIGURE 14.6. Hanumān. Temple of the Emerald Buddha, Bangkok. Photo by Tirthankar Bose.

the great artist who painted both the *Rāmāyaṇa* and the *Gīta Govinda* (1651 C.E.). The paintings are remarkable examples of the transformation of the verbal (not just episodic, but also metaphorical) text into pictorial image. The Devanagari text is by Hiranand, which follows the Vālmīki *Rāmāyaṇa* more closely than the Tulsīdās *Rāmāyaṇa*. Other sets appear in the late seventeenth and early eighteenth centuries in Madhya Pradesh (Malwa), to be followed by two splendid sets from Basohli and Kulu and one from Kangra. In addition, there is an illustrated Tulsī *Rāmāyaṇa* in the collections of the Maharaja of Banaras belonging to the nineteenth century. In the east, the tradition continued in Assam, Orissa, and Bengal. By the twentieth century, scroll painting and *paṭa* took over. Contemporary history penetrated into the paintings, and the visual discourse continued on multiple planes of mythical, historical, and contemporary experience.

Brief as it is, the survey offered here indicates the perennial fascination of the *Rāmāyaṇa* over vast areas. In the course of its travels it invited countless

FIGURE 14.7. An eighteenth-century gold leaf on lacquer painting from Ayutthya depicts Śatrughna's fall from the serpent's clutches as Garuḍa wins his battle. Photo by Julie Mehta.

attempts to re-interpret, refashion, even remake its themes, characters, and ethical contents. Yet through its sometimes radical variations the *Rāmāyaṇa* retained its distinct identity and indeed its integrity as a narrative. How may one account for the constant reappearance of the story in its main plot line and with the major episodes generally intact in so many versions? How, for that matter, did so many versions come to be written in different parts of India, Thailand, Burma, and elsewhere from early eighteenth century onward, even in the absence of an authoritative source text? In my view, we have to turn to the oral tradition for an answer. The widespread popularity of *Rāmāyaṇa* themes in the visual, plastic, and performing arts suggests the conservation of the story in the oral traditions of South and Southeast Asia, ready to be drawn upon. When some political or social need impelled kings and their officials to turn to the *Rāmāyaṇa* as a storehouse of didactic or political wisdom, it had to be anchored down to the written word, copied, and disseminated.

Thus, whether as a written text or a visual or performed one, the *Rāmāyaṇa* continues to command our attention. As a cultural theme in Asia it finds artistic expression on a number of levels:

1. On the level of ritualistic and institutionalized religion, it exists in the form of a highly sanctified ritual where Rāma is considered an incarnation of god and is worshiped.
2. It is found in the life cycle of the agricultural calendar of many socie-

ties in this region, from India to Indonesia, and from Nepal to Sri Lanka, where a particular time of the year is associated with the birth of Rāma. The forms of the commemoration of the story of the birth and death of this hero vary. It may be in the form of the Navarātra, as in Gujarat and in Nepal; or it may be in the form of the worship of Lakṣmī, seen as the goddess form of Sītā; or in the form of a plain narration of the episode of the hero's life; or as tableaux, as in the Dussehra festival popular in different regions of India, particularly Kulu, Varanasi, and Mysore. Narration through pageantry and festival is also known in other parts of Asia, as in the cart-play tradition or the *Nibhatkhin* tradition of Burma that has influenced the Thai *Rāmākien* tradition. The mobile theater or the theater with a moving locale is almost confined to the Rāma theme in other countries.

3. The *Rāmāyaṇa* also appears in plain ballad singing or recitation at all levels of public life, the most unsophisticated as well as the most sophisticated. The *cāraṇas*, as they are known, are minstrels who move from one part to another and gather around themselves audiences who hear in rapture the story of Rāma. The story is sometimes recited with a book in hand, but more often only to the accompaniment of a stringed instrument. The ballad singer, or the minstrel narrator, is known to all parts of Asia, including India, Sri Lanka, Thailand, Burma, Cambodia, Laos, and Nepal. He may be considered the precursor of the present puppeteer or the *dhalang* of the Asian tradition.
4. The *Rāmāyaṇa* theme appears in the form of drama proper as spoken word in the *Wayang Wong* tradition of Indonesia and in the many forms of folk and traditional theater of India, such as the *yātrā*, the *tāmaśā*, the *bhāvāi*, the *yakṣagāna*, the *nauṭaṅkī*. The spoken word is primary here as the groundwork of theater, in which the recitative line forms the basis of the interpretation.
5. It is in the dance-drama traditions, however, that the Rāma theme achieves its full glory. The forms of the *khon* play based on the *Rāmāyaṇa* in Thailand and in Cambodia and the *zat-pwe* of Burma, along with the innumerable forms found in India, such as *kūṭiyāṭṭam*, the *bhāgavata melā*, the *aṅkiā naṭ* of Assam, the Mayurbhanja chhau *Rāmāyaṇa*, the Purulia *Rāmāyaṇa*, and finally the sophisticated kathakali, is theater at its finest and most chiselled. A purposeful denial of stage scenery and of realism on the one hand, and an equally deliberate use of stylization, abstraction, poetry, a complex musical orchestra, and an articulation through a codified system of evocative pose and gesture characterize this sophisticated total theater. Here the elements of the literary, the plastic, and the visual arts, in conjunction with the emotive vibrations of the musical systems come together to make an integral whole.
6. Perhaps the last step in abstraction and sophistication in these traditions is seen in several forms of shadow and puppet theater known to practically all countries of South and Southeast Asia. It has

> been argued by some scholars that the *wayang* preceded live theater. It is not our purpose here to establish a chronology of the origin of the shadow and puppet theater as opposed to the live theater. In form, the range presented in the shadow and puppet theater is almost as extensive as in live theater. In its most sophisticated forms, such as the *nang sbek thom* of Cambodia, the *nang yai* of Thailand, *wayang kulit*, and the *wayang purwa* of Indonesia, one can easily discern the heights of abstraction and articulation to which this art can be taken. In India also there are many varieties of the puppet tradition ranging from marionette to glove, rod, and shadow puppets, all revolving around the Rāma theme. The *tolapāvakuṭhu* of Kerala and *Rāvaṇa chāya* of Orissa are outstanding examples.

This multilayered presence of the *Rāmāyaṇa* in Asia shows a remarkably resilient tradition, whose continuation depends upon its constant recreation and reinvention. With and without state patronage or social pressure, writers and artists, choreographers, and creators of drama, dance drama, and musical operas have been attracted by this theme and have reinterpreted it through a modern idiom. Practically all twentieth-century choreographers of dance and dance drama in India have attempted to present ballets based on the *Rāmāyaṇa* theme. Many playwrights have also tried to reinterpret the *Rāmāyaṇa* theme in India, Burma, Thailand, and Sri Lanka. Modern novels on the theme are considerable in number.

What conclusions can be drawn from this pervasive artistic activity around a single pivot? What maintains the unity of such diverse explorations and expressions of the *Rāmāyaṇa*? Instead of enunciating a fully formed theory or even advancing a hypothesis, perhaps it would be pertinent to identify some key common elements at the level of fundamental principles of worldview and life philosophy. In doing so we must bear in mind that these common features have to be set against the distinctive features of specific versions, texts that are unique to time, place, region, locality, and level of society, if we are to understand the relationship between the root and the branches.

The first question is whether the content and form of the Rāma story presents a vision of life that cuts across all versions. A close look at the core theme and its varied treatments does point to a similar if not identical basic approach to life, which negates death as a finality. Whether Rāma is human or divine, king or god, he is by explicit statements in most versions and by implication in all others an incarnation of divinity or capable of reincarnation. This is explicitly stated in the versions in which he is seen as the reincarnation of Viṣṇu, the creator principle, in all others by implication. Although the forces of light and power, good and evil, natural and supernatural confront each other, often seeming to pull the world into the realm of death, there is a continuity of life, ever renewing and rejuvenating itself. No character works toward a destiny that ends in "Death." It is significant that even in the versions in which Rāma is supposed to vanish into the Sarayū River (Burmese and Indian versions), he does not die. Also, appropriately in concrete terms, Rāma is con-

FIGURE 14.8. The *Rāmāyaṇa* in performance. Rāma fights Rāvaṇa: Rāmlīlā performance in the late 1950s in Delhi. Photo courtesy of Hiren Kundu, principal dancer.

ceived as ever young and ageless: the convention of making young boys or girls portray Rāma in stage versions has deep-rooted philosophical and cultural significance, and is not a matter of mere chance or expediency or the fancy of stage directors in the casting of roles.

The life-death continuum was shared by Buddhist and Jain thought alike, and thus even when the Rāma story was conceived as the *Daśaratha Jātaka,* or the stories of Jain Tirthankaras, this was a basic premise. This hypothesis or vision is shared by all of the participating cultures. Would it be too much to conclude that the power of the Rāma theme continued and will continue until such time as this unspoken premise of the life-death continuum is abandoned? This premise also accounts for the capacity for most modern Asians to feel at home in myth and legend, which move freely between the celestial and terrestrial planes: they continue to have the capacity to see magic ritual and life together, to share in one breath the life of spirit and man, of dream and reality. Dream and reality, the microcosm and the macrocosm, are not opposite forces or experiences pitched against each other; instead they are interconnected facets of existence continually playing upon one another. The interplay of the living and the dead is accepted as a fact deep down in the psyche, buried as it may be under many layers of rational thinking. No wonder these cultures have

FIGURE 14.9. The *Rāmāyaṇa* in performance. Four brothers: Rāmlīlā performance in the late 1950s in Delhi. Photo courtesy of Hiren Kundu, principal dancer.

been termed the cultures of encapsulation, where the kernel has remained unaltered and only further shells and sheaths have been added.

Related to this and almost more fundamental is the concept of time. Time does not have only a linear dimension of progression, where each successive stage of development is vertically higher and obliterates the earlier stage. Instead, the rhythm of the universe is conceived in terms of a cyclical movement where repetitive moments occur as in a wheel. There is also coiling and recoiling. Often it is conceived as a still center holding together a large circumference: within it many moments of historical time can coexist. A cyclic view of life and time poses no resistance to the repetition of the old and the gradual permeation of the new. Movements in art do not grow by a constant self-conscious revolt against the immediately preceding movement; they move in a well-set rhythm and tempo of circles, where themes, symbols, and motifs recur, all the while acquiring new significance. The pattern that emerges within specific regions and among differing regions is not one of the annihilation of earlier levels or replacement of indigenous, national, or local character by an alien influence; it is instead a pattern of partially overlapping circles arranging themselves in an order of interconnection, which makes for both sharing and overlapping as well as distinct untouched autonomous areas, within the periphery of any given circle. The centers of all circles are distinct, separate entities. The theory of waves of influence states only a partial truth of this phenomenon in South and Southeast Asia and not the whole truth. The Rāma theme, resonating through its journey in time and its impregnation in space, provides an excellent illustration of the life-death continuum and cyclic time vision.

Rāma occurs again and again, acquiring new meaning and validity. So does Sītā, not only as a beautiful woman born to suffer but also as the primeval force of terrestrial energy and its purification. Rāvaṇa and the forces he represents also occur again and again, acquiring new meaning and validity by a ready flexibility of the mind to understand present events through the power of the myth. Tradition and modernity, tradition and contemporaneity are thus not clashing with each other: they are mingling and merging and supporting each other. Here again is the potential for reversal and inversion.

The two main principles enunciated above may encourage us to move toward the theories and principles that govern artistic creation. In such a vision, the framework of the dramatic unities of time and place is irrelevant; character development as linear progression, arising out of inner conflict, is also irrelevant. The artistic form of the *Rāmāyaṇa*, whether as epic narrative, or as Sanskrit drama, or as one of the dance dramas of Southeast Asia, exhibits this disregard for the unities of time and place and of character development. Rāvaṇa, Hanumān, and a host of other characters go through a variety of ordeals, sufferings, privations, defeats, and victories, but none questions the singularity of his purpose or his individual path of action. Thus life is abstracted into recurring states and moments; characters become symbolic of deep philosophical and spiritual meaning, and not just particular human beings in states of mental conflict and of action arising out of that conflict at a single moment in time. Individual characters represent qualities, moods, shades of meaning, color and line, all symbolic at their best, stereotyped conventional characters at their worst. Forms and techniques acquire a chiseled sophistication and refinement at their highest, dull repetitive forms at their lowest. In all cases, the artist never aims at particularity or uniqueness.

The capacity for abstraction finds a concrete manifestation in a variety of artistic forms and techniques, common to the region under consideration. Whether it is the *wayang wong* or *orang* or the *khol* or *khon* or the Rāmlīlā of Varanasi or kathakali, abstraction and stylization is the essence. Plurality arises out of the methods of abstraction adopted and not from adherence to different principles of artistic creation.

Also, a look at the development of the theme of the *Rāmāyaṇa* reveals that in each of these regions no watertight compartments exist between levels of artistic creation. The categorization of the levels into folk and classical becomes almost an impossibility. The degree of stylization indicates the level of refinement or sophistication, but there is no such thing as the drama of realism as opposed to the drama of idealism or stylization. A mobility between sophisticated and unsophisticated (or what would be termed as elitist and popular) is discernible in all regions. There is both an upward and downward movement, not only a filtering through of an elitist culture to popular levels. This interdependence is a key characteristic of representations of the *Rāmāyaṇa* in all regions.

Perhaps it is this flexibility of response—a flexibility allowed, indeed compelled by the narrative, ethical, and philosophical core values of the *Rāmāyaṇa*—that nurtures the interdependence and interrelationship of the literary, performing, and visual arts in which it lives on, creating a connected yet elastic cultural system. The growth and sustenance of that system has been facilitated by the mobility of peoples between contiguous and distant regions of Asia. This cultural flow has led to creations that represent at once many moments of history and facets of culture which, even when they are mutually contradictory, nevertheless fall into a consistent whole when held together in an art form. Within that whole both the diffusionist tendencies and the autochthonous character of regional cultures and art styles remain distinct even as they interact with one another by a variety of negotiating strategies that we may identify as specific influences.

These comments are admittedly broad generalizations, but they are warranted in the context of the *Rāmāyaṇa*. Beginning with the central figure, we see that the character of Rāma undergoes modifications and changes as it cycles through different cultures, but nevertheless remains recognizable as Rāma. True, the differences in portraiture within a common frame of reference are not insignificant. In India, although he began as a hero, he was deified between the twelfth and sixteenth centuries; this aspect of his character is stressed in practically all Indian versions, although shades of meaning and color vary. In Burma, the character is invested with the hues of the "bodhisattva" or the hero symbolizing moral and ethical good. The preliminaries before the play are suggestive of the extra artistic importance given to him. In Thailand, Cambodia, and Java, he is a hero no doubt, but not a god following a predetermined path of action. Often he is portrayed as a romantic hero, especially in versions in which he exiles Sītā in a fit of jealousy after she paints a portrait of Rāvaṇa on the fan. But in all versions he is the embodiment of good and is recognized as such.

Sītā's character also goes through many transformations and changes. The one consistent and invariable element is her association with the earth. In all versions, she comes from the earth, is discovered there and goes back to it. The symbolism initially attached to the myth may get lost, or may be superimposed by others, but the undertones continue. In Vālmīki's *Rāmāyaṇa* she is a strong, proud woman who is an equal match for Rāma. The conversation between Rāma and Sītā just before the fire ordeal is powerful and profoundly significant. Tulsīdās's Sītā is the long-suffering medieval, unquestioning woman. In both cases, however, she is faithful to the last and dignified in every step of her conduct. In the Cambodian version, which has Sītā allowing Rāvaṇa to enter into the hut, some of the drama is lost and so is the irony. She remains, however, the faithful wife who confronts a villain and therefore feels free to rebuke and slap him. The conception of Sītā changes in some other versions, particularly in Balinese narratives, where she is deified as Devī Sintā, but de-

FIGURE 14.10. Hanumān saving Sītā. Bas-relief at Wat Po. Photo by Julie Mehta.

spite this elevation her human characteristics do not change, nor the emphasis on her wifely virtue.

The most consistent character is that of Hanumān, who epitomizes calm, solid loyalty. In all versions, he is connected with the wind god, the son of Vāyu, and is the last word in friendship and faithfulness. However, Hanumān's character has a wide range. He is a confirmed bachelor and a celibate in most Indian versions, but the moment he crosses the shores of India he is an amorous hero, father of sons begot with *apsaras*es and nymphs, as in the Thai version. On the stage he is heavy-footed in Indian versions, light and sprightly in Southeast Asian versions. But nowhere is his basic character as the epitome of active loyalty lost. The character of Rāvaṇa also changes with regions. He is portrayed as a powerful ascetic in his previous birth in all versions, but his character changes from a cultivated and dignified king to a despot drunk with power in some representations, to a simple evil villain in others.

As we look at these varied treatments in the performing arts, the differences in forms and techniques become quite evident. Yet common threads run through all strategies of presentation. For example, the performer who recites the story—rather, declaims it—is a common figure who holds together the narrative line. So is the ballad singer whose narrative parallels representations in bas-relief, murals, pageants, and tableaux. The earliest versions in Thailand, Burma, and India confirm this view. Whether the shadow and puppet theater preceded or followed the stage version of Rāma remains a question mark. In all forms there is a close relationship between the declaimed verse, sung poetry, the music, the visual manifestation, and the stage presentation. Forms of shadow and puppet theater and stage plays or dance dramas are only different dimensions of the same genre rather than different art forms. The close interrelationship between the artistic expressions of a particular region is evident in all the *Rāmāyaṇa* presentations. Parallel runs the connection of a specific form or genre among regions. Thus, methods of manipulation in puppet theater, especially the rods, are common to most regions. Cambodia and Thailand are very similar; the Andhra *bomalāṭṭam* and the Kerala puppets are close seconds. The theater of the *khol* and *khon* of the Burmese *zat*, and of the Purulia dancers of India are comparable in their use of masks, even though Indian masks, particularly those of Purulia, are quite different from Thai, Burmese, Laotian, and Cambodian masks, which have much in common. Dance techniques and musical models also have strong affinities despite their distinctiveness. The principle of the stylized pose and gesture is followed in all traditions. In some cases the pose is more significant, as in the Thai and Khmer traditions; in others, facial miming and gesticulation with the words, as in kathakali and bharatanatyam.

A basic color symbolism is also common. Green is always associated with Rāma, white with Hanumān, red and black with Rāvaṇa. The difference lies in the particulars, such as patterns of costuming and décor, and techniques of making and designing masks, which are distinctive to each region, although even there close similarities exist, as between Thailand and Cambodia. Also distinctive to each tradition are the musical compositions, both in the orchestration pattern and the modes and tunes used. Yet these too share the technique of the repetitive melodic line and a rhythm, both cyclic and circular in structuring.

Above all, there is the phenomenon of the amazing tenacity of the oral traditions which has facilitated the survival and continuance of the traditions in contemporary Asia. Even when the theme seems to run into a dry sand bed, it never dies, for the oral tradition sustains it. The oral tradition has also supported, supplemented, and complemented the traditions of the written word and of brick, mortar, clay, stone, color, and paint. It was also responsible for facilitating processes of assimilation and for creating the basis of integration. The worldview, the affirmation of a life-death continuum, the adherence to a concept of cyclic time, through a method of transmission which was a total integrated approach, have led to artistic creations on the *Rāmāyaṇa* theme in all times, including the present. Each encapsulates many dimensions in time. A single sculpture, painting, or spectacle has elements in it that can be traced back not to one moment of historical time but to several: it has other elements that echo cultures of distant lands; and yet the creation is new and contemporary, with a distinct identity and personality. It is not an artificial resurrection of a dead language, a piece of antiquity, but a living being of the present.

That is why more vistas and avenues of exploration await the interest of creative minds and artists. Kampaṉ, the Tamil poet, begins his *Rāmāyaṇa* with the words: "As a cat standing on the shores of the ocean of milk thinks it can lick up the whole ocean, I hope to retell the Rāma story already told by Vālmīki." This may seem a superhuman undertaking but such is the fascination of the *Rāmāyaṇa* that it has never ceased to attract its refashioners. From Kampaṉ to

Gandhi in India, from the rulers of Champa to Maha Eisey in Khmer, from the rulers of Srivijayan to Prince Dhani Nivat, creative minds across Asia have been drawn to this epic of all epics.

NOTES

1. *Epigraphica Indica* 8, p. 42.
2. Ibid. 6, p. 6.
3. *Rāmāyaṇa* 6.110. 83–84.
4. *South Indian Inscriptions* 1, p. 9.
5. A film made sometime ago, now unavailable, correlated the *rāmanāṭṭam* performance with the murals.
6. See studies of the set by Asoke K. Das, formerly director of the Khasmahal Museum at the palace of the maharaja of Jaipur. His comprehensive work on the set is as yet unpublished.

REFERENCES

Epigraphica Indica. n.d. Delhi: Motilal Banarsidass.
South Indian Inscriptions. 1890–. New Delhi: Archaeological Survey of India.
Vālmīki Rāmāyaṇa. 1960–. Edited by J. M. Mehta, et al. Critical edition. Baroda: Oriental Institute.

APPENDIX I

The *Rāmāyaṇa* in Asia

Date	Rāma Tales in Sanskrit and Other Indian Languages	Buddhist and Jain Works, and Purāṇas	Related Artistic Material	Literary Versions Outside India
Pre-600 B.C.E.	Rāma, Janaka, Sītā as names			
600 B.C.E.	Ākhyāna kāvya			
400–300 B.C.E.		*Daśaratha Jātaka*		
300 B.C.E.	*Vālmīki Rāmāyaṇa*			
200 B.C.E.			Earliest date for Bharata's *Nāṭyaśāstra*	
100 B.C.E.	*Rāmopakhyāna, Bālakāṇḍa*	*Anāmaka Jātaka*		
100 C.E.				
200–300	*Uttarakāṇḍa*	*Daśaratha Jātaka* (Chinese sources)		
300–400	*Pratimā nāṭaka & Abhiṣekha Nāṭaka*	*Brahmāṇda Purāṇa* & *Viṣṇu Purāṇa*		
400–500	*Raghuvaṁśa* by Kalidasa	*Daśaratha Jātaka*, Chinese *Jātaka, Harivaṁśa Purāṇa, Vāyu Purāṇa*	Deogarh temple, Nachna temple	
500–700	*Rāvaṇavadha, Bhaṭṭi kāvya*	*Matsya Purāṇa, Bhāgavata Purāṇa, Kūrma Purāṇa*	Virūpākṣa temple	*Jānakīharaṇa* (Sri Lanka), Tibetan and Khotanese *Rāmāyaṇa*
700–800	*Mahāvīra Caritam, Uttararāmacarita* of Bhavabhūti		Kailasa temple, Ellora	
800–900	*Jānakīharaṇam, Kundamālā*	*Agnipurāṇa, Skandapurāṇa*	*Rāmāyaṇa* in Nāgeśvara temple, Kumbhakonam;	*Kakawin Rāmāyaṇa*
900–1000	*Anargha Rāghava, Bāla Rāmāyaṇa, Āścaryacūḍāmaṇi*	*Garuḍa Purāṇa, Brahma Purāṇa, Nāradīya Purāṇa*	Prambanan temple; Lara Jongprang; Aihole Pattadakal; Papanath	

(*continued*)

The *Rāmāyaṇa* in Asia

Date	Rāma Tales in Sanskrit and Other Indian Languages	Buddhist and Jain Works, and Purāṇas	Related Artistic Material	Literary Versions Outside India
1000–1100	*Mahānāṭaka, Rāmāyaṇamañjarī, Kathāsaritsāgar, Campā Rāmāyaṇa* (Kerala), *Pampā Rāmāyaṇa* (Kannada)	*Mahābhāgavata, Devī Purāṇa, Kālikā Purāṇa*	Viṣṇu temple; Pagan Burma; Bamphon Mountains	
1100–1200	*Dvipada Rāmāyaṇa* (Telugu), *Kamban Rāmāyaṇa* (Tamil)		Angkor Vat; Bamphon Mountains; Hoyśaleśvara Temple, Halebid;	
1200–1300	*Uttara Rāmāyaṇa* (Telugu), *Jivana Sambodhanam* (Kannada), *Raṅganātha Rāmāyaṇa* (Telugu)		Banteay Seri, Lopburi period; Candi Singasari (East Java)	Prose version in Sri Lanka
1300	*Uttararāghava, Unmattarāghava, Adhyātma Rāmāyaṇa* (Kerala), *Adbhuta Rāmāyaṇa, Bhāskara Rāmāyaṇa* (Telugu), *Gīti Rāmāyaṇa* (Assamese), *Rāmapadas* by Rāmānanda		Chola bronzes; Sukhathai bronzes of Viṣṇu; sculptural reliefs of Majapahit period; Candi Panataran (East Java)	
1400–1500	*Rāmābhuyudaya, Ānanda Rāmāyaṇa,* Kṛttivāsa's *Rāmāyaṇa* (Bengali), *Kannasse Rāmāyaṇa* (Malyayalam) *Rāma Viraha* (Gujrati)	*Padma Purāṇa, Śiva Purāṇa*	Hazara Rāma temple; Nang Sbek Wayang forms; Chola and Pallava sculpture; Ayutthya (Thailand)	*Hikayet Seri Rāma*
1500–1600	Śrīdhara's *Rāmāyaṇa* (Marathi), Balarāmadāsa's *Rāmāyaṇa* (Orissa), *Rāghavanaiṣadhīya, Rāmakṛṣṇa Vilomakāvya, Jānakīharaṇam, Rāmaliṅgāmṛta,* Vasudeva's *Yādava Rāghavīya Rāmakathā, Vicitra Rāmāyaṇa* (Orissa), *Molla Rāmāyaṇa* (Telugu)	*Agniveśa Rāmāyaṇa, Mahā Rāmāyaṇa, Hanuman Saṁhitā*	Two sets of *Rāmāyaṇa* in miniature paintings (Akbar period in India); beginning of Wayang Gedong Golek	Andhra murals at Hampi, Lepakshi (Andhra); Rāmakaliṅga, (Java); *Reamker* (Cambodia); Deat

				Kanda (Java); illustrated manuscripts of Nepal
1600–1700	*Toravai Rāmāyaṇa* (Kannada), Kumaragam's *Rāmakathā*, Ezchuttan's *Adhyātma Rāmāyaṇa* (Malayalam), *Bhāgavata Rāmāyaṇa, Rāvaṇa Mandodarī,* Tulsīdās's *Rāmcaritmānas* (Hindi), *Uttara Rāmāyaṇa, Rāmayajña* (Gujrati) Nabhadās's *Rāmacarita* (Hindi), Keśavdās's *Rāmacandrikā* (Hindi), *Lakṣmanāyan* (Rajasthani), *Hanumāncandrikā* (Jaina version), *Avadhivilās* (Avadhi), *Kavitā Ratnākar* (Brajbhāṣā)		Thai murals; Bali Wayangpurwa; miniature painting traditions of Moghul school, Mewar, Malwa (India); murals at Mattancheri Palace (Cochin), Tiruvanchikulam	
1700–1800	*Rāmanāṭṭam* (Kerala), *Rāmanāṭaka, Kīrtanaigal* (musical work in Tamil), Kashmiri *Rāmāyaṇa*		Reliefs in Wat Po (Bangkok); murals in Cambodia; reliefs in Burma; *Rāmāyaṇa* in Pahari, Basholi, Kulu, Deccani, Orissan; Tanjavur schools of paintings, scroll paintings and in illustrated manuscripts; murals at Trichur; beginning of kathakali, revival of bharatanāṭyam	Burmese *Rāma Thagyin*, Thai *Rāmākien*

(continued)

Date	Rāma Tales in Sanskrit and Other Indian Languages	Buddhist and Jain Works, and Purāṇas	Related Artistic Material	Literary Versions Outside India
1800–1900	Thiagayya songs on Rāma in Telugu, musical work in Marathi, Bengali, Assamese, Kannada, Gujrati, Hindi		Murals in Emerald Buddha Temple, murals and paintings in Cambodia, reliefs in Burma, scroll paintings in Orissa, illustrated palm-leaf in Orissa, *pat* paintings in Bengal, *Rāmāyaṇa* in traditional theaters in India; Jatra, Nautanki, Ankia Nat, Terukuthu, Yaksagana, ballad singing Daskatha (Orissa) Veeragasay (Andhra), etc.; shadow theater of India, Malayasia, Cambodia, Thailand;	*Rāmāyaṇa* by U. Toe (Burma), *Rāmakien* by Rāma II (Thailand), operatic work in Cambodia
1900–late 20th c.	*Bhūmi Kanyā* (Marathi), *Sāket* (Maithili Saran Gupta's Hindi), *Rāma kī Śakti Pūje* (Hindi), *Ramā Vaidehivanavās* (Sāket Ūrmilā, 1963), *Rāma Story* (C. Rajagopalachari, English), *Rāma Story Retold* (A. Menon, English), *Rāma, A Play* (Gopal Sharman)		Revival of Khol, Khon, Nang Sbek; Fine Arts University, Nangyei, Khon-Chud Burmese marionettes; Javanese, Sudanese, Balinese versions, kalakshetra *Rāmāyaṇa*, kathakali *Rāmāyaṇa*, Uday Shaknar's shadow *Rāmāyaṇa*, Shanti Bardhan's *Rāmāyaṇa*, Narendra Sharma's *Rāmlīla*, Sachin Shankar's *Rāmlīla*, *Rāmāyaṇa* based on Mayurbhanj Chau	*Rāmāyaṇa* in Burma, 1910; *Rāmāyaṇa* by Dhani Nivat (Thai and Cambodian versions), English novel based on the *Rāmāyaṇa* in Sri Lanka

APPENDIX 2

Variant Names of Main Characters

Indian	Khmer Laotian	Thai	Burmese	Malaysian	Javanese	Balinese
Rāma	Rām	Phrā Rāma	Rāma	Seri Rāma	Rāma	Rāma
Sītā	Sitā	Sidā		Sitā Devī	Sintā Devī	Sintā
Rāvaṇa	Rāb	Tosakānth	Dasagiri	Rāvaṇa	Rāhwana	Rāhwana
Hanumān	Hanumān	Hanumān	Hanumān	Ānomān	Ānomān	Ānomān
Bharata	Bharut	Phrut	Bharata	Berdan	Berata	Barata
Śūrpanakhā	Surupnakhā	Sarunakhā	Gāmbi	Suna Pandeki	Surupnakhā	Surupnakhā
Trijaṭā	Punukay	Benyāki		Devī Seri Jāli	Trijaṭā	Trijaṭā

Index

Abhijñānaśakuntalā 254–55
Abhinavagupta 50–51, 78, 256
Abhiṣeka Nāṭaka 243–45, 247–48, 255–56, 355
Ācārya, Nārāyaṇa Rām 45
Adbhuta Rāmāyaṇa 10, 88–89, 96, 109, 114, 119, 140, 356
Adbhutācārya 89, 92, 96, 105, 119
adharma 11, 22, 26, 126
adharmya 25
Adhyātma Rāmalilā 100, 104, 119, 156
Adhyātma Rāmāyaṇa 10, 71, 81, 89, 93–96, 100–103, 109, 119, 140, 147, 156, 159, 171, 207, 209, 356–57
Ādi kavi 89, 272
Ādikāṇḍa 89–90
Ādikāvya 20, 336
Ādiśaṅkarācārya 26
Aditi 67
Aditjondro, G. J. 305, 310, 316, 319
Advaitin 157–58
Aeneid 305, 318
Agastya 62–63
Agni 67, 70–71, 80, 112, 245
agniparīkṣā 51–54, 113, 173
Agnipurāṇa 81, 355
Agniveśa Rāmāyaṇa 356
Ahalyā 39, 70–73, 76, 81, 186, 271, 337, 339–40
Ahirāvaṇa 93, 108, 153–56, 157–62
Aihole 338, 355
Airāvaṇa 153
Aitarak 309
Aithal, P. 146
Ajgaonkar, Vasant 273
Akashwani 263
Ākhyāna kāvya 355
Aklujkar, Vidyut 13–14, 207
Alambuṣā Jātaka 79
Alap-alapan Sukesi 276, 285
Albert, Michael 317
Ālhākhaṇḍ 159
al-Hallaj 283
Alter, Joseph 160, 162
Amba karna 279
Ambegaonkar, Shobha 265
Amonkar, Kishori 264
amṛta 67
Amṛtamanthana 68, 70
Anāmaka Jātaka 355
Ānanda Rāmāyaṇa 89, 153, 356
Ānandavardhana 50–51, 78, 82
Ananta Kandalī 90
Anargha Rāghava 355
Anasūyā 168, 174, 177, 194, 208, 244–45, 337
Anderson, Benedict 288, 291
Andhra-Jyoti 234
Aṅgada 93, 96, 98, 109, 221, 250, 270, 272

Aṅgada Rāybara 88, 93, 98, 109
Angkor Vat 305, 311, 313, 325, 327, 331–32, 342, 356
Angsarwa 279
Aṅkiyā Nāṭ 89, 96, 346, 358
ANMEFTIL 307
Ānomān 359
Āpastamba Śatapathabrāhmaṇa 79
Āpastamba Śrautasūtra 81
apsaras 61, 67, 269, 330, 352
Apte, V. S. 82
Araṇisena 98–99, 101
Araṇyakāṇḍa 34, 46, 63
Aristocrat (company) 313
Arjuna 27, 43, 159, 257
Arjunasasrabahu 280–81, 283, 285, 289, 292
Arjunawijaya Kakawin 277–78, 281, 292
Armstrong, Charles 313–14, 319–320
artha 188, 205
Arundale, Rukmini Devi 16
Arundhatī 228, 239
Aru Sea 300
Āryadeśa 330
Aryan, K. C. 82
Āścaryacūḍāmaṇi 243–44, 250, 253, 255, 355
Ashbery, John 305
Aṣṭāvakra 92, 108
asura 153, 157
aśvamedha 48–49, 51, 55, 58–60, 79
Aśvins 127
Ātā, Ananta Ṭhākur 88
Atharva Veda 58
Atikāya 98
Atri 168, 337, 340
Australia 310, 313–14
Avadānakalpalatā 79
Avadh 213
Avadhi 153
Avadhivilās 357
avatar 74, 158, 170, 208, 323
Ayodhyā 17, 29–32, 39, 49, 55–56, 60–64, 72, 74–75, 96–97, 101, 116, 120, 151, 159, 167, 175, 177–78, 183–84, 191, 194–96, 199, 203, 212, 217, 225, 239, 243, 251, 269–70
Ayodhyākāṇḍa 24, 46, 76, 168, 175, 177
Āyurveda 85
Ayutthya 323, 329, 345, 356
Babhruvāhana 27
Bailey, Greg 45
Bakhshi, G. 206, 209
Bakhtin, Mikhail 319–20
Bālakāṇḍa 26, 45, 47–49, 54–56, 58–61, 63, 66–68, 70, 72, 76–77, 168, 171, 177, 355
Balarāmadāsa 91, 93–95, 104, 106, 356
Bāla Rāmāyaṇa 355
Balasiri 336
Bali 295, 298, 300, 304, 306–7
Bāli (also see Vāli) 248, 250
Balinese *Rāmāyaṇa* 318
Bali Post 298–99
Bālivadham 248
Bamphon 356
Bāṇa 211
Bandopadhyaya, Ajit Kumar 104–5
Bandopadhyaya, Balarāma 119
Bandopadhyaya, Lakshmana 119
Banteay Seri 325, 328, 332, 342, 356
Baphoun 342
Bapuji, Sunita 266
barāt 177–78, 181–82, 184–85, 189, 191, 195, 197, 202, 207, 213, 215, 217–18
Barata 359
Bardhan, Shanti 16, 358
Basabalingaiah 139–43, 146
Basu, Rajnarayan 16, 111
Batara Guru (Siwa) 280, 282–83
Batara Indra 316
baṭ-talā 108
Becker, A. L. 289, 291, 316, 318, 320
Bedekar, V. M. 81–82
Belo, Bishop Carlos 293–94, 296, 309
Benjakai 328
Benyāki 359
Berata 359
Berdan 359
Bessinger, Margaret 319–20
Betari Durga 282
Bhabha, Homi 315, 319–20
Bhadrakalāvadāna 79
Bhagavadajjukīya 254
bhāgavata melā 346
Bhāgavata Purāṇa 13, 81–82, 98, 200, 355
Bhāgavata Rāmāyaṇa 357
Bhagīratha 92, 108
Bhagwat, Kamala 273

Bhagwat, Kumud 273
bhakta 112, 119, 170, 202
bhakti 10, 17–18, 93, 107, 119, 121, 142, 173, 178, 182–83, 186, 195, 201–3, 208, 256
Bhañja, Upendra 87–88
Bharat Kala Bhavan 338
Bharata 29, 33–35, 42, 97, 101, 159, 176, 180–81, 197, 207, 210, 212–15, 218, 224, 243–44, 247, 252, 254, 269–72, 355, 359
Bharatamañjarī 79, 82
bharatanatyam 253, 266, 357
Bhāratavarṣa 159
Bharatayudha 300
Bhārgava Rāma 72, 76, 167, 196
Bhārgavas 45
Bharhut 337
Bharut 359
Bhāsa 243–44, 254–57, 336
Bhāskara Rāmāyaṇa 356
Bhat, U. 273
Bhatia, Sooraj 16
Bhatt, G. H. 45, 58, 78–79, 81–82
Bhattacharya, Ashutosh 105
Bhattacharya, T. 103–5
Bhattacharya, Vaasoo 264
Bhaṭṭi Kāvya 342, 355
Bhavabhūti 37, 45, 125, 138, 140, 145, 147, 223–24, 226–28, 239–40, 336, 355
bhāvagīta 268, 272
bhāvāi 346
Bhavānanda 92
Bhavānī 154
Bhāvārtha Rāmāyaṇa 262
Bhima Suci 275, 288
Bhīma 159, 288
Bhīṣma 27
Bhogavatī 153
Bhūmi Kanyā 357
Bhuśuṇḍi Rāmāyaṇa 93, 96, 342
Bhuvaneśvara 93
Biardieu, Madeleine 45
Bibisana 279
Bilaṅkā Rāmāyaṇa 96–97
Bima 285
Bipra (Vipra) Harivara 94
Bisa Warna 279
Blackburn, Stuart 17, 240, 254–56
Bodhāyana 254
bodhisattva 351
Bollywood 182
bomalāṭṭam 353
Bonnemaison, S. 16, 17
Borges, Libania 310
Borges, Manuela 310
Bose, Mandakranta 10, 19, 45, 105, 209, 334
Bose (Basu), Rajshekhar (also *see* Parashuram) 114–15, 122
Brahmā 52, 78, 98–101, 108, 120, 184–86, 188, 214–15, 243, 249–50, 324
brahmacarya 60
Brahmadatta 65–66
brahmahatyā 26, 58
Brāhmaṇa 77
Brahmāṇḍa Purāṇa 82, 355
Brahmapurāṇa 81–82
brahmāstra 136–37, 141, 143, 222
Brahmavaivarta Purāṇa 81–82
Brajbhāṣā/Brajabhāṣā 87
Brama 278
Brama Raja 279–80
Brama Sudarga 278–79
Brama Tama 278–79
Bramani Wati 278
Brandes, J. L. A. 288, 291
Bratayuda 289
Bṛhadāraṇyaka Upaniṣad 78
Bṛhaddharmapurāṇa 96
Bṛhan Mahārāṣṭra Vṛtta 274
Bṛhaspati 97, 104
Bṛhat-kathā 237
Bṛhat-kathā-śloka-saṁgraha 237
Brockington, John 15, 17, 41, 45, 47, 77, 82, 199–200, 206, 209
Brockington, Mary 41, 45
Brown, W. Norman 80, 82
Brückner, H. 254, 256
Buddha 324, 326, 329, 336, 343, 344, 358
Buddhist 276, 324, 329, 348
Bui Lailua 296
Bulke, Camille 16, 79, 82, 150, 162
Buniyad 167
Burmese *Rāmāyaṇa* 358
Butalia, Urvashi 208, 210

Cabolek 275, 292
Caitanya 93

Cākyār 246–47, 249, 251–52, 254–55
Cākyār, A. M. 247
Cākyār, Kuṭṭan 247
Cākyār, M. K. 247
Callistraus 318
Campā Rāmāyaṇa 356
Cañcarīka 116–17
Cāndāinī 238, 240
Caṇḍī 97
Caṇḍī Maṅgala 92
Candi Pantaran 356
Candi Singasari 356
Candra Bhāratī 160
Candrāvatī, 8, 11, 17, 88, 109–11, 119–22
Candrāvatī Rāmāyaṇa 110, 120
Canosian 309, 316
Carabaulo Tetum 296, 306, 308–9, 314
Carakasaṃhitā 80, 82, 121
cāraṇa 346
Cekarāppāvalar 145
Chachu Cākyār Madhom 248
Chakravarti, R. 103–5
Chakri dynasty 324
Chalam, V. 232, 234–35, 240–41
Chalukya 338–39
Cham 311, 313
Champa 279, 323, 354
Chandrashekhara, B. 146
Chatterji, Ashoke 79, 82, 104–5
Chatterji (Chattopadhyaya), Suniti Kumar 16–17, 122
Chattopadhyaya, Bankimchandra 206
Chaudari, T. Ramasvami 127–30, 133, 142–45, 147
Chavan, Y. 264
Chavji, S. 271, 274
Cheleder Rāmāyaṇa 115, 123
Chitra Bahar 279–80
Chitrakūṭa 269
Chola 339, 356
Chomsky, Noam 317
Chopra, Ramchand 166
Christ Rei 314, 316
Cilappatikāram 246
Cilimpā 116–17
Coburn, T. 162
Coomaraswamy, Radhika 319
Creed, Barbara 80, 82
Cūlin 65
dāija 190
daitya 157
Dai Viet 311
Dakṣiṇī Rāmāyaṇa 91, 93
dalit 126, 139, 144
Dalmia-Luderitz, V. 16, 17, 174, 206, 209
Damayantī 238
Daṇḍaka 303, 337–38, 340
Daṇḍī Rāmāyaṇa 92, 95
Dange, S. A. 81–82
Das, Ashoke K. 354
Das, Maheswar 91, 93, 104–5
Das, Rahul Peter 121
Das, Rāmgovinda 119
Dasagiri 359
Daśamahāvidyā 328
Dasamuka 279, 284
Daśaratha 23–28, 30–31, 33–34, 49, 55–58, 60–61, 72, 74–76, 79, 92, 94, 101, 110, 117, 120, 175–80, 183–86, 188–91, 194–95, 198, 208, 210–14, 216–18, 227–28, 243–44, 270–71, 274, 341
Daśaratha Jātaka 151, 336–37, 348, 355
Dāśarathi 72, 74, 76
Daśāvatāra 339
Daskatha 358
Dastān-e-amīr-Hamzah 159
dāsya 202–3
dāsyabhakti 203
Datar, Narendra 266, 273
Datar, S. 273
Datta, B. N., 16, 18
Datta, Hirendranāth 90, 104
Datta (Dutt), Michael Madhusudan 5, 11, 16, 111–13, 120–22, 152
Datta, P. K. 16, 17
Daugherty, D. 255–56
Davis, R. H. 16, 17
Day, J. A. 283, 289, 291
de Bruin, H. 254, 256
Demak 283
Denpasar 298, 318
Deogarh 337–39, 355
Dev Sen, Nabaneeta 16–17
deva 157
devadāsī 332
devarāja 323, 328
Devī (*devī*) 10, 154–55, 162, 186, 339
Devī Māhātmya 97

Devīpurāṇa 356
Devī Seri Jāli 359
Devī Sintā 351
Devnārāyan 238
Dewaruci 275, 286–88
Dewi S'rati 279
Dewi Sri 306
dhalang 287, 346
Dhanapati 281–82
Dhanaraj 282
dhanuṣyagya 168–69, 210
dharma 24–8, 30, 34–9, 52, 101, 125–26, 131, 160, 175, 187–88, 201–2, 205
dharmaśāstra 36, 38, 83, 128, 130, 205, 209
Dhṛtarāṣṭra 280
Dhruva 89
Dhvanyāloka 82
Diana (Princess of Wales) 308–9
Dido 318
Dīkṣit, Rājeś 162
Dili 294–95, 303–4, 307–8, 310, 312, 314, 318–19
Dilīpa 89, 92, 227
Dimock, Edward 17, 122–23
Diñgnāga 224, 226–29, 237, 240
Diti 67–71, 81
Divya Śrī Caritra 94–95
Diwali 262
Djambumangli 289
Doordarshan 4, 59, 172, 203
Dowry 190, 203, 217
Draupadī 13, 31, 45–46, 162, 238
Dravida Kazhagam 129, 132–33
Drewes, G. W. J. 289–91
Droṇa 43
Duḥśanta 44
Dundubhi 249–50
Durbala 94, 97
Durga 282, 338
Durgā Pūjā 89, 96, 338
Durgāsaptaśati 183, 188, 215
Durgāvara 88, 93, 110–11
Duryodhana 244
Dutt, Utpal 16
Dvija, Dayārām 96, 104
Dvija, Durgarām 119
Dvija, Pañcānana 88
Dvipada Rāmāyaṇa 356
Dyaus-pitṛ 158
East Timor 14, 293–99, 302, 304–7, 309–12, 314–19
Ekalavya 144
ekapatnīvrata 165, 167, 200, 218
Eknāth 262, 267
Ekphrasis 305, 316, 318
Ellora 339, 355
Em Theay, Madam 333
Emerson, C. 320
Endra 314
Entwistle, A. 183, 209
Ezchuttan 357

Florida, Nancy 289–91
Flueckiger, Joyce B. 240
Fontain, J. 318, 320
Ford, Gerald 314, 317
Foucault, Michel 275, 288, 291
Francisco, J. R. 16
Funan 331

Gadgil, Vasant 273
Gādhi 80
Gadimā, (see also Madgulkar, G. D.) 260, 263, 265, 267–68, 272
Gail A. 81–82
Gāmbi 359
Gaṇapati 184
Ganapati Sastri, T. 243, 254
Gandawajriran 286
Gandhamādan Baiṭhak 122
Gandhamādana Parvata 114–15
gandharva 269, 339
gāndharva vivāha 204, 206
Gandhi (Mahatma) 354
Gandhi, Rajiv 209
Gaṇeśa 172–73, 215, 262
Gaṅgā 66, 79, 239–40, 339
Gaṅgādhara 94
gārī 184
Garuḍa 89, 160, 303, 308, 345
Garuḍamahāpurāṇa 82
Gaurī 184, 215
Gautama 70–73, 78, 186
Geertz, C. 293, 316, 320
Gerow, Edwin 254, 256
Ghosh, Ramananda 108–9, 119
Girnar 336
Gītā 27, 210
Gīta Govinda 344

Gita Press 153, 155, 162, 188, 206
Gīta-Rāṁyaṇa 13, 259–73
Gīti Rāmāyaṇa 88, 93, 356
godāna 183, 214, 216
Gokhale 273
Goldman, Robert P. 9, 10, 15, 19, 41–45, 59, 63, 77–82, 149, 158, 162, 178, 185, 206–9
Golgotha 314
gopa 101
Gopalakrishnamurti, S. 239–40
gopī 13
Gosvami, Madhusudan 119
Gosvami, Raghunandan 95, 108–9, 119
Goswami, Chinmanlal 209
Goswamin 255
Govindarāja 50–51, 62, 69, 78–79, 81
Gross, Kenneth 16, 319–20
Guha 269
Gunung Kawi 290
Gupta, Dindayal 162
Gupta, Maithili Saran 357
Gupta Period 337
Gusmao, Jose "Xanana" 297

Haberman, D. 255–56
Habibie, B. J. 294
Haksar, A.N.D. 254, 256
Halebid 356
Ham Log 167
Hampi 337, 339–40, 342–43, 356
Han, U Than 16
Hanumān 10, 12–13, 88, 96–97, 102–3, 112, 114–17, 120, 122, 134, 149, 152–55, 157–63, 220–22, 247, 249–50, 252, 269, 271, 326–30, 337, 342–44, 350, 352–53, 359
Hanumān Candrikā 357
Hanumān Mahimā 162
Hanumān Nāṭaka 324, 342
Hanumān Rāmāyaṇa 163
Hanumān Saṁhitā 356
Hanumānāyana 161
Hanumāner Svapna 114, 116–18, 120, 122
Hardjanta, Pak 290–91
Harivaṁśa 92, 355
Harrison, Seligh 147
Harṣa 254
Hart, George 16–17, 151, 162
Hazara Rama 339, 342–43, 356
Heffernan, James 305, 309–11, 318, 320
Heifetz, Hank 16–17, 151, 162
Hekamedos (Academus) 296
Hertel, B. R. 17
Het Javaansche Tooneel 290–91
Hicks, David 308, 317, 320
hijra 140
Hikayat Seri Rāmāyṇa 342, 356
Hiltebeitel, Alf 44–45, 159, 162
Himalaya 66
Hiranand 344
hlādini śakti 158
Holquist, M. 320
Holt, Claire 318, 320
Holtzmann, Adolf 77, 83
Homer 11, 305
Hopkins, Edward W. 16
Horace 296
Hoskins, Janet 296, 317, 320
Hospital, Clifford 16
Hoyasaleśvara 356
Hum aapke hain kaun? 16, 205
Humes, C. A. 17
Hyang Girinata (Lord Siwa) 284

Ikṣvāku 33, 67, 243
Iliad 305
Imagines 318
Indonesian *Rāmāyaṇa* 318, 342
Indra 67–71, 81, 89, 98, 158, 186, 282, 324
Indra, D. R. 234
Indrajit 111, 154, 160
Indrapuri 279
Irāmāvatāram 4, 149
Irāmāyaṇappattiraṅkal 147
Irāmāyaṇatiṉ Āpācam 145
Iriyan Jaya 300, 319
iṣṭadeva 158
itihāsa-purāṇa 157
Iyengar, K. R. Srinivasa 5, 16, 18, 150, 162
Iyengar, Venkatesha (also see Masti) 137–38
Iyer, R. 254

Jacobi, Hermann 55, 79, 83
Jaffrelot, C. 209

Jagadambikā 169
Jagadram 10, 108, 119
Jagamohana Rāmāyaṇa 91, 105
Jagat Jananī 170, 210
Jāhṇavī 66
Jaimini Aśvamedhaparvan 94
Jaimini Bhārata 94
Jaina/Jain 94, 151, 348
Jakarta 294, 302, 306–7, 315, 317, 319
Jāmbuvān/Jāmbavān 114–15, 271, 279
Jamison, Stephanie 79, 80, 83
Janaka 31, 44, 51, 63, 73, 98, 120, 167–68, 171, 175, 177–78, 180–82, 184–91, 193–95, 198, 202–3, 210–17, 227, 336, 355
Jānakīharaṇa 355–56
Jānakīmaṅgal 206
Jarwa Dhusak 280
Jātaka 83, 336
Jaṭāyu 243, 249, 271, 303, 308, 311, 338, 340
jāti 144
Java 306
Javanese *Rāmāyaṇa* 275–76, 318
Jayabhaya 277
Jayagopāl 91
Jīvana 137
Jīvana Sambodhanam 356
Jogati 140
Jogjakarta 291
Johns, A. H. 284, 289–91
Jones, C. 254–56
Joshi, Bhimsen 264
Jṛmbhaka 239
Jusuf, General M. 302

K. G. P. A. A. Mangkunegara 289, 291
Kabandha 342
Kaca 81
Kadhiri 277
Kaikayī 269–72, 274
Kaikesī 277
Kaikeyī 25, 28–30, 33–34, 38, 94, 110, 120, 160, 176, 191, 196, 200, 207, 210, 212, 215–16, 218, 269–72, 274
Kailasa 152, 325, 338–39, 341, 355
Kailasnath 339
Kakar, S. 159, 162
kakawin 277–78, 282, 284–85, 292, 342, 355
Kākutstha 28, 51
Kalaksetra *Rāmāyaṇa* 358
Kālamṛgayā 120
Kālanemi 159
Kalangwan 292
Kalbuadi 316
Kālī 96, 103, 108, 252
Kālidāsa 84, 224, 251, 254–55, 336, 355
Kālikā Purāṇa 356
Kalyānasugandhikā 254
kāma 62, 80, 188, 205
Kāmadeva 66–67, 251
Kamadjaja 289
Kāmarūpī 160
Kamasan 298–300, 302
Kamath 273
Kambu 330
Kambu Svayambhuva 330
Kambuja 330
Kamma *jāti* 127, 144
Kampaṇ 4, 17, 149, 151, 156, 162, 223, 353, 356
Kāñcana Mṛga 266
Kāñcana Sītā 144
Kanchipuram 339
Kaṇḍu 26
Kane, P. V. 58, 79, 83, 167, 175, 177, 181–83, 187–88, 206, 209
Kannesse Rāmāyaṇa 356
kanyādāna 206, 216
kanyādhana 190, 217
kanyāpakṣa 167, 177, 191, 216
Kapp, David 153
Kapur, Anuradha 16–17, 184, 208–9
Karṇabhāra 256
Karnad, Girish 145–47
Kārttikeya 67–70, 89
karuṇarasa 22, 39, 50, 202
karuṇā 193–95
Kashmiri *Rāmāyaṇa* 357
Kāśyapa 25
Kataka 50, 78–79
Katamaraju 238, 240
Kathā 237
kathakali 8, 255, 346, 350, 357
kathakali *Rāmāyaṇa* 358
Kathāsaritsāgara 13, 237–38, 356
Kathāvācak Rādheśyām 209
Katidja Wp., U. J. 289

Kats, J. 290–91
Kātyāyana Śrautasūtra 79, 84
Kausalya/Kauśalyā 24–26, 28–30, 33, 38, 58, 77, 97, 160, 176–77, 183, 191, 196, 198, 210, 213, 215–16, 218, 268, 271
Kauśika 23
Kaustubha 67
kautukamaṅgala 185, 215
Kavitā Ratnākar 357
Kāvye Upekṣitā 121
kawi miring 281
Kawthalkar, Sudhakar 274
Keats, John 319
Keilhorn, F. 45
kejawen 276, 283, 287, 289
Kerala Kalamandalam 248, 255
Keśavadāsa 357
keta-mate 297
Ketkar, Kamala 273
Khala 93–95, 97
Khan, Sanjay 4
Khara 249
Khmer 311, 313, 323, 325–29, 331–33, 342, 353
khol 350, 353, 358
khon 324, 329, 331, 346, 350, 353, 358
khon chud 358
Khotanese *Rāmāyaṇa* 355
Khuṇṭia, Visvanātha 89
Kibe, M. V. 16
King Borom Trailokanath 329
King Jayavarman II 329, 332
King Norodom 329
King Rāma 324–25
King Sūryavarman II 311, 325
Kirfel, Willibald 81, 84
Kishwar, Madhu 206, 209, 236, 239–40
Kiṣkindhā 249
Kissinger, Henry 314, 317
Klungkung 298, 300
Kodi of Sumba 296
kohabara 189, 197, 216
Kondke, Dada 264
Kopytoff, Igor 317, 320
krauñca 49–54, 57, 78
KRI Macan Tutul 300
Krishnankutty 144, 147
Kṛṣṇa/Krishna xv, 27, 59, 158, 183, 203, 209, 254–55, 262
Kṛṣṇabhakti 199, 203, 208
Kṛṣṇa Yajurveda 336
kṛtayuga 67
Kṛttivāsa (Kṛttibāsa) 4, 10, 17, 90–97, 103–5, 107–9, 112, 115, 118–19, 121–23, 153, 160, 229
Kṛttivāsī Rāmāyaṇa 105, 107, 121–22, 356
kṣatradharma 25, 27–28, 37
kṣatriya/kshatriya 27, 35, 57, 61, 64, 74–76, 79, 101, 129, 199, 206, 271
kṣatriyadharma 37, 40
Kṣemendra 82
Kukuyā 110, 120–21
Kulaśekhara Varman 254, 257
Kumar, Nita 16–17
Kumaragam 357
Kumārasaṃbhava 84
Kumbakarna 277, 282
Kumbhakarṇa 271–72, 277
Kumbhakonam 341–42, 355
Kundamālā 226, 228, 239–40, 355
Kūrma Purāṇa 355
Kuśa 48–49, 51, 53, 88, 94, 225, 228–29, 267–69, 333
kuśa 68
Kuśadhvaja 171, 181, 211, 214
Kuśalava-kuccala-kathā 229
Kuśalavopākhyāna 94
Kuśanābha 64–65, 67, 70–72, 76, 80
kuṭiyāṭṭam xii, 7, 13, 243, 246–48, 250–57, 346
Kuttaccākkaiyan, Paryar 246
kuttambalam 246, 256
Kuvempu, K. V. 133–47
Kuvera 341

Lakhon Lueng 332–33
Lakon 285
Lakṣmaṇa 24–25, 27–28, 31, 34, 37–38, 42, 44–45, 73, 92, 94, 96–97, 111, 114–15, 117, 120–21, 130, 151–52, 154, 158–59, 162, 169, 171, 179–81, 197, 210–14, 221, 223–27, 229, 235, 243–44, 249–51, 270–72, 303, 326, 329, 337, 339
Lakṣmaṇāyaṇ 357
Lakṣmaṇera Śaktiśela 109, 114, 119–20, 123
Lakṣmī 100, 171, 194, 217, 244, 346
Lalitā 250–51
Laṅkā 10, 16, 32, 39, 78, 95–96, 98–99, 102, 120, 134, 144, 152–55, 157–58, 220–

22, 230–31, 247, 262, 269, 303, 310–12, 314–15, 338
Laṅkākāṇḍa 109, 122, 153
Laṅkālaksmī nāṭakam 16
Lankesh Patrike 146
Lara Joreng 342, 355
Larson, Gerald J. 255–56
Lava 48–49, 51, 53, 88, 94, 225, 228–29, 267–69
Lavakuśara Yuddha 94, 103
Lavakuśopākhyāna 105
Lefeber, R. 43, 45
Lepakshi 356
Limaye, V. P. 46
Lokapala 280–1, 285–86
lolon 297
Lomaśa 116
Lopaburi 356
Lor 289
Lorenzen, D. 18
Lutgendorf, Philip 12, 16–17, 144, 147, 150, 157, 161–62, 207, 209

Macan Tutul 300
macapat 281–82, 285
Maccavallapan 155
Macy, C. 16–17
Madgulkar, Anand 265, 272–74
Madgulkar, G. D. (see also Gadimā) 260–61, 263, 267–72
Madgulkar, Vidya 263, 274
Mādhava 45
Mādhava Kandalī 90, 93–95, 103, 105
Mādhavadeva 90, 92
Mādhavī 54
Madhukaiṭabha 89
madhuparka 178
Maha Eisey 354
Mahā Rāmāyaṇa 356
Mahābhāgavatapurāṇa 96, 356
Mahābhārata vii, xvi, 13–14, 20–21, 26–27, 41–46, 50, 76, 79–81, 84, 89, 93, 96, 98, 148, 159, 236–38, 245–46, 253–54, 256, 277–78, 280–81, 285, 288, 291, 300, 302, 331, 336, 339
Mahābhāṣya 42, 45
Mahādevī 328
Mahākṣatrapa Rudradaman 336
Mahānaṭaka 208, 356
Mahānta, Raghunāth 88
mahāpātaka 26, 58
Mahāvīra (Hanumān) 116
Mahāvīra (Jaina) 336
Mahāvīracaritam 355
Mahāyogin 160
Mahendravikrama Pallava 254
Maheśvara 62, 340
Maheśvara Dāsa 91, 93
Mahīrāvaṇa 91–93, 98, 103, 105, 108, 153, 157, 160, 163
Mahīrāvaṇavadha 153
Mahīrāvaṇavadha Nāṭaka 153
Mahispati 281
Mahiṣāsuramardinī 328
maikā 193, 215
Mailirāvaṇa 153, 157
Mailirāvaṇa Katai 153, 155
Mairāvaṇa 93, 153
Mairāvaṇacarita 153
Maithilī xvi, 33, 53
Majapahit 277, 284, 342, 356
Makaradhvaja 154–55, 160, 162
makarī 159
Mambai 295–96
Manasā 88
Mandodarī 11, 50, 110, 120, 151, 154, 249
Mangeshkar, Lata 270
Mangliawan 279, 289
Maṇi-pravālam 245
Mankekar, P. 167, 203, 206, 209
Mannika, Eleanor 311, 319–20
Mantharā 94, 207, 215
Marathe, Gopal 265, 272–73
Maria 310
Mārīca 60, 62–63, 244, 249, 340
Mārīca Kāśyapa 68
maruts 69
maryādā 158, 170, 174, 202, 204, 215
maryādāpuruṣa 200
Maryyada Purushottam 4
Maspero, Georges 319–20
Masson, J. L. 43, 45, 78, 80, 84
Masti (*see also* Iyengar, Venkatesha) 137–38
Mataṅga 250
Mataram 283
Matsya Purāṇa 80–81, 84, 355
Mattavilāsa 254
māyā Sītā 156
Mayurbhanja chau *Rāmāyaṇa* 346, 358

Māruta 70
McCarthy, Terry 310, 319
McDonald, Hamish 313, 319
McGowan, K. M. 14, 302, 320
Meghanada 120, 152, 154
Meghanādavadha Kāvya 5, 11, 16, 111, 120, 152
Mehta, J. L. 241, 354
Mehta, Julie 14, 206, 334
Mehtha, C. C 145, 147
Menakā 61
Menon, A. 357
Menon, K. P. 255–56
Menon, K. P. S. 256
Meyer, John 44, 46
Miller, Barbara S. 254, 256
Mishra, Rudradatta 273
Miśra, B. S. 161–62
Miśra, Jvālāprasād 153–55, 157–59, 162–63
Miśra, V. P. 149
Misra Warna 279
Mitchell, W. J. T. 305
Mithilā 31, 51, 55, 60, 63–64, 66, 70–73, 167, 174, 177–78, 181, 191, 212–13
mithyāpratijñaḥ 23
Mizokami, T. 170, 173, 206, 209
Moerdani 316, 318
Moertono, S. 288, 291
Molla Rāmāyaṇa 356
Moropant 262, 267
Mpu Tantular 277, 284, 292
Mughal *Rāmāyaṇa* 343
Mukhopadhyaya, Harekrishna 121–22
Mukhopadhyaya, Sukhamaya 90, 104–5
Mukteshvar 267
Mukundarāma 92
Mulyono, I. S. 290–91
Munilal 104–5
Murtiyasa, B. 285–86, 290–91
Muses 296

Nabhadās 357
Nabi Adam 278, 292
Nachna 337–38, 355
Nag, Sujitkumar 122
naga 153, 158–60, 330
Nāgānanda 254
Nāga Pañcamī 160
Nagarjunakonda 337
Nagesvara 341, 355
Nāgojibhaṭṭa 78
Naidu, Namini S. 234
Naik period 343
Naik, Sudnya 266
nakha-śikha 169, 189, 202, 210
Nalanikā Jātaka 79
Nandini, K. R. 145
nāndīśrāddha 183
nang 329, 358
nang sbek thom 347, 358
nang sbek wayang 356, 358
nang talung 325
nang yai 323, 325, 329, 334, 347
nangiar koothu 256
Nangyar 246, 251, 254–56
Nara Nārāyaṇa 338
Nārada 21–22, 49, 171, 181, 278
Narakāsura 262
Naramedhayajña 103
Narang, Nouth 330
Narang, S. P. 46
Narasimhan, C. V. 289, 291
Narasiṁharāman 339
Nārāyaṇa 100, 188
Narayana Rao, V. 13, 16, 129, 144–45, 147, 239–40
Narendra, Vikrama 89
Nasik Cave 336
Naṭāṇkuśa 252–56
Nath, Lala Baij 147
Nāṭyaśāstra 244, 247–48, 252, 254–55, 257, 355
nauṭaṅkī 346, 358
Naval Kishore 159
Navaratra 346
Nawangsih 282
Nayar, C. N. Srikantan 16, 144
Neang Seta 329–30
Nehru, Jawaharlal 133, 145
nelmu wirasat (Arab. *ilmu 'l-firasa*) 284
Ngalenka 281–82, 289
Ngamarta 281
Ngastina 281
Ngayodya 281
Nibhatkhin 346
Nigam, Vijay 16
Nīla 102
Nīlakaṇṭha 254
Niranjana, Tejaswini 147

nirguṇa 158
nirvahaṇa 246, 250, 253
Niṣāda 49, 78–79, 81

Obeysekare, G. 20, 41, 46
O'Connor, Stanley J. 318
odissi 253
O'Flaherty, Wendy Doniger 80, 84
ogoh-ogoh 298
Oki 313
Olthof, W. L. 288, 291
orang 350
Orr, Leslie 334

Padmanabhan, K. 45
Padmapurāṇa 71, 79, 81, 84, 92, 94, 105, 356
Padmapuspita, J. 288, 291
pakem 278
Pakubuwana 283, 289
Pallava 339, 356
Pampā 338
Pampā Rāmāyaṇa 356
Panataran 342
Panchal, G. 254–56
pāñcālī 109, 123
Pañcatīrtha 102
Pañcavaṭī 151
Pāṇḍava 26
Pandjangmas 290–91
Pāṇḍu/ Pandu 50, 280, 285
Pandu Papa 285
Pangeran Panggung 283
pāṇigraha 188, 208, 215
Panikkar, N. 255–56
Pāpanatha 338, 355
Parāśara, J. 162–63
Parashuram (also *see* Rajshekhar Bose) 114, 120, 122
Paraśurāma 76, 103, 167, 207, 212, 217
Parkhill, Thomas 16, 18
Pārvatī 62, 66–67, 80, 89, 172, 188, 197, 216, 227, 341
parwa 277
pasisir 284
Paśupati 98
Pātāla 154–55
Pātāla Devī 162
Pātāla Loka 153–56, 159–60
Pātālakhaṇḍa 79, 94
Pātālī Kāṇḍa 88
Patañjali 42, 45
Pathabhi 232–35, 240–41
pativratā 188, 193, 204, 216, 220–21, 225, 229, 231, 234–35, 237–38
pātivrātya 230, 236
Pattadakal 341, 355
Paulose, K. G. 254–56
Paumacariya 94, 151, 336
Pauwels, Heidi 12–13, 205, 208–9
Pavana 99
Pavananandana 102
Pavanaputra 162
Pepakem 278
Phadke, Sudhir (Bābujī) 260–61, 263–65, 271–72, 274
phalgunī 181–82, 214
Philomela 319
Philostratus 318
Phitsanu (Lord Viṣṇu) 324
Phnom Penh 329
Phra Lak 327
Phra Narai 324, 329
Phra Rām (Rāma) 324, 326–29, 359
Phrut 359
phulvārī 170, 181, 209
Pigeaud, Theodore 285, 288–91
Pines, Jim 320
pitṛkārya 183
Plato 296, 317
Plosokuning 306
Poddar, Hanumanprasad 209
Poerbatjaraka 282, 285, 289–91
Pollock, Sheldon 16, 18, 42–44, 46
Pol Pot 332
Porter, David 318
Prajāpati Bhaga 181
prakṛti 180
Prambanan 342, 355
Pramilā 120
Prasanna 145
Prasant Au 342
Prasat Phanom Rung 324
Prasravaṇa 158
Pratimā Nāṭaka 243–44, 256, 355
Preah Lak 329
Preah Ram 329–30
Prem, Sri Svami 161, 163
Prichett, F. 159, 163
Prince Bidyalongkorn 324

Prince Damrong Rajanubhav 324
Prince Dhani Nivat 354, 358
Prince Kittiyakar Krommophra Chandavurinarunath 324
Princess Buppha Devi 333
Princess Maha Chakri Sirinidhorn 324
Probohardjono 286
Proeung Chheng 333
Progymnasmata 305
Pṛthivī 81
pujangga 280
Pulakesi 338
Punukay 359
purāṇa 96, 101, 160, 246, 262, 331, 355
Purāṇic 47–48, 157
Purulia *Rāmāyaṇa* 346
puruṣakāra 28
pūrvapakṣa 22, 33, 38, 168, 180
Puṣkara 96
Puṣkarakāṇḍa 108
Puttappa, K. V. 146–47
putreṣṭi 55, 58–59

Rab (Rāvaṇa) 329, 359
Rādhā 203
Rādheśyām Rāmāyaṇa 184–85, 209
Rafferty, Ellen 321
Raffles, Sir Thomas S. 278, 283, 288–89, 291
Rāghava 115, 207, 274
Rāghavan, V. 16, 18, 54, 64, 73, 150, 163
Rāghavanaiṣadhiya 356
Raghu 135, 227, 232
Raghu-rājā 268
Raghukula 178, 182
Raghunathan, N. 144, 147
Raghunāyaka 97
Raghupati 172
Raghuvaṁśa 251, 355
Raghuvara 172
Raghuvira 16, 18
Rahwana 276–77, 278–84, 286–87, 289, 359
Raja Annamalaipuram 147
Raja, Kunjunni 254–56
rājadharma 38, 112
Rajagopalachari, C. 133, 358
Rajagopalan, L. S. 254–56
rājasvapna 114
rākṣasa / raksasa 23, 32, 34–35, 50–52, 60, 62, 108, 111–112, 116, 120, 156–57, 220, 239, 277, 279, 283, 286, 298
rākṣasī 62–63, 239
Rām 359
Rāma xi–xii, xv, 5, 7–19, 22–45, 47–51, 54, 58–64, 66–67, 70–76, 78–79, 87–92, 94–101, 103–4, 108–21, 125–32, 134–38, 140–41, 143–45, 150–55, 157–62, 165–76, 179–81, 184, 186–91, 194–97, 219–37, 239–40, 243–45, 248–53, 260–62, 267–72, 292, 303, 310–11, 324, 326–29, 336–43, 345–46, 348, 350–51, 353, 355–59
Rāma, A Play 359
Rāma Jāmadagnya 26, 49, 73–76, 167, 217
Rāma kī Śakti Pūje 358
Rāma Story 358
Rāma Story Retold 358
Rāma Thagyin 357
Rāma Vaidehi Vanavās 358
Rāma Viraha 356
Rāmābhyudaya 356
Ramacami, I. Ve. 145, 147
Rāmacandrikā 357
Rāmacarita 357
Rāmakaliṅga 356
Rāmakathā/ Rāmkathā 10–11, 18, 34, 110, 126, 133–34, 140, 142, 150, 162, 260–62, 267–68, 271–72, 357
Rāmakathāra Prāk-Itihāsa 16, 18
Ramakien 323–27, 329–31, 342, 346, 357–58
Rāmalingāmṛta 356
Rāmānanda 356
Rāmanāṭaka 357
Rāmanāṭṭam 343, 357
Rāmanavamī 261, 264, 266, 271
Ramanujan, A. K. 150–52, 219
Rāmapadas 356
Rāmarājya/ *Rāmrāj* 113, 118, 131, 200, 235, 324
Ramasami, E. V. 129–30, 132, 145, 150–51, 161
Rāmāśvamedha 94
Rāmāthibodhi I 323
Rāmavijaya 262
Rāmayajña 357

Rāmāyaṇa vii–xi, xii, xiv–xvi, 3–21, 26–27, 33–34, 37–46, 58, 61–63, 66, 71, 76–79, 81, 84–85, 87–97, 103–5, 107–10, 112–22, 125–26, 129–30, 133, 137–38, 140, 142–53, 156–63, 165–68, 170–71, 173–79, 183–87, 189, 199–200, 203–10, 219–20, 223–25, 229, 231–37, 239–41, 243–45, 251, 253, 260, 262–63, 266–70, 274, 276–78, 280–81, 287–89, 292, 295, 300, 302, 305, 307, 320, 323–26, 328–51, 354–58
Rāmāyaṇa Nāṭakam 129–30, 132, 148
Rāmāyaṇamañjarī 356
Rāmāyaṇī 153
Rāmāyaṇīkathā 15, 153
Rambhā 61
Rāmcaritmānas 13, 17, 37, 149, 153, 159, 165–79, 182–92, 194–200, 203–13, 216–18, 262, 357
Rāmdas 262
Rāmera Vanagamana o Sitāharaṇa 119
Rameshwaram 152
Rāmlīlā 16–18, 109, 119, 153, 184, 207–8, 348–50, 358
Rāmmohan 118–19
Rāmnagar Rāmlīlā 184, 207–9
Rām-nām 158
Rāmopākhyāna 93, 355
Rāmprasāda/Ramprasad 10, 95, 118–19
Rāmprasādī Jagadrāmī Rāmāyaṇa 95–96, 104–5, 123
Ramseyer, Urs. 320
Raṅganātha Rāmāyaṇa 356
Rangayana 139, 142, 146, 148
Ranggawarsita 280
Rangnath, H. K. 146–47
rasa 246–47, 253, 255
rasātala 54
Rashtrakuta 339
Rashtriya Swayamsevak Sangha (RSS) 145, 234
Rāslīlā 208
Rās-Pañcādhyāyī 209
Ratnam, Kamala 16
Rattanakosin 325
Rāvaṇa 5, 8, 10, 13–14, 16, 32, 38–39, 50, 78–79, 88, 91, 93–97, 99, 102, 108–11, 114–15, 117, 120–21, 129, 136, 151–55, 157, 159–62, 211, 220–22, 224, 228, 230–35, 244, 247–49, 269–72, 276–77, 295, 300, 303, 305–8, 310–11, 325–26, 329, 337–38, 340–43, 348, 350–53, 359
Rāvaṇa chāyā 347
Rāvaṇa Josyam 234
Rāvaṇa Kāppiyam 145
Rāvaṇamandodarī 357
Rāvaṇavadha 109, 119, 355
Ray, B. 103–5
Ray, Dasarathi (Dasu) 107–9, 111–12, 119, 122–23
Ray, Jagdram 108, 121, 123
Ray, Ramprasad 108, 118, 121, 123
Ray, Sukumar 114, 120, 122–23
Ray Chowdhury, Upendra Kishore 115, 123
Reamker 323, 325–27, 329, 332, 356
rejeki 302
Renetil Youth Congress 316
Reṇukā 76, 146
Resi Tama 279–80
Revatī 266
Ṛgveda 59, 336
Richman, Paula 10–11, 16, 18–20, 46, 118, 122–23, 144, 147, 150–51, 161, 163, 240–41
Richmond, F. 254, 257
Ricklefs, M. C. 280, 288–91
Robson, O. 318, 320
Romapāda 56–57, 61
Rudal Scud 298
Rudra 70
Rudrasaṃhitā 80
Ṛśyaśṛṅga/ Ṛṣyaśṛṅga 55–58, 60–61, 73, 75–77, 80, 93

Saaptaahik Sakaal 274
Śabala 61
Sachin Sankar 358
Saddam Hussein 317
Sagar (Sāgar), Ramanand 4, 13, 37, 59, 165–79, 181–206, 209, 259
Sagara 26, 60, 67
sahadharmacārī 188
Sahai, S. 16, 18
Sahibadin 343
Sahitya Akademi 4, 18, 144
Śaiva 152
Śaivaite 61, 143, 276, 278, 284, 325, 331
Śaivism 143, 256
Sāket 358

Sāket Ūrmilā 358
Sako, Yugo 16
Śakra 68–69, 177
śākta 10, 96–97, 107, 109, 119, 157–58
Śakti 108, 173, 328
Śaktibhadra 243–44
śaktiśela 114–16
Śakuntalā 44, 121, 123
Śakuntalā o Sītāra Vanavāsa 121, 123
Śakuntalopākhyānam 44
Salatiga 299
Sāma 59
samāvartana 183
Sambar Prei Kuk 323
Śambūka Vadha 127–31, 144
Śambūka 11, 125–30, 132–34, 136–45
Samudaya 139
sanātanī 158
Sanchi 337
sang stryahajong 284
Sang Yang Guru 279
sañjīvanī 158
Śaṅkara Kavicandra 96, 98–100, 105, 108–9, 119
Śaṅkarācārya 215
Śaṅkaradeva 88–90, 104–5, 110–19, 121
Śaṅkaradigvijayam 42, 45
Saṅkaṭamocan 328
Śāntā 56, 79
śānti 202
Santoso, Soewito 342
Sapiro, Virginia 305, 319–20
Saptakāṇḍa Rāmāyaṇa 105, 122
Sarabhai, Mallika 17
Saraladāsa 93–4, 96, 104–5
Sarasvatī 78–79, 95
Sarayū 49, 62, 347
Sarkar, H. B. 16, 342
Sarkar, Tanika 208, 210
Śarmā, N, 161–63
Śārṅgadharapaddhati 80
Śārṅgadharasaṃhitā 80, 84
Sarpa kanaka 279
Sarpadnuke, Chamlong 16
Sarunakhā 359
Sarup, L. 254, 257
Sasmitaningsih 282
Ṣaṣṭhīvara 119
sastra harjendra 282, 289
sastra harjeng 284
sastra rancan 284
sastrajendra 282, 284–87, 289, 290, 292
sasural 167, 176, 181, 193
Śatānanda 73, 175, 181–82, 185, 191, 210, 213–14, 217
Śatapathabrāhmaṇa 77, 81, 84
Śataskandha Rāvaṇa Vadha 96, 103
satī 170, 172, 211, 232
Śatrughna 29, 176, 180–81, 210, 212–14, 224, 345
Śatruñjaya 88
satyapratiśravaḥ 23
Śavarī/Śabarī 94–95, 144, 147, 271
Sāvitrī 32, 238
Sax, William 16–18
Schechner, Richard 16, 18
Schoebel, Charles 81
Schreiner, Peter 45
Scott, Grant F. 318, 320
Sears, Laurie 14, 288–89, 292, 321
Seely, Clint 16, 152, 163
Seh Siti Jenar 287, 290
Sekar, I Made 298–300, 302–3, 305–10, 313–15, 318
Sen, Dinesh Chandra 16, 18, 105, 119, 123, 157
Sen, Gaṅgādās 119
Sen, Nilmadhav 16
Sen, Sukumar 16, 18
Sena Rodra 285
Sengupta, Subodhchandra 123
Serat Cabolek 283
Serat Darmagandul 284
Serat Kandha 278, 280, 283–86, 289
Serat Kandhaning Ringgit Purwa 278, 291
Serat Lokapala 281, 285–86, 292
Serat Pakem Ringgit Purwa 278
Serat Suluk 283
Seri Rāma 359
Śeṣa 153, 160
Śeṣaśāyī 338
Shah, U. P. 45
Shahani, Rita 273
Shaikh Among Raga 283
Shaikh Sit Jenar 283
Shakespeare, W. 139, 146
Shalom, Stephen R. 317
Sharma, Narendra 358
Sharma, R. K. 80
Sharman, Gopal 358

Shasrabuddhe, P. 263
Shastri, H. P. 288, 292
Shivarudrappa, G. 139, 145
shudra/śudra xi, 125–26, 130, 132–33, 136–37, 144, 147
Shulman, David 144, 147, 157
Sidā 359
Siddappa, K. M. 145
siddhāntapakṣa 22, 33
Śikhika 10
Śilparatna 256
Siṁha, S. 161, 163
Siṁhikā 154, 158–59
Sindusastra 283–86, 290, 292
Singh, K. S. 16, 18
Sintā 359
Sītā 3, 8, 10–14, 17, 24, 26, 28–35, 37–41, 44, 46, 50–52, 54, 64, 66, 73–74, 76–79, 85, 88, 90, 92, 95–97, 100, 102, 105, 108–12, 115–17, 120–21, 134–35, 140, 147, 151–52, 158, 162, 165–75, 177, 179–81, 183–84, 187–89, 192–216, 218–41, 243–44, 247, 249, 253, 262, 267–72, 293, 295, 300–301, 303, 305–8, 310–12, 314–16, 324, 326–30, 336–38, 340, 350–51, 355, 359
Sītā Agnipraveśam 231, 241
Sītā Anveṣaṇa 119
Sītāra Bāromāsī 120
Sītāra Vanavāsa (*Banabāsa*) 94, 112, 120–121, 123
Sītāyana 17
Śiromaṇi 69, 81
Śiva 62, 66–68, 72–75, 80–81, 89, 91, 154, 158, 168, 172, 184–86, 188, 197, 215–16, 227, 324, 327–28, 331, 339–41
Śiva Maṅgala 98
Śiva Purāṇa 80–81, 84, 356
Śiva Rāmera Yuddha 88, 98, 103
Śivaliṅga 152, 329
Śivasahāya 44
Sivasagar 148
Siwa 281
Skanda Purāṇa 80–81, 84, 355
Smith, W. L. 10, 16, 18, 46, 103–5, 123, 153–55, 157, 160, 162–63, 206
smṛti 127–28
Smṛtikathā 120
Soebardi, S. 282–83, 288–89, 291–92
Solo 285, 290
somana kunita 141
Śoṇā 64
Sousa, Nica 308–9
Śravaṇā Sundarī 95
Śrī/Sri 50, 79, 188, 279, 289, 306
Sri Gati 279
Śrī Rāmāyaṇa Darśanam 133, 147
Śrīdhara 262, 356
Śrīrāmacandrera Vivāha 119
Śrīrāmakīrtana 88
Śrīrāmalīlā 89
Śrīrāmarasāyaṇa 109, 119
Śrīvaiṣṇavism 39
Srivijayan 354
śṛṅgār 196, 199, 215
śṛṅgārarasa 199, 202–3
Śruti 127–28
śrutikā 259
Staffeld, Bill 300–301, 308, 312, 316
Stasik, D. 206, 210
Steenbrink, K. A. 289, 292
Stein, B. 148
Stewart, Tony 17, 122–23
strīvadha 102
Stutterheim, W. 342
Subāhu 60, 63, 98
Subbiah, G. V. 145
Subhadrā xvi, 257
Subhadrā Dhanañjaya 254, 257
Sudarso, Josaphat 299–300, 302
Śudra Tapasvī 133–34, 137–43, 146, 148
Sugrīva 35, 38, 43, 96, 101, 111, 116–17, 221, 244, 248–50, 270–71, 310–11, 329, 337–38
Suharto 294, 300, 314, 317, 319
Sukarnaputri, Megawati 294
Sukarno (President) 316
Śuka-saptati 237
Sukesi 276, 279–83, 285–86, 289–90
Sukhathai 356
Śukra 81
Sukthankar, V. S. 46, 81, 84
Sullivan, Bruce 254–55, 257
Sulocanā 152
Sumāli 277, 279–82, 286, 289
Sumantra 213, 216
Sumeru 89
Sumitrā 215–16
Suna Pandeki 359
Sunandā 215

Sunardi, D. M. 290, 292
Sunayanā 171–72, 177, 181, 187, 190, 192–95, 198, 204, 211–12, 216–17
Sunda 62
Sundara 158
Sundarakāṇḍa 10, 41, 52, 79, 158, 219–20, 223, 238–39
Suppanamacha 328
Supomo, S. 278, 284, 288–89, 292
Surabhi 94
Surakarta 280–81, 289, 291
Suralaya 279–80
Surasā 10, 158
Surpanakā 277, 282, 359
Śūrpanakhā 117, 120, 130, 151, 156, 230, 249–53, 271–72, 277, 337, 359
Surupnakhā 359
Suśrutasaṃhitā 80, 84–85
Suta Ashram 145
Sutherland-Goldman, Sally 10, 42, 46, 77, 79, 80–81, 83, 85
sūtradhāra 249, 251
svadharma 27, 30
Svargakhaṇḍa 92, 105
svayaṁvara 167–69, 171, 174–75, 204, 206–7, 209–10
Swami Tapasyānanda 209
Swāmi Viśveś Tīrth 209
Swāmy, Gangadhar 145
Swann, D. 257
Sweeny, Amin 16, 342
Sydney Morning Herald 313, 319

Tagore, Abanindranath 17
Tagore, Rabindranath 5, 16, 18, 114, 120–21, 123
Taittirīya Brāhmaṇa 336
Taittirīya Upaniṣad 42
Tajussalatin 284
Takṣaka 153
Tamasā 22, 346
Tambe, K. 273
Tankaraju, T. K. (also *see* Thangaraju, T. K.) 144–45, 148
Tantrasamuccaya Śilpa Bhāgam 256
tapas 126, 130–31, 135–36, 143
tapasyā 154, 193
Tapatī-Saṁvaraṇa 254, 257
Tārā 116–17, 337–38
Taraṇīsena 96, 98, 101, 108
Taraṇīsena Vadha 119
Taraṇīsenera Yuddha 88, 104
Tarlekar, G. H. 254, 257
Tāṭakā 60, 62–63, 67, 71–72, 76, 338, 343
Taylor, John G. 295, 317, 319–20
Tejasvi, Poornachandra 137–38, 146
tembang gede 281
Terukuthu 358
Tetum 297, 316, 320
Thakkar, H. 273
Thakkar, Menaka 17
Thangaraju, T. K. (also *see* Tankaraju, T. K.) 129–33, 142–45, 147
Thapar, Romila 16–17, 144, 148
The Australian 319
The Legend of Prince Rama: Ramayana 16
Theravadin 7
Thiagayya 358
Thiel-Horstmann, Monica 16–18, 46, 150, 163, 209
Thomas, Nicholas 318, 320
Tibetan Rāmāyaṇa 355
Ṭikā Rāmāyaṇa 91, 93, 105
Tilak, Bal Gangadhar 262
Tilakasiri 16
Tilakaṭīkā 69, 78–79, 81
Timaeus 317
Time Asia 310, 319
Timor Loro Sa'e 294, 297, 312–13, 315
Tirthankara 348
Tirucchirapalli 133
Toe, U 358
Tofakhane, B. H. 273
tolapāvakuthu 7, 347
Toraṇa Yuddham 247
Toravai Rāmāyaṇa 357
Tosakanth 326, 359
Traube, Elizabeth 295, 317, 320
Trijaṭā 359
Tripurāsura 89
Triveṇīsaṅgama 162
Tulsīdās 4–5, 8, 10, 12–13, 17, 37, 92, 94, 109, 149, 151, 153, 155–56, 158, 162, 165–66, 169–74, 176, 178–79, 181–202, 204–7, 262, 267, 344, 351, 357
Tulsīdāsī 4, 6, 8, 12, 344
Tumba 116
Tungabhadra 116

TVRāmāyaṇa (*TVR*) 165–205, 207–10, 259
Tyāgarāja 231, 239
Tylus, J. 319–20

Uccaiśravas 67
Udayshankar 16, 358
Umā 66, 79
uma lolon 297
Uma Mutuk 310
Umāpati 62, 80
Unmattarāghava 356
Unni, N. P. 248, 254–55, 257
UNTAET 307, 312
Upadhye, S. 273
upanayana 79
Upaniṣad 46, 77, 128
upapurāṇa 89
upodghāta 21–22, 39
Ūrmilā 73, 121, 152, 181
Ursekar, Mr. 273
Ūrubhaṅga 244, 256
Uttara Kandha 277
Uttara Rāghava 356
Uttara Rāmāyaṇa 356–57
Uttarakāṇḍa 11, 48–49, 51–53, 77, 89–90, 97, 104–5, 111, 122–23, 125, 219, 223–25, 277, 355
Uttararāmacarita 45, 125, 140, 145, 226, 239–40, 336, 355

Vāc 77
Vadekar, Ācārya V. P. 46
Vadekar, R. D. 46
vāgdāna 181
Vaideha 31
Vaidehī 53
Vaidehī Vilāsa 87
Vaikuṇṭha 94
Vaiṣṇava 37–38, 90, 96, 109, 119, 157, 158
Vaiśravaṇa 277
Vajpayi, Atal Bihari 133, 264
vajra 69
Vāli 35–38, 43, 88–89, 100–101, 111, 130, 135, 145, 162, 233, 244, 249, 271, 337–38
Vālivadha 37
Vālmīki 4–6, 8–11, 13, 15–16, 19–22, 27–28, 36–55, 59–62, 77–79, 84–85, 87, 89–91, 93–94, 99–101, 103, 107–9, 112, 115, 117, 120, 122–23, 125, 128, 133–34, 138, 140, 142–43, 147, 149–51, 159–60, 165–66, 168–69, 171, 173–79, 181–90, 194, 196, 198–200, 203–5, 207–10, 219–20, 224–30, 233–35, 239, 251, 253, 267–70, 272, 276–77, 292, 305, 318, 323, 334, 336, 338, 353
Vālmīki Pratibhā 120
Vālmīki Rāmāyaṇa 106, 118, 122–23, 162, 165–69, 171, 181–83, 185–87, 198–200, 204, 207–9, 210, 213, 216, 223, 241, 251, 259, 262, 270, 277, 292, 336, 339, 344, 351, 354–55
Vāmadeva 176
Vāmanapurāṇa 80, 85
van Buitenen, J. A. B. 146, 148, 240–41
Van der Veer, Peter 16, 18
vanaparva 93
vānara 51
vāṇīniścaya 181
Varadacharya, V. M. 273
Varāhapurāṇa 80, 85
varapakṣa 167, 177, 179, 191, 216
varṇa 20, 22, 57, 126, 131–32, 144
varṇāśramadharma 20, 23, 38, 125
Varuṇa 98, 244
Vāruṇī Surā 67
Vasiṣṭha 24, 33, 60–61, 92, 135, 160, 176, 178, 180–86, 187–88, 196–98, 204–5, 210, 212–15, 217–18
Vasiṣṭha Rāmāyaṇa 92
Vasudeva 356
Vāsuki 153
vātsyalya bhāva 176
vātsyalya rasa 199
Vatsyayan, Kapila 15, 206
Vaudeville, Charlotte 78, 85, 169, 206–7, 210
Vāyu 64–67, 70–71, 80–81, 352
Vāyu Purāṇa 81, 85, 355
Veda 29, 79, 81, 128, 132, 183, 187
Vedavatī 65, 228
Vellāla 131
Venu, G. 254–55, 257
Vetālacaṇḍī 160
Vetālapañcaviṁśati 237
Vibhāṇḍaka 56–57
Vibhāvasu 228
Vibhiṣaṇa 39, 96, 98–99, 111, 114, 116, 122, 154, 160, 277

Vicitra Rāmāyaṇa 89, 356
Videha 31, 192–93, 208, 214
vidhātā 180, 213
Vidura 280
vidūṣaka 245
Vidyasagar, Iswarchandra 112, 120–21, 123
Vietnam 311
Vijayanagar 337, 339–40, 342–43
Vikramāṇka 237
Vilomakāvya 356
Vimalasūri 94, 336
Virabāhu 95, 98, 104, 108
Virāṅganā Kāvya 120
Virgil 11, 305
Virupākṣa 338, 341, 355
Viśālā 67, 70
Viṣṇu 73–74, 89–90, 94, 98, 108, 158, 160, 171, 244, 262, 268, 323–24, 326, 328–29, 331, 337–39, 347, 356
Viṣṇu Purāṇa 81, 85, 324, 355
Viṣṇu Sahasranāma 188, 216
Viṣṇudharmottarapurāṇa 81, 85
Viṣṇupurī Rāmāyaṇa 97–99, 104, 119
Viśvāmitra 23–24, 55, 60–64, 66–67, 70–73, 75–77, 80, 103, 160, 169, 171, 175, 179, 181, 184, 190–91, 198, 207, 210–14, 216–17, 271, 338–40
Viśravas 277
Viswanatha Satyanarayana 223, 232
Viṭhobā 262
Viṭṭhala 337, 340
Vṛtra 89
Vyas, Hari Narayan 273
Vyas, Hariram 208–9
Vyas, R. 104, 106
Vyāsa 89, 104, 106
Vyāsa (Abiyasa) 280

Wahhabi 288
Wahhabism 284
Waisrawana 277
Walter, E. V. 294, 296, 317, 320
Warta Wayang 290, 292
Washbrook, David 145, 148
Wat Phra Keo 324, 325
Wat Po 343, 352
Waterson, Roxana 317, 320
wayang 280, 284–87, 290, 342, 347
wayang gedong golek 356
wayang kulit 342, 347
wayang purwa 278, 357
wayang wong 346, 350
Welty, Eudora 317, 320
West Timor 294, 297, 316
Wheatley, Paul 316, 321
Whitlam, Gough 314
Wibisana 277, 282
Wijaya, Putu 313, 319, 321
Willeman, Paul 320
Winichakul, Thongchai 295, 317, 321
Winter, C. F. 289, 292
Wisnu 279, 289
Wisrawa/Wisrawana 277, 281–84, 286–87, 289–90
Wofford, S. 319–20
Woltors, Oliver W. 304, 316, 318, 321
Wonoboyo 306
Woolner, A. C. 254, 257
Wujastyk, Dominik 80, 85
Wulff, Donna 255, 257
Wuruk, Hayam 277

Yādava Rāghavīya Rāmakathā 356
Yajurveda 59, 182, 186, 188, 213, 215–16
yakṣa 62
Yakshagana 141, 346, 358
Yama 115
yamadūta 114
Yamamoto, Chikiyo 16, 18
Yamunā 339
Yarlamma 140
Yasadipura 280–87
yātrā/jātrā 114, 346, 358
Yengoyan, A. A. 291
Yogiswara 318
Yogya 314
Yogyakarta 281
Yosuf, Mohammed 342
Yuddhakāṇḍa 32, 51–53, 123, 262
Yudhājit 207

Z Magazine 317
Zain, Ki. Shaikh 275
Zarkasi, H. E. 290, 292
Zarrilli, P. 257
zat-pwe 346, 353
Zaw, U Khin 16
Zoetmulder, P. J. 277, 288, 292
Zvelebil, Kamil V. 104, 106, 153–55, 157–58, 163